Lecture Notes in Computer Science

Lecture Notes in Artificial Intelligence   14546

Founding Editor

Jörg Siekmann

The series Lecture Notes in Artificial Intelligence (LNAI) was established in 1988 as a topical subseries of LNCS devoted to artificial intelligence.

The series publishes state-of-the-art research results at a high level. As with the LNCS mother series, the mission of the series is to serve the international R & D community by providing an invaluable service, mainly focused on the publication of conference and workshop proceedings and postproceedings.

Ana Paula Rocha · Luc Steels ·
Jaap van den Herik
Editors

Agents and
Artificial Intelligence

15th International Conference, ICAART 2023
Lisbon, Portugal, February 22–24, 2023
Revised Selected Papers

 Springer

Editors
Ana Paula Rocha
LIACC, University of Porto
Porto, Portugal

Luc Steels
ICREA, Institute of Evolutionary Biology
Barcelona, Spain

Jaap van den Herik
Leiden Institute of Advanced Computer
Science
Leiden, The Netherlands

ISSN 0302-9743   ISSN 1611-3349 (electronic)
Lecture Notes in Artificial Intelligence
ISBN 978-3-031-55325-7   ISBN 978-3-031-55326-4 (eBook)
https://doi.org/10.1007/978-3-031-55326-4

LNCS Sublibrary: SL7 – Artificial Intelligence

This Springer imprint is published by the registered company Springer Nature Switzerland AG
The registered company address is: Gewerbestrasse 11, 6330 Cham, Switzerland

Paper in this product is recyclable.

Preface

The present book includes extended and revised versions of a set of selected papers from the 15th International Conference on Agents and Artificial Intelligence (ICAART 2023), held in Lisbon, Portugal, from 22–24 February 2023.

ICAART 2023 received 306 paper submissions from 52 countries, of which 23 papers were included in this book.

The papers were selected by the event chairs and their selection was based on a number of criteria that included the classifications and comments provided by the program committee members, the session chairs' assessment and also the program chairs' global view of all papers included in the technical program. The authors of selected papers were then invited to submit revised and extended versions of their papers having at least 30% innovative material.

The purpose of the International Conference on Agents and Artificial Intelligence is to bring together researchers, engineers and practitioners interested in theory and applications in the areas of Agents and Artificial Intelligence. Two simultaneous related tracks were held, covering both applications and current research work. One track focused on Agents, Multi-Agent Systems and Software Platforms, Distributed Problem Solving and Distributed AI in general. The other track focused mainly on Artificial Intelligence, Knowledge Representation, Planning, Learning, Scheduling, Perception Reactive AI Systems, Evolutionary Computing and other topics related to Intelligent Systems and Computational Intelligence.

The papers selected to be included in this book contribute to the understanding of relevant trends of current research on Agents and Artificial Intelligence, including: Machine Learning, Deep Learning, Neural Networks, Multi-Agent Systems, Agent Models and Architectures, Simulation, Autonomous Systems, Industrial Applications of AI, Planning and Scheduling and Big Data.

We would like to thank all the authors for their contributions and also all reviewers who have helped to ensure the quality of this publication.

February 2023

Ana Paula Rocha
Luc Steels
Jaap van den Herik

Organization

Conference Chair

Jaap van den Herik   Leiden University, The Netherlands

Program Co-chairs

Ana Paula Rocha   LIACC/FEUP, University of Porto, Portugal
Luc Steels   Barcelona Supercomputing Center, Spain

Program Committee

Vicki Allan	Utah State University, USA
Klaus-Dieter Althoff	German Research Center for Artificial Intelligence/University of Hildesheim, Germany
Frédéric Amblard	IRIT - Université Toulouse 1 Capitole, France
Ilze Andersone	Riga Technical University, Latvia
Anastassia Angelopoulou	University of Westminster, UK
Alla Anohina-Naumeca	Riga Technical University, Latvia
Patricia Anthony	Lincoln University, New Zealand
Marcelo Armentano	ISISTAN Research Institute (CONICET-UNICEN), Argentina
Wudhichai Assawinchaichote	King Mongkut's University of Technology Thonburi, Thailand
Jean-Michel Auberlet	IFSTTAR (French Institute of Science and Technology for Transport, Development and Networks), France
Hadi Banaee	Örebro University, Sweden
Necaattin Barisci	Gazi University, Turkey
Maria Barron-Estrada	Instituto Tecnológico de Culiacán, Mexico
Montserrat Batet	Universitat Rovira i Virgili, Spain
Rafael Berlanga	Universitat Jaume I, Spain
Heder Bernardino	Federal University of Juiz de Fora, Brazil
Carole Bernon	University of Toulouse III, France

Adriana Birlutiu	1 Decembrie 1918 University of Alba Iulia, Romania
Stefano Bistarelli	University of Perugia, Italy
Marcin Blachnik	Silesian University of Technology, Poland
Carlos Bobed Lisbona	University of Zaragoza, Spain
Hamid Boubertakh	University of Jijel, Algeria
Lars Braubach	City University of Hamburg, Germany
Joerg Bremer	University of Oldenburg, Germany
Edward Brent	University of Missouri, USA
Paolo Bresciani	Fondazione Bruno Kessler, Italy
Daniela Briola	Università degli Studi Di Milano-Bicocca, Italy
Paola Britos	National University of Río Negro, Argentina
Aleksander Byrski	AGH University of Science and Technology, Poland
Giacomo Cabri	Università di Modena e Reggio Emilia, Italy
Patrice Caire	Stanford University, USA
Valérie Camps	IRIT - Université Paul Sabatier, France
Javier Carbó Rubiera	Universidad Carlos III de Madrid, Spain
Henrique Lopes Cardoso	Universidade do Porto, Portugal
Cristiano Castelfranchi	Institute of Cognitive Sciences and Technologies - National Research Council, Italy
Wen-Chung Chang	National Taipei University of Technology, Taiwan, Republic of China
Amitava Chatterjee	Jadavpur University, India
Chandreyee Chowdhury	Kolkata University, India
Davide Ciucci	Università degli Studi di Milano-Bicocca, Italy
Leandro Coelho	Pontifícia Universidade Católica do Paraná, Brazil
Stéphanie Combettes	IRIT - Universite Paul Sabatier - Toulouse III, France
Flavio Correa da Silva	University of São Paulo, Brazil
Paulo Cortez	University of Minho, Portugal
Erzsébet Csuhaj-Varjú	Eötvös Loránd University, Hungary
Riccardo De Benedictis	CNR-Italian National Research Council, Italy
Fernando de Souza	Universidade Federal de Pernambuco, Brazil
Carmelo Del Valle	Universidad de Sevilla, Spain
Bruno Di Stefano	Nuptek Systems Ltd., Canada
João Dias	Universidade do Algarve, Portugal
Dragan Doder	Utrecht University, The Netherlands
Michel Dojat	Université Grenoble Alpes, France
Rafal Drezewski	AGH University of Science and Technology, Poland
Viktor Eisenstadt	University of Hildesheim, Germany

Thomas Eiter	Technische Universität Wien, Austria
Hojjatollah Farahani	Tarbiat Modares University, Iran
Catherine Faron	Université Côte d'Azur, France
Edilson Ferneda	Catholic University of Brasilia, Brazil
Alexander Ferrein	MASCOR Institute, FH Aachen University of Applied Sciences, Germany
Oscar Fontenla-Romero	University of A Coruña, Spain
Agostino Forestiero	ICAR-CNR, Italy
Katsuhide Fujita	Tokyo University of Agriculture and Technology, Japan
Alfredo Garro	Università della Calabria, Italy
Benoit Gaudou	University Toulouse 1 Capitole, France
Andrey Gavrilov	Novosibirsk State Technical University, Russian Federation
Gianfranco Giulioni	University of Chieti-Pescara, Italy
Janis Grundspenkis	Riga Technical University, Latvia
Bertha Guijarro-Berdiñas	Universidade da Coruña, Spain
James Harland	RMIT University, Australia
Hisashi Hayashi	Advanced Institute of Industrial Technology, Japan
Alexis Heloir	Polytechnic University of Hauts-de-France, France
Pedro Henriques	University of Minho, Portugal
Ramon Hermoso	University of Zaragoza, Spain
Vincent Hilaire	UTBM, France
Hanno Hildmann	TNO, The Netherlands
Rolf Hoffmann	Darmstadt University of Technology, Germany
Wei-Chiang Hong	Asia Eastern University of Science and Technology, Taiwan, Republic of China
Ales Horak	Masaryk University, Czech Republic
Takashi Ikegami	University of Tokyo, Japan
Arti Jain	Jaypee Institute of Information Technology, India
Fethi Jarray	LimTic, Tunisia
Agnieszka Jastrzebska	Warsaw University of Technology, Poland
Francisco José Domínguez Mayo	University of Seville, Spain
Norihiro Kamide	Nagoya City University, Japan
Ashwin Viswanathan Kannan	Amazon Labs, USA
Geylani Kardas	Ege University International Computer Institute, Turkey
Mohd Shareduwan Mohd Kasihmuddin	Universiti Sains Malaysia, Malaysia
Petros Kefalas	CITY College, University of York Europe Campus, Greece

Koichi Moriyama	Nagoya Institute of Technology, Japan
Gildas Morvan	Université d'Artois, France
Bernard Moulin	Université Laval, Canada
Muhammad Marwan Muhammad Fuad	Coventry University, UK
Hien Nguyen	University of Information Technology, VNU-HCM, Vietnam
Antoine Nongaillard	Lille University, France
Nadim Obeid	University of Jordan, Jordan
Michel Occello	Université Grenoble Alpes, France
Michael O'Grady	University College Dublin, Ireland
Andrei Olaru	University "Politehnica" of Bucharest, Romania
Joanna Isabelle Olszewska	University of the West of Scotland, UK
Eva Onaindía de la Rivaherrera	UPV, Spain
Stanislaw Osowski	Warsaw University of Technology, Poland
Andrew Parkes	University of Nottingham, UK
Daniel Paternain	Public University of Navarre, Spain
Danilo Pianini	Università di Bologna, Italy
Sébastien Picault	INRAE, France
Maria Silvia Pini	University of Padova, Italy
Jamshid Piri	Independent Researcher, Iran
Agostino Poggi	University of Parma, Italy
Dawid Polap	Silesian University of Technology, Poland
Horia Pop	Babes-Bolyai University, Romania
Filipe Portela	University of Minho, Portugal
Roberto Posenato	Università degli Studi di Verona, Italy
Anas Quteishat	Al-Balqa' Applied University, Jordan
Abdellatif Rahmoun	École supérieure en informatique de Sidi Bel Abbès, and Graduate School of Computer Science, Algeria
Riccardo Rasconi	National Research Council of Italy, Italy
Ramesh Rayudu	Victoria University of Wellington, New Zealand
Lluís Ribas-Xirgo	Universitat Autònoma de Barcelona, Spain
Patrizia Ribino	ICAR-CNR, Italy
Rui Rocha	University of Coimbra, Portugal
Fátima Rodrigues	Polytechnic Institute of Porto, Portugal
Juha Röning	University of Oulu, Finland
Ruben Ruiz	Universidad Politécnica de Valencia, Spain
Francesco Santini	Università di Perugia, Italy
Fabio Sartori	University of Milano-Bicocca, Italy
Jurek Sasiadek	Carleton University, Canada
Stefan Schiffer	RWTH Aachen University, Germany

Dmitriy Serdyuk	Google, USA
Emilio Serrano	Universidad Politécnica de Madrid, Spain
Gerardo Simari	Universidad Nacional del Sur, Argentina
Aleksandra Sojic	National Research Council (CNR), Italy
Bernd Steinbach	Freiberg University of Mining and Technology, Germany
Darko Stipanicev	FESB University of Split, Croatia
Thomas Stützle	Université Libre de Bruxelles, Belgium
Sivarao Subramonian	Universiti Teknikal Malaysia Melaka, Malaysia
Ron Sun	Rensselaer Polytechnic Institute, USA
Zhaohao Sun	Federation University Australia, Australia and PNG University of Technology, Papua New Guinea
Olarik Surinta	Mahasarakham University, Thailand
Yasuhiro Suzuki	Nagoya University, Japan
Gábor Szucs	Budapest University of Technology and Economics, Hungary
Ryszard Tadeusiewicz	AGH University of Science Technology, Poland
Zaiyong Tang	Salem State University, USA
Andrea Tettamanzi	Université Côte d'Aazur, Inria, I3S, UMR 7271, France
Satoshi Tojo	Japan Advanced Institute of Science and Technology, Japan
Pei-Wei Tsai	Swinburne University of Technology, Australia
Leo van Moergestel	HU Utrecht University of Applied Sciences, The Netherlands
Harko Verhagen	Stockholm University, Sweden
Jørgen Villadsen	Technical University of Denmark, Denmark
Emilio Vivancos	Universitat Politècnica de València, Spain
Wojciech Waloszek	Gdansk University of Technology, Poland
Frank Wang	University of Kent, UK
Bozena Wozna-Szczesniak	Jan Dlugosz University in Czestochowa, Poland
Seiji Yamada	National Institute of Informatics, Japan
Hongji Yang	University of Leicester, UK
Chung-Hsing Yeh	Monash University, Australia

Additional Reviewers

Victor David	University of Perugia, Italy
Hércules do Prado	Catholic University of Brasília, Brazil
Yu-Lin Huang	University of Luxembourg, Luxembourg

Ricardo Martins   Universidade do Minho, Portugal
Corrado Mio   EBTIC, Khalifa University of Science and
                             Technology, UAE
Carlo Taticchi   University of Perugia, Italy
Joaquin Taverner   Universitat Politècnica de València, Spain

Invited Speakers

Philippe Codognet   JFLI - CNRS/Sorbonne University,
                             France/University of Tokyo, Japan
Valentina Presutti   University of Bologna, Italy
Michael Spranger   Sony AI, Japan
Aldo Gangemi   University of Bologna, Italy

Contents

Agents

Bees, Bats and Glowworms: Swarm Algorithms for Optimizing Industrial Plants from the Bottom-Up

M. Umlauft⬛, M. Gojkovic, K. Harshina, K. Majbour, and M. Schranz(✉)⬛

Lakeside Labs GmbH, Klagenfurt, Austria
{umlauft,gojkovic,harshina,majbour,schranz}@lakeside-labs.com

Abstract. The scheduling problem in production plants with diverse product ranges is NP-hard, posing challenges in finding optimal solutions. To overcome this, we propose a novel approach utilizing three bio-inspired optimization algorithms: artificial bee colony (ABC), bat, and glowworm algorithm. We apply these algorithms to address the job-shop scheduling problem and overcome computational barriers associated with traditional methods. Unlike previous studies, our approach departs from using these algorithms for global optimization within the solution space. Instead, we adopt a bottom-up strategy, directly applying them as verbatim swarm intelligence algorithms. Focusing on a semiconductor production plant, we employ agent-based modeling in the NetLogo simulation platform. By mapping bees, bats, and glowworms to plant entities like lots and machines, we establish direct correspondences. Agents interact with each other and the environment based on local rules, resulting in the emergence of desired global behavior—the industrial plant optimization. To evaluate performance, we compare our approach to a baseline algorithm employing engineered heuristics like First-In-First-Out (FIFO) and filling fullest batches first. Through this comparison, we assess the effectiveness of the bottom-up algorithms. Our results show promising performance improvements achieved with these algorithms, which rely on low-effort local calculations.

Keywords: Swarm intelligence · Bio-inspired algorithm · Artificial bee algorithm · Bat algorithm · Glowworm algorithm · Flexible job-shop scheduling · Agent-based modeling

1 Introduction

In today's production plants organized by the job-shop principle we face an increased complexity in scheduling due to the dynamics of customized, flexible, on-demand production combined with a high product diversity. Throughout this paper, we consider the semiconductor manufacturer Infineon Technologies Austria AG[1] that deals with comparatively low-volume production runs[2] of integrated circuits in the logic and power

---

[1] Infineon Technologies, https://www.infineon.com/.
[2] Compared to memory and CPU manufacturers.

ⓒ The Author(s), under exclusive license to Springer Nature Switzerland AG 2024
A. P. Rocha et al. (Eds.): ICAART 2023, LNAI 14546, pp. 3–25, 2024.
https://doi.org/10.1007/978-3-031-55326-4_1

sector where they produce 1500 products in around 300 process steps using up to 1200 stations [18,33]. These characteristics lead to an NP-hard problem where linear optimization methods reach their limits for a global plant optimization due to the excessive computation time [22]. Centrally pre-computed swarm intelligence algorithms have already been used for the optimization of industrial production plants. Due to their impressive performance, these methods are frequently employed as substitutes or enhancements for linear optimization techniques. For a detailed examination, readers are directed to the comprehensive review by Gao et al. [9]. Nevertheless, they face the same problems in terms of calculation time and complexity [18]. As proposed in [33], we use the novel approach to model the production plant as a self-organizing system of agents, using local rules, local knowledge and local interactions. This transfers the problem of computing an overall solution to engineering a distributed algorithm that produces a solution from the bottom-up. An optimization from the bottom-up is able to dynamically react on changing environmental conditions (e.g., tool downs, product priorities) and to produce near-optimal solutions for NP-hard problems.

In this paper, honeybees, microbats, and glowworms serve as inspiration to derive three distributed swarm intelligence algorithms. Honeybees live in a colony, search for pollen, and transport it back to their hive. To attract other bees for the same food source, they perform a waggle dance that shows the direction and distance to the food source. They also use pheromones to communicate a possible attack. Microbats use echolocation signals to search for nearby prey. They update the loudness, rate of pulse and the frequency of the signal based on the distance of the bats to the prey. Glowworms use luminescence to attract prey or mates. By employing the bioluminescence phenomenon to indicate location quality in terms of resources, each worm is attracted to the brightest glowing worm in its neighbourhood and moves toward it. Our contribution is related to exactly this natural bee, bat, and glowworm behaviour originally designed as the artificial bee colony algorithm (ABC) [15], the bat algorithm [44], and the glowworm algorithm [2], but engineered onto the problem of the semiconductor production plant. For the first time, the ABC, bat and glowworm algorithms are not used as centrally computed optimization approaches, but rather the rules are adapted and used as local rules to perform the optimization from the bottom-up in this setting. With the glowworm algorithm and additional evaluation results for all algorithms, this chapter presents an extensions to the paper Umlauft et al. [39].

We state the problem to optimize and describe our model of the production plant in Sect. 2 and give an overview of the relevant related work in Sect. 3. We show our novel algorithm designs of the three bio-inspired algorithms used in a bottom-up manner, describing the respective inspiring algorithms and our adapted versions in detail in Sects. 4, 5, and 6. To evaluate the performance of our algorithms, we use the NetLogo simulation platform where we have implemented a flexible framework containing a model of our production plant. As comparison we use an engineered baseline algorithm that uses simple FIFO queues and the fill-least-empty-batch first principle, see Sect. 7. The paper is closed out with the conclusion in Sect. 8.

2   Problem Statement and Model

The overall goal is to optimize the production of products in a plant with the main key performance indicator being **makespan** (the total time it takes to produce all products). A secondary performance indicator is the time wasted by products waiting in machine queues, which can be measured as flow factor or as tardiness. In addition, machine utilization should also be monitored (see Sect. 7 for a detailed description).

We model the production plant as follows: there are a number of products, called **lots** $L^t = \{l_1^t, l_2^t, \dots\}$ which need to be produced. To produce a lot of a certain product type t, its respective **recipe** R^t must be followed. The recipe describes which **process steps** P_i^m must be performed in which order $R^t = \{P_1^m, P_2^n, \dots\}$. A process step P^m can be performed on any **machine** M^m in the plant. I.o.w., there is a $1 : 1$ relationship between process type m and machine type m. The plant has a (potentially large) number of machines M and each machine M_i^m has a queue Q_i^m. Machines of the same type m are grouped into a **workcenter** $W^m \subset M$. For every process type m to be performed, at least one workcenter W^m containing at least one machine M^m of type m must exist. As there typically are multiple machines per workcenter, for each necessary process step $P^m \in R^t$ a lot l_n^t must decide which of the suitable machines $M_i^m \in W^m$ to use.

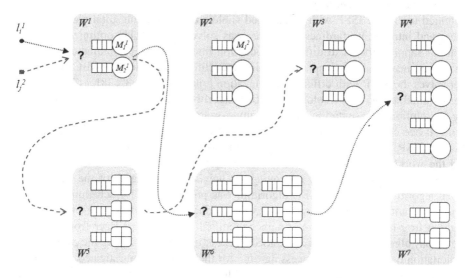

Fig. 1. Fab model showing two lots of different types with their respective recipes going through the workcenters and machines of the fab. Machines shown in workcenters $W^1 \dots W^4$ are single-step machines, while machines in workcenters $W^5 \dots W^7$ are batch machines.

Figure 1 shows the concept: two lots l_i^1, l_j^2 of types $t = \{1, 2\}$ follow their recipes (dotted and dashed edges respectively) through the production plant. At each workcenter $\{W^1, \dots, W^7\}$ a lot has to decide at which of the possible machines to enqueue. Depending on the used algorithm, machines can also re-order their queues. Machines can be one of two kinds: either **single-step** which process one lot after the other, or

batch-oriented (such as a furnace) which can process a batch of several lots of the same type t at once. Whenever there are switches between machine kinds, this makes optimization difficult as theory suggests that for single-step machines, uniform arrival times are optimal [37]. An incoming wave of lots from a preceding batch machine disrupts this flow, though. Conversely, the filling of batches at batch machines can be delayed if all the necessary lots of the same type t are enqueued at the same preceding single-step machine.

3   Related Work

There has been extensive research on applying the **ABC (artificial bee colony)** algorithm to the job-shop scheduling problem (JSSP): [15] optimized multivariable functions which outperform other evolutionary algorithms. [11,46] proposed the improved artificial bee colony (IABC) algorithm with an enhanced convergence rate. [10] were able to efficiently solve JSSP by implementing additional mutation and crossover operator of GA in the classical ABC algorithm. Another ABC adaptation is given in [21], named Crossover-based ABC (CbABC). This solution strengthens the exploitation phase of ABC as crossover enhances the exploration of search space. ABC algorithm was also successfully applied to the JSSP [48] with the objective of minimizing total weighted tardiness. JSSP with equal-sized sublots by minimizing total weighted earliness and introducing tardiness penalties was solved in [31]. [1] optimized the raw material supply process to different production lines in a local manufacturing plant. There have been multiple proposals of a discrete artificial bee colony (DABC) algorithm that solves the JSSP with different optimization criteria [25,26,32,38]. [47] proposed the modified artificial bee colony (M-ABC) algorithm with random key-based encoding for solution representation and a new multi-search strategy. Enhanced Pareto-based artificial bee colony (EPABC) algorithm is introduced in [41] for the multi-objective flexible JSSP with the maximum completion time, the total workload of machines, and the workload of the critical machine as optimization criteria. Tabu search (TS) has been further exploited for improving the neighborhood search of the newly proposed algorithms [24,25]. TABC algorithm was proposed [7] for scheduling and rescheduling with new job insertion(s). [36] introduced a hybrid version of ABC and shuffled frog-leaping algorithm. Another modified ABC, named Beer froth artificial bee colony algorithm [35], solves the JSSP successfully by maintaining the exploration-exploitation balance. Fuzzy processing time for the FJSP was investigated in [8]. Proposed ABC in [51] outperforms other algorithms (GA, PSO, ant colony optimization, and cuckoo) for the JSSP with two sequence-dependent setup times. ABC variations for data clustering-related applications are given in [20]. For a further literature overview, the reader is referred to [16,17].

Over the past decade, the **bat algorithm** and its various versions have been utilized to tackle the JSSP, following the algorithm's initial introduction in [44]. In [30], a bat algorithm based scheduling tool was developed to solve multi-stage multi-machine multi-process scheduling problems. The bat algorithm was also applied in [29] to address the multi-stage hybrid flow shop (HFS) scheduling problem, while [28] introduced the discrete bat algorithm to optimize the permutation flow shop scheduling problem. In [43], an improved bat algorithm was proposed to handle the dual flexible job-shop scheduling problem (DFJSP), whereas [50] presented a modified bat algorithm to solve the multi-objective JSSP. To address JSSP [4] proposed an optimization algorithm that runs parallel versions of the bat algorithm, random-key encoding scheme, and makespan scheme. [27] was the first to apply the bat algorithm to the low-carbon JSSP, and more recently, [3] proposed another improved bat algorithm to speed up convergence and determine the optimal global solution for JSSP. [45] provided a comprehensive review of different variants of the bat algorithm and their applications, including various case studies. A more recent review in [12] focused on the bat algorithm's usage and application in optimizing various engineering problems.

Using the **glowworm metaphor** was introduced in 2005 to solve the optimization problem of multiple optima as a variant of the ant colony algorithm. The proposed scenario was exploring the resources in terms of food by employing a set of autonomous robots who coordinate and communicate by emitting and detecting light [19]. In 2011, [34] introduced a variant of the glowworm algorithm called firefly algorithm. [13] presented an improved glowworm swarm optimization algorithm to solve the planning problems of job-shop production planning referring to a model of a tobacco production company. Each glowworm or firefly represented a solution in the solution space, where the improved algorithm showed favorable results by applying the exchange and mutation to avoid falling in local optima. Another work in [6] improved the glowworm swarm algorithm by supporting the bunching, communication, and an adaptive step to solve the flow shop scheduling problem of a watt-hour metres production line. It showed a higher speed of convergence comparing to the ABC and basic glowworm algorithms. In [23], the glowworm algorithm is used to derive the optimal solution of mathematical models created to optimize the smart charging process of electrical vehicles concerning the power grid constraints. [49] proposed a variant of glowworm swarm optimization with Levy variation for solving vehicle scheduling problem in a logistic system of iron and steel plants, and compared its performance with PSO, GSO, and ant-colony algorithms.

4   The ABC Algorithm

4.1   Inspiration

The artificial bee colony (ABC) algorithm draws inspiration from the foraging behavior of honeybees [14] and was originally designed to solve numerical optimization problems. To solve the problem, the ABC algorithm converts it into the problem of finding the best parameter vector and minimizes an objective function. The ABC algorithm as a global optimizer has the following steps (for more formal details, the reader is referred to [39]):

In the vast literature on the ABC algorithm applied to the JSSP (see Sect. 3), the population of bees always represent a solution space, i.e., the algorithm is calculated centrally. Our contribution consists of opting for the bottom-up approach, where bees represent agents (instead of solutions) that follow local rules from which a global behavior (the optimal schedule) emerges. Thus, we present a completely new approach to the ABC algorithm application.

Algorithm 1. ABC as global optimizer.

1: Initialization Phase (population of the food source)
2: **repeat**
3:     Employed Bees Phase
4:     Onlooker Bees Phase
5:     Scout Bees Phase
6:     Memorize the best solution
7: **until** Cycle = Maximum Cycle Number or a Maximum CPU time

---

4.2   The ABC Algorithm in a Bottom-Up Approach

To model the ABC algorithm to optimize the production scheduling, the following mapping has been placed [39]:

- food source = machine, $M_i^m \in W^m, i = 1, 2, \ldots, I$
- bee = lot from one product, $l_n^t \in L^t, n = 1, 2, \ldots, N$

where an individual machine M_i^m is grouped with other machines of the same m type to form a workcenter W^m. Each lot l_n^t follows a recipe R^t related to its type t that contains a sequence of process steps P^m necessary for the lot l_n^t to finish its production.

Since lots must select a suitable machine $M_i^m \in W^m$ to perform a process $P^m \in R^t$, it can be distinguished between lots modeled as onlooker bees l_{OB} and those modeled as scout bees l_{SB}. At the beginning of our simulation, there is no a priori knowledge of any machine, thus the first lots to arrive at a machine are l_{SB}. Therefore the first phase of the bottom-up ABC is the Scout Bees Phase. Lots modeled as l_{SB} explore the W^m (search area) by randomly selecting one machine $M_i^m \in W^m$ to perform the necessary process P^m prescribed by the recipe R^t. Upon finished process, l_{SB} will evaluate the quality of the selected machine $Q(M_i^m)$ by taking into account the total waiting time w_{SB}, i.e., how long the l_{SB} waited in machine's queue, in addition to the processing time of the machine M_i^m (Eq. 1):

$$Q(M_i^m) = \frac{1}{w_{SB}} \qquad (1)$$

Once l_{SB} has finished its process P^m, the Onlooker Bees Phase starts, as l_{OB} lots can now use the quality information provided by l_{SB} to probabilistically [14] select the best $M_i^m \in W^m$ as in Eq. 2:

$$P_r(M_i^m) = \frac{fit(M_i^m)}{\sum_{i=1}^{I} fit(M_i^m)} \qquad (2)$$

Each machine $M_i^m \in W^m$ has the probability $P_r(M_i^m)$ of being selected by the l_{OB} which is a relation of its own fitness $fit(M_i^m)$ and the sum of fitness values of all machines belonging to the same workcenter W^m. Once the l_{SB} provide the quality information of a machine $Q(M_i^m)$ and the probability $P_r(M_i^m)$ is calculated, the l_{OB} will have enough information to choose the best machine in the workcenter.

After the l_{OB} have chosen the best $M_i^m \in W^m$, the Employed Bees Phase starts. In our simulation, lots only move forward in the factory by following their recipes, there is no hive concept as in the original ABC algorithm. Therefore we only model some of the functionalities of the original Employed Bees Phase: Instead of sharing the food source information with other bees in the hive, l_{SB} notifies the machine M_i^m of the assessment (Eq. 1). This information is stored in the machine and is available to the l_{OB} who will make their decision based on it. Thus, instead of direct communication among lot agents, our model uses stigmergy for self-coordination and communication.

Another function of the Employed Bees Phase regarding generating a new solution in the neighborhood and applying greedy selection is in the bottom-up ABC modeled as follows: The neighborhood consists of lots waiting in Q_i^m of a chosen M_i^m. By default, M_i^m will select the first enqueued lot to process. However, it might happen that some other lot in Q_i^m has the next P^m corresponding to a batch machine. Therefore processing such lot first (instead of following the First-In-First-Out algorithm), can improve the performance of the batch machine and overall production time [39]. If in Q_i^m there are such lots, the M_i^m will process the one that can contribute to the most full batch in the following process step of the lot.

The last functionality modeled is food source abandonment due to poor quality. A food source can have poor quality initially or due to excessive exploitation. This is modeled with a predefined limit value l that serves as a machine's timeout. Namely, when a certain number of l_{OB} chooses the best $M_i^m \in W^m$, the total waiting time w_{OB} of each enqueued lot will increase, and therefore the initial quality $Q(M_i^m)$ will change. Each time l_{OB} chooses this machine M_i^m, its limit value l will decrease. When it becomes $l = 0$, the machine will lose its evaluated tag, and this will make it attractive to other l_{SB} that will come to re-evaluate it.

With everything aforementioned, Algorithm 2 [39] displays phases of our bottom-up ABC that change as lot l^t changes process steps $P^m \rightarrow P^n$ in its recipe R^t:

Initialization Phase. In the first phase of the algorithm, values like limit l, a certain number of lots, machines, and their memory get initialized.

Case 0 to SingleStep. The first lots to arrive at a machine are modeled as l_{SB} and thus, a random machine $M_i^m \in W^m$ will be selected. After these lots finish the process P^m, lots will evaluate the corresponding machine. Once all machines $M_i^m \in W^m$ are evaluated, the Onlooker Bees Phase can start.

Case 0 to Batch. If a lot's recipe R^t starts with P^m performed by a batch machine, the l_{SB} will be randomly allocated. Lots modeled as l_{OB} will firstly search the workcenter W^m for machines already having lots of the same type t in their queues. If there are no such machines, l_{SB} will be selected randomly. However, if there are such machines $M_i^m \in W^m$, the lot will count the number of free places n_{fs} (until the full batch) of each machine. Finally, it will select the machine with the least missing places—the best machine will be the one with $n_{fs} = 1$. If more such machines exist, the best will be the one with the shortest remaining time $t_{M_i^m}$ before the machine processes this semi-filled batch. If no such machine exists, the lot will search for one with $n_{fs} = 2$, etc.

Case SingleStep to SingleStep. Following the selection rules described for the two previous cases will eventually cause overpopulation of queues of the best-rated machines $M_i^m \in W^m$. This will lead to an extended total waiting time in the machine's queue.

Algorithm 2. Bottom-up ABC.

1: Initialization Phase (population of lots and machines)

2: **repeat**
3: **switch** $m_{prev} \rightarrow m_{next}$ **do**

4: **case** $0 \rightarrow SingleStep$:
  Scout Bees Phase
  Onlooker Bees Phase

5: **case** $0 \rightarrow Batch$:
  Scout Bees Phase
  Onlooker Bees Phase

6: **case** $SingleStep \rightarrow SingleStep$:
  Scout Bees Phase
  Onlooker Bees Phase

7: **case** $SingleStep \rightarrow Batch$:
  Employed Bees Phase

8: **case** $Batch \rightarrow Batch$:
  Scout Bees Phase
  Onlooker Bees Phase

9: **case** $Batch \rightarrow SingleStep$:
  Scout Bees Phase

10: **until** all lots have found their last machine

To maintain the correct information, each machine $M_i^m \in W^m$ gets assigned a limit l which decreases each time a lot selects this particular machine $M_i^m \in W^m$. When $l = 0$, the machine M_i^m will lose its "evaluated" status. This will attract new l_{SB} to select and re-evaluate the machine. In this manner, new incoming l_{OB} will have an updated quality $Q(M_i^m)$ information to make the correct decision. The newly l_{SB} will be coming from the decision process of l_{OB} modeled lots. As the l_{OB} chooses the best machine $M_i^m \in W^m$ probabilistically, if the decision falls into the $1 - P_r(M_i^m)$ case, the l_{OB} will change its status completely to a l_{SB} modeled lot, and will choose its next machine randomly.

Case SingleStep to Batch. All lots that have a transition in their recipe P^t from a process performed by a single-step machine to a process performed by a batch machine will enter the Employed Bees Phase. When enqueued, lots await their turn to be processed by a machine M_i^m. By default, the single-step machine M_i^m follows the First-In-First-Out algorithm. However, if there are lots with the next recipe step corresponding to a process performed by a batch machine in the machine's queue Q_i^m, all these lots will enter the comparison procedure. The single-step machine will apply the greedy selection and process the lot that has the minimum values from the set $[\, n_{fs}, t_{M_i^m}]$, as in the case "0 to Batch". This will reduce the idling of lots that could have prevented semi-filled batch processing, as this is influencing production performance drastically.

Case Batch to Batch: The concept of selecting the next machine is similar to the case of "0 to Batch". As the already formed batch of lots needs to move to another batch machine, the machine selection will be performed on a whole group of lots, instead of individually.

Case Batch to SingleStep. Once a batch machine finishes processing lots that have the next P^m step at a single-step machine, it is important to distribute them across the corresponding workcenter W^m, as these lot waves introduce disturbances in the production performance. To prevent queue overload, the finished batch enters the Scout Bees Phase. Lots get randomly distributed over all machines $M^m \in W^m$.

5 The Bat Algorithm

5.1 Inspiration

Initially introduced in [44], the bat algorithm draws inspiration from the hunting patterns of microbats that rely on echolocation to detect and capture their prey. As most other metaheuristic algorithms inspired by behaviors encountered in nature, the bat algorithm is primarily applied to optimization problems, focusing on the top-down approach, as opposed to the bottom-up. The three fundamental principles derived from the behavior of microbats form the main idea behind the algorithm:

1. The first principle concerns the fact that bats use echolocation signals to determine the distance to their prey.
2. Bats move with a certain velocity (v_i) while occupying a specific position (x_i) with a fixed frequency (f_{min}). They can modify the loudness (A_0) and pulse rate $(r \in [0, 1])$ of their signal based on their proximity to the prey.
3. The loudness of the signal they emit ranges between maximum (A_0) and minimum (A_{min}), depending on how close the bat is to the prey.

After the initialization of the first bat population, new solutions are generated by adjusting the positions, frequencies, and velocities of the bats. The update happens at every time step. After the current best global solution is identified, a new local solution is generated around the best solution. The local solution is achieved through a random walk. Afterward, the loudness and the pulse rate of the signal are adjusted. The closer the bat is to the prey, the quitter the signal is (loudness decreases). However, the pulse rate of the signal increases with the proximity to the prey. Finally, the best overall solution is selected. Algorithm 3. provides a description of the pseudo-code for the original bat algorithm.

The standard bat algorithm is utilized as a global optimizer for problems in the solution space. However, adjustments have been made to the algorithm to adapt it to the bottom-up approach required for our specific objective.

5.2 The Bat Algorithm in a Bottom-Up Approach

We propose a mapping for the bottom-up bat algorithm to the production scheduling problem [39], similar to the approach used in the ABC algorithm:

- bats = machine, $M_i^m \in W^m, i = 1, 2, \ldots, I$
- prey = lot from one product, $l_n^t \in L^t, n = 1, 2, \ldots, N$

In this mapping, the M_i^m is associated with a workcenter $W^m \subset M$ which is a subset of all machines in the fab. The lots $l_n^t \in L^t$ in the algorithm have access to their corresponding R^t (sequence of process steps P^m), which indicates the required machine types for producing each lot.

Algorithm 3. Bat algorithm as global optimizer.

1: Initialization Phase (initialization of the bat population x_i, objective function f(x), frequency f_i at x_i, pulse rate r_i, velocity v_i and loudness A_i)
2: **repeat**
3:      Generate new solutions by adjusting position x_i, frequency f_i and velocity v_i
4:      Evaluate solutions and select the best one
5:      Generate new local solution around the best solution
6:      Generate new random solution (random fly)
7:      Adjust loudness A_i and pulse rate r_i
8:      Select the best solution x_*
9: **until** Cycle = Maximum Cycle Number or a Maximum CPU time

---

The original bat algorithm follows and models the swarm behavior of microbats searching for the nearest prey. The algorithm depends on various variables such as the frequency, position, and velocity of the bat population. The microbats emit an echolocation signal with which they orient themselves within their surroundings. The echolocation signal of the microbats is formalized through the pulse rate and the loudness. After the initialization of the parameters, solutions are produced with each new iteration of the algorithm by fine-tuning the parameters. The solutions are then assessed and the best one is chosen.

The original bat algorithm has undergone some substantial changes while being adapted to the bottom-up approach. The main adjustment that needed to be implemented was concerning the mobility of the agents. The original bat algorithm formalizes the movement of the bats with equations describing the position and the velocity of the bat population. When mapping the algorithm to the production scheduling problem the bats are mapped onto the machines that process the lots and the lots become the prey that the bats are searching for. However, since the machines in the factory are static, there is no need to use equations related to the movement of the bats. Instead, we reimagine the problem statement of the original algorithm from the bats using their echolocation signal to discover and reach nearby prey to the bats, now static, attracting/luring the prey towards them.

The distance between the bat and the prey is calculated using Eq. 3.

$$Dist = min \sum (\alpha \cdot P_{distr} + \beta \cdot Q_{distr}) \tag{3}$$

The equation represents the minimum value of the combined product (P_{distr}) and queue (Q_{distr}) distributions for a particular workcenter in the production process. It is calculated prior to the lot selecting a queue at the current workcenter based on the lot's recipe.

The weights of the equation, α and β, represent the parameters that are applied to the product and queue distributions, respectively. The values of the parameters α and β were assigned after testing, and based on testing it was determined that the values are 0.7 (for α) and 0.3 (for β).

The augend of the equation is the product distribution. Product distribution describes the distribution of lots of the same product type at a particular machine and within a workcenter, where the workcenter is the term to describe a group of machines that perform the same processing step in the fab. In Eq. 4 the nominator of the product distribution represents the quantity of the lots of a particular product type for a machine in the workcenter. The product type corresponds to the product type of the lot that is in the process of choosing the most optimal machine for processing. The denominator describes the sum of the lots with the before-mentioned product type for the entire workcenter.

$$P_{distr} = \frac{\sum_{j=1}^{num(M_i^m)} l_j^t}{\sum_{k=1}^{I} l_k^t} \tag{4}$$

The addend of the distance equation is the queue distribution. Queue distribution describes the distribution of queues at a particular machine and within a workcenter. Queues consist of lots waiting to be processed at a certain machine. In Eq. 5 the nominator of the queue distribution represents the length of the queue for an individual machine in the workcenter. The denominator describes the sum of all the queues within the workcenter.

$$Q_{distr} = \frac{qlen(M_i^m)}{\sum_{j=1}^{I} qlen_j(M_i^m)} \tag{5}$$

Product and queue distributions are calculated for every machine in the workcenter. The memory of each machine in the workcenter stores both the product and the queue distributions. After both distributions are computed for every machine, following Eq. 3, they are multiplied by their weights, summed up, and stored in memory, resulting in a list of values for each machine. The machine with the lowest distribution value within the workcenter is then selected to process the lot.

The solution outlined above is intended for a workcenter with single-step machines, machines that are able to process one lot at a time. For selecting the optimal machine in a workcenter with batch machines, which are able to process multiple lots of the same product type at once, we use the same mechanism as described in the Algorithm 2 for the "0 to Batch" and "Batch to Batch" cases in the bottom-up ABC.

The pseudo-code for the bottom-up bat algorithm can be seen in Algorithm 4.

6 The Glowworm Algorithm

6.1 Inspiration

The glowworm swarm algorithm presented in [2], is inspired by the phenomenon of bioluminescence that has been discovered in nature among several groups of insects such as Lampyridae, a family of beetles. It can be summarized under the umbrella of social algorithms that simulate the behaviour of organisms in terms of foraging, mating, warning, etc. The glowworm algorithm puts reliance on the capability of worms to produce light as a communication mechanism used for attracting prey or mates. The luminescence quantity that results from the chemical interactions inside the body of a worm, is associated with the worm as an indicator of its location quality in terms of the locally available resources. The brighter the worm is glowing, the closer to food resources or potential mates it is. Consequently, the glowworm is attracted to the brightest glowing worm in its neighbourhood and moves toward it. The glowworm algorithm is composed of four phases which are as follows:

Algorithm 4. Bottom-up bat algorithm.

1: Initialization Phase (initialization of the alpha, beta parameters, memory)
2: **repeat**
3:     **switch** $m_{singleStep} \rightarrow m_{batch}$ **do**

4:         **case** *SingleStep*:
        Calculate Q_{distr} for the WC;
        Calculate P_{distr} for the WC;
        Save Q_{distr} and P_{distr} to the memory of each machine of the WC;
        Calculate the weighted sum of the queue and product distributions for each machine in the WC;
        Save the weighted sum of the distributions (the distance) to memory of each machine of the WC;
        Choose the machine with the minimum weighted sum value (Choose the bat with the minimum distance to the prey);

5:         **case** *Batch*:
        Analogous to bottom-up ABC cases "case 0 → Batch" and "case Batch → Batch";

6: **until** all lots have found their last machine

Luminescence Value Update. The glow or luminescence value τ of each glowworm is a positive value that changes in every iteration t with respect to the quality of the current location of the worm and its previous luminescence value using the following formula:

$$\tau_j(t+1) = \max\{0, (1-\rho) \cdot \tau_j(t) + \gamma \cdot J_j(t+1)\} \tag{6}$$

where $\tau(t)$ is the past glow value, $\tau(t+1)$ the current glow value, and $J_j(t+1)$ presents the objective function, which is defined based on the context of the implementation, representing the cost of being moved to the current position. Additionally, γ describes the influence of updating the location, and ρ the evaporation constant that represents the impact of the past position on the current move. γ and ρ can take any value between 0 and 1 to preserve a harmony in the glowworm's steps.

Finding Glowing Neighbours. Since the intense luminosity reveals the location superiority of a glowworm, worm i explores if there are glowing worms within its neighbourhood and how bright these worms are, then the worm will be attracted to one of these glowing neighbouring worms j which is brighter than itself $\tau_i(t) < \tau_j(t)$.

Local Decision Range Update. Around each glowworm, two ranges are defined. The ranges are the local decision range r_d^i and the sensor range r_s^i. The sensor range, which is the maximum range that can be reached for finding neighbours, remains fixed during the execution time of the algorithm, whereas the local decision range that is used to control the size of the neighbourhood $N_i(t)$ around each worm shrinks or enlarges over time based on the number of surrounding glowworms in the worm's neighbourhood.

Location Update. The worm opts one of these brighter glowing neighbours stochastically and moves toward it. The probability that glowworm i moves towards a brighter neighbour j is given by:

$$P_{j(t)} = \frac{\tau_{j(t)} - \tau_{i(t)}}{\sum_{k \in N}(\tau_{k(t)} - \tau_{i(t)})} \qquad (7)$$

where $j \in N_i(t), d_{ij}(t)$ presents the Euclidean distance distance between glowworms i and $j, and \quad N_i(t) = \{j : d_{i,j}(t) < r_d^i(t) \text{ and } \tau_i(t) < \tau_j(t)\}$.

The pseudo-code of glowworm algorithm is illustrated in Algorithm 5.

Algorithm 5. Glowworm as global optimizer.

1: Initialize (the glowworm population with equal luminescence $\tau_i(0)$, local-decision range radius $r_d^i(0)$, and sensor range radius r_s^i)
2: **repeat**
3:    Luminescence value update
4:    Finding glowing neighbours
5:    Location update
6:    Local decision range update
7: **until** Cycle = Maximum cycle number or a maximum CPU time

---

6.2 The Glowworm Algorithm in a Bottom-Up Approach

To meet the requirements of the job-shop scheduling problem that is addressed in Sect. 2, the glowworm algorithm is adapted and introduced in a new design for a bottom-up approach as done with ABC and bat algorithms. For exploiting the glowworm algorithm in the explained model, the following mapping is proposed:

- Glowworms = Lots, $l_n \in L, n = 1, 2, \ldots, N$
- Resources = Machines, $M_i^m \in W^m, i = 1, 2, \ldots, I$
- Possible locations = Queues, $Q_{(M_i^m)}$

In the glowworm algorithm, the brighter glowworms attract other faded glowworms. Thus, a few groups of glowworms can cluster around available resources which is not desired in all cases of the production. The bottom-up approach glowworm algorithm is designed to tackle the difference between the encountered cases in the given model. For a good utilization, a fair usage of a single-step machine workcenter is recommended. Therefore, a dispersing mode is presented in this approach in order to spread the lots over the workcenter of single-step machines. Moreover, grouping of lots of the same product type in a queue of a batch machine is needed. Hence, the luminescence of the glowworms is given as a set of different colours which are used for the purpose of location update. The colour of the luminescence refers to the product type whereas there is no equivalent to the luminescence in the model. The glowworms of the same colour aim to form clusters seeking out the core concept of the glowworm algorithm in workcenters of batch machines, and to some extent try to be distributed in workcenters of single-step machines. The mapping is continued as follows:

- Colour = Product type
- Dispersing mode = Single step machines
- Clustering mode = Batch machines

The bottom-up approach glowworm algorithm is designed by retaining three main phases which are luminescence value update, finding glowing neighbours, and location update. The phase of local decision range update is not used because the lot only sees one step ahead. Accordingly, the local decision remains fixed equalling the vision range which is one step ahead in the recipe. The dynamics of this bottom-up approach are explained through the three phases as follows:

1. **Finding Glowing Neighbours.** The lots or the glowworms represent the active agents in the given model, whereas the machines are static agents. After the simulation is initialized, each lot $l^t \in L^t$ follow its recipe $R^t = \{P_1^m, P_2^n, \dots\}$. The type of the machine M^m that preforms the process p^m defines how the lot l^t finds its way to it. For single-step machines, the queue length of each machines in the workcenter is calculated. An empty workcenter means that the queue length of all single-step machines of this workcenter is 0. Therefore, the lot goes randomly to any of these machines. If the workcenter is not empty, the luminescence value τ of all lots with the same product type l^t on each queue is averaged using Eq. 10. Each queue is associated with its length and the average glow of the occupying lots of a specific product type l^t. Moreover, the queue length of the specific product type of each machine in the workcenter of batch machines is calculated. If the work-center does not contain any queue of this product type, the lot goes randomly to any machine. If the workcenter contains queues with the needed product type, each queue is associated with its length and the average glow of the occupying lots which is also calculated using Eq. 10.

2. **Location Update.** After the lot l^t explored the available positions or the possible queues, the likelihood of a queue to be chosen by the lot is based on two factors which are its length and the average luminescence value of its lots of the same product type. The queues are ranked. For queues of single step machine, the rank for each queue q is calculated as follows:

$$Rank_{(q)} = \alpha \cdot AVG(glow_{(q)}) - \beta \cdot Length_{(q)} \tag{8}$$

and for queues of batch machine, the rank is calculated as follows:

$$Rank_{(q)} = -\alpha \cdot AVG(glow_{(q)}) - \beta \cdot Length_{(q)} \tag{9}$$

with

$$AVG(glow_{(q)}) = \frac{1}{J} \sum_{j=1}^{J} \tau_j^t(t) \tag{10}$$

and α as the influence of the average luminescence on queue rank, and β as the influence of queue length influence on queue rank.

After the queues are ranked, the lot updates its location by choosing the queue with the highest rank.

3. **Luminescence Value Update.** The luminescence value update comes after the lot finishes its process and just before starting a new one. The lot updates the luminescence according to the chosen queue quality using Eq. 11. However, the objective function $J_j(t+1)$ is called correction factor in the bottom-up approach glowworm

algorithm. The target of the correction factor is to review the lot decision. It is calculated differently for the both types of machines: For single-step machines, the lots try to be dispersed. Therefore, if the lot finds no other lots of its product type in the queue of its processing machine, no correction is needed, so the correction factor takes its default value 1. But if the lot finds other lots of its product type, the correction is needed where the factor is calculated using Eq. 12. For batch machines, the lot of the same type need to cluster. If the lot is processed in a full batch, no correction is needed and the correction factor takes its default value 1. But if the lot is not processed in a full batch, the correction is needed where the factor is calculated using Eq. 13.

$$\tau_j(t+1) = \max\{0, (1-\rho) \cdot \tau_j(t) + \gamma \cdot CF\} \tag{11}$$

For single-step machines the correction factor is

$$CF_s = (2 - \frac{\sum l^t(q)}{max \sum l^t(q_{wc})}) \tag{12}$$

where $\sum l^t(q)$ presents the sum of lots of product type t of the queue of the processing machine, and $max \sum l^t(q_{wc})$ the maximum sum of lots of product type t of a queue in the workcenter. For batch machines the correction factor is

$$CF_b = (1 - \frac{\sum l^t}{BS}) + 1 \tag{13}$$

where $\sum l^t$ presents the sum of processed lots, and BS the batch size.

The pseudo-code of the bottom-up approach glowworm algorithm is illustrated in Algorithm 6. Table 1 is used to initialize the parameters of the bottom-up approach glowworm algorithm.

Table 1. Parameter setting for the bottom-up approach of the glowworm algorithm.

Parameter	Value
$\tau_i(0)$	random (0.1)
γ	0.5
ρ	0.5
α	0.5
β	0.5

7   Evaluation and Results

7.1   Simulation Environment

We use the free agent-based simulation platform NetLogo [42] on top of which we implemented a simulation framework SwarmFabSim that models the production plant

---

Algorithm 6. Bottom-up glowworm algorithm.

1: Initialization Phase using Table 1
2: **repeat**
3: | **switch** machine type **do**

4: | **case Single Step**:
    calculate $Length_{(q)}$;
    calculate $AVG(glow_{(q)})$ using (10);
    rank all queues using (8);

5: | **case Batch**:
    calculate $Length_{(q)}$;
    calculate $AVG(glow_{(q)})$ using (10);
    rank all queues using (9);

6: | Choose a machine: choose the q of the highest $rank_q$
7: | Luminescence value update using (11)
8: **until** all lots have finished their last process at the machine

---

with its machines, queues, and lots to be produced which are all realized as different types of agents. Our framework supports plugging in and evaluating different optimization algorithms. We use NetLogo BehaviorSpace to control the simulation runs and the R statistics package to post-process the resulting log files. A detailed description of our simulation framework can be found in [40]. The source code and necessary configuration files can be obtained at our GitHub repository[3]. In overview, our simulation works as follows: once per time tick, the main simulation loop is run and drives the movement of lots through the factory:

– First, each lot that is not currently being processed, in a queue, or already finished gets to choose the next queue/machine via the *choose-queue* callback to the currently active algorithm.
– Secondly, every machine that is not currently processing chooses the next lot (or, in case of a batch machine, a set of lots) from its respective queue via the *take-from-queue* callback to the currently active algorithm.
– Thirdly, the *move-out* callback is called after the lot(s) has/have finished processing, to enable the algorithm to communicate information or perform other updates before the lot(s) move to the next queue.
– Finally, two more algorithm callbacks (*tick-start, tick-end*) enable updates such as, e.g., the degradation of pheromones at the beginning and/or end of every tick.

7.2   The Baseline Algorithm

For performance comparison, we provide an algorithm called "Baseline". This algorithm uses simple heuristics and, for comparability to the swarm algorithms, only local information to make its decisions. Ideally, one would like to calculate an optimal schedule as a comparison, but since we want to consider large problem sizes, calculating an

---

[3] https://swarmfabsim.github.io.

optimal global solution is infeasible. In real-world production plants, such as the one from Infineon Technologies Austria AG, of course more sophisticated approaches are used; these typically contain corporate secrets and involve sophisticated re-scheduling of machine queues based on several levels of lot priorities and other constraints (e.g., taking lot deadlines into account).

Baseline has two modes: For single-step oriented machines, it chooses the machine with the shortest queue from the workcenter that is able to perform the required next processing step. It also does not re-schedule lots in the queue. I.o.w. in this mode, baseline uses a simple shortest queue/FIFO heuristic.

For batch machines, the aim is to assign lots to machines in such a way that batches are filled as fast and as full as possible before a process is started. This way, the machine will run at maximum capacity, neither with a semi-filled batch nor sit idle. We therefore adapted the real-world strategy of waiting for a time WT to try and fill up a batch before starting a batch machine. When assigning a lot to a batch machine, the baseline algorithm checks all potential machines whether they already have a semi-filled batch of the same product type in their queue. If there are several semi-filled batches, the lot is assigned to the batch with the least missing lots. Once a batch fills up, an idling machine does not have to wait for the WT timer to finish and can immediately start processing that batch. Therefore, this strategy reduces idle times on batch machines. If there is not yet a semi-filled batch of the correct product type, the algorithm starts a new batch at the machine with the least overall sum of lots in the queue. If no batch fills up during the waiting time WT, the machine processes the largest semi-filled batch available. In case of contention, when either several full batches or several semi-filled batches of the same size are available in the queue when the batch machine gets to take from its queue (after finishing processing the previous batch), a batch is chosen at random.

In our version of baseline, we deliberately keep the information horizon as small as possible and therefore do neither implement communications with other machines nor consider the interplay between single-step machines and batch machines.

7.3 Simulation Settings

We use a small (SFAB), a medium-sized (MEDIUM), and a large (LFAB) scenario of a fab with different numbers of machines and machine types. Parameter details are given in Table 2.

Table 2. Parameters used to create the three evaluation scenarios. Table reproduced from [39].

Parameter	SFAB	MEDIUM	LFAB
Mach. types	25	50	100
Mach./type	$U(2,5)$	$U(2,10)$	$U(2,10)$
Product types	50	50	100
Recipe length	$U(90,110)$	$U(90,110)$	$U(90,110)$
Lots per type	$U(1,10)$	$U(1,10)$	$U(2,10)$

The parameters used to create the machines are shown in Table 3. For raw process time, $N(\mu,\sigma^2)$ denotes the Normal Distribution. Negative values from the normal distribution have been capped as process time can not be negative. For batch size and waiting time at batch machines, $U(a, b)$ denotes the uniform distribution.

Table 3. Machine parameters used in the simulation. Table reproduced from [39].

Machine Parameter	Value
Raw process time	$N(\mu,\sigma^2)$ with $\mu = 1.16$, $\sigma^2 = 0.32$
Probability batch machine	50%
Batch size batch machines	$U(2, 8)$
Waiting time batch machines	$U(1, 2)$

7.4 Results and Discussion

In the following, we evaluate the performance of the developed algorithms according to the following metrics:

- Makespan (MS): the time (in simulation ticks) it takes to produce all lots ordered from the plant, from start to finish. The lots are all introduced into the fab at the start of the simulation.
- Flow Factor (FF): the factor between the time incurred to actually produce a lot over the time it would theoretically take to produce (I.o.w. pure production time without any waiting times in queues). We calculate the average flow factor over all lots produced.
- Tardiness (TRD): our model does not contain deadlines for the production of lots. Therefore, in our model tardiness is not calculated w.r.t. to a deadline but rather describes how late (in simulation ticks) a lot is w.r.t. to the time it would have taken to produce if zero queue waiting times had been incurred. We calculate the average tardiness over all lots produced.
- Machine Utilization (UTL): is calculated as the percentage of time ticks machines are used on average w.r.t. to the total number of simulation time ticks (normalized by the number of machines).

Tables 4, 5, and 6 depict a comparison between the performance of the reference algorithm "Baseline" and the ABC, bat, and glowworm-inspired algorithms. For the evaluation, each scenario setting has been run 30 times, and averaged.

The performance evaluation shows that the ABC algorithm performs slightly worse than Baseline for the SFAB and LFAB scenarios and worse in the MEDIUM scenario. For the bat algorithm, SFAB and LFAB scenarios depict very promising improvements, while the MEDIUM scenario performs worse. The glowworm algorithm improves the utilization in all scenarios compared to Baseline. However, it performs slightly worse in SFAB and much worse in MEDIUM and LFAB with regards to the other key performance indicators. Additionally, the glowworm algorithm has been tested with eight different parameters settings, but the parametric study showed negligible differences in outcomes.

Table 4. Small Scenario (SFAB). Changes in %, positive values denote improvement over Baseline. Table reproduced from [39] and extended.

	Baseline	ABC	Change	Bat	Change	Glow	Change
MS	10398	10838	−4.2%	9851	5.3%	12004.6	−15.45%
FF	6.51	6.55	−0.6%	5.24	19.6%	7.10	−8.96%
TRD	6971.1	7031.5	−0.9%	5312.5	23.8%	7689.83	−10.31 %
UTL	35.90	33.74	6.0%	32.58	9.2%	31.98	10.90%

Table 5. Medium Scenario (MEDIUM). Changes in %, positive values denote improvement over Baseline. Table reproduced from [39] and extended.

	Baseline	ABC	Change	Bat	Change	Glow	Change
MS	4536	5403	−19.1%	5604	−23.5%	9629.13	−112.27%
FF	3.21	3.36	−4.9%	3.30	−2.8%	6.48	−101.91%
TRD	2481.8	2656.0	−7.0%	2576.9	−3.8%	6152.07	−147.89 %
UTL	23.87	19.58	18.0%	19.34	19.0%	12.72	46.73%

Table 6. Large Scenario (LFAB). Changes in %, positive values denote improvement over Baseline. Table reproduced from [39] and extended.

	Baseline	ABC	Change	Bat	Change	Glow	Change
MS	6207	6528	−6.0%	5790	6.7%	10319.2	−66.25 %
FF	3.47	3.54	−1.9%	2.78	20.0%	5.84	−68.28 %
TRD	3126.8	3210.38	−2.7%	2244.0	28.2%	6124.50	−95.87 %
UTL	22.71	20.37	10.3%	23.94	−5.4%	15.58	31.40 %

As described in Sect. 2, our understanding is that the job shop problem is exacerbated by the switch between single-step oriented and batch machines. Therefore, an algorithm like Baseline, that pursues a strategy to best fill semi-filled batches (and therefore reduces idling time and inefficient use of batch machines) is hard to beat by algorithms that only employ local calculations to decide queue assignment. This has also been observed in our previous work [40], where we show how a hormone algorithm [5] that spreads information (in the form of artificial hormones) back several machines is able to consistently beat Baseline while an ant algorithm that uses only local pheromones (at the current workcenter) is not. In general, an optimal algorithm for this problem should take these switches from single-step to batch machines and vice versa explicitly into account. We are therefore planning to improve on the proposed algorithms in the future by increasing the size of the local neighborhood by looking several machines "ahead" and anticipating switches between machine kinds.

8 Conclusion

This chapter has proposed the use of three bio-inspired algorithms, namely the artificial bee colony (ABC), the bat, and the glowworm algorithm in a bottom-up manner to tackle the problem of optimization for a semiconductor fab using the job-shop manufacturing principle. In contrast to prior approaches that utilize these algorithms for global optimization within the solution space, we diverge by adopting a bottom-up strategy. We directly implement these algorithms as verbatim swarm intelligence algorithms, without applying them to solutions within the solution space. In our approach, the active agents, such as artificial bees, bats, and glowworms, are mapped to actual entities present in the production plant. These agents rely exclusively on information from their local neighborhood to make decisions, and through their interactions, the global solution naturally emerges. To assess the performance of the proposed algorithms in comparison to an engineered baseline algorithm, we conducted simulations of the fab using the NetLogo platform. Four key performance indicators, namely makespan, flow factor, tardiness, and machine uptime utilization, were employed for evaluation. The results obtained indicate that these algorithms, when implemented in a bottom-up fashion, exhibit promising performance enhancements. Despite relying on low-effort local calculations, they demonstrate the potential to improve various aspects of the production process. The simulation environment's implementation has been openly released in a Git repository[4], allowing for easy access, collaboration, and contribution from other researchers and interested community.

Future work will concentrate on investigating what we think are the two most promising areas for improvement: 1) the impact of the size of the local neighborhood used for calculations in the respective algorithms (eg. by looking ahead or back several machines) and 2) especially on adaptations to explicitly address the switching between single-step oriented machines and batch machines as we believe this to be the core of the problem. This is due to the fact that batch machines create waves of product when they finish processing a batch. These waves then negatively influence subsequent single-step oriented machines because they disrupt the uniform arrival times that would be optimal according to queueing theory. In turn, single-step oriented machines can delay the accumulation of a complete batch at later batch machines if all lots "belonging" to a batch are stuck in the same queue. This would then lead to batch machines either idle-waiting for a batch to fill up or running with semi-filled batches. Our hypothesis is that an optimal algorithm would use a strategy of actively dispersing a wave of lots coming from a batch machine over several, parallel single-step oriented machines and later collect these lots again into a full batch at subsequent batch machines.

Acknowledgements. This work was performed in the course of project ML&Swarms supported by KWF-React EU under contract number KWF-20214|34789|50819, and SwarmIn supported by FFG under contract number 894072.

---

[4] https://swarmfabsim.github.io.

References

1. Alvarado-Iniesta, A., Garcia-Alcaraz, J.L., Rodriguez-Borbon, M.I., Maldonado, A.: Optimization of the material flow in a manufacturing plant by use of artificial bee colony algorithm. Expert Syst. Appl. **40**(12), 4785–4790 (2013)
2. Brabazon, A., O'Neill, M., McGarraghy, S.: Natural computing algorithms. In: Rozenberg, G., Bäck, T., Kari, L., Stepney, S. (eds.) Natural Computing Series, pp. 201–205. Springer, Heidelberg (2015). https://doi.org/10.1007/978-3-662-43631-8
3. Chen, X., Zhang, B., Gao, D.: An improved bat algorithm for job shop scheduling problem. In: 2019 IEEE International Conference on Mechatronics and Automation (ICMA), pp. 439–443. IEEE (2019)
4. Dao, T.K., Pan, T.S., Pan, J.S., et al.: Parallel bat algorithm for optimizing makespan in job shop scheduling problems. J. Intell. Manuf. **29**(2), 451–462 (2018)
5. Elmenreich, W., Schnabl, A., Schranz, M.: An artificial hormone-based algorithm for production scheduling from the bottom-up. In: Proceedings of the 13th International Conference on Agents and Artificial Intelligence. SciTePress (2021)
6. Fang, Y., Tang, M.: Scheduling optimization of watt-hour meters' automatic production line based on improved GSO method. In: 11th IEEE International Conference on Control & Automation (ICCA), pp. 1045–1049 (2014). https://doi.org/10.1109/ICCA.2014.6871064
7. Gao, K.Z., Suganthan, P.N., Chua, T.J., Chong, C.S., Cai, T.X., Pan, Q.K.: A two-stage artificial bee colony algorithm scheduling flexible job-shop scheduling problem with new job insertion. Expert Syst. Appl. **42**(21), 7652–7663 (2015)
8. Gao, K.Z., Suganthan, P.N., Pan, Q.K., Tasgetiren, M.F., Sadollah, A.: Artificial bee colony algorithm for scheduling and rescheduling fuzzy flexible job shop problem with new job insertion. Knowl.-Based Syst. **109**, 1–16 (2016)
9. Gao, K., Cao, Z., Zhang, L., Chen, Z., Han, Y., Pan, Q.: A review on swarm intelligence and evolutionary algorithms for solving flexible job shop scheduling problems. IEEE/CAA J. Autom. Sinica **6**(4), 904–916 (2019)
10. Gupta, M., Sharma, G.: An efficient modified artificial bee colony algorithm for job scheduling problem. Int. J. Soft Comput. Eng. (IJSCE) **1**(6) (2012)
11. Han, Y.Y., Pan, Q.K., Li, J.Q., Sang, H.Y.: An improved artificial bee colony algorithm for the blocking flowshop scheduling problem. Int. J. Adv. Manuf. Technol. **60**(9–12), 1149–1159 (2012)
12. Jayabarathi, T., Raghunathan, T., Gandomi, A.H.: The bat algorithm, variants and some practical engineering applications: a review. In: Yang, X.-S. (ed.) Nature-Inspired Algorithms and Applied Optimization. SCI, vol. 744, pp. 313–330. Springer, Cham (2018). https://doi.org/10.1007/978-3-319-67669-2_14
13. Jing, L., Song, H., Lv, X.: Research and application on job shop planning based on improved glowworm swarm optimization algorithm. In: 2013 5th International Conference on Intelligent Human-Machine Systems and Cybernetics, vol. 2, pp. 139–143 (2013). https://doi.org/10.1109/IHMSC.2013.180
14. Karaboga, D.: Artificial bee colony algorithm. Scholarpedia **5**(3), 6915 (2010)
15. Karaboga, D., Basturk, B.: A powerful and efficient algorithm for numerical function optimization: artificial bee colony (ABC) algorithm. J. Global Optim. **39**(3), 459–471 (2007)
16. Karaboga, D., Gorkemli, B., Ozturk, C., Karaboga, N.: A comprehensive survey: artificial bee colony (ABC) algorithm and applications. Artif. Intell. Rev. **42**(1), 21–57 (2014)
17. Khader, A.T., Al-betar, M.A., Mohammed, A.A.: Artificial bee colony algorithm, its variants and applications: a survey. J. Theor. Appl. Inf. Technol. **47**(2), 434–459 (2013)
18. Khatmi, E., et al.: Swarm intelligence layer to control autonomous agents (SWILT). In: STAF (Co-Located Events), pp. 91–96 (2019)

19. Krishnanand, K., Ghose, D.: Detection of multiple source locations using a glowworm metaphor with applications to collective robotics. In: Proceedings 2005 IEEE Swarm Intelligence Symposium, SIS 2005, pp. 84–91 (2005). https://doi.org/10.1109/SIS.2005.1501606
20. Kumar, A., Kumar, D., Jarial, S.: A review on artificial bee colony algorithms and their applications to data clustering. Cybern. Inf. Technol. **17**(3), 3–28 (2017)
21. Kumar, S., Sharma, V.K., Kumari, R.: A novel hybrid crossover based artificial bee colony algorithm for optimization problem. arXiv preprint arXiv:1407.5574 (2014)
22. Lawler, E.L., Lenstra, J.K., Kan, A.H.R., Shmoys, D.B.: Sequencing and scheduling: algorithms and complexity. Handb. Oper. Res. Manage. Sci. **4**, 445–522 (1993)
23. Lei, J., Xiaoying, Z., Labao, Z., Kun, W.: Coordinated scheduling of electric vehicles and wind power generation considering vehicle to grid mode. In: 2017 IEEE Transportation Electrification Conference and Expo, Asia-Pacific (ITEC Asia-Pacific), pp. 1–5 (2017). https://doi.org/10.1109/ITEC-AP.2017.8081021
24. Li, J.Q., Pan, Q.K.: Solving the large-scale hybrid flow shop scheduling problem with limited buffers by a hybrid artificial bee colony algorithm. Inf. Sci. **316**, 487–502 (2015)
25. Li, J.Q., Pan, Q.K., Tasgetiren, M.F.: A discrete artificial bee colony algorithm for the multi-objective flexible job-shop scheduling problem with maintenance activities. Appl. Math. Model. **38**(3), 1111–1132 (2014)
26. Liu, Y.F., Liu, S.Y.: A hybrid discrete artificial bee colony algorithm for permutation flow-shop scheduling problem. Appl. Soft Comput. **13**(3), 1459–1463 (2013)
27. Lu, Y., Jiang, T.: Bi-population based discrete bat algorithm for the low-carbon job shop scheduling problem. IEEE Access **7**, 14513–14522 (2019)
28. Luo, Q., Zhou, Y., Xie, J., Ma, M., Li, L.: Discrete bat algorithm for optimal problem of permutation flow shop scheduling. Sci. World J. **2014** (2014)
29. Marichelvam, M., Prabaharan, T., Yang, X.S., Geetha, M.: Solving hybrid flow shop scheduling problems using bat algorithm. Int. J. Logist. Econ. Glob. **5**(1), 15–29 (2013)
30. Musikapun, P., Pongcharoen, P.: Solving multi-stage multi-machine multi-product scheduling problem using bat algorithm. In: 2nd International Conference on Management and Artificial Intelligence, vol. 35, pp. 98–102. IACSIT Press, Singapore (2012)
31. Pan, Q.K., Tasgetiren, M.F., Suganthan, P.N., Chua, T.J.: A discrete artificial bee colony algorithm for the lot-streaming flow shop scheduling problem. Inf. Sci. **181**(12), 2455–2468 (2011)
32. Pan, Q.K., Wang, L., Li, J.Q., Duan, J.H.: A novel discrete artificial bee colony algorithm for the hybrid flowshop scheduling problem with makespan minimisation. Omega **45**, 42–56 (2014)
33. Schranz, M., Umlauft, M., Elmenreich, W.: Bottom-up job shop scheduling with swarm intelligence in large production plants. In: Proceedings of the 11th International Conference on Simulation and Modeling, Methodologies, Technologies and Applications (SIMULTECH), pp. 327–334 (2021)
34. Senthilnath, J., Omkar, S., Mani, V.: Clustering using firefly algorithm: performance study. Swarm Evol. Comput. **1**(3), 164–171 (2011). https://doi.org/10.1016/j.swevo.2011.06.003
35. Sharma, N., Sharma, H., Sharma, A.: Beer froth artificial bee colony for job-shop scheduling problem. Appl. Soft Comput. **68**, 507–524 (2018)
36. Sharma, T.K., Pant, M.: Shuffled artificial bee colony algorithm. Soft. Comput. **21**(20), 6085–6104 (2017)
37. Stidham, S., Jr.: Analysis, design, and control of queueing systems. Oper. Res. **50**(1), 197–216 (2002)
38. Tasgetiren, M.F., Pan, Q.K., Suganthan, P., Oner, A.: A discrete artificial bee colony algorithm for the no-idle permutation flowshop scheduling problem with the total tardiness criterion. Appl. Math. Model. **37**(10–11), 6758–6779 (2013)

39. Umlauft, M., Gojkovic, M., Harshina, K., Schranz, M.: Bottom-up bio-inspired algorithms for optimizing industrial plants. In: Proc. 15th International Conference on Agents and Artificial Intelligence (ICAART). INSTICC, SciTePress (2023)
40. Umlauft, M., Schranz, M., Elmenreich, W.: SwarmFabSim: a simulation framework for bottom-up optimization in flexible job-shop scheduling using netlogo. In: Proceedings of the 12th International Conference on Simulation and Modeling Methodologies, Technologies and Applications (SIMULTECH), vol. 1, pp. 271–279. INSTICC, SciTePress (2022). https://doi.org/10.5220/0011274700003274
41. Wang, L., Zhou, G., Xu, Y., Liu, M.: An enhanced pareto-based artificial bee colony algorithm for the multi-objective flexible job-shop scheduling. Int. J. Adv. Manuf. Technol. **60**(9–12), 1111–1123 (2012)
42. Wilensky, U.: Netlogo. Webpage (1999). Center for Connected Learning and Computer-Based Modeling, Northwestern University, Evanston, IL. http://ccl.northwestern.edu/netlogo/
43. Xu, H., Bao, Z., Zhang, T.: Solving dual flexible job-shop scheduling problem using a bat algorithm. Adv. Prod. Eng. Manage. **12**(1) (2017)
44. Yang, X.S.: A new metaheuristic bat-inspired algorithm. In: González, J.R., Pelta, D.A., Cruz, C., Terrazas, G., Krasnogor, N. (eds.) Nature Inspired Cooperative Strategies for Optimization (NICSO 2010). Studies in Computational Intelligence, vol. 284, pp. 65–74. Springer, Heidelberg (2010). https://doi.org/10.1007/978-3-642-12538-6_6
45. Yang, X.S., He, X.: Bat algorithm: literature review and applications. Int. J. Bio-Inspir. Comput. **5**(3), 141–149 (2013)
46. Yao, B.Z., Yang, C.Y., Hu, J.J., Yin, G.D., Yu, B.: An improved artificial bee colony algorithm for job shop problem. In: Applied Mechanics and Materials, vol. 26, pp. 657–660. Trans Tech Publ (2010)
47. Yurtkuran, A., Emel, E.: A modified artificial bee colony algorithm for-center problems. Sci. World J. **2014** (2014)
48. Zhang, R., Song, S., Wu, C.: A hybrid artificial bee colony algorithm for the job shop scheduling problem. Int. J. Prod. Econ. **141**(1), 167–178 (2013)
49. Zhao-Ming, L., Fan, Z., Wen-Zhe, L., Peng-Cheng, W.: An improved glowworm swarm optimization for vehicle scheduling in the iron and steel plant logistics. In: 2018 24th International Conference on Automation and Computing (ICAC), pp. 1–6 (2018). https://doi.org/10.23919/IConAC.2018.8749065
50. Zhu, H., He, B., Li, H.: Modified bat algorithm for the multi-objective flexible job shop scheduling problem. Int. J. Perform. Eng. **13**(7), 999 (2017)
51. Zhuang, Z., Huang, Z., Lu, Z., Guo, L., Cao, Q., Qin, W.: An improved artificial bee colony algorithm for solving open shop scheduling problem with two sequence-dependent setup times. Procedia CIRP **83**, 563–568 (2019)

Estimating the Spread of COVID-19 Due to Transportation Networks Using Agent-Based Modeling

Ruturaj Godse[1(✉)] , Shikha Bhat[1] , Shruti Mestry[1] , and Vinayak Naik[1,2(✉)]

[1] CSIS, BITS Pilani, Sancoale, Goa, India
{f20190002,f20190063,2020proj031,naik}@bits-pilani.ac.in
[2] APPCAIR, BITS Pilani, Sancoale, Goa, India

Abstract. Governments worldwide have faced unprecedented challenges in managing the COVID-19 pandemic, particularly in implementing effective lockdown policies and devising transportation plans. As infections continue to surge exponentially, the need for carefully regulating travel has become paramount. However, existing research has struggled to address this issue comprehensively for India, a country characterized by diverse transportation networks and a vast population spread across different states. This study aims to fill this crucial research gap by analyzing the spread of infection, recovery, and mortality in the state of Goa, India, over a twenty-eight-day period. Through the use of agent-based simulations, we investigate how individuals interact and transmit the virus while utilizing trains, flights, and buses in two key scenarios: unrestricted and restricted local movements. By conducting a detailed comparison of all transportation modes in these two distinct lockdown settings, we examine the speed and intensity of infection spread. Our findings reveal that trains contribute to the highest transmission rates within the state, followed by flights and then buses. Notably, the combined effect of all modes of transport is not merely additive, emphasizing the urgent need for analysis to prevent infections from surpassing critical thresholds.

Keywords: Agent-based simulation · COVID-19 · Artificial intelligence

1 Introduction

The Severe Acute Respiratory Syndrome CoronaVirus 2 (SARS-CoV-2), popularly known as COVID-19, has unleashed unprecedented challenges upon the world in recent years. Within a mere three months, the virus managed to spread like wildfire to over a hundred countries, prompting the World Health Organization to declare it a global pandemic. The primary mode of transmission for this highly contagious disease is through respiratory droplets and physical contact between infected individuals. With the urgency to prevent a similar catastrophic spread, it becomes imperative to delve into the study of disease transmission using advanced epidemiological modeling techniques.

Traditional mathematical models, while useful, rely on fixed values that produce a singular outcome. However, in order to capture the complexity of real-life scenarios,

---

R. Godse and S. Bhat—These authors contributed equally to this work.

A. P. Rocha et al. (Eds.): ICAART 2023, LNAI 14546, pp. 26–47, 2024.
https://doi.org/10.1007/978-3-031-55326-4_2

stochastic computer simulations utilizing agent-based models have emerged as a more effective approach. Agent-based models depict autonomous entities (agents) interacting within an environment, thus reflecting the dynamics of real-world systems. In this context, our research focuses on investigating the spread of COVID-19 in the state of Goa, India, by employing an agent-based simulation developed in the NetLogo software. This simulation incorporates spatial data related to population and transportation networks, enabling us to estimate the impact of railway, road, and airway travel on the disease's dissemination.

Through the simulation, individual agents traverse the transportation networks, mirroring human behavior and interactions. By introducing various factors, such as different transportation frequencies and imposing restrictions on local movements, we observe the escalation of infections and recoveries within the population over time. The simulation provides invaluable insights into critical aspects, such as determining the minimum number of vehicles required to curtail the spread, analyzing the rate of infection growth, and evaluating the effectiveness of movement restrictions, such as lockdown measures. Consequently, the model helps individuals comprehend the range of scenarios that can occur under different degrees of movement, enabling policymakers to formulate effective strategies to mitigate the disease's transmission.

To ensure the credibility of our research, we validate the simulation by comparing its results with real-world data. In the subsequent sections, we discuss prior research endeavors in pandemic modeling, outline the problem statements addressed in this study, and elucidate the methodology employed to tackle the research questions. Furthermore, we provide a comprehensive account of the implementation details of our simulation model and present the results obtained from our experimentation. Finally, the conclusion offers a summary of the paper's findings and explores potential avenues for further extension and exploration of the presented work.

In this study, we make several significant additions to the existing research on the impact of transportation on the spread of COVID-19. Specifically, we incorporate new findings that contribute to a deeper understanding of the subject matter. This is an extended version of the paper that appeared in ICAART'23 [4]. These additions include the following.

1. Quantifying the total number of deaths: We introduce an analysis that focuses on quantifying the total number of deaths by manipulating the frequency of each vehicle. By examining the relationship between vehicle frequency and mortality rates, we gain valuable insights into the severity of the disease spread in different transportation scenarios.
2. Analyzing the time to reach the peak of infections: Another crucial aspect we investigate is the number of days required to reach the peak of infections. By varying the frequencies of each transport mode, we analyze the temporal dynamics of the disease. This information aids in understanding the speed and intensity of the disease spread under different transportation conditions.
3. Comparative analysis of restricted and unrestricted movements: Additionally, we conduct a comprehensive comparison between the scenarios of restricted and unrestricted movements of people. By examining the number of infections in these distinct movement scenarios, we gain insights into the effectiveness of local movement

restrictions in mitigating the spread of the disease. This analysis allows us to evaluate the impact of different policy measures and guide decision-making processes for implementing effective control strategies.

4. A summary of results: We have a table for a summary of results for a quick understanding of the quantitative estimates and conclusions drawn from the simulations.

By incorporating these novel elements into our research, we contribute to the existing body of knowledge by providing a more comprehensive and nuanced understanding of the interplay between transportation, movement restrictions, and disease transmission. These findings have significant implications for public health policies and interventions aimed at minimizing the spread of COVID-19.

2   Literature Review

Analyzing how the infection spreads among people and observing the emerging patterns have become crucial in understanding the global COVID-19 pandemic. Researchers have explored various approaches to modeling the spread of the virus, with a focus on implementing effective lockdown policies and non-pharmaceutical interventions. Mathematical modeling has played a crucial role in understanding the COVID-19 outbreak. Previous studies have utilized various deterministic approaches, ranging from simple mathematical equations [11] to complex nonlinear differential equations [7] and even fractional order mathematical modeling [2]. These deterministic models, such as the Susceptible, Exposed, Infected, and Recovered (SEIR) model, have proven to be valuable tools in epidemiology. [8] However, incorporating realistic population networks into these models can be challenging. To address this limitation, the integration of stochastic parameters with the SEIR techniques has been proposed, aiming to develop a more comprehensive and accurate representation of the real-world situation. Notably, agent-based models with stochastic parameters present a compelling avenue [6]. Such models delve into the intricate movements and interactions of individuals, thereby capturing the essence of the spreading phenomenon. An exemplary contribution by Wilder et al. [12] manifests in their stochastic SEIR agent-based model, which scrutinizes the influence of age distribution and family structure. Burman [5] created an agent-based model for disease spread applicable to any geographical location and socio-economic structure. To extend the understanding of this global predicament, our study adopts an agent-based modeling approach to investigate the transmission of the disease within local communities and among individuals traversing diverse transportation systems.

Barat et al. [3] proposed an agent-based model that captures movements within and between places. Our study delves into various such aspects, such as the geospatial representation of a state, local movement restrictions, and the influence of different vehicular travel on disease transmission. Despite the significance of transportation networks in COVID-19 spread, limited research has explored this phenomenon in the Indian context. In our study, we employ time-specific restrictions during lockdown scenarios, utilizing software such as QGIS and NetLogo to create a simulated geospatial environment in Goa. Previously, Talekar et al. [10] implemented cohort strategies within a city-scale agent-based epidemic simulator, investigating the impact of grouping agents during travel on Mumbai railways. In contrast, our simulation-based model treats each agent as an independent entity residing in both restricted and unrestricted lockdown scenarios. By separately modeling trains, flights, and buses, we uncover substantial disparities in terms of infection transmission among these modes of transport. In contrast to Talekar et al.'s [10] focus solely on the effect of creating cohorts for train travel, our study takes a broader approach. We aim to enhance transportation and lockdown policies within a state by leveraging insights gleaned from our agent-based simulation.

3   Problem Statements

To enable the resumption of socio-economic activities, it is crucial to comprehend the spread of infection through transportation networks. This understanding will aid in formulating effective lockdown measures and offer insights into predicting future outbreaks. Therefore, the simulation study aims to achieve the following objectives -

1. Quantify the total infections by changing the frequency of each vehicle.
2. Quantify the total number of deaths by changing the frequency of each vehicle.
3. Determine an upper limit on the number of allowed transport vehicles while ensuring the maximum number of infections remains below 20%.
4. Find the number of days taken to attain a peak in the number of infected people with varying frequencies of each transport mode.
5. Compare the number of infections in the scenarios of restricted and unrestricted movements of people.
6. Assess the model's validity by comparing and establishing correlations with real-world data.

4   Research Methods

In this section, we provide a comprehensive description of our research methodology and elaborate on how our simulation works.

The key components of our simulation model encompass the agents, the environment they inhabit and traverse, and the interactions between agents that facilitate the transmission of the disease.

4.1   Agents

In order to replicate the transmission of the COVID-19 disease among the human population in Goa, we establish a simulation framework using agents that represent individuals within the GIS space. To maintain scalability, we create a downscaled population model of Goa, generating a proportional number of agents for each district. These agents have the ability to move within and across districts, utilizing various modes of transportation, such as trains, flights, or buses. Consequently, they can become exposed to the disease and subsequently infect others.

Within the simulation, we classify individuals currently present in the state as a category of *persons*, while those in transit via train, flight, or bus are categorized as *passengers*. Each person is associated with a specific district variable, enabling us to track their district of origin. On the other hand, passengers possess a vehicle variable, such as a flight or train number, which determines their location as it corresponds to the vehicle's movement.

4.2 SEIRD Framework

Our model adopts the SEIRD framework, which stands for Susceptible - Exposed - Infected - Recovered - Deceased, to illustrate the progression of the disease within individual agents. Among the various epidemic modeling approaches available, the SEIRD framework offers a comprehensive understanding by encompassing every stage of the disease.

In our simulation, individuals are permitted to travel and interact with one another, facilitating potential disease transmission. Each individual is assigned a variable that tracks their disease progression status, following the S-E-I-R-D categories. At the initiation of the simulation, certain individuals are already infected, while others remain susceptible to the disease. As individuals move and come into contact with others, they can become exposed to the disease. Over time, and subject to infection probabilities, exposed individuals may transition into the infected state. Following a designated recovery period, infected individuals have the chance to either recover or continue to remain infected, based on individualized recovery probabilities. Moreover, the simulation incorporates the evaluation of mortality probabilities. If infected individuals meet the criteria for death, they are subsequently removed from the simulation.

4.3 Simulation Environment

Data Collection. To establish the transportation networks in Goa, we utilize datasets obtained from OpenStreetMap through the QGIS software [9] and generate specific shapefiles for our model. These shapefiles encompass vector point data representing nine railway stations along the Konkan railway route, one airport at Dabolim, and four border-crossing points on the national highways. The locations of these stops for all three modes of transportation are depicted in Fig. 1.

For the variable values required in our model, such as the maximum number of trains or the passenger count, we gather relevant data from various sources [1]. This data encompasses rail-related information, such as train numbers, routes, timings, and frequency. Similarly, airway-related data includes details of all the airlines operating in Goa, including flight timings and frequency. Additionally, we collect road-related data, which entails the number of buses running from Goa to Maharashtra and Goa to Karnataka through different entry points. To ensure realistic movement within the GIS space, we employ vector polygon datasets representing administrative boundaries.

To calibrate and validate our model, we incorporate COVID-19 statistics and the timeline of nationwide lockdown policies, obtained from available sources. These data play a crucial role in fine-tuning our simulation.

Geographic Information System. This research focuses on constructing a simulated environment that closely resembles the intricate transportation network of Goa, encompassing railways, roadways, and air travel. To achieve this, we integrate vector datasets depicting administrative boundaries, railway stations, airports, and highway checkpoints into the simulation. These datasets play a crucial role in accurately reproducing the transportation infrastructure of Goa. Additionally, we incorporate state boundaries to confine the movement of agents within the simulated geographic space.

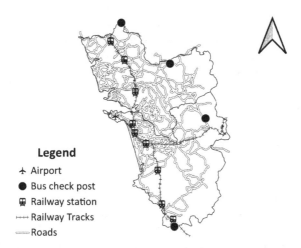

Fig. 1. A map with the distribution of airports, bus checkposts, railway stations, and the intricate transportation networks within Goa [4].

Specifically, we define the train routes along the Konkan Railway, stretching from Pernem station in the North Goa district to Loliem station in the South Goa district. As for air travel, we designate Dabolim airport as the primary hub for flight arrivals and departures. Moreover, we identify highway checkpoints as entry points at the Goa border, facilitating the movement of buses.

To ensure consistency and accurate spatial representation, we employ the EPSG:7779 projected coordinate system specifically tailored for the state of Goa. This choice guarantees a standardized framework for spatial referencing throughout the simulation.

4.4   How It Works

We employ a comprehensive simulation encompassing three primary modes of transportation – trains, flights, and buses, both individually and in various combinations. The simulation commences by initializing the vehicles and their respective starting locations. Subsequently, individuals within the district are transformed into passengers who embark on these vehicles. To ensure accuracy, we regularly update the positions of both the vehicles and passengers, considering an hourly interval. The passengers interact with one another utilizing the SEIRD model, while new passengers board the vehicles and existing passengers disembark at different stations or ports. Those who disembark then continue their journey homeward. A visual representation of the simulation process for a vehicle is presented in Fig. 2. Multiple vehicles are concurrently operate from diverse stations and at different times, adhering to the gathered transportation data.

Beyond the confines of the vehicles, individuals residing in the district intermingle haphazardly and engage in interactions that can facilitate the transmission of infections within a specific radius. We simulate the movement of people using two distinctive approaches. In the first scenario, known as *unrestricted movement*, individuals are at liberty to traverse within the state and exploit the available transportation networks for inter-state travel. The second scenario, labeled *restricted movement*, permits inter-state travel while imposing limitations on local movement. These two types of movements were officially sanctioned in India during the COVID-19 period. Consequently, our simulation focuses solely on monitoring individuals within the state and excludes those who travel outside the state through flights and buses.

5   Implementation Details

5.1   Software

For our modeling platform, we chose the NetLogo software developed by Uri Wilensky due to its versatile features and toolset. One notable aspect of NetLogo is its GIS extension, which enables our model to handle both vector and raster GIS data. Our model is designed as an object-oriented agent-based model, where each agent represents an object within the simulation. Throughout the simulation, the monitors, GIS space, and plots are updated at each tick, with the results being carefully tracked. In our context, each tick corresponds to an hour. To execute the model efficiently, we run it on a Red Hat Linux server without utilizing the graphical user interface (GUI). We leverage the power of BehaviorSpace, an integrated tool in NetLogo, which allows us to run multiple simulations concurrently through threading. By employing a NetLogo-headless batch file executed via the command line, each simulation is run with different sets of parameters, and the output is exported as CSV files. To ensure robustness and reliable results, we perform three runs of each experiment and calculate the average results. The obtained data is then utilized for plotting graphs using MATLAB R2021b, aiding us in the interpretation of the outcomes.

5.2   Variables

Table 1. Parameters for the agent-based simulation [4].

Parameter	Value
Time period	28 days
Population	15,000
Chances of exposure	70%
Exposure radius	0.001 units ($\sim$33.85 m)
Incubation period	4 days
Illness period	10 days
Chances of infection	70%
Chances of recovery	80%
Chances of death	5%

In order to investigate the impact of different transportation networks on the spread of the disease, we conduct separate simulations for railways, airways, and roadways, as

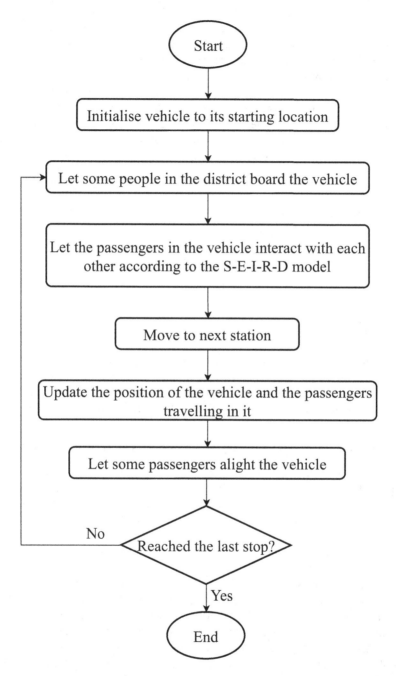

Fig. 2. Flowchart depicting the sequential steps for simulating the movement of a single vehicle [4]. Multiple vehicles, each with distinct starting locations and departure times, operate simultaneously in parallel.

well as a combined simulation incorporating all three networks. To ensure accuracy and realism, we obtain the actual numbers of vehicles and passengers from real-world data. To effectively simulate the population of Goa, we scale it down to 1%, resulting in a model population of 15, 000 individuals. The number of individuals in each vehicle is further scaled down by a factor of 10 to maintain proportionality. Our simulation spans a duration of twenty-eight days, allowing us to capture the subsequent recovery and fatality rates. The parameters governing the simulation, along with the corresponding values for the vehicles, are provided in Table 1 and 2. These parameters serve as crucial inputs for our simulation, ensuring the accurate representation of the various factors influencing the spread of the disease.

Table 2. Parameters for each mode of transport in the simulation [4].

Mode of Transport	Number of Vehicles	Number of Passengers
Trains	[1, 2, 3, 4, 5, 6, 7, 8, 9, 10, 11, 12]	50
Flights	[10, 20, 30, 40, 50, 60, 70, 80, 90, 100]	9
Buses	[30, 60, 90, 120, 150, 180, 210, 240, 270, 300]	5

6 Findings

By employing agent-based models, we comprehensively simulate various modes of transportation, including trains, flights, buses, and a combination of these networks. To ensure robustness, we perform three separate simulations for each mode, employing different seed values, and subsequently calculate the average outcomes.

6.1 Cumulative Infections with Varying Frequencies of Transportation Modes

The spread of COVID-19 through transportation networks reveals compelling insights. The impact of various movement scenarios on cumulative infections becomes evident.

As demonstrated by Fig. 3, unrestricted movement, ranging from 8% to 50% of daily trains, leads to infection rates of 45% to 89% across the population. Interestingly, an increase in trains up to 25% corresponds to a 17% rise in cumulative infections. Beyond that threshold, the rate of increase declines to 3.3%. Remarkably, when more than 50% of trains operate per day, the infection rate stabilizes at 87% to 89%. Conversely, implementing restrictions on local movement significantly reduces cumulative infections. Combining local movement restrictions with 100% train operations lowers the cumulative infections to 38%. These findings underscore the crucial role of operating trains with restricted local movement to effectively mitigate the spread of COVID-19.

For flights (Fig. 4), altering the percentage of flights significantly impacts the proportion of the population contracting the infection within twenty-eight days. As flights increase, the cumulative number of infections rises, reaching up to 63%. Surprisingly, unlike trains, the rate of increase for flight-related infections remains relatively low, at approximately 1% when the percentage ranges from 10% to 30%. However, this rate jumps to 8.2% when flights surpass 30%. Meanwhile, restricted local movement paired

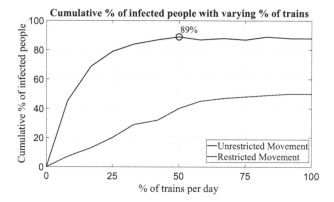

Fig. 3. The cumulative percentage of infected individuals as the number of trains running per day increases, considering both unrestricted and restricted movements [4]. In the case of unrestricted movement, this trend reaches a saturation point of 89% when the percentage of trains exceeds 50% per day.

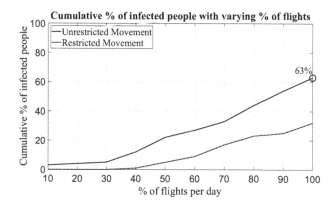

Fig. 4. The cumulative percentage of infected individuals as the number of flights flying per day increases, considering both unrestricted and restricted movements [4]. Under unrestricted movement conditions, the number of infections continues to rise, eventually reaching a maximum of 63%.

with varying flight percentages keeps the cumulative number of infections below 1%, except when flights reach 40%, infecting approximately 1% of the population. Escalating flight percentages to 100% results in a staggering 32% infection rate. Notably, maintaining restrictions on local movement alongside flights over 50% demonstrates the continued benefits of mitigating disease spread compared to trains. The difference between unrestricted and restricted movements becomes more pronounced as flights increase, emphasizing the crucial role of local movement restrictions.

In Fig. 5, we see that the cumulative number of infections associated with buses, as compared to other modes of transportation, appears to be relatively lower. Under the scenario of unrestricted movement, the percentage of the population contracting the disease ranges from 3% to 27% depending on the percentage of buses operating, varying

36   R. Godse et al.

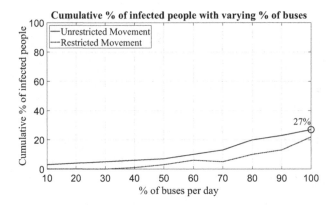

Fig. 5. The cumulative percentage of infected individuals as the number of busses running per day increases, considering both unrestricted and restricted movements [4]. Under unrestricted movement conditions, the number of infections steadily increases, reaching a maximum of 27%.

from 10% to 100%. Notably, there is a gradual increase of 1% in the cumulative number of infections when the percentage of buses increases from 10% to 50%.

Similar to flights, when local movement is restricted, the cumulative number of infections remains below 1% for 10% to 30% of buses. Considering that the cumulative percentage of infections with unrestricted movement is 27%, it is evident that operating buses at full frequency without local restrictions would pose a significant risk and lead to a higher number of cumulative infections.

The combined simulation of all transport modes reveals the most severe scenario in terms of the infected population. In Fig. 6, it can be observed that under unrestricted movement, a high percentage of the population becomes infected. For instance, with 10% of vehicles, 90% of the population contracts the infection, and when 40% of vehicles are in operation, the entire population becomes infected. Even with restrictions on local movement, the cumulative number of infections remains alarmingly high. With just 10% of vehicles and restricted local movement, approximately 68% of the population gets infected. Although the restriction on local movement helps to lower the cumulative percentage of infections, it is not sufficient to effectively contain the spread of the disease. Notably, when more than 50% of vehicles are in operation, the entire population is affected by the disease. This highlights that operating the transport network simultaneously contributes significantly to the transmission of the infection.

These findings underscore the critical role of implementing stringent measures and regulations in controlling the spread of the disease when multiple transport modes are operational simultaneously.

6.2 Maximum Deaths with Varying Frequencies of Transportation Modes

In the case of unrestricted movement for trains, we observe the maximum number of deaths when ~33% of trains, i.e., four to five trains running per day. It is 0.31% of the total population as shown in Fig. 7. Initially, the number of deaths increases rapidly with an increase in the number of trains, starting from 0.12% with 8% of trains, i.e., one

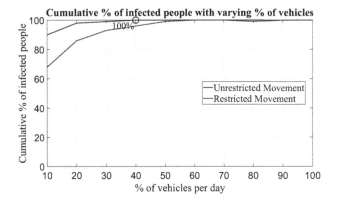

Fig. 6. The cumulative percentage of infected individuals as the number of vehicles running per day increases, considering both unrestricted and restricted movements [4]. With unrestricted movement, the number of infections escalates rapidly, reaching 100% when the percentage of vehicles exceeds 40%.

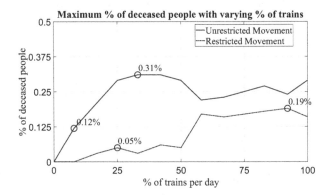

Fig. 7. The maximum number of deaths with increasing trains running per day for unrestricted and restricted movements scenarios. The number of deaths increases rapidly up to 0.31% for four to five trains per day, after which it remains fairly constant. In the restricted movement, we see a sudden rise in deaths when 50% of trains run daily.

train per day, and going up to 0.31% for 33% to 42% of trains per day, i.e., four to five trains per day, after which it remains almost constant. The restricted movement sees a sudden rise in the number of deaths, from 0.05% for 50% of trains, i.e., six trains per day, to 0.19% for 92% of trains, i.e., eleven trains per day.

In Fig. 8 for flights, we observe the maximum number of deaths to be 0.22% of the total population, with 100% flights, i.e., a hundred flights running per day in the case of unrestricted movement. From 10% to 20% of flights per day, we see 0.01% deaths for the case of unrestricted movement and very low or no deaths for the case of restricted movement. We observe a sudden rise in the number of deaths when we increase the number of flights from 70% to 80% per day. As compared to trains, we see fewer deaths for twenty-eight days.

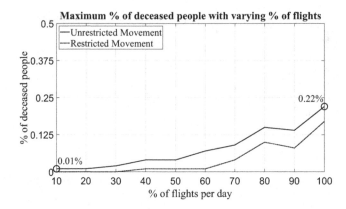

Fig. 8. The maximum number of deaths with an increasing number of flights running per day for unrestricted and restricted movements. We see a sudden rise in the number of deaths when we increase the number of flights from 70% to 80%.

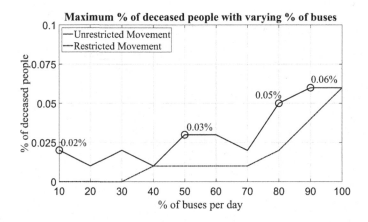

Fig. 9. The maximum number of deaths with an increasing number of buses running per day for unrestricted and restricted movements. As compared to the case of trains and flights, we see a significantly fewer number of deaths over twenty-eight days.

For buses, we observe the maximum number of deaths to be 0.06% of the total population, with 100% buses, i.e., three hundred buses running per day for both unrestricted and restricted movements as seen in Fig. 9. The deceased population stays constant at 0.02–0.03% till 70% of buses, i.e., two hundred and ten buses per day, after which it shoots up to 0.06% for more number of buses in the case of unrestricted movement. We see a similar sudden increase in the case of restricted movement. As compared to the case of trains and flights, we see a significantly fewer number of deaths over twenty-eight days.

In Fig. 10, we see the maximum number of deaths to be 1.2% of the total population after 60% of total vehicles, i.e., eight trains, sixty flights, and one-hundred and eighty buses running per day in the case of unrestricted movement. The number of deaths keeps increasing as we increase the frequency of transportation. The difference in the number of deaths for unrestricted and restricted movement remains consistent at 0.1–0.2%.

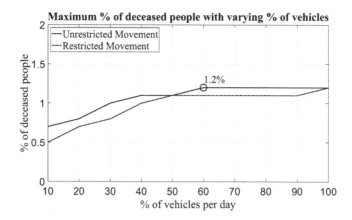

Fig. 10. The maximum number of deaths are observed from eight trains, sixty flights, and one hundred and eighty buses running per day for the case of unrestricted movement. It is 1.2% of the total population.

6.3 Upper Limit on the Number of Vehicles to Ensure Infections Remain Below a Threshold of 20%

Our study reveals crucial findings regarding the upper limits on the number of vehicles allowed to prevent infections from exceeding a 20% threshold.

By analyzing the data, we see that in unrestricted movement, even 8% of trains per day leads to alarming consequences, with the maximum number of infections reaching a staggering 36% as seen in Fig. 11. Thus, it becomes evident that train travel in unrestricted movement must be curtailed to maintain cases below the desired threshold of 20%. However, in scenarios where movement is restricted, a tolerable range of up to 25% of trains per day can be allowed.

Similarly, our investigation into flights demonstrates that up to 50% of flights per day can operate without surpassing the 20% infection threshold in unrestricted scenarios (Fig. 12). In restricted movement, the maximum number of infections always remains below 20%, reassuring the feasibility of regulating flight frequencies.

Turning our attention to buses, the analysis indicates that in the absence of restrictions, infections stay below 20% until 90% of buses are operational (Fig. 13). However, the maximum frequency of buses elevates infections slightly to 23%. Nevertheless, under restricted movement, the maximum number of infections remains below 20%, even with the highest possible bus frequency.

Finally, when considering the combination of minimal frequencies for each mode of transportation—three trains, ten flights, and thirty buses-the minimum number of infections is 57% for unrestricted movement and 40% for restricted movement. So, a combination of all vehicles cannot be allowed if we want to maintain the 20% threshold. Findings from Fig. 14 emphasize the criticality of carefully regulating vehicle numbers in transportation networks to control the spread of COVID-19 and minimize the impact on public health.

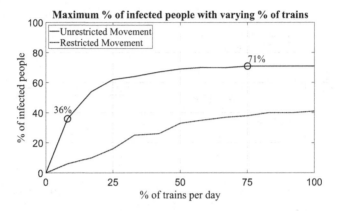

Fig. 11. With an increase in the daily number of trains, both for unrestricted and restricted movements, we observe a gradual rise in the total number of infected individuals [4]. The infection rate continues to escalate until it reaches a saturation point of 71%, which occurs when the percentage of trains allowed exceeds 75% per day.

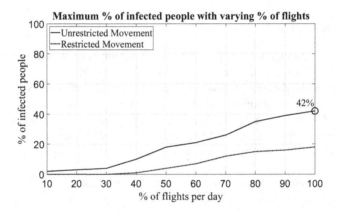

Fig. 12. For the scenarios of both unrestricted and restricted movements, the number of infections continues to rise over twenty-eight days, with each increment of ten flights per day resulting in a significant increase of approximately 5% in cases [4].

6.4 Peak in Number of Infections

In Table 3, we observe that 8% to 33% of trains with unrestricted movement do not show a peak in the number of infected people within twenty-eight days. We see a peak in the number of infected people for 42% of trains on the twenty-fifth day. The day of peak arrival does not show a uniform trend with the increase in the frequency of trains. On average, the number of infected people attains a peak on the twenty-fifth day with unrestricted movement.

Similarly, in the case of restricted movement, the number of infected people does not reach a peak for up to 50% of trains. 58% of trains show a peak occurring on the twenty-fifth day. As the frequency of trains increases further, the peak occurs as early

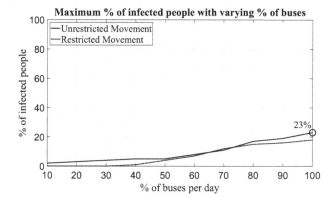

Fig. 13. In the case of buses, the infection count steadily rises over a span of twenty-eight days, showcasing a compelling trend. Remarkably, with each 10% increase in bus frequency, the infection rate shows a steady rise of approximately 1%. However, as the number of buses surpasses ∼50% (150), a significant spike in infections becomes evident [4].

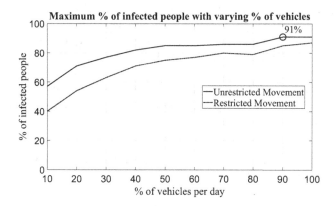

Fig. 14. In both scenarios of unrestricted and restricted movement, we unveil the highest count of infected individuals with a combination of all vehicles. Our findings indicate that a mere combination of twelve trains, hundred flights, and three hundred buses per day in unrestricted movement contributes to a shocking 91% of the total population being infected [4].

as the twenty-second day with the maximum frequency of trains. The occurrence of an early peak suggests that the infection spreads faster as the frequency of trains increases.

The number of infected people per day does not attain a peak for any frequency of flights with both restricted and unrestricted movements. Similar to the case of flights, the number of infected people does not reach a peak with any frequency of buses.

In Table 4, we observe that all of the combinations, with and without restrictions in the local movement, attain a peak in the number of infected people within twenty days. The day of peak shows a downward trend with an increase in the frequency of vehicles. The unrestricted movement with 10% of vehicles shows a 57% of a peak on the twentieth day. As the frequency of vehicles increases, the peak occurs on the

Table 3. Simulation days when we observe a peak in the number of infections with increasing frequency of trains.

% of trains per day	8%	17%	25%	33%	42%	50%	58%	67%	75%	83%	92%	100%
Day with unrestricted movement	NA	NA	NA	NA	25	24	26	25	27	25	25	25
Day with restricted movement	NA	NA	NA	NA	NA	NA	25	25	24	23	21	22

Table 4. Simulation days when we observe a peak in the number of infections with increasing frequency of the combination of vehicles.

% of vehicles per day	10%	20%	30%	40%	50%	60%	70%	80%	90%	100%
Day with unrestricted movement	20	19	19	18	18	18	15	15	15	14
Day with restricted movement	19	18	18	18	18	17	16	16	15	15

eighteenth day with 50% of vehicles. The maximum frequency of vehicles shows a peak as early as the fourteenth day.

Similarly, in the case of restricted movement, 10% of vehicles show the number of infected per day, attaining a peak on the nineteenth day. The case of 50% of vehicles with restrictions results in a peak on the eighteenth day. The maximum frequency of vehicles with restricted movement shows a peak in the number of people on the fifteenth day.

The simultaneous operation of trains, buses, and flights increases the number of people traveling and exposed to the disease. Thus, even the restrictions on this simulation do not significantly minimize the number of infected people.

6.5   A Comparison Between Unrestricted and Restricted Movements in Terms of of Number of Infections

We observe in Table 5 that the ratio of the maximum number of infected people per day for unrestricted and restricted movement per day decreases with an increase in the frequency of trains.

Table 5. Ratio of the maximum number of infected people per day for unrestricted and restricted movement with increasing frequency of trains.

% of trains per day	8%	17%	25%	33%	42%	50%	58%	67%	75%	83%	92%	100%
Ratio	6	5.4	3.9	2.6	2.6	2.1	2	1.9	1.9	1.8	1.8	1.7

With 8% of trains, the ratio for unrestricted and restricted movement is 6. Till 25% of trains, the ratio remains above 4. This shows that the infection spreads faster in the case of unrestricted movement. Beyond 25% of trains, the ratio ranges from 2.6 to 1.7 as the trains reach their maximum frequency. This shows that as the frequency of trains increases, the effectiveness of restrictions decreases.

Table 6. Ratio of the maximum number of infected people per day for unrestricted and restricted movement with increasing frequency of flights.

% of flights per day	10%	20%	30%	40%	50%	60%	70%	80%	90%	100%
Ratio	NA	NA	NA	10	4.5	3	2.2	2.3	2.4	2.3

Similar to trains, the ratio of maximum infected people per day with unrestricted and restricted movement, as shown in Table 6, decreases with an increase in the frequency of flights. The ratio for 10% to 30% of flights is absent because the number of infected people with restrictions is less than 1% of the population. The case of 40% of flights has a ratio of 10, which becomes 4.5 with 50% of flights and 3 with 60% of flights. Further increase in the frequency of flights shows a nearly constant ratio in the range of 2.2 to 2.4. This decrease in the ratio shows that as the frequency of flights increases, restrictions' effectiveness decreases.

Table 7. Ratio of the maximum number of infected people per day for unrestricted and restricted movement with increasing frequency of buses.

% of busses per day	10%	20%	30%	40%	50%	60%	70%	80%	90%	100%
Ratio	NA	NA	NA	5	2.5	1.6	2.8	1.9	1.7	1.4

For the case of buses as shown in Table 7, the ratio of maximum infected people for 10% to 30% is not assigned because the number of infected people per day with restricted movement is less than 1% of the population. The case of 40% of buses shows a ratio of 5 for the unrestricted and restricted movements that becomes 2.5 with 50% of buses. The maximum frequency of buses shows a ratio of 1.4. So a lesser number of buses is effective in reducing the spread.

Table 8. Ratio of the maximum number of infected people per day for unrestricted and restricted movement with increasing frequency of the combination of vehicles.

% of vehicles per day	10%	20%	30%	40%	50%	60%	70%	80%	90%	100%
Ratio	1.4	1.3	1.2	1.2	1.1	1.1	1.1	1.1	1.1	1

The ratio of the maximum number of infected people per day for unrestricted and restricted movement decreases with an increase in the frequency of vehicles. The ratio ranges from 1.4 to 1 for 10% to 100% of vehicles, respectively as shown in Table 8. This shows that restrictions do not have a positive effect in lowering the number of infected people.

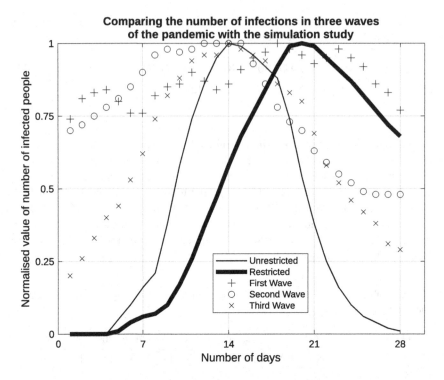

Fig. 15. A comparison plot of the simulation results with all modes of transport combined to the three waves of COVID-19 in Goa [4]. Remarkably, the simulation results reveal a striking resemblance between the second wave's peak, characterized by unrestricted movement, and the peak of the third wave, which witnessed restricted movement. Such similarity provides a promising validation of our simulation's accuracy, as the number of cases escalated at a less rapid pace for the third wave-akin to the scenario with restricted movement.

6.6   Validating the Model: Correlations with Real-World Data

Comparing our simulation observations with real-world COVID-19 data in Goa, we unveil a fascinating pattern - the spread of infections through combined transportation follows a bell-shaped curve. In Fig. 15, we present the results, analyzing twenty-eight days of data for all three pandemic waves. We plot the number of infections normalized individually per the maximum number of infections. The first wave, starting in early November 2020, is followed by the second wave in early May 2021, and the third wave commences in the second week of January 2022. Remarkably, as we progress from the first wave to the third, the rate of infection transmission diminishes. Examining the unrestricted scenario, we observe that the curve reaches its peak simultaneously with the second wave, while the curve for the restricted scenario exhibits peak points during both the first and third waves. This can be attributed to the varying levels of restrictions imposed during these waves, with the second wave experiencing comparatively lesser constraints.

Table 9. Summary of results.

Findings	Trains	Flights	Buses	Combination
Maximum number of infections as a % of total population (cumulative)	89%	63%	27%	100%
Maximum number of deaths as a % of total population	0.31%	0.22%	0.06%	1.2%
Upper limit on vehicles allowed (per day) while keeping the infections less than 20%	Unrestricted: 0% Restricted: 25% Total Passengers: 150	Unrestricted: 50% Restricted: 100% Total Passengers: 900	Unrestricted: 90% Restricted: 100% Total Passengers: 1500	N.A.
Average number of days to attain peak in the number of infections	Unrestricted: 25 Restricted: 27	Unrestricted: 28 Restricted: 28	Unrestricted: 28 Restricted: 28	Unrestricted: 17 Restricted: 17
Max. ratio of number of infections between unrestricted and restricted movements	6%	10%	5%	1.4%

7   Discussion

The transmission dynamics of COVID-19 are governed by various factors. This study aims to investigate the dissemination of infections through transportation networks in two distinct scenarios of permissible movement. To accomplish this, we utilize agent-based simulation modeling in NetLogo, integrating geospatial data to represent Goa, including its railway stations, airports, and bus stops. The complete source code and data files for this study can be accessed publicly through a GitHub repository[1], ensuring transparency and facilitating further exploration and research in this area.

In a closely related study conducted by Talekar et al. (reference: [10]), the impact of transportation on the spread of the disease was examined with a specific focus on the effectiveness of creating cohorts of people. In contrast, our approach diverges as we consider each individual as a distinct entity and evaluate the influence of their movements through various modes of transportation on the spread of the disease. By adopting this individual-centric perspective, we aim to provide a comprehensive understanding of how the transportation choices of individuals contribute to the transmission dynamics of the disease.

We measure the rise in infections and deaths while varying the frequency of trains, buses, and flights. We observe that trains cause the maximum number of infections (71%) and deaths (0.31%) at a rapid rate in the state because they move interstate and have the highest number of passengers. On the other hand, buses minimize the spread of infection in the state (23%) and cause much fewer deaths (0.06%). Our study also highlights an upper bound on all these modes of transport to keep infections less than 20%. It is interesting to see that the combined effect of trains, flights, and buses on the number of infection cases is not additive. A combination causes many more infections and levels off faster, causing the peak to occur earlier. A summary of our results can be found in Table 9. In our previous study, we made several noteworthy findings.

---

[1] https://github.com/Networked-Systems-Lab/Simulating-COVID-19-Using-ABM.

Firstly, we examine the relationship between transportation frequency and the number of recoveries, providing insights into the impact of transportation policies on recovery rates. Additionally, we analyze the rate of change in the number of infections over time, revealing patterns and trends throughout the outbreak. Lastly, we identify an equivalence point between unrestricted and restricted movements, highlighting the effectiveness of local movement restrictions in controlling the spread of the disease [4]. We validate the same with the three big waves of COVID-19 in Goa as we find a similar bell curve. We make a detailed comparison for all transportation modes in unrestricted and restricted movement settings regarding speed and intensity of infection spread.

In future iterations, it is conceivable to expand this simulation to encompass multiple states, thereby incorporating inter-state travel as well as international travel. Additionally, by implementing more precise tracking mechanisms for road movements, it would be possible to identify potential exposures to the virus with greater accuracy. However, it is worth noting that such an extension would necessitate significantly greater computational power, as individual-level tracking of both people and vehicles would be required.

Furthermore, the simulation can be enhanced by incorporating the presence of vaccinated individuals, who would either possess immunity or have reduced susceptibility to the disease. This addition would enable a more comprehensive analysis of the impact of vaccination on the spread of the virus and aid in evaluating the efficacy of vaccination campaigns in controlling the outbreak.

While these future extensions would introduce additional complexities and computational requirements, they hold the potential to provide valuable insights into the dynamics of disease transmission across regions, the influence of international travel, and the effectiveness of vaccination strategies.

References

1. Transportation - department of tourism, government of Goa. https://goatourism.gov.in/transportation/
2. Ahmad, S., Ullah, A., Al-Mdallal, Q.M., Khan, H., Shah, K., Khan, A.: Fractional order mathematical modeling of COVID-19 transmission. Chaos Solitons Fractals **139**, 110256 (2020). https://doi.org/10.1016/j.chaos.2020.110256, https://www.sciencedirect.com/science/article/pii/S0960077920306524
3. Barat, S., et al.: An agent-based digital twin for exploring localized non-pharmaceutical interventions to control COVID-19 pandemic. Trans. Indian Natl. Acad. Eng. **6** (2021). 10.1007/s41403-020-00197-5
4. Bhat, S., Godse, R., Mestry, S., Naik, V.: Studying the impact of transportation during lockdown on the spread of COVID-19 using agent-based modeling. In: Proceedings of the 15th International Conference on Agents and Artificial Intelligence - Volume 1: ICAART, pp. 80–92. INSTICC, SciTePress (2023). https://doi.org/10.5220/0011733400003393
5. Burman, A., Chatterjee, S., Ghosh, P., Mukhokadhyay, I.: A flexible agent-based model to study covid-19 outbreak – a generic approach (2021). https://doi.org/10.48550/ARXIV.2106.11070, https://arxiv.org/abs/2106.11070
6. Cuevas, E.: An agent-based model to evaluate the COVID-19 transmission risks in facilities. Comput. Biol. Med. **121**, 103827 (2020). https://doi.org/10.1016/j.compbiomed.2020.103827

7. Iboi, E., Sharomi, O.O., Ngonghala, C., Gumel, A.B.: Mathematical modeling and analysis of COVID-19 pandemic in Nigeria. medRxiv (2020). https://doi.org/10.1101/2020.05.22.20110387, https://www.medrxiv.org/content/early/2020/07/31/2020.05.22.20110387

8. Paoluzzi, M., Gnan, N., Grassi, F., Salvetti, M., Vanacore, N., Crisanti, A.: A single-agent extension of the sir model describes the impact of mobility restrictions on the COVID-19 epidemic. Sci. Rep. **11** (2021). https://doi.org/10.1038/s41598-021-03721-x

9. QGIS Development Team: QGIS Geographic Information System. QGIS Association (2022). https://www.qgis.org

10. Talekar, A., et al.: Cohorting to isolate asymptomatic spreaders: an agent-based simulation study on the Mumbai suburban railway (2020). https://doi.org/10.48550/ARXIV.2012.12839, https://arxiv.org/abs/2012.12839

11. Tang, Y., Wang, S.: Mathematic modeling of COVID-19 in the united states. Emerg. Microbes Infect. **9**(1), 827–829 (2020). https://doi.org/10.1080/22221751.2020.1760146. pMID: 32338150

12. Wilder, B., et al.: The role of age distribution and family structure on COVID-19 dynamics: a preliminary modeling assessment for Hubei and Lombardy. SSRN Electron. J. (2020). https://doi.org/10.2139/ssrn.3564800

Dealing with the Unpredictability of Physical Resources in Real-World Multi-agent Systems

Nilson Mori Lazarin[1,2(✉)] [ID], Carlos Eduardo Pantoja[1,2] [ID], and José Viterbo[1] [ID]

[1] Institute of Computing – Fluminense Federal University (UFF), Niterói, RJ, Brazil
viterbo@ic.uff.br
[2] Federal Center for Technological Education Celso Suckow da Fonseca (Cefet/RJ),
Rio de Janeiro, RJ, Brazil
{nilson.lazarin,carlos.pantoja}@cefet-rj.br

Abstract. Although Multi-Agent Systems (MAS) can handle various problems in heterogeneous environments, unknown problems may arise at runtime due to their inherent heterogeneity when dealing with cyber-physical systems. Therefore, designers of intelligent cyber-physical systems must adopt approaches that enable adaptability and fault tolerance at runtime. This work proposes techniques for dynamically adding, removing, and swapping resources (sensors or actuators) in Embedded MAS at runtime. These approaches utilize the BDI model and a customized agent architecture capable of perceiving the availability of microcontrollers integrated into the system through serial communication. A case study was conducted to analyze five scenarios that an embedded MAS can deal with, starting from where there are no existing physical resources and new resources must be added at runtime and a scenario where failures, replacement, and the need for upgrade scenarios occur. Our approach was evaluated and tested in three different BDI frameworks, demonstrating that swapping resources at runtime is a promissory feature to guarantee the adaptability of intelligent cyber-physical systems.

Keywords: Multi-agent systems · Embedded multi-agent systems · Embedded systems

1 Introduction

Distributed Artificial Intelligence is a field of Science dedicated to studying, constructing, and applying autonomous systems capable of achieving objectives or performing some set of tasks [28]. A Multi-Agent System (MAS) comprises software agents that can perceive or act autonomously in a real or a virtual environment where they are situated; besides, these agents are cognitive, autonomous, proactive, and have social ability since they can interact with other agents from the MAS to compete or collaborate toward their individual or system goals [29]. Agents can assume cognitive abilities by adopting a cognitive model. One of the most adopted cognitive models is the Belief-Desire-Intention model (BDI) [6]. This model is based on understanding the practical human reasoning that decides, moment by moment, what action to take to achieve goals based on plans that beliefs, desires, and intentions can activate [30].

A. P. Rocha et al. (Eds.): ICAART 2023, LNAI 14546, pp. 48–71, 2024.
https://doi.org/10.1007/978-3-031-55326-4_3

These MAS have been applied in several domains due to their advantages that allow an increase in speed and efficiency due to their parallel nature and asynchronous operation, in addition to allowing scalability and flexibility [2]. These systems differ from conventional systems by presenting additional characteristics such as independence since its operation or existence does not depend on other agents; proactivity, as it acts on the environment, on its initiative; collaboration, as it communicates with other agents to organize their actions; cognition, as it draws up action plans to achieve a goal; and adaptability because in case of failure, it looks for executing alternative plans.

An Embedded MAS is a system running on top of devices, where cognitive agents are physically connected to resources to perceive and act in the real world and communicability with other devices [5]. By definition, these systems can deal with different problems in heterogeneous environments. However, unknown problems, and consequently, those not foreseen at design time, may be presented to the MAS at runtime, and there may be no agents in the system capable of dealing with the presented problem. Thus, due to the natural heterogeneity of real environments and the adaptability of agents, the designer must adopt an approach that makes the Embedded MAS adaptable and fault-tolerant at runtime, allowing the maintenance and replacement of resources that are damaged, or even the addition of new resources, to deal with new problems. One of them is to employ an Open MAS that allows mobility. Then, an agent with the necessary skills could be invited to join the society [8]. Besides, a MAS could also dispatch a duplicate capable of dealing with the problem [24].

The resources of an Embedded MAS are defined only at design time. The designer must define them before assembling the device, and, once defined, it is impossible to change them at runtime. For this, the Embedded MAS must be stopped, and the MAS reprogrammed. The swapping of resources—addition or removal—is an interesting feature in the development of Embedded MAS because it adds adaptability at runtime for agents. The system does not need to be turned off, and agents could reason about the availability of resources. In this way, an autonomous agent can be adaptable, continuing to perform actions to achieve its goals in case of hardware failure, for example. Considering the extant BDI agent-oriented languages and frameworks [3,4,9,22], they do not initially provide access to physical resources. Argo is a customized architecture that allows agents to interface with hardware resources but is also not prepared to deal with the swapping of resources [21].

This work introduces a novel functionality that enables the dynamic swapping of physical resources within an Embedded MAS. Consequently, an embedded system with existing physical resources can now have new resources attached or removed, with the agents automatically detecting these additions or absences. As the Embedded MAS uses the serial port to govern the microcontroller, the agent becomes aware of its availability each time it attempts to access it during perception or action. The primary objective is to enhance the MAS's adaptive capacity and facilitate the development process of embedded systems. To achieve this, we extend Argo agents by incorporating a modified version of Javino [16], a serial interface responsible for message exchange between the microcontroller and agents. Javino can now identify added or removed resources, effectively notifying the agent about these changes.

Adding resources at runtime could be achieved by adopting an Open MAS and agent mobility allowing agents to enter and leave its system anytime [1]. In Jason, this is possible by adopting bio-inspired protocols for moving agents from one Embedded MAS to another [26]. Then, one resource could be added, and one agent with proper plans could be sent to control this resource. However, it is important to note that even with agent mobility, the agents cannot currently identify when a resource has been removed.

In this extended version of the paper [14], we also provide packages of Argo to work along with JaCaMo and Jason using command line interface (CLI). JaCaMo [3] integrates three MAS dimensions—organizational, environmental, and agency—combining Moise [12], CArtAgO [23], and Jason framework [4]. JaCaMo-CLI and Jason-CLI allows the creation of MAS using terminal commands without graphical interfaces. Besides, we assembled a new study case using a single-board computer hosting the Embedded MAS and some microcontrollers managing sensors and actuators considering Jason Embedded [19] using the ChonIDE [13], JaCaMo-CLI, and Jason-CLI. The Embedded MAS is developed using Jason interpreter, the extended Argo agents and packages, and Javino.

The contributions of this work are a novel feature to swap resources in Embedded MAS using BDI agents at runtime, an extended version of Argo agents and Javino for Jason framework, and packages for working with JaCaMo. This paper is structured as follows: Sect. 2 discusses some related work; In Sect. 3, we present the swap approach; The swap feature is tested in Sect. 4, and finally, we present the Conclusions and the References.

2 Related Work

From a practical point of view, the swap of physical resources at runtime could facilitate the process of maintaining and expanding an Embedded MAS since it does need to be stopped to add a new resource or to remove an existing one. If the domain is critical, undesirable stops must be avoided at the most, and turning it off is not an option.

The Argo [21] architecture is a BDI agent capable of capturing and filtering the perceptions [27] coming from the sensors that sense the environment. It is also capable of sending commands to activate and deactivate actuators. Argo processes the perceptions directly as beliefs, and it can reduce the amount of perceptions by activating runtime filters, so the agent can focus only on those necessary to achieve its goals. Argo uses Javino [16] as the serial interface for accessing the device's resources. Considering the various layers and steps of the development process of an embedded system, Argo facilitates MAS programming because it abstracts the technological issues of interfacing hardware. The agent just needs to know what serial port it is handling. Argo and Javino do help in the development of MAS, but they do not offer a mechanism to identify if the port the agent is handling is available or not. In fact, several solutions allow to define and employ the devices' resources at design-time [11,18,25]. In none of these solutions, the designer adds or removes the resources without stopping the system.

The Resource Management Architecture (RMA) [20] enables the addition of new devices at the edge of an IoT system at runtime. A device using the RMA can use an Embedded MAS to control microcontrollers, and all information gathered could be forwarded to be published using the Sensor as a Service model. In addition, Physical Artifacts using CArtAgO [23] can be used as a resource with or without a dedicated MAS [17]. These devices can be added or removed from the RMA at any time. However, although the dynamism of this IoT architecture, devices can only be added to the network if it is online. Furthermore, swapping the devices' resources is only possible during design time, and it is still impossible to add or remove any resource without stopping the MAS. Besides, it depends on an available IoT network for communicating.

The bio-inspired protocols [26] for moving agents allow an Embedded MAS of a device to take control of another device by moving all its agents and their respective mental states. However, the target device must be identical to the source device for effective hardware control. So, it is still possible to add additional resources to the target device at runtime and move agents with proper plans to handle these new resources. As an Embedded MAS uses a physical architecture with boards running an OS with serial interfacing between agents and microcontrollers, it is possible to add resources at runtime. Then, once agents can communicate and move from one MAS to another using bio-inspired protocols, it is possible to program the agent at design time and move it at runtime, adopting a protocol that does not eliminate the target MAS. In this way, knowing the serial port where the new device is connected and sending the agent prepared to handle it, it is possible to add a resource accessible by BDI agents at runtime in an Embedded MAS. However, removing agents is not yet possible, and the solution depends on the available communication infrastructure.

In our approach, the serial interface informs the agent about the port availability it is trying to access. Then, whenever the agent has a new resource connected to the Embedded MAS, it perceives which port it is connected to. If the resource is removed, the next time the agent tries to gather the perceptions or act, it updates its mental state with the unavailability of the resource. In this new version of Argo, the agent receives this information each time (in the beginning) its reasoning cycle is performed. It is also updated at the end of the cycle if it tries to perform an action using any resource. With this perception, the agent can deliberate whether or not to pursue an intention that might be unreachable.

3   Methodology

When acting in a dynamic physical environment, agents must be prepared to reason regarding the availability of information and resources. Agents can use their own physical resources to gather information and act upon this environment. Still, as with any physical component, these resources could be damaged, unavailable, or changed by improved technologies. Then, agents must follow the adaptive ability to be aware of which resources are available when it needs to use them. Besides, embedded agents must also be fault tolerant and decide what to do when a resource is not available or damaged. So, swapping devices at runtime is a desired feature for any Embedded MAS. In this section, we review the architecture for constructing a cognitive device using Embedded MAS and the new feature for swapping physical resources using the Jason framework and Argo agents.

It is necessary to observe a four-fold architecture to construct a device managed by an Embedded MAS:

1. **Hardware.** It comprises all available resources of a device. They are physically connected to a microcontroller. These sensors and actuators are responsible for gathering the environment's perceptions and acting upon them. All microcontrollers employed in the device must also be connected in serial ports of a single-board computer (or any micro-processed platform).
2. **Firmware.** It represents the microcontroller programming where the perceptions are mounted and sent to the Embedded MAS based on the agent-programming language or framework adopted. The commands that activate the actuators are also programmed in response to serial messages.
3. **Serial Communication.** All messages exchanged between agents and resources use serial communication. This layer uses a serial interface to manage the message flow between agents and different microcontrollers. Agents need to know which serial port the resources are connected to.
4. **Reasoning.** It includes the Embedded MAS programming running on the single-board computer. Agents are programmed to automatically understand the perceptions of sensors as beliefs; afterward, they can deliberate and send commands back to activate actuators.

This architecture makes it possible to exchange resources at runtime on an already-designed device since all layers are low coupled. New sensors or actuators can be added to the system anytime since they are connected to a microcontroller. After this, they can be connected to a serial port. So, for any agent to interface these new resources, it would only need to know which port to access at runtime. However, it could not know how to manipulate it and would need to learn these skills some other way.

In this paper, we present an approach that allows Argo agents to test the availability of serial ports. Then it can deliberate whether or not to continue pursuing the goals associated with an unavailable resource. Besides, when it becomes available again or a new resource is inserted at runtime, the agent is aware of the availability of the serial port. We define the swapping of resources as the ability to add, remove, or exchange physical components to the device at runtime. This novel ability of BDI agents guarantees that agents could be adaptive and fault-tolerant regarding hardware resources. The Embedded MAS—and, consequently, the device—does not need to be turned off for predictive, preventive, or corrective maintenance. This characteristic could reduce risks and increase profits in some domains, such as industrial applications.

Any Argo agent interfaces the hardware resources using Javino by accessing which port the microcontroller is connected to the single-board computer. So, when connecting a new microcontroller with new resources in a device managed by an Embedded MAS (or when removing), Javino verifies if the port is accessible or not and informs to the Argo agent who is trying to access it by sending a belief with the port information and if it is *on*, *off*, or *timeout*. Otherwise, when the resource is removed or fails, it can deliberate to drop its intentions related to the disconnected resources, for example. Figure 1 shows the four-fold architecture and the belief representing the port availability (i.e., port(name, status)).

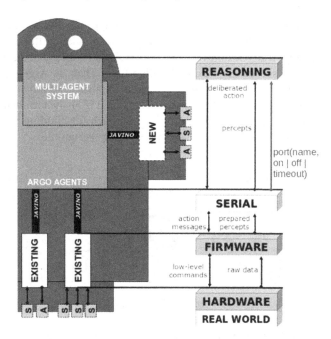

Fig. 1. The four-fold architecture for programming Embedded MAS on top of hardware devices [14].

When connecting a new resource in the system, three possible approaches can occur: an agent needs to learn how to deal with this new resource, a new agent can be employed to handle it, or any agent can already know how to use it. For the first case, the designer must program an external MAS and use an IoT network [10] infrastructure to transfer the knowledge (plans) or the agent. At first, the designer can send the plans directly to a Communicator agent that redirects the plans to the Argo agent that controls the serial port. For this, Jason Embedded is employed. At last, a new Argo agent with the new desired abilities is transferred to the Embedded MAS using the bio-inspired Protocols [26]. Once the agent arrives at the destination, it can control the new resources and interact with the existing agents in that system. If no communicability or mobility is available, the designer can program the agent's behavior at design time to deal with possible new resources connected at runtime. However, adding totally unknown resources is still an open issue in the domain.

The practical intention is to create cognitive devices where agents are not dependent on resource availability. Agents can be stuck in pursuing goals that could be momentarily or permanently unreachable since the resources are not available anymore. In the worst case, the agent could deliberate based on wrong information, or the whole Embedded MAS could crash with malformed beliefs.

In order to ensure runtime adaptability in Embedded MAS, particularly for adding new resources or updating existing ones, it is essential to design the system with a communicator agent connected to an IoT server when using Jason Embedded. In this way, the system can receive new plans for an Argo agent that already manipulates a resource or can receive a new Argo agent capable of manipulating the resource to be added. When using the Argo packages for JaCaMo or Jason, some agent that knows how to deal with the new resource must exist at design time. Then, in Argo packages, the agent should exist when starting the system since it is impossible to move or create it at runtime. Alternatively, adding new agents at runtime direct from the terminal is possible using Jason-CLI. Figure 2 presents the proposed approach for building an Embedded MAS capable of adding, removing, or changing resources at runtime.

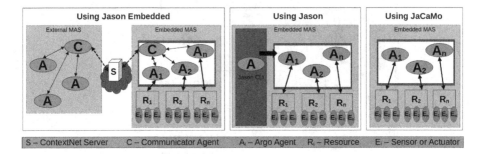

Fig. 2. The swapping methodology for Embedded MAS.

3.1   The Swap Feature in Argo Agents

Argo agents is a customized architecture from Jason's framework for interfacing hardware resources. All the information gathered from sensors is interpreted as perceptions by Argo. Then, when programming Argo agents at design time, the designer needs to inform the serial port that the agent interfaces to the perceptions flow directly to the agent's belief base. It is important to remark that this process still occurs when resources fail or become unavailable. As said before, the agent is unaware of the port availability, which could lead to undesired behaviors.

Argo has the ability to change the serial port it is accessing and block the flow of perceptions at any time. If Argo is aware that a serial port is not answering anymore, it could try to reach another port or simply block the perceptions from that port. Then, when swapping resources, Argo agents need to access the status of the port which is trying to reach. For this, we defined a belief *port(Name, Status)*, where the name identifies the serial port name, and the status indicates if it is *on*, *off* or *timeout*. For example, when removing a resource located at serial port name *ttyACM0*, the agent receives directly in its belief base *port(ttyACM0, off)*.

Every BDI agent from Jason performs a well-defined reasoning cycle where the agent executes an expected behavior in each step. Argo has an extended reasoning cycle that modifies two distinct steps at the beginning of the cycle, when the agents perceive the real environment to gather perceptions, and at the end, when it acts, sending commands to actuators. The remaining steps are inspired by the Practical Reasoning System (PRS) [7]. It defines which events will trigger plans and intentions to define the sequence of actions to be performed.

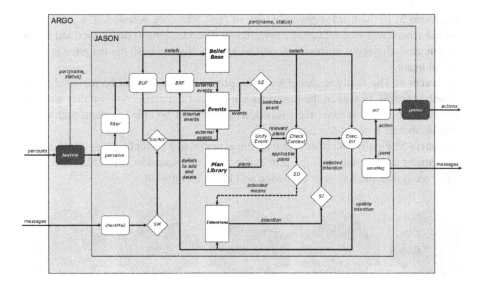

Fig. 3. The Argo's extended reasoning cycle [14].

In the perceive step of an Argo's reasoning cycle, the Javino is the serial interface responsible for gathering the perceptions from sensors and forwarding them to the Belief Update Function (BUF). Javino requests the perceptions by accessing the microcontroller whenever the agent performs a cycle. In this step, we modified Javino to inform whether or not the serial port the agent is trying to connect to is available.

In the same way, at the end of the cycle, the agent performs actions that can reflect in commands to be sent to actuators. In this step, Javino is also responsible for sending serial commands to the microcontroller. In this case, we modified the internal action named *act* to update the agent's belief base by adding the *port(Port, off)* belief in case the serial port is unavailable anymore. Javino tries to access the port, and in case of failure, it returns the aforementioned belief. The modified reasoning cycle of Argo agents is presented in Fig. 3.

4   Case Study

This case study involves the analysis of five possible scenarios at runtime considering an Embedded MAS that avoids obstacles. We considered the following scenarios (Fig. 4):

– **Scenario 1:** The first scenario presents an Embedded MAS controlling a prototype with no sensor or actuator. In this scenario, there are no goals to achieve by agents, but the MAS must be ready if new resources are added.
– **Scenario 2:** In the second scenario, two new resources (a sensor and an actuator) will be added to the prototype. In this case, the Embedded MAS must identify the type of resource received and find an agent to control it.

– **Scenario 3:** In the third scenario, a case of fault tolerance is tested. The previously added sensor will stop reporting environmental perceptions to the Embedded MAS. In this case, the agent must stop acting to avoid collisions until the resource is functional again.
– **Scenario 4:** The faulty resource from the previous scenario will be replaced in the fourth scenario. However, the new resource will not maintain compatibility with the removed one. In this case, the Embedded MAS must be able to adapt, and agents still deliberate without any change.
– **Scenario 5:** Finally, the fifth scenario, the actuator will be replaced by another type of actuator compatible with the previous one. In this scenario, the Embedded MAS must recognize the resource exchange and fulfill its mission.

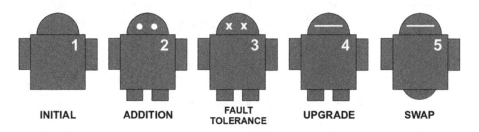

INITIAL   ADDITION   FAULT   UPGRADE   SWAP
                                   TOLERANCE

Fig. 4. The scenarios of proposed case study.

To fulfill the proposed scenarios, we implemented an Embedded MAS, which runs and controls the following physical devices: a single-board computer to host the reasoning layer and some microcontrollers to host the firmware layer. USB ports provide serial communication from the reasoning layer to the firmware layer. Finally, in the hardware layer, the actuators accountable for moving the robot were a biped platform and a wheeled robotic chassis; moreover, the sensors accountable for environmental perceptions used were an infrared sensor and an ultrasonic distance sensor.

4.1 Reasoning Implementation

A MAS was idealized to deal with the unpredictability of physical resources and meet the proposed scenarios, basically containing a coordinator agent for the embedded system and operator agents for dealing with physical resources when they exist. The behavior of these agents is standard, regardless of the framework used, be it Jason Embedded, Jason-CLI, or JaCaMo. Thus, this subsection presents the plans of these agents before presenting each scenario.

Coordinator Agent. The coordinator agent initially aims to test the system's serial ports. For this, three achievement goals were implemented, one for each serial port that triggers a plan to validate serial communication connectivity every five seconds and a contingency plan for when the ports are found, and he can achieve the objective of walking around.

The plan to validate connectivity tries to use the serial port and get the exogenous environment's perceptions. Two plans were implemented to meet these perceptions about the serial port's status. One to abort if the port is in an unknown state. The second is to trigger a plan for employing an operator agent when the serial port is online.

If the employing plan fails, a contingency plan is created to wait until an agent capable of handling the resource arrives at the MAS. In addition, a plan to deal with possible problems informed by the operator agents was implemented so that when a resource fails, the coordinator agent will order all agents in the system using a serial port to stop acting or perceiving. So it will again start the testing serial ports achievement plan.

Finally, when the serial ports are connected and controlled by an operator agent, the coordinator will try to achieve the objective of walking around. For this, three achievement plans were created. First, if the coordinator agent does not have perceptions about obstacles, it will order all agents to inform the exogenous perceptions. In the second, if the coordinator has received information that there is no obstacle, it will order the agents to act. Finally, if it has received information about an obstacle, it will order stopping acting. The coordinator agent code is presented in Code 1.1.

Code 1.1. coordinator.asl.

```
1  /* Initial goals */
2  !testPorts.
3
4  /* Plans */
5  +!testPorts: not using(ttyUSB0) <- !search(ttyUSB0); .wait(5000); !testPorts.
6  +!testPorts: not using(ttyUSB1) <- !search(ttyUSB1); .wait(5000); !testPorts.
7  -!testPorts <- +ready; !walkAround.
8
9  +!search(Port) <- argo.port(Port); argo.limit(2500); argo.percepts(open).
10 +port(P,S): P = unknown <- argo.percepts(close); .abolish(_[source(percept)]).
11 +port(P,S): S=on & resource(R) <- argo.port(none); !newResource(P,R).
12
13 +!newResource(Port,RN)[source(self)]: operator(Ag,R) & R = RN <-
14    .abolish(_[source(percept)]);
15    +using(Port);
16    .send(Ag,achieve,work(Port)).
17 -!newResource(Port,RN) <- .wait(operator(Ag,R)); !newResource(Port,RN).
18 +!offResource(N)[source(LayerAg)]: operator(A,R) & R = N & Ag = A <-
19    .drop_desire(walkAround);
20    .abolish(using(_));
21    .broadcast(achieve,leavePort);
22    !!testPorts.
23
24 +!walkAround: not obstacle(O) & using(ttyUSB0) & using(ttyUSB1)<-
25    .broadcast(askOne,obstacle(R));
26    .wait(obstacle(X));
27    !walkAround.
28 +!walkAround: obstacle(O) & O = no & using(ttyUSB0) & using(ttyUSB1) <-
29    .broadcast(achieve,task(front));
30    .abolish(obstacle(_)[_]);
31    !walkAround.
32 +!walkAround: obstacle(O) & O = yes & using(ttyUSB0) & using(ttyUSB1)<-
33    .broadcast(achieve,task(stop));
34    .abolish(obstacle(_)[_]);
35    !walkAround.
```

Resource Operator Agent. All resource operator agents initially aim to inform the coordinator agent of their abilities. An achievement goal was implemented to meet this objective that sends a message to the coordinator containing the agent's name and the resource's name.

In addition, these agents have a plan that the coordinator agent can trigger to start the serial port control activities. When connecting to the port, agents receive perceptions about serial port status. Two plans were programmed. The first one, if the serial port is on, the agent adds a mental notation that it is ready. Conversely, if the serial port is off, the agent removes the mental notation and sends a message informing the coordinator that the resource is unavailable.

Finally, four plans were implemented: the first was an achievement goal to disconnect from the serial port at the coordinator's request, and the last three were contingency plans. The operator agents' standard code is presented in Code 1.2.

Code 1.2. common/argoAgents.asl.

```
1  /* Initial goals */
2  !infoCoordinator.
3
4  /* Plans */
5  +!infoCoordinator: myResource(R) <- .my_name(N);
       .send(coordinator,tell,operator(N,R)).
6
7  +!work(Port)[source(coordinator)] <- argo.port(Port); argo.percepts(open);
       !conf.
8  +port(Port,Status)[source(percept)]: Status = on & myResource(R) <- +ready.
9  +port(Port,Status)[source(percept)]: Status = off & myResource(R) <
10     -ready;
11     argo.port(none);
12     .abolish(_[source(percept)]);
13     .send(coordinator,achieve,offResource(R)).
14
15 +!leavePort[source(coordinator)] <- !disconf; argo.percepts(close);
       argo.port(none).
16 -!task(T).
17 -!conf.
18 -!disconf.
```

Below are presented the specific behaviors of each resource operator agent used in the study case.

– **Operator Agent 1:** Initially, the agent has a belief about the resource that it can operate. In addition, it has seven achievement goals: the first configures the resource perception cycle to occur every two seconds. The following five are responsible for managing the sending of actuation commands to the resource's microcontroller. The last stops the actuator before releasing the serial port communication. The first operator agent code is presented in Code 1.3.

Code 1.3. resourceOperator1.asl.

```
1  /* Initial goals */
2  myResource(biped).
3
4  /* Plans */
5  +!conf <- argo.limit(2000).
6
7  +!task(T)[source(coordinator)]: not acting & ready & T=front & not
       status(walk) <- !platformOtto(walk).
8  +!task(T)[source(coordinator)]: not acting & ready & T=left & not
       status(turnL)<- !platformOtto(turnL).
9  +!task(T)[source(coordinator)]: not acting & ready & T=right & not
       status(turnR)<- !platformOtto(turnR).
10 +!task(T)[source(coordinator)]: not acting & ready & T=stop & not
       status(stop) <- !platformOtto(stop).
11 +!platformOtto(Op) <- +acting; argo.act(Op); .wait(3000); -acting.
12
13 +!disconf: status(S) & S \== stop <- !platformOtto(stop); !disconf.
14
15 { include("common/argoAgents.asl") }
```

- **Operator Agent 2:** Like the previous one, this agent has an initial belief about the resource it can operate. Moreover, an achievement goal is to carry out the configuration of perception. Finally, it has four plans that manipulate a mental notation regarding the existence or not of an obstacle ahead. The second operator agent code is presented in Code 1.4.

Code 1.4. resourceOperator2.asl.

```
1  /* Initial goals */
2  myResource(obstacleIR).
3
4  /* Plans */
5  +!conf <- argo.limit(1000).
6
7  +left(L): right(R) & R=1 & L=1 <- -+obstacle(no).
8  +right(R): left(L) & R=1 & L=1 <- -+obstacle(no).
9
10 +right(R): left(L) & (R=0 | L=0) <- -+obstacle(yes).
11 +left(L): right(R) & (R=0 | L=0) <- -+obstacle(yes).
12
13 { include("common/argoAgents.asl") }
```

- **Operator Agent 3:** This agent has two initial beliefs, the first referring to the resource it is capable of operating and the second referring to the minimum limit in centimeters to consider that there is an obstacle ahead. Finally, it has two plans that manage a mental notation about the existence of an obstacle ahead. The third operator agent code is presented in Code 1.5.

Code 1.5. resourceOperator3.asl.

```
1  /* Initial goals */
2  myResource(ultrasonicSensor).
3  minimalDistance(20).
4
5  /* Plans */
6  +!conf <- argo.limit(1000).
7
8  +distance(N): minimalDistance(D) & N <= D <- -+obstacle(yes).
9  +distance(N): minimalDistance(D) & N > D <- -+obstacle(no).
10
11 { include("common/argoAgents.asl") }
```

– **Operator Agent 4:** Like the others, the last operator agent has an initial belief about
the resource it operates and a plan for configuring the perception cycle. The following four achievement plans manage the actuator. The final plan is responsible for
stopping the action when the coordinator agent requests the release of the serial
port. The code of the fourth resource operator agent is presented in Code 1.6.

Code 1.6. resourceOperator4.asl.

```
1  /* Initial goals */
2  myResource(wd).
3
4  /* Plans */
5  +!conf <- argo.limit(1000).
6
7  +!task(T)[source(coordinator)]: ready & T=front & not status(running)<-
       argo.act(goAhead).
8  +!task(T)[source(coordinator)]: ready & T=left & not status(turnL)<-
       argo.act(goLeft).
9  +!task(T)[source(coordinator)]: ready & T=right & not status(turnR)<-
       argo.act(goRiht).
10 +!task(T)[source(coordinator)]: ready & T=stop & not status(stop)<-
       argo.act(stop).
11
12 +!disconf: status(S) & S \== stop <- argo.act(stop); .wait(2000); !disconf.
13
14 { include("common/argoAgents.asl") }
```

4.2   Scenario 1: Initial Embedded MAS

In this scenario, the Embedded MAS has no sensor or actuator. Resources are not initially used for acting or perceiving the physical environment. The reasoning, in turn,
runs on a Raspberry Pi Zero W, powered by a 5200 mAh (5 V, 1.0 A) portable battery.
However, the system must be prepared to receive a new resource at anytime. Thus, an
OTG cable and a USB hub are used in the serial communication layer to allow receiving new resources to the system at runtime. Figure 5 shows the necessary hardware to
host the Embedded MAS. Additionally, we deploy an image of ChonOS [15] (*chonos-
beta-RPI-Zero-W*) in a memory card, insert the card into the device, boot the system,
connect it to the network, run the update of all system packages, and restart the device.

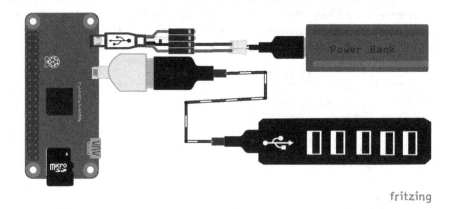

Fig. 5. Schematic of the necessary hardware to host the Embedded MAS.

- Reasoning Layer with *Jason Embedded*. It was necessary to program an Embedded MAS with two initial agents, to fulfill the first scenario using the Jason Embedded. For this, we use the IDE that comes with the ChonOS installation (Fig. 6). The first agent is the coordinator with an Argo architecture, presented in Code 1.1 from Sect. 4.1. The second agent is the telephonist with a Communicator architecture, responsible for managing MAS communications through an IoT gateway.

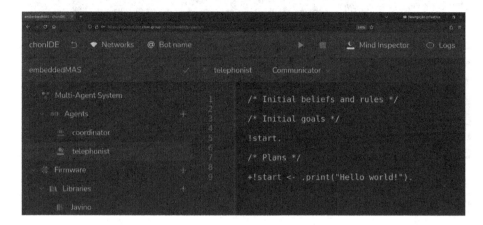

Fig. 6. Developing the Embedded MAS using ChonIDE [13].

The telephonist agent (Code 1.7) has initial beliefs that represent the address of a gateway and its identification in the IoT network. Its initial goal is to stay connected to the network, and for that, an achievement goal was implemented to use *.connectCN* internal action. Two plans are implemented to allow communication management with other MAS: the first is to answer to the sender's attempt of connection, informing that the communication is ready; the second is to forward the received message to one internal agent in the MAS.

Code 1.7. telephonist.asl.

```
1  /* Initial beliefs and rules */
2  myID("10348514-519f-439b-afd7-7330027f4b70").
3  srv("skynet.chon.group",5500). //public IoT gateway address
4
5  /* Initial goals */
6  !connect.
7
8  /* Plans */
9  +!connect: myID(ID) & srv(S,P) <- .connectCN(S,P,ID).
10
11 +communication(trying)[source(X)] <- .sendOut(X,tell,communication(ok)).
12
13 +!retransmit(Dest,Force,Content)[source(X)] <- .send(Dest,Force,Content).
```

A MAS developed with Jason Embedded is an Open MAS. This way, new agents can be added at runtime. Adding operator agents in the initial scenario is unnecessary, and the MAS is easily adaptable to other scenarios.

- Reasoning Layer with *Jason-CLI*. It was necessary to program an Embedded MAS with one initial agent, to fulfill the first scenario using the Jason. For it, we installed the ChonOS Jason-CLI package[1]; after that, an initial project was created, and finally, it was necessary to import the Argo package[2] into the project libraries directory. Figure 7 shows the Jason-CLI environment preparation process.

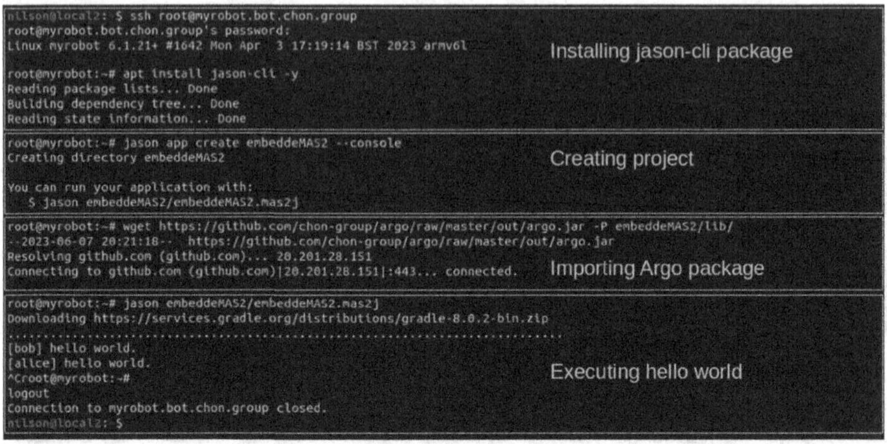

Fig. 7. Developing the MAS using Jason [4] through CLI.

The initial project was changed to serve the scenario, according to Code 1.8. The initial MAS has the coordinator agent, presented in Code 1.1 from Sect. 4.1, which now uses the Argo architecture.

Code 1.8. embeddedMAS2.mas2j.

```
1  MAS embeddedMAS2 {
2      agents: coordinator agentArchClass jason.Argo;
3      aslSourcePath: "src/agt";
4  }
```

- Reasoning Layer with *JaCaMo*. It was necessary to program an Embedded MAS with all agents, to fulfill the first scenario using the JaCaMo. For it, we installed the ChonOS JaCaMo-CLI package[3]; after that, an initial project was created, and finally, it was necessary to import the Argo-jcm package[4] into project file. Figure 8 shows the jacamo-cli environment preparation process.

The initial project was changed to serve the scenario, according to Code 1.8. The initial MAS has the coordinator agent, presented in Code 1.1 and operator agents, presented in Codes 1.3–1.6 from Sect. 4.1, which now uses the Argo architecture.

---

[1] https://github.com/chon-group/dpkg-jason.

[2] https://github.com/chon-group/argo.

[3] https://github.com/chon-group/dpkg-jacamo.

[4] https://github.com/chon-group/argo-jcm.

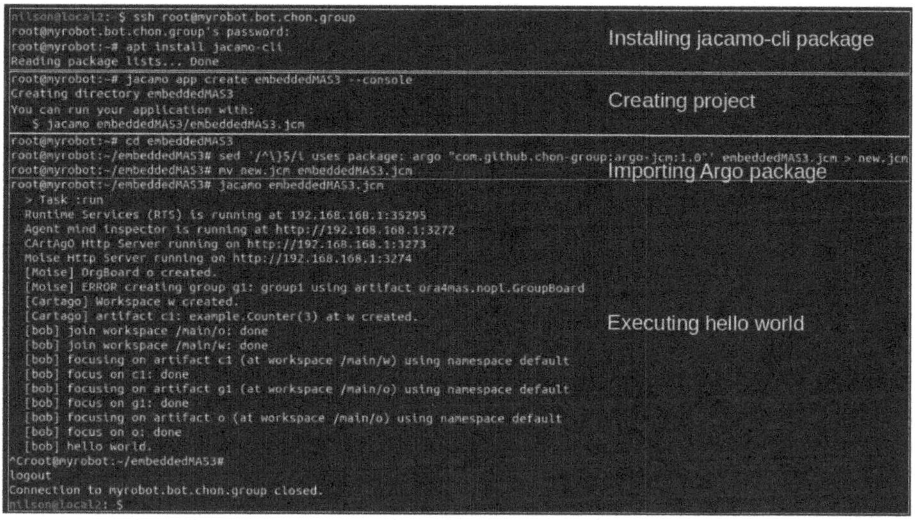

Fig. 8. Developing the MAS using JaCaMo [3] through CLI.

Code 1.9. embeddedMAS3.jcm.

```
1  mas embeddedMAS3 {
2    agent resourceOperator1 { ag-arch: jason.Argo
3    }
4    agent resourceOperator2 { ag-arch: jason.Argo
5    }
6    agent resourceOperator3 { ag-arch: jason.Argo
7    }
8    agent resourceOperator4 { ag-arch: jason.Argo
9    }
10   agent coordinator { ag-arch: jason.Argo
11   }
12   uses package: argo "com.github.chon-group:argo-jcm:1.0.1"
13 }
```

4.3 Scenario 2 - Addition

All interventions performed in the four layers to meet the second scenario will be described in this subsection.

Hardware Layer. For this scenario, two resources were assembled and connected to the USB hub of the prototype at runtime. The first, shown in Fig. 9, is an actuator (biped platform) formed by four Micro Servo 9g SG90 TowerPro. The second, shown in Fig. 10, is an obstacle sensor formed by two IR Sensor Modules.

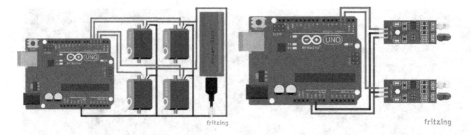

Fig. 9. Schematic of the resource 1. **Fig. 10.** Schematic of the resource 2.

Firmware and Serial Layer. We used the Otto Library to program the microcontroller of the first resource. The microcontroller receives commands (walk, turnL, or turnR) to act in the environment. Besides, it sends two beliefs to the agent, one is the platform's status, and the other is the resource name. Code 1.10 presents the firmware programming of the resource.

Code 1.10. bipcd.ino.

```
1 #include <Javino.h> //https://github.com/chon-group/javino2arduino
2 #include <Otto.h> //https://github.com/OttoDIY/OttoDIYLib
3 Javino javino;
4 Otto Otto;
5 String strStatus = "stop";
6
7 void serialEvent(){javino.readSerial();}
8
9 void setup(){javino.start(9600); Otto.init(4, 5, 2, 3, true, 0);}
10
11 void loop(){if(javino.availableMsg()){
12   if(javino.getMsg()=="getPercepts"){javino.sendMsg("resource(biped);status("+
13     strStatus+");");}
14   else{strStatus = javino.getMsg();}}
15   delay(100);
16   action(strStatus);
17 }
18
19 void action(String strCMD){
20   if(strCMD == "walk"){Otto.walk(1,1000,1);}
21   else if (strCMD == "turnL"){Otto.turn(1,1000,1);}
22   else if (strCMD == "turnR"){Otto.turn(1,1000,-1);}
23 }
```

The microcontroller of the second resource sends three beliefs to the agent, one is the resource name, and the next two are the status of the obstacle ahead. Code 1.11 presents the firmware programming of the second resource.

Code 1.11. obstacle.ino.

```
1 #include <Javino.h> //https://github.com/chon-group/javino2arduino
2 Javino javino;
3
4 void serialEvent(){javino.readSerial();}
5
6 void setup(){javino.start(9600); pinMode(3, INPUT); pinMode(2, INPUT);}
```

```
 7
 8  void loop() {
 9   if(javino.availableMsg()){if(javino.getMsg() == "getPercepts"){
10      javino.sendMsg("resource(obstacleIR);left(" +
11      String(digitalRead(3))+");right(" + String(digitalRead(2))+");");}
12   }
13  }
```

In both cases, the Javino library for Arduino provides the integration of the firmware layer with the reasoning layer.

Reasoning Layer. This layer had different implementations for each of the frameworks used. The operator agent for resource 1 was described in Code 1.3 and the operator agent for resource 2 was described in Code 1.4, both in Sect. 4.1.

- **Using Jason Embedded:** In this case, it was necessary to program a Communicator agent in an external MAS to send the operator. This agent has plans to test communication with the operator agent running on the Embedded MAS. After confirming the connection, the agent executes a plan responsible for sending the operator using the mutualism protocol. Finally, an execution request plan is triggered so that the operator agent, newly arrived at the MAS, informs the coordinator agent. Code 1.12 presents the sender agent plans.

Code 1.12. sender.asl.

```
 1  embMAS("10348514-519f-439b-afd7-7330027f4b70"). /* Initial belief */
 2  !start.            /* Initial goal */
 3  /* Plans */
 4  +!start <-
 5     .connectCN("skynet.chon.group",5500,"19566fee-4bc6-45eb-8f72-455552d50116");
 6     +connected; !testComm.
 7
 8  +!testComm: communication(ok) <- !transmit.
 9  +!testComm : connected & not communication(ok) & embMAS(E)<-
10     .sendOut(E, tell, communication(trying)); .wait(3000); !testComm.
11
12  +!transmit <-
13     !sendAgent(operator1); !requestExecution(operator1, infoCoordinator);
14     !sendAgent(operator2); !requestExecution(operator2, infoCoordinator);
15     .disconnectCN; .stopMAS.
16  +!sendAgent(Agent): embMAS(E) <- .moveOut(E,mutualism,Agent).
17  +!requestExecution(Receiver, Operation): embMAS(E) <-
18     .sendOut(E, achieve, retransmit(Receiver,achieve,Operation)).
```

- **Using Jason:** In this case, shell access to the operating system that hosts the Embedded MAS is required. So, the developer must input the agents into the running MAS using Jason-CLI. Code 1.13 presents the necessary terminal commands.

Code 1.13. jason-cli terminal commands.

```
 1  root@myrobot:~# cd embeddedMAS2/
 2  root@myrobot:~/embeddedMAS2# jason agent start operator1
        --ag-arch=jason.Argo
 3  root@myrobot:~/embeddedMAS2# jason agent load-into
        --source=newAgents/op1.asl operator1
 4  root@myrobot:~/embeddedMAS2# jason agent start operator2
        --ag-arch=jason.Argo
 5  root@myrobot:~/embeddedMAS2# jason agent load-into
        --source=newAgents/op2.asl operator2
```

4.4   Scenario 3 - Fault Tolerance

This scenario is accomplished by the port plan (+*port(Port,Status)*) common to all Argo agents, described in Code 1.2 (in Sect. 4.1). If some communication problem arises with the reasoning layer (*Status=off* context), the agent sends a message to the coordinating agent(*.send(coordinator,achieve,offResource(R))*).

The coordinator agent, in turn, gives up on reaching the goal of walking around (*.drop_desire(walkAround)*), asks all agents to release the serial ports (*.broadcast(achieve,leavePort)*), clears its beliefs about the use of ports (*.abolish(using(_))*) and start testing the serial ports again, and then employ the operator agents. The Code1.1, described in Sect. 4.1, presents the coordinating agent's plans to deal with this scenario of failure in communication with the resources.

4.5   Scenario 4 - Upgrade

Interventions performed in the four layers to meet scenario 4 are described in this subsection.

Hardware Layer. A distance sensor was made to meet this scenario. It consists of an ultrasonic sensor HC-SR04. Besides, resource 2 was removed from the USB port, and resource 3 has been plugged into its place. The resource schematic is shown in Fig. 11.

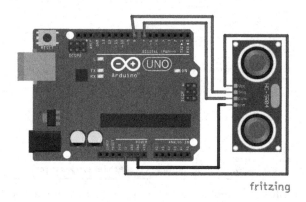

Fig. 11. Schematic of the resource 3.

Firmware and Serial Layer. To program the firmware for this resource, we used the HCSR04 library. The microcontroller informs the operator agent of the distance in centimeters and the resource's name. To allow communication between the layers, the Javino library for Arduino was used. The resource schedule is presented in the Code 1.14.

Code 1.14. ultrasonic.ino.

```
1  #include <Javino.h> //Available at:
        https://github.com/chon-group/javino2arduino
2  #include <HCSR04.h> //Available at:
        https://www.arduinolibraries.info/libraries/hcsr04
3  Javino javino;
4  HCSR04 hc(8, 7);
5
6  void serialEvent(){javino.readSerial();}
7
8  void setup() {javino.start(9600); pinMode(7, INPUT); pinMode(8, OUTPUT);}
9
10 void loop(){if(javino.availableMsg()){
11    if(javino.getMsg()=="getPercepts"){javino.sendMsg("distance("
12    +String(hc.dist())+");resource(ultrasonicSensor);");}}
13 }
```

Reasoning Layer. In the reasoning layer, using Jason Embedded, it was necessary to implement a MAS to send the coordinator agent in the same way as performed in scenario number 2 (Code1.12). The only difference in this scenario is that only one agent is sent. Operator agent 3, described in Code1.5 (Sect. 4.1). Similarly, when using Jason, the developer must have access to the operating system hosting the MAS to run the terminal commands, add an empty agent to the SMA, and later load the plans described above.

4.6 Scenario 5 - SWAP

Interventions performed in the four layers to meet scenario 5 are described in this subsection.

Hardware Layer. In this scenario, a 2WD robotic platform was used. Resource 1 has been removed from the USB port, and this resource has been plugged into its place. The schematic of resource 4 is shown in Fig. 12.

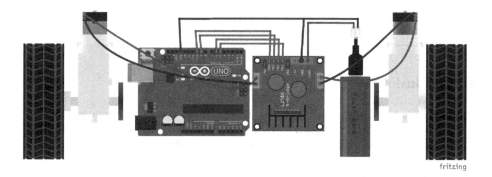

Fig. 12. Schematic of the resource 4.

Firmware and Serial Layer. The microcontroller of resource 4 receives the commands (goAhead, goLeft, goRight, or stop) sent by the operator agent to act in the environment. In addition, the microcontroller reports the actuators' status to the agent. The Javino library for Arduino provides communication between the agent and the resource. The programming is presented in Code 1.15.

Reasoning Layer. In the reasoning layer, using Jason Embedded, it was necessary to implement a MAS to send the coordinator agent in the same way as performed in scenarios 2 and 3 (Code 1.12). This operator agent is described in Code 1.6, in Sect. 4.1. Similarly, when using Jason, the developer must have access to the operating system hosting the MAS, to run the terminal commands to add an empty agent to the SMA and later load the plans described above.

Code 1.15. 2WD.ino.

```
#include <Javino.h> //Available at: https://github.com/chon-group/javino2arduino
Javino javino;
String strMotorStatus;

void serialEvent(){ javino.readSerial(); }

void setup(){javino.start(9600); pinMode(5, OUTPUT); pinMode(6, OUTPUT);
            pinMode(9, OUTPUT); pinMode(10, OUTPUT);}

void loop(){
if(javino.availableMsg()){
  String strMsg = javino.getMsg();
  if(strMsg=="getPercepts")javino.sendMsg("resource(wd);motor("+strMotorStatus+");");
    else if(strMsg=="stop")stopRightNow();
    else if(strMsg=="goLeft")turnLeft();
    else if(strMsg=="goRight")turnRight();
    else if(strMsg=="goAhead")goAhead();
  }
}

void stopRightNow(){digitalWrite(5, LOW); digitalWrite(6, LOW); digitalWrite(9,
    LOW);
                    digitalWrite(10, LOW); strMotorStatus="stopped";}

void goAhead(){stopRightNow(); digitalWrite(6, HIGH); digitalWrite(10, HIGH);
    strMotorStatus="running";}

void turnRight(){stopRightNow(); digitalWrite(5, HIGH); digitalWrite(10, HIGH);
    strMotorStatus="turningRight";}

void turnLeft(){stopRightNow(); digitalWrite(6, HIGH); digitalWrite(9, HIGH);
    strMotorStatus="turningLeft";}
```

5 Conclusions

This work presented three approaches to adding, removing, and swapping resources (sensors or actuators) in Embedded MAS at runtime using a customized agent architecture capable of perceiving the availability of microcontrollers integrated into the system via serial communication. The first approach uses an IoT infrastructure to receive or send agents able to operate resources unknown by a society of agents. In this approach, we used Jason Embedded and ChonIDE.

Considering the access to the CLI of the operating system that hosts the Embedded MAS, the second approach uses the developer's ability to create and include new agents capable of operating a new resource in the runtime. In this approach, we used Jason-CLI.

In the third approach, we developed an Embedded MAS using JaCaMo-CLI. However, in this approach, the creation or reception of new agents at runtime is still open; therefore, all possible resources to be added at runtime must exist at design time.

A case study with five possible runtime scenarios with an embedded MAS was conducted to analyze the proposed approaches, demonstrating that swapping resources at runtime is a promissory feature to guarantee the adaptability of intelligent cyber-physical systems.

Adding resources allows an Embedded MAS to be updated and improved at runtime without stopping it. Stopping a MAS can lead to some undesired situations, for example, in a mission-critical domain, which could generate failures because of the absence of information. Besides, when adding a new resource, it would be necessary to modify the physical structure of the device, offering some continuity and availability risks of the service that the device is running. Until recently, any resource addition forces the device to be turned off, limiting the adaptability inherent to a Cognitive MAS.

This discussion can also be expanded toward replacing and removing resources at runtime. In embedded systems, it is not uncommon for components to be damaged when interacting with the real world, given their unpredictability. In the presented approaches, the replacement could be performed without risks to the Embedded MAS if the damaged resource is replaced by another one of the same logical structure connected to the same serial port. Removing a resource (whether damaged or intentionally removed) leads to readapting the Embedded MAS to avoid pursuing intentions and objectives that can no longer be achieved due to the absence of interfacing. In this case, mechanisms for removing intentions, objectives, or plans are necessary.

Swapping resources at runtime still requires a multidisciplinary effort from the designer team since it has to know several areas (electronics, operating systems, object-oriented and agent-oriented programming). Besides, adding an totally unknown resource is still an open issue in the domain. In future works, a mechanism is needed for the dynamic management of resources in Embedded MAS so that, when adding a new resource, the MAS would automatically recognize the device and its functionalities without transferring agents from other systems or searching the necessary plans to operate the resource.

References

1. Artikis, A., Pitt, J.: Specifying open agent systems: a survey. In: Artikis, A., Picard, G., Vercouter, L. (eds.) ESAW 2008. LNCS (LNAI), vol. 5485, pp. 29–45. Springer, Heidelberg (2009). https://doi.org/10.1007/978-3-642-02562-4_2
2. Balaji, P.G., Srinivasan, D.: An introduction to multi-agent systems. In: Srinivasan, D., Jain, L.C. (eds.) Innovations in Multi-Agent Systems and Applications - 1. Studies in Computational Intelligence, vol. 310, pp. 1–27. Springer, Heidelberg (2010). https://doi.org/10.1007/978-3-642-14435-6_1
3. Boissier, O., Bordini, R.H., Hübner, J.F., Ricci, A., Santi, A.: Multi-agent oriented programming with jacamo. Sci. Comput. Program. **78**(6), 747–761 (2013). https://doi.org/10.1016/j.scico.2011.10.004. Special section: The Programming Languages track at the 26th ACM

Symposium on Applied Computing (SAC 2011) & Special section on Agent-oriented Design Methods and Programming Techniques for Distributed Computing in Dynamic and Complex Environments

4. Bordini, R., Hübner, J., Wooldridge, M.: Programming Multi-agent Systems in AgentSpeak Using Jason. Wiley Series in Agent Technology. Wiley (2007)

5. Brandão, F.C., Lima, M.A.T., Pantoja, C.E., Zahn, J., Viterbo, J.: Engineering approaches for programming agent-based IoT objects using the resource management architecture. Sensors **21**(23) (2021). https://doi.org/10.3390/s21238110

6. Bratman, M.E.: Intention, Plans and Practical Reasoning. Cambridge Press, Cambridge (1987)

7. Bratman, M.E., Israel, D.J., Pollack, M.E.: Plans and resource-bounded practical reasoning. Comput. Intell. **4**(3), 349–355 (1988)

8. Demazeau, Y., Costa, A.R.: Populations and organizations in open multi-agent systems. In: Proceedings of the 1st National Symposium on Parallel and Distributed AI, pp. 1–13 (1996)

9. Dennis, L.A., Farwer, B.: Gwendolen: a BDI language for verifiable agents. In: Proceedings of the AISB 2008 Symposium on Logic and the Simulation of Interaction and Reasoning, Society for the Study of Artificial Intelligence and Simulation of Behaviour, pp. 16–23 (2008)

10. Endler, M., et al.: ContextNet: context reasoning and sharing middleware for large-scale pervasive collaboration and social networking. In: Proceedings of the Workshop on Posters and Demos Track, PDT 2011. Association for Computing Machinery, New York (2011). https://doi.org/10.1145/2088960.2088962

11. Hamdani, M., Sahli, N., Jabeur, N., Khezami, N.: Agent-based approach for connected vehicles and smart road signs collaboration. Comput. Inform. **41**(1), 376–396 (2022). https://doi.org/10.31577/cai_2022_1_376

12. Hubner, J.F., Sichman, J.S., Boissier, O.: Developing organised multiagent systems using the MOISE+ model: programming issues at the system and agent levels. Int. J. Agent-Oriented Softw. Eng. **1**(3–4), 370–395 (2007). https://doi.org/10.1504/IJAOSE.2007.016266

13. Souza de Jesus, V., Mori Lazarin, N., Pantoja, C.E., Vaz Alves, G., Ramos Alves de Lima, G., Viterbo, J.: An ide to support the development of embedded multi-agent systems. In: Mathieu, P., Dignum, F., Novais, P., De la Prieta, F. (eds.) PAAMS 2023. LNCS, vol. 13955. pp. 346–358. Springer, Cham (2023). https://doi.org/10.1007/978-3-031-37616-0_29

14. Lazarin., N., Pantoja., C., Viterbo., J.: Swapping physical resources at runtime in embedded multiagent systems. In: Proceedings of the 15th International Conference on Agents and Artificial Intelligence - Volume 1: ICAART, pp. 93–104. INSTICC, SciTePress (2023). https://doi.org/10.5220/0011750700003393

15. Lazarin, N., Pantoja, C., Viterbo, J.: Towards a toolkit for teaching AI supported by robotic-agents: proposal and first impressions. In: Anais do XXXI Workshop sobre Educação em Computação, pp. 20–29. SBC, Porto Alegre (2023). https://doi.org/10.5753/wei.2023.229753

16. Lazarin, N.M., Pantoja, C.E.: A robotic-agent platform for embedding software agents using raspberry pi and arduino boards. In: 9th Software Agents, Environments and Applications School (2015)

17. Manoel, F., Pantoja, C.E., Samyn, L., de Jesus, V.S.: Physical artifacts for agents in a cyber-physical system: a case study in oil & gas scenario (EEAS). In: SEKE, pp. 55–60 (2020)

18. Michaloski, J., Schlenoff, C., Cardoso, R., Fisher, M., et al.: Agile Robotic Planning with Gwendolen (2022)

19. Pantoja, C.E., de Jesus, V.S., Lazarin, N.M., Viterbo, J.: A spin-off version of Jason for IoT and embedded multiagent systems. In: Naldi, M.C., Bianchi, R.A.C. (eds.) BRACIS 2023. LNCS, vol. 14195, pp. 382–396. Springer, Cham (2023). https://doi.org/10.1007/978-3-031-45368-7_25

20. Pantoja, C.E., Soares, H.D., Viterbo, J., Alexandre, T., Seghrouchni, A.E.F., Casals, A.: Exposing IoT objects in the internet using the resource management architecture. Int. J. Softw. Eng. Knowl. Eng. **29**(11n12), 1703–1725 (2019). https://doi.org/10.1142/S0218194019400175

21. Pantoja, C.E., Stabile, M.F., Lazarin, N.M., Sichman, J.S.: ARGO: an extended Jason architecture that facilitates embedded robotic agents programming. In: Baldoni, M., Müller, J.P., Nunes, I., Zalila-Wenkstern, R. (eds.) EMAS 2016. LNCS (LNAI), vol. 10093, pp. 136–155. Springer, Cham (2016). https://doi.org/10.1007/978-3-319-50983-9_8

22. Pokahr, A., Braubach, L., Lamersdorf, W.: Jadex: A BDI reasoning engine. In: Bordini, R.H., Dastani, M., Dix, J., El Fallah Seghrouchni, A. (eds.) Multi-Agent Programming. MSASSO, vol. 15, pp. 149–174. Springer, Boston, MA (2005). https://doi.org/10.1007/0-387-26350-0_6

23. Ricci, A., Piunti, M., Viroli, M., Omicini, A.: Environment programming in CArtAgO. In: El Fallah Seghrouchni, A., Dix, J., Dastani, M., Bordini, R.H. (eds.) Multi-Agent Programming, pp. 259–288. Springer, Boston (2009). https://doi.org/10.1007/978-0-387-89299-3_8

24. Shehory, O., Sycara, K., Chalasani, P., Jha, S.: Agent cloning: an approach to agent mobility and resource allocation. IEEE Commun. Mag. **36**(7), 58–67 (1998). https://doi.org/10.1109/35.689632

25. Silva, G.R., Becker, L.B., Hübner, J.F.: Embedded architecture composed of cognitive agents and ROS for programming intelligent robots. IFAC-PapersOnLine **53**(2), 10000–10005 (2020). https://doi.org/10.1016/j.ifacol.2020.12.2718. 21st IFAC World Congress

26. Souza de Jesus, V., Pantoja, C., Manoel, F., Alves, G., Viterbo, J., Bezerra, E.: Bio-inspired protocols for embodied multi-agent systems. In: Proceedings of the 13th International Conference on Agents and Artificial Intelligence - Volume 1: ICAART, pp. 312–320. INSTICC, SciTePress (2021). https://doi.org/10.5220/0010257803120320

27. Stabile, M.F., Jr., Pantoja, C.E., Sichman, J.S.: Experimental analysis of the effect of filtering perceptions in BDI agents. Int. J. Agent-Oriented Softw. Eng. **6**(3–4), 329–368 (2018)

28. Weiss, G.: Multiagent Systems: A Modern Approach to Distributed Artificial Intelligence, 1st edn. MIT Press, Cambridge (2000)

29. Wooldridge, M.: An Introduction to MultiAgent Systems. Wiley, Hoboken (2009)

30. Wooldridge, M.: Intelligent agents. In: Multiagent Systems: A Modern Approach to Distributed Artificial Intelligence, 1st edn. MIT Press, Cambridge (2000)

Coalition Alternating-Time Temporal Logic: A Logic to Find Good Coalitions to Achieve Strategic Objectives

Davide Catta[1], Angelo Ferrando[2], and Vadim Malvone[1(✉)]

[1] LTCI, Telecom Paris, Institut Polytechnique de Paris, Palaiseau, France
{davide.catta,vadim.malvone}@telecom-paris.fr
[2] Department of Informatics, Bioengineering, Robotics and Systems Engineering,
University of Genoa, Genoa, Italy
angelo.ferrando@unige.it

Abstract. Alternating-time Temporal Logic (ATL) extends the temporal logic CTL, permitting quantification over coalitions of agents. During the model checking process, the coalitions defined in a given formula are predetermined, operating under the assumption that the user possesses knowledge about the specific coalitions under exam. However, this presumption is not universally applicable. The outcome of this paper is twofold. Initially, we introduce CATL, a modified version of ATL which empowers users to define coalition quantifiers based on two key attributes: the number of agents involved within the coalitions and the methodology for grouping these agents. Subsequently, we show the incorporation of CATL into MCMAS, a widely recognized tool dedicated to ATL model checking. Additionally, we provide details of this extension accompanied by empirical experiments.

Keywords: Logics for strategic reasoning · Alternating-time Temporal logic · Coalition of agents · Formal verification

1 Introduction

It is difficult to fully trust software systems. When considering the reliability of a software system, it is therefore crucial to ensure certain guarantees are in place for the end user. Out of these guarantees is demonstrating the correctness of the system under exams, and it poses a particularly challenging task. For this very reason, the formal verification of Multi-Agent Systems (MAS) has become an important research field in both theoretical and applied computer science during the last decades. Reactive, autonomous, and distributed systems have become ubiquitous nowadays, and as a result, the need to verify the correctness of such systems has emerged. One of the main contributions in formal verification of MAS is model checking: to verify if a MAS satisfies a given property of interest, a mathematical model (usually a graph-like entity) of the MAS is defined and the property of interest is expressed as a formula in some logical language (usually temporal logic). To ensure that the MAS satisfies the property, we check whether the mathematical representation of the MAS is a *model* (in the logical sense) of the logical formula expressing the property of interest. Agents of a MAS are

A. P. Rocha et al. (Eds.): ICAART 2023, LNAI 14546, pp. 72–94, 2024.
https://doi.org/10.1007/978-3-031-55326-4_4

often conceived as players of a concurrent game: they act synchronously, they have a goal, and they can pursue the latter either alone or by forming coalitions with other agents. For this reason, logics that are used to specify the properties of interest are usually strategic logics [1, 17]. In particular, one of the most popular logics that is used to specify desired properties of a MAS is Alternating-time Temporal Logic (ATL) [1]. This latter logic is an extension of Computation Tree Logic (CTL) obtained by substituting the path quantifiers "there is a path" and "for all paths" of CTL with two strategic operators, $\langle\langle \Gamma \rangle\rangle$ and $[\![\Gamma]\!]$, whose meaning can be spelled out as "there exists a joint strategy for the coalition of agents Γ" and "for all strategies for the coalition of agents Γ", respectively. In this context, a strategy is a generic conditional plan that at each step of the game prescribes an action. With more detail, there are two main classes of strategies: memoryless and memoryfull. In the former case, agents choose an action by considering only the current state while, in the latter case, agents choose an action by considering the full history of the MAS.

From a practical point of view, the most popular tool for the model checking of Multi-Agent Systems is MCMAS [16]. In this tool, the Multi-Agent System is formally modeled as an interpreted system that is a product of local models, one for each agent involved in the multi-agent system to represent its visibility. MCMAS provides the specification of properties via CTL, ATL [1], Strategy Logic [17], and some of their extensions/fragments. The tool handles the model checking problem by using a Binary Decision Diagram (BDD) representation for models and formulas.

Notice that, in the model checking process, both from a theoretical and practical viewpoint, the coalitions in the strategic operators need to be fixed before the verification process. The latter constraint is not always well-known by the developers/users called to verify the Multi-Agent System. In the following, we analyze the main features related to our extension.

Coalitions as Variables. To automatically generate the coalitions in an ATL formula φ, it is first necessary to have a way to uniquely identify each coalition inside the formula. In more detail, given an ATL formula φ, we can annotate each strategic operator with a corresponding variable. Just to make an example. Let us assume the ATL formula φ is as follows: $\langle\langle a, b \rangle\rangle F \langle\langle b, c \rangle\rangle G \langle\langle a, c \rangle\rangle X p$; with $\{a, b\}$, $\{b, c\}$, and $\{a, c\}$ three coalitions, and p an atomic proposition. The formula becomes $\langle\langle \Gamma_1 \rangle\rangle F \langle\langle \Gamma_2 \rangle\rangle G \langle\langle \Gamma_3 \rangle\rangle X p$, where Γ_1, Γ_2, and Γ_3 are three variables, which will be replaced by the automatically generated coalitions. Note that, in all strategic operators we may add the same Γ variable. In such a case, we would enforce to use the same coalition in the three strategic operators of φ.

In the following, we report the kind of rules we want to enforce over the coalitions. Such rules guide the coalitions' generation, so that all coalitions proposed by our approach both make φ satisfied in the formal model and respect all the guidelines.

Two types of features could be of interest in our investigation: the number of agents and how to group the agents.

Number of Agents in Coalition. The first analysis concerns the size of the coalitions to generate. In more detail, we want to enforce the minimum (resp. maximum) number of agents per coalition. This is very important, because it relates to possible real-world limitations. For instance, there might be scenarios where coalitions with less than n

or more than m agents are not reasonable, because to create a coalition of less than n or more than m agents is too expensive for its gain. For this reason, a min (resp. max) constraint can be specified to rule out all Γ coalitions such that $min \leq |\Gamma|$ (resp. $|\Gamma| \leq max$).

Agents in the Same/Different Coalition. Another relevant group of features concerns which agents can (or not) be in the same coalition. Again, this finds its motivation in real-world applications, where it is common to have limitations on how some agents can be grouped. For instance, considering that the agents are commonly situated in an environment, it may be possible that some of them are close (or not) to each other. For this reason, there might be interest in not having in the same coalition agents that are far from each other (for technological and practical reasons), while there might be interest in having in the same coalition agents that are local to each other. For this reason, a $[a \rightarrow\leftarrow b]$ (resp. $[a \leftarrow\rightarrow b]$) constraint can be specified to keep all Γ coalitions s.t. $a \in \Gamma \iff b \in \Gamma$ (resp. $a \in \Gamma \implies b \notin \Gamma$ and $b \in \Gamma \implies a \notin \Gamma$); where a and b can be any agent.

In this paper, we propose a methodology to tackle the above mentioned rules. To do so, we first introduce a variant of ATL (which we call Coalition ATL) in which the following specifications can be expressed:

1. there is a coalition Π which includes all the members of Γ and all those of Δ such that the member of Π can realize φ by coordinating their actions;
2. there is a coalition Π which includes all the members of Γ and no member of Δ such that the members of Π can realize φ by coordinating their actions;
3. there is a coalition Π counting at most n agents such that the members of Π can realize φ by coordinating their actions;
4. there is a coalition Π counting at least n agents such that the members of Π can realize φ by coordinating their actions;

where Γ and Δ are two coalitions of agents, n is a natural number, and φ is a formula expressing a desired property of the MAS.

Coalition ATL (or CATL for short) is obtained by considering four new strategic operators whose intuitive semantics is expressed in the four above statements. We study the formal properties of this logic. In particular, we show that CATL and ATL have the same expressive power, but CATL can express some ATL properties in an exponentially more concise manner.

After having introduced CATL, we detail an implementation of it in MCMAS. More precisely, we present an extension of MCMAS in which we give the ability to the end user to characterize the coalitions in the strategy quantifiers with respect to two main features: the *number of agents* involved in the coalitions and *how to group* the agents. That is, we ask the user to give some information on the coalitions involved in each strategic operator by considering them as a variable of the problem. With more detail, the user can input a minimum and maximum number of agents involved in the coalitions and give guidelines with respect to the agents that have to (resp., cannot) stay in the same coalitions. After that, our tool extracts all coalitions of agents that respect the user's guidelines. Then, for each valid coalition, our tool verifies the formal specification over the Multi-Agent System. Finally, the coalitions that make the formal specification satisfied in the Multi-Agent System are returned to the user. We consider our work as a first stone on the development of a more generalized tool for the verification of multi-agent systems.

Differently from [13], in this work we introduce the formal machinery to verify parametric ATL formulas w.r.t. the generated coalitions. To achieve this, we introduce CATL, a variant of ATL that we prove to be as expressive as ATL, but whose formulas are exponentially more succinct. In addition, we provide additional experimental results on some CATL formulas.

Structure of the Work. The paper is structured as follows. In Sect. 2 we give some related works on formal verification of multi-agent systems. In Sect. 3 we define CATL, we prove that CATL and ATL have the same expressive power, and we study the model checking for our logic. In Sect. 4 we recall the definition of interpreted systems, which are the mathematical models used in practice. To exemplify our approach, we present a variant of the Train Gate Controller in Sect. 5. Then, in Sect. 6 we provide the algorithms to solve CATL model checking via ATL model checking. Finally, we give the details of our extension for MCMAS in Sect. 7 and, in Sect. 8, provide experimental results on a parameterised version of the Train Gate Controller scenario. We conclude in Sect. 9 by recapping our work.

2 Related Work

In the introduction, we mentioned another important logic for the strategic reasoning called Strategy Logic (SL) [17]. The latter is a powerful formalism for strategic reasoning. As a key aspect, this logic treats strategies as *first-order objects* that can be determined by means of the existential $\exists x$ and universal $\forall x$ quantifiers, which can be respectively read as *"there exists a strategy x"* and *"for all strategies x"*. Therefore, in Strategy Logic, these strategies are not intrinsically glued to a specific agent, but an explicit binding operator (a, x) allows to link an agent a to the strategy associated with a variable x. Unfortunately, the high expressiveness of SL comes at a price. Indeed, it has been proved that the model checking problem for SL becomes non-elementary complete [17] and the satisfiability undecidable [18]. To gain back elementariness, several fragments of SL have been considered. Among the others, Strategy Logic with Simple-Goals [5] considers SL formulas in which strategic operators, bindings operators, and temporal operators are coupled. It has been shown that Strategy Logic with Simple-Goals strictly subsumes ATL and its model checking problem is PTIME-COMPLETE, as it is for ATL [1]. Note that, none of these fragments, nor SL, explicitly allow to parameterize over the coalition of agents.

To conclude this section, we want to focus on the agents' information. Specifically, we distinguish between *perfect* and *imperfect* information [20]. The former corresponds to a basic setting in which every agent has full knowledge about the MAS. However, in real-life scenarios it is common to have situations in which agents have to play without having all relevant information at hand. In computer science these situations occur for example when some variables of a system are internal/private and not visible to an external environment [8, 15]. In MAS, the imperfect information is usually modeled by setting an indistinguishability relation over the states of the system [15, 19, 20]. This feature deeply impacts on the model checking complexity. For example, ATL becomes undecidable in the context of imperfect information and memoryful strategies [10]. To overcome this problem, some works have either focused on an approximation to perfect information [3, 7], developed notions of bounded memory [2, 6], or developed hybrid techniques [11, 12, 14]. Note that, even though in this work we focus on the perfect information scenario, our results hold in the imperfect one as well. We decided to tackle the former case to simplify the presentation and help the reader to fully understand the contribution of the work.

3   Coalition ATL

In this section, we introduce Coalition ATL (CATL for short). Before detailing the syntax and semantics of CATL, let us fix some notation and terminology that we shall use along the paper.

Preliminary Notions. If V is a set and $U \subseteq V$, we denote by $\overline{U}$ the complementary $V \setminus U$ of U in V. If v is a (finite or infinite) sequence over U, we denote by $|v|$ its length (which is ω if v is infinite), by v_i its i-th element, by $v_{\leq i}$ the finite prefix $v_1, \ldots, v_i$ of v and by $v_{\geq i}$ the (possibly infinite) suffix of v starting at v_i. If v is a finite sequence, $last(v)$ denotes the last element $v_{|v|}$ of v. We fix once and for all a finite set Ap of atomic propositions or atoms (the letters $p, q, r, \ldots$ will range over this set) and a finite set $\mathsf{Ag} = \{1, \ldots, n\}$ of agents. A subset of Ag will be called a coalition and we will use the Greek Letters $\Gamma, \Delta, \Pi \ldots$ to range over them. If $l = \langle x_1, \ldots, x_n \rangle$ is a tuple, we denote by $l[i]$ the i-th component x_i of the tuple.

3.1   Syntax

We now define the syntax of CATL.

Definition 1. *State φ and path ψ formulas are defined by mutual induction using the following grammar:*

$$\varphi ::= \top \mid p \mid \neg\varphi \mid \varphi \vee \varphi \mid \langle\!\langle \Gamma \rangle\!\rangle \psi \mid \langle\!\langle \Gamma {\rightarrow} {\leftarrow} \Delta \rangle\!\rangle \psi \mid \langle\!\langle \Gamma \to \Delta \rangle\!\rangle \psi \mid \langle\!\langle \leq_n \rangle\!\rangle \psi \mid \langle\!\langle \geq_n \rangle\!\rangle \psi$$

$$\psi ::= \mathsf{X}\,\varphi \mid \varphi\,\mathsf{U}\,\varphi \mid \varphi\,\mathsf{R}\,\varphi$$

where p is an atom, Γ and Δ are coalitions, and $n \leq |\mathsf{Ag}|$ is a natural number. The boolean connectives $\to$ and $\wedge$, and the temporal connectives F and G can be defined as usual. We define $\langle\!\langle \Gamma {\leftarrow}{\rightarrow} \Delta \rangle\!\rangle \psi$ as $(\langle\!\langle \Gamma \to \Delta \rangle\!\rangle \psi) \vee (\langle\!\langle \Delta \to \Gamma \rangle\!\rangle \psi)$. Formulas of CATL are all and only state formulas. Formulas of ATL are CATL formulas in which no occurrences of the operators $\langle\!\langle \Gamma {\rightarrow}{\leftarrow} \Delta \rangle\!\rangle$, $\langle\!\langle \Gamma \to \Delta \rangle\!\rangle$, $\langle\!\langle \leq_n \rangle\!\rangle$, and $\langle\!\langle \geq_n \rangle\!\rangle$ appear for any Γ, Δ, and n.

The size of a formula is the height of its construction tree, the formal definition follows.

Definition 2. *The size* $|\theta|$ *of a formula* θ *is recursively defined as follows:*

- *if* θ *is an atom then* $|\theta| = 0$;
- *if* θ *is* $\theta_1 \star \theta_2$ *with* $\star \in \{\wedge, \vee, \mathsf{U}, \mathsf{R}\}$, *then* $|\theta| = max(|\theta_1|, |\theta_2|) + 1$;
- *if* θ *is* $\circ\theta_1$ *with* $\circ \in \{\mathsf{X}, \langle\!\langle\Gamma\rangle\!\rangle, \langle\!\langle\Gamma\rightarrow\leftarrow\Delta\rangle\!\rangle, \langle\!\langle\Gamma\rightarrow\Delta\rangle\!\rangle, \langle\!\langle\leq_n\rangle\!\rangle, \langle\!\langle\geq_n\rangle\!\rangle\}$, *then* $|\theta| = |\theta_1| + 1$.

3.2 Semantics

We specify the meaning of CATL formulas by means of Concurrent Game Structures (CGS for short). Intuitively, a CGS is a labeled directed graph that represents the possible evolution of a given Multi-Agent System with respect to simultaneous choices of actions of a group of (autonomous) agents. Both states and edges are labeled by members of two disjoints alphabets. States are labeled by atomic propositions. These atomic propositions represent the properties that are true at a given state. Each edge is labeled by a tuple, and each member of a given tuple represents an action that is available for a given agent at the source state of the edge. The formal definition follows.

Definition 3. *Given a set* Ap *of atomic proposition, and a set* Ag $= \{1, \ldots, k\}$ *of agents, A Concurrent Game Structure with Imperfect Information (iCGS for short) constructed over* Ap *and* Ag *is a tuple* $M = \langle S, s_I, \{Act_i\}_{i \in \mathsf{Ag}}, P, T, \{\sim_i\}_{i \in \mathsf{Ag}}, \mathcal{L}\rangle$, *where:*

- S *is a finite set of states and* $s_I \in S$ *is the initial state.*
- Act_i *is a finite non-empty set of actions for any* $i \in$ Ag; *we denote by* ACT *the product set* $\Pi_{i \in \mathsf{Ag}} Act_i$ *and we call elements of this set* joint actions.
- $P : S \times Ag \rightarrow (2^{Act_i} \setminus \emptyset)$ *is the protocol function which assigns a non empty-subset of actions* $P(s, i)$ *of* Act_i *to any agent* i *and state* s. *The set* $P(s, i)$ *represents the set of actions that are available at the state* s *to the agent* i.
- $T : S \times ACT \rightarrow S$ *is the (partial) transition function. Such function associates to any state* s *and joint action* $\mathbf{a} = \langle a_1, \ldots, a_k\rangle$ *such that for all* $i \in$ Ag, $\mathbf{a}[i] \in P(s, i)$, *a state* $s' = T(s, \mathbf{a})$.
- *for each* $i \in$ Ag, $\sim_i \subseteq S \times S$ *is an equivalence relation dubbed* indistinguishability *relation.*
- $\mathcal{L} : S \rightarrow 2^{Ap}$ *is the labeling function, assigning each state* s *to a (possibly empty) subset of* Ap.

Given an iCGS M, we say that M is a CGS when the indistinguishability relation $\sim_i$ is the identity for any $i \in$ Ag.

A path ρ is an infinite sequence of states of M, $\rho = s_1, s_2, s_3, \ldots$ respecting the following constraints: for every $i \geq 1$, there is a joint action $\mathbf{a}$ such that $T(s_i, \mathbf{a}) = s_{i+1}$. We denote paths by ρ, τ, and π. An history h is a finite prefix of some path ρ. We use H to denote the set of histories. Given two histories h and h', we say that h and h' are indistinguishable for the agent i (denoted by $h \equiv_i h'$) when they have the same length m and $\langle h_j, h'_j\rangle \in \sim_i$ for all $j \leq m$.

Definition 4. *A uniform strategy (strategy for short) for an agent* i *is a function* $\sigma_i : H \rightarrow Act_i$ *such that:*

1. *for every $h \in H$ we have that $\sigma_i(h) \in P(last(h), i)$.*
2. *For every pair of histories h and h', $h \equiv_i h'$ implies $\sigma_i(h) = \sigma_i(h')$.*

A strategy is memoryless when for every pair of histories h and h' we have that $last(h) = last(h')$ implies $\sigma(h) = \sigma(h')$.

As usual, we can see a memoryless strategy for an agent as a function whose domain is the set of states of the iCGS and whose co-domain is the set of agents actions.

Given a coalition Γ, a uniform strategy for Γ, or simply Γ-strategy, is a collection σ_Γ of uniform strategies comprising one strategy σ_i for each $i \in \Gamma$. Given a path ρ, we say that ρ is σ_Γ-compatible iff for every $j \geq 1$, $\rho_{j+1} = T(\rho_j, \mathbf{a})$ for some joint action $\mathbf{a}$ such that for every $i \in \Gamma$, $\mathbf{a}[i] = \sigma_i(\rho_{\leq j})$, and for every $k \in \overline{\Gamma}$, $\mathbf{a}[k] \in P(\rho_j, k)$. We denote with $Out(s, \sigma_\Gamma)$ the set of all σ_Γ-compatible paths whose first state is s.

Finally, given a natural number $n \leq$ Ag, and two coalitions Γ and Δ we define $\mathrm{Ag}_{\Gamma,\Delta}^{\rightarrow\leftarrow} = \{\Pi \in 2^{\mathrm{Ag}} \mid \Gamma \cup \Delta \subseteq \Pi\}$, $\mathrm{Ag}_{\Gamma,\Delta}^{\rightarrow} = \{\Pi \in 2^{\mathrm{Ag}} \mid \Gamma \subseteq \Pi \wedge \Pi \subseteq \overline{\Delta}\}$, $\mathrm{Ag}_n^{\leq} = \{\Gamma \in 2^{\mathrm{Ag}} \mid |\Gamma| \leq n\}$, and $\mathrm{Ag}_n^{\geq} = \{\Gamma \in 2^{\mathrm{Ag}} \mid |\Gamma| \geq n\}$.

We now have all the needed ingredients to specify CATL semantics.

Definition 5. *Given a iCGS M, a state s of M, and a state formula φ, the satisfaction relation $M, s \models \varphi$ is defined by structural induction on φ as follows:*

- $M, s \models p$ *iff* $p \in \mathcal{L}(s)$;
- $M, s \models \neg\varphi_1$ *iff it is not the case that* $M, s \models \varphi_1$ *(noted $M, s \not\models \varphi$);*
- $M, s \models \varphi_1 \vee \varphi_2$ *iff* $M, s \models \varphi_1$ *or* $M, s \models \varphi_2$;
- $M, s \models \langle\!\langle \Gamma \rangle\!\rangle \psi$ *iff there is a Γ-strategy σ_Γ such that for all $\rho \in Out(s, \sigma_\Gamma)$ we have that $M, \rho \models \psi$;*
- $M, s \models \langle\!\langle \Gamma \!\rightarrow\!\leftarrow\!\Delta \rangle\!\rangle \psi$ *iff there is a coalition $\Pi \in \mathrm{Ag}_{\Gamma,\Delta}^{\rightarrow\leftarrow}$ and there is a Π-strategy σ_Π such that for all $\rho \in Out(s, \sigma_\Pi)$ we have that $M, \rho \models \psi$;*
- $M, s \models \langle\!\langle \Gamma \rightarrow \Delta \rangle\!\rangle \psi$ *iff there is a coalition $\Pi \in \mathrm{Ag}_{\Gamma,\Delta}^{\rightarrow}$ and there is a Π-strategy σ_Π such that for all $\rho \in Out(s, \sigma_\Pi)$, $M, \rho \models \psi$;*
- $M, s \models \langle\!\langle \leq_n \rangle\!\rangle \psi$ *iff there is a coalition $\Gamma \in \mathrm{Ag}_n^{\leq}$ and there is a Γ-strategy σ_Γ such that for all $\rho \in Out(s, \sigma_\Gamma)$, $M, \rho \models \psi$;*
- $M, s \models \langle\!\langle \geq_n \rangle\!\rangle$ *iff there is a coalition $\Gamma \in \mathrm{Ag}_n^{\geq}$ and there is a Γ-strategy σ_Γ such that for all $\rho \in Out(s, \sigma_\Gamma)$ we have that $M, \rho \models \psi$.*

Given a iCGS M, a path ρ of M, and a path formula ψ, the satisfaction relation is defined as follows:

- $M, \rho \models \mathsf{X}\varphi$ *iff* $M, \rho_2 \models \varphi$
- $M, \rho \models \varphi_1 \mathsf{U} \varphi_2$ *iff there is an $i \geq 1$ such that $M, \rho_i \models \varphi_2$ and $M, \rho_j \models \varphi_1$ for all $1 \leq j < i$;*
- $M, \rho \models \varphi_1 \mathsf{R} \varphi_2$ *iff either $M, \rho_i \models \varphi_2$ for all $i \geq 1$ or there is an $i \geq 1$ such that $M, \rho_i \models \varphi_1$ and $M, \rho_j \models \varphi_2$ for all $1 \leq j \leq i$.*

The memoryless satisfaction relation $\models_r$ is obtained by substituting "memoryless strategy" to "strategy" in the clauses for the strategic operators. For a CATL formula φ we write $M \models \varphi$ and we say that M is a model of φ whenever $M, s_I \models \varphi$.

We can now define the model checking problem for CATL.

Definition 6. *Given a iCGS M and a CATL formula φ, the model checking problem is solved by determining whether $M \models \varphi$.*

Remark 1. Since each ATL formula is a CATL formula and since the model-checking problem for ATL over iCGS with uniform strategies is undecidable, we have the same result for CATL.

In what follows, we show that CATL is a variant of ATL, that is: every CATL formula φ can be expressed as an ATL formula φ' and these two formulas are semantically equivalent.

3.3 From CATL to ATL

There is an intuitive translation from CATL formulas to ATL formulas. For instance, suppose that $\langle\langle \Gamma \rightarrow \leftarrow \Delta \rangle\rangle \psi$ is a CATL formula such that ψ does not contain any occurrence of one of the new strategic operators that we introduced. Given a state s of a model M, we have that $M, s \models \langle\langle \Gamma \rightarrow \leftarrow \Delta \rangle\rangle \psi$ if and only if $M, s \models \langle\langle \Pi_1 \rangle\rangle \psi \vee \cdots \vee \langle\langle \Pi_n \rangle\rangle \psi$ where the $\Pi_1, \ldots, \Pi_n$ are all the coalitions in Ag that contains all elements of both Γ and Δ. Following this intuition, we can define $(-)^\bullet$ as follows:

$$
\begin{aligned}
(\top)^\bullet &= \top \\
(p)^\bullet &= p \\
(\neg\varphi)^\bullet &= \neg(\varphi)^\bullet \\
(\varphi_1 \vee \varphi_2)^\bullet &= (\varphi_1)^\bullet \vee (\varphi_2)^\bullet \\
(\langle\langle \Gamma \rangle\rangle \psi)^\bullet &= \langle\langle \Gamma \rangle\rangle (\psi)^\bullet \\
(\langle\langle \Gamma \rightarrow \leftarrow \Delta \rangle\rangle \psi)^\bullet &= \bigvee\nolimits_{\Pi \in \mathsf{Ag}^{\rightarrow\leftarrow}_{\Gamma,\Delta}} \langle\langle \Pi \rangle\rangle (\psi)^\bullet \\
(\langle\langle \Gamma \rightarrow \Delta \rangle\rangle \psi)^\bullet &= \bigvee\nolimits_{\Pi \in \mathsf{Ag}^{\rightarrow}_{\Gamma,\Delta}} \langle\langle \Pi \rangle\rangle (\psi)^\bullet \\
(\langle\langle \leq_n \rangle\rangle \psi)^\bullet &= \bigvee\nolimits_{\Gamma \in \mathsf{Ag}^{\leq}_{n}} \langle\langle \Gamma \rangle\rangle (\psi)^\bullet \\
(\langle\langle \geq_n \rangle\rangle \psi)^\bullet &= \bigvee\nolimits_{\Gamma \in \mathsf{Ag}^{\geq}_{n}} \langle\langle \Gamma \rangle\rangle (\psi)^\bullet \\
(\mathsf{X}\,\varphi)^\bullet &= \mathsf{X}\,(\varphi)^\bullet \\
(\varphi_1 \mathsf{U}\,\varphi_2)^\bullet &= (\varphi_1)^\bullet \mathsf{U}\,(\varphi_2)^\bullet \\
(\varphi_1 \mathsf{R}\,\varphi_2)^\bullet &= (\varphi_1)^\bullet \mathsf{R}\,(\varphi_2)^\bullet
\end{aligned}
$$

From the above, we can notice that, given the translation $(-)^\bullet$ and a CATL formula φ, we can obtain an exponentially bigger representation of φ in ATL (in the worst case).

By using our translation we can obtain the following result.

Proposition 1. *For every CATL formula φ, for every iCGS M, and state s of M, we have that:*

$$
M, s \models \varphi \text{ if and only if } M, s \models (\varphi)^\bullet
$$

Proof. The proof is by induction on the size of φ. When φ is an atom, the result is clear. When the main connective of φ is boolean, the result follows directly by induction hypothesis. All the cases for the strategic operators follow exactly the same pattern, therefore we detail only some of them.

If φ is $\langle\!\langle \Gamma \!\rightarrow\!\leftarrow\! \Delta \rangle\!\rangle \psi$ and ψ is $\mathsf{X}\varphi_1$:

For the ($\Rightarrow$)-direction, suppose that $M, s \models \langle\!\langle \Gamma \!\rightarrow\!\leftarrow\! \Delta \rangle\!\rangle \mathsf{X}\varphi_1$. This means that there is a coalition $\Pi \in \mathsf{Ag}_{\Gamma,\Delta}^{\rightarrow\leftarrow}$ and a Π-strategy σ_Π such that for all $\rho \in Out(s, \sigma_\Pi)$ we have that $M, \rho_2 \models \varphi_1$. By induction hypothesis, we obtain that $M, \rho_2 \models (\varphi_1)^\bullet$, and this for every $\rho \in Out(s, \sigma_\Pi)$. We thus conclude that $M, s \models \langle\!\langle \Pi \rangle\!\rangle \mathsf{X}(\varphi_1)^\bullet$, and by the semantics of $\vee$ we deduce that $M, s \models \bigvee_{\Pi \in \mathsf{Ag}_{\Gamma,\Delta}^{\rightarrow\leftarrow}} \langle\!\langle \Delta \rangle\!\rangle \mathsf{X}(\varphi)^\bullet$ which is exactly $(\varphi)^\bullet$.

For the ($\Leftarrow$)-direction. Suppose that $M, s \models (\varphi)^\bullet$. By the definition of $(-)^\bullet$, this means that $M, s \models \bigvee_{\Pi \in \mathsf{Ag}_{\Gamma,\Delta}^{\rightarrow\leftarrow}} \langle\!\langle \Pi \rangle\!\rangle \mathsf{X}(\varphi_1)^\bullet$ which is the same as $M, s \models \langle\!\langle \Pi \rangle\!\rangle \mathsf{X}(\varphi_1)^\bullet$ for some $\Pi \in \mathsf{Ag}_{\Gamma,\Delta}^{\rightarrow\leftarrow}$. We thus deduce that there is a Π-strategy σ_Π such that $M, \rho_2 \models (\varphi_1)^\bullet$ for all $\rho \in Out(s, \sigma_\Pi)$. By induction hypothesis $M, \rho_2 \models \varphi_1$ for any $\rho \in Out(s, \sigma_\Pi)$. Since σ_Π is a Π-strategy and $\Pi \in \mathsf{Ag}_{\Gamma,\Delta}^{\rightarrow\leftarrow}$, we can conclude that $M, s \models \langle\!\langle \Gamma \!\rightarrow\!\leftarrow\! \Delta \rangle\!\rangle \mathsf{X}\varphi_1$ as we wanted.

If φ is $\langle\!\langle \leq_n \rangle\!\rangle \psi$ and ψ is $\varphi_1 \mathsf{R} \varphi_2$:

For the ($\Rightarrow$) direction, suppose that $M, s \models \langle\!\langle \leq_n \rangle\!\rangle \varphi_1 \mathsf{R} \varphi_2$, then there is a coalition $\Gamma \in \mathsf{Ag}_n^{\leq}$ and a Γ-strategy σ_Γ such that for all $\rho \in Out(s, \sigma_\Gamma)$ either $M, \rho_i \models \varphi_2$ for all $i \geq 1$ or there is a $j \geq 1$ such that $M, \rho_j \models \varphi_1$ and $M, \rho_i \models \varphi_2$ for all $1 \leq i \leq j$. We use the induction hypothesis, and we conclude that for all $\rho \in Out(s, \sigma_\Gamma)$ we either have that $M, \rho_i \models (\varphi_2)^\bullet$ for all $i \geq 1$, or $M, \rho_j \models (\varphi_1)^\bullet$ for some $j \geq 1$, and $M, \rho_i \models (\varphi_2)^\bullet$ for all $1 \leq i \leq j$. We thus conclude that $M, s \models \langle\!\langle \Gamma \rangle\!\rangle (\varphi)_1^\bullet \mathsf{R} (\varphi_2)^\bullet$ and by the semantics of $\vee$ we deduce that $M, s \models \bigvee_{\Gamma \in \mathsf{Ag}_n^{\leq}} \langle\!\langle \Gamma \rangle\!\rangle (\varphi)_1^\bullet \mathsf{R} (\varphi_2)^\bullet$ which is exactly $(\langle\!\langle \leq_n \rangle\!\rangle \varphi_1 \mathsf{R} \varphi_2)^\bullet$.

For the ($\Leftarrow$) direction, suppose that $M, s \models (\varphi)^\bullet$ this means that for some $\Gamma \in \mathsf{Ag}_n^{\leq}$ $M, s \models \langle\!\langle \Gamma \rangle\!\rangle (\varphi_1)^\bullet \mathsf{R} (\varphi_2)^\bullet$, thus there is a Γ-strategy σ_Γ such that for all $\rho \in Out(s, \sigma_\Gamma)$ we either have that $M, \rho_i \models (\varphi_2)^\bullet$ for all $i \geq 1$, or there is a $j \geq 1$ such that $M, \rho_j \models (\varphi_1)^\bullet$, and $M, \rho_i \models (\varphi_1)^\bullet$ for all $1 \leq i \leq j$. We use the induction hypothesis, and we conclude that for all $\rho \in Out(s, \sigma_\Gamma)$ we either have that $M, \rho_i \models \varphi_2$ or there is a $j \geq 1$ such that $M, \rho_j \models \varphi_1$ and $M, \rho_i \models \varphi_1$ for all $1 \leq i \leq j$. Since $\Gamma \in \mathsf{Ag}_n^{\leq}$ we conclude that $M, s \models \langle\!\langle \leq_n \rangle\!\rangle \varphi_1 \mathsf{R} \varphi_2$ as we wanted.

If φ is $\langle\!\langle \geq_n \rangle\!\rangle \psi$ and ψ is $\varphi_1 \mathsf{U} \varphi_2$:

For the ($\Rightarrow$) direction, suppose that $M, s \models \langle\!\langle \geq_n \rangle\!\rangle \varphi_1 \mathsf{U} \varphi_2$ thus there is a coalition $\Gamma \in \mathsf{Ag}_n^{\geq}$ and a Γ-strategy σ_Γ such that for all $\rho \in Out(s, \sigma)$ there is a $j \geq 1$ such that $M, \rho_j \models \varphi_2$ and $M, \rho_i \models \varphi_1$ for all $1 \leq i < j$. We use induction hypothesis and conclude that for all $\rho \in Out(s, \sigma_\Gamma)$ there is a $j \geq 1$ such that $M, \rho_j \models (\varphi_2)^\bullet$ and $M, \rho_i \models (\varphi_1)^\bullet$ for all $1 \leq i < j$. Thus, we have that $M, s \models \langle\!\langle \Gamma \rangle\!\rangle (\varphi_1)^\bullet \mathsf{U} (\varphi_2)^\bullet$ and by the semantics of $\vee$ we deduce that $M, s \models \bigvee_{\Gamma \in \mathsf{Ag}_n^{\geq}} \langle\!\langle \Gamma \rangle\!\rangle (\varphi)_1^\bullet \mathsf{U} (\varphi_2)^\bullet$ which is exactly $(\langle\!\langle \geq_n \rangle\!\rangle \varphi_1 \mathsf{U} \varphi_2)^\bullet$.

For the ($\Leftarrow$) direction, suppose that $M, s \models (\varphi)^\bullet$, thus $M, s \models \langle\!\langle \Gamma \rangle\!\rangle (\varphi_1)^\bullet \mathsf{U} (\varphi_2)^\bullet$ for some $\Gamma \in \mathsf{Ag}_n^{\geq}$. This means that there is a Γ-strategy σ_Γ and for all

$\rho \in Out(s, \sigma_\Gamma)$ we have that there is a $j \geq 1$ such that $M, \rho_j \models (\varphi_2)^\bullet$ and $M, \rho_i \models (\varphi_1)^\bullet$ for all $1 \leq i < j$. We use induction hypothesis and we conclude that for all $\rho \in Out(s, \sigma_\Gamma)$ we have that there is a $j \geq 1$ such that $M, \rho_j \models \varphi_2$ and $M, \rho_i \models \varphi_1$ for all $1 \leq i < j$. Since $\Gamma \in \text{Ag}_n^\geq$ we have that $M, s \models \langle\langle \geq_n \rangle\rangle \varphi_1 \, U \, \varphi_2$ as we wanted.

□

Given the above result, we can conclude that CATL and ATL have the same expressive power. So, we may derive the following result.

Corollary 1. *The satisfaction relation $\models$ and the memoryless satisfaction relation $\models_r$ coincides over CGSs, that is, for every CATL formula φ, for every CGS M, and state s:*

$$M, s \models \varphi \text{ if and only if } M, s \models_r \varphi$$

We now study the complexity of the model checking problem for CATL with respect to CGSs.

Theorem 1. *Given a formula φ and a CGS M the problem of determining the set $[\![\varphi]\!] = \{s \in S \mid M, s \models \varphi\}$ is in $\Delta_2^P = P^{NP}$ with respect to the size of φ and M.*

Proof. We know that given an ATL formula λ, $[\![\lambda]\!]$ can be computed in polynomial time w.r.t. the size of λ and M. Consider a subformula φ' of φ that contains exactly one strategic operator $\langle\langle \Gamma \rightarrow\leftarrow \Delta \rangle\rangle$, or $\langle\langle \Gamma \rightarrow \Delta \rangle\rangle$, or $\langle\langle \leq_n \rangle\rangle$, or $\langle\langle \geq_n \rangle\rangle$. By Proposition 1 we know that φ' is equivalent to a finite disjunction $\varphi_1 \vee \cdots \vee \varphi_n$ of ATL formulas. Thus given a state s, a certificate consists in an ATL formula φ_i i.e., for the considered φ' checking whether $M, s \models \varphi'$ is in the NP class. We then use the classic bottom-up approach to evaluate each subformula of φ on M: we order the subformulas of φ by their size (in ascending order). For each subformula φ_1 having exactly one of the four above-mentioned strategic operators, we create a new atom p_{φ_1}, we substitute p_{φ_1} to φ_1 in each subformula φ_2 that contains φ_1, and we add p_{φ_1} to the set of satisfied atoms of each state s such that $M, s \models \varphi_1$. This means that we use an NP oracle over a polynomial procedure for each strategic operator in φ and each state s of M. Summing up, the total complexity of determining $[\![\varphi]\!]$ is P^{NP}.   □

We now study the complexity of the model checking problem for CATL with respect to iCGSs in which agents use memoryless-strategies.

Theorem 2. *Given a formula φ and an iCGS M the problem of determining the set $[\![\varphi]\!] = \{s \in S \mid M, s \models_r \varphi\}$ is in Δ_3^P with respect to the size of φ and M.*

Proof. We know that the same problem with respect to ATL formulas is in Δ_2^P [21]. We simply remark that, to solve our problem, we can use another NP oracle $|S|$ times to guess the good coalitions needed to satisfy a CATL formula as we do in Theorem 1. From the above the result follows.

3.4   Fragments

In this subsection, we present a fragment of CATL where we have the same complexity of ATL model checking. The intuition behind the resulting approach is to generalize the coalitions involved in the CATL strategic operators. Specifically, we achieve this by replacing $\langle\!\langle \Gamma {\rightarrow}{\leftarrow} \Delta \rangle\!\rangle$ and $\langle\!\langle \geq_n \rangle\!\rangle$ with $\langle\!\langle \mathsf{Ag} \rangle\!\rangle$.

Before doing this, let us recall a classic result that holds in ATL and that will be fundamental in our translation.

Proposition 2. *For any pair of coalitions Γ and Δ, for any iCGS M and state s of M, and for any path formula ψ, we have that, if $\Gamma \subseteq \Delta$ then:*

$$M, s \models \langle\!\langle \Gamma \rangle\!\rangle \psi \text{ implies } M, s \models \langle\!\langle \Delta \rangle\!\rangle \psi$$

Proof. See [9].

Let CATL$^{\blacktriangledown}$ be the subset of CATL formulas constructed using all CATL connectives but $\langle\!\langle \Gamma \rightarrow \Delta \rangle\!\rangle$ and $\langle\!\langle \leq_n \rangle\!\rangle$. Let $(-)^\circ$ to be a function from CATL$^{\blacktriangledown}$ formulas to ATL formulas, such that:

$$
\begin{aligned}
(\top)^\circ &= \top\\
(p)^\circ &= p\\
(\neg\varphi)^\circ &= \neg(\varphi)^\circ\\
(\varphi_1 \vee \varphi_2)^\circ &= (\varphi_1)^\circ \vee (\varphi_2)^\circ\\
(\langle\!\langle \Gamma \rangle\!\rangle \psi)^\circ &= \langle\!\langle \Gamma \rangle\!\rangle (\psi)^\circ\\
(\langle\!\langle \Gamma {\rightarrow}{\leftarrow} \Delta \rangle\!\rangle \psi)^\circ &= \langle\!\langle \mathsf{Ag} \rangle\!\rangle (\psi)^\circ\\
(\langle\!\langle \geq_n \rangle\!\rangle \psi)^\circ &= \langle\!\langle \mathsf{Ag} \rangle\!\rangle (\psi)^\circ\\
(\mathsf{X}\,\varphi)^\circ &= \mathsf{X}\,(\varphi)^\circ\\
(\varphi_1 \,\mathsf{U}\, \varphi_2)^\circ &= (\varphi_1)^\circ \,\mathsf{U}\, (\varphi_2)^\circ\\
(\varphi_1 \,\mathsf{R}\, \varphi_2)^\circ &= (\varphi_1)^\circ \,\mathsf{R}\, (\varphi_2)^\circ
\end{aligned}
$$

We can prove the following result.

Proposition 3. *For every CATL$^{\blacktriangledown}$ formula φ, for every iCGS M, and every state s of M, we have that:*

$$M, s \models \varphi \text{ if and only if } M, s \models (\varphi)^\circ$$

Proof. The proof is by induction on the size of φ. When φ is an atom, the result is clear. When the main connective of φ is boolean, the result follows directly by induction hypothesis. As in Proposition 1, all the cases for the strategic operators follow exactly the same proof pattern. Thus, we only detail the case in which φ is $\langle\!\langle \Gamma {\rightarrow}{\leftarrow} \Delta \rangle\!\rangle \psi$ and ψ is $\mathsf{X}\,\varphi_1$.

For the ($\Rightarrow$)-direction, suppose that $M, s \models \langle\!\langle \Gamma {\rightarrow}{\leftarrow} \Delta \rangle\!\rangle \mathsf{X}\,\varphi_1$. By the CATL semantics, this means that there is a Π such that $\Gamma \cup \Delta \subseteq \Pi$ and a Π-strategy σ such that for all $\rho \in Out(s, \sigma)$ we have that $M, \rho_2 \models \varphi_1$. By induction hypothesis, we conclude that for all $\rho \in Out(s, \sigma)$ we have that $M, \rho_2 \models (\varphi_1)^\circ$, which is the same as $M, s \models \langle\!\langle \Pi \rangle\!\rangle \mathsf{X}\,(\varphi_1)^\circ$. Since $\Pi \subseteq \mathsf{Ag}$, we conclude by Proposition 2 that $M, s \models \langle\!\langle \mathsf{Ag} \rangle\!\rangle \mathsf{X}\,(\varphi_1)^\circ$ which is exactly $((\langle\!\langle \Gamma \cup \Delta \rangle\!\rangle \mathsf{X}\,\varphi_1)^\circ$.

For the $(\Leftarrow)$-direction, suppose that $M, s \models \langle\langle \mathsf{Ag} \rangle\rangle \mathsf{X} (\varphi_1)^\circ$, thus for all $\rho \in Out(s, \sigma)$ we have that $M, \rho_2 \models (\varphi_1)^\circ$ for some Ag-strategy σ. By induction hypothesis, we have that $M, \rho_2 \models \varphi_1$ for all $\rho \in Out(s, \sigma)$ and since $\Gamma \cup \Delta \subseteq \mathsf{Ag}$ we can conclude that $M, s \models \langle\langle \Gamma {\rightarrow} {\leftarrow} \Delta \rangle\rangle \mathsf{X} \varphi_1$.

$\square$

Since the ATL model checking problem is PTIME [1] with respect to CGS, we immediately obtain the following corollary.

Corollary 2. *For any CATL$^\mathbf{\triangledown}$ formula φ and any CGS M, the problem of determining $[\![\varphi]\!]$ is in PTIME with respect to the size of φ and M.*

Since the ATL model checking problem is Δ_2^P [21] with respect to iCGS with memoryless strategies, we immediately obtain the following corollary.

Corollary 3. *For any CATL$^\mathbf{\triangledown}$ formula φ and any iCGS M, the problem of determining $[\![\varphi]\!]$ is in Δ_2^P with respect to the size of φ and M.*

In the following sections, we exemplify the formal machinery introduced so far by providing an example.

4   Interpreted Systems

The semantics of a strategic logic, such as ATL or CATL, can be specified, equivalently, by resorting to either CGSs or Interpreted Systems. As the reader has probably noticed, we have chosen to resort to the first alternative by defining the semantics of CATL through CGSs. This choice is due to the fact that CGSs have a simple and intuitive definition. Essentially, they are directed and labeled graphs in which the edge relation is serial and in which edges are labeled by tuples of agent's actions. As intuitive as this definition is, the MCMAS verification tool operates on interpreted systems. So, for the sake of completeness, we now introduce the formal definition of interpreted systems. Then, in the next section, we will present this latter formal model through an example to guide the reader.

An interpreted system, like a CGS, is a formal description of the computations carried out by a set of agents. More specifically, an interpreted system is given by a set of agents. Each of these agents operates on local states, representing the information that they have about the system under exam. The system itself is represented as the product of the local states of the agents: in any of its local states, an agent can perform a fixed set of actions, and the global state of the system evolves with respect to the product of the actions of all the agents. We now state the formal definitions. First, we define agents.

Definition 7 (Agent). *Let* $\mathsf{Ag} = \{1, \dots, k\}$ *be a finite set of agent indexes. An* agent *is a tuple* $i = \langle L_i, act_i, P_i, t_i \rangle$, *where:*

- L_i *is the finite non-empty set of local states.*
- Act_i *is the finite non-empty set of individual actions. We denote by ACT the product set* $\Pi_{i \in \mathsf{Ag}} Act_i$ *and we call its elements* joint actions.

- $P_i : L_i \rightarrow (2^{Act_i} \setminus \emptyset)$ *is the local protocol function associating to any local state a non-empty set of actions representing the actions available to the agent at that state.*
- $t_i : L_i \times ACT \rightarrow L_i$ *is the local transition function. Such function takes an agent's state l and a joint action $\mathbf{a} = \langle a_1, \ldots, a_k \rangle$ and outputs an agent's state. The function $t_i(l_i, \mathbf{a})$ is defined if and only if we have that $\mathbf{a}[i] \in P_i(l_i)$. Remark that, the output of the transition function depends on a joint action $\langle a_1, \ldots, a_k \rangle$, but we only require that the i-th component of this joint action belongs to the set of actions that are available for the considered agent at the considered state.*

By the above definition, an agent i is situated in a local state $l \in L_i$ representing the information it has about the system. At any state, the agent can perform the actions in Act_i according to the protocol function P_i. A joint action determines a change in the state of the agent according to the transition function t_i.

If Ag is a set of agents of length k, a **global state** $s \in G$ is a tuple $s = \langle l_1, \ldots, l_k \rangle$ where each l_i is an i agent's state for $i \leq k$. A **history** is a finite sequence $h = s_1, \ldots, s_n$ of global states. We denote by H_G the set of histories of global states. Two global states s and s', are **equivalent** for the agent i whenever $s[i] = s'[i]$. We denote such notion by $s \sim_i s'$. Two histories h and h' are equivalent for the agent i whenever they have the same length m and $h_j \sim_i h'_j$ for any $j \leq m$.

Definition 8. *Given a set of atomic propositions Ap, an interpreted system is a tuple $I = \langle \mathsf{Ag}, s_0, T, \Pi \rangle$ where Ag is a set of agents, $s_0 \in G$ is the (global) initial state, $T : G \times ACT \rightarrow G$ is the global transition function such that $T(s, \mathbf{a}) = s'$ iff for every $i \in \mathsf{Ag}$, $t_i(s[i], \mathbf{a}[i]) = s'[i]$. Finally, $\Pi : G \rightarrow 2^{\mathsf{Ap}}$ is the labeling function, associating to any global state an (eventually empty) set of atomic propositions.*

A strategy for an agent i, is a function from the set of local histories H_G to the set of actions act_i of the agent i defined exactly as in Definition 4. Joint strategies and paths that are compatible with joint strategies are also defined as the corresponding notions for iCGSs. The semantics of CATL formulas on interpreted systems is defined exactly as in Definition 5, the only difference is that we use an interpreted system I instead of a iCGS M in such a definition.

5   Train Gate Controller Scenario

In this section, we exemplify the formal apparatus introduced in the previous section through an example. We consider a revised version of the Train Gate Controller by [1, 3, 4, 7] in which there are two trains and a controller. The aim of the two trains is to pass a gate. To do this, they need to coordinate with the controller. The trains are initially placed outside the gate and to ask to go in the gate they need to do a request (action req). If the controller accepts the request (actions ac_1 and ac_2, respectively), the train has the grant to pass through the gate. Note that, to perform the physical action of passing through the gate, the train has to select the action in. Then, it stays in the gate until it does the action out. What we want to show in this game is the fact that the trains need the accordance of the controller to achieve their objectives (*i.e.* to pass the gate).

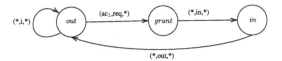

Fig. 1. Local model for train 1 [13].

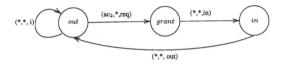

Fig. 2. Local model for train 2 [13].

More formally, this game can be represented as the Interpret System $I = \langle \text{Ag}, s_0, T, \Pi \rangle$, such that:

- Ag = { $Train_1$, $Train_2$, $Controller$};
- $Act_{Train_1} = Act_{Train_2} = \{req, in, out, i\}$, where by action req they do a request, by action in they go in the gate, by action out they go outside the gate, and by action i they do nothing. $Act_{Controller} = \{ac_1, ac_2, i\}$, where by action ac_j the $Controller$ gives the access to train $j \in \{1, 2\}$, and by action i it does nothing.

The local model for $Train_1$ is given in Fig. 1, the local model for $Train_2$ is given in Fig. 2, and the local model of the $Controller$ is given in Fig. 3. The global initial state, the transition function, and the labeling function are given in Fig. 4. In particular, each global state is represented as a rectangle where the tuple (l_c, l_{t_1}, l_{t_2}) includes the Controller's local state (l_c), the Train 1's local state (l_{t_1}), and the Train 2's local state (l_{t_2}). Furthermore, by the tuple of local states, we can consider as atomic propositions true in each state the names of the local states and, in accordance to them, define the labeling function. Notice that, in the figures, we denote any available action with the symbol $*$.

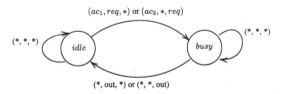

Fig. 3. The local model for the controller [13].

The property the Train 1 has a winning strategy to achieve the gate can be represented as follows:

$$\varphi_1 = \langle\langle Train_1 \rangle\rangle \mathsf{F}\, in_1$$

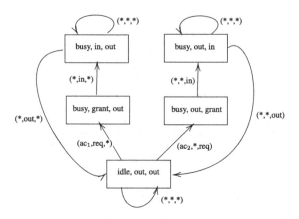

Fig. 4. The interpreted systems IS, where $s_0 = (idle, out, out)$ [13].

We observe that φ_1 is false since to make the property true the Train 1 needs the agreement of the Controller. By consequence, the property that can be satisfied is the following:

$$\varphi_1 = \langle\!\langle Train_1, Controller \rangle\!\rangle \mathsf{F}\, in_1$$

Analysis over Coalitions. Considering our example, a possible guideline over the size of the coalitions could be $min : 2$. With such feature, we would enforce the generation of coalitions with at least two agents. This could be guided by the fact that we know that no agent in isolation can achieve its own goals in the train gate controller example. Another possible constraint could be $[Train_1 \rightarrow\!\leftarrow Controller]$, where we enforce $Train_1$ and $Controller$ to be in coalition. For similar reasons, we may add the constraint $[Train_1 \leftarrow\!\rightarrow Train_2]$ and enforce the two trains to not be in coalition. Remark that such constraints precisely corresponds to the CATL operators $\langle\!\langle \Gamma\rightarrow\!\leftarrow\Delta \rangle\!\rangle$ and $\langle\!\langle \Gamma\leftarrow\!\rightarrow\Delta \rangle\!\rangle$[1].

6   Verification

In this section, we present the algorithms to solve, in practice, the model checking problem for CATL. To do so, we exploit the MCMAS model checker, and its verification engine for ATL formulas. Note that, as proved previously in the paper (see Proposition 1), CATL and ATL share the same semantics; because of that, the actual verification of CATL formulas can be obtained through the standard verification of ATL ones.

Once an interpreted system I has been defined, we can unleash our approach. Starting from such model, we can verify for which coalitions of agents an ATL formula φ is verified in I. Specifically, differently from standard ATL, we do not want to explicitly state each Γ coalition in φ; instead, we want to automatically generate such coalitions. Naturally, not all coalitions are always of interest; this of course depends on the domain

---

[1] Remark that this operator can be defined in terms of $\langle\!\langle \Gamma \rightarrow \Delta \rangle\!\rangle$ see Definition 1.

of use. Thus, even though a coalition makes a formula φ satisfied by a model I, it does not necessarily mean such coalition is a good one (*i.e.*, a usable one).

Now, we move forward and present how our approach uses the pre-processing steps to perform the actual formal verification on MAS. Specifically, this is obtained through two algorithms. Let us explore them in detail.

Algorithm 1. GenCoalitions(Ag, min, max, T, S).

1: $\Gamma_{valid} = \emptyset$
2: **for** $k \in [min, max]$ **do**
3:     **for** $\Gamma \in \Gamma_k^{\text{Ag}}$ **do**
4:         **if** $\exists [\Gamma_1 \rightarrow\leftarrow \Gamma_2] \in T : \{\Gamma_1, \Gamma_2\} \not\subseteq \Gamma \wedge \{\Gamma_1, \Gamma_2\} \cap \Gamma \neq \emptyset$ **then continue**
5:         **if** $\exists [\Gamma_1 \longleftrightarrow \Gamma_2] \in S : \{\Gamma_1, \Gamma_2\} \subseteq \Gamma$ **then continue**
6:         Add Γ to Γ_{valid}
7: **return** Γ_{valid}

Algorithm 2. MCMAS$_{co}$($I, \varphi, min, max, T, S, num\_coalitions$).

1: Ag = $GetAgents(I)$
2: $\Gamma_{good} = \emptyset$
3: $\Gamma_{valid} = GenCoalitions(\text{Ag}, min, max, T, S)$
4: **for** $\Gamma \in \Gamma_{valid}$ **do**
5:     **if** $I \models \varphi^{\Gamma}$ **then**
6:         Add Γ to Γ_{good}
7:     **if** $|\Gamma_{good}| = num\_coalitions$ **then**
8:         **return** Γ_{good}
9: **return** Γ_{good}

Algorithm 1. It reports the steps required to generate a set of valid coalitions, *i.e.*, coalitions that respect the user's guidelines. Algorithm 1 takes in input the set of agents Ag, and the user's guidelines, such as the minimum/maximum number of agents to be in the coalitions, and the set of agents that have to (resp., cannot) stay in the same coalition T (resp., S). At line 1, the set of valid coalitions is initialized to the empty set. Then, at line 2, a value k is selected for any integer value between min and max (both included). After that, the algorithm loops over all possible values of k (lines 3–6); with k denoting the current size of the considered coalitions. Naturally, there are multiple k coalitions that can be formed over a set Ag of agents. In more detail, they correspond to all possible combinations of k agents taken from the set Ag; this is expressed by the set Γ_k^{Ag}. For each of these coalitions, the algorithm checks whether the constraints hold or not. First, it checks if all agents that are required to be together in the coalition are as such (line 4). If for at least one couple $[\Gamma_1 \rightarrow\leftarrow \Gamma_2]$, we find only one subset of agents in the coalition, then we skip to the next possible coalition to evaluate. In the same way, the algorithm checks for the agents that are not meant to be together (lines 5). This again is achieved by checking whether for some couple both the subset of agents are in the coalition. If that is the case, then the algorithm moves on to the next coalition to evaluate. At the end of the algorithm, the set Γ_{valid} contains all coalitions respecting the user's guidelines.

Algorithm 2. It performs the actual verification considering all valid agents' coalitions. Algorithm 2 takes in input the model I, the ATL formula to verify φ, and the user's guidelines. At line 1, the set of agents is extracted from I. These are the agents involved in the model. At line 2, the set of good coalitions is initialized to the empty set. By the end of the algorithm, such set will contain the coalitions that respect the user's guidelines and make φ satisfied in I. At line 3, Algorithm 1 is called. In this step, all valid coalitions respecting the user's guidelines are returned. After that, the algorithm loops over such valid coalitions (lines 4–8). For each of them, the model checking is performed (line 5). In here, with φ^{Γ} we denote φ where the coalition has been replaced with the currently selected one (*i.e.*, Γ). If the model checking returns true, *i.e.*, model I satisfies formula φ^{Γ}, then Γ is added to the set of good coalitions Γ_{good} (line 6). After that, if the number of required coalitions has been found (the number of good coalitions in Γ_{good} is equal to $num\_coalitions$), then the coalitions are returned (lines 7–8). Otherwise, the algorithm evaluates all the valid coalitions, and returns the good ones at the end (line 9). Note that, in Algorithm 2, we only show the case with one strategic operator in φ, that is, only one Γ coalition is replaced in φ. We decided to do so in order to improve the readability of the procedure. However, in case multiple Γ coalitions are used, the same reasoning is followed, where for each one of them a set of valid coalitions is generated (using Algorithm 1). Then, instead of performing model checking only once (Algorithm 2, line 5), the algorithm would perform the latter for every possible permutation.

Remark 2. Given a CATL formula φ and a model I, to solve the model checking problem through our procedure (Algorithm 2), we need to set $num\_coalitions$ to 1. This is done to enforce the algorithm to terminate as soon as a good coalition is found (in accordance to the CATL strategic operators' semantics). Furthermore, given the CATL strategic operators involved in the formula φ, we need to determine the values for the different parameters: min, max, T, and S. On one hand, suppose that we have a CATL formula $\varphi = \langle\!\langle \leq_n \rangle\!\rangle \mathsf{X} p$ (resp., $\varphi = \langle\!\langle \geq_n \rangle\!\rangle \mathsf{X} p$), then the parameters passed to Algorithm 2 are set as follows: $min = 0$, $max = n$, $T = \emptyset$, and $S = \emptyset$ (resp., $min = n$, $max = |\mathrm{Ag}|$, $T = \emptyset$, and $S = \emptyset$). On the other hand, suppose that we have a CATL formula $\varphi = \langle\!\langle \Gamma_1 {\rightarrow}{\leftarrow} \Gamma_2 \rangle\!\rangle \mathsf{X} p$ (resp., $\varphi = \langle\!\langle \Gamma_1 {\leftarrow}{\rightarrow} \Gamma_2 \rangle\!\rangle \mathsf{X} p$), then the parameters passed to Algorithm 2 are set as follows: $min = 0$, $max = |\mathrm{Ag}|$, $T = \{[\Gamma_1 {\rightarrow}{\leftarrow} \Gamma_2]\}$, and $S = \emptyset$ (resp., $min = 0$, $max = |\mathrm{Ag}|$, $T = \emptyset$, and $S = \{[\Gamma_1 {\leftarrow}{\rightarrow} \Gamma_2]\}$).

7   Implementation

A prototype of our approach has been implemented in Python[2]. The prototype gets in input an interpreted system I, specified in terms of an ISPL file (the formalism supported by the MCMAS model checker), an ATL formula to verify φ, and generates

---

[2] https://github.com/AngeloFerrando/mcmas-multi-coalitions.

all coalitions of agents which make $I \models \varphi$. To understand the tool, first, we need to describe its pillar components.

The model checker we use is MCMAS [16], which is the *de facto* standard model checker of strategic properties on MAS. MCMAS expects in input an interpreted system specified as an ISPL file. In such a file, the interpreted system is defined along with the formal property of interest to verify. From the viewpoint of a MCMAS user, our tool can be seen as an extension of MCMAS that allows the user to, not only perform the verification of ATL properties as usual, but to extract which coalitions of agents make such properties verified in the model.

Since MCMAS expects a fully instantiated ATL formula, in order to extract which coalitions of agents are good candidates, our tool performs a pre-processing step. In such step, as described previously in the paper, all coalitions which follow the user's guidelines are generated (Algorithm 1) and tested on MCMAS (Algorithm 2). In each run, MCMAS returns the boolean result corresponding to the satisfaction of the ATL formula over the interpreted system. The coalitions for which MCMAS returns a positive verdict are then presented as output to the user. To help the reader to understand the whole machinery see Fig. 5.

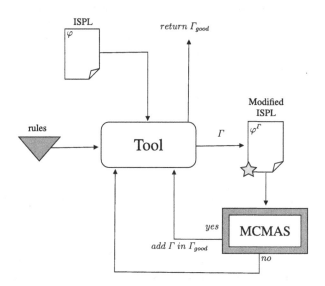

Fig. 5. Overview of the tool.

The generation of all agents' coalitions has been implemented in Python, as well as its enforcement over the ISPL file. In fact, for each coalition following the user's guidelines, our tool updates the ISPL in the following way. Considering Algorithm 2, this step is implicitly performed in line 5, where the model checking is performed. However, at the implementation level, the actual verification through MCMAS requires to explicitly modify the ISPL file w.r.t. the Γ coalition of interest (*i.e.*, each coalition generated by Algorithm 1). To achieve this technical step, first, the tool searches all occurrences of

Γ coalitions in the ISPL file. This can be done by looking for the `groups` keyword (which is the one used in MCMAS to define the agents belonging to each coalition used in the ATL formula). After that, the tool replaces each coalition with a coalition following the user's guidelines. Naturally, in case of multiple Γ coalitions in the ATL formula, all possible permutations of valid coalitions are considered. Once the ISPL file has been properly modified with valid coalitions, MCMAS is called to perform the actual verification.

8 Experiments

We tested our tool over the train gate controller scenario, on a machine with the following specifications: Intel(R) Core(TM) i7-7700HQ CPU @ 2.80 GHz, 4 cores 8 threads, 16 GB RAM DDR4. We carried out various experiments on our running example. But, we have not only considered the case with two trains. Instead, we experimented with larger number of trains as well, to better evaluate our tool's performance. Tables 1, 2 and 3 report the results we obtained.

Table 1. Number of good coalitions generated in our experiments. 1st column reports number of trains. 2nd column, no guidelines are given. 3rd to 5th column minimum number of agents per coalition is required. 6th to 8th column maximum number of agents per coalition is required. 9th to 12th columns guidelines on which agents can stay (or not) in coalition with [13].

N	−	≥ 2	≥ 3	≥ 4	≤ 2	≤ 3	≤ 4	$\exists! i.[T_i \rightarrow\leftarrow C]$	$\forall i.[T_i \rightarrow\leftarrow C]$	$\exists!(i,j).[T_i \leftarrow\rightarrow T_j]$	$\forall(i,j).[T_i \leftarrow\rightarrow T_j]$
2	3	3	1	0	2	3	3	2	1	2	2
4	15	15	11	5	4	10	14	8	1	11	4
6	63	63	57	42	6	21	41	32	1	47	6
8	255	255	247	219	8	36	92	128	1	191	8
10	1023	1023	1013	968	10	55	175	512	1	767	10

Let us start with Table 1. It contains the number of coalitions we found through experiments. In more detail, the table is so structured. The first column reports the number of trains used in the experiments (from 2 to 10 trains). Then, the rest of the columns correspond to the results we get w.r.t. some specific guidelines. Going from left to right. First, we find the case where no guidelines have been passed to the tool. In such case, the tool reports all good coalitions, without any filter. This would correspond to a scenario where we would not have any sort of resource limitation and to group agents. Then, we have three different scenarios where we set the minimum number of agents per coalition (*i.e.*, we pass the *min* guideline). We do so for *min* equals to 2, 3, and 4. That is, we request only coalitions containing at least 2, 3, and 4 agents, respectively. Here, we can note how with *min* : 2, the number of coalitions does not change w.r.t. the case with no guidelines. This is due to the fact that, as expected, no coalitions with less than 2 agents can satisfy the property of interest; which we remind being $\varphi = \langle\!\langle \Gamma \rangle\!\rangle F\,in$. Instead, the other two cases have a fewer number of coalitions. This does not come as a surprise, since we are requesting only larger coalitions (we filter out all coalitions with 2 and 3 agents, respectively). After that, we find similar cases, where instead the max guideline is used. First, by enforcing the maximum number of agents in each coalition to be 2, then 3, and finally 4. W.r.t. the previous cases, here we can note how the choice of limiting the maximum number of agents in the coalitions is much more effective in reducing the number of good coalitions proposed. This again is reasonable, because we are filtering out the larger coalitions. Finally, we find the last four columns, which are focused on guidelines on which agents can stay with whom in the coalitions. First, we find the case where we request one single train to be in coalition with the controller. Note that, we do not decide such train a priori; it can be any of the available trains. In such case, the number of good coalitions is reduced, but not too much. This is due to the fact that requesting only one train to be in coalition with the controller is not a strong guideline (indeed, other trains can be in coalition as well). Then, the next case consists in requesting all trains to be in coalition with the controller. In this case, we obtain only one good coalition (no matter the number of trains). Since we are requesting all agents to be in coalition, this result is in line with the expectations. In the second to last column, we find a case where we request two trains not to be in coalition. As before, we are not interested in which trains, as long as only two are required not to be in coalition. As expected, this guideline does not affect much the number of good coalitions generated. Indeed, asking to not having just two trains in coalition does not filter out many viable alternatives. Last column presents the same scenario, but where all trains are requested to not be in the same coalition. So, each train cannot collaborate with any other train. This produces a number of coalitions equivalent to the number of trains used in the experiments. This again does not come as a surprise, since the only possible good coalitions are the ones with one train and the controller (no other trains involved).

Table 2. Execution time (in seconds) to generate the set of good coalitions in our experiments. 1st column reports number of trains. 2nd column, no guidelines are given. 3rd to 5th column minimum number of agents per coalition is required. 6th to 8th column maximum number of agents per coalition is required. 9th to 12th columns guidelines on which agents can stay (or not) in coalition with [13].

N	-	≥ 2	≥ 3	≥ 4	≤ 2	≤ 3	≤ 4	$\exists!i.[T_i \rightarrow\leftarrow C]$	$\forall i.[T_i \rightarrow\leftarrow C]$	$\exists!(i,j).[T_i \leftarrow\rightarrow T_j]$	$\forall(i,j).[T_i \leftarrow\rightarrow T_j]$
2	0,06	0,03	0,01	0,00018	0,05	0,05	0,05	0,03	0,01	0,04	0,04
4	0,28	0,23	0,15	0,06	0,13	0,22	0,36	0,13	0,02	0,2	0,09
6	8,87	8,33	6,88	4,62	1,99	4,34	6,9	4,45	0,08	6,68	0,89
8	53,41	51,11	47,4	38,88	4,5	12,49	24,69	25,18	0,1	37,99	1,77
10	382,18	380,66	369,09	340,04	12,03	40,58	99,93	186,9	0,19	304,06	3,94

Moving on with Table 2, we find the same kind of experiments of Table 1. Nonetheless, instead of reporting the number of good coalitions generated, Table 2 reports the execution time required to extract such coalitions. The execution time comprises both the generation of the valid coalitions, and their verification through MCMAS. The columns are the same as in Table 1, but we can observe how much time the tool required to extract the coalitions. Naturally, we can observe that stronger are the guidelines, less is the execution time (since less are the valid coalitions that need to be verified in MCMAS). One important aspect to point out is that our experiments required less than

1 min when considering the scenarios with at most 8 trains and less than 6 min (or so) for 10 trains. This is encouraging, since our approach handles even scenarios where the resulting model is far from being trivial (or small).

Table 3. Execution time (in seconds) to verify CATL formulas in our experiments. 1st column reports number of trains. 2nd column, no guidelines are given. 3rd to 5th column minimum number of agents per coalition is required. 6th to 8th column maximum number of agents per coalition is required. 9th to 11th columns guidelines on which agents can stay (or not) in coalition with. Note that T stays for the whole set of trains.

N	$\langle\langle\geq_0\rangle\rangle$	$\langle\langle\geq_2\rangle\rangle$	$\langle\langle\geq_3\rangle\rangle$	$\langle\langle\geq_4\rangle\rangle$	$\langle\langle\leq_2\rangle\rangle$	$\langle\langle\leq_3\rangle\rangle$	$\langle\langle\leq_4\rangle\rangle$	$\langle\langle T_1{\to}{\leftarrow}C\rangle\rangle$	$\langle\langle T{\to}{\leftarrow}C\rangle\rangle$	$\langle\langle T_1{\leftarrow}{\to}T_2\rangle\rangle$
2	0,06	0,03	0,01	0,00018	0,05	0,05	0,05	0,03	0,01	0,04
4	0,12	0,05	0,05	0,04	0,12	0,12	0,12	0,05	0,02	0,09
6	1,16	0.47	0,41	0,32	0,99	0,99	0,99	0,48	0,08	0,97
8	1,28	0,87	0,76	0,65	1,95	1,95	1,85	0,86	0,1	1,84
10	5,02	2,06	1,75	1,55	4,35	4,08	4,02	2,19	0,19	4,26

In Table 3, we provide the results for the CATL formula $\varphi = \langle\langle-\rangle\rangle F\ in_1$, in which for each column we use the corresponding strategic operator. Notice that, for all the cases our tool returns $\top$, but row 2 column 5. In the latter case, the procedure returns $\perp$ because there are no coalitions with more than 4 agents. In fact, in the above mentioned case, we have only two trains and one controller (*i.e.*, the maximum number of agents is 3). Furthermore, we have removed the 12th column since it is semantically equivalent to column 6th. Another relevant aspect is that our procedure performs better in the case of CATL formulas. This is due to the fact that our algorithm needs to search for only one good coalition (*i.e.*, $num\_coalitions = 1$); while in the experiments carried out in Table 1 and Table 2, all good coalitions are returned (*i.e.*, $num\_coalitions = \infty$).

9   Conclusions

In this paper, we have presented a variant of ATL, called CATL, in which we can reason upon coalitions. We have proved that CATL has the same expressive power of ATL, but it is exponentially more succinct than ATL. We also studied the model checking complexity of CATL in case of both imperfect and perfect information. Furthermore we implemented an extension of MCMAS in which the users can characterize the coalitions in the strategy quantifiers. To do this, we have considered coalitions as variables of the problem. In particular, we have shown how to give the power to a user to handle two main features: the number of agents involved in the coalitions and how to create coalitions by considering who have to play together and who have to play against. This tool is a first stone to develop a more generalized verification approach for MAS.

References

1. Alur, R., Henzinger, T., Kupferman, O.: Alternating-time temporal logic. J. ACM **49**(5), 672–713 (2002)

2. Belardinelli, F., Lomuscio, A., Malvone, V.: Approximating perfect recall when model checking strategic abilities. In: KR18 (2018)
3. Belardinelli, F., Lomuscio, A., Malvone, V.: An abstraction-based method for verifying strategic properties in multi-agent systems with imperfect information. In: Proceedings of AAAI (2019)
4. Belardinelli, F., Ferrando, A., Malvone, V.: An abstraction-refinement framework for verifying strategic properties in multi-agent systems with imperfect information. Artif. Intell. **316**, 103847 (2023). https://doi.org/10.1016/j.artint.2022.103847
5. Belardinelli, F., Jamroga, W., Kurpiewski, D., Malvone, V., Murano, A.: Strategy logic with simple goals: tractable reasoning about strategies. In: Kraus, S. (ed.) Proceedings of the Twenty-Eighth International Joint Conference on Artificial Intelligence, IJCAI 2019, Macao, China, 10–16 August 2019, pp. 88–94. ijcai.org (2019). https://doi.org/10.24963/ijcai.2019/13
6. Belardinelli, F., Lomuscio, A., Malvone, V., Yu, E.: Approximating perfect recall when model checking strategic abilities: theory and applications. J. Artif. Intell. Res. **73**, 897–932 (2022). https://doi.org/10.1613/jair.1.12539
7. Belardinelli, F., Malvone, V.: A three-valued approach to strategic abilities under imperfect information. In: Calvanese, D., Erdem, E., Thielscher, M. (eds.) Proceedings of the 17th International Conference on Principles of Knowledge Representation and Reasoning, KR 2020, Rhodes, Greece, 12–18 September 2020, pp. 89–98 (2020). https://doi.org/10.24963/kr.2020/10
8. Bloem, R., Chatterjee, K., Jacobs, S., Könighofer, R.: Assume-guarantee synthesis for concurrent reactive programs with partial information. In: Baier, C., Tinelli, C. (eds.) TACAS 2015. LNCS, vol. 9035, pp. 517–532. Springer, Heidelberg (2015). https://doi.org/10.1007/978-3-662-46681-0_50
9. Demri, S., Goranko, V., Lange, M.: Temporal Logics in Computer Science: Finite-State Systems, 1st edn. Cambridge University Press, Cambridge (2016)
10. Dima, C., Tiplea, F.: Model-checking ATL under imperfect information and PerfectRecall semantics is undecidable. Technical report, arXiv (2011)
11. Ferrando, A., Malvone, V.: Strategy RV: a tool to approximate ATL model checking under imperfect information and perfect recall. In: Dignum, F., Lomuscio, A., Endriss, U., Nowé, A. (eds.) AAMAS 2021: 20th International Conference on Autonomous Agents and Multiagent Systems, Virtual Event, United Kingdom, 3–7 May 2021, pp. 1764–1766. ACM (2021). https://doi.org/10.5555/3463952.3464230, https://www.ifaamas.org/Proceedings/aamas2021/pdfs/p1764.pdf
12. Ferrando, A., Malvone, V.: Towards the combination of model checking and runtime verification on multi-agent systems. In: Dignum, F., Mathieu, P., Corchado, J.M., de la Prieta, F. (eds.) PAAMS 2022. LNCS, vol. 13616, pp. 140–152. Springer, Cham (2022). https://doi.org/10.1007/978-3-031-18192-4_12
13. Ferrando, A., Malvone, V.: How to find good coalitions to achieve strategic objectives. In: Rocha, A.P., Steels, L., van den Herik, H.J. (eds.) Proceedings of the 15th International Conference on Agents and Artificial Intelligence, ICAART 2023, Lisbon, Portugal, 22–24 February 2023, vol. 1, pp. 105–113. SCITEPRESS (2023). https://doi.org/10.5220/0011778700003393
14. Ferrando, A., Malvone, V.: Towards the verification of strategic properties in multi-agent systems with imperfect information. In: Agmon, N., An, B., Ricci, A., Yeoh, W. (eds.) Proceedings of the 2023 International Conference on Autonomous Agents and Multiagent Systems, AAMAS 2023, London, United Kingdom, 29 May–2 June 2023, pp. 793–801. ACM (2023). https://doi.org/10.5555/3545946.3598713, https://dl.acm.org/doi/10.5555/3545946.3598713

15. Kupferman, O., Vardi, M.Y.: Module checking revisited. In: Grumberg, O. (ed.) CAV 1997. LNCS, vol. 1254, pp. 36–47. Springer, Heidelberg (1997). https://doi.org/10.1007/3-540-63166-6_7

16. Lomuscio, A., Qu, H., Raimondi, F.: MCMAS: a model checker for the verification of multi-agent systems. Softw. Tools Technol. Transf. (2015). https://doi.org/10.1007/s10009-015-0378-x, https://dx.doi.org/10.1007/s10009-015-0378-x

17. Mogavero, F., Murano, A., Perelli, G., Vardi, M.: Reasoning about strategies: on the model-checking problem. ACM Trans. Comp. Log. **15**(4), 34:1–34:47 (2014). https://doi.org/10.1145/2631917, https://doi.acm.org/10.1145/2631917

18. Mogavero, F., Murano, A., Perelli, G., Vardi, M.Y.: Reasoning about strategies: on the satisfiability problem. Log. Methods Comput. Sci. **13**(1) (2017). https://doi.org/10.23638/LMCS-13(1:9)2017

19. Pnueli, A., Rosner, R.: Distributed reactive systems are hard to synthesize. In: FOCS, pp. 746–757 (1990)

20. Reif, J.H.: The complexity of two-player games of incomplete information. J. Comput. Syst. Sci. **29**(2), 274–301 (1984)

21. Schobbens, P.Y.: Alternating-time logic with imperfect recall. Electron. Notes Theor. Comput. Sci. **85**(2), 82–93 (2004)

Holonic Energy Management Systems: Towards Flexible and Resilient Smart Grids

Ihab Taleb$^{(\boxtimes)}$ ⓘ, Guillaume Guerard ⓘ, Frédéric Fauberteau ⓘ, and Nga Nguyen ⓘ

Léonard de Vinci Pôle Universitaire, Research Center, 92 916 Paris La Défense, France
{ihab.taleb,guillaume.guerard,
frederic.fauberteau,nga.nguyen}@devinci.fr

Abstract. The increasing global warming and soaring fossil fuel prices have made energy generation minimization a crucial objective. As a result, the relevance of smart grids has significantly grown, especially in the context of regulating energy demand based on available resources. This necessitates the implementation of Demand Side Management (DSM) tools for effective regulation. While various models and architectures have been developed for smart grids, the utilization of holonic architectures remains limited in existing literature. In this paper, we propose a holonic architecture specifically tailored for smart grids, which proves to be highly advantageous. Holonic architectures are particularly valuable in smart grids as they enable seamless operation among different actors, even during technical challenges. Our proposed model consists of interconnected agents forming holons, with five agents working in tandem to ensure flexibility across multiple aspects. We have tested this model in three different scenarios. The first scenario represents a healthy grid. The second scenario simulates a grid with production mismanagement. Lastly, the third one simulates a grid experiencing a region-specific blackout. Results show how the grid distributes the available energy depending on the available production, storage (if any) and the assurance of the distribution across the various requesting holons.

Keywords: Smart grid · Holarchy · Holon · Multi Agent System (MAS) · Energy Management System (EMS)

1 Introduction

In 2015, the Paris Agreement was accepted by 196 countries as a commitment to limit global climate change resulting from global warming to be less than 2°C, primarily through the reduction of fossil fuel usage [29]. In line with this, the European Union is funding projects aimed at developing solutions to mitigate greenhouse gas emissions. One such project is MAESHA, which includes the contributions discussed in this article, focusing on decarbonizing the French island of Mayotte.

Energy production infrastructures play a significant role in climate change, and early projects have revealed that relying on natural gas for electricity production is not an ideal solution. Firstly, natural gas is a fossil fuel, meaning its energy generation still

This project has received funding from the European Union's Horizon 2020 research and innovation programme under grant agreement No. 957843.

contributes to pollution. Secondly, the availability of natural gas is not uniform across all countries, and transportation issues, whether due to accidents or political conflicts, can lead to dramatic price increases.

Consequently, it is essential to explore alternative solutions that are more accessible and manageable. To this end, transition policies away from coal and other fossil fuels have been discussed in [26], proposing an increased integration of Renewable Energy Sources (RESs) such as Photovoltaic (PV) panels. Although RES installations are currently more costly compared to conventional energy sources, the study in [4] estimates that the Return Of Investment (ROI) will improve over time, eventually matching that of fossil fuels. However, a significant challenge associated with RESs is their dependency on weather parameters like sunlight, temperature, and wind, making it difficult to control energy generation.

Another challenge arises from the increasing number of Electric Vehicles (EVs) and the subsequent higher demand for charging, which increases the risk of grid instability and potential blackouts [12]. Nevertheless, with proper control over EVs charging processes (such as delaying or advancing the charging time) and utilizing their batteries for discharging when necessary, it becomes possible not only to prevent blackouts but also to leverage these batteries as energy storage units during peak hours-a concept known as Vehicle to Grid (V2G) [13,18]. Given the uncontrollable nature of energy generation and the controllable aspects of EVs charging and discharging, demand becomes the only parameter that can be managed through Demand Side Management (DSM). DSM aims to delay, flatten, or plan energy demand and utilize battery storage during periods of high demand and excess energy production [16]. Therefore, upgrading traditional Electrical Grids (EGs) to Smart Grid (SG) is necessary to enable intelligent energy usage and efficient energy routing, thereby maximizing the benefits of DSM.

The concept of SGs as known today was defined by Amin and Wollenberg [2]. It represents an upgraded version of traditional EGs that aims to enhance various aspects such as measurements, predictions, data registry and analytics, control, and communication. SGs address a wide range of challenges and requirements within the grid system, including consumers, producers, energy distribution, and blackout management. By improving communication and distributed control among different actors, including consumers, producers, storage facilities, EVs, and the emergence of prosumers [8], SGs facilitate the integration of RESs. Prosumers, who can generate energy using RES, contribute to the grid by either satisfying or supplementing their own energy demands based on factors like weather conditions (sun radiation) and the energy availability on both the grid and EV side.

To fully utilize RESs, batteries, and EVs, SGs necessitate bidirectional energy routing, enabling users to not only consume but also produce and feed surplus energy back into the grid during peak hours [25]. However, to optimize the performance of prosumers, accurate measurements and predictions for the near future are crucial. Predictive capabilities allow SG actors to plan their energy demands or offerings in advance, enabling more effective energy routing with reduced losses and lower transmission costs. It also allows for the possibility of delaying certain demands before peak hours occur. Several deep learning methods have been proposed for energy demand prediction in a flexible and reusable manner. Studies such as [6,15] have introduced deep learning models for demand prediction in different regions, while [15,22] have focused on different time ranges. Additionally, [27] has proposed a flexible deep learning approach that ensures adaptability to both time ranges and regional domains.

Numerous architectures and models have been proposed for SGs. However, one architecture that remains insufficiently tested and defined in the domain of SGs is the holonic architecture. This paper aims to address this gap by introducing a holonic SG architecture, in response to the suggestion put forth by Howell et al. [14].

The holonic architecture is characterized by the aggregation of a universal entity known as a holon. A holon possesses the ability to function autonomously as a whole entity while also being part of a larger entity of the same type [20]. In the context of a holonic SG, a holon can be conceptualized as the aggregation of multiple microgrids, each of which is further comprised of smaller microgrids, ultimately extending to the level of individual houses or electric devices.

The proposed model in this paper aims to simulate the behavior of holons within the SG framework. Holons encompass a variety of agents that can be modified to simulate diverse scenarios. For instance, the model can incorporate different energy pricing schemes (e.g., flat prices, dynamic prices, carbon-based prices) and energy management strategies (including load curtailment, peak and load reduction, peak clipping, valley filling, etc.), as well as encompass various technologies. Scenarios within the model encompass a wide range of disturbances that can affect the grid, including those related to its structure, behaviors, or external factors.

By adopting the holonic architecture, the proposed model presents a novel approach to SGs, allowing for the exploration of complex interactions and behaviors within the system. It provides a platform to study and evaluate different energy pricing strategies, energy management techniques, and the impact of disturbances on the grid. Through this holistic approach, the holonic SG architecture holds promise for enhancing the efficiency and resilience of future SGs.

In this paper, we present an extended version of the paper [28]. The present version contains a mathematical model that includes costs, energy storage via Battery Energy Storage System (BESS) and the concept of energy curtailment. It also distinguishes between the Energy Management System (EMS), that is, the root holon (the deciding holon) and the aggregator holons that can play the role of EMS in case of grid faults to prevent blackouts. The paper starts with a literature review of holons and Holonic Multi-Agent System (HMAS) in Sect. 2. Section 3 describes the proposed model as both a single holon model, a holarchic model, as well as a control method based on cost optimization. In Sect. 4, the materials and methods used for the simulations are discussed, along with the three test cases used on the proposed model. Conclusion and future work are given in Sect. 5.

2 Literature Review and Gaps

The concept of holons and holarchy, where holons are organized in a hierarchical architecture, was first introduced by Arthur Koestler in his book "The Ghost in the Machine" in 1967 [17]. The concept of HMASs was then introduced by Gerber, Siekmann, and Vierke [10], where an agent can be an aggregation of multiple lower domain agents.

This concept has been applied to various domains, including automation, manufacturing, and transportation systems [19].

While different architectures have been proposed for SGs, the most interesting ones are based on holarchies as they provide greater flexibility to the different actors within the grid, such as consumers, producers, prosumers, storage facilities, and distribution points [21]. These architectures benefit from both decentralized decision-making and a top-down hierarchical organization or surveillance. [11] has proposed to compose the SG of two layers: physical layer where all the connections to all physical devices happen, and aggregation layer where all holons from the first layer merge or aggregate to form the SG. [3] has defined their SG based on low and medium voltages: a first level designs smart homes and energy resources, than the higher levels are for low voltage feeders, medium voltage feeders, medium voltage substations, etc. up to the highest level that contains the EMS holon that is responsible for managing the whole system.

Many papers have discussed the various control methods and architectures for EMSs. However, the most relevant architectures and solution are the ones that focus on hierarchical EMSs and EMS aggregators [7]. Indeed, EMS aggregators have been discussed for different objectives and in different roles such as demand response aggregators [5], load aggregators [24], and microgrid aggregators [23].

In terms of holonic architecture, Ferreira et al. [9] introduced the concept of single holon modeling, where a holon can manage anything from a physical device to an apartment, building, or even micro-grids. They also proposed a multi-threaded holon, with separate threads for negotiation with peers, negotiation with children, and local behaviors. The application of holonic SGs for self-healing purposes has been discussed in [1], highlighting the potential, challenges, and requirements of SGs in a holonic architecture. Another framework based on holonic architectures has been proposed, consisting of historical data collection, prediction (Forecasting of Resources for Dynamic Optimization - FRODO), and decision or strategy selection (Optimal Load and Energy Flow - OLAF) [30].

The existing modeling of SGs has some limitations and challenges. One of the main drawbacks is the lack of flexibility in the architecture, which often leads to rigid and centralized control systems. This limits the ability of different actors within the grid to make autonomous decisions and adapt to changing conditions. Additionally, traditional SG models often struggle to handle the complexity and scalability of large-scale systems, making it difficult to incorporate diverse energy sources, accommodate fluctuations in supply and demand, and ensure efficient grid operation.

This is where the holonic model can provide significant benefits. The holonic architecture offers a more flexible and decentralized approach to SG modeling. By organizing the SG as a hierarchy of holons, where each holon can function as an autonomous unit while being part of a larger entity, the holonic model enables more distributed decision-making and control. This allows for greater adaptability, resilience, and self-organization within the SG.

Furthermore, the holonic model supports modularity and reusability. Holons can be easily composed and recomposed to form different configurations of the SG, accommodating various energy sources, devices, and actors. This modularity facilitates system expansion, integration of new technologies, and easier maintenance and upgrade processes.

The holonic model also addresses the challenge of scalability. By breaking down the SG into smaller holonic units, such as microgrids, and then aggregating them into larger holonic structures, the model can effectively manage the complexity of large-scale SGs. This hierarchical organization allows for efficient coordination and communication between different levels, ensuring smooth operation and effective resource management.

Overall, the holonic model overcomes the limitations of traditional SG modeling by offering greater flexibility, decentralization, modularity, and scalability. It empowers individual actors within the grid while enabling coordinated behavior and optimal system performance.

In the next sections we will discuss a new proposed single holon model that is composed of multiple agents. The main goal of this model is to provide the highest possible flexibility in terms of the definition of the SG architecture, its reuse and blackouts avoidance.

3   The Proposed Model

In this section, we propose a holonic architecture that is composed of flexible and resilient holons, organized as a hierarchical bidirectional rooted tree. Holons represent their connected actors and their subholons, they are able to control them or to communicate with upper level entities that take care of the control and they are composed of five interconnecting agents: measurement agent, data agent, prediction agent, control agent and communication agent. These holons, their functionality, as well as their composing agents will be discussed in details in the following subsections.

3.1   Holarchic Architecture

A holarchy, or holarchic architecture, is a hierarchical arrangement of holons. Unlike traditional hierarchies where parts rely on the whole and cannot function individually, holons are autonomous units that can operate both independently or as a part of their corresponding roots.

The proposed holarchic architecture offers flexibility in three aspects: control and communication, space, and time. It allows holons to represent and control various actors in the SGs, such as physical devices, storage facilities, EVs, or even micro-grids. The measurement agent facilitates communication with different devices or smart meters, while the communication agent enables interactions with other holons representing smaller or larger micro-grids. This ensures the flow of data from devices and other holons to the control agent.

Holons are created and distributed on different levels based on regional considerations. For example, the top-level holon represents an entire country or an island. The second level consists of holons representing regions or actors with similar power demand or generation capacity, like a thermal power plant. The third level represents villages or equivalent actors involved in power trading, such as renewable energy, facilities or storage units. This architecture can extend to lower levels, depending on the configuration, reaching down to simple smart devices like heating devices. At each time step, holons check for connections to physical devices or subholons to provide or obtain the required energy.

Holons should also be capable of providing predictions at different regional scales, whether for a large region, a small group of buildings, or even a single device. In this paper, holons are connected only to their upper holon, lower holons, and associated devices. They do not communicate directly with other holons at the same level but rely on feedback from their upper holon, which has broader information.

Furthermore, holons need to adapt to various time ranges depending on their level and the physical actors and holons they interact with. A data agent stores relevant data for future steps, including predictions and decision-making, while a prediction agent generates predictions for multiple time ranges according to the control agent's requirements.

Figure 1 shows an example of how a holarchy looks like for the SG while Fig. 2 shows a sequence diagram for the five agents of a holon, with social agents of its connected holons.

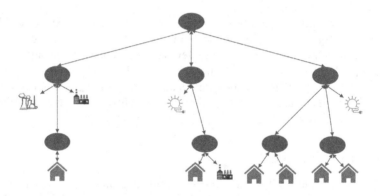

Fig. 1. The holarchic architecture. In this image, we can see that the holarchy is composed of three levels whereas it can be extended to as many levels as needed [28].

3.2   The Holon: Composition and Functionality

In this subsection we will discuss the details of the main element of the holarchy: the holon. Holons in the proposed model can have two different roles. The first role is the global EMS (called root holon) and the second role is the aggregator role.

Holons Roles

Aggregator Holons represent a part of the EG, a region or a micro-grid. They apply basic control algorithms only to provide the necessary data and information to the root holon (or EMS). They also take care of forwarding or sending the result of the decision that they receive from their upper holon. In case of grid faults or disturbance, in order to

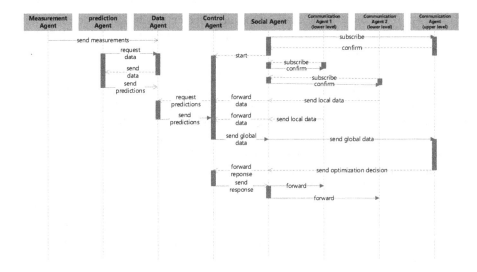

Fig. 2. The interaction between the various agents of the holon and the social agents of their connected holons. In this diagram, we considered that the holon is connected to only 2 subholons while this number can be less or more in other cases [28].

ensure the highest resilience possible, aggregator holons can temporarily play the role of a root holon in their local holarchy, and thus act as a separate holarchy until the grid problems get fixed.

Root Holon is the highest level holon that has a global reach to all its subholons demands, generations, available BESS and possible charging. It applies a relatively complicated algorithm that aims to ensure a global convergence while ensuring the priority of RESs and cost minimization. Section 3.3 provides more details on how this holon performs its optimization.

It is worth mentioning that while the architecture proposed in this paper is similar to the original paper [28], the main difference, in addition to introducing BESS and load curtailment and generation and demand costs, is in the behaviours or roles of the various holons, namely: the aggregator and the root roles. The advantage of having these two roles compared to the original paper is that in the first proposition, subholons could prioritize their self consumption and do not send their generation information to higher levels, while in the current version aggregator holons should declare or inform the root holon which can take decisions considering the global interests of the grid. This helps to avoid any conflict of interest between the local decisions and the global decision.

Composing Agents. The previously mentioned holon, is composed of five agents that are similar to the original proposition of the [28], except for the control agent which has different behaviours that can change depending on the needs of the grid. They are shown in Fig. 3, and are defined as follows:

Measurement Agent handles the data and the measurements by handling the communication with physical devices (IoT devices, smart meters, etc.) and the transmission of these data to the Data Agent.

Prediction agent handles the forecasting the energy generation and/or demands using historical data that is stored in the data agent and other data like holidays and weather forecasts. In this paper, prediction agent implements the hybrid deep learning algorithm described in [27], which is able to make flexible predictions on both time scale and spatial scale. For the spatial scale, this method can provide predictions on a whole island scale as well as on the scale of a small group of buildings without the need of any modifications in the method. On the time scale, this method can also provide predictions on different time ranges (real-time, daily and weekly predictions) with minor changes in the preprocessing phase.

Data agent is the agent that handles and stores the data sent by data agent to provide them later to the prediction agent. The data agent also stores the energy forecasts made by the prediction agent to be sent for control agent upon request.

Communication agent is the agent responsible for the communications with other holons via their respective communication agents, it uses the Agent Communication Language (ACL) specifications for the communications with other agents. It also ensures that lower holons are in synchronization with its current time-step.

Control agent is the decision making unit inside the holon in the case of decentralized or distributed decisions (in the case of the original proposition), and it is the representative of the interests of its lower holons and itself in the case of centralized control systems that implements the concept of centralized EMS (in the case of the current proposition). It takes its decision depending on two flows of information. The first is the prediction data made by prediction agent and stored with data agent. The second is the ensemble of requests and/or offers sent from lower holons and the feedback received from the upper holon (in a holarchic architecture). Details about the control algorithm are provided in Sect. 3.3.

3.3 Control Method

In this section, we will discuss the algorithm and behaviour of the control agent in more details. The first part of this section will discuss the algorithm of this agent, while the second part will discuss the details of the mathematical representation and the optimization model proposed for the decision making in the control agent of the root holon.

Control Algorithm. Control agent is the brain of its corresponding holon. It takes the role of the root or aggregator holon depending on its position in the holarchy and on potential problems in the SG. It also takes care of informing and of decision making for the demands, generation and storage. Algorithm 1 shows the steps followed by this agent in order to ensure the well functionality in the holon.

The PSO() method is Particle Swarm Optimization (PSO) that has been applied to the optimization algorithm described in Sect. 3.3.

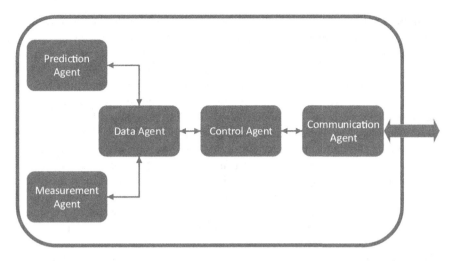

Fig. 3. The structure of the proposed holon, composed of five interconnecting agents as defined in [28].

Algorithm 1. Control Algorithm.

1: $T \leftarrow T_{max}$
2: $UPPER\_HOLON$ = READ_UPPER_INFO()
3: $HOLON\_STATE$ = READ_HOLON_STATE()
4: **while** $T \leq T_{max}$ **do**
5:     RECEIVE_DATA_FROM_LOWER_LEVELS()
6:     RECEIVE_LOCAL_PREDICTIONS()
7:     CHECK_AVAILABLE_STORAGE()
8:     CHECK_AVAILABLE_THERMAL_GENERATION()
9:     **if** $UPPER\_HOLON \neq NUll$ & $CHECK\_UPPER\_CONNECTION() = True$ **then**
10:         SET_STATE(Aggregator)
11:         SEND_AGGREGATION_TO_UPPER_HOLON()
12:         WAIT_FEEDBACK()
13:         RECEIVE_FEEDBACK()
14:     **else if** $UPPER\_HOLON \neq NUll$ & $CHECK\_UPPER\_CONNECTION() = False$ **then**
15:         SET_STATE(EMS)
16:         PSO()
17:     **else if** $UPPER\_HOLON = NUll$ **then**
18:         PSO()
19:     **end if**
20:     SEND_FEEDBACK_TO_LOWER_HOLONS()
21:     $T \leftarrow T + 1$
22: **end while**

Mathematical Model. In this paper, we represent the smart grid as a holarchy, which can also be viewed as a rooted tree structure where each node is connected to a single parent node. A smart grid can be described using a tuple (V, E, r), where V represents the set of nodes, E denotes the communication links between holons, and r is the root node that represents the entire island and that plays the role of the EMS. The links between holons symbolise the bidirectional communication for exchanging data and decisions between lower and upper holons. While r plays the role of EMS, other nodes are considered as aggregation holons that can play the role of EMS in case of need (grid fault, communication problems, etc.). Holons, or nodes, within the smart grid handle specific segments of the grid, such as regions. They encompass themselves, their subholons (representing villages within the region), and any actor directly associated with them (such as a solar park). Therefore, a holon h can be associated to a 3-tuple (G_h, S_h, H_h), where G_h denotes the subset of generation points, S_h represents the subset of battery energy storage systems (BESS), and H_h represents the subset of subholons connected to holon h.

Let $G_{h,g}(t)$ be the energy generated in the holon h, by the generator g, at the period of time t. Let $S_{h,s}(t)$ be the amount of energy stored in holon h, inside the BESS s, at time t. $\delta S_{h,s}(t)$ is the amount of energy charged or discharged from time t to $t+1$. Let D_h is the amount of energy demanded or needed by the holon h from the grid.

$$Minimize \sum_{g \in G} C_{h,g} G_{h,g}(t) + \sum_{s \in S} C_{h,s} \delta S_{h,s}(t) + \sum_{h} C_D D_h(t) + \sum_{h} C_{LC} LC_h(t)$$

$$\forall h \in H, t \in T \quad (1)$$

subject to:

$$\sum_{g \in G} G_{h,g}(t) + \sum_{s \in S} \delta S_{h,s}(t) + \sum_{h} D_h(t) + \sum_{h} LC_h(t) = 0$$

$$\forall h \in H, t \in T \quad (2)$$

and

$$\delta S_{h,s}(t) = S_{h,s}(t+1) - S_{h,s}(t) \qquad \forall h \in H, s \in S, t \in T \quad (3)$$

and

$$S_{h,s}^{Min} \leq S_{h,s}(t) \leq S_{h,s}^{Max} \qquad \forall h \in H, s \in S, t \in T \quad (4)$$

and

$$G_{h,g}^{Min} \leq G_{h,g}(t) \leq G_{h,g}^{Max} \qquad \forall h \in H, g \in G, t \in T \quad (5)$$

where T is the hourly index in the simulation, H is the set of holons (nodes in the rooted tree), G is the set of generation points (generators), S is the set of BESS, D is the total energy demand needed for the holon (energy consumption).

$LC_h(t)$ is the load curtailment required to ensure the satisfaction of the clients. It is the result of the energy demand that could not be satisfied with the generated energy or with the stored energy in the BESS, during the time period t, and that has been delayed for later hours.

$G_{h,g}$, $S_{h,s}$, D_h and LS_h are all positive variables while $\delta S_{h,s}$ can be positive (recharging) or negative (discharging).

$C_{h,g}$, $C_{h,s}$, C_D, C_{LS} are the respective costs for the generation for each generator g that belongs to the holon h, energy storage for each BESS s that belongs to the holon h, the demand tariff and the load curtailment cost. In the proposed model, we estimate that battery charging and discharging is always more costly that energy production while it is always less costly that load curtailment.

4 Model Validation

The simulation has been made using JAVA as a programming language and JAVA Agent DEvelopment Framework (JADE) for the development of holons and their composing agents. It exploits the optimization method proposed in Sect. 3.3.

4.1 Data and Approach

In this paper, the data used for the simulations are for the island of Mayotte, and it has been provided by the MAESHA project. The simulation utilized weather forecasts, holiday data, and historical data on energy demand and renewable energy production with a time granularity of 60 min. Mayotte's energy landscape comprises two thermal power plants, various renewable energy sources (PV parks) and two BESS. The simulation implemented a 3-level holarchy architecture, with the root holon representing the entire island at the first level and playing the role of the EMS, the 17 regions at the second level, and the villages within each region at the third level playing the role of aggregator holons.

In this simulation, second-level holons represent their corresponding regions and encompasses the thermal power plants, renewable energy facilities (PV parks), energy demands of big consumers and BESSs. Third-level holons represent the villages, each responsible for initiating energy demands (excluding big consumer demands, that are represented by second level holons), that will then propagate to the second level. Second-level holons aggregate the data from third-level holons with its own demands (big consumers), generation, and energy storage offers and demands. The aggregated data will be then sent to first-level holon or the EMS. The EMS applies the control method defined in Sect. 3.3, and provides its feedback to lower level holons, this feedback propagates until it reaches the specific holons responsible for the demands. The proposed control method ensures the use of BESS for discharging during peak-hours and for charging during off-peak hours, as well as the stability in case of grid faults.

The architecture described in Sect. 3 was tested in three scenarios. We have applied the PSO algorithm on the optimization method of Sect. 3.3. The cost of RES has been considered as only O&M costs (without installation costs, to ensure the low cost for RES and thus to give it a higher priority in the optimization algorithm). The cost for energy storage has been considered as a very low cost to ensure that the BESS will be properly charged when grid faults happen. The cost for diesel is the average cost for the year 2020 in the island of Mayotte. Finally, to ensure that the model will only resort to load curtailment when needed (in case it is impossible to deliver energy during grid faults), we have considered that the cost of load curtailment is very high compared to other costs. This can be justified by the fact that not providing energy can have bad effects on the economy.

Due to the large number of holons on the island, the simulation results were presented for one specific holon, Mamoudzou, representing a region in the island that has its own PV park and BESS ensuring that even in the case of disconnection (as demonstrated in Sect. 4.4), it could still demand energy from its region's holon (its own) and compensate its lack of sufficient generation with the energy that is already stored in the BESS. Regions or villages capable of either producing their own energy or requesting energy from connected holons should exhibit similar behavior as demonstrated in the second scenario. However, it should be noted that holons or groups of holons that are disconnected from the grid with zero production or energy storage will be unable to satisfy their demands due to the lack of energy availability. It is worth mentioning that the simulation scenarios in this paper are similar to those in [28]. However they have been applied to another control algorithm that provides more flexibility and introduces the aspects of energy costs, energy storage and load curtailment.

4.2 Standard Scenario

In the standard scenario, all holons across the three levels described in Sect. 4.1 are properly connected, and thermal production operated optimally to meet all energy demands throughout the grid while BESSs have all the needed energy to stay charged during the simulation. Energy requests and availability propagate from the third level (lowest level) to higher levels. Once the highest-level holon (EMS) received all the requests, it provides its feedback for the demands ranging from 0 (no available energy) to 1 (the full demanded energy can be fulfilled), as well as feedback for the storage ranging from -1 (to discharge all the energy that is stored and available with respect to the batteries characteristics into the grid) to +1 (to charge the batteries to the maximum that is possible during the one hour time-step). Figure 4 illustrates that the energy demanded by Mamoudzou was successfully received in this standard scenario.

4.3 Disrupted Plant

This scenario considers the case where a thermal power plant (a large energy provider) experiences disruptions or undergoes maintenance, leading to its temporary shutdown. In this test case, the power plant located in **Koungou** stops working between the timestep 5 and 14, leading to a decrease in the energy generation while only the second thermal power plant located in **Badamiers** is working along side the PV parks and

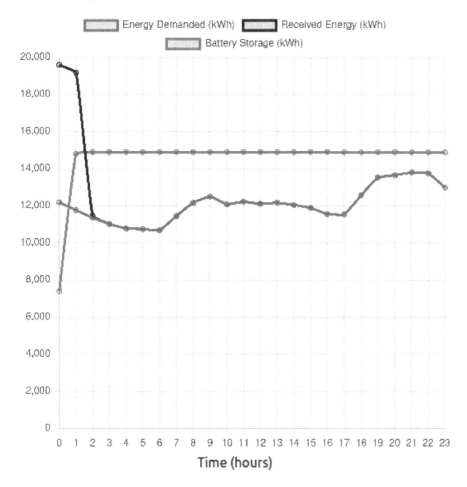

Fig. 4. Energy received by a holon representing a region in the island, in the standard scenario where all the holons and actors across the whole grid are properly connected.

BESSs. Figure 5 shows that the energy received is higher than the energy demanded in the beginning of the simulation due to the charging of the BESS. Between time steps 5 and 10, even though the thermal power plant has been shut down, the region still received all its requested energy because the PV generation with the other power plant was still enough to satisfy all demands. Starting from time-step 10 up to time step 13, BESSs starts discharging to compensate the insufficiency of energy generation compared to the peak in the demand side. After energy generation in the **Koungou** plant restarts, energy demands start to be fully received in the grid and BESSs start receiving energy for recharging. It is worth mentioning that in this scenario all holons keep their respective role as aggregators with the root holon plays the role of the EMS.

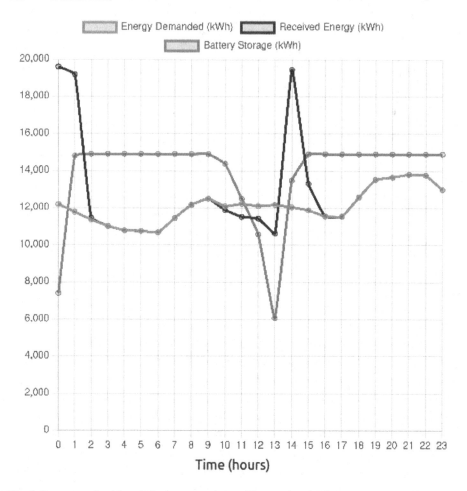

Fig. 5. Energy received by a holon representing a village on level 3, in a scenario where only one thermal power plant is operating.

4.4 Disconnected Region

In this section, the simulation explores the effects of a grid fault that causes a disconnection between the region of **Mamoudzou** and the rest of the grid. In this case, the grid functions normally until time-step 5, when the grid fault occurs. After that, the representing holon of this region starts acting as its own EMS, separately from the rest of the grid, while relying solely on available energy generation sources, namely photovoltaic (PV) generation and energy storage in the BESS. Any unsatisfied energy demand during this period is treated as load curtailment. Subsequently, at time-step 14, the grid recovers from its fault, the holon reestablishes its connection with the rest of the grid and it goes back to playing the role of an aggregator. Consequently, the region regains access to the grid generation, starting to recharge its batteries and to fulfill its demands. Figure 6 shows the results of this simulation test.

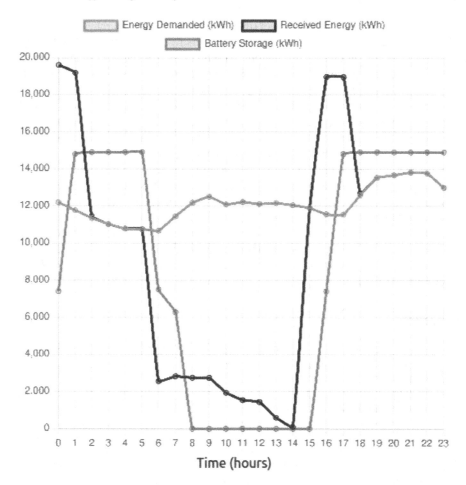

Fig. 6. Energy received by a holon representing region in the island, in a scenario where it is disconnected from the grid and the only energy and storage available are the energy produced and the storage available locally in the region.

5   Conclusion and Future Work

In this paper, we proposed a holonic smart grid architecture following the concept of single holon modelling, where holons can take the role of an EMS or an aggregator. Holons represent geographical zones starting from small villages up to the whole grid as a whole thanks to its flexibility on the regional, spatial and functional aspects. In this paper, we have discussed the composing components (agents) of this holon, the interactions between the agents in the same holon, and between the various connected holons as well as the optimization and control method applied at the highest level holon (the EMS) and the role of other holons as aggregators. We then applied this architecture to the French island of Mayotte, forming a 3 levels holarchy. The first level consists of the highest holon which represents the island. The second level represents the 17 regions of the island and the third level (the lowest level in the holarchy) is composed of 72 holons. Each of these holons is connected to its respective upper holon. We then tested this holarchy on three test scenarios. The first one is a standard scenario where the energy flow and the connection between holons are working as supposed to be. The second scenario is a test where a thermal power plant is disconnected from the grid due to disruption or maintenance problems. The third scenario is a disconnection scenario where a holon is disconnected from the main grid and it has to deal with the energy generation and storage that it has without going into a blackout. The simulations have proven this architecture to be flexible and resilient in the three tested scenarios. Finally, the paper has focused mainly on the proposition of this new architecture, its feasibility and its flexibility in all aspects, while introducing the EMS element, the aggregator holon that can change to EMS depending on the needs, the energy storage using BESSs and load curtailment to ensure the well functioning of the grid in all situations while aiming to the highest satisfaction of the clients. In future works, more advanced control and communication algorithms will be introduced to get the most benefits of the available resources like generation and storage while introducing the concepts of Virtual Power Plants (VPPs) and load shifting.

References

1. Abdel-Fattah, M., Kohler, H., Rotenberger, P., Scholer, L.: A review of the holonic architecture for the smart grids and the self-healing application, pp. 1–6 (2020). https://doi.org/10.1109/EPE51172.2020.9269182
2. Amin, S.M., Wollenberg, B.F.: Toward a smart grid: power delivery for the 21st century. IEEE Power Energy Mag. 3(5), 34–41 (2005)
3. Ansari, J., Kazemi, A., Gholami, A.: Holonic structure: a state-of-the-art control architecture based on multi-agent systems for optimal reactive power dispatch in smart grids. IET Gener. Transmission Distrib. 9 (2015). https://doi.org/10.1049/iet-gtd.2014.1183
4. Brockway, P.E., Owen, A., Brand-Correa, L.I., Hardt, L.: Estimation of global final-stage energy-return-on-investment for fossil fuels with comparison to renewable energy sources. Nat. Energy 4(7), 612–621 (2019). https://doi.org/10.1038/s41560-019-0425-z
5. Di Somma, M., Graditi, G., Siano, P.: Optimal bidding strategy for a der aggregator in the day-ahead market in the presence of demand flexibility. IEEE Trans. Ind. Electron. 66(2), 1509–1519 (2019). https://doi.org/10.1109/TIE.2018.2829677
6. Dudek, G., Pełka, P., Smyl, S.: A hybrid residual dilated LSTM and exponential smoothing model for midterm electric load forecasting. IEEE Trans. Neural Netw. Learn. Syst. 33, 2879–2891 (2021)
7. Elmouatamid, A., Ouladsine, R., Bakhouya, M., El Kamoun, N., Khaidar, M., Zine-Dine, K.: Review of control and energy management approaches in micro-grid systems. Energies 14(1), 168 (2020)
8. Espe, E., Potdar, V., Chang, E.: Prosumer communities and relationships in smart grids: a literature review, evolution and future directions. Energies 11(10) (2018). https://doi.org/10.3390/en11102528. https://www.mdpi.com/1996-1073/11/10/2528
9. Ferreira, A., Ângela Ferreira, Cardin, O., Leitão, P.: Extension of holonic paradigm to smart grids. IFAC-PapersOnLine 48(3), 1099–1104 (2015). https://doi.org/10.1016/j.ifacol.2015.06.230. https://www.sciencedirect.com/science/article/pii/S2405896315004693
10. Gerber, C., Siekmann, J., Vierke, G.: Holonic multi-agent systems (1999). http://dx.doi.org/10.22028/D291-24979

11. Ghorbani, S., Unland, R.: A holonic multi-agent control system for networks of micro-grids. In: Klusch, M., Unland, R., Shehory, O., Pokahr, A., Ahrndt, S. (eds.) MATES 2016. LNCS (LNAI), vol. 9872, pp. 231–238. Springer, Cham (2016). https://doi.org/10.1007/978-3-319-45889-2_17

12. Green, R.C., Wang, L., Alam, M.: The impact of plug-in hybrid electric vehicles on distribution networks: a review and outlook. Renew. Sustain. Energy Rev. **15**(1), 544–553 (2011). https://doi.org/10.1016/j.rser.2010.08.015. https://www.sciencedirect.com/science/article/pii/S1364032110002674

13. Hannan, M., et al.: Vehicle to grid connected technologies and charging strategies: operation, control, issues and recommendations. J. Clean. Prod. **339**, 130587 (2022). https://doi.org/10.1016/j.jclepro.2022.130587. https://www.sciencedirect.com/science/article/pii/S0959652622002281

14. Howell, S., Rezgui, Y., Hippolyte, J.L., Jayan, B., Li, H.: Towards the next generation of smart grids: semantic and holonic multi-agent management of distributed energy resources. Renew. Sustain. Energy Rev. **77**, 193–214 (2017). https://doi.org/10.1016/j.rser.2017.03.107. https://www.sciencedirect.com/science/article/pii/S1364032117304392

15. Huang, Y., Hasan, N., Deng, C., Bao, Y.: Multivariate empirical mode decomposition based hybrid model for day-ahead peak load forecasting. Energy **239**, 122245 (2022). https://doi.org/10.1016/j.energy.2021.122245. https://www.sciencedirect.com/science/article/pii/S0360544221024932

16. Kanakadhurga, D., Prabaharan, N.: Demand side management in microgrid: a critical review of key issues and recent trends. Renew. Sustain. Energy Rev. **156**, 111915 (2022). https://doi.org/10.1016/j.rser.2021.111915. https://www.sciencedirect.com/science/article/pii/S1364032121011801

17. Koestler, A.: The Ghost in the Machine. Macmillan, New York (1967)

18. Liu, C., Chau, K.T., Wu, D., Gao, S.: Opportunities and challenges of vehicle-to-home, vehicle-to-vehicle, and vehicle-to-grid technologies. Proc. IEEE **101**(11), 2409–2427 (2013). https://doi.org/10.1109/JPROC.2013.2271951

19. Mařík, V., Lastra, J.L.M., Skobelev, P. (eds.): HoloMAS 2013. LNCS (LNAI), vol. 8062. Springer, Heidelberg (2013). https://doi.org/10.1007/978-3-642-40090-2

20. Mella, P.: The holonic revolution holons, holarchies and holonic networks. In: The Ghost in the Production Machine (2009). https://doi.org/10.13140/2.1.1954.5922

21. Negeri, E., Baken, N., Popov, M.: Holonic architecture of the smart grid. Smart Grid Renew. Energy **04**, 202–212 (2013). https://doi.org/10.4236/sgre.2013.42025

22. Pallonetto, F., Jin, C., Mangina, E.: Forecast electricity demand in commercial building with machine learning models to enable demand response programs. Energy AI **7**, 100121 (2022). https://doi.org/10.1016/j.egyai.2021.100121. https://www.sciencedirect.com/science/article/pii/S2666546821000690

23. Pei, W., Du, Y., Deng, W., Sheng, K., Xiao, H., Qu, H.: Optimal bidding strategy and intra-market mechanism of microgrid aggregator in real-time balancing market. IEEE Trans. Ind. Inf. **12**(2), 587–596 (2016). https://doi.org/10.1109/TII.2016.2522641

24. Rahmani-Andebili, M., Venayagamoorthy, G.K.: Investigating effects of changes in power market regulations on demand-side resources aggregators. In: 2015 IEEE Power & Energy Society General Meeting, pp. 1–5 (2015). https://doi.org/10.1109/PESGM.2015.7286312

25. Ramchurn, S., Vytelingum, P., Rogers, A., Jennings, N.: Putting the 'Smarts' into the smart grid: a grand challenge for artificial intelligence. Commun. ACM - CACM **55**, 86–97 (2012). https://doi.org/10.1145/2133806.2133825

26. Spencer, T., Berghmans, N., Sartor, O.: Coal transitions in China's power sector: a plant-level assessment of stranded assets and retirement pathways. Coal Trans. **12/17**, 21 (2017)

27. Taleb, I., Guerard, G., Fauberteau, F., Nguyen, N.: A flexible deep learning method for energy forecasting. Energies **15**(11), 3926 (2022). https://doi.org/10.3390/en15113926. https://www.mdpi.com/1996-1073/15/11/3926

28. Taleb., I., Guerard., G., Fauberteau., F., Nguyen., N.: A holonic multi-agent architecture for smart grids. In: Proceedings of the 15th International Conference on Agents and Artificial Intelligence, vol. 1: ICAART, pp. 126–134. INSTICC, SciTePress (2023). https://doi.org/10.5220/0011803300003393

29. The Paris Agreement | UNFCCC (2021). https://unfccc.int/process-and-meetings/the-paris-agreement/the-paris-agreement

30. Wallis, A., Hauke, S., Egert, R., Mühlhäuser, M.: A framework for strategy selection of atomic entities in the holonic smart grid (2020)

Artificial Intelligence

Predictive Explanations for and by Reinforcement Learning

Léo Saulières[(✉)] [iD], Martin C. Cooper [iD], and Florence Dupin de Saint-Cyr [iD]

IRIT, University of Toulouse III, Toulouse, France
leo.saulieres@irit.fr

Abstract. In order to understand a reinforcement learning (RL) agent's behavior within its environment, we propose an answer to 'What is likely to happen?' in the form of a predictive explanation. It is composed of three scenarios: best-case, worst-case and most-probable which we show are computationally difficult to find (W[1]-hard). We propose linear-time approximations by considering the environment as a favorable/hostile/neutral RL agent. Experiments validate this approach. Furthermore, we give a dynamic-programming algorithm to find an optimal summary of a long scenario.

Keywords: Explainable artificial intelligence · Reinforcement learning

1 Introduction

The need for explanations of black-box Artificial Intelligence models, highlighted by researchers [7, 16] but also by legislators [8], has become an important topic during the last few years. As a consequence, the research field of eXplainable Artificial Intelligence (XAI) has developed, with the aim of building trustworthy AI models. These models can be then used in a wider range of applications, including high-risk or safety-critical ones. The aim of this paper is to explore new avenues of explanations in Reinforcement Learning (RL). RL can be summarized as follows. An agent learns while making a sequence of decisions consisting of actions within an environment. At each time-step, the information available to the agent defines a state. In a state, the agent chooses an action, and so arrives in a new state, determined by a transition function (which is not necessarily deterministic), and receives a reward (a negative reward being rather a punishment). The agent aims at maximizing its reward, while striking a balance between exploration (discover new ways to face the problem) and exploitation (use already learnt knowledge). The agent's strategy is learnt in the form of a policy, which maps each state to either an action (if the policy is deterministic) or a probability distribution over actions (if the policy is stochastic).

The subfield of XAI which focuses on RL models is eXplainable Reinforcement Learning (XRL). Researchers used key RL features to explain agent's decisions. As an example, the VIPER algorithm [2] learns a Decision Tree policy which is a surrogate for the actual policy given by a deep neural network. The surrogate policy is easier to verify concerning different properties such as safety, stability and robustness. With

A. P. Rocha et al. (Eds.): ICAART 2023, LNAI 14546, pp. 115–140, 2024.
https://doi.org/10.1007/978-3-031-55326-4_6

states considered as images, [10,22] explain agent's decisions in different ways. Grey-danus *et al.* use a perturbation-based approach to generate a saliency map, i.e. parts of an image that lead the agent to choose an action [10]. Given a state s and a selected action a, a GAN produce a counterfactual state s', to show the user in which settings the agent would select an action b instead of a [22]. Another approach is reward decomposition [15] which focuses on the reward function and is used when an agent has multiple objectives. This XRL method expresses a reward through a vector of scalars instead of a simple scalar. This makes it easier to understand why an agent performs an action, and to identify its objective in choosing this action.

In their survey, Milani *et al.* emphasize the need for explanations that capture the concepts of RL [19]. Our study tries to meet this need by proposing a predictive XRL method based on the sequential aspect of RL. The aim of this method is to answer the question *"What is likely to happen from the state s with the current policy of the agent?"*. To this end, we compute three different state-action sequences (called scenarios), starting from the current state s. This method allows us to explain a policy by giving pertinent examples of scenarios from s, hence the name of the explainer: Scenario-Explanation, shortened to SXp. It provides information about future outcomes by looking forward N time-steps according to three different scenarios: a worst-case scenario, a most-probable scenario and a best-case scenario. To avoid an exhaustive search over all possible scenarios, we propose approximations based on learning policies of hostile/favorable environments. Our approximate SXp's are computed using transition functions learnt by treating the environment as an RL agent. The advantage is that this can be achieved by using the same technology and the same computational complexity as the learning of the agent's policy. We tested our approximate SXp on two problems: Frozen Lake, an Open AI Gym benchmark problem [3], and Drone Coverage, a problem we designed.

This paper is an extended version of the paper [23]. The main additional contributions are a representativeness score and a method for summarizing the Scenario-Explanation. This last addition allows us to consider SXp's with a large N and thus to have a long term vision of what can happen, while keeping the explanations concise.

This paper first gives a theoretical justification for Scenario-Explanation and introduces new metrics for quantifying their quality and representativeness, before describing experimental results on two RL problems. For each problem, short and long scenarios explanations are computed, the long scenarios are summarized thanks to a quadratic algorithm. We then survey related work on XRL, before discussing the efficiency and usefulness of SXp.

2   Scenario-Explanation

Before describing our XRL method, we need to introduce some notation. An RL problem is described by a Markov Decision Process (MDP) [26]. An MDP is a tuple $\langle S, A, R, p \rangle$ where S and A are respectively the state and action space, $R : S \times A \to \mathbb{R}$ is the reward function, $p : S \times A \to Pr(S)$ is the transition function of the environment which provides a distribution over reachable states: given an action $a \in A$ and a state $s \in S$, $p(s'|s, a)$ denotes the probability of reaching the state s' when a is performed in the state s. For a deterministic policy $\pi : S \to A$, $\pi(s)$ denotes the action the agent performs in s whereas for a stochastic policy $\pi : S \to Pr(A)$, $\pi(a|s)$ denotes the probability that the agent performs action a in s.

Our aim is to answer the question: *"What is likely to happen from the state s with the current policy of the agent?"*. We choose to do this by providing three specific scenarios using the learnt policy π. By scenario, we mean a sequence of states and actions, starting with s. Scenarios are parameterised by their length, denoted by N, which we consider as a parameter determined by the user. We provide a summary of all possible scenarios via the *most-probable*, the *worst-case* and the *best-case* scenarios starting from s.

When considering possible scenarios, we may choose to limit our attention to those which do not include highly unlikely transitions or actions. The following technical definition based on two thresholds α and β allows us to restrict the possible transitions and actions. We do not filter out all transitions with probability less than a certain threshold, but rather those whose probability is small (less than a factor of α) compared to the most likely transition. This ensures that at least one transition is always retained. A similar remark holds for the probability of an action. We filter out those actions whose probability is less than a factor of β from the probability of the most probable action.

Definition 1. *Given $N \in \mathbb{N}^*$, $\alpha, \beta \in [0,1]$, an MDP $\langle S, A, R, p \rangle$ and a stochastic policy π over S, an (α, β)-credible length-N scenario is a state-action sequence $s_0, a_0, s_1, a_1, \ldots, a_{N-1}, s_N \in (S \times A)^N \times S$ which satisfies: $\forall i \in \{0, \ldots, N-1\}$, $\pi(a_i|s_i)/\pi^* \geq \beta$ and $p(s_{i+1}|s_i, a_i)/p^* \geq \alpha$, where $\pi^* = \max_{a \in A} \pi(a|s_i)$ and $p^* = \max_{s \in S} p(s|s_i, a_i)$.*

In a $(1,1)$-credible length-N scenario, the agent always chooses an action among it's most likely choices and we only consider the most probable transitions of the environment. At the other extreme, in a $(0,0)$-scenario, there are no restrictions on the choice of actions or on the possible transitions of the environment.

The following definition is parameterised by $\alpha, \beta \in [0,1]$ and an integer N. For simplicity of presentation, we leave this implicit and simply write credible scenario instead of (α, β)-credible length-N scenario. In the following definition, $R(\sigma)$ denotes the reward of a credible scenario σ. By default $R(\sigma)$ is the reward attained at the last step of σ.

Definition 2. *For an MDP $\langle S, A, R, p \rangle$ and a policy π over S, a scenario-explanation for π from a state s is a credible scenario $\sigma = s_0, a_0, s_1, a_1, \ldots, a_{N-1}, s_N$ such that $s_0 = s$. σ is a most-probable scenario-explanation for π from s if its probability given s, denoted $Pr(\sigma)$, is maximum, where*

$$Pr(\sigma) = \prod_{i=1}^{N} \pi(a_{i-1}|s_{i-1})p(s_i|s_{i-1}, a_{i-1})$$

σ is a best-case scenario-explanation for π from s if it maximises the reward $R(\sigma)$. σ is a worst-case scenario-explanation from s if it minimizes the reward $R(\sigma)$.

In the best (worst) case, the environment always changes according to the best (worst) transitions for the agent, i.e., the environment maximises (minimises) the agent's reward after N steps. Not surprisingly, finding such scenarios is not easy, as we now show.

Proposition 1. *For any fixed values of the parameters $\alpha, \beta \in [0,1]$, the problem of finding a best-case or worst-case length-N scenario-explanation, when parameterized by N, is W[1]-hard. Finding a most-probable length-N scenario-explanation is W[1]-hard provided $\alpha < 1$.*

The detailed proof of Proposition 1 can be found in [23].

2.1 Approximate Scenario-Explanation

In view of Proposition 1, we consider approximations to scenario-explanations which we obtain via an algorithm whose complexity is linear in N, the length of the SXp. Indeed, since determining most-probable/worst/best scenarios is computationally expensive, we propose to approximate them. For this purpose, it can be useful to imagine that the environment acts in a deliberate manner, as if it were another agent, rather than in a neutral manner according to a given probability distribution. In this paper, as a first important step, we restrict our attention to approximate SXp's that explain deterministic policies π. An *environment policy* π_e denotes a policy that models a specific behavior of the environment.

There are different policies π_e for the most-probable, worst and best cases which correspond to policies of neutral, hostile and favorable environments respectively. In the case of a hostile/favorable environment, π_e denotes an environment policy that aims at minimizing/maximizing the reward of the agent. The policy of a neutral environment is already given via the transition probability distribution p. On the other hand the policies of hostile or favorable environments have to be learnt. We propose to again use RL to learn these two policies. Compared to the learning of the agent's policy, there are only fairly minor differences. Clearly, in general, the actions available to the environment are not the same as the actions available to the agent. Another technical detail is that as far as the environment is concerned the set of states is also different, since its choice of transition depends not only on the state s but also on the action a of the agent.

Recall, from Definition 1, that in a (1,1)-scenario a most-probable action and a most-probable transition are chosen at each step. Of course, for deterministic policies or transition functions there is no actual choice.

Definition 3. *A probable scenario-explanation (P-scenario) of π from s is a (1,1)-scenario for π starting from s.*

A favorable-environment scenario-explanation (FE-scenario) for π from s is a (1,1)-scenario, in which the transition function (p in Definition 1) is a learnt policy π_e of a favorable environment.

A hostile-environment scenario-explanation (HE-scenario) for π from s is a (1,1)-scenario, in which the transition function p is a learnt policy π_e of a hostile environment.

A length-N P-scenario is computed by using an algorithm that simply chooses, at each of N steps starting from the state s, the action determined by π and a most-probable transition according to p. In the case of the FE/HE scenario, p is replaced by the environment policy π_e which is learnt beforehand. The same RL method that was used to learn the agent's policy π is used to learn π_e (which hence is deterministic since we assume that π is deterministic). The fact that the learnt environment policy

π_e is deterministic means that scenario-explanations can be produced in linear time. In the favorable-environment (FE) case the reward for the environment is R (the same function as for the agent) and in the hostile-environment (HE) case the reward function is (based on) $-R$.

Proposition 2. *Consider an MDP* $\langle S, A, R, p \rangle$ *for which we learn by RL a deterministic policy* π. *Producing length-N P/HE/FE scenario-explanations does not increase the asymptotic worst-case (time and space) complexity of the training phase. Moreover the computation of the explanation only incurs a cost which is linear in N.*

The proof of Proposition 2 can be found in [23]. Having shown that our algorithm is efficient in time, hence avoiding the complexity issue raised by Proposition 1, in Sect. 3 we describe experiments which indicate that the returned results are good approximations of the most-probable, best and worst explanations.

2.2 Scenario-Explanation Rendering

The length of an SXp is parameterized by N, as already mentioned. Accordingly, the SXp's rendering to the user will depend on it. On one hand, for N relatively low, we simply display each scenario (FE-scenario/HE-scenario/P-scenario) to the user by assuming that the amount of information does not impact the user's understanding of the explanation. So, the SXp provides a summary of what is likely to happen in the short term. On the other hand, for N high, the SXp provides more information on the agent's future interaction with the environment. In this case, displaying the three scenarios can give rise to an important cognitive load for the user, thus making the explanation inefficient. In order to avoid this, we propose to summarize the scenarios for large values of N. Before describing how to summarize such scenarios, we define which goals the summary must achieve to be of good quality.

First, a scenario summary has to highlight the most important states within it. We call *state importance* the notion introduced by Clouse [4]. This notion is used to provide explanations in the form of a policy summary in [1]. Formally, given a Q function and a state s, the importance of s is defined as the difference between the best and worst Q value in s by performing an action a:

$$I(s) = \max_a Q(s, a) - \min_a Q(s, a)$$

Secondly, the summary should cover the entire scenario as well as possible. In other words, the selected states should be distributed as uniformly as possible along the scenario. We achieve this by minimizing the sum of the squares of the distances between consecutive selected states. The following definition expresses the *summary problem* discussed above through an objective function.

Definition 4. *Let* $\sigma = (s_1, a_1, s_2, a_2, \dots, a_{N-1}, s_N)$ *be a length-N scenario and* $I(s_1), \dots, I(s_N)$ *the corresponding state importance scores. For given constants* $M \leq N$ *and* $\lambda \geq 0$, *the summary problem consists in finding a sample of M states*

$s_{i_1}, \ldots, s_{i_M}$, with $1 = i_1 < i_2 < \ldots < i_M = N$ such that the following objective function is maximised:

$$f_N(\sigma, i_1, \ldots, i_M) = \sum_{j=1}^{M} I(s_{i_j}) - \lambda \sum_{k=1}^{M-1} (i_{k+1} - i_k)^2$$

The spread-regularity score is given by the negation of the sums of the squares of the differences between consecutive values, i.e. $- \sum_{k=1}^{M-1} (i_{k+1} - i_k)^2$. Observe that maximizing this score is equivalent to minimizing the variance of these differences, since their average $\mu = \frac{1}{M-1} \sum_{k=1}^{M-1} (i_{k+1} - i_k) = \frac{1}{M-1}(i_M - i_1) = (N-1)/(M-1)$ is a constant and their variance $\frac{1}{M-1} \sum_{k=1}^{M-1} (i_{k+1} - i_k - \mu)^2 = \frac{1}{M-1} \sum_{k=1}^{M-1} ((i_{k+1} - i_k)^2 - 2(i_{k+1} - i_k)\mu + \mu^2) = \frac{1}{M-1} \sum_{k=1}^{M-1} (i_{k+1} - i_k)^2 - \mu^2$.

Thus, with the objective function given in Definition 4, we want a sample of M states which have high state importance scores and are evenly spread. The summary problem can be solved using dynamic programming with the following equations.

Definition 5. *For $2 \leq m \leq n \leq N$ and a length-N scenario σ, let $g_\sigma(m, n)$ be the optimal value of $f_n(\sigma, i_1, \ldots, i_m)$ such that $i_1 = 1$ and $i_m = n$. We can calculate all values of $g(m, n)$ using dynamic programming via the equations*

$$g_\sigma(m, n) = \max_{p \in \{m-1, \ldots, n-1\}} \left(g_\sigma(m-1, p) + I(s_n) - \lambda(n-p)^2 \right) \ (2 < m \leq n \leq N)$$

$$g_\sigma(2, n) = I(s_1) + I(s_n) + \lambda(n-1)^2 \qquad (2 \leq n \leq N)$$

Once we have calculated $g_\sigma(M, N)$, we can determine for which values of p the maximum is reached: this gives us the values of $i_{M-1}, \ldots, i_2$, thus the states $s_{i_{M-1}}, \ldots, s_{i_2}$.

Note that the value of λ has a significant impact on the summary. Indeed, the higher the value is, the more evenly spread out the summary states are. On the contrary, a small value can lead to summaries which only maximize the sum of the importance of the states in the summary.

We normalize the two terms of the objective function f_N to lie in the interval $[0, 1]$ to have the two terms within the same amplitude (hence f_N lies in the interval $[-\lambda, 1]$) whatever the amplitude of the Q-values and the scenario length. The normalization of a value b that is obtained by a function h is performed by means of the *norm* function which requires b, the value to be normalized, together with h_{min} and h_{max}, the extrema of the function h. Formally, we have: $norm_h(b) = (b - h_{min})/(h_{max} - h_{min})$. For the sum of the importance scores, we perform a normalization of the importance scores. In this context, the extrema used are the minimum and maximum importance score reachable in a scenario. To keep the sum of the importance scores of M states selected among N in the range $[0,1]$, the following formula is used: $\frac{1}{M} \sum_{s \in S^M} norm_I(I(s))$, where S^M is the set of M selected states.

Lemma 1. *The complexity of the normalization of the sum of importance scores is in $O(N)$.*

Proof. It is the complexity of finding the maximal and minimal importance scores. □

Lemma 2. *The complexity of calculating the normalization factor for the spread-regularity term is in O(1).*

Proof. To normalize the sum of the squares of the gaps $i_{k+1} - i_k$, we have to determine the extrema as a function of M and N. With $\sigma = (s_1, a_1, s_2, a_2, \ldots, a_{N-1}, s_N)$ a length-N scenario, these extrema are attained for a sample of $M \leq N$ states $s_{i_1}, \ldots, s_{i_M}$ such that the following equation is maximised/minimised:

$$\sum_{k=1}^{M-1} (i_{k+1} - i_k)^2$$

$$\text{s.t.} \quad i_1 = 1, i_M = N \text{ and } i_k < i_{k+1} \text{ for } k \in [1, .., M-1]$$

By elementary methods, we find that the maximum value is: $(M-2)(1)^2 + (N-M+1)^2$. With $v = (N-1)/(M-1)$ and $w = (v - \lfloor v \rfloor) \times (M-1)$, the minimum value is: $w \times (\lceil v \rceil)^2 + (M-1-w) \times (\lfloor v \rfloor)^2$. Therefore, the complexity of this calculation is in $O(1)$. □

Proposition 3. *The complexity of solving the summary problem is in $O(MN^2)$.*

Proof. Based on Definition 5, and Lemmas 1 and 2, it is easy to see that the complexity of solving the summary problem is in $O(MN^2)$. Indeed, with the negligible complexity of the normalization step, the complexity depends on the complexity of the dynamic programming algorithm.

It is important to specify that the normalizations mentioned above do not impact this complexity (the extraction of the minimal and maximal importance scores being performed before the use of the dynamic programming method). Note that the summary problem would be more difficult with a different objective function. Indeed, minimizing redundancy between all pairs of states would make the summary problem NP-hard, as observed by McDonald [18].

In several different experiments, we noticed that scenarios can contain loops, i.e. repeating sub-sequences of state-actions. This inevitably leads to a redundancy in the explanation. So, before producing a summary of a scenario, we perform a pre-processing step to detect such loops in order to display to the user only one iteration. It is interesting to note that when the agent is in a loop, it can never get out of it if the environment response is deterministic, as stated in the following proposition:

Proposition 4. *Given a deterministic policy of the agent π, a deterministic response of the environment π_e, consider a length-N scenario $\sigma = s_0, a_0, s_1, \ldots, s_{N-1}, a_{N-1}, s_N$, corresponding to π and π_e. Suppose that $s_j = s_k$ where $0 \leq j < k \leq N$ and that (j, k) is the lexicographically smallest pair with this property. Then σ is a periodic sequence from rank j.*

Proof. By design, the agent's choice and environment response are deterministic, hence the produced scenario σ is also deterministic. A loop starting at time-step j, always repeats. Thus, this ensures the sequence periodicity of σ from rank j. □

As a reminder, with SXp we are interested in explaining deterministic policies. Moreover, in the case of FE-scenarios and HE-scenarios, the environment policy π_e is deterministic. The proposition therefore holds for them. For P-scenarios, the response of the environment depends on its transition function p.

Corollary 1. *Let σ^j be a loop in a P-scenario σ_P, and $tr_b(s, a)$ be the highest environment transition probability from (s, a). Proposition 4 holds for a P-scenario iff:*

$$\forall (s, a) \in \sigma, \quad card(\{s' \in S \text{ and } p(s'|s, a) = tr_b(s, a)\}) = 1$$

where card is the cardinality of a set.

In other words, the existence of a non-deterministic transition in a scenario invalidates Proposition 4.

The method described in Definition 5 thus provides a solution to the selection of M states among a set of size N. In practice, for the generation of SXp summaries, the value of M cannot be fixed beforehand, as the length-N scenario may contain subsequences to be summarized (in the case of loop detection). It is therefore necessary to introduce a ratio that defines the number of elements to be extracted. Thus, μ defines the compression ratio, i.e. the number of states to be summarized into a single one. Consequently, with μ fixed, the number of states m to be extracted for any sequence of length n is defined by: $m = \lfloor n/\mu \rfloor$.

The summarizing of a scenario, taking into account the loops, is described in Algorithm 1 where the function $findLoop$ looks for a loop and its starting index in the scenario (it is only performed when Proposition 4 holds), and the function $summarize$ returns the elements to display to the user according to a set of states and the compression ratio μ. When Algorithm 1 is executed, depending on the values of N and μ, a length-N scenario is either summarized or simply displayed. If a loop is detected, the scenario is split into two sub-sequences, and each part is summarized according to its length and μ. Finally, states are displayed to the user.

Algorithm 1. Scenario summary.

Input: $\sigma = s_0, a_0, s_1, \ldots, s_{N-1}, a_{N-1}, s_N, \quad \mu \in \mathbb{N}$

1: $states \leftarrow [s_0]$
2: $loop, j \leftarrow findLoop(\sigma)$
3: **if** $loop$ **then**
4:      **if** $j > 1$ **then**   ▷ Summarize first part of σ
5:          $states.add(summarize([s_1, \ldots, s_{j-1}], \mu))$
6:      **end if**
7:      $states.add(summarize(loop, \mu))$ ▷ Summarize the loop
8: **else**
9:      $states.add(summarize([s_1, \ldots, s_{n-1}], \mu))$ ▷ Summarize the scenario σ
10: **end if**
11: $states.add(s_n)$
12: $display(states)$

Proposition 5. *The complexity of summarizing an SXp is in $O(MN^2)$.*

Proof. Summarizing an SXp consists of the *summary problem* (Definition 4) and loop detection. Since loop detection can be carried out in $O(N^2)$ time (even $O(N)$ with an appropriate data structure), the complexity of summarizing an SXp is in $O(MN^2)$ by Proposition 3. □

Although the linearity of the time complexity of producing explanations is not preserved when the length of the scenario requires a summary, explaining nevertheless remains efficient.

2.3 Metrics

Since SXp is an original approach to provide explanations, we did not find in the literature a way to evaluate them. Therefore, we introduce three scores related to the quality of SXp which we used in a validation phase. Moreover, in order to provide additional information to the user, we introduce a score of how representative the displayed scenarios are. For example, whereas the quality of an HE-scenario measures how good of an approximation it is to the true worst-case scenario, its representativeness measures how likely it is.

SXp's Quality. To measure the quality of the SXp produced, we implemented three simple scores to answer the question: *"How good is the generated Scenario-Explanation?"*. Let the function q denote the quality evaluation function of a scenario σ; $q(\sigma)$ can vary depending on the application domain and the quality aspect we choose to measure. By default it is equal to the reward $R(\sigma)$, but may be refined to incorporate other criteria for technical reasons explained later. $q(\sigma_F)$ and $q(\sigma_H)$ are respectively the quality of a FE-scenario σ_F and a HE-scenario σ_H. They are used to measure to what extent the scenario is similar to a best-case or worst-case scenario respectively. The resulting *FE-score/HE-score* is *the proportion of k randomly-generated scenarios that have a not strictly better/worse quality (measured by q) than the FE/HE-scenarios themselves* (hence the score lies in the range $[0, 1]$). For the P-scenario, the *P-score* is *the absolute difference between the normalized quality $q(\sigma_P)$ of a P-scenario σ_P and the normalized mean of $q(\sigma)$ of k randomly-generated scenarios* (hence lies again in the range $[0, 1]$). Formally, given a FE-scenario σ_F, a HE-scenario σ_H and a P-scenario σ_P from s:

$$\text{FE-score}(\sigma_F) = \frac{card(\{\sigma \in S_s^k \text{ and } q(\sigma) \leq q(\sigma_F)\})}{k}$$

$$\text{HE-score}(\sigma_H) = \frac{card(\{\sigma \in S_s^k \text{ and } q(\sigma) \geq q(\sigma_H)\})}{k}$$

$$\text{P-score}(\sigma_P) = \left| norm_q(q(\sigma_P)) - norm_q\left(\sum_{\sigma \in S_s^k} q(\sigma)/k\right) \right|$$

where S_s^k is a set of k randomly-generated scenarios s.t. $\forall \sigma = (s_0, a_0, \ldots, s_N) \in S_s^k$, $s_0 = s$. The closer the HE-score, FE-score of a HE/FE-scenario is to 1, the closer it is respectively to the worst/best-case scenario because no other, among the k scenarios produced, is worse/better. A P-score close to 0 indicates that the P-scenario is a good approximation to an average-case scenario. In each case, the scenarios randomly-generated for comparison are produced using the agent's learnt policy π and the transition function p. As mentioned above, by default, the function q is the last-step reward of a scenario, i.e. $q(\sigma) = R(s_{N-1}, a_{N-1})$.

It is important to specify that these quality scores are only used to validate the SXp, given learnt agent and environment policies. These scores are not calculated for each SXp requested by the user but rather upstream during the validation phase of the explainer. On the contrary, the following metric is computed for each SXp to provide additional information to the user.

SXp's Representativeness. The objective of this score is to measure the representativeness of a scenario. For each SXp, it is computed and displayed to the user next to the scenarios. This score aims at answering the question: *"How representative is this scenario of all possible scenarios starting at state s and with a horizon of N ?"*. This information is important because it indicates, as an example, which scenario is the most representative at horizon N between the FE-scenario and the HE-scenario and to what extent. If the representativeness score is low for the HE-scenario (resp. FE-scenario), it may reassure (resp. alert) the user because this scenario is not very representative. On the contrary, if its score is high, the HE-scenario (resp. FE-scenario) is representative and it may alert (resp. reassure) the user.

To compute this score, it is first necessary to obtain the probability of the FE-scenario, HE-scenario and P-scenario. The agent's policy being deterministic, the probability of a scenario $\sigma = s_0, a_0, s_1, \ldots, s_{N-1}, a_{N-1}, s_N$, denoted $Pr(\sigma)$, is defined by: $Pr(\sigma) = \prod_{i=1}^{k} p(s_i | s_{i-1}, a_{i-1})$. The P-scenario being an approximation of the most probable scenario, it is considered the most representative. Therefore, the representativeness score is simply the ratio between the probability of a scenario σ and the probability of the P-scenario σ_P.

Definition 6. *Given a P-scenario σ_P, the representativeness score of a scenario σ is:*

$$rep(\sigma, \sigma_P) = \min(1, Pr(\sigma)/Pr(\sigma_P))$$

The score lies in range $[0, 1]$. A score of 1 means that the scenario is at least as representative as the P-scenario and a score close to 0 reflects a scenario with little representativeness. The *min* operation limits the result to 1. If the ratio is higher, it can mean two things. First meaning: the HE/FE-scenario length is smaller than that of the P-scenario, which may make the HE/FE-scenario more likely. This can occur if the agent reaches a terminal state in less time in the HE/FE-scenario than in the P-scenario. Second meaning: the HE/FE-scenario is the same length as the P-scenario but it is a better approximation of the *most-probable* scenario than the P-scenario. This latter case was not encountered during the experiments.

3   Experimental Results

The Frozen Lake (FL) and Drone Coverage (DC) problems illustrate, respectively, a single and a multi-agent context. Furthermore, the training process was managed by two distinct algorithms, respectively Q-learning [30] and a Deep-Q-Network [21]. Recall that the algorithm used to train environment-agents is similar to the one used to train the agent. The exploration/exploitation trade-off is achieved by using an ϵ-greedy action selection where ϵ is a probability to explore. For short SXp, the hyper-parameter N (scenario-length) is set to 5 and 6 respectively for the FL and DC problems. For long SXp's, it is set respectively to 20 and 50 for the FL and DC problems. The compression ratio μ is set to 5 for both problems. FL experiments were run on an ASUS GL552VX, with 8 GB of RAM and a 2.3 GHz quad-core i5-6300HQ processor and DC experiments were carried out using a Nvidia GeForce GTX 1080 TI GPU, with 11 GB of RAM (source code available at: https://github.com/lsaulier/SXp-ICAART23). Each SXp presented in this section (see e.g. Fig. 2) is displayed as follows. On the left, there is the starting state, from which the SXp is generated. On the right, there are 3 lines, each representing a scenario, which are in order the FE-scenario, HE-scenario and P-scenario. Next to each scenario is displayed its representativeness score. The explanation quality scores in Tables 1 and 2 are based on $k = 10000$ to reduce the randomness of score calculation. The Avg_i and σ_i columns show the average and standard deviation of explanation scores based on i different states, or configurations (i.e. states of all agents in a multi-agent problem such as DC).

3.1   Frozen Lake (FL)

Description. The FL problem is an episodic RL problem with discrete state and action spaces. The agent (symbolized in Fig. 2 by a blue dot) moves in a 2D grid world, representing the surface of a frozen lake, with the aim to reach an item in a specific cell of the grid (marked with a star). There are holes in the frozen lake (symbolized by blue cells in the map) and the others cells are solid ice. When an agent falls into a hole, it loses. The agent's initial state is at the top-left corner cell of the map.

A state is represented by a single value, corresponding to the agent's position in the map, $S = \{1, \ldots, l \times c\}$ with, l, c the map dimensions. For the sake of readability, in the results a state is denoted by the agent's coordinates *(line,column)*, where $(1, 1)$ is the top left cell and $(4, 4)$ is the bottom right cell which are respectively the initial state of the agent and its goal on the 4×4 map in Fig. 2. The action space is $A = \{left,down,right,up\}$. The reward function is sparse and described as follows: for $s \in S, a \in A$, s' denoting the state reached by performing action a from s, and s^g being the goal state:

$$R(s, a) = \begin{cases} 1, & \text{if } s' = s^g. \\ 0, & \text{otherwise.} \end{cases}$$

The transition function p is the same from any state. Because of the slippery nature of the frozen lake, if the agent chooses a direction (e.g. *down*), it has 1/3 probability to go on this direction and 1/3 to go towards each remaining direction except the opposite one (here, 1/3 to go *left* and 1/3 to go *right*).

To solve this RL problem, we use the tabular Q-learning method because the state and action space is small. The end of an episode during training is characterized by the agent reaching its goal or falling into a hole.

As stated in the proof of Proposition 2, an environment-agent's state contains an extra piece of information compared to an agent's state: the action executed by the agent from this position, according to its policy π. As the environment-agent reflects the transitions of the environment, there are only 3 actions available and they depend on the agent's choice of action. The reward function of the favorable agent is similar to the agent's reward function. The hostile agent receives a reward of 1 when the agent falls into a hole, of -1 if the agent reaches its goal and a reward of 0 otherwise.

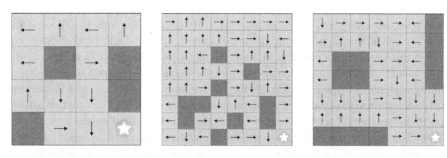

Fig. 1. Agent's learnt policies for the 4×4 and 8×8 maps and a safe 7×7 grid [23].

Results

Short SXp. In order to test our approximate SXp on different environment sizes, we used a 4×4 map and a 8×8 map, the ones presented in OpenAI Gym [3]. Since the reward is sparse (0 except in goal states), FE/HE/P-scores computed purely with $q(\sigma) = R(s_{N-1}, a_{N-1})$ are uninformative (when the number of steps N is not large enough to reach the goal). Accordingly, the quality evaluation function was defined as follow: $q(\sigma) = R(\sigma) + \lambda Q(\sigma)$, where $Q(\sigma) = \max_{a_N \in A} Q(s_N, a_N)$ is the maximum last-step Q-value, $R(\sigma) = R(s_{N-1}, a_{N-1})$ is the reward of scenario σ and $\lambda < 1$ is a positive constant. Another particularity of this problem, is that since the transitions are equiprobable, many P-scenarios are possible.

The agent's learnt policy for the 4×4 map is represented in Fig. 1. Each arrow represents the action performed by the agent from this state. We note that the agent learns to avoid to enter the top-right part of the map (i.e. the two first lines without the first column), which is the most dangerous part, due to the $(2,3)$ state. In the remaining parts of the map, the only dangerous state is $(3,3)$ since the agent action choice is *down*, so it has a probability of $\frac{1}{3}$ to fall into a hole.

The SXp calculated starting from the state $(2,1)$ is shown in Fig. 2. The P-scenario is one scenario among many, and it highlights the difficulty for the agent to succeed in this particular grid with a few steps. The hostile agent exploits well its only way to *force* the agent to fall into a hole given the agent's policy (Fig. 1) which is to push it towards the hole located at $(3,4)$. The favorable agent also learns well and provides an

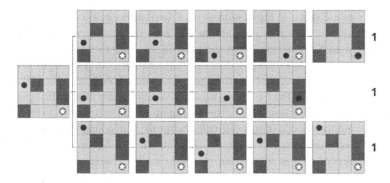

Fig. 2. Scenario-Explanations (from top to bottom: FE-scenario, HE-scenario, P-scenario) from a specific state in the 4×4 map [23].

FE-scenario where the agent reaches its goal in the minimum number of steps. The *HE-score* and *FE-score* of SXp's from state $(2, 1)$ are presented in Table 1. These are perfect scores (equal to 1). Moreover, since the *P-score* is close to 0, the provided P-scenario is a good approximation. We computed SXp's based on the same agent's policy π but starting from 7 reachable states, i.e. states that can be reached following the policy π (Fig. 1) and which are neither holes nor the goal. Results are reported in the Avg_7 column of Table 1. Hostile and favorable agents learnt perfectly.

Table 1. Quality scores for Scenario-Explanation in the 4×4 map and 8×8 map [23].

	4×4 map			8×8 map		
	State $(2, 1)$	Avg_7	σ_7	State $(3, 6)$	Avg_{20}	σ_{20}
FE-score	1	1	0	1	0.824	0.281
HE-score	1	1	0	1	0.828	0.346
P-score	0.081	0.211	0.115	0.031	0.08	0.09

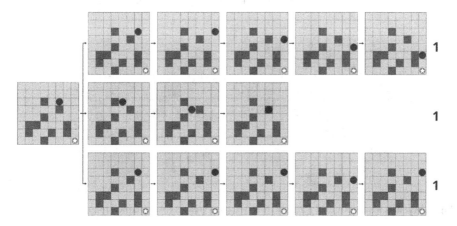

Fig. 3. Scenario-Explanations from a specific state in the 8×8 map [23].

The SXp method was also tested with an 8×8 map. As we can see in Fig. 1, the agent has learned to avoid as much as possible the left zone of the map which is dangerous. Figure 3 depicts an SXp starting from the state $(3, 6)$. Due to the agent's policy, the hostile agent can't just push the agent down from state $(3, 6)$, but it manages to push the agent along a path which ensures that the agent falls into a hole, hence the HE-scenario ends after only 3 steps. In the FE-scenario, the favorable agent brings the agent closer to its goal over the $N = 5$ time-steps. The P-scenario again provides evidence that the agent is likely not to succeed in this difficult environment in a small number of steps.

From the scores presented in Table 1 concerning the 8×8 map, we can again conclude that the 3 produced scenarios are of good quality. The scores presented in the Avg_{20} column were obtained by SXp from 20 randomly-chosen starting states. The average score is lower than 1 but note that 1 is achieved for respectively more than 75% and 60% of HE-scenarios and FE-scenarios. Hence, apart from some randomly-generated starting states located in the little explored left-zone of the map, the scores indicate that HE/FE-scenarios are good approximations of worst/best scenarios.

The representativeness scores are similar for each scenario in Fig. 2 and Fig. 3. This is due to the fact that each transition is equiprobable in the FL problem. In addition, the time horizon of the displayed HE/FE-scenarios do not exceed that of the P-scenarios. This is why all scenarios are equally representative.

In order to check the impact of the agent's policy on the environment-agents' learning process, we designed a 7×7 map, shown in Fig. 1, in such a way that if the agent learns well, it can avoid falling into a hole. Once the learning phase is over, we noticed that the hostile agent learns nothing. Since the agent learns an optimal policy π, the hostile agent can't push the agent into a hole. Accordingly, it can't receive any positive reward and therefore can't learn state-action values. *This is strong evidence that the agent's policy is good.*

Long SXp. The summarized SXp's were tested on two maps of size 10×10 to show the usefulness of summaries with a relatively large scenario-length. The maps and their policies are shown in Fig. 4 (named map A and map B respectively). The agents for the 2 maps have learned well to reach the objective, avoiding as much as possible to

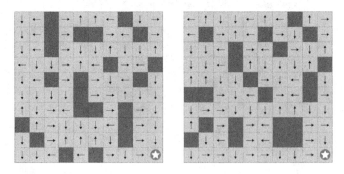

Fig. 4. Agent's learnt policies for two 10×10 maps (respectively named map A and map B).

fall into the holes. However, there are still many opportunities for the hostile agent to make the agents fall. The scenario length is large ($N = 20$) to have a long term view of what can happen from a given state. λ is set to 1.0 for the calculation of the objective function f_N of the summary problem (Definition 4). This means that we consider as equally important the importance of the states and the distribution of the displayed states. Figure 5 and 6 show summarized SXp's for respectively map A and B beginning in the agent's initial state. Each number shown between states (such as 4, 4, 5, 1 in the FE-scenario of Fig. 5) represent the number of omitted states.

In Fig. 5, the hostile agent succeeds in causing the agent to fall into the nearest reachable hole from its starting point. The HE-scenario summary gives a good idea of what happened. It is more difficult to understand what happened in the P-scenario by looking at its summary. This is due to the problem difficulty of the agent reaching the goal; non-deterministic transitions can cause the agent to stagnate in a region of the map for a long time. The favorable agent is successful in helping the agent achieve the objective and the FE-scenario summary is of good quality. Indeed, the states are sufficiently spread out for the user to understand how the scenario unfolds. In the FE-scenario, the last states displayed are relatively close in terms of distance. Importance scores for states near the goal are higher than those far from it; as a result, the summary is impacted. These remarks are also relevant for the SXp summarized in Fig. 6. Similarly to the presented short SXp, the scenarios are equally representative.

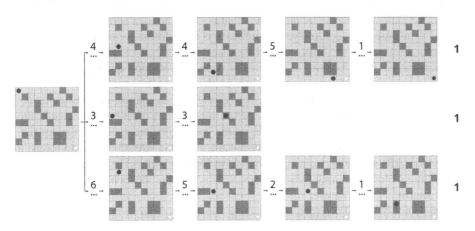

Fig. 5. Scenario-Explanations from a specific state in map A.

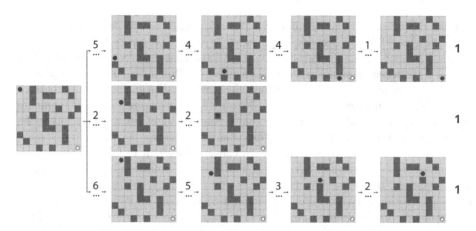

Fig. 6. Scenario-Explanations from a specific state in map B.

We now focus on the FE-scenario in Fig. 5 and vary the value of λ to observe its impact on the scenario summary provided. The different summarized FE-scenarios are displayed in Fig. 7. The values of λ are respectively 1, 0.5 and 0. With $\lambda = 0$, the uniformity of the gaps between the selected states is not taken into account. Note that the associated summary only displays the last elements, because they are the most decisive for achieving the objective. The problem is that we have no idea about what happened during 14 time-steps. Accordingly, this summary is not informative enough. This justifies taking into account the uniformity of the distribution of selected states in selecting SXp summaries. The other two summaries provided are of good quality, with a more evenly spread summary for the summary provided with $\lambda = 1$.

In the experiments, no loops were detected for the FE-scenarios and HE-scenarios. This makes sense since both the hostile and favorable agents must bring the agent into specific states to obtain a reward. In other words, looping between different states (i.e. positions on the map) does not bring any reward, which is why there are no loops in FE-scenarios/HE-scenarios (assuming they have learned well). The P-scenarios have probability *zero* of containing infinite loops. This is because the environment response is non-deterministic. Whatever the state s and the action a chosen from s, transitions are non-deterministic. Therefore, Proposition 4 does not hold in this problem for P-scenarios.

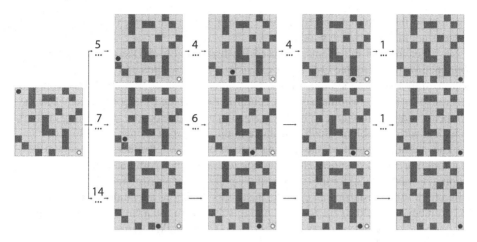

Fig. 7. Summarized FE-scenarios from a specific state in map A.

3.2 Drone Coverage (DC)

Description. The DC problem is a novel multi-agent, episodic RL problem with discrete state and action spaces. The agents' goal is to cover the largest area in a windy 2D grid-world containing trees (symbolized by a green triangle in Fig. 8). The coverage of each drone (represented as a dot) is a 3×3 square centered on its position. A drone is considered as lost and indeed disappears from the grid if it crashes into a tree or another drone.

A state for an agent is composed of the contents of its neighbourhood (a 5×5 matrix centered on the agent's position) together with its position on the map. The action space is $A = \{left, down, right, up, stop\}$. The reward function R of an agent is impacted by its coverage, its neighbourhood, and whether it has crashed or not (the reward is -3 in case of $crash$): if there is no tree or other drone in the agent's 3×3 coverage, it receives a reward (called $cover$) of $+3$ and $+0.25 \times c$ otherwise, where c is the number of free cells (i.e. with no tree or drone) in its coverage; the agent receives a $penalty$ of -1 per drone in its 5×5 neighbourhood (since this implies overlapping coverage of the two drones). With s' the state reached by executing action a from s, the reward function is as follows: for $s \in S, a \in A$,

$$R(s, a) = \begin{cases} -3, & \text{if } crash \\ cover(s') + penalty(s'), & \text{otherwise} \end{cases}$$

As there are 4 drones, the maximum cumulative reward (where cumulative reward means the sum of all agents rewards in a given configuration) is 12 and the minimum is -12. The transition function p, which represents the wind, is similar in each position and is given by the following distribution: $[0.1, 0.2, 0.4, 0.3]$. This distribution defines the probability that the wind pushes the agent respectively $left, down, right, up$. After an agent's action, it moves to another position and then is impacted by the wind. As an additional rule, if an agent and wind directions are opposite, the agent *stays in its new position*, so the wind has no effect. After a *stop* action, the drone does not move and hence is not affected by the wind.

In order to train the agents, we used the first version of Deep-Q Networks [21] combined with the Double Q-learning extension [12]. The choice of this algorithm was motivated by two factors. First, we wanted to investigate our XRL method's ability to generalise to RL algorithms, such as neural network based methods, used when the number of states is too large to be represented in a table. Secondly, this setting enables us to deal with a problem which is scalable in the number of drones and grid size.

The end of an episode of the training process occurs when either one agent crashes, or a time horizon is reached. This time horizon is a hyper-parameter fixed before the training; it was set to 22 for the training of the policy which is explained in the following subsection. When restarting an episode, the agents' positions are randomly chosen. This DC problem is a multi-agent problem, and to solve it, we use a naive approach without any cooperation between agents. Only one Deep-Q Network is trained with experiences from all agents. The reward an agent receives is only its own reward; we do not use a joint multi-agent reward.

Concerning the implementation of the hostile and favorable environment: the extra information in the environment-agent's state is the action performed by the agent in its corresponding state. Actions are similar to the agents' except that there is no *stop* action. The favorable-agent reward function is similar to the one of the agent's and the reward function of the hostile agent is exactly the opposite.

Results

Short SXp. For the sake of simplicity, each drone has an associated color in Fig. 8. Above each map, there is a list of colored arrows, or stop symbols, corresponding to each colored drone's action which leads them to the configuration displayed in the map. A colored cell means that the area is covered by the drone of the same color and a dark

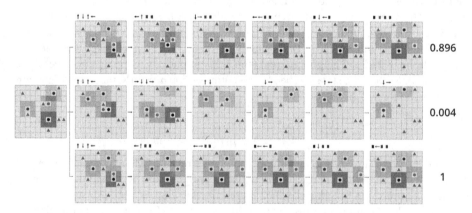

Fig. 8. Scenario-Explanation of a specific configuration of the DC problem [23]. (Color figure online)

grey cell indicates an overlap of the coverage of different drones. To compute the SXp quality scores, we use $q(\sigma) = \sum_i R_i(s_{N-1}, a_{N-1})$ with R_i denoting the reward of agent i (i.e. q is the last-step aggregate reward). Note that the policy to be explained is good, but not optimal. Measuring the performance of a policy by the average of the cumulative rewards obtained at the end of the last hundred training episodes, the performance is 11.69 (out of 12).

The SXp for a particular configuration, denoted as *configuration A*, is shown in Fig. 8. The hostile agent succeeds in crashing two drones and positioning the remaining drones in bad covering positions. The P-scenario demonstrates well the most probable transition (the wind pushes the drones to the *right*) and the favorable agent manages to reach a perfect configuration in only 5 steps. The representativeness scores reassure the user for this SXp. Indeed, the catastrophic HE-scenario is not representative at all while the successful FE-scenario is. SXp quality scores are given in Table 2 where the last columns show the average and standard deviation of scores obtained from 30 random configurations. These results indicate good approximate SXp's. Moreover experiments showed that 19 *HE-scores* are higher than 0.95 and 24 *FE-scores* are perfect (equal to 1). The quality of the learnt policy is also attested by the fact that a maximum reward is attained in 21 out of 30 P-scenarios.

Table 2. Quality scores for Scenario-Explanation in 10×10 map, showing the mean and standard deviation over 30 trials [23].

	Configuration A	Avg_{30}	σ_{30}
FE-score	1	0.919	0.198
HE-score	1	0.936	0.08
P-score	0.073	0.034	0.04

Long SXp. The DC problem is a multi-agent one. This means that a new *configuration importance score* must be expressed to summarize SXp. Since a configuration is the aggregation of each drone's state, the *configuration importance* is simply the average importance score of drone states. With C denoting the set of states of a configuration, the *configuration importance score* I_{config} is defined by:

$$I_{\text{config}}(C) = \frac{1}{card(C)} \sum_{s \in C} I(s)$$

An example of an SXp summary based on the same policies as the short SXp is shown in Fig. 9. λ is set to 1.0 for the computation of the objective function f_N of the *summary problem* (Definition 4). Scenario-length is voluntarily large because, during the experiments, we noticed that the drones looped quite quickly between one or several states. Therefore, loop handling is useful for SXp. Moreover, Proposition 4 holds for P-scenarios since the environment response is deterministic. Indeed, at each time step,

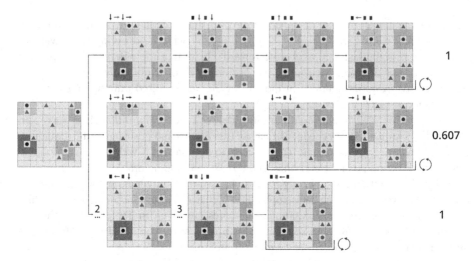

Fig. 9. A long Scenario-Explanation of a specific configuration of the DC problem.

whatever the state is, there is only one most probable transition (push the agent to the *right*).

In the long SXp shown in Fig. 9, each scenario ends with a loop (of length 1, 2 and 1, respectively). The hostile agent definitively prevents 3 out of 4 drones from having a perfect coverage by 'blocking' them in a loop of two configurations. The P-scenario shows a scenario where drones quickly reach a perfect configuration that they maintain. The summary of the first part of the P-scenario allows the user to deduce the drones' movements (despite the compression ratio of $\mu = 3$). The FE-scenario presents a scenario where drones reach a perfect configuration faster. For the FE/HE-scenario, there is no need to summarize the part before the loop because there are few states. In each scenario, loop management allows us to keep SXps both concise and easily comprehensible.

We now focus on the FE-scenario and vary the value of λ in order to observe its impact on the scenario summary. λ takes a value among 0, 0.5 and 1 and the compression ratio μ is set to 3. In Fig. 10, the summary only has an impact on the first part of the scenario. The different scenarios are of good quality, except for the third one in which the gap between the configurations is not taken into account ($\lambda = 0$). In this summarized FE-scenario, only the first states, considered important, are displayed. Therefore, it is more difficult to understand how the drones reached the loop configuration. Again, these experiments confirm that the default value $\lambda = 1$ is a sensible choice.

Results obtained in the FL and DC problems show that, whether the agent's policy is optimal or not, we can obtain interesting information via our SXp. Furthermore, this XRL method does not increase asymptotic complexity of RL. The user can choose to display short-term scenarios or long-term scenarios. These latter are summarized by a combination of loop detection and a dynamic programming algorithm to find the best balance between the importance of states and their uniform spread over the scenario.

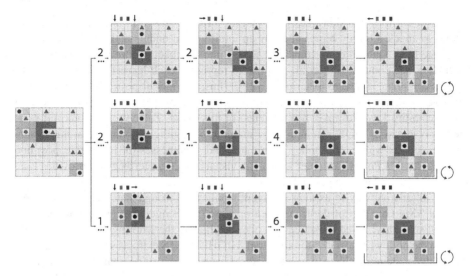

Fig. 10. Summarized FE-scenarios from a specific configuration of the DC problem.

4   Related Work

XRL methods use different key features of Reinforcement Learning to provide explanations. As an example, we can cite the interpretable reward proposed in [15]. Using
exclusively agent's states which are images, Greydanus *et al.* present a method to produce saliency maps for Atari agents [10]. By adding object recognition processing, Iyer
et al. produce object saliency maps from states to gain more insights about the agent's
decisions [14]. Olson et al. and Hubert et al. answer the question 'Why perform action
a rather than action *b* from the state *s*?' in a counterfactual fashion [13,22]. To do so, a
state s' close to s is generated using a GAN, which leads to the choice of action *b*. In
order to focus on causal relationship between action and state variables, Madumal *et al.*
[17] build an action influence model (AIM) used for explanation. Yu et al. extend the
use of AIM to problems with continuous action space, without the need of prior knowledge of the environment causal structure [32]. Additional information can be collected
during the agent's training process, including XRL methods [5] which extract success
probabilities and number of transitions, or methods which learn a belief map [31]. All
these XRL methods allow one to essentially explain the choice of an action in a specific state. For policy-level explanations, EDGE highlights the most critical time-steps,
states, given the agent's final reward in an episode [11]. Policy explanations can be used
to improve the policy. As an example, the ReCCoVER algorithm shows to developers
the spurious correlations between critical states features which impact the generalisa-
tion of the agent's policy and proposes a revision [9].

Several works aim at making the policy interpretable, i.e. making it understandable
for the user. A fairly common approach consists in training a black-box policy represented by a NN and approximating it, or even outperforming it, with an interpretable
model also called a *surrogate model*. The VIPER algorithm results in verifiable poli-

cies in the form of decision trees [2]. With the PIRL framework, the NDPS algorithm allows to check a policy represented by an intuitive and understandable programming language [28]. Danesh et al. transform RNNs into compact Moore machines [6]. In a multi-task RL context, Shu et al. propose to represent each learned policy for a sub-task as a human language description [25]. Thus, the global policy is directly interpretable. Rather than obtaining an interpretable policy by design, some works add an interpretability layer to black-box policies. In this sense, Zahavy et al. interpret policies represented by DQN's in a post hoc manner, by highlighting the hierarchical state aggregation, as well as the policy's strengths and weaknesses [33]. Another post-hoc explainer tool is PolicyExplainer which is a visual analytic interface that provides a set of tools to understand the policy [20].

An alternative way to explain the agent's policy is through state-action sequences, like our SXp. One part of the framework proposed by Sequeira and Gervasio provides a visual summary, based on sequences obtained during the learning phase, to globally explain the policy [24]. With the same goal, HIGHLIGHTS extracts sequences based on a notion of state importance to provide a summary of the agent's learnt behaviour [1]. In a context of MDP, the method implemented in [27] computes sequences that differ in at most n actions from the sequence to explain, as counterfactual explanations. Explaining a sequence in a contrastive way, is achieved in [29] by producing a contrastive policy from the user question and then comparing both sequences. These XRL methods do not solve the same problem as our SXp. Indeed, [24] and [1] provide high-level policy explanation through summaries in a general context of the agent's interaction with the environment. [27] and [29] explain the policy in a counterfactual way; the problem is to generate a sequence in which actions differ from π. Thus, these approaches are incomparable with our SXp, which explain the policy from a particular state, by producing scenarios using the policy π.

5   Discussion

The experiments illustrate the different possible uses of SXp. Apart from understanding policies, SXp also provide a way to evaluate them. Indeed, even if the policy π learnt is not optimal, HE-scenarios and FE-scenarios provide useful information. If from multiple starting states and by varying the scenario-length N, an FE agent cannot bring the agent closer to its goal, this is a proof that the policy π is inadequate. Conversely, an HE agent which cannot prevent the agent from reaching its goal is a evidence of a good policy π. Concretely, in the FL problem this means that the agent has learnt not to give a hostile environment the opportunity to force it to fall into a hole, and in the DC problem the agent has learnt to stay sufficiently far away from trees and other drones. To ensure that the scenario-length is not impacting the results, a more complete study could be carried out by increasing N and using summarized SXp in order to examine the generated scenarios. In other words, our XRL method can also be used as a *debugging tool*.

The experiments have also taught us some valuable lessons. Since we use the same RL method and the same resources to learn π_e as were used to learn π (in order not to increase asymptotic time and space complexity), we cannot expect the quality of explanations to be better than the quality of the original policy π. For example, when states are represented by a simple index in a table, as in Q-learning, π_e can provide no useful information concerning states which were not visited during the learning of π_e. Indeed, whatever the RL method used, since π_e is learnt after (and as a function of) the agent's policy π, the latter will be of better quality on (states similar to) states visited more frequently when following the agent's policy π. A higher/lower quality of explanation for those states that are more/less likely to be visited is something the user should be aware of. If it is important that quality of explanations should be independent of the probability of a state, then the training phase of π_e should be adapted accordingly. This is an avenue of future research.

We should point out the limitations of our method. The three scenarios which are produced are only approximations to the worst-case, best-case and most-probable scenarios. Unfortunately, approximation is necessary due to computational complexity considerations, as highlighted by Proposition 1. We should also point out that the distinction between these three scenarios only makes sense in the context of RL problems with a stochastic transition function. Moreover, the transition function must be known or approximated using model-based methods and SXp summaries require Q-values for the *importance score* computation. Finally, due to the relative novelty of the notion of scenario-explanation, no metric was found in the literature to evaluate the quality of SXp's.

6   Conclusion

In this paper, we describe an RL-specific explanation method based on the concept of transition in Reinforcement Learning. To the best of our knowledge, SXp is an original approach for providing predictive explanations. This predictive XRL method explains the agent's deterministic policy through scenarios starting from a certain state. Moreover, SXp is agnostic concerning RL algorithms and can be applied to all RL problems with a stochastic transition function. An SXp is composed of 3 scenarios: HE-scenario, FE-scenario and P-scenario. They respectively give an approximation of a worst-case scenario-explanation, a best-case scenario-explanation and a most-probable scenario explanation. Experiments indicate that these approximations are informative according to SXp quality scores. In the FL and DC problems, SXp provides a good answer to the question *"What is likely to happen from the state s with the current policy of the agent?"*. Of course, in any new application, experimental trials would be required to validate this XRL method and evaluate its usefulness. Our 3-scenario-based method appears promising and can be used in more complex problems: we only require that it is possible to learn policies for hostile/favorable environments.

SXp's are parameterized by the length N of the scenarios generated. This parameter must be entered by the user in order to look at the short- or long-term future of the agent's interactions in the environment. The greater the N, the longer the scenarios, and therefore the more long-term the vision. A large N results in a high cognitive load for the user. To eliminate this cognitive overload, we have introduced summarized SXp. It summarizes HE-scenario, FE-scenario and P-scenario according to two criteria: the importance of a state and its position in the scenario. We consider that an optimal summary should display important states that are well distributed along the scenario. We have developed a dynamic programming solution to generate these summaries. We use the parameter λ to modulate the importance of the spread of states displayed in the summary produced. Summarized SXp provides a concise and effective way of seeing what can happen in the long term.

An avenue of future work would be to focus on the probabilistic aspect of stochastic policies and provide specific approximate SXp definitions. Another avenue of future work would be to provide SXp's for 2-person games (e.g. Connect 4) where the presence of an opponent player makes the environment stochastic. In this context, the environment policies would simply be opposing player policies. The hostile environment can be seen as a player who is good and the favorable environment as a bad player who gives the agent plenty of opportunities. To provide the P-scenario, one would have to determine the likely behavior of an average opponent. Another idea would be to provide the user with more tools to understand the agent's policy in detail. This could be achieved by learning several environment policies, based on more refined properties than the agent's success or failure in achieving its goal, such as the risk or safety of the agent's policy. An avenue of future research would be to study possible theoretical guarantees of SXp performance.

In a nutshell, after introducing a theoretical framework for studying predictive explanations in RL, we presented a novel practical predictive-explanation method. A pleasing aspect of our method is that explanation employs the same tools as the original reinforcement learning method. In addition, when scenarios are too long to be displayed to the user, we provide a dynamic programming solution that enables us to generate scenario summaries in which a compromise is made between displaying the most important states and evenly covering the scenario steps.

Acknowledgements. The authors would like to thank Arnaud Lequen for his valuable suggestions that have led to the improvement of this paper. This work was supported by the AI Interdisciplinary Institute ANITI, funded by the French program "Investing for the Future - PIA3" under grant agreement no. ANR-19-PI3A-0004.

References

1. Amir, D., Amir, O.: HIGHLIGHTS: summarizing agent behavior to people. In: André, E., Koenig, S., Dastani, M., Sukthankar, G. (eds.) Proceedings of the 17th International Conference on Autonomous Agents and MultiAgent Systems, AAMAS, pp. 1168–1176. International Foundation for Autonomous Agents and Multiagent Systems/ACM (2018). http://dl.acm.org/citation.cfm?id=3237869
2. Bastani, O., Pu, Y., Solar-Lezama, A.: Verifiable reinforcement learning via policy extraction. In: Bengio, S., Wallach, H.M., Larochelle, H., Grauman, K., Cesa-Bianchi, N., Garnett, R. (eds.) NeurIPS, pp. 2499–2509 (2018). https://proceedings.neurips.cc/paper/2018/hash/e6d8545daa42d5ced125a4bf747b3688-Abstract.html
3. Brockman, G., et al.: OpenAI gym. arXiv preprint arXiv:1606.01540 (2016)
4. Clouse, J.A.: On integrating apprentice learning and reinforcement learning. University of Massachusetts Amherst (1996)
5. Cruz, F., Dazeley, R., Vamplew, P.: Memory-based explainable reinforcement learning. In: Liu, J., Bailey, J. (eds.) AI 2019. LNCS (LNAI), vol. 11919, pp. 66–77. Springer, Cham (2019). https://doi.org/10.1007/978-3-030-35288-2_6

6. Danesh, M.H., Koul, A., Fern, A., Khorram, S.: Re-understanding finite-state representations of recurrent policy networks. In: Meila, M., Zhang, T. (eds.) Proceedings of the 38th International Conference on Machine Learning, ICML 2021, 18–24 July 2021, Virtual Event. Proceedings of Machine Learning Research, vol. 139, pp. 2388–2397. PMLR (2021). http://proceedings.mlr.press/v139/danesh21a.html
7. Darwiche, A.: Human-level intelligence or animal-like abilities? Commun. ACM **61**(10), 56–67 (2018). https://doi.org/10.1145/3271625
8. European Commission: Artificial Intelligence Act (2021). https://eur-lex.europa.eu/legal-content/EN/TXT/?qid=1623335154975&uri=CELEX%3A52021PC0206
9. Gajcin, J., Dusparic, I.: ReCCoVER: detecting causal confusion for explainable reinforcement learning. In: Calvaresi, D., Najjar, A., Winikoff, M., Främling, K. (eds.) EXTRAAMAS 2022. LNCS, vol. 13283, pp. 38–56. Springer, Cham (2022). https://doi.org/10.1007/978-3-031-15565-9_3
10. Greydanus, S., Koul, A., Dodge, J., Fern, A.: Visualizing and understanding Atari agents. In: Dy, J.G., Krause, A. (eds.) ICML. Proceedings of Machine Learning Research, vol. 80, pp. 1787–1796. PMLR (2018). http://proceedings.mlr.press/v80/greydanus18a.html
11. Guo, W., Wu, X., Khan, U., Xing, X.: EDGE: explaining deep reinforcement learning policies. In: Ranzato, M., Beygelzimer, A., Dauphin, Y.N., Liang, P., Vaughan, J.W. (eds.) NeurIPS, pp. 12222–12236 (2021). https://proceedings.neurips.cc/paper/2021/hash/65c89f5a9501a04c073b354f03791b1f-Abstract.html
12. Hasselt, H.: Double Q-learning. In: Advances in Neural Information Processing Systems, vol. 23 (2010)
13. Huber, T., Demmler, M., Mertes, S., Olson, M.L., André, E.: GANterfactual-RL: understanding reinforcement learning agents' strategies through visual counterfactual explanations. CoRR abs/2302.12689 (2023). https://doi.org/10.48550/arXiv.2302.12689
14. Iyer, R., Li, Y., Li, H., Lewis, M., Sundar, R., Sycara, K.P.: Transparency and explanation in deep reinforcement learning neural networks. In: Furman, J., Marchant, G.E., Price, H., Rossi, F. (eds.) Proceedings of the 2018 AAAI/ACM Conference on AI, Ethics, and Society, AIES, pp. 144–150. ACM (2018). https://doi.org/10.1145/3278721.3278776
15. Juozapaitis, Z., Koul, A., Fern, A., Erwig, M., Doshi-Velez, F.: Explainable reinforcement learning via reward decomposition. In: IJCAI/ECAI Workshop on Explainable Artificial Intelligence, p. 7 (2019)
16. Lipton, Z.C.: The mythos of model interpretability. Commun. ACM **61**(10), 36–43 (2018). https://doi.org/10.1145/3233231
17. Madumal, P., Miller, T., Sonenberg, L., Vetere, F.: Explainable reinforcement learning through a causal lens. In: The Thirty-Fourth AAAI Conference on Artificial Intelligence, AAAI 2020, pp. 2493–2500. AAAI Press (2020). https://ojs.aaai.org/index.php/AAAI/article/view/5631
18. McDonald, R.: A study of global inference algorithms in multi-document summarization. In: Amati, G., Carpineto, C., Romano, G. (eds.) ECIR 2007. LNCS, vol. 4425, pp. 557–564. Springer, Heidelberg (2007). https://doi.org/10.1007/978-3-540-71496-5_51
19. Milani, S., Topin, N., Veloso, M., Fang, F.: A survey of explainable reinforcement learning. CoRR abs/2202.08434 (2022). https://arxiv.org/abs/2202.08434
20. Mishra, A., Soni, U., Huang, J., Bryan, C.: Why? Why not? When? Visual explanations of agent behavior in reinforcement learning. CoRR abs/2104.02818 (2021). https://arxiv.org/abs/2104.02818
21. Mnih, V., et al.: Human-level control through deep reinforcement learning. Nature **518**(7540), 529–533 (2015). http://www.nature.com/articles/nature14236
22. Olson, M.L., Neal, L., Li, F., Wong, W.: Counterfactual states for Atari agents via generative deep learning. CoRR abs/1909.12969 (2019). http://arxiv.org/abs/1909.12969

23. Saulières, L., Cooper, M.C., Dupin de Saint Cyr, F.: Reinforcement learning explained via reinforcement learning: towards explainable policies through predictive explanation. In: 15th International Conference on Agents and Artificial Intelligence (ICAART 2023), pp. 35–44 (2023)

24. Sequeira, P., Gervasio, M.T.: Interestingness elements for explainable reinforcement learning: understanding agents' capabilities and limitations. Artif. Intell. **288**, 103367 (2020). https://doi.org/10.1016/j.artint.2020.103367

25. Shu, T., Xiong, C., Socher, R.: Hierarchical and interpretable skill acquisition in multi-task reinforcement learning. CoRR abs/1712.07294 (2017). http://arxiv.org/abs/1712.07294

26. Sutton, R.S., Barto, A.G.: Reinforcement Learning: An Introduction. MIT Press, Cambridge (2018)

27. Tsirtsis, S., De, A., Rodriguez, M.: Counterfactual explanations in sequential decision making under uncertainty. In: Ranzato, M., Beygelzimer, A., Dauphin, Y.N., Liang, P., Vaughan, J.W. (eds.) NeurIPS 2021, pp. 30127–30139 (2021). https://proceedings.neurips.cc/paper/2021/hash/fd0a5a5e367a0955d81278062ef37429-Abstract.html

28. Verma, A., Murali, V., Singh, R., Kohli, P., Chaudhuri, S.: Programmatically interpretable reinforcement learning. In: Dy, J.G., Krause, A. (eds.) Proceedings of the 35th International Conference on Machine Learning, ICML 2018. Proceedings of Machine Learning Research, vol. 80, pp. 5052–5061. PMLR (2018). http://proceedings.mlr.press/v80/verma18a.html

29. van der Waa, J., van Diggelen, J., van den Bosch, K., Neerincx, M.A.: Contrastive explanations for reinforcement learning in terms of expected consequences. CoRR abs/1807.08706 (2018). http://arxiv.org/abs/1807.08706

30. Watkins, C.J., Dayan, P.: Q-learning. Mach. Learn. **8**(3), 279–292 (1992)

31. Yau, H., Russell, C., Hadfield, S.: What did you think would happen? Explaining agent behaviour through intended outcomes. In: Larochelle, H., Ranzato, M., Hadsell, R., Balcan, M., Lin, H. (eds.) NeurIPS (2020). https://proceedings.neurips.cc/paper/2020/hash/d5ab8dc7ef67ca92e41d730982c5c602-Abstract.html

32. Yu, Z., Ruan, J., Xing, D.: Explainable reinforcement learning via a causal world model. CoRR abs/2305.02749 (2023). https://doi.org/10.48550/arXiv.2305.02749

33. Zahavy, T., Ben-Zrihem, N., Mannor, S.: Graying the black box: understanding DQNs. In: Balcan, M., Weinberger, K.Q. (eds.) Proceedings of the 33nd International Conference on Machine Learning, ICML 2016. JMLR Workshop and Conference Proceedings, vol. 48, pp. 1899–1908. JMLR.org (2016). http://proceedings.mlr.press/v48/zahavy16.html

Effects of Feature Types on Donor Journey

Greg Lee[1]([✉])[ID], Ajith Kumar Raghavan[2][ID], and Mark Hobbs[2][ID]

[1] Acadia University, Wolfville, NS B4P 2R6, Canada
glee@acadiau.ca
[2] Fundmetric, 1526 Dresden Row #502, Halifax, NS B3J 3K3, Canada
{ajith,mark}@fundmetric.com
http://www.acadiau.ca

Abstract. A donor journey is the series of actions taken by a fundraising institution and one of its donors that leads to a donation. This journey can take place over a few seconds or a few years and can involve one action (donation) or hundreds of actions, ending with a donation. Ultimately, fundraising institutions are most interested in the *next* best action to take that will lead to a significant donation. In the past, research has been done on this topic to discover which combination of features of actions and constituents can be used to best predict which series of actions will lead to a donation. This research involves the use of temporally capable deep learning algorithms (e.g., Recurrent Neural Networks) and other forms of deep learning (e.g., Convolutional Neural Networks). We extend this work by combining constituent features with time-based features and show that the combination leads to machine learned models with lower MAEs than previously created models, ultimately resulting in a model with an MAE of $22 for a wildlife charity.

Keywords: Deep learning · Artificial neural networks · Charitable giving

1 Introduction

All donations made to fundraising institutions involve a donor journey. This journey may be short - a constituent may simply decide to donate to a cause on a whim, or this journey may involve a series of actions (sent emails, received emails, website visits, and more) before a donation is made. A sample solicitation email is shown in Fig. 1. In the past, the process of determining which action should be taken next in order to maximize donations (and minimize attrition) was typically done by hand, but deep learning has been able to create models that are accurate to approximately $25 [6].

In order to model the donor journey, we build datasets of actions taken by the constituent (e.g., visiting the fundraising institution's website) and by the fundraising institution with respect to the constituent (e.g., sending an email to the constituent) and arrange them in chronological order. These datasets vary from 1 action (the last action taken) to 25 actions in length in our experiments, providing machine learning algorithms with varying amounts of past activity to consider when trying to model how much a constituent will donate when the next action is taken, as chosen by the fundraising institution and fed as a query to the learned model. The goal is to discover the model

A. P. Rocha et al. (Eds.): ICAART 2023, LNAI 14546, pp. 141–163, 2024.
https://doi.org/10.1007/978-3-031-55326-4_7

that minimizes the mean absolute error (MAE) in terms of predicted donation amount, while also discovering which types of data, data combination, and window sizes are best used to learn this model.

The experiments conducted have shown that using a CNNLSTM withall email, subject line, and constituent features and a window size of 6 leads to a model that has a $22 MAE for a wildlife fundraising institution, which is a lower MAE than models built in previous research with fewer features. This helps to show that the donor journey is not a simple process, but one that can be informed by the sequence of actions involving the constituent, features describing the constituent, and features describing the emails sent to the constituent. Using time features, models are able to reach an MAE of $23, showing that the length of time between actions can be used by machine learning algorithms to build accurate models as well.

The remainder of this chapter is organized as follows. We next consider research related to this work, and then formulate the problem. This is followed by a description of our approach and empirical results. We conclude with a discussion of how the new results help fundraising institutions to understand the donor journey.

2   Related Research

Donor journey advice prior to this line of research has been mostly limited to bullet points listed on fundraising institution advice webpages [8]. We aim to automate and machine learn the donor journey and avoid anecdotal evidence being used to try to guide fundraising institutions' actions towards their donors.

A Red Cross direct mail experiment showed that enrollment cards can lead to repeat donations, but sending donors gifts actually hurt retention as this creates a *transactional* donation, where there can be confusion about whether the donor is seeking a reward from the fundraising institution, or actually seeking to help the organization. Machine learning for predicting the *customer* journey is commonplace in the for-profit industry, and customer loyalty programs are one of the main drivers of the data used for these purposes [7]. Fundraising institutions are now adopting similar practices and the research described in this chapter is an example of this.

The donor journey itself has been studied extensively [4,6], including experiments that make use of constituent features (e.g., *maximum donation*), time-based features(e.g., *time between two actions*), and email features (e.g., *number of words in subject line*). These experiments have been carried out using various deep learning algorithms (e.g., recurrent neural networks (RNNS)) on datasets for fundraising institutions from various domains, such as disease and universities. More specific charitable predictions have also been studied extensively, such as "who has given one gift and is likely to become a repeat donor?", and models have been built to provide fundraising institutions with a ranked list of prospects for these type of predictions [3]. While these predictions have their use, they are not temporally useful, in the sense that they do not tell fundraising institutions what to do *now*.

Recurrent neural networks (RNNs) are artificial neural networks that are capable of modelling temporal data. Using long short-term memory (LSTM) units, RNNs can keep track of relevant events from the past while also discarding events that are not of any

Fig. 1. A sample email solicitation, redacted to maintain anonymity.

use for an accurate model. Bidirectional RNNs (BDLSTMs) are RNNs that work in two directions (with events being modelled in both chronological and reverse chronological order). RNNs and BDLSTMs have been used extensively in the for-profit industry, with the modelling of customer churn (customers stopping purchasing) being the most similar problem to predicting donations in the non-profit sector [9].

Convolutional neural networks (CNNs) were not designed to model temporal data, but have been shown to create accurate models with this type of data regardless [4,6, 10]. CNNs are typically used for object recognition and video classification, but their ability to map internal features of sequences to the convolutional layer from previous network layers allows them to create accurate models for problems with time series data as well. CNNs are effective for deriving features from a fixed length segment of the overall dataset [2].

In this research, we continue to experiment with RNNs, BDLSTMs, CNNs, and CNN LSTMs in order to see which algorithm can produce the best models for predicting the next best action to take in the donor journey, in terms of maximizing donations, when adding constituent features to time and email features.

3   Problem Formulation

The problem at hand is to accurately model the donor journey so that any potential next action taken with respect to a fundraising institution constituent (or by a constituent) can be properly evaluated in terms of its effect on the potential donation made by said constituent. Put more plainly, we seek a model that can be queried with a past set of actions taken with respect to a constituent and a potential next action that (accurately) answers the question - given this set of past actions {X} taken with respect to the constituent and a potential next action Y, how much will this constituent donate to the fundraising institution if action Y is taken? Put even more plainly, the fundraising institution's goal is to raise more money and having an accurate understanding of the donor journey helps.

The donor journey is generally implicitly modelled by the fundraising institution, in that they consider what has been recently done with respect to a constituent (e.g., "we sent them 2 emails, they opened both, so we should ..."); we seek to formalize this process by presenting machine learning algorithms with an ordered list of actions in order to model the donor journey. The rules developed "by hand" by fundraising institutions likely do raise substantial funds in many cases, but we seek to be able to replicate and maximize this process, as well as understand *why* certain sequences of actions lead to more and higher donations.

The actions involved in the donor journey for every fundraising institution we consider are shown in Table 1. Note that all of these actions are taken by the constituent except for *Delivered* which is the fundraising institution sending an email to the constituent and having it arrive and *no action* (which is, of course, taken by neither the constituent nor the fundraising institution). Table 2 shows extra actions tracked in the donor journey by one of the educational fundraising institutions for which we have data, labelled initially as C5 and later as F2 in the empirical evaluation section (Table 3).

Table 1. The list of all actions used in our experiments for every fundraising intitution.

Action	Description
No Action	Used to fill an action when no action has happened
Delivered	A successfully delivered email
Opened	Constituent opens an email
Pageview	Constituent views the donation portal
Donated	Constituent makes a donation to the fundraising institution
Clicked	Constituent clicked on a link in an email
Complained	Constituent reported an appeal email as spam
Dropped	Email did not reach the constituent
Bounced	Email was blocked by the constituent
Unsubscribed	Constituent unsubscribed from a mailing list

Table 2. The list of all actions used in our experiments exclusively for a university foundation (C5) [6].

Action	Description
Virtual Response	Made a social media comment
Attended	Attended a university event
Prospect Visit	A major gift officer visited the constituent
Volunteer Member	Volunteered for a foundation committee
Purchased	Purchased an event ticket
Recurring signup	Signed up for the same activity 2+ times
Volunteer	General volunteering
Participant	Participated in an advisory circle
Staff	Foundation staff action
Current	Continued volunteering
Mentors	Participated in accelerator mentoring
Ex Officio	Historic trustee action
Trustee Term	Alumnus trustee action
Participating Host	Off-campus event
Suppressed	Unknown email error
Opt out	Opted out of some email options
Failed	Email did not reach constituent
Trustee Liaison	Relevant board participation
Former	Former board member action

4   Our Approach

To model the donor journey, we consider the last X actions taken by the constituent or the fundraising institution with respect to the constituent, where X typically varies in our experiments from 1 to 25. We arrange the actions in chronological order and *describe* each action with a set of features, with this set varying depending upon the experiment. If we set X to 3, a set of actions could be {delivered, opened, delivered}.

Table 3. Variable email parameters [6].

Parameter	Description
Words	Number of words
Paragraphs	Number of paragraphs
Images	Number of images
Links	Number of HTML links
Blocks	Number of sections
Divs	Number of HTML content division elements
Editable Content Divs	Number of editable HTML divs

A_1	A_3	A_2	A_2	A_6	A_3

A_1	A_2	A_3	...	A_{10}	E_1	E_2	E_3	E_4	...	E_7
1	0	0		0	0	0	0	0		0
0	0	1		0	191	5	4	10		16
0	1	0		0	191	5	4	10		16
0	1	0		0	281	8	16	4		11
0	0	0		0	281	8	16	4		11
0	0	1		0	115	6	2	3		1

Fig. 2. An example set of six actions used as training data for deep learning models. The actions are one-hot encoded and have their corresponding email features appended.

We one-hot encode the actions since there is no "order" to them, in the sense that action 3 is not 2 more than action 1. We then append to each action all associated features. Which type of features that are appended depends on the experiment at hand, but for all experiments in this work, email features are appended to actions. All actions except "no action" have an associated email (the data used is from email appeals), thus we can append the features of that email to each action (e.g., number of words). For "no action", we give these features all the value 0.

In Fig. 2, the donor journey consists of $\{A_1, A_3, A_2, A_2, A_6, A_3\}$, which is shown at the top of the figure. The bottom of the figure shows the same set of actions one-hot encoded with email features appended (E_i). A_1 is the "no action" action, which is why its associated email features all have value 0. The second action taken (A_3) is a true action and has associated email features (e.g., E_4 is 10 here, which could be the number of paragraphs in the email.). The next two actions taken chronologically are A_2, which could be opening an email. Since the associated email features are different (e.g., E_1 is 191 for the first A_2 and 281 for the second A_2), this would mean the constituent opened two different emails. The fifth action, A_6 has the same email features as the fourth action, meaning it involves the same email. Finally, the sixth action is A_3, which is the same action as the second action, and could indicate the delivery of a different email (since the second and sixth actions have different email parameter values). In some experiments each action also is appended with time features (e.g., *time since*

Table 4. Best performing RNN architectures for three fundraising institutions.

	F1	F2	F3
LSTM Layer 1	64	64	
LSTM Layer 2	32	32	
Dropout	0.2	0.2	
Learning Rate	0.001	0.001	
Momentum	0.9	0.9	
Activation Function	ReLU	ReLU	

Table 5. Best performing CNN architectures for three fundraising institutions.

	F1	F2	F3
Layer 1			
Kernel Size	3	3	
Maxpooling	1	1	
Filters	128	128	
Layer 2			
Kernel Size	3	3	
Maxpooling	1	1	
Filters	128	128	

last action), subject line features (e.g., *number of words in subject*) and/or constituent featuers (e.g., *maximum donation*).

As in previous experiments, we use each of RNNs, BDLSTMs, CNNs and CNN LSTMs in an effort to both find the best model for the donor journey and to understand what makes a good model of the donor journey, especially in terms of which feature sets are provided to these algoirithms. Architectures for these algorithms are kept the same as in previous work [5] and given in Tables 4, 5, 6 and 7. The best architectures are shown graphically in Fig. 4.

Table 6. Best performing BDLSTM architectures for three fundraising institutions.

	Value
BDRNN Layer 1	64
BDRNN Layer 1	32
Dropout	0.2
Learning Rate	0.001
Momentum	0.9
Activation Function	ReLU
Merge Mode	concat
Optimizer	SGD

Table 7. Best performing CNNLSTM architectures for three fundraising institutions.

	Value
Conv1D (Layer 1)	32
Kernel Size	1
Maxpooling (Layer 1)	1
LSTM (Layer 1)	64
Conv1D (Layer 2)	64
Kernel size	1
Maxpooling (Layer 2)	1
LSTM (Layer 2)	32
Dropout	0.2
Learning Rate	0.001
Momentum	0.9
Activation	ReLU
Merge Mode	concat
Optimizer	Adam

We created and added some features to previous experiments and those features are listed in Table 8. These features add context to actions by describing how much time has elapsed between actions and by describing the subject line of emails associated to action, which is generally the section of an email first seen by the reader and has been shown to have strong effects on whether the recipient reads the email or not [1]. We track both the number of characters and number of words in the subject line, as well as the number of variables. Here a variable holds a place for a value associated with the reader – typically their first name, as in "Hi *Maria*, we thought you might like to know...".

Other new features include the font and background colours of the email, as well as how many special characters are used. These can be seen as a measure of how *complicated* the email is, with more simple emails sometimes being better at delivering a message to constituents. Constituent features are used in some experiments and are also listed in Table 8.

Table 8. The new features added to training data. These are divided into time features, subject line features, email features, and constituent features, for clarity.

Feature	Description
Time Features	
Time Since Last Action	Time in seconds since last action
Time Since Last Same Action	Time in seconds since last same action
Subject Line Features	
Subject Line Characters	Number of chars in the subject line
Subject Line Words	Number of words in the subject line
Subject Line Variables	Number of variables in the subject line
Email Features	
Special Characters	Number of special chars
Font Colours	The number of fonts
Background Colours	The number of background colours
Constituent Features	
Solicitation	Presence of/permission to contact by email/phone/address
Donation summary	Max/min/mean/total/count of/stdev of donations
Donation times	Time since last/first donation and span of giving
Donation Methods	Donated by cash/credit/stock/electronic transfer
Threshold donations	Donations within 10/20/30/40/50% of a major gift
Best designations	ID of campaign/appeal/designation with highest donation
LYBUNT/SYBUNT	Donated Last/Some Year But Unfortunately Not This year
Small Gifts	Count of gifts below $50 and below $25
Line of Best Fit	Slope and intercept of line of best fit of donations
Wealth	Estimates of income/investment/net worth
Engagement stats	Number of emails opened, clicks, videos watched/started/stopped
Last interaction	Number of days since last interaction with the charity

Figure 3 shows the same set of actions as Fig. 2 but with time features appended. Both the time since the last action (TA) and the time since the last same action (TSA) are added. TA and TSA are related of course, as the TSA for the second instance of A_3 (the sixth action taken) is the sum of the TA values since the previous A_3 (the second action), being 1 day + 2 h + 2 days + 22 h = 4 days. Comparing Fig. 3 to Fig. 2 shows how much more information is provided by the time features. Without the last two columns of Fig. 2, there is no way for the machine learning algorithms to know how much time has elapsed between actions, meaning the second action could have been 1 s later than the first action or ten years later, which are very different situations in terms of the donor journey.

A₁	A₂	A₃	...	A₁₀	E₁	E₂	E₃	E₄	...	E₇	TA	TSA
1	0	0		0	0	0	0	0		0	0	0
0	0	1		0	191	5	4	10		16	0	3 days
0	1	0		0	191	5	4	10		16	1 day	1 year
0	1	0		0	281	8	16	4		11	2 hours	2 hours
0	0	0		0	281	8	16	4		11	2 days	10 days
0	0	1		0	115	6	2	3		1	22 hours	4 days

Fig. 3. The action set from Fig. 2 with TA (Time since last action) and TSA (Time since last same action) added.

5 Empirical Evaluation

We first add time and email features to previous data sets to see the effect of their addition without constituent features, to try to isolate how much they can help deep learning algorithms model the donor journey. We then add constituent features to this data in order to see if we can lower the mean absolute error of these models further. All experiments involved the use of four deep learning algorithms: CNNs, CNN LSTMs, RNNs and BDLSTMs. All experiments involve the use of one particular fundraising institution's data for both training and testing (distinct sets).

All results are averaged across 25 cross validation runs with each cross validation run having a balanced number of donors and non donors. We accomplish this balancing by selecting all of the smaller set (which in this case is always the donor set) and selecting an equal random number from the larger (non donor) set, with this random set changing at each fold. We divide the data into donors and non-donors despite this being a regression problem (how much will a donor donate?) since non-donors are an important special case of a $0 donation. Training data was 75% of the available data, while 25% of the data was used for testing. In all tables, bold numbers represent the lower MAE in comparing two data sets and italics represent the lowest MAE for a given fundraising institution.

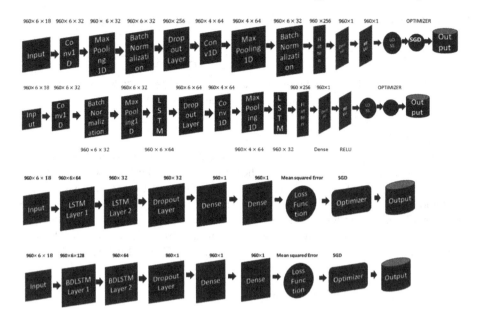

Fig. 4. The best deep learning architectures discovered empirically and used in our experiments. From top to bottom they are: CNN, CNN LSTM, RNN, and BDLSTM [6].

5.1 Preliminary Experiments

We first experimented with all the data used in previous experiments [4,5], which is described in Table 9. These fundraising institutions are C1: a wildlife fundraising institution, C2: a disease fundraising institution, C3: a youth sports fundraising institution, C4: a mental health fundraising institution and C5: a university fundraising institution. The data used is provided by Fundmetric (www.fundmetric.com) a company that uses machine learning to discover patterns in fundraising data that can be used to predict future donor behaviour.

Table 9. Summary of training data from five fundraising institutions [6].

	C1	C2	C3	C4	C5
Donors	640	229	316	27	70
Non-Donors	184000	195688	50811	60	6880
Total Raised	$54,387	$55,952	$130,034	$6,285	$364,133
Mean Don.	$85	$245	$409	$233	$290
Median Don.	$50	$100	$100	$100	$100
Standard Dev.	$105	$514	$1520	$585	$1,035
Min Don.	$5	$1	$1	$10	$1
Max Don.	$1,000	$5,000	$10,000	$3,000	$500

152   G. Lee et al.

Table 10. Preliminary experiment using all 5 fundraising intitutions, with window size 20 and a CNN [6].

	C1	C2	C3	C4	C5
Without Time Features	**$26**	$490	$195	$59	**$46**
With Time Features	$35	**$290**	**$138**	**$57**	$52

Table 10 shows typical results when using a deep learning algorithm with the data previously described. The algorithm used here is a CNN and the window size is 20, but the results are typical of any combination of learner and window size. C4 is too small of a fundraising institution for which to trust the results (it only has 27 donors) and the errors for C2 and C3 are too high to use in a model used to suggest email parameters, so the remaining experiments do not make use of data from C2, C3, or C4. We also rename the remaining fundraising institutions for clarity- C1 to F1 and C5 to F2.

Table 11. Summary of training data for F3.

	F3
Donors	425
Non-Donors	8175
Total Raised	$126125.72
Mean Don	$296.76
Median Don	$200
Standard Dev	$302.44
Min Don	$1
Max Don	$1,000

Data for another university fundraising institution, which we call F3, also became available and we use this data in further experiments. F3 is described in Table 11. These experiments include adding time features (Sect. 5.2), adding subject line features and more email features (Sect. 5.3), adding constituent features (Sect. 5.4), and adding constituent features with other features (Sect. 5.5).

5.2 Experiment 1: Adding Time Features

In our first full experiment, we added two time features to the previously available data - the time elapsed since the previous action involving the constituent, and the time elapsed since the previous *same* action taken involving the constituent. Tables 12, 13, 14 and 15 show the change in MAE when the two time features are added to the F1–F3 data compared to the MAE without these features using four different deep learning algorithms.

Time features help RNNs and BDLSTMs to lower their MAE on prediction donation amounts for almost every window size. CNNs, on the other hand, actually have
their MAEs increase when provided with time features. While recurrent neural networks benefitting more than convolutional neural networks from temporal data is logical, convolutional neural networks actually being hurt by temporal data is surprising.

For F1, the lowest MAE for any model was \$24, which always involved a data set
with time features and was achieved by RNNs and BDLSTMs. For F2, the lowest MAE
for any model was \$38, which always involved a data set with time features and was
achieved by RNNs and BDLSTMs. For F3, the lowest MAE for any model was \$121,
which involved a data set with time features and was achieved by BDLSTMs.

Table 12. Comparing the performance of CNNs with new added time features to data without
these features."TF" stands for time features being added to the data.

Window Size	1	3	6	10	15	20	25
F1	**\$32**	**\$33**	*\$26*	**\$34**	**\$29**	**\$27**	**\$27**
F1TF	\$43	\$42	\$44	\$43	\$39	\$41	\$40
F2	**\$49**	**\$49**	**\$44**	\$49	**\$49**	**\$50**	\$57
F2TF	\$52	\$52	\$46	*\$41*	\$52	\$52	**\$50**
F3	**\$146**	**\$138**	\$163	**\$163**	**\$163**	*\$129*	*\$129*
F3TF	\$151	\$163	**\$149**	\$163	\$163	\$163	\$147

Table 13. Comparing the performance of CNN LSTMs with new added time features to data
without these features. "TF" stands for time features being added to the data.

Window Size	1	3	6	10	15	20	25
F1	**\$41**	**\$41**	**\$36**	*\$35*	**\$36**	\$42	**\$33**
F1TF	**\$41**	\$42	\$43	\$41	\$40	**\$39**	\$39
F2	**\$49**	*\$46*	**\$47**	\$48	\$47	**\$49**	*\$46*
F2TF	\$53	\$52	\$52	\$53	\$53	\$52	\$53
F3	*\$163*	**\$164**	*\$163*	*\$163*	**\$164**	**\$164**	**\$164**
F3TF	*\$163*	**\$164**	*\$163*	\$164	**\$164**	**\$164**	**\$164**

5.3 Experiment 2: Adding Subject Line Features and More Email Features

After adding time features, subject line and new email features were added to see their
effect. Tables 16, 17, 18 and 19 show MAEs for the four deep learning algorithms with
this data added.

For CNNs and CNNLSTMs, adding subject line and new email features increased
the error for F1 and F2. For F3 these features generally made no difference to model
accuracy. For RNNs and BDLSTMS, F1 and F2 errors were decreased for most window
sizes with the addition of the new email and subject line features. For F3, the features
did not help except for larger window sizes for RNNs.

Table 14. Comparing the performance of RNNs with new added time features to data without these features. 'TF' stands for time features being added to the data.

Window Size	1	3	6	10	15	20	25
F1	$43	$31	$30	$28	$27	$26	$27
F1TF	**$25**	*$24*	*$24*	*$24*	**$25**	*$24*	*$24*
F2	$55	$55	$55	$54	$55	$50	$48
F2TF	**$44**	*$38*	**$40**	**$41**	**$40**	**$40**	**$41**
F3	$163	$138	$163	$183	$184	**$163**	**$183**
F3TF	**$133**	**$136**	**$135**	**$136**	*$129*	$184	$184

Table 15. Comparing the performance of BDLSTMs with new added time features to data without these features. "TF" stands for time features being added to the data.

Window Size	1	3	6	10	15	20	25
F1	$43	$31	$29	$28	$27	$28	$25
F1TF	**$28**	**$25**	**$28**	*$24*	**$25**	**$26**	*$24*
F2	$53	$52	**$42**	$41	$43	**$40**	$50
F2TF	**$39**	*$38*	$48	**$40**	**$40**	**$40**	*$38*
F3	$135	**$135**	$138	$186	$138	$164	$181
F3TF	**$133**	*$121*	**$133**	**$135**	**$122**	**$127**	**$125**

For F1, the lowest MAE for any model was $24, which always involved a data set with subect line and new features and was achieved by RNNs and BDLSTMs. For F2, the lowest MAE for any model was $36, which involved a data set with subject line and new features and was achieved by BDLSTMs. For F3, the lowest MAE for any model was $124, which involved a data set with time features and was achieved by BDLSTMs. This shows that adding subject line and new features helps more accurate models achieve a lower MAE in the best case, but that it may prevent less accurate models (the F3 model) from achieving as low an MAE.

Table 16. Comparing the performance of CNNs with new features (time and new email features) to without new features."NewF" stands for new email and subject line features being added to the data.

Window Size	1	3	6	10	15	20	25
F1	**$32**	**$33**	*$26*	**$34**	**$29**	**$27**	**$27**
F1NewF	$40	$42	$42	$39	$40	$39	$38
F2	**$49**	**$49**	*$44*	**$49**	**$49**	**$50**	**$57**
F2NewF	$52	$58	$52	$53	$52	$52	$51
F3	**$151**	$163	$149	**$163**	**$163**	**$163**	**$147**
F3NewF	$163	**$154**	*$140*	**$163**	**$163**	**$163**	$163

Table 17. Comparing the performance of CNN LSTMs with new features (time and new email features) to without new features. "NewF" stands for new email and subject line features being added to the data.

Window Size	1	3	6	10	15	20	25
F1	**$41**	**$41**	**$36**	**$35**	**$36**	**$42**	*$33*
F1NewF	**$41**	$42	$42	$42	$42	**$42**	$41
F2	**$49**	*$46*	**$47**	**$48**	**$47**	**$49**	*$46*
F2NewF	$51	$50	$52	$53	$54	$53	$53
F3	**$163**	**$164**	**$163**	**$164**	**$164**	**$164**	**$164**
F3NewF	**$163**	**$164**	$164	**$164**	**$164**	**$164**	**$164**

5.4   Experiment 3A: Adding Constituent Features and Time Features

In previous experiments [4] constituent features have been shown to add useful information to the feature set for machine learning the donor journey, leading to lower MAEs for learned donor journey models. We thus experimented with adding constituent features to the base data without the subject line and email features, but with time features, to see their effect with the time features added.

Table 18. Comparing the performance of RNNs with new features (time and new email features) to without new features. "NewF" stands for new email and subject line features being added to the data.

Window Size	1	3	6	10	15	20	25
F1	$43	$31	**$30**	$28	$27	$26	$27
F1NewF	*$24*	*$24*	$32	*$24*	*$24*	*$24*	*$24*
F2	$55	$55	$55	$54	$55	$50	**$48**
F2NewF	**$44**	*$39*	**$41**	**$40**	**$44**	**$46**	**$48**
F3	$133	$136	$135	$136	**$129**	$184	$184
F3NewF	$133	$135	$145	$184	$139	$141	**$131**

Table 19. Comparing the performance of BDLSTMs with new features (time and new email features) to without new features. "NewF" stands for new email and subject line features being added to the data.

Window Size	1	3	6	10	15	20	25
F1	$43	$31	**$29**	**$28**	$27	$28	$25
F1NewF	**$25**	**$25**	$30	$29	*$24*	**$25**	*$24*
F2	$53	$52	**$42**	**$41**	$43	**$40**	$50
F2NewF	*$36*	**$41**	$43	**$41**	**$41**	$42	**$41**
F3	$133	**$121**	$133	$135	$122	$127	$125
F3NewF	$133	$132	$129	$133	**$124**	$127	$163

Tables 20, 21, 22 and 23 show the results of adding constituent features to the base data.

For F1, the lowest MAE for any model was $22, which involved a data set with constituent features but not time features and was achieved by CNNLSTMs. For F2, the lowest MAE for any model was $34, which involved a data set with constituent features but not time features and was achieved by RNNs. For F3, the lowest MAE for any model was $106, which involved a data set with time features and was achieved by BDLSTMs. These results show that constituent features can help with or without time features, since the lowest MAEs achieved with constituent features in the data set are lower than those achieved without the constituent features.

5.5   Experiment 3B: Adding Constituent Features with Subject Line and New Email Features

We next compared data sets with constituent features, subject line features and new email features but no time features to the base set with constituent features, subject line features and new email features *and* time features – what we call the *full set*.

Tables 24, 25, 26 and 27 show the results of adding constituent features to the base data.

Table 20. Comparing the performance of CNNs with constituent features and time features to data without the time features."TF" stands for time features being added to the data.

Window Size	1	3	6	10	15	20	25
F1	$42	$42	$95	*$23*	$42	$42	$42
F1TF	$43	$25	$42	$42	$51	$42	*$23*
F2	$52	$52	$52	$52	$52	$52	$43
F2TF	$52	$42	$52	$52	*$39*	$52	$52
F3	$163	$163	$163	*$127*	$132	*$127*	$163
F3TF	$152	$163	$163	$168	$163	$148	$165

Table 21. Comparing the performance of CNNLSTMs with constituent features and time features to data without the time features."TF" stands for time features being added to the data.

Window Size	1	3	6	10	15	20	25
F1	$24	$23	*$22*	$23	*$22*	$23	$23
F1TF	$24	$29	$24	$30	$25	$32	$23
F2	$45	*$44*	*$44*	*$44*	$45	*$44*	$45
F2TF	$46	*$44*	$51	$46	$45	$45	$46
F3	*$163*	$164	$164	*$163*	$164	$164	$164
F3TF	*$163*	$164	$164	$164	$164	$164	$164

Table 22. Comparing the performance of RNNs with constituent features and time features to data without the time features."TF" stands for time features being added to the data.

Window Size	1	3	6	10	15	20	25
F1	**$25**	$24	**$24**	*$23*	*$23*	$24	*$23*
F1TF	**$25**	*$23*	$25	$24	$24	*$23*	$24
F2	**$37**	$40	**$40**	**$37**	$41	*$34*	**$37**
F2TF	$41	**$39**	$41	$40	**$39**	$36	$38
F3	*$114*	**$115**	$139	$165	**$139**	$168	**$160**
F3TF	$130	**$115**	*$114*	**$121**	$145	**$142**	$183

Table 23. Comparing the performance of BDLSTMs with newly added constituent features and time features to data without the time features."TF" stands for time features being added to the data.

Window Size	1	3	6	10	15	20	25
F1	*$23*	**$24**	**$24**	**$24**	*$23*	**$24**	**$24**
F1TF	$24	**$24**	$26	$26	$25	$25	**$24**
F2	$39	*$36*	$41	**$39**	**$38**	$39	$40
F2TF	**$38**	$38	**$40**	$41	**$38**	**$38**	*$36*
F3	**$113**	**$113**	**$109**	$112	$111	$117	$114
F3TF	$127	$121	*$106*	*$106*	**$110**	**$112**	**$109**

For F1, the lowest MAE for any model was $23, which was achieved by CNNs, CNNLSTMs and RNNs with both the full data set and the set without the time features. For F2, the lowest MAE for any model was $36, which was achieved by RNNs and BDLSTMs with both the full data set and the set without the time features. For F3, the lowest MAE for any model was $104, which involved the full data set and was achieved by BDLSTMs.

Table 24. Comparing the performance of CNNs with constituent features, subject line features, and new email features to data with the time features (the"full set"). "F" stands for "full set".

Window Size	1	3	6	10	15	20	25
F1	$43	**$25**	$42	**$42**	$51	$42	*$23*
F1NewF	**$42**	**$42**	**$36**	**$42**	**$42**	*$23*	$25
F2	**$52**	**$42**	$52	$52	*$39*	$52	**$52**
F2NewF	**$52**	$52	**$51**	**$51**	**$50**	$52	**$52**
F3	**$152**	**$163**	$163	**$168**	$163	**$148**	$165
F3NewF	$163	**$163**	**$158**	**$163**	**$152**	$163	*$144*

Table 25. Comparing the performance of CNNLSTMs with constituent features, subject line features, and new email features to data with the time features (the"full set"). "F" stands for "full set".

Window Size	1	3	6	10	15	20	25
F1	**$24**	**$29**	**$24**	$30	**$25**	$32	*$23*
F1NewF	**$24**	$30	**$24**	**$26**	$35	**$26**	$26
F2	**$46**	*$44*	$51	**$46**	$45	**$45**	**$46**
F2NewF	**$46**	$45	**$50**	$52	*$44*	**$45**	$48
F3	**$163**	**$164**	**$164**	**$164**	**$164**	**$164**	$164
F3NewF	**$163**	**$164**	**$164**	**$164**	**$164**	**$164**	*$151*

Table 26. Comparing the performance of RNNs with constituent features, subject line features, and new email features to data with the time features (the"full set"). "F" stands for "full set".

Window Size	1	3	6	10	15	20	25
F1	$25	*$23*	$25	**$24**	**$24**	*$23*	**$24**
F1NewF	**$24**	*$23*	**$24**	**$24**	**$24**	*$23*	**$24**
F2	$41	**$39**	$41	**$40**	**$39**	*$36*	**$38**
F2NewF	*$36*	$41	**$39**	$42	**$39**	*$36*	$39
F3	**$130**	**$115**	$114	**$121**	$145	$142	$183
F3NewF	$132	$119	*$108*	$123	**$114**	**$125**	**$130**

5.6   Experiment 4: Querying the Most Accurate Models

In order to use the models produced in our experiments to suggest actions, data sets with previous actions needed to be created, but without the final action. This involved "shifting all actions" back by 1 position, as shown in Fig. 5. Doing so allows us to try every possible action at the last position and query the model with this set of actions to see how large of a donation it predicts (with the possibility of $0, of course). The last action that when appended to the shifted data set produces the largest predicted donation amount can then be deemed the best possible next action to take for a given series of actions.

Using the best models discovered in Sect. 5, we performed some experiments to see which actions were generally deemed the next best actions. The actions most often "chosen" as the best action were *pageview*, *donated*, and *delivered*, which are positive actions. Negative actions such as *complained* never resulted in the highest prediction donation amount, which we interpret to mean the model has learned that negative actions do not help and positive actions are best to take, which is logical.

Table 27. Comparing the performance of BDLSTMs with constituent features, subject line features, and new email features to data with the time features (the"full set"). "F" stands for "full set".

Window Size	1	3	6	10	15	20	25
F1	*$24*	*$24*	$26	$26	**$25**	**$25**	*$24*
F1NewF	$26	$25	**$25**	**$25**	$26	$25	*$24*
F2	**$38**	**$38**	**$40**	$41	**$38**	**$38**	*$36*
F2NewF	$43	$45	**$39**	**$39**	$39	**$39**	$39
F3	**$127**	$121	**$106**	**$106**	**$110**	**$112**	$109
F3NewF	$131	**$117**	*$104*	$108	$117	$114	**$105**

Action 1	Action 2	Action 3	Action 4	Action 5	Action 6
Action 2	Action 3	Action 4	Action 5	Action 6	**New action**

Fig. 5. When querying the models, all actions are shifted back by 1 and a new action is inserted into the last position. The model is then queried for a predicted donation amount with this set of actions. Email and time features are included, but are not shown here.

While it is useful to know what action should be taken next even if it is a constituent action, the fundraising institution can only take one action in the set with which we experiment – *delivered*. In order to discover which email feature values are best to use, we queried the best models from Sect. 5 with a range of values for each email parameter and noted which values led to the highest predicted donation amount, all with the delivered action. We show these results in Tables 28 and 29 for F1 and F2, since their data sets generated the most accurate models. A window size of 20 was used for BDLSTMs since this was the best window size for this algorithm, empirically.

BDLSTMs suggested a larger number of paragraphs for F2 than F1 which may be explained by F1 being a university foundation and F2 being a wildlife fundraising institution, with the former's constituents perhaps being affiliated with a university makes them more interested in longer text. This would also help explain shorter subject line words suggested for F1 than for F2, with this length calculated by considering the number of characters suggested (20 vs 38) while for each institution 5 words were suggested.

Another difference is the number of background colours suggested - 15 for F1 and 5 for F2. This suggests that the BDLSTM learned that F1 consitituents prefer shorter emails with more colours and F2 constituents prefer longer emails with less colour variation. For both fundraisiing institutions, 0 subject line variables were suggested, meaning the BDLSTM has learned not to put the constituent's name in the subject line for any fundraising institution.

Table 28. Summary of email parameter values chosen by BDLSTMs for F1.

	Mode	Median	Mean	St. Dev.
Words	150	150	134.43	132.47
Paragraphs	18	18	15.03	6.43
Images	15	15	13.54	3.32
Links	35	35	34.14	2.1
Blocks	9	9	9	0
Special chars	5	5	6.76	3.8
Font colours	5	5	5.14	1.18
Background colour	15	15	12.52	4.32
Divs	41	41	44.64	6.4
Editable Content	9	9	10.17	2.3
Subject line words	5	5	5.69	2.7
Subject line characters	20	20	22.53	5.74
Subject line variables	0	0	0.4	0.49

Table 29. Summary of email parameter values chosen by BDLSTMs for F2.

	Mode	Median	Mean	St. Dev.
Words	150	150	124.8	56.23
Paragraphs	1	1	1	0
Images	15	15	13.4	3.3
Links	35	35	33.9	2.2
Blocks	9	9	9	0
Special chars	5	5	8.23	4.7
Font colours	5	5	9.9	5.03
Background colour	5	5	9.9	5.03
Divs	56	56	53.4	5.6
Editable Content	15	15	13.05	2.8
Subject line words	5	5	5	0
Subject line characters	38	38	29.12	9.06
Subject line variables	0	0	0.05	0.23

Despite the fact that the F3 models were less accurate, we queried the most accurate F3 model for comparison as well, with the results shown in Table 30. For F3, the BDLSTM suggested fewer, longer paragraphs as it did for F2 and the same number of HTML divs as F2, but shorter subject line words like F1 and a variable in the subject line, which was not the case for F1 or F2.

Table 30. Summary of email parameter values chosen by BDLSTMs for F3.

	Mode	Median	Mean	St. Dev.
Words	150	150	155.33	60.19
Paragraphs	3	3	2.851	0.626
Images	6	6	5.83	1.22
Links	28	28	26.981	5.342
Blocks	8	8	7.72	1.53
Special chars	20	20	18.55	4.78
Font colours	25	25	23.14	6.01
Background colour	10	10	9.48	2.02
Divs	56	56	53.64	10.81
Editable Content	15	15	14.11	3.11
Subject line words	8	8	7.92	0.77
Subject line characters	28	28	27.73	2.7
Subject line variables	1	1	0.99	0.09

6   Conclusions and Future Work

The experiments in this chapter help to further understand what types of data, machine learning algorithms and window size are best used in order to model the donor journey. Building on previous research [4–6], time features, subject line features, new email features (relavive to [4]) and constituent features are added to previously used data to study both the impact of these features on their own and their combination.

Time features provide machine learning algorithms context for how much time has passed between actions. Subject line features provide a description of what is generally the first part of an email consumed by a constituent. Constituent features provide information about the constituent taking the actions in a particular donor journey, which we hypothesized should affect what is the next best action in a donor journey.

In general, models benefit from more types of data, with all of time, subject line, (new) email, and constituent features generally being better to have in a dataset for any given machine learning algorithm to model the donor journey. Table 31.

Table 31. ML Parameters for lowest MAEs for each fundraising institution. Here "FI" represents "fundraising institution", "CF" represents "Constituent Features", "NF" represents "New email Features", and "SF" represents "Subject line Features".

FI	Algorithm	Window Size	Dataset	Error
F1	CNNLSTM	6	CF, NF, SF	$22
F2	BDLSTM	20	CF, NF, SF	$34
F3	BDLSTM	6	full	$104

162   G. Lee et al.

Compared to previous research using data for F1 and F2, the lowest MAEs have been further lowered, with the best error for F1 being \$22 and the best error for F3 being \$34. Both of these errors allow for trust in models to be used to suggest next best actions as described in Sect. 5.6. F3 models had higher errors, but this may be have been caused by them having a larger range of donation amounts (\$999) than F2, while having much less data than F1. Generally, adding in data of various types helps to build more accurate models, but how to do so varies across the type of machine learning algorithm. Ultimately, the most accurate machine learning algorithm is likely to be chosen to build a donor journey model (which in this case has been BDLSTMs), but it is important to understand the performance of other algorithms as data may change and more types of data may become available.

We queried the most accurate models for F1, F2, and F3. BDLSTMs suggest short emails with many colours for a F1's emails, while suggested the opposite for a F2's emails. For both, it suggests not including the constituent's name (a variable) in the email subject. For F3, there were some similarities to the F2 parameter values, but also to F1. This model is less trustworthy since it is less accurate.

In the future, we hope to anonymously combine data across fundraising institution verticals and even across any combination of fundraising institutions to see what lessons can be learned with more data, and if the data being similar (i.e., from the same vertical) makes a difference. An example of a "vertical" is "disease fundraising institutions".

We would also like to learn why certain features matter, such as the length of words, while other features do not seem to matter at all. We have arrived at some hypothesis in this chapter based on features that vary in range of suggested values by accurate models, but analyzing these features more deeply should yield more solid results. Comparing these results to what constituents tell us directly via conducting a survey would also be interesting,.

Emails to charities are generally sorted into four types - {acquisition, solicitation, stewardship, cultivation}. Acquisition emails are sent to non-donors to try and elicit a first donation. Solicitation emails are sent to donors in an attempt to have them donate again. Stewardship emails are sent mainly as thank yous to show appreciation to the donor and to show them the results of their donations. Cultivation emails generally have as their purpose to try and move donors along a *donor pipeline*, from one-time donors to planned givers (constituents who make a plan for a gift to be given after they pass). We would like to categorize emails with these types and use the types as data to see what can be learned about what types of emails should be sent, and when.

References

1. Janke, R.: Effects of mentioning the incentive prize in the email subject line on survey response. Evid. Based Libr. Inf. Pract. **9**(1), 4–13 (2014)
2. Kim, Y.: Convolutional neural networks for sentence classification. In: Proceedings of the 2014 Conference on Empirical Methods in Natural Language Processing (EMNLP), pp. 1746–1751. Association for Computational Linguistics, Doha (2014). https://doi.org/10.3115/v1/D14-1181. https://aclanthology.org/D14-1181
3. Lee, G., Adunoor, S., Hobbs, M.: Machine learning across charities. In: Proceedings of the 17th Modeling Decision in Artificial Intelligence Conference (2020)

4. Lee, G., Raghavan, A.K., Hobbs, M.: Deep learning the donor journey with convolutional and recurrent neural networks. In: Wani, M.A., Raj, B., Luo, F., Dou, D. (eds.) Deep Learning Applications, Volume 3. AISC, vol. 1395, pp. 295–320. Springer, Singapore (2022). https://doi.org/10.1007/978-981-16-3357-7_12

5. Lee, G., Raghavan, A.K.V., Hobbs, M.: Improving the donor journey with convolutional and recurrent neural networks. In: Wani, M.A., Luo, F., Li, X.A., Dou, D., Bonchi, F. (eds.) 19th IEEE International Conference on Machine Learning and Applications, ICMLA 2020, Miami, FL, USA, 14–17 December 2020, pp. 913–920. IEEE (2020). https://doi.org/10.1109/ICMLA51294.2020.00149

6. Lee, G., Raghavan, A.K.V., Hobbs, M.: Adding time and subject line features to the donor journey. In: 15th International Conference on Agents and Artificial Intelligence, ICAART 2022, Lisbon, Portugal, 22–24 February 2023, pp. 45–54. IEEE (2023)

7. Lemon, K.N., Verhoef, P.C.: Understanding customer experience throughout the customer journey. J. Mark. **80**(6), 69–96 (2016). https://doi.org/10.1509/jm.15.0420. http://journals.sagepub.com/doi/10.1509/jm.15.0420

8. McLellan, T.: Mapping the donor journey - part one: five reasons to consider it (2022). http://www.finelinesolutions.com/academy/blogs/18-non-profits-learn-here/129-mapping-the-donor-journey-part-one-why-is-mapping-a-good-idea.html

9. Sudharsan, R., Ganesh, E.N.: A swish RNN based customer churn prediction for the telecom industry with a novel feature selection strategy. Connect. Sci. **34**(1), 1855–1876 (2022). https://doi.org/10.1080/09540091.2022.2083584

10. Xia, J., Kiguchi, K.: Sensorless real-time force estimation in microsurgery robots using a time series convolutional neural network. IEEE Access **9**, 149447–149455 (2021). https://doi.org/10.1109/ACCESS.2021.3124304

Data-Efficient Offline Reinforcement Learning with Approximate Symmetries

Giorgio Angelotti[1,2(✉)] ⓘ, Nicolas Drougard[1,2] ⓘ, and Caroline P. C. Chanel[1,2] ⓘ

[1] ANITI, University of Toulouse, Toulouse, France
[2] ISAE-Supaero, University of Toulouse, Toulouse, France
{giorgio.angelotti,nicolas.drougard,
caroline.chanel}@isae-supaero.fr

Abstract. The performance of Offline Reinforcement Learning (ORL) models in Markov Decision Processes (MDPs) is heavily contingent upon the quality and diversity of the training data. This research furthers the exploration of expert-guided symmetry detection and data augmentation techniques by considering approximate symmetries in discrete MDPs, providing a fresh perspective on data efficiency in the domain of ORL. We scrutinize the adaptability and resilience of these established methodologies in varied stochastic environments, featuring alterations in transition probabilities with respect to the already tested stochastic environments. Key findings from these investigations elucidate the potential of approximate symmetries for the data augmentation process and confirm the robustness of the existing methods under altered stochastic conditions. Our analysis reinforces the applicability of the established symmetry detection techniques in diverse scenarios while opening new horizons for enhancing the efficiency of ORL models.

Keywords: Offline reinforcement learning · Approximate symmetries · Data augmentation

1 Introduction

Offline Reinforcement Learning (ORL) aims to obtain a performing policy for an agent, using only a fixed data set of pre-collected experiences and hence without further interaction with the environment [2, 15, 24]. The mathematical framework upon which the ORL framework is defined is that of Markov Decision Processes (MDPs) [18].

Learning or directly solving an MDP from data may not be straightforward [15]. Notwithstanding, sometimes the state-action space of the sequential decision-making problem is endowed with a particular structure that allows putting sets of states and actions into peculiar classes of equivalence. Once these classes of equivalence have been established, one could consider a *simpler* (smaller) MDP whose state-action pairs are just representatives of the said classes. The simpler MDP is called an *abstraction* (see Fig. 1). Planning in the abstraction would be easier than planning in the original model. Moreover, up to an appropriate transformation, by construction, every policy obtained in the abstraction can be deployed into the original decision process without loss in performance.

A. P. Rocha et al. (Eds.): ICAART 2023, LNAI 14546, pp. 164–186, 2024.
https://doi.org/10.1007/978-3-031-55326-4_8

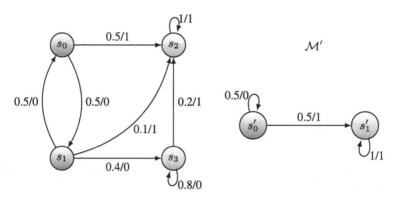

Fig. 1. Representation of an MDP $\mathcal{M}$ (left) and its abstraction $\mathcal{M}'$ (right). Both MDPs have different number of states but the same number of actions. The states s_0 and s_1 of $\mathcal{M}$ are mapped to s_0' in $\mathcal{M}'$ (blue) while s_2 and s_3 are mapped to s_1' (red). Transition between states are shown with black arrow and probability of transition with respect to the two actions are displayed aside the arrows. The probability of transition with the first action is displayed in blue and the probability of transition with the second action is shown in red. The same reward is assigned to states and actions of the same combination of *colors*. Planning in $\mathcal{M}'$ provides the same optimal policy than planning in $\mathcal{M}$ after lifting. (Color figure online)

The interest in abstraction schemes rose with the hope of reducing a complex, continuous states MDP into a discrete more tractable one [5,20,21,32].

Several schemes of abstraction have been proposed during the years [16], among many we mention:

1. abstractions preserving the complete model, *e.g. homomorphisms* [8], *symmetries* [25] and *bisimulation* [11];
2. abstractions that approximate the original model up to a given error, *e.g. approximate homomorphisms* [26] and *bisimulation metrics* [10].

As far as it concerns the first class, the works in [8,11] introduced the notions of MDP homomorphism (structure-preserving maps between the original MDP and one characterized by a factored representation) and stochastic bisimulation to automatically partition the state space of an MDP and to find aggregated and factored representations. For those of the second class, [25] extended the previous works on state abstractions to include the concept of symmetry. Subsequently, the work in [26] considered approximate homomorphisms. It is worth reporting the definition of homomorphism in an MDP.

Definition 1 (MDP Homomorphism). *An MDP homomorphism* h *[26] from an MDP* $M = \langle \mathcal{S}, \mathcal{A}, T, R, \gamma \rangle$ *to an MDP* $M' = \langle \mathcal{S}', \mathcal{A}', T', R', \gamma \rangle$ *is a surjection from* $\mathcal{S} \times \mathcal{A}$ *to* $\mathcal{S}' \times \mathcal{A}'$ *, defined by a tuple of surjections* (f, g)*, with* $h(s, a) = \big(f(s), g(a)\big)$*, where* $f : \mathcal{S} \to \mathcal{S}'$ *and* $g : \mathcal{A} \to \mathcal{A}'$ *such that* $\forall (s, s') \in \mathcal{S}^2, a \in \mathcal{A}$:

$$T'\big(f(s), g(a), f(s')\big) = \sum_{s'' \in [s']_f} T(s, a, s''), \tag{1}$$

$$R'\big(f(s), g(a)\big) = R(s, a). \tag{2}$$

where $[s']_f = f^{-1}\big(\{f(s')\}\big)$, i.e. $[s']_f$ is the set of states for which the application of f results in the state $f(s') \in \mathcal{S}'$.

Later on, [22] showed that the fully automatic discovery of symmetries in a discrete MDP is as hard as verifying whether two graphs are isomorphic. Concurrently, [29] relaxed the notion of bisimulation to allow for the attainment of performance bounds for approximate MDP homomorphisms. Approximate homomorphisms are of particular interest in continuous state MDPs where a hard mapping to an aggregated representation could be impractical. In this context, [10] developed a bisimulation pseudometric to extend the concept of bisimulation relation. The automatic discovery of representations using the bisimulation pseudometric has been investigated in recent years using DNNs and obtaining theoretical guarantees for such a methodology [1,7,27]. From a different perspective, [17] developed an algorithm that aims to cluster MDPs states in a Bayesian sense to solve the MDP in a more data-efficient way, even when an underlying homomorphic or symmetric structure is not present. Recently, [30] used a contrastive loss function that enforces action equivariance on a to-be-learned representation of an MDP. Their approach resulted in the automatic learning of a structured latent space which can be used to plan in a more data-efficient fashion. Finally, [31] introduced MDP Invariant Networks, a specific class of DNN architectures that guarantees by construction that the optimal MDP control policy obtained through other Deep RL approaches will be invariant under some set of symmetric transformations and hence providing more sample efficiency to the baseline when the symmetry is present.

In the context of offline learning, knowledge of these structures prior to training can be exploited by practitioners to improve and augment the batch [2,3]. Information extrapolated from some transitions could be valid for all state-action pairs in the same class of equivalence, including those unexplored in the batch. Therefore, a method to detect a homomorphism or symmetry, even if not fully automatic, could be a useful tool [2,3]. Let us provide a definition of symmetry in an MDP.

Definition 2 (MDP Symmetry). *Given an MDP $\mathcal{M}$, let k be a surjection on $\mathcal{S} \times \mathcal{A} \times \mathcal{S}$ such that $k(s, a, s') = \big(k_\sigma(s, a, s'), k_\alpha(s, a, s'), k_{\sigma'}(s, a, s')\big) \in \mathcal{S} \times \mathcal{A} \times \mathcal{S}$. Let $(T \circ k)(s, a, s') = T\big(k(s, a, s')\big)$. k is a symmetry if $\forall (s, s') \in \mathcal{S}^2$, $a \in \mathcal{A}$ both T and R are invariant with respect to the image of k:*

$$(T \circ k)(s, a, s') = T(s, a, s'), \tag{3}$$

$$R\big(k_\sigma(s, a, s'), k_\alpha(s, a, s')\big) = R(s, a). \tag{4}$$

If $k_\sigma = k_{\sigma'}$ then an MDP symmetry is also an MDP homomorphism. On one hand, the studies by [30,31] demonstrated that constraining the learning process of the obtainable Q-value function using a valid symmetry results in convergence of the estimate with fewer samples. However, in this approach, valid symmetries were provided by an oracle. On the other hand, it has been established that the fully automatic discovery of homomorphisms in a finite MDP constitutes a graph isomorphism complete problem [22].

In this context, the research questions that we answered in previous works [3,4] were the following:

1. *Is it possible to develop a method for expert-guided detection of alleged symmetries in the context of offline learning?*
2. *Is Data Augmentation exploiting a detected symmetry beneficial to the learning of an MDP policy in the offline context?*

Contribution. The contribution of this work is to show that the method proposed in our previous works [3,4], based on Density Estimation statistical techniques to validate the presence of an *expert-given, alleged* symmetry in an MDP to subsequently augment the data set before offline learning, can not only work with *approximate* symmetries but is also stable with respect to variations in the probabilities of transitions of the stochastic environment tested in our previous work [4].

To clarify the motivations, we present an intuitive example below.

One of the most emblematic examples is checking whether or not a dynamical system is symmetric with respect to a specific transformation of the system of reference. Consequently, we aim to exploit this symmetry for more efficient learning. For instance, consider the well-known CartPole domain of the OpenAI's Gym Learning Suite [6]. In CartPole, the purpose of the automated agent is to prevent a rotating pole situated on a sliding cart from falling due to gravity. The state of the system is expressed as a tuple $s = (x, v, \alpha, \omega)$ where x is the position of the cart with respect to a horizontal track upon which it can slide, v is its longitudinal velocity, α is the angle between the rotating pole and the axis pointing along the direction of the gravitational acceleration, and ω the angular velocity of the pole. The agent can push the cart left ($\leftarrow$) or right ($\rightarrow$) at every time step (in the negative or positive direction of the track) providing to the system a fixed momentum $|p|$. A pictorial representation of a state-action pair (s_t, a_t) can be found in Fig. 2.

Let us suppose there exists a function $h : \mathcal{S} \times \mathcal{A} \rightarrow \mathcal{S} \times \mathcal{A}$ that maps a state-action pair (s_t, a_t) to $(k_\sigma(s_t), k_\alpha(a_t))$, where $k_\sigma : \mathcal{S} \rightarrow \mathcal{S}$ and $k_\alpha : \mathcal{A} \rightarrow \mathcal{A}$, such that the dynamics of the pair (s, a) is the same as the one of $h(s, a)$. Note that in this example, the system dynamics is symmetric with respect to a flip around the vertical axis. In other words, its dynamics is invariant by multiplication by minus one, assuming that if $a =\leftarrow$ then $k_\alpha(a) = -a =\rightarrow$ and vice versa. Indeed, if the state-action pair (s_t, a_t) leads to the state s_{t+1}, this property will imply that $h(s_t, a_t) = (-s_t, -a_t)$ leads to $k_\sigma(s_{t+1}) = -s_{t+1}$.

When learning the dynamics from a finite batch of experiences (or trajectories), resulting in a set of transitions $\mathcal{D} = \left\{ (s_i, a_i, s_i') \right\}_{i=1}^n$ with $n \in \mathbb{N}$ being the size of the batch, we might, for instance, fit a function to predict the next state in a transition $\hat{s}(s, a) = s'$ to minimize a loss, *e.g.* the Mean Squared Error. However, imagine that in the batch $\mathcal{D}$ there were many transitions regarding the part of the state-action space with $x > 0$ and very few with $x < 0$. Unfortunately, we may learn a good model to forecast what will happen when the cart is at the right of the origin and a very poor model at its

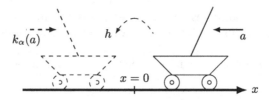

Fig. 2. The cart in the right is a representation of a CartPole's state s_t with $x_t > 0$ and action $a_t = \leftarrow$. The dashed cart in the left is the image of (s_t, a_t) under the transformation h which inverses state $k_\sigma(s) = -s$ and action $k_\alpha(a) = -a$. Example taken from the work in [3].

left side. We can then suppose that also a control policy will perform well when $x > 0$ and poorly when $x < 0$. Nevertheless, if it were possible to be confident of the existence of the symmetry $k_\sigma(s, a, s') = -s$ and $k_\alpha(s, a, s') = -a$ (where the opposite of the action a is the transformation stated above), we might extend the batch of experiences without additional interaction with the system, and then improve the accuracy of the model also to the regions where $x < 0$.

With this motivation in mind, in the next section, we present density estimation methods that assist in learning the likelihood of any transition given the starting data set.

2   Density Estimation Methods and Normalizing Flows

To verify the presence of a symmetry, a preliminary estimate of the transition model is needed. More specifically, we first perform a probabily mass function (pmf) estimation or a pdf estimation of the transitions in the batch $\mathcal{D}$ depending on the typology of the MDP we are tackling (respectively discrete or continuous). In the discrete case, this amounts to learning a set of discrete distributions. In the continuous case, we can use approaches of the literature to approximate the transition function, such as Normalizing Flows [9,13]. A Normalizing Flow is a DNN architecture that allows us to approximate a pdf while being able to compute an analytically estimated density value for new samples.

In this way, once a pmf/pdf has been estimated from the batch of transitions $\mathcal{D}$, we can compute the probability of an alleged symmetric transition that is supposed to be sampled from the same distribution. When the probability (or the density in the continuous case) is greater than a given threshold for a high fraction of samples, we decide to *trust* in the presence of this alleged symmetry and augment the batch by including the symmetric transitions. In the end, the dynamics of the model is learned over the augmented data set. When the approach detects a symmetry that is present in the true environment, the accuracy of the learned model increases; otherwise, the procedure could also result in detrimental effects.

Probability Mass Function Estimation for Discrete MDPs. Let $\mathcal{D} = \{(s_i, a_i, s_i')\}_{i=1}^n$ be a batch of recorded transitions. Performing mass estimation over $\mathcal{D}$ amounts to compute the probabilities that define the unknown discrete transition distribution T by estimating the frequencies of transition in $\mathcal{D}$. In other words, we compute

$$\hat{T}(s,a,s') = \frac{\sum_{i=0}^{N} \delta_{s_i,s}\delta_{a_i,a}\delta_{s_{i+1},s'}}{\sum_{j=0}^{N} \delta_{s_j,s}\delta_{a_j,a}}.\tag{5}$$

Probability Density Function Estimation for Continuous MDPs. Performing density estimation over $\mathcal{D}$ amounts to finding an analytical expression for the probability density of a transition (s,a,s') given $\mathcal{D}$: $\mathcal{L}(s,a,s'|\mathcal{D})$. Normalizing flows [9,13] allow defining a parametric flow of continuous transformations that reshapes a known pdf (*e.g.* a multivariate Gaussian) to one that best fits the data. Since the transformations are known, the Jacobians are computable at every step and the probability value can always be assessed [9].

3 Proposed Paradigm and Flowchart

In our previous works [3,4], we proposed a paradigm to check whether the dynamics of a to-be-learned (i) discrete MDP (see Algorithm 1) or (ii) a continuous MDP (see Algorithm 2) are endowed with the invariance with respect to some transformation. A pseudo representation of the flow chart of the algorithms is shown in Fig. 3.

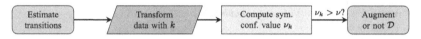

Fig. 3. Pseudo flow chart of Algorithms 1 and 2.

Paradigm Summary. The paradigm can be summarized as follows:

1. An expert presumes that a to-be-learned model is endowed with the invariance of T with respect to a transformation k;
2. She/He computes the probability function estimation based on the batch $\mathcal{D}$:
   (a) (discrete case) She/He computes $\hat{T}$, an estimate of T, using the transitions in a batch $\mathcal{D}$ by applying 5;
   (b) (continuous case) She/He performs Density Estimation over $\mathcal{D}$ using Normalizing Flows;
3. She/He applies k to all transitions $(s,a,s') \in \mathcal{D}$ and then checks whether the symmetry confidence value ν_k
   (a) (discrete case) using 12 is smaller than the confidence threshold ν;
   (b) (continuous case) of probability values $\mathcal{L}$ evaluated on $k(\mathcal{D})$ exceeds a threshold θ that corresponds to the $q-$order quantile of the distribution of probability values evaluated on the original batch. The quantile order q is given as an input to the procedure by an expert (see Algorithm 2);
4. If the last condition is fulfilled, then $\mathcal{D}$ is augmented with $k(\mathcal{D})$.

   Notice that

$$0 < d_k(s,a,s') \le 1 \quad \forall (s,a,s') \in \mathcal{S} \times \mathcal{A} \times \mathcal{S}.\tag{6}$$

It is worth noting that since $\nu_k \in [0, 1]$, it can be interpreted as the probability that k is a symmetry. Therefore, one could consider ν as a classification threshold and set it, for example, to 0.5 (binary classification). Moreover, keep in mind that once a transformation k is detected as a symmetry, the data set is potentially augmented with transitions that are not present in the original batch, injecting hence unseen and completely novel information into the data set.

Explanation of the Procedure. Let $\mathcal{M}$ be a deterministic MDP, let $\mathcal{D}$ be a batch of pre-collected transitions, and let k be an alleged symmetric transformation of $\mathcal{M}$'s dynamics.

Algorithm 1. Symmetry detection and data augmenting in a discrete MDP.

    Input: Batch of transitions $\mathcal{D}$, k alleged symmetry
    Output: Possibly augmented batch $\mathcal{D} \cup \mathcal{D}_k$
1 $\hat{T} \leftarrow$ Most Likely Categorical pmf from $\mathcal{D}$
2 $\nu_k = 1 - \dfrac{1}{|\mathcal{D}|} \displaystyle\sum_{(s,a,s') \in \mathcal{D}} d_k(s, a, s')$ *(where d_k is defined in Equation 11)*
3 **if** $\nu_k > 0.5$ **then**
4 | $\mathcal{D}_k = k(\mathcal{D})$ *(alleged symmetric samples)*
5 | **return** $\mathcal{D} \cup \mathcal{D}_k$ *(the augmented batch)*
6 **else**
7 | **return** $\mathcal{D}$ *(the original batch)*
8 **end**

In order to check whether k can be considered or not as a symmetry of the dynamics, in the discrete case, we will first estimate the most likely set of transition distributions $\hat{T}$ given the batch of transitions (Line 1, Algorithm 1) while in the continuous case we will estimate the density of transition in the batch obtaining the probability density value $\mathcal{L}(s, a, s'|\mathcal{D})$ (Line 1, Algorithm 2). In the continuous case, we will then compute the density value of every transition $(s, a, s') \in \mathcal{D}$, resulting in a set of real values from $\mathcal{L}$ denoted by Λ (Line 2, Algorithm 2). We will select the q-order quantile of Λ to be a threshold $\theta \in \mathbb{R}$ (Line 3, Algorithm 2) that will determine whether we can trust the symmetry to be present, and hence to augment or not the starting batch. Next, we will map any $(s, a, s') \in \mathcal{D}$ to its alleged symmetric image $\big(k_\sigma(s, a, s'), k_\alpha(s, a, s'), k_{\sigma'}(s, a, s')\big)$ (Line 4, Algorithm 2). The map of $\mathcal{D}$ under the transformation k will be denoted as $\mathcal{D}_k$. Let then, $\forall (s, a, s') \in \mathcal{D}_k$, $\mathcal{L}(s, a, s'|\mathcal{D})$ be the probability density of the symmetric image of a transition in the batch. We will assume that the system dynamics is invariant under the transformation k if ν_k, the percentage of transitions whose density is greater than θ, is bigger than the percentage threshold ν (Lines 5–10, Algorithm 2). In the discrete case, a complex estimate of a distance between probability distributions is needed to assess if the sampled transitions would be likely to have been generated also after the application of an alleged symmetric transformation (see Subsect. 4.1 for more details and Line 2 in Algorithm 1). If data augmenting is performed, the boosted batch $\mathcal{D} \cup \mathcal{D}_k$ will be returned as output.

This proposed paradigm offers a systematic way to check for the invariance of dynamics with respect to a given transformation, potentially allowing for improved learning and more efficient exploration of the state and action spaces. By identifying symmetries and augmenting the dataset with novel information, this method can contribute to more effective reinforcement learning algorithms and ultimately better decision-making processes in complex environments.

Algorithm 2. Symmetry detection and data augmenting in a continuous MDP with detection threshold $\nu = 0.5$.

    Input: Batch of transitions $\mathcal{D}$, $q \in [0, 1)$ order of the quantile, k alleged symmetry

    Output: Possibly augmented batch $\mathcal{D} \cup \mathcal{D}_k$

1 $\mathcal{L} \leftarrow$ Density Estimate $(\mathcal{D})$ *(e.g. with Normalizing Flows)*

2 $\Lambda \leftarrow$ Distribution $\mathcal{L}(\mathcal{D})$ *($\mathcal{L}$ evaluated over $\mathcal{D}$)*

3 $\theta = q$-order quantile of Λ

4 $\mathcal{D}_k = k(\mathcal{D})$ *(alleged symmetric samples)*

5 $\nu_k = \dfrac{1}{|\mathcal{D}_k|} \displaystyle\sum_{(s,a,s') \in \mathcal{D}_k} \mathbb{1}_{\{\mathcal{L}(s,a,s'|\mathcal{D}) > \theta\}}$

6 **if** $\nu_k > 0.5$ **then**

7 | **return** $\mathcal{D} \cup \mathcal{D}_k$ *(the augmented batch)*

8 **else**

9 | **return** $\mathcal{D}$ *(the original batch)*

10 **end**

---

4 Expert-Guided Symmetry Discovery

4.1 Discrete MDPs

For the method to work in both deterministic and stochastic environments, we need to measure the distance between distributions. Estimating a distance in distribution is considered in the version of the approach that addresses continuous environments, as learning a distribution over transitions represented by their features is independent of the nature of the dynamics. However, when dealing with categorical states, the notion of distance between features cannot be exploited.

We propose to compute the percentage ν_k relying on a distance between discrete probability distributions. Since the transformation k is a surjection on transition tuples, we do not know a-priori the correct mapping $k_{\sigma'}(s, a, s') \; \forall s' \in \mathcal{S}$. In other words, we can compute $k_{\sigma'}$, the symmetric image of s', only when we receive the entire tuple (s, a, s') as input, as an inverse mapping might not exist.

Therefore, as prescribed in our previous work [4], we will resort to computing a *pessimistic* approximation of the Total Variational Distance (proportional to the L^1-norm). Specifically, given (s, a, s'), we aim to calculate the Chebyshev distance (the L^∞-norm) between $T(s, a, \cdot)$ and $T(k_\sigma(s, a, s'), k_\alpha(s, a, s'), \cdot)$. Recall that given two vectors of dimension d, x and y both $\in \mathbb{R}^d$, $||x - y||_\infty \leq ||x - y||_1$.

Let us then define the following four functions:

$$m(s, a, s') = \min_{\bar{s} \in \mathcal{S} \setminus \{s'\} : \hat{T} \neq 0} \hat{T}(s, a, \bar{s}) \tag{7}$$

$$M(s, a, s') = \max_{\bar{s} \in \mathcal{S} \setminus \{s'\}} \hat{T}(s, a, \bar{s}), \tag{8}$$

$$m_k(s, a, s') = \min_{\substack{\bar{s} \in \mathcal{S} \text{ s.t.} \\ \bar{s} \neq k_{\sigma'}(s,a,s') \\ \text{and } \hat{T} \circ k \neq 0}} \hat{T}\big(k_\sigma(s, a, s'), k_\alpha(s, a, s'), \bar{s}\big), \tag{9}$$

$$M_k(s, a, s') = \max_{\substack{\bar{s} \in \mathcal{S} \text{ s.t.} \\ \bar{s} \neq k_{\sigma'}(s,a,s')}} \hat{T}\big(k_\sigma(s, a, s'), k_\alpha(s, a, s'), \bar{s}\big) \tag{10}$$

where m (M) and m_k (M_k) are the minimum (maximum) of the probability mass function (pmf) $\hat{T}$ when evaluated respectively on an initial state and action (s, a) and $\big(k_\sigma(s, a, s'), k_\alpha(s, a, s')\big)$ for which $\hat{T} \neq 0$.

To make Eqs. 7 to 10 work even on deterministic or sparse $\hat{T}$, instead of excluding zero values we add a small pseudo-count $0 < \varepsilon \leq 10^{-6}$ to all possible transitions before normalization when learning $\hat{T}$ (line 1 of Algorithm 1).

To approximate the Chebyshev distance between $\hat{T}(s, a, \cdot)$ and $\hat{T}(k_\sigma(s, a, s'), k_\alpha(s, a, s'), \cdot)$, we define a pessimistic approximation d_k as follows:

$$d_k(s, a, s') = \max \Big\{ \underbrace{\big|M(s, a, s') - m_k(s, a, s')\big|}_{(I)},$$

$$\underbrace{\big|M_k(s, a, s') - m(s, a, s')\big|}_{(II)}, \tag{11}$$

$$\underbrace{\big|\hat{T}(s, a, s') - (\hat{T} \circ k)(s, a, s')\big|}_{(III)} \Big\}.$$

For the moment, consider $\hat{T}(s, a, \cdot)$ and $\hat{T}(k_\sigma(s, a, s'), k_\alpha(s, a, s'), \cdot)$ just as two sets of numbers. Remove the value corresponding to s' from the first set and the one corresponding to $k_{\sigma'}(s, a, s')$ from the second set. Taking the max between (I) and (II) just equates to selecting the maximum possible difference between any two values of these modified sets. Equation 11 tells us to select the worst possible case since we do not know which permutations of states we should compare when computing the Chebyshev distance.

We remove s' from $\hat{T}(s, a, \cdot)$ and $k_{\sigma'}(s, a, s')$ from $\hat{T}(k_\sigma(s, a, s'), k_\alpha(s, a, s'), \cdot)$ because we hypothesize that k maps (s, a, s') to $(k_\sigma(s, a, s'), k_\alpha(s, a, s'), k_{\sigma'}(s, a, s'))$, and thus, we can compare those values directly (III).

In detail, the symmetry confidence value ν_k used in Line 2 of Algorithm 1 is defined as:

$$\nu_k(\mathcal{D}) = 1 - \frac{1}{|\mathcal{D}|} \sum_{(s,a,s') \in \mathcal{D}} d_k(s, a, s'). \tag{12}$$

Extreme Case Scenario. Is Eq. 11 *Too Pessimistic?* Consider that for a given state action couple $(\bar{s}, \bar{a})$, we have a transition distributed over 3 states $s \in \mathcal{S} = \{One, Two, Three\}$ with probabilities $T(\bar{s}, \bar{a}, One) = 0.01$, $T(\bar{s}, \bar{a}, Two) = 0.01$ and $T(\bar{s}, \bar{a}, Three) = 0.98$. Now, assume the estimate of the transition function is perfect. Does the distance in Eq. 11 converge to 0? Not always, but what matters for the detection of symmetries is the average of the distances over the entire batch (Eq. 12). Suppose that these probabilities were inferred from a batch with the transition $(\bar{s}, \bar{a}, One)$ once, $(\bar{s}, \bar{a}, Two)$ once and $(\bar{s}, \bar{a}, Three)$ ninety-eight times. Consider $(\bar{s}, \bar{a}, Three)$. $M(\bar{s}, \bar{a}, Three) = M_k(\bar{s}, \bar{a}, Three) = m(\bar{s}, \bar{a}, Three) = m_k(\bar{s}, \bar{a}, Three) = 0.01$. Following 11, $d_k(\bar{s}, \bar{a}, Three) = 0$. However, $d_k(\bar{s}, \bar{a}, One) = d_k(\bar{s}, \bar{a}, Two) = 0.97$, which is a too pessimistic estimate. Nonetheless, let us calculate ν_k (Eq. 12). For this state-action pair $(\bar{s}, \bar{a})$, the average over the batch is: $(d_k(\bar{s}, \bar{a}, One) + d_k(\bar{s}, \bar{a}, Two) + 98d_k(\bar{s}, \bar{a}, Three))/100 = 0.0194$. If the estimation is the same for other pairs (s, a), then $\nu_k = 1 - 0.0194 = 0.9806$. This is a value close to 1, suggesting k is a symmetry.

4.2 Continuous MDPs

Figure 4 provides an intuition about Algorithm 2. The intuition behind the approach in the continuous case is that if in the original batch $\mathcal{D}$ the density of transitions that are *"not so different"* from some of the symmetric images $\mathcal{D}_k$ of $\mathcal{D}$, then $\mathcal{L}(\mathcal{D}_k|\mathcal{D})$ will not be *"too small"*. How small is small when we are considering real-valued, continuous pdf? In order to insert a comparable scale, we take the threshold θ to be a q-quantile of the set of the estimated density values of the transitions in the original batch $\mathcal{D}$, *i.e.* $\{\mathcal{L}(s, a, s' \mid \mathcal{D}) \mid (s, a, s') \in \mathcal{D}\}$. It goes without saying that since the purpose of

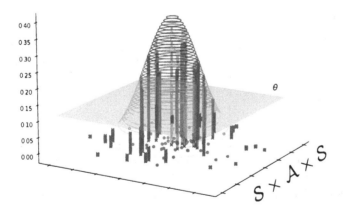

Fig. 4. Intuition for the continuous case [3]. The xy plane is the space of transitions $\mathcal{S} \times \mathcal{A} \times \mathcal{S}$, the z axis is $\mathcal{L}$, the value of the probability density of a given transition. The red points represent $\mathcal{D}$, the blue crosses $\mathcal{D}_k$ for a given transformation k. We display as a red contour plot the pdf $\mathcal{L}$ learned in Line 1 of Algorithm 2. The orange hyperplane has height θ which is the threshold computed in Line 3 of Algorithm 2. The blue vertical bars have as height the value of $\mathcal{L}$ evaluated for that specific transition. The algorithm counts the fraction ν_k of samples (blue crosses) that have a vertical bar higher than the hyperplane. (Color figure online)

Algorithm 2 is to perform data augmentation, it is necessary to select a small q-order quantile; otherwise, the procedure would bear no meaning. It would be pointless to augment the batch with transitions that are already very likely in the original one (see Fig. 5). In this case, we would not insert any new information.

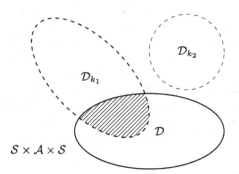

Fig. 5. Representation of the support in $\mathcal{S}^2 \times \mathcal{A}$ of the of $\mathcal{D}$, $\mathcal{D}_{k_1}$ and $\mathcal{D}_{k_2}$. k_1 and k_2 are two different alleged transformations. The shape and position of the sets are determined by the log-likelihood of the density estimate $\mathcal{L}$ and the quantile threshold θ. It is worth noting that $\mathcal{D}_{k_1} \cap \mathcal{D} \neq \varnothing$ and $\mathcal{D}_{k_2} \cap \mathcal{D} = \varnothing$. If the user-chosen percentage threshold ν is taken into account, then k_1 may be detected as a symmetry while k_2 is not. If k_1 is indeed detected as a symmetry, then augmenting the data in $\mathcal{D}$ with $\mathcal{D}_{k_1}$ involves training the model on the combined dataset $\mathcal{D} \cup \mathcal{D}_{k_1}$. It is important to note that the data in $\mathcal{D}_{k_1} \setminus \mathcal{D}$ are not present in the original batch $\mathcal{D}$. Figure taken from the work in [3].

5   Experiments

We test the algorithm in one discrete grid environment, with and without periodic boundary conditions, and in a *stochastic* version of two famous environments of OpenAI's Gym Learning Suite: CartPole and Acrobot.

5.1   Environments

In the next subsections, we describe the environments and the proposed transformations k. It is worth noting that sometimes we use a contracted notation to indicate k_α. Let a_1, a_2, a_3, a_4 represent some actions $\in \mathcal{A}$, for semplicity we denote $g(a_1, a_2, \dots) = (a_3, a_4, \dots)$ to indicate $k_\alpha(s, a_1, s') = a_3, k_\alpha(s, a_2, s') = a_4, \dots$, etc.

Discrete Environments

Stochastic Toroidal Grid. In this environment, the agent can move along fixed directions over a torus by acting with any $a \in \mathcal{A} = \{\uparrow, \downarrow, \leftarrow, \rightarrow\}$. However, when intending to head towards a chosen direction, the agent could slip and end up somewhere else (with a fixed probability), *i.e.* in the opposite direction, to its left, or to its right. We

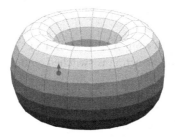

Fig. 6. Representation of the Grid Environment. The red dot is the position of a state s on the torus. The displacement obtained by acting with action $a = \uparrow$ is shown as a red arrow. (Color figure online)

Table 1. Stochastic Toroidal Grid: transition probabilities for the four variants.

Variant	Intended direction	Opposite direction	Orthogonal direction
1	60%	20%	10%
2	75%	15%	5%
3	90%	5%	2.5%
4	100%	0%	0%

conducted the experiments in four different variants of this environment characterized by different transition probabilities (see Table 1). In the first variant, when performing an action, the agent has a 60% chance of moving to the intended direction, a 20% chance to move to the opposite one, and a 10% chance along an orthogonal direction. In the second variant, when acting, the agent has a 75% chance of moving to the intended direction, a 15% chance to move to the opposite one, and a 5% chance along an orthogonal direction. In the third variant, the probabilities are, respectively, 90%, 5%, and $2, 5\%$. In the fourth variant, the agent does not slip and always can move to the wanted direction with a 100% probability. For every variant, we collect $z = 10$ sets of $M = 100$ batches, with respectively $N = 1000 \times i_z$ steps in each batch (i_z going from 1 to z). The positions on the torus are the states $s = (i, j)$, and the set S is represented as a grid of fixed side $l = 10$ and periodic boundary conditions (see Fig. 6). Since there are no obstacles, this environment is endowed with many symmetric transformations and therefore can serve as a useful proof-of-concept.

We tested Algorithm 1 with six different alleged transformations k in a Grid with size $l^2 = 100$ over $N = 50$ different simulations.

1. **Time Reversal Symmetry with Action Inversion (TRSAI).** Assuming that $\downarrow$ is the reverse of $\uparrow$ and $\leftarrow$ is the reverse of $\rightarrow$, we proposed the following transformation: $k = \big(k_\sigma(s, a, s') = s', g(\uparrow, \downarrow, \leftarrow, \rightarrow) = (\downarrow, \uparrow, \rightarrow, \leftarrow), k_{\sigma'}(s, a, s') = s\big)$.
2. **Same Dynamics with Action Inversion (SDAI).** $k = \big(k_\sigma(s, a, s') = s, g(\uparrow, \downarrow, \leftarrow, \rightarrow) = (\downarrow, \uparrow, \rightarrow, \leftarrow), k_{\sigma'}(s, a, s') = s'\big)$.
3. **Opposite Dynamics and Action Inversion (ODAI):** $k = \big(k_\sigma(s, a, s') = s, g(\uparrow, \downarrow, \leftarrow, \rightarrow) = (\downarrow, \uparrow, \rightarrow, \leftarrow), k_{\sigma'}(s, a, s) = s' \mp (2, 0) \vee (0, 2)\big)$. In other words,

we revert the action but also the final state is changed to reproduce the correct destination.

4. **Opposite Dynamics but Wrong Action (ODWA).** The alleged transformation is like the one of Point 3, but the action is switched on the wrong axis, *e.g.* $g(\uparrow) = \rightarrow$).

5. **Translation invariance (TI).** $k = \left(k_\sigma(s, a, s') = s', g(\uparrow, \downarrow, \leftarrow, \rightarrow) = (\uparrow, \downarrow, \leftarrow, \rightarrow), k_{\sigma'}(s, a, s') = s' \pm (1, 0) \vee (0, 1)\right)$.

6. **Translation Invariance with Opposite Dynamics (TIOD).** In this case, the action is the same as Point 5, but the agent returns to the previous state.

The said transformations are resumed in Table 2.

Table 2. Stochastic Toroidal Grid: proposed transformations and label.

k	Label
$k_\sigma(s, a, s') = s'$ $k_\alpha(s, a = (\uparrow, \downarrow, \leftarrow, \rightarrow), s') = (\downarrow, \uparrow, \rightarrow, \leftarrow)$ $k_{\sigma'}(s, a, s') = s$	**TRSAI**
$k_\sigma(s, a, s') = s$ $k_\alpha(s, a = (\uparrow, \downarrow, \leftarrow, \rightarrow), s') = (\downarrow, \uparrow, \rightarrow, \leftarrow)$ $k_{\sigma'}(s, a, s') = s'$	SDAI
$k_\sigma(s, a, s') = s$ $k_\alpha(s, a = (\uparrow, \downarrow, \leftarrow, \rightarrow), s') = (\downarrow, \uparrow, \rightarrow, \leftarrow)$ $k_{\sigma'}(s, a = (\uparrow, \downarrow, \leftarrow, \rightarrow), s') =$ $(s' - (0, 2), s' + (0, 2), s' + (2, 0), s' - (2, 0))$	**ODAI**
$k_\sigma(s, a, s') = s$ $k_\alpha(s, a = (\uparrow, \downarrow, \leftarrow, \rightarrow), s') = (\rightarrow, \leftarrow, \uparrow, \downarrow)$ $k_{\sigma'}(s, a = (\uparrow, \downarrow, \leftarrow, \rightarrow), s') =$ $(s' - (0, 2), s' + (0, 2), s' + (2, 0), s' - (2, 0))$	ODWA
$k_\sigma(s, a, s') = s'$ $k_\alpha(s, a, s') = a$ $k_{\sigma'}(s, a = (\uparrow, \downarrow, \leftarrow, \rightarrow), s') =$ $(s' + (0, 1), s' - (0, 1), s' - (1, 0), s' + (1, 0))$	**TI**
$k_\sigma(s, a, s') = s'$ $k_\alpha(s, a, s') = a$ $k_{\sigma'}(s, a, s') = s$	TIOD

Deterministic Grid with Boundaries. This environment is a classic deterministic Grid with side $l = 10$ and $l^2 = 100$ the number of cells. As in the previous case, the agent can move along fixed directions by acting with any $a \in \mathcal{A} = \{\uparrow, \downarrow, \leftarrow, \rightarrow\}$. The outcome of the actions is deterministic, *i.e.* every action has a 100% probability of success. It is worth noting that this grid has boundaries, and therefore when the agent will try to cross any boundaries, it will instead stay in the same spot. The valid symmetries proposed for the Stochastic Grid environment are, in this scenario, only approximately valid, since they are broken for states next to the boundaries, but valid anywhere else. After collecting data in the same fashion as for the Stochastic Toroidal Grid environment, we tested Algorithm 1 with the very same six different alleged transformations k over $N = 50$ different simulations.

Continuous Environments

Stochastic CartPole. As previously stated, the dynamics of CartPole is invariant with respect to the transformation $k = (k_\sigma(s, a, s') = -s, k_a(s, a, s') = -a, k_{\sigma'}(s, a, s') = -s) \forall (s, a, s') \in \mathcal{S} \times \mathcal{A} \times \mathcal{S}$. In order to use Algorithm 2, we first map the actions to real numbers: $\leftarrow = -1.5$ and $\rightarrow = 1.5$. We then normalize every state feature in the range $[-1.5, 1.5]$. The dynamics of Stochastic CartPole is similar to that of CartPole [6], however, the force that the agent uses to push the cart is sampled from a normal distribution with mean f (the force defined in the deterministic version) and standard deviation $\tilde{\sigma} = 2$. We tested Algorithm 2 with four different alleged transformations k over $N = 5$ different simulations, a batch of size $|\mathcal{D}| = 10^3$ collected with a random policy, and a quantile order to compute the thresholds $q = 0.1$.

1. **State and Action Reflection with Respect to an Axis in $x = 0$ (SAR).** Assuming that $\leftarrow$ is the reverse of $\rightarrow$ we proposed the following transformation: $k = \left(k_\sigma(s, a, s') = -s, g(\leftarrow, \rightarrow) = (\rightarrow, \leftarrow), k_{\sigma'}(s, a, s') = -s'\right)$.
2. **Initial State Reflection (ISR).** We then tried the same transformation as before but without reflecting the next state s': $k = \left(k_\sigma(s, a, s') = -s, g(\leftarrow, \rightarrow) = (\rightarrow, \leftarrow), k_{\sigma'}(s, a, s') = s'\right)$.
3. **Action Inversion (AI).** What about reversing only the actions? $k = \left(k_\sigma(s, a, s') = s, g = (\leftarrow, \rightarrow) = (\rightarrow, \leftarrow), k_{\sigma'}(s, a, s') = s'\right)$.
4. **Single Feature Inversion (SFI).** We also tried to reverse only one single feature of the starting state: $k = \left(k_\sigma(s = (x, v, \alpha, \omega), a, s') = (-x, v, \alpha, \omega), g(\leftarrow, \rightarrow) = (\leftarrow, \rightarrow), k_{\sigma'}(s, a, s') = s'\right)$.
5. **Translation Invariance (TI).** We translated the position of the initial state x and that of the final state x' by an arbitrary value (0.3): $k = \left(k_\sigma(s = (x, v, \alpha, \omega), a, s') = (x + 0.3, v, \alpha, \omega), g(\leftarrow, \rightarrow) = (\leftarrow, \rightarrow), k_{\sigma'}(s, a, s' = (x', v', \alpha', \omega')) = (x' + 0.3, v', \alpha', \omega')\right)$.

The proposed transformations are resumed in Table 3.

Table 3. Stochastic CartPole. Proposed transformations and labels.

k	Label
$k_\sigma(s, a, s') = -s$ $k_a(s, a = (\leftarrow, \rightarrow), s') = (\rightarrow, \leftarrow)$ $k_{\sigma'}(s, a, s') = -s'$	**SAR**
$k_\sigma(s, a, s') = -s$ $k_a(s, a, s') = a$ $k_{\sigma'}(s, a, s') = s'$	ISR
$k_\sigma(s, a, s') = s$ $k_a(s, a = (\leftarrow, \rightarrow), s') = (\rightarrow, \leftarrow)$ $k_{\sigma'}(s, a, s') = s'$	AI
$k_\sigma(s = (x, ...), a, s') = (-x, ...)$ $k_a(s, a, s') = a$ $k_{\sigma'}(s, a, s') = s'$	SFI
$k_\sigma(s = (x, ...), a, s') = (x + 0.3, ...)$ $k_a(s, a, s') = a$ $k_{\sigma'}(s, a, s' = (x', ...)) = (x' + 0.3, ...)$	**TI**

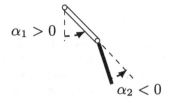

Fig. 7. Representation of a state of the Acrobot environment [3].

Stochastic Acrobot. The Acrobot environment consists of two poles linked with a rotating joint at one end. One of the poles is pinned to a wall with a second rotating joint (see Fig. 7). The system is affected by gravity and hence the poles are hanging down. An agent can apply a negative torque to the lower pole ($a = -1$), a positive one ($a = 1$), or do nothing ($a = 0$). The goal is to push the lower pole as high as possible. The state consists of the sine and cosine of the two rotational joint angles (α_1, α_2) and the joint angular velocities (ω_1, ω_2) : $s = (\sin\alpha_1, \cos\alpha_1, \sin\alpha_2, \cos\alpha_2, \omega_1, \omega_2)$. The dynamics is invariant under the transformation $k = (k_\sigma(s = (\alpha_1, \alpha_2, \omega_1, \omega_2), a, s') = (-\alpha_1, -\alpha_2, -\omega_1, -\omega_2)$ and $k_\alpha(s, a, s') = -a$,

$$k_{\sigma'}(s, a, s' = (\alpha_1', \alpha_2', \omega_1', \omega_2')) = (-\alpha_1', -\alpha_2', -\omega_1', -\omega_2')) \quad \forall (s, a, s') \in \mathcal{S} \times \mathcal{A} \times \mathcal{S}.$$

To apply Algorithm 2 we first normalize the state features and the action in the interval $[-3, 3]$. Stochastic Acrobot is the very same Acrobot of [6] but at every time step a noise ϵ is sampled from a uniform distribution on the interval $[-0.5, 0.5]$ and added to the torque. We tested Algorithm 2 with four different alleged transformations k over $N = 5$ different simulations, a batch of size $|\mathcal{D}| = 10^3$ collected with a random policy, and a quantile order to compute the thresholds $q = 0.1$. The label of the transformations hereafter explained are resumed in Table 4.

Table 4. Acrobot. Proposed transformations and labels.

k	Label
$k_\sigma\left(s = (s_1, s_2, \omega_1, \omega_2, \dots), a, s'\right)$ $= (-s_1, -s_2, -\omega_1, -\omega_2, \dots)$ $k_\alpha(s, a = (-1, 0, 1), s') = (1, 0, -1)$ $k_{\sigma'}\left(s, a, s' = (s_1', s_2', \omega_1', \omega_2', \dots)\right)$ $= (-s_1', -s_2', -\omega_1', -\omega_2', \dots)$	**AAVI**
$k_\sigma\left(s = (c_1, c_2, \omega_1, \omega_2, \dots), a, s'\right)$ $= (-c_1, -c_2, -\omega_1, -\omega_2, \dots)$ $k_\alpha\left(s, a = (-1, 0, 1), s'\right) = (1, 0, -1)$ $k_{\sigma'}\left(s, a, s' = (c_1', c_2', \omega_1', \omega_2', \dots)\right)$ $= (-c_1', -c_2', -\omega_1', -\omega_2', \dots)$	**CAVI**
$k_\sigma(s, a, s') = s$ $k_\alpha\left(s, a = (-1, 0, 1), s'\right) = (1, 0, -1)$ $k_{\sigma'}(s, a, s') = s'$	**AI**
$k_\sigma(s, a, s') = -s$ $k_\alpha\left(s, a, s'\right) = a$ $k_{\sigma'}(s, a, s') = s'$	**SSI**

1. **Angles and Angular Velocities Inversion (AAVI).**
$$k = \big(k_\sigma(s = (\sin\alpha_1, \sin\alpha_2, \cos\alpha_1, \cos\alpha_2, \omega_1, \omega_2), a, s')$$
$$= (-\sin\alpha_1, -\sin\alpha_2, \cos\alpha_1, \cos\alpha_2, -\omega_1, -\omega_2),$$
$$k_\alpha(s, a, s') = -a, k_{\sigma'}(s, a, s' = (\sin\alpha_1', \sin\alpha_2', \cos\alpha_1', \cos\alpha_2', \omega_1', \omega_2'))$$
$$= (-\sin\alpha_1', -\sin\alpha_2', \cos\alpha_1', \cos\alpha_2', -\omega_1', -\omega_2')\big).$$

2. **Cosines and Angular Velocities Inversion (CAVI).**
$$k = \big(k_\sigma(s = (\sin\alpha_1, \sin\alpha_2, \cos\alpha_1, \cos\alpha_2, \omega_1, \omega_2), a, s')$$
$$= (\sin\alpha_1, \sin\alpha_2, -\cos\alpha_1, -\cos\alpha_2, -\omega_1, -\omega_2),$$
$$k_\alpha(s, a, s') = -a, k_{\sigma'}(s, a, s' = (\sin\alpha_1', \sin\alpha_2', \cos\alpha_1', \cos\alpha_2', \omega_1', \omega_2'))$$
$$= (\sin\alpha_1', \sin\alpha_2', -\cos\alpha_1', -\cos\alpha_2', -\omega_1', -\omega_2')\big).$$

3. **Action Inversion (AI).**
$$k = \big(k_\sigma(s, a, s') = s, k_\alpha(s, a, s') = -a, k_{\sigma'}(s, a, s') = s'\big).$$

4. **Starting State Inversion (SSI).**
$$k = \big(k_\sigma(s, a, s') = -s, k_\alpha(s, a, s') = a, k_{\sigma'}(s, a, s') = s'\big).$$

5.2 Setup

We first collect a batch of transitions $\mathcal{D}$ by acting in the environment with a uniform random policy. We suppose the presence of a symmetry k and we try to detect it using Algorithm 1 or Algorithm 2. We report $\overline{\nu}_k$, the average value plus or minus the standard deviation of the quantity ν_k, computed over an ensemble of N different iterations of the procedure (using N distinct batches $\mathcal{D}$). We set the confidence threshold $\nu = 0.5$ since ν_k is normalized between 0 and 1, and can be interpreted as the binary probability of detecting or not a symmetry. However, distinct thresholds ν may yield varying results.

We show the real gain in performance when the policies computed for the model learned using the (augmented) data set eventually deployed in the real environment. The performance metrics are defined in the next paragraphs.

Evaluation of the Performance (Discrete Case). In the end, let ρ be the distribution of initial states $s_0 \in S$ and let the performance u^π of a policy π be $u^\pi = \mathbb{E}_{s \sim \rho}[V^\pi(s)]$. We consider as performance difference the quantity $\Delta U = u^{\hat{\pi}_k} - u^{\hat{\pi}}$. In *discrete* environments, the policies are obtained with Policy Iteration and evaluated with Policy Evaluation.

Evaluation of the Performance (Continuous Case). In *continuous* environments, Offline Learning is not trivial. With the aim of showing that batch augmentation through symmetry detection is beneficial, we resort to two Model-Free Deep RL architectures: DQN [19] and CQL [14] of the d3rlpy learning suite [28] to obtain a policy starting from the batches. The first method originally established the validity of Deep RL and is used in online RL, while the second was specifically developed to address offline RL problems. Convergence of Deep RL training is heavily dependent on hyperparameter tuning, which in turn relies on both the environment and the batch [23]. Therefore, we apply DQN and CQL using the default parameters provided by d3rlpy, adhering more closely to an offline learning setting. This implies that the learning may not always converge to a good policy. We find this philosophy more honest than showing the results obtained with the best seed or the finest-tuned hyperparameters. Each architecture is trained for a number of steps equal to fifty times the number of transitions present in the batch.

5.3 Results

Discrete Environments

Stochastic Toroidal Grid. Detection Phase (ν_k). The proposed algorithm perfectly manages to identify the real symmetries of the environment (see Fig. 8): $\nu_k > 0.5$, $\forall k \in \{\text{TRSAI}, \text{ODAI}, \text{TI}\}$. Moreover, there are no false positives: $\nu_k < 0.5$, $\forall k \in \{\text{SDAI}, \text{ODWA}, \text{TIOD}\}$. We observe that in the first variant, ν_k for a true symmetry saturates around 0.7 as the batch size increases, while ν_k is slightly less than 0.5 for incorrect symmetries (see Fig. 8a). Increasing the probability of moving in the right direction raises the saturation level of ν_k for correct symmetries: 0.75 for the second variant (see Fig. 8b), 0.8 for the third variant (see Fig. 8c), and 1 in the case of a deterministic environment (see Fig. 8d). Similarly, ν_k for an incorrect symmetric transformation decreases when the probability of moving in the right direction increases. In the deterministic variant, $\nu_k = 0$ for all k that are not symmetries.

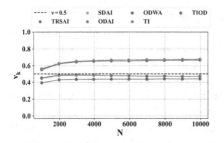

(a) First variant: movement in the intended direction with 60% probability.

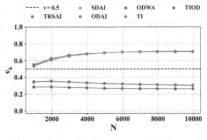

(b) Second variant: movement in the intended direction with 75% probability.

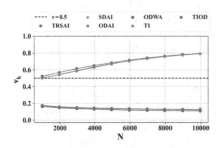

(c) Third variant: movement in the intended direction with 90% probability.

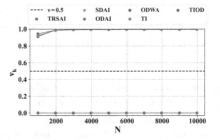

(d) Fourth variant: deterministic environment.

Fig. 8. Stochastic Toroidal Grid Environment. ν_k for every variant and for every transformations k computed over sets of 100 different batches of size N. Points are mean values and bars standard deviations.

Evaluation of Performance Gain (ΔU). The difference in the performance of the deployed policies, ΔU, aligns well with the expected behavior. When k is a symmetry,

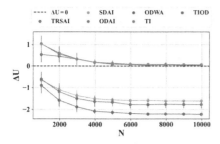

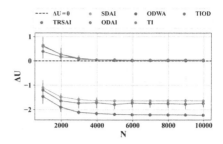

(a) First variant: movement in the intended direction with 60% probability.

(b) Second variant: movement in the intended direction with 75% probability.

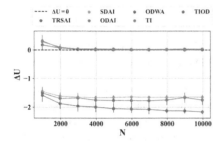

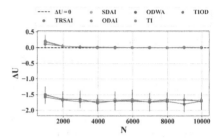

(c) Third variant: movement in the intended direction with 90% probability.

(d) Fourth variant: deterministic environment.

Fig. 9. Stochastic Toroidal Grid Environment. Performance difference ΔU. The threshold at $\Delta U = 0$ is displayed as a dashed line. $\Delta U > 0$ means that data augmenting leads to better policies.

$\Delta U > 0$ and approaches 0 as N increases. Conversely, when k is not a symmetric transformation of the dynamics, $\Delta U < 0$ and continues to decrease with N (see Fig. 9a). In the low samples regime, the performance gain is the highest for the environment with the less deterministic transformations, as more samples would be needed to estimate the correct transition function. In this case, data augmentation using valid symmetric samples has the most significant impact on the performance of the learned policy.

Deterministic Grid with Boundaries Detection Phase (ν_k). Fig. 10a demonstrates that the symmetries which are only approximately valid, such as TRSAI, ODAI, and TI, are detected with a lower ν_k compared to their "deterministic toroidal counterpart" (see Fig. 8d). This result is not surprising, considering the manner in which ν_k is computed.

Evaluation of Performance Gain (ΔU). Although the algorithm identifies TRSAI, ODAI, and TI as valid symmetries, Fig. 10b shows that using data augmentation with symmetric transitions to enhance planning performance in this environment is, on average, detrimental. We hypothesize that while data augmentation reduces the distributional shift for state-action pairs far from the grid borders, it actually increases the error for state-action pairs at the border. This effect leads to an overall decrease in performance if the computed policy relies on the negatively affected state-action pairs.

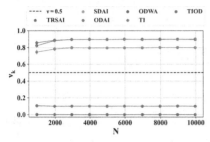

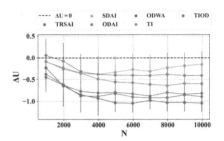

(a) Deterministic Grid with boundaries. Probability of symmetry ν_k. The threshold at $\nu = 0.5$ is displayed as a dashed line. $\nu_k > 0.5$ means that the transformation is detected as a symmetry.

(b) Performance difference ΔU. The threshold at $\Delta U = 0$ is displayed as a dashed line. $\Delta U > 0$ means that data augmenting leads to better policies.

Fig. 10. Deterministic Grid with boundaries. Detection phase and evaluation of performance gain.

Continuous Environments. The experiments in continuous environments were performed in our previous work [4], and are reported here for the sake of completeness.

Stochastic CartPole. Detection Phase (ν_k) In Stochastic CartPole, the algorithm fails to detect the symmetry $k = TI$. This could be because the translation invariance symmetry in this case is fixed for a specific value (see TI in Table 3 where the translation is set at 0.3). If the translation is too small, the neural network struggles to discern the transformation from the noise. The algorithm correctly classifies $k = SAR$ as a symmetry and the remaining transformations as non-symmetries (see Fig. 11a).

Evaluation of Performance Gain (ΔU). Results are displayed in Table 5. Offline RL is highly unstable and sensitive to the choice of hyperparameters. Furthermore, the training is conducted for a fixed number of epochs. We observe that on average, across different batch sizes, $\Delta U > 0$ for DQN and SAR, and SFI transformations. While SAR is a valid symmetry, SFI is not. A more conservative algorithm like CQL more readily exploits SAR. The performance difference for TI, both for DQN and CQL, is so close to zero that we believe augmenting the data set with this symmetry might not provide a significant advantage over using only the information contained in the original batch.

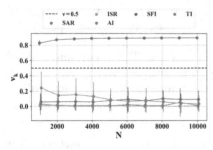

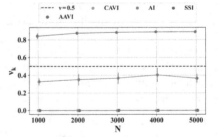

(a) Stochastic CartPole. Probability of symmetry ν_k. The threshold at $\nu = 0.5$ is displayed as a dashed line. $\nu_k > 0.5$ means that the transformation is detected as a symmetry.

(b) Stochastic Acrobot. Probability of symmetry ν_k. The threshold at $\nu = 0.5$ is displayed as a dashed line. $\nu_k > 0$ means that the transformation is detected as a symmetry.

Fig. 11. ν_k, for the transformations k computed over sets of different batches of size N in Stochastic CartPole (up) and Stochastic Acrobot (down). Points are mean values and are a bit shifted horizontally for the sake of display. Standard deviation is displayed as a vertical error bar.

Table 5. ΔU for every alleged symmetry in Stochastic CartPole with two baselines and different batch sizes N [4].

k	Baseline	N (number of transitions in the original batch)						Average ΔU
		5000	10000	15000	20000	25000	30000	
SAR	DQN	−7.3	25.4	41.8	7.2	9.0	3.4	**13.3**
	CQL	37.4	−2.5	−4.1	20.1	17.9	−9.0	**10.0**
ISR	DQN	−1.3	−48.5	−29.9	−78.7	−107.8	−29.1	−49.2
	CQL	6.4	1.6	−2.2	−22.3	−10.3	−25.9	−8.8
AI	DQN	26.9	−48.5	−43.7	−74.6	−41.3	−84.6	−44.3
	CQL	−13.1	−7.6	−29.8	−6.5	−22.3	−15.3	−15.8
SFI	DQN	−33.4	17.9	21.4	45.4	−6.9	−0.1	7.4
	CQL	−5.5	−2.1	7.4	−3.9	−3.6	−18.5	−4.4
TI	DQN	36.9	−28.1	34.5	15.7	6.1	−9.1	−0.2
	CQL	7.6	−1.3	−2.1	11.8	−16.5	5.2	**0.8**

Stochastic Acrobot Detection Phase (ν_k). In this environment, the only real symmetry of the dynamics, *AAVI*, gets successfully detected by the algorithm with $q = 0.1$. Non-symmetries yield a $\nu_k < 0.5$ (Fig. 11b).

Table 6. ΔU for every alleged symmetry in Stochastic Acrobot with two baselines and different batch sizes N [4].

k	Baseline	N				Average ΔU
		10000	20000	30000	40000	
AAVI	DQN	24.7	−17.5	−63.4	−10.6	−16.7
	CQL	−2.8	10.5	−9.5	213.3	**52.9**
CAVI	DQN	8.9	−9.3	−24.6	−48.0	−12.2
	CQL	−8.8	0.5	4.4	1.1	−0.7
AI	DQN	−377.3	−399.3	−386.8	−388.5	−388.0
	CQL	−25.6	235.3	−88.2	−49.9	17.9
SSI	DQN	265.7	−408.2	−334.9	−396.3	−218.4
	CQL	35.8	4.0	11.9	−22.8	7.2

Evaluation of Performance Gain (ΔU). Results are displayed in Table 6 and indicate that the training in Stochastic Acrobot is more challenging than in Stochastic CartPole. Even with a large data set, the algorithms sometimes fail to learn a good policy. In particular, while CQL manages to learn appropriate behavior in the environment by exploiting the **AAVI** symmetry (average $\Delta U = 52.9$), DQN still struggles with every k, both correct and incorrect. However, CQL also benefits from augmenting the data set with wrong symmetries, albeit to a lesser extent. We suspect that this effect is due to the instability in Offline RL training.

6 Conclusions

Data efficiency in the offline learning of MDPs is highly coveted. Exploiting the intuition of an expert about the nature of the model can help to learn dynamics that better represent reality.

In this work, we used a semi-automated tool that can aid an expert in providing a statistical data-driven validation of her/his intuition about some properties of the environment [3,4]. Correct deployment of the tool could improve the performance of the optimal policy obtained by solving the learned MDP. Indeed, our results suggest that the proposed algorithm can effectively detect a symmetry of the dynamics of an MDP with high accuracy and that exploiting this knowledge can not only reduce the distributional shift but also provide performance gain in an envisaged optimal control of the system. The approach is stable in stochastic environments with respect to perturbations of the transition probabilities and can also help detect approximate symmetries in a deterministic environment. However, exploiting the knowledge of symmetry in the deterministic environment could eventually lead to detrimental performances when considering long-term planning. When applied to Offline RL environments with DNN, all the prescriptions (and issues) about hyperparameter fine-tuning well known to Offline RL practitioners persist.

Besides its pros, the proposed paradigm is still constrained by several limitations. We note that the quality of the approach in continuous MDPs is greatly affected by the architecture of the Normalizing Flow used for Density Estimation and, more generally, by the state-action space preprocessing. In detail, sometimes an environment is endowed by symmetries that an expert can not straightforwardly perceive in the default representation of the state-action space and a transformation would be required (imagine the very same CartPole, but with also the linear speed and position of the car expressed in polar coordinates).

Future perspectives could include: (i) expanding this approach by trying out more recent Normalizing Flow architectures like FFJORD [12]; (ii) considering combinations of multiple symmetries.

References

1. Abel, D., Umbanhowar, N., Khetarpal, K., Arumugam, D., Precup, D., Littman, M.: Value preserving state-action abstractions. In: International Conference on Artificial Intelligence and Statistics, pp. 1639–1650. PMLR (2020)
2. Angelotti, G., Drougard, N., Chanel, C.P.C.: Offline learning for planning: a summary. In: Proceedings of the 1st Workshop on Bridging the Gap Between AI Planning and Reinforcement Learning at the 30th International Conference on Automated Planning and Scheduling, pp. 153–161 (2020)
3. Angelotti, G., Drougard, N., Chanel, C.P.C.: Expert-guided symmetry detection in markov decision processes. In: Proceedings of the 14th International Conference on Agents and Artificial Intelligence, vol. 2: ICAART, pp. 88–98. INSTICC, SciTePress (2022). https://doi.org/10.5220/0010783400003116
4. Angelotti, G., Drougard, N., Chanel, C.P.C.: Data augmentation through expert-guided symmetry detection to improve performance in offline reinforcement learning. In: Proceedings

of the 15th International Conference on Agents and Artificial Intelligence, vol. 2: ICAART, pp. 115–124. INSTICC, SciTePress (2023). https://doi.org/10.5220/0011633400003393

5. Bertsekas, D.P., Tsitsiklis, J.N.: Neuro-dynamic programming: an overview. In: Proceedings of 1995 34th IEEE Conference on Decision and Control, vol. 1, pp. 560–564. IEEE (1995)
6. Brockman, G., et al.: Openai gym (2016). arXiv:1606.01540
7. Castro, P.S.: Scalable methods for computing state similarity in deterministic markov decision processes. In: Proceedings of the AAAI Conference on Artificial Intelligence, vol. 34, pp. 10069–10076 (2020). https://doi.org/10.1609/aaai.v34i06.6564
8. Dean, T., Givan, R.: Model minimization in markov decision processes. In: AAAI/IAAI, pp. 106–111 (1997)
9. Dinh, L., Krueger, D., Bengio, Y.: NICE: non-linear independent components estimation. In: Proceedings of the 3rd International Conference on Learning Representations (2015). http://arxiv.org/abs/1410.8516
10. Ferns, N., Panangaden, P., Precup, D.: Metrics for finite markov decision processes. In: Conference on Uncertainty in Artificial Intelligence, vol. 4, pp. 162–169 (2004)
11. Givan, R., Dean, T., Greig, M.: Equivalence notions and model minimization in Markov decision processes. Artif. Intell. **147**(1–2), 163–223 (2003)
12. Grathwohl, W., Chen, R.T.Q., Bettencourt, J., Sutskever, I., Duvenaud, D.: FFJORD: free-form continuous dynamics for scalable reversible generative models. In: Proceedings of the 7th International Conference on Learning Representations (2019). https://openreview.net/forum?id=rJxgknCcK7
13. Kobyzev, I., Prince, S., Brubaker, M.: Normalizing flows: an introduction and review of current methods. IEEE Trans. Pattern Anal. Mach. Intell. **43**, 3964–3979 (2020)
14. Kumar, A., Zhou, A., Tucker, G., Levine, S.: Conservative q-learning for offline reinforcement learning. Adv. Neural Inf. Process. Syst. **34**, 20132–20145 (2020)
15. Levine, S., Kumar, A., Tucker, G., Fu, J.: Offline reinforcement learning: tutorial, review, and perspectives on open problems (2020). arXiv:2005.01643
16. Li, L., Walsh, T.J., Littman, M.: Towards a unified theory of state abstraction for MDPS. In: Proceedings of the Ninth International Symposium on Artificial Intelligence and Mathematics, pp. 531–539 (2006)
17. Mandel, T., Liu, Y.E., Brunskill, E., Popovic, Z.: Efficient bayesian clustering for reinforcement learning. In: Proceedings of the 25th International Joint Conference on Artificial Intelligence, pp. 1830–1838 (2016)
18. Mausam, N., Kolobov, A.: Planning with Markov decision processes: an AI perspective. Synth. Lect. Artif. Intell. Mach. Learn. **6**(1), 1–210 (2012)
19. Mnih, V., et al.: Human-level control through deep reinforcement learning. Nature **518**(7540), 529–533 (2015). https://doi.org/10.1038/nature14236
20. Munos, R.: Error bounds for approximate policy iteration. In: Proceedings of the 20th International Conference on International Conference on Machine Learning, vol. 3, pp. 560–567 (2003)
21. Munos, R., Moore, A.: Variable resolution discretization in optimal control. Mach. Learn. **49**(2), 291–323 (2002)
22. Narayanamurthy, S.M., Ravindran, B.: On the hardness of finding symmetries in Markov decision processes. In: Proceedings of the 25th International Conference on International Conference on Machine Learning, pp. 688–695 (2008)
23. Paine, T.L., et al.: Hyperparameter selection for offline reinforcement learning (2020). arXiv:2007.09055
24. Prudencio, R.F., Maximo, M.R., Colombini, E.L.: A survey on offline reinforcement learning: taxonomy, review, and open problems. IEEE Trans. Neural Netw. Learn. Syst. (2023)
25. Ravindran, B., Barto, A.G.: Symmetries and Model Minimization in Markov Decision Processes. Technical report, USA (2001)

26. Ravindran, B., Barto, A.G.: Approximate homomorphisms: a framework for non-exact minimization in Markov decision processes. In: International Conference on Knowledge Based Computer Systems (2004)
27. Ruan, S.S., Comanici, G., Panangaden, P., Precup, D.: Representation discovery for mdps using bisimulation metrics. In: Twenty-Ninth AAAI Conference on Artificial Intelligence (2015)
28. Takuma Seno, M.I.: d3rlpy: an offline deep reinforcement library. In: NeurIPS 2021 Offline Reinforcement Learning Workshop (2021)
29. Taylor, J., Precup, D., Panagaden, P.: Bounding performance loss in approximate MDP homomorphisms. Adv. Neural Inf. Process. Syst. **21** (2009). https://proceedings.neurips.cc/paper/2008/file/6602294be910b1e3c4571bd98c4d5484-Paper.pdf
30. van der Pol, E., Kipf, T., Oliehoek, F.A., Welling, M.: Plannable approximations to MDP homomorphisms: equivariance under actions. In: Proceedings of the 19th International Conference on Autonomous Agents and MultiAgent Systems, pp. 1431–1439 (2020)
31. van der Pol, E., Worrall, D., van Hoof, H., Oliehoek, F., Welling, M.: MDP homomorphic networks: group symmetries in reinforcement learning. Adv. Neural Inf. Process. Syst. **33**, 4199–4210 (2020). https://proceedings.neurips.cc/paper/2020/file/2be5f9c2e3620eb73c2972d7552b6cb5-Paper.pdf
32. Whitt, W.: Approximations of dynamic programs, i. Math. Oper. Res. **3**(3), 231–243 (1978)

Dynamic Communities: A Novel Recommendation Approach for Individuals and Groups

Sabrine Ben Abdrabbah[1]([⊠]), Sabrine Mallek[2], and Nahla Ben Amor[3]

[1] Pôle R&D, Audensiel, 93 rue Nationale, 92100 Boulogne-Billancourt, France
s.benabdrabbah@audensiel.fr
[2] ICN Business School, CEREFIGE, Université de Lorraine, Nancy, France
sabrine.mallek@icn-artem.com
[3] LARODEC, ISG Tunis, Université de Tunis, Tunis, Tunisie
nahla.benamor@gmx.fr

Abstract. As user preferences rapidly and continually evolve, it becomes crucial to incorporate these temporal dynamics in the design of recommender systems. This paper proposes a novel dynamic and overlapping community-based recommender system framework, which considers the evolving nature of users' preferences to suggest items distinctly for both individuals and groups. Using temporal networks to capture the dynamic interplay of users' interests, we apply dynamic community detection techniques to identify similar items, thereby addressing scalability issues. To cater to group recommendation scenarios, the framework leverages users' satisfaction with similar items, thereby mitigating data sparsity and delivering a broad range of recommendations. Experimental results show that the proposed system outperforms state-of-the-art approaches in terms of recommendation accuracy for both individual and group recommendations.

Keywords: Recommendation systems · Group Recommendation · Dynamic community detection · Overlapping communities · Dynamic networks

1 Introduction

The abundant content available on the internet presents a challenge in terms of delivering relevant and personalized content to users. Recommender systems (RSs) have been developed to address the information overload dilemma. Predictive techniques are used to cross users' data on historical behaviours, personal profiles, social relationships, and other relevant information to suggest personalized content such as ads and products, among others [23]. Recently, RSs have become an essential business tool in e-commerce to engage in personalisation and innovation and provide individualized shopping experiences to customers [16]. They offer firms in the electronic marketplace a competitive advantage by facilitating up- and cross-sales, reducing consumers' search time, and enabling innovative bundling of digital content and products [18].

RSs have predominantly been designed to recommend items to individual users, using techniques such as collaborative filtering, content-based methods, and hybrid

A. P. Rocha et al. (Eds.): ICAART 2023, LNAI 14546, pp. 187–201, 2024.
https://doi.org/10.1007/978-3-031-55326-4_9

approaches [1,3,24]. However, there is an increasing need for systems that can effectively recommend items to groups of users, considering their collective interests and preferences. For instance, these systems would be beneficial in situations where items are consumed collectively, such as gym-goers seeking music playlists, family members looking for a restaurant for a shared dining, a group of friends trying to choose a movie to watch, or organizing a trip that aligns with everyone's preferences. Yet, the task of providing group recommendations presents its own set of challenges. While current methods focus on either aggregating individual preferences or individual recommendations [3], these methods rely heavily on user ratings which are often sparse. This can bring two significant shortcoming: (i) the produced recommendations may satisfy many, but not all the members of the group and (ii) it is less likely to generate unexpected and novel items.

To overcome these challenges, community-based recommendation methods have been proposed. These methods leverage the community structure of the network to identify sets of similar items or users, thus enabling a more targeted approach to recommendations [12,25,28]. However, these methods are often static and do not take into account the temporal evolution of users' preferences, which is a critical aspect given the rapidly changing nature of user interests [33].

In this paper, we present a novel recommendation system based on dynamic and overlapping community structures in data that addresses the limitations of existing methods. Our proposed framework extends the methodology presented in [1], evolving it into a more sophisticated recommendation system capable of providing recommendations for both individuals and groups. The new system is configurable; it allows for specific adjustments depending on the input, for individual or group recommendations. This ensures optimal performance by adapting the underlying mechanisms according to the context, offering an adaptable and robust solution to address varying recommendation scenarios. It uses dynamic and overlapping community detection techniques to identify similar items. By leveraging these techniques, the framework considers the temporal dynamics of user preferences and ensures that the recommendations made are not only accurate but also computationally efficient. This efficiency is achieved by focusing on predetermined communities within the network, rather than conducting an exhaustive exploration of the entire network.

The remainder of this paper is structured as follows. Section 2 provides an overview of individual and group recommendation, community detection, and community detection-based RSs. Section 3 outlines the different components of our proposed framework. Section 4 presents experimental results of the framework along with a comparison with traditional methods. Concluding remarks are covered in Sect. 5.

2 Related Work

2.1 Individual and Group Recommendation

RSs are typically organized into three primary classes: collaborative filtering (CF), content-based, and hybrid methodologies [3]. CF methods use a user-item rating matrix to anticipate unknown entries and, accordingly, propose suitable items. CF methods can be further classified into two sub-categories: item-based and user-based approaches.

Item-based strategies generate recommendations by analyzing items that have been favorably rated by the user in the past, while user-based approaches rely on the preferences of similar users to make suggestions. Content-based strategies, use the characteristics of previously liked items to recommend items with comparable features. Hybrid methodologies leverage the benefits of both content representation and user rating information, drawn from content-based and CF techniques, to formulate recommendations.

Although most RSs make suggestions for individual users, in many circumstances the selected items (e.g., movies) are not intended for personal usage but rather for consumption in groups. Extant literature that focuses on group recommendation strategies fall into two categories: (i) Merging profiles strategy, also called virtual user strategy since it aggregates group members' prior ratings into a single virtual user profile and makes recommendations to that user, and (ii) Merging recommendations strategy, which computes each group member's individual recommendations and merges them to produce a single list for the group. The key idea is to merge all user profiles into a unique common user profile using total distance minimization in order to generate a common program recommendation list. We can also mention other research studies, that are not necessarily application-oriented, like the one in [6] proposing a group recommender system that uses a local-search algorithm for aggregating users' ratings into a single consensus ordering (Kemeny-optimal ordering). If group members have an unequal importance weight, which reflects the situation that some users have more influence on the group, a weighted average can be used as aggregation method to take the relative importance of each group member into account [30, 36]. Group recommendation systems based on *Merging recommendations* highly depend on the aggregation methods. Different techniques have been explored, namely Average (AVG), Average without misery (AvgWM), Least misery (LM), Most pleasure (MP). The influence of the aggregation method on the accuracy of the group recommendations was investigated in [5, 11] showing that the effectiveness of a group recommendation is not necessarily influenced by the aggregation method but rather by the group size and the inner group similarities. Other group attributes have been incorporated in aggregation strategies, namely behavioural tendency, power balance among members [29], social relationship interactions [13]. Using multiple qualitative aspects (accuracy, diversity, coverage, and serendipity) with different state-of-the-art recommendation algorithms, [11] shows that there exists no 'overall-best' recommendation algorithm and merging strategy. Clearly, all combinations basically rely on members' individual preferences which may not be completely available when the rating matrix is sparse or when groups are large. To mitigate this limitation, we introduce a strategy that employs community detection algorithms. This approach allows us to harness the network community structure of similar items, enabling a deeper and more accurate understanding of the collective group behaviour.

2.2 Community Detection

The process of identifying structured interconnections within complex networks is often conducted through community detection. This technique plays a crucial role in unveiling densely connected communities and capturing the hidden structure of the network by partitioning the entities into subsets of highly interconnected groups, providing valuable insights into the underlying structure and shared characteristics of these groups. Communities are typically regarded as clusters/groups of nodes that maintain strong interconnections while only loosely connecting with the rest of the network [15]. By analyzing the emerging community structure in complex networks, we can gain insights into the collective behaviour of their entities and thereby enhance our understanding of the systems being modeled. Traditional methods [19,22] concentrated on identifying communities within static networks, these being constructed by aggregating all observed data of static graphs. However, with the rise of Web 2.0, new challenges have surfaced for community detection, namely the overlapping of communities and the temporal evolution of data - dynamic networks [4]. Static community detection algorithms fall short when confronted with these issues as they fail to account for the temporal information necessary to the understanding of the dynamics at play within these networks. To address these problems, numerous algorithms have recently been proposed [9,20,31] that effectively manage dynamic networks.

2.3   Community-Based Recommendation

Basic entities of RSs are largely grouped into users and items. The underlying community structure can be used to represent items or users with similar characteristics. The emphasis of much of the existing research has been on identifying communities of users, given the natural tendency of individuals to form communities in their real-life interactions. For instance, [28] leveraged the multiple dimensions of social networks to unearth latent user communities by implementing the principal modularity maximization method, thereby helping RSs mitigate the cold start problem that arises when a user's rating history is nonexistent. A Multi-label propagation algorithm for static community detection was employed by [24] in a bipartite network made up of users and items, with recommendations generated based on the active user's communities via the collaborative filtering recommendation method. In contrast, other studies, such as [14,25,27], have focused on identifying communities of items and integrating these findings into recommendation models. These studies construct item-specific networks, apply community detection algorithms such as CFinder and Louvain [7], and leverage the detected communities to deliver diverse recommendations to users.

Nevertheless, a limitation of these studies is the neglect of the temporal dimension of users' preferences in recommendation generation. The time factor is critical to accurately identify users' current needs based on recent data as most data collected from RSs are time-stamped. To address this limitation, [2] proposed employing fuzzy k-means clustering periodically to capture user preferences dynamically when identifying communities, and these are then utilized to predict the active user's preferences for unseen items. Similar approaches that consider the temporal aspect have been proposed by [17] and [32]. Despite these advances, existing community-based recommendation methods continue to rely on static community detection algorithms, which are incapable of coping with the dynamic nature of users' preferences. Such static detection does not account for changes in network topology and hence fails to portray an accurate representation of network partitions. Consequently, using these communities in preference prediction could potentially reduce the performance of the generated recommendations

[34]. This highlights the necessity of new approaches capable of dealing with the temporal changes in user preferences, ensuring recommendations remain relevant and valuable to the end user.

3   Dynamic Communities for Enhanced Individual and Group Recommendations

In this paper, we introduce a novel framework, termed as dynamic and overlapping community-based recommendation system for distinctly individual users and groups of users (denoted for short by DO2IG). The proposed framework, depicted in Fig. 1, aims to provide a an effective recommendation system for individual users and groups, by considering temporal aspects, community structure, and user preferences. The framework is divided into three major steps: dynamic network construction and community detection, individual and group profile construction, and recommendation generation.

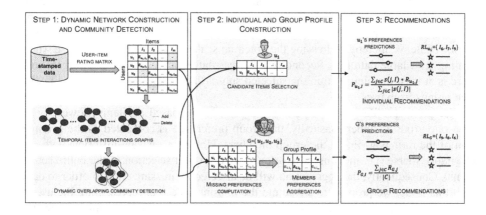

Fig. 1. Architecture of the proposed DO2IG framework.

3.1   Step 1: Dynamic Network Construction and Community Detection

The first step in the framework involves constructing a temporal network, which captures the dynamic aspect of users' interests in items based on their interactions over time. Unlike snapshot-based representations, this approach is designed to handle rapidly evolving data in RSs. The process begins by representing the items as nodes and establishing edges to represent relationships between items. We analyze the timestamped data of users' ratings to build the graph of interactions between items. Items interactions are modeled based on the co-ratings relationship derived from users' profiles. An item-item interaction occurs when a user rates two items simultaneously with the same rating. This indicates that the user has a similar interest in both of these items. It is obvious that a pair of items can interact more than once over time. Therefore, it is crucial to take into account both the frequency of item interactions and the timeframe in which these interactions occurred to gain a better understanding of the evolution of users' preferences. To construct the temporal network, two parameters, denoted as N for the number of interactions and T for the number of days, are defined. More details regarding the dynamic network construction are given in [1].

Next, a dynamic and overlapping community detection algorithm such as TILES [26] can be utilized to analyse the temporal network and detect overlapping communities. Actually, overlapping communities reflect the reality that a single item may meet the interests of various user groups. Consider the example of movie preferences: users who enjoy both 'Maleficent' and 'Aladdin' may also derive satisfaction from viewing 'Spider-Man'. Similarly, fans of 'Taken' and 'Transporter' might find 'Spider-Man' appealing as well. Thus, 'Spider-Man' can effectively cater to the tastes of multiple user groups, each with distinct preferences.

3.2   Step 2: Individual and Group Profile Construction

The second step involves using the community structure detected in the first step to construct individual and group profiles. For individual profiles, candidate items that align with the user's recent preferences are identified. These candidate items are detected by assessing the communities of the recently appreciated item of the active user. This approach addresses two significant outcomes. First, we alleviate the need to explore all the unviewed items, thereby addressing the potential scalability challenges that arise when dealing with large data sets. Second, we address data sparsity, as our method ensures there is at least one item within the selected subset that has previously received favorable ratings from user.

For group profiles, we compute group preferences based on items viewed by at least one group member. Basically, the group preference is computed as the average sum of the ratings given by the group members. However, relevant historical data are inevitably sparse (i.e. most users have only rated a small selection of the entire set of items). Consequently, the aggregation will be affected by missing data. In order to deal with this issue, we propose to substitute the missing data (i.e. representing the user's interest for the item) by the most recent feedback given by the group member to similar items. Obviously, user's preferences are changing over time and we cannot rely on the old data that cannot reflect the actual interest of the user. Thus, instead of considering all user's ratings for similar items, we propose to consider only the most recent rating left by the active user.

Example 1. *Let us consider the user-movie rating matrix of Table 1. We start by determining the list of items interactions when T is set to 3 (shown in Table 2). By applying the TILES algorithm with ttl $= 8$ and obs $= 30$ on the items interactions list, we get the community structure C composed of three film communities: $C_1 = \{Jocker, Aquamen, Batman, Jumanji\}$, $C_2 = \{King\text{-}Kong, Jumanji, Mowgli\}$ $C_3 = \{Lion, Jumanji\}$. Let us now consider the rating matrix of the group members in Table 3 for a group of 3 friends $G = \{Nicolas, Colin, Victor\}$. Table 3 details the new user-item matrix after replacing the missing data. For instance, $R_{Nicolas,Lion} = R_{Nicolas,Jumanji} = 4$ because Jumanji is the only movie rated by Nicolas in C_3 and $R_{Colin,Aquaman} = R_{Colin,Jocker} = 5$ given that it is the most recent rating compared to $R_{Colin,Jumanji}$. So that, the group profile computed as the average of all the group members is given in the same table.*

Table 1. User-item rating matrix.

UserID	ItemID	Rating	Timestamp
Colin	Jumanji	2	16/12/2022
Victor	Lion	5	16/12/2022
Rayan	Mowgli	4	17/12/2022
Rayan	Jumanji	4	17/12/2022
Nadine	Mowgli	5	17/12/2022
Nadine	King−Kong	5	18/12/2022
Victor	Jocker	3	18/12/2022
Victor	Jumanji	5	19/12/2022
Nicolas	Jumanji	4	19/12/2022
Lina	Aquaman	4	19/12/2022
Nicolas	King−Kong	4	20/12/2022
Victor	Aquamen	3	20/12/2022
Lina	Jocker	5	20/12/2022
Eli	Jocker	4	20/12/2022
Lina	Batman	5	21/12/2022
Eli	Jumanji	4	22/12/2022
Rayan	Jumanji	5	22/12/2022
Rayan	Aquaman	5	22/12/2022
Lina	Batman	4	22/12/2022
Nicolas	Jocker	3	23/12/2022
Colin	Jocker	5	23/12/2022

Table 2. Item-item interaction list ($T = 3$).

Movie1	Movie2	Timestamp
Mowgli	Jumanji	17/12/2022
Mowgli	King−Kong	18/12/2022
Jumanji	Lion	19/12/2022
Jocker	Aquaman	20/12/2022
Jumanji	King−Kong	20/12/2022
Jocker	Batman	21/12/2022
Jocker	Jumanji	22/12/2022
Jumanji	Aquaman	22/12/2022
Batman	Aquaman	22/12/2022

Table 3. Group members rating matrix.

	Jocker	King-Kong	Lion	Jumanji	Aquamen
Nicolas	2	4	**[4]**	4	**[3]**
Colin	5	4	**[2]**	2	**[5]**
Victor	3	**[5]**	5	5	3
G	3.33	4.33	3.66	3.66	3.66

3.3 Step 3: Recommendation Generation

The final step involves generating recommendations based on the constructed profiles. For individual recommendations, we compute the active user's preference towards each candidate item, which is then employed to get the top-k list of recommendations, optimizing the user's experience by presenting the most promising selections.

$$P_{u,i} = \frac{\sum_{j \in C} s(i,j)\, r_{u,j}}{\sum_{j \in C} |s(i,j)|} \tag{1}$$

C represents the set of items belonging to the communities of the item i. The rating assigned by the currently active user u to the item j is represented as $r_{u,j}$ and $s(i,j)$ is the similarity between items i and j. Details about this step are given in [1].

For group recommendations, the framework predicts group preferences for unseen items based on the members interest in similar items. Assuming that the group is often interested in novel recommendations that are not yet discovered by any of its members, it would be worthwhile to predict the preference of the group on the set of items which are not yet evaluated by any of its member. The group preference for an unseen item is then defined based on the group interest for similar items. In other words, the recommendation process is based on the similarity between items which is measured according to the similarity of the users behaviour pattern. Formally, the group preference prediction $P_{G,i}$ for item i is computed as the average of the group interests on items pertaining to the same communities of i:

$$P_{G,i} = \frac{\sum_{j \in C} R_{G,j}}{|C|} \tag{2}$$

where C is the set of items pertaining to the communities of i, $R_{G,j}$ is the group rating to the item j. Once the group preference predictions computed for unseen items, we select the ones having the highest values in the group recommendation list RL.

Example 2. *We compute the group preference prediction for each unseen item* $\{Batman, Mowgli\}$. $P_{G,Batman}$ *(resp.* $P_{G,Mowgli}$*) is equal to* $(3.33 + 3.66 + 3.66)/3 = 3.55$ *(resp.* $(4.33 + 3.66)/2 = 4$*). Thus, the most relevant recommendation for the group G is item* $Mowgli$.

Recommendations are presented as a list, prioritizing items with the highest predicted preferences at the top. This approach facilitates easy decision-making for users and encourages the discovery of new items that align with their evolving tastes.

4   Experimental Results

In this section, we detail the experimental study carried out to evaluate the proposed framework DO2IG. The experimental protocol used for this study remains the same as the one detailed in [1]. Experiments are conducted on the 1M MovieLens[1] dataset, a widely-used resource extracted from a movie recommender system, encompassing one million ratings collected from 6,000 users for 4,000 movies between 2000 and 2003. The dataset ensures robustness as each user has provided ratings for at least 20 items, with ratings ranging from 1 to 5 on a discrete scale. In group recommendation scenarios, a key challenge is evaluating collective satisfaction, given the absence of datasets with both individual and group ratings. This can be addressed through either online or offline evaluation approaches. The online evaluation technique measures the

---

[1] https://movieLens.umn.edu.

effectiveness of group recommendations by synthesizing individual member feedback into a collective evaluation or by asking direct group feedback. On the other hand, offline evaluation compares generated recommendations against the existing dataset for each group member. In this study, we follow an offline approach.

We apply the k-nearest neighbors algorithm (kNN) from the scikit-learn library to identify high inner groups composed of the most p similar members (i.e. $[2, 5, 10, 20, 60]$). The community-based group recommendation algorithm is executed for these different group sizes. For each size, a quality metric is calculated across 50 groups, and the average is taken as an estimate of the recommendation quality. To better evaluate the quality of the predicted ratings, only items evaluated by every member in the testing set are selected. The true group rating is calculated as the average of all member ratings for these items. Otherwise, the remaining items (i.e. items rated by at least one group member) are used to build the group profile and calculate the group predicted rating.

Evaluating the performance of the recommender system is essential to determine how well the generated recommendations align with the individual and group's collective interests and expectations. In this study, the Mean Absolute Error (MAE) is used to assess the accuracy of both group and individual recommendations by measuring the average absolute deviation of predicted ratings from the actual ratings. Each predicted rating denoted P_i (e.g., for a user or group of users), for an item i is compared to the true rating, denoted R_i, which is the rating of the same user or the average of the true ratings of all group members. The MAE is computed for both cases according to the system configuration (e.g., individual or group recommendations), and a lower MAE indicates higher accuracy in the recommendations. The formula for MAE is as follows:

$$MAE = \frac{\sum_{i=1}^{m} |R_i - P_i|)^2}{m} \qquad (3)$$

where m is the total number of items rated by the group or individual user, respectively.

4.1   Parameters Tuning

We started by analyzing the user-item rating matrix in order to determine the list of the timestamped interactions of items. An item-item interaction is established when a user assigns identical ratings to both items over a time span of T days. To capture the values that allow us to detect communities with the most effective size and internal structure, we computed, for each items pair, the number of interactions N and the corresponding period T. Then, we tested different values for these parameters. We found that $171,787$ pairs of movies interacted together. A temporal network was built for each possible combination between T and N (i.e., 4^2 temporal networks). We applied *TILES* [26] algorithm[2] to detect dynamic communities for each temporal network. The resulting communities were then used to compute recommendations. We kept only the valid temporal network of items (i.e., with existing links and non-empty community structure) as it is difficult to find connections that exist between nodes if N is maximal and/or T is minimal. We found that maximum recommendation accuracy is achieved

---

[2] https://github.com/GiulioRossetti/TILES.

when N is fixed to 2 and P is fixed to 1035. In light of this observation, we choose to set the parameter T to 1035 (i.e. the maximum number of days between co-ratings in data) in order to consider a large number of items' interactions and to avoid outliers, and we set N to 2.

We tested the impact of *TILES* parameters on the quality of the detected communities and the proposed method. The parameters representing the optimum values are then fixed to be used for the rest of the experiment. There are two basic parameters to consider in *TILES* including *obs* (i.e. specifies the number of days from a community observation to the subsequent one) and *ttl* (i.e. specifies the edge time to live in days) which are very sensitive to the data sets. These parameters highly depend on data characteristics (e.g. number of users, number of items, number of ratings). It is obvious that when $ttl = 0$ an edge disappears immediately after its creating producing an empty network at each new step, when $ttl = +\infty$, we fall into a static graph which is constructed by aggregating all observed interactions. We set the temporal observation of the network to 900 days (i.e. $obs = 1000$ representing all the period of items interactions) and we varied ttl values from 30 to 680. Table 4 shows the MAE of DO2IG for different ttl values. As illustrated, the prediction accuracy reached its maximum when ttl was fixed to 340 and *obs* was set to 1000. Hence, we used these values in the rest of the experiments.

Table 4. The impact of ttl on recommendation quality in terms of MAE ($obs = 1000$).

Group Size	ttl = 30	ttl = 180	ttl = 340	ttl = 680
Individual	1.03	0.98	**0.58**	1.05
2	1.064	1.008	**0.6**	1.072
5	0.864	0.856	**0.456**	0.888
10	0.816	0.784	**0.368**	0.896
20	0.768	0.76	**0.328**	0.792
60	0.736	0.72	**0.32**	0.776

Next, we compared the proposed framework DO2IG to the following state-of-the-art group recommendation methods:

- Group recommendation based on preferences predictions aggregation [35] (denoted as $RAIKM$) which consists in applying the basic user-based CF to predict members ratings on those individual non-rated items. The group preferences predictions are then computed as the weighted average of all the members preference predictions.
- Group recommendation based on preferences aggregation [10] (denoted as $PAIKM$) which consists in combining the ratings of the members to build the group profile for items already seen by at least one member. Then, the basic user-based CF is applied to suggest the top k most interesting items to the group.
- Group recommendation based on users' preferences on similar items [8] (denoted by $PRAIKM$) which consists in evaluating users' similarities to create communities

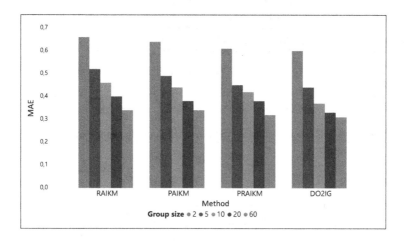

of users. Then, the group preferences prediction for items rated by enough members is computed as the mean of the members' true ratings. While for the remaining items, the group ratings prediction is computed as the mean of the members' predicted ratings which are generated based on their interests for similar items. Figure 2 shows MAE results of group recommendations produced by the different algorithms according to different group sizes.

Fig. 2. MAE results compared to group recommendation methods.

We compared the recommendation accuracy of the individual recommendations component of DO2IG with the following existing approaches for single recommendations:

- The static community-based collaborative filtering approach [14], denoted by S.community. Here communities of movies are extracted utilizing the Louvain method.
- The static clustering-based collaborative filtering approach [21], denoted by S.cluster, employs the average link clustering algorithm to group items into clusters, this is based on a similarity matrix.
- The dynamic clustering-based collaborative filtering [17], denoted by D.cluster, integrates a time weight parameter in the item-item similarity measure. This serves to reduce the influence of historical data, thereby considering the evolving nature of an active user's purchasing habits.
- TimeSVD++ [33], which is a time-sensitive algorithm that factors in temporal information in addition to the rating matrix. This approach introduces time-variant biases for each user and item, with the core concept being to decrease the weight of a user's older ratings, ensuring they have a negligible effect on their current state.

Figure 3 illustrates MAE results over extant literature individual recommendation methods.

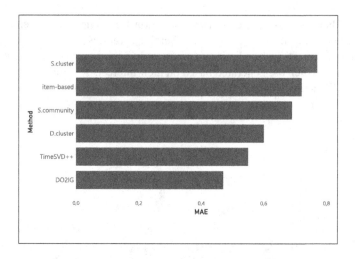

Fig. 3. MAE results compared to individual recommendation methods.

4.2 Discussion

This study examined a dynamic overlapping community-based individual and group recommendation approach using the MovieLens data set, and demonstrated improved accuracy in terms of MAE compared to other methods. The use of temporal observation and the implementation of the dynamic community detection algorithm in creating network communities revealed a significant impact on the quality of both individual and group recommendations. Additionally, a key advantage of this system is that it is naturally adjustable, allowing for custom changes depending on the type of recommendations sought: for individuals or groups. This inherent adaptability ensures optimal performance by calibrating the system mechanisms according to the context.

The first synthesis to point out from Fig. 2 is that the MAE values are enhanced when the group size grows for all methods since the number of items that have been seen by enough members becomes more important with large groups. In fact, when the group size increases the items already seen by at least one group member increases and since we work with high inner groups, the group profile can be induced from some few members unlike the randomly constructed groups. The second synthesis is that the MAE of RAIKM is less effective than PAIKM when the group size is small and it is the same when the group size is large (i.e. more than 20 members). This can be explained by the fact that aggregating the preferences of the group members provides optimal results than computing preferences prediction since this latter can be affected by the missing data especially with small groups. However, the compensatory effect provoked by missing data is less important with large high inner groups. Moreover, we note that PRAIKM gives the best MAE results compared to PAIKM for the different group sizes. This is justified by the fact that the missing data can affect the group profile since this latter cannot be correctly determined by aggregating insufficient individual preferences. Finally, the proposed DO2IG provides the most accurate recommendations compared to all the comparing methods for all the group size. This is can be justified by the fact that capturing the temporal changes of users' interests leads to extract very effective communities that reveal the most recent partitions of similar items. This underlying community structure is used in order to identify items capturing the present taste of the group members.

As corroborated by literature [1], the individual recommendation component of the proposed framework, outperfoms all other methods by achieving the lowest MAE values (as illustrated in Fig. 3). This can be attributed to its consideration of both temporal variations in user interests and the overlapping nature of items. Consequently, the communities detected are better positioned to represent recent, related neighbors, which in turn enhances recommendation accuracy.

5   Conclusion

In this study, we proposed a novel recommendation system, DO2IG. This framework is designed to deliver real-time, relevant recommendations to both groups and individual users by modeling the fluid evolution of user preferences in a dynamic network of items. By employing a community detection algorithm, DO2IG identified dynàmic and overlapping groups of items, allowing us to provide diverse recommendations that accurately reflect the current tastes of users.

This research highlighted the importance of accounting for changes in network topology and the overlapping nature of item memberships. The experimental results showed that (i) the compensatory effect of the missing data presented over the user-item matrix was not important with large high inner groups, (ii) the group preference prediction was better captured when the group size was large, and (iii) the proposed DO2IG framework provided the most accurate recommendations compared to basic individual and group recommendation strategies. Furthermore, results based on the MovieLens dataset demonstrated that our proposed framework, DO2IG, is capable of efficiently handling large-scale data and mitigating issues related to data sparsity.

As part of our future work, we aim to explore the dynamics of social interactions within groups. This exploration will focus on addressing specific scenarios pertinent to group recommendations, such as evaluating how an item's value varies amongst diverse groups, understanding the evolving roles of group members in decision-making, and assessing how the dominance of an authoritative member can affect the preferences of others.

References

1. Abdrabbah, S.B., Amor, N.B., Ayachi, R.: A new dynamic community-based recommender system. In: Rocha, A.P., Steels, L., van den Herik, H.J. (eds.) Proceedings of the 15th International Conference on Agents and Artificial Intelligence, ICAART 2023, Lisbon, Portugal, 22–24 February 2023, vol. 2, pp. 125–136. SCITEPRESS (2023). https://doi.org/10.5220/0011641300003393
2. Abrouk, L., Gross-Amblard, D., Cullot, N.: Community detection in the collaborative web. Int. J. Managing Inf. Technol. (IJMIT) 2(4) (2010). https://doi.org/10.5121/ijmit.2010.2401

3. Adomavicius, G., Tuzhilin, A.: Toward the next generation of recommender systems: a survey of the state-of-the-art and possible extensions. IEEE Trans. Knowl. Data Eng. **17**(6), 734–749 (2005)
4. Aston, N., Hertzler, J., Hu, W.: Overlapping community detection in dynamic networks. J. Softw. Eng. Appl. **7**(10), 872–882 (2014). https://doi.org/10.4236/jsea.2014.710078
5. Baltrunas, T., Makcinskas, F., Ricci, F.: Group recommendations with rank aggregation and collaborative filtering. In: 4th ACM Conference on Recommender Systems, pp. 119–126 (2010)
6. Baskin, J., Krishnamurthi, S.: Preference aggregation in group recommender systems for committee decision-making. In: 3rd ACM Conference on Recommender Systems, pp. 337–340 (2009)
7. Blondel, V.D., Guillaume, J.L., Lambiotte, R., Lefebvre, E.: Fast unfolding of communities in large networks. J. Stat. Mech: Theory Exp. **2008**(10), P10008 (2008). https://doi.org/10.1088/1742-5468/2008/10/P10008
8. Boratto, L., Carta, S., Chessa, A., Agelli, M., Clemente, M.: Group recommendation with automatic identification of users communities. In: IEEE/WIC/ACM International Conference on Web Intelligence and International Conference on Intelligent Agent Technology - Workshops, pp. 547–550 (2009)
9. Cazabet, R., Amblard, F.: Simulate to detect: a multi-agent system for community detection. In: 2011 IEEE/WIC/ACM International Conference on Web Intelligence and Intelligent Agent Technology (WI-IAT), vol. 2, pp. 402–408 (2011). https://doi.org/10.1109/WI-IAT.2011.50
10. Christensen, I., Schiaffino, S.: Entertainment recommender systems for group of users. Expert Syst. Appl. **38**(11), 14127–14135 (2011)
11. De Pessemier, T., Dooms, S., Martens, L.: Comparison of group recommendation algorithms. Multimedia Tools Appl. **72**, 2497–2541 (2014)
12. Deng, W., Patil, R., Najjar, L., Shi, Y., Chen, Z.: Incorporating community detection and clustering techniques into collaborative filtering model. In: The 2nd International Conference on Information Technology and Quantitative Management (ITQM 2014), vol. 31, pp. 66–74 (2014). https://doi.org/10.1016/j.procs.2014.05.246
13. Fang, G., Su, L., Jiang, D., Wu, L.: Group recommendation systems based on external social trust networks. Wirel. Commun. Mobile Comput. (2018)
14. Fatemi, M., Tokarchuk, L.: A community based social recommender system for individuals and groups. In: 2013 International Conference on Social Computing (SocialCom), pp. 351–356 (2013). https://doi.org/10.1109/SocialCom.2013.55
15. Fortunato, S.: Community detection in graphs. Phys. Rep. **486**(3), 75–174 (2010)
16. Gao, Y., Liu, H.: Artificial intelligence-enabled personalization in interactive marketing: a customer journey perspective. J. Res. Interact. Mark. 1–18 (2022), https://doi.org/10.1108/JRIM-01-2022-0023
17. Hamzaoui, N., Sedqui, A., Lyhyaoui, A.: Multi-criteria collaborative recommender. Int. J. Comput. Linguist. Res. **3**(3) (2012)
18. He, A.Z., Zhang, Y.: Ai-powered touch points in the customer journey: a systematic literature review and research agenda. J. Res. Interact. Mark. 1–20 (2022), https://doi.org/10.1108/JRIM-03-2022-0082
19. Newman, M.E.J., Girvan, M.: Finding and evaluating community structure in networks. Phys. Rev. E **69**(2) (2004). https://doi.org/10.1103/PhysRevE.69.026113
20. Nguyen, N.P., Dinh, T.N., Tokala, S., Thai, M.: Overlapping communities in dynamic networks: their detection and mobile applications. In: Proceedings of the 17th Annual International Conference on Mobile Computing and Networking, pp. 85–96 (2011). https://doi.org/10.1145/2030613.2030624

21. O'Connor, M., Herlocker, J.: Clustering items for collaborative filtering. In: Proceedings of the ACM SIGIR Workshop on Recommender Systems: Algorithms and Evaluation (2001)
22. Palla, G., Farkas, I., Vicsek, T.: Uncovering the overlapping community structure of complex networks in nature and society. Nature **435**, 814–818 (2005). https://doi.org/10.1038/nature03607
23. Peng, S., et al.: A modern recommendation system survey in the big data era. In: Park, J.S., Yang, L.T., Pan, Y., Park, J.H. (eds.) Advances in Computer Science and Ubiquitous Computing, pp. 577–582. Springer, Singapore (2023). https://doi.org/10.1007/978-981-99-1252-0_77
24. Qiang, H., Yan, G.: A method of personalized recommendation based on multi-label propagation for overlapping community detection. In: The 3rd International Conference on System Science Engineering Design and Manufacturing Informatization, vol. 1, pp. 360–364 (2012). https://doi.org/10.1109/ICSSEM.2012.6340748
25. Qin, S., Menezes, R., Silaghi, M.: A recommender system for youtube based on its network of reviewers. In: The IEEE International Conference on Social Computing, pp. 323–328 (2010). https://doi.org/10.1109/SocialCom.2010.53
26. Rossetti, G., Pappalardo, L., Pedreschi, D., Giannotti, F.: Tiles: an online algorithm for community discovery in dynamic social networks. Mach. Learn. J. **106**, 1213–1241 (2016)
27. Rostami, M., Farrahi, V., Ahmadian, S., Mohammad Jafar Jalali, S., Oussalah, M.: A novel healthy and time-aware food recommender system using attributed community detection. Expert Syst. Appl. **221**, 119719 (2023). https://doi.org/10.1016/j.eswa.2023.119719. https://www.sciencedirect.com/science/article/pii/S0957417423002208
28. Sahebi, S., Cohen, W.: Community-based recommendations: a solution to the cold start problem. In: Workshop on Recommender Systems and the Social Web (RSWEB) (2011)
29. Seko, S., Yagi, T., Motegi, M., Muto, S.: Group recommendation using feature space representing behavioral tendency and power balance among members. In: RecSys, pp. 101–108 (2011)
30. Wang, W., Zhang, G., Lu, J.: Member contribution based group recommender system. Decis. Supp. Syst. **87**, 80–93 (2016)
31. Xie, J., Chen, M., Szymanski, B.K.: Labelrankt: incremental community detection in dynamic networks via label propagation. CoRR (2013)
32. Xin, L., Haihong, E., Junde, S., Meina, S., Junjie, T.: Book recommendation based on community detection. In: Pervasive Computing and the Networked World, pp. 364–373 (2014)
33. Yehuda, K.: Collaborative filtering with temporal dynamics. In: Proceedings of the 15th ACM SIGKDD International Conference on Knowledge Discovery and Datamining, pp. 447–456 (2009). https://doi.org/10.1145/1557019.1557072
34. Yin, B., Yang, Y., Liu, W.: Exploring social activeness and dynamic interest in community-based recommendation system. In: Proceedings of the 23rd International Conference on World Wide Web, pp. 771–776 (2014). https://doi.org/10.1145/2567948.2579237
35. Yuan, C., Lv, T., Chen, X.: An adaptive group recommender based on overlapping community detection. In: IEEE International Conference on Granular Computing, pp. 402–407 (2013)
36. Yuan, Q.: Com: a generative model for group recommendation. In: 20th ACM SIGKDD International Conference on Knowledge Discovery and Data Mining, pp. 163–172 (2014)

Towards Improving Multivariate Time-Series Forecasting Using Weighted Linear Stacking

Konstandinos Aiwansedo$^{(\boxtimes)}$ [ID], Jérôme Bosche [ID], and Wafa Badreddine [ID]

University of Picardy Jules Verne, 33 rue Saint-Leu, Amiens, France
{konstandinos.aiwansedo,jerome.bosche,
wafa.badreddine}@u-picardie.fr

Abstract. In this day and age, the emergence of Big Data, has made a substantial amount of data accessible across various fields. In particular, time-series data has sparked interest, with researchers and practitioners developing approaches and models in an attempt to accurately forecast such type of data. Amongst the three main forecasting approaches, that is, the Separate Model Forecasting Approach (SMFA), the Global Model Forecasting Approach (GMFA) and the Cluster-Based Forecasting Approach (CBFA), studies have showed that GMFA is the least accurate but also the least time-consuming forecasting approach. We propose a Weighted Linear Stacking (WLS) technique for increasing accuracy in the three forecasting approaches, with the highest increase observed by the GMFA, thus becoming the most accurate and viable approach for multivariate time-series forecasting. In addition, we propose two novel forecasting models, a multivariate variant of the N-BEATS model (M-N-BEATS) and a hybrid Transformer-N-BEATS (TRANS-BEATS) model, both for multivariate multi-step ahead time-series forecasting. The proposed models outperform their rivals and their forecasting performance is evaluated by multiple evaluation metrics.

Keywords: Artificial intelligence · Machine learning · Deep neural networks · Time-series forecasting · Clustering algorithms · transformer model · Multivariate Time-Series Forecasting (MTSF) · Weighted linear stacking

1 Introduction

The advent of the information age has allowed for massive data collection and storage across various fields such as finance, weather forecasting, energy, and health sector, etc. A particular type of data collected is time-series data. A time series is defined as a collection of observations obtained through repeated measurements over time. Analyzing time-series data results in a better understanding of the underlying causes that drive different processes that may change over time. Being able to accurately extract useful knowledge from such data structures enables better decision-making strategies, allows for proactive planning, and helps to anticipate upcoming events. Researchers and practitioners alike have been heartily developing various forecasting tools and techniques in order to precisely and accurately model both complex univariate and multivariate time-series sequences and design management systems that can produce robust data

A. P. Rocha et al. (Eds.): ICAART 2023, LNAI 14546, pp. 202–222, 2024.
https://doi.org/10.1007/978-3-031-55326-4_10

processing in distributed parallel computing systems. A specific field where time-series data is conventionally made use of is the energy sector, which heavily relies on time-based predictions for planning purposes. Accurately modeling load consumption over time is paramount when it comes to efficiently allocating resources and planning ahead. This is all the more important given the current geopolitical climate, with the war in Ukraine and the goals set by the European Union in terms of energy efficiency.

When it comes to time-series forecasting, the conventional way of achieving it is to implement a local statistical or deep learning model for each time series, capable of accurately modeling the time series in question. Over the years, this traditional approach has been improved upon in various ways in an attempt to increase forecasting accuracy. Ensemble techniques have been proposed by researchers, consisting of combining the results of either multiple instances of the same forecasting model or the forecasts of multiple distinct forecasting models in an attempt to ameliorate the accuracy of the target variable. Other studies have also proposed combining the weights of the forecasting models instead of the results.

Research has also been carried out on the different forecasting approaches available when dealing with multivariate time series forecasting. In [2], the authors highlight three main approaches for multivariate multi-step ahead time-series forecasting. The study focuses on three forecasting approaches: a Separate Model Forecasting Approach (SMFA), a Global Model Forecasting Approach (GMFA), and a Cluster-Based Forecasting Approach (CBFA). The main takeaway of the study concerning the three forecasting approaches is the necessity of a trade-off between accuracy, execution time, and dataset size is to be made when it comes to determining the finest forecasting approach for a particular dataset. The authors also compared the performance of 6 deep learning architectures when dealing with both univariate and multivariate time-series datasets for multi-step ahead time-series forecasting, across 6 benchmark datasets.

We propose a follow-up study that implements the three aforementioned forecasting approaches on a new benchmark dataset, made up of 14 times series, across more recent deep learning architectures. In addition, we propose two novel forecasting models, the first consists of a modified variant of the Neural Basis Expansion Analysis for Time Series (N-BEATS) model denominated Multivariate-N-BEATS (M-N-BEATS) capable of multivariate forecasting, and the second model is a multivariate hybrid architecture dubbed Transformer-N-BEATS (TRANS-BEATS). Furthermore, we also propose a weighted linear stacking technique for increasing the accuracy of load forecasting.

The remainder of the paper is structured as follows. Section 2 describes the related work found in the literature, while Sect. 3 explains the methodology of our study. Section 4 details the experimental framework of our paper, Sect. 5 exhibits and discusses the results obtained, and finally Sect. 6 concludes on the results and on the overall study and describes what the future work entails.

2   Related Work

2.1   Multivariate Multi-step Time-Series Forecasting Approaches

Local Deep Learning Models for Time-Series Forecasting. When aiming to forecast multiple time series in a dataset, one's traditional approach would be to individually model each time series present in the dataset. Such an approach is dubbed a local approach and exploits univariate time-series datasets. In such regressive cases, time-series future values only depend on past observations. There has been a lot of research done on using deep learning models to regressively forecast univariate time series. In [9], a performance evaluation of multiple deep learning models such as long short-term memory (LSTM), recurrent Neural networks (RNNs), convolutional neural networks (CNNs), bidirectional LSTM (BiLSTM), is conducted. These models are implemented on univariate time series and a multi-step ahead forecasting scheme is implemented is carried out on benchmark datasets. The study concluded that bidirectional networks and encoder-decoder LSTM outcompeted their rivals in terms of accuracy for both simulated and real-world time series problems. In [24], a univariate time-series forecasting study is presented. In the study, temperature and precipitation are forecasted using both machine learning (ML) and statistical methods. Problems associated with univariate time-series forecasting such as lagged variable selection, hyperparameter selection, and performance comparison between machine learning and classical algorithms are explored and dealt with.

Global Deep Learning Models for Time-Series Forecasting. A unique universal function approximator can also be used for multivariate time-series forecasting. In such scenarios, a unique deep learning model takes multiple time series as input at once, processes them in parallel and outputs predictions for each time series. In [20], the local and global principles are studied, implementing both statistical and deep learning models on benchmark datasets. According to this study, as the length of a series increases so does the complexity of local models, which is not the case with global models. The authors showed that global models with an increased complexity outperformed local state-of-the-art models on most datasets, with way fewer parameters. Nonetheless, they argued that the benefits of one principle over the other depend on the context. Their findings underline the necessity of further research in the field of time-series forecasting. In [27], a hybrid model is proposed, capable of thinking globally but acting locally. The model achieves such a feat by leveraging its convolution layers, which capture both local and global time-series properties in a dataset. The proposed model outperformed its contenders on 4 benchmark datasets. In [34], a novel multivariate temporal convolutional network is proposed for multivariate time-series forecasting and compared to existing widely used models for such tasks, such as LSTMs, CNNs, and multivariate attention-based models. In [14], a novel attention-based encode-decoder framework is introduced for multivariate time-series forecasting, with the proposed model outperforming the baseline methods.

Clustering-Based Time-Series Forecasting. When dealing with multiple time-series forecasting problems, several approaches have been put forward over the years in an effort to ameliorate time-series forecasting accuracy. One of these approaches entails a clustering paradigm, whose advantages have been detailed in [4,5,25]. In [5] a clustering approach was evaluated on two different datasets: CIF2015 and NN5. On the CIF2015 dataset, the proposed clustering model outperformed the other models with respect to the specific evaluation metrics used in the competition. On the NN5 dataset, a model based on the clustering method was the best-performing contender in terms of the average rankings, over the evaluated error measures. A similar clustering method was put forward in [31], where the clustering approach results indicated overall forecasting improvements in terms of accuracy and execution time. In [25], the clustering approach was implemented on a financial dataset so as to address noise and non-stationarity. The experimental results were promising for one-step-ahead forecasting, with multi-step-ahead forecasting being a more difficult task. In [28], a clustering method was implemented for pattern recognition on separate datasets.

2.2 Deep Neural Networks Architectures for Time-Series Forecasting

When it comes to time-series forecasting, one has multiple avenues for achieving it. Traditionally, statistical models such as autoregressive integrated moving average ARIMA model had been the default choice. In [10], such a model is used for short-term load forecasting. The ARIMA model is a generalization of a simple autoregressive moving average (ARMA) model capable of modeling sequential data. In [3], an ARIMA model was used for short-term load forecasting and although this was outperformed by an SVM model on a non-linear dataset, it gave better results on a linear type of load. Despite the good results demonstrated by statistical approaches such as ARIMA, they display some notable drawbacks when it comes to dealing with multiple variables, long-term load forecasting and larger datasets. As a result machine learning approaches were introduced as a way of curtailing the problem. In [7], a comparative study of both statistical and machine learning approaches was carried out on time-series forecasting and it showed that on larger and more complex datasets, machine learning approaches tend to yield better results than traditional statistical methods.

A variety of machine learning methods have been proposed for load forecasting such as neural networks [39], support vector regressor machines (SVR) [6], Decision Trees [12], etc. Amongst all machine learning approaches, neural networks in particular have earned quite a reputation in recent years. With regards to load forecasting, the first variants of neural networks proposed were Artificial Neural Networks (ANNs). In [13] and [29], ANNs produced great results on short-term load forecasting and started garnering attention as extremely useful tools for forecasting. However, ANNs were later on supplanted by recurrent neural networks (RNNs), which were more suited for sequential data, as they were able to model sequentiality and learn long-term dependencies in data. Such recurrent networks include Elman Recurrent Networks (ERNNs) [37], Long Short-Term Memory (LSTM) [17] and Gated Recurrent Units(GRU) [36], tailor-made for processing sequential data.

Besides RNNs, convolutional neural networks (CNN) have also surprisingly proved to use extremely suitable for processing sequential data, as they are quite adept at extracting spatial and temporal information in temporal data. In [11], a CNN architecture was used for load forecasting on relying of historical consumption data and outperformed support Vector Machines (SVM) and achieved comparable results to ANNs.

Hybrid models based on a combination of statistical and deep learning models have also recently emerged. In [40] results show that a merging of the two models significantly resulted in reduction in the overall forecasting error, with the hybrid model being able to capture concurrently both linear and nonlinear patterns in the dataset. Hybrid models based solely on combination of machine learning models have also been widely studied and democratized. In [23, 30, 38] and [26], a hybrid CNN-GRU model is utilized for resolving various tasks such as, water level prediction, license plate recognition, oil soil moisture prediction and residential short-term residential load forecasting respectively.

Despite the state-of-art performance of recurrent neural networks and hybrid models, a new family of neural network models have been developed fairly recently, based the self-attention mechanism, called Transformers [33]. Such transformer-based architectures include Informer model in [15], temporal fusion transformers in [18], transformer-based model in [19] and probabilistic transformer for time-series forecasting in [32]. The main advantages of transformer-based architectures compared to recurrent neural network architectures are the elimination of the time-dependant aspect related to recurrent networks, thus allowing for parallelization, the capability of modeling long-term dependencies in long sequences and their ability to selectively focus on the most relevant features of the input by weighting and computing attention scores.

2.3   Linear Combination for Time-Series Forecasting

Several linear combination schemes for increasing forecasting accuracy can be found in literature. In [1], a linear combination framework for time series forecasting that applies an Artificial Neural Network (ANN) model to combine the weights of individual models trained on in-samples datasets. The results of the study showed the proposed methodology increased accuracy and produced better results than the component models. In [35], the results of four statistical forecasting models were combined through various combination schemes and the results showed that although the combination techniques do not always lead the most accurate results when compared to the results of individual models, the combination techniques considerably result in a reduction of forecasting failure and thus tend to be more reliable. In [16], a study carried out on the M3-competition dataset of over 3000 time-series showed that the advantage of combining forecasts resides in the fact that it is less risky in practice to combine forecasts than to select an individual forecasting method.

3   Methodology

In this section, we detail the methodology of our study. The three forecasting approaches and the 2 proposed forecasting models are presented as well as the Weighted Linear Stacking (WLS) technique for increase accuracy in load data.

3.1   Forecasting Approaches

In aiming to achieve multivariate forecasting by implementing various deep learning neural network models, one must first determine the most suitable forecasting approach at their disposal and determine the factors that hold the highest significance for each approach, in order to obtain optimal results. The three forecasting approaches described in [2] are presented below and allow for both univariate and multivariate multi-step ahead time-series forecasting, by implementing a Multi Input Multi Output scheme (MIMO).

The Separate Model Forecasting Approach (SMFA). As shown in Fig. 1, consists of employing distinct models to process each time series within a dataset individually. In this approach, the forecasts for a specific time-series variable are generated by solely processing lagged values of that particular variable, without considering the data from other time-series variables. This methodology follows an autoregressive process, where the values of a time series are explained by its previous values rather than those of other time-series variables.

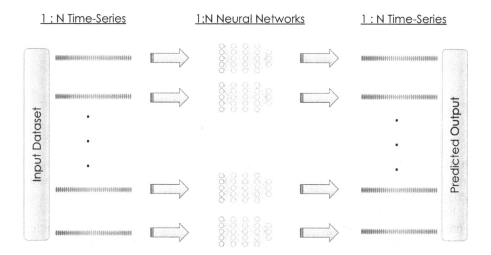

Fig. 1. Separate Model Forecasting Approach (SMFA) described in [2].

The Global Model Forecasting Approach (GMFA). As shown in Fig. 2, utilizes cross-series information sharing, employing a singular global model to simultaneously process all time-series within the dataset. In this scenario, the exchange of information across series becomes crucial and impactful, as the predictions of a specific time-series are the results of processing not only its historical data but also the historical data of other time-series present in the dataset.

The Cluster-Based Forecasting Approach (CBFA). As shown in Fig. 3, comprises two distinct stages: clustering and forecasting. The clustering stage involves identifying similarities amongst dataset elements with the purpose of forming homogeneous groups, also referred to as clusters, by partitioning the dataset. Subsequently, during the forecasting stage, an instance of deep neural network models is applied to each cluster identified in the clustering stage, in order to forecast the elements of each cluster.

3.2 Proposed Forecasting Models

In our study, we propose two novel deep learning models for time-series forecasting. The first model is a modified variant of the N-BEATS model introduced in [21] for multivariate time-series dubbed M-N-BEATS. The second proposed model is a hybrid model, made up of a Transformer model introduced in [33] and an N-BEATS model [21], dubbed TRANS-BEATS also for multivariate time-series forecasting.

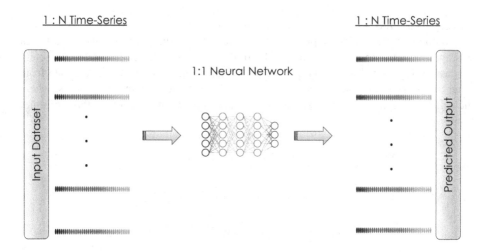

Fig. 2. Global Model Forecasting Approach (GMFA) described in [2].

Multivariate N-BEATS (M-N-BEATS) Model: is based on the N-BEATS architecture but tailored for multiple time-series processing. The N-BEATS is a basis expansion method for modeling non-linear relationships and is trained to determine the appropriate basis expansion method for accurately modeling the data for forecast purposes. It presents several advantages over existing deep learning models, such as training faster, multi-step-ahead forecasting, inherently leveraging the advantages of boosting and ensemble learning, and not suffering from the vanishing gradient problem. It has been notably used in [22] for mid-term electricity forecasting.

The N-BEATS model is composed of blocks, with each block containing 4 fully connected layers and producing two outputs. The first output, the backcast, tries to rebuild the block's input, while the second, the forecast, tries to predict the desirable forecast horizon. The N-Beats architecture leverages the potential of residual connections by adding skip connections between the blocks to capture information that was missed by previous blocks. Several aligned blocks form a stack, with the final output of a specific stack being the summed-up element-wise forecast outputs of its comprising blocks. When multiple stacks are piled up, the final predictions are obtained by summing up element-wise the outputs of all stacks.

Although a similar model to the N-BEATS architecture has been introduced for multivariate time-series, named Neural Hierarchical Interpolation for Time Series Forecasting (N-hits) presented in [8], which introduces hierarchical interpolation and multi-rate data sampling techniques for time-series forecasting, we decided to stick with the initial model and modify its architecture in order to be able to simplify its merger with a transformer model.

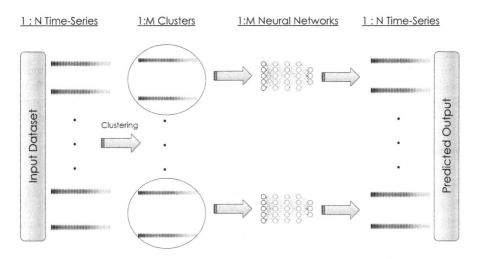

Fig. 3. Cluster-Based Forecasting Approach (CBFA) described in [2].

TRANS-BEATS Forecasting Model: is a fusion of a Transformer model and our proposed M-N-BEATS model. The intuition behind this merger is to combine the multi-headed self-attention mechanism of a Transformer model with the advantages of boosting and ensemble learning techniques associated with an M-N-BEATS model.

The transformer model is a natural language processing model initially intended for tasks such as text summarization and translation, but giving its dominance in the field of NLP and its expanding usage in other fields such as computer vision, music generation, time-series forecasting, and image recognition and generation.

It is two main advantages: a self-attention mechanism that weighs the importance of each part of the input data differently and its ability to parallelize processing during training. It is based on an encoder-decoder structure, with the encoder mapping the input to a sequence of continuous representations and the decoder receiving the encoder's output as well as the decoder's previous time step's output before generating an output sequence. The encoder and decoder modules can be stacked on each other several times to capture more complex patterns and relationships in the data, effectively model long-range dependencies and improve hierarchical feature extraction.

3.3 Proposed Weighted Linear Stacking Technique

Section 3.1 presents three different forecasting approaches: SMFA, GMFA, and CBFA. Previous studies in the literature show that amongst the three forecasting approaches, the Separate Model Forecasting Approach (SMFA) seems to produce the most accurate results but is also the most computationally expensive approach. Conversely, the Global Model Forecasting Approach (GMFA) tends to lead to poorer performance in terms of accuracy but it is the most time-efficient approach. As for the Cluster-Based Forecasting Approach (CBFA), it appears to be an acceptable compromise between accuracy and time efficiency. Each of these approaches can be implemented by N models whose architecture and dimension can impact the quality of the forecasts. With that in mind, Sect. 3.2 presents two novel deep learning models (M-N-BEATS and TRANS-BEATS models).

In an attempt to furthermore increase accuracy, Fig. 4 illustrates a Weighted Linear Stacking (WLS) technique that can be applied indiscriminately regardless of the forecasting approach (SMFA, GMFA, or CBFA). The main goal is to predict the load data set for the year 2019. It is therefore assumed that load data corresponding to the period from January 1, 2015, to December 31, 2018, is available. Accordingly, this technique consists of 3 steps:

- **Step 1:** From the load data available until the end of 2017, the N models (M_1, M_2,...,M_N) are established and produce N data forecasts for 2018: $f_1, f_2,...,f_n$. At this point, it is clear that these N forecasts are distinct from each other, with some being more accurate and others. It is then possible to assess the quality of these forecasts since the load data for the year 2018, denoted f^{2018}, is also known.
- **Step 2:** From the N forecasts f_i^{2018}, $\forall i \in \{1,..,N\}$ obtained during step 1, the objective is to determine the function $\hat{f}^{2018}$ defined in (1) that minimizes the square difference between f^{2018} and $\hat{f}^{2018}$.

$$\hat{f}^{2018} = \sum_{i=1}^{N} a_i.f_i^{2018} \tag{1}$$

Let's consider the time-series f^{2018} of dimension k such as $f^{2018} \in \mathbf{R}^{k \times 1}$, with our task involving addressing following optimization problem:

$$\min_{a_1, a_2, .., a_N} \frac{1}{k}e^T.e \text{ such as } f^{2018} = a_1.f_1^{2018} + a_2.f_2^{2018} + ... + a_N.f_N^{2018} \tag{2}$$

with

$$\{e = f^{2018} - \hat{f}^{2018} \,|\, e \in \mathbf{R}^{k \times 1}\} \tag{3}$$

A solution can be directly determined by the expression (4).

$$\begin{bmatrix} a_1 & a_2 & ... & a_N \end{bmatrix}^T = (VV^T)^{-1}.V.f^{2018} \tag{4}$$

with

$$V = \begin{bmatrix} f_1^{2018} & f_2^{2018} & ... & f_N^{2018} \end{bmatrix}^T \tag{5}$$

- **Step 3:** From the load data available until the end of 2018, N data forecasts are computed for 2019: f_1^{2019}, f_2^{2019},...,f_n^{2019}. The final forecast for 2019 consists of a weighted linear combination of the N forecasts from the different models such that:

$$\hat{f}^{2019} = \sum_{i=1}^{N} a_i.f_i^{2019} \tag{6}$$

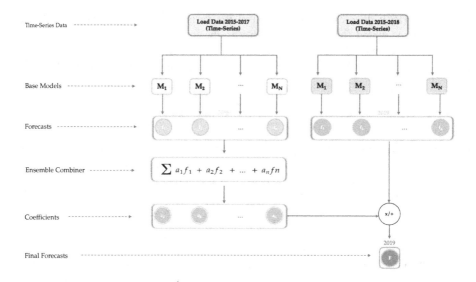

Fig. 4. Weighted Linear Stacking Technique (WLS).

4   Experimental Framework

In this section, we detail the experimental setup, such as the benchmark dataset used, the evaluation metrics, the deep neural networks' hyperparameters tuning, and the hardware requirements.

4.1   Dataset

The European Network of Transmission System Operators for Electricity (ENTSO-E) Transparency Platform allows users to access data related to electricity generation, transportation, and consumption in the pan-European market. This platform includes information provided by different transmission system operators (TSOs) across Europe.

The dataset[1] used is comprised of load consumption data from the following countries: Specifically, consumption data for Western European countries such as Austria, Belgium, Switzerland, Denmark, Germany, Spain, France, the UK, Italy, Ireland, the Netherlands, Norway, Portugal, and Sweden has been obtained. The load consumption is given in Megawatts (MW), is available at a time resolution of 1 h, and goes from January 2015 up to August 2020.

4.2   Evaluation Metrics

In order to address the limitations of individual forecasting metrics, multiple evaluation measures are employed. In doing so, we account for various shortcomings associated with specific metrics, such as sensitivity to outliers, balancing between penalizing over-predictions and underpredictions, handling homogeneous and heterogeneous samples, and distinguishing between small and large errors.

---

[1] Dataset available at: https://transparency.entsoe.eu.

R-Squared (R^2): denotes the proportion of the variability in the dependent variable that can be accounted for by the variability in the independent variable. When R^2 is high, it indicates that the model's variability is comparable to that of the actual values, whereas a low R^2 value implies a weak relationship between the two sets of values.

$$R^2 = 1 - \frac{\sum_{i=1}^{n}(y_i - \hat{y}_i)^2}{\sum i = 1^n (y_i - \bar{y})^2} \tag{7}$$

Root Mean Absolute Percentage Error (RMSE): is the standard deviation of the residuals (forecasting errors). The residuals measure the deviation between the data points and the regression line. The RMSE metric is a measure of the spread of these residuals.

$$RMSE = \sqrt{\frac{\sum_{i=1}^{n}(y_i - \hat{y}_i)^2}{n}} \tag{8}$$

Mean Absolute Error (MAE): is defined as the average of the absolute difference between forecasted and actual values. MAE measures only the magnitude of the errors and does not take into account the direction of the error.

$$MAE = \frac{1}{n}\sum_{i=1}^{n}|y_i - \hat{y}_i| \tag{9}$$

Weighted Absolute Percentage Error (WAPE): is a metric used to measure the accuracy of a forecast by calculating the average of the absolute percentage errors, with each error weighted by the corresponding actual value.

$$WAPE = \frac{\sum_{i=1}^{n}|y_i - \hat{y}_i|}{\sum i = 1^n y_i} \tag{10}$$

4.3   Deep Neural Networks' Hyperameters

(See Tables 1 and 2).

Table 1. Deep Learning Models' Shared Hyperparameters.

Hyperparameters	Values
Batch size	32
Learning Rate	0.01
Past History	30 Timesteps
N of epochs	1400
Forecast Horizon	20
Dropout	0.2
Normalisation (ED)	Minmax
Optimizer	Adam
Forecasting scheme	Multi-Input Multi-Output (MIMO)

Table 2. Deep Learning Models' Hyperparameters.

Models	Hyperparameters	Values
M-N-BEATS	$N°$ of stacks	11
	$N°$ of blocks	1
	FC stacks layers	4
	FC hidden units	64
	Block sharing	false
Transformer	$N°$ of encoders	3
	$N°$ of attention heads	5
	Dimensionality	15
	Hidden size	6, 64
Bi-GRU	Layers	3
	Units	32, 32, 24
	Return sequences	True, True
TRANS-BEATS	$N°$ of encoders	3
	$N°$ of attention heads	5
	Dimensionality	15
	Hidden size	6, 64
	$N°$ of stacks	11
	$N°$ of blocks	1
	FC stacks layers	4
	FC hidden units	64
	Block sharing	false
CNN-GRU	Layers	2
	Filters - Units	32–14
	Pool size	1
	Return sequences	True

4.4 Hardware Requirements

In order to evaluate the three forecasting approaches across 5 distinct deep neural network architectures, a specialized hardware setup was necessary for the experimentation. For this purpose, we employed our laboratory's distributed memory system. The system comprises 2320 computing cores, and 20 GPUs, providing a computing power of 225 teraFLOPS, along with 19.4 TB of memory. Additionally, a visualization node with 1 GPU is included. The platform also incorporates 3D scanners, humanoid robots, and customized software tools.

5 Results and Discussions

This section presents the experimental results from our study, focusing on the assessment of the three forecasting approaches (SMFA, GMFA, CBFA.SOM, CBFA.OPTICS,

CBFA.K-MEANS) detailed in Sect. 3.1. We also evaluate the accuracy of our forecasting architectures. Figure 5 provides a visual comparison of all approaches in relation to the forecasting models with respect to the 1-R^2 metric. The closer the point is to the center of the plot, the more precise and accurate the approach and forecasting model is. We also present the results obtained from the weighted linear stacking technique for increasing forecasting accuracy.

5.1 Cluster Generation and Selection Phases' Results

Similarly to the study in [2], before assessing the performance of the clustering approach (CBFA), a cluster generation phase and selection phase preceded. The clustering algorithms, K-Means, OPTICS, and SOM, used in [2], were also implemented for this study. During the clustering phase, the hyperparameters of these clustering algorithms were varied, with each variation leading to the formation of different clusters. Following the clustering generation phase, the cluster selection phase involved identifying the optimal cluster amongst those previously generated for each clustering algorithm. The results are displayed in Table 3.

Table 3. Clustering Results.

Clustering Algorithms	Clusters	Execution Time (seconds)
SOM	4	292.318
K-MEANS	8	0.054
OPTICS	3	0.059

5.2 Forecasting Approaches' Evaluation Results

To evaluate the performance of a forecasting approach, various evaluation metrics are calculated for each time-series in the dataset and for each forecasting model, that is, M-N-BEATS, Transformer, Bi-GRU, TRANS-BEATS, and CNN-GRU. The overall error for each forecasting approach is determined by taking the average error across all series for a specific forecasting model and then averaging the results across the forecasting models. Figure 5 displays the results obtained with respect to the R^2 metric when attempting to forecast the electricity consumption for the year 2019.

Out of the three variants of the clustering approach (CBFA), the one involving the SOM algorithm achieves better results when compared to CBFA.OPTICS and CBFA.K-MEANS clustering approaches. The SOM clustering algorithm has been able to accurately cluster the series in the dataset in comparison to the K-MEANS and OPTICS clustering algorithms. It is also worth noting that the performance of the SOM algorithm could be partly explained by its execution time (Table 3), which is significantly longer than the execution time of the K-MEANS and OPTICS algorithms, thus allowing for more processing to take place. As a result, we'll be only presenting the results of this approach (CBFA.SOM) and comparing it to the SMFA and GMFA approaches.

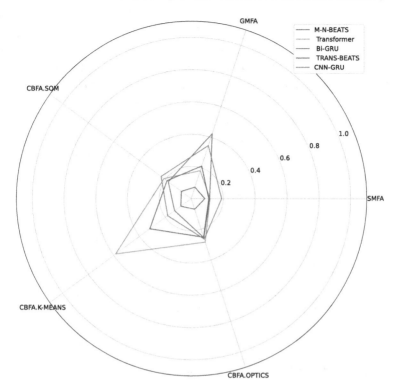

Fig. 5. R^2 Load Forecasting Results For 2019.

Table 4. Average Scores Across All Models.

Metrics	R^2	RMSE	MAE	WAPE
SMFA	**87.64%**	**1308.14**	**931.97**	**0.0430**
GMFA	75.22%	1669.34	1255.97	0.0591
CBFA.SOM	*82.33%*	*1537.28*	*1140.12*	*0.0539*
CBFA.K-MEANS	74.11%	1836.70	1374.62	0.0633
CBFA.OPTICS	77.48%	1686.90	1268.39	0.0611

Table 4 shows the results obtained per forecasting approach. Amongst all forecasting approaches and with respect to all four evaluation metrics used, the SMFA approach ranks first with an overall R^2 score of 87.64%, with the second most accurate forecasting approach being a clustering approach CBFA.SOM, with an R^2 score of 82.33%. The GMFA approach generally comes in last among all forecasting approaches.

It is important to point out that these results corroborate the findings of [2] pertaining to the accuracy of the three forecasting approaches: Separate Model Forecasting Approach (SMFA), Global Model Forecasting Approach (GMFA) and Cluster-Based Forecasting Approach (CBFA). Indeed, [2] found that overall the SMFA and CBFA approaches tend to yield better results than the GMFA, which is also the case in our study.

Table 5. SMFA Scores.

Metrics	R^2	RMSE	MAE	WAPE
M-N-BEATS	**91.49%**	**1074.13**	**717.09**	**0.0342**
Transformer	88.26%	1262.87	881.74	0.0409
Bi-GRU	88.48%	1310.45	950.12	0.0435
TRANS-BEATS	89.02%	1244.22	884.92	0.0410
CNN-GRU	80.97%	1649.03	1225.97	0.0554
Average	87.64%	1308.14	931.97	0.0430

Table 6. GMFA Scores.

Metrics	R^2	RMSE	MAE	WAPE
M-N-BEATS	**92.52%**	**950.70**	**624.47**	**0.0307**
Transformer	81.81%	1361.84	996.84	0.0499
Bi-GRU	57.61%	2174.34	1707.95	0.0779
TRANS-BEATS	78.77%	1558.87	1128.05	0.0547
CNN-GRU	65.42%	2300.93	1822.52	0.0823
Average	75.22%	1669.34	1255.97	0.0591

5.3 Forecasting Models' Evaluation Results

Tables 5, 6 and 7 condense the results displayed in the radar plot Fig. 5 and display the results obtained for the forecasting models with respect to all 4 evaluation metrics. As for the SMFA approach (Table 5), the proposed M-N-BEATS model outperforms any other model with an R^2 score of 91.49%. This also seems to be the case for the GMFA (Table 6) and CBFA (Table 7) where M-N-BEATS occupies once again the first position in the rankings, with an R^2 score of 92.52% and 92.41% respectively. The second proposed model TRANS-BEATS is the second-ranked forecasting model for the SMFA approach, regardless of the evaluation metric used, with the Transformer model securing the third position. However, when it comes to the GMFA approach, it is the Transformer model that claims the second spot with the TRANS-BEATS model holding the third position. As for the CBFA approach, the TRANS-BEATS model claims the second spot but only with respect to the R^2 and WAPE metrics and third when considering the RMSE and MAE metrics. Consequently, for the CBFA, the Transformer model takes second place with respect to the RMSE and MAE metrics and secures third place when only taking into account the R^2 and WAPE evaluation metrics.

The average scores of all forecasting models across all 3 forecasting approaches are depicted in Table 8, with respect to all evaluation metrics. Once again, the forecasting model producing the best scores, regardless of the chosen evaluation metric, tends to be the M-N-BEATS forecasting model with an average R^2 score of 92.14% across the three forecasting approaches. The TRANS-BEATS model ranks second when considering the R^2 metric score but third with respect to RMSE and MAE metrics. Consequently, the Transformer model ranks third and fourth, with respect to the R^2 and RMSE and MAE metrics respectively.

Table 7. CBFA.SOM Scores.

Metrics	R^2	RMSE	MAE	WAPE
M-N-BEATS	**92.41%**	**999.36**	**666.47**	**0.0322**
Transformer	78.96%	1541.42	1161.55	0.0599
Bi-GRU	82.33%	1629.81	1219.51	0.0565
TRANS-BEATS	81.26%	1588.65	1185.09	0.0574
CNN-GRU	76.72%	1927.15	1467.96	0.0637
Average	82.33%	1537.28	1140.12	0.0539

In general, amongst all forecasting models, the proposed M-N-BEATS model is undoubtedly the highest-performing forecasting model across all forecasting approaches and regardless of the evaluation metric employed. The M-N-BEATS model seems to produce better results for GMFA and CBFA.SOM approaches (92.51% and 92.41%) than the SMFA (91.49%) The second-highest performing forecasting model is either the second proposed hybrid model TRANS-BEATS or Transformer model, depending on the forecasting approach or evaluation metric taken into account. The least accurate forecasting model seems to be the hybrid CNN-GRU model. However, the CNN-GRU model had been the highest performing model in the study carried out in [2], when compared to traditional deep learning models, such as MLP, LSTM, GRU, and CNN. This outlines the recent advances made in the field of time-series forecasting, with the new generation of time-series forecasting models being even more robust and accurate compared to the models of the previous generations.

Table 8. Average Scores Across All Approaches.

Metrics	R^2	RMSE	MAE	WAPE
M-N-BEATS	**92.14%**	**1008.07**	**669.34**	**0.032**
Transformer	83.01%	*1388.71*	*1013.38*	*0.050*
Bi-GRU	76.14%	1704.86	1292.53	0.059
TRANS-BEATS	*83.02%*	1463.91	1066.02	0.051
CNN-GRU	74.37%	1959.04	1505.48	0.067

5.4 Average Execution Time

The average execution time for both the forecasting approaches and models are depicted in Fig. 6. The completion time of forecasting model is calculated by summing up the execution time for all the time-series (14 time-series) in the dataset. The overall time completion of a forecasting model across all forecasting approaches can be computed by summing up the completion time of each approach. In doing so, the most time-intensive forecasting model is the Bi-GRU model with an execution time of 17.19 h, followed by the TRANS-BEATS model with a completion time of 6.72 h, then the

Transformer model with an execution time of 5.16 h, the penultimate M-N-BEATS model with a completion time of 2.44 h and the least time-consuming model, which is the CNN-GRU model with an execution time of 1.83.

The total execution time for a forecasting approach can be estimated by the addition of the execution time of all forecasting models to belonging that approach. By doing so, we observe that the most time-consuming forecasting approach is the Separate Model Forecasting Approach (SMFA), with an overall execution time of 26.73 h, followed by the Cluster-Based Forecasting Approach(CBFA.SOM), with a completion time of 4.15 h and unsurprisingly, the least time-consuming approach is the Global Model Forecasting Approach (GMFA), with a completion time of 2.46 h.

5.5   Weighted Linear Stacking (WLS) Results

The results obtained by applying a weighted linear stacking (WLS) technique on the load forecasts for the year 2019 are presented in Table 9. This scheme involves linearly combining the results of forecasting models' predictions in an attempt to increase accuracy for each forecasting approach. The results show that after having applied WLS, the accuracy increases across the board in all approaches, irrespective of the evaluation metric used. Amongst all forecasting approaches, the Global Model Forecasting Approach (GMFA) produces the finest results with an R^2 score of 93.29%, followed by a Cluster-Based Forecasting Approach (CBFA.SOM) with an R^2 score of 92.75% and the Separate Model Forecasting Approach (SMFA) securing the last position with an R^2 score of 92.05%.

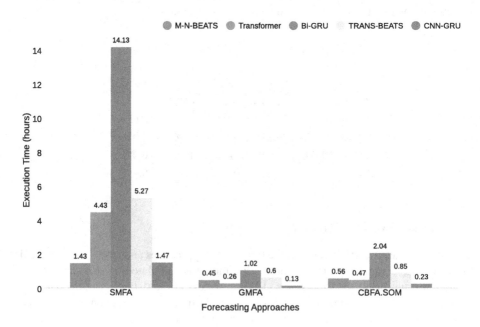

Fig. 6. Average Execution Time.

Table 9. WLS Evaluation Results.

Metrics	R^2	RMSE	MAE	WAPE
SMFA	92.05%	1035.55	700.56	0.0332
GMFA	93.29%	918.64	615.66	0.0300
CBFA.SOM	92.75%	982.37	661.15	0.0318

The study carried in [2], showed that among the three forecasting approaches, the GMFA had been the least accurate but also the least time-consuming approach, which was also confirmed by the results of our study by Table 4 and by Fig. 6. However, after having implemented the WLS technique, the results in Table 9, the Global Model Forecasting Approach (GMFA) becomes the most accurate approach among the three, while also being the most time-efficient approach, followed by a Cluster-Based Forecasting Approach (CBFA.SOM) and finally the Separate Model Forecasting Approach (SMFA). Consequently, the results indicate that the Global Model Forecasting Approach (GMFA) can be considered a viable forecasting approach when dealing with multivariate multi-step time-series forecasting.

6   Conclusion

In this study, we evaluated the results obtained after implementing the 3 main forecasting approaches, that is the Separate Model Forecasting Approach (SMFA), the Global Model Forecasting Approach (GMFA), and the Cluster-Based Forecasting Approach (CBFA), on an electricity consumption dataset, by applying multiple recent state-of-the-art forecasting models, which allowed us to validate the results obtained by a previous evaluation study [2], pertaining to the efficacy of the three forecasting approaches. We also proposed two different multivariate forecasting models, one being a modified variant of the N-BEATS model for multivariate time-series forecasting, dubbed M-N-BEATS and the second one being a hybrid Transformer M-N-BEATS model, dubbed TRANS-BEATS, with the M-N-BEATS model producing the best results amongst all forecasting models and the TRANS-BEATS model achieving the second or third best performance depending on the evaluation metric taken into consideration. In addition, we also proposed a weighted linear stacking (WLS) technique for increasing accuracy in load forecasting. In future work, we intend to evaluate the performance of the two proposed forecasting models on more datasets. In addition, we also plan to apply Weighted Linear Stacking (WLS) technique for increasing accuracy, on datasets originating from various fields, such as finance, the healthcare and the weather sectors, and retail. Another interesting work, given the good and promising results obtained by multi-attention-based models, would be to compare the performance of various transformer-based models, such as the Informer, the Temporal Fusion Transformer (TFT), the LogTrans, and the Reformer forecasting models, by applying the three forecasting approaches. Such a study would help determine the strengths and weaknesses associated with each transformer model in relation to the three forecasting approaches.

Acknowledgements. We would like to express our deepest appreciation to Teleric, a prominent company based in Amiens, France, specializing in connected traceability in the cleaning market. We would also like to extend our deepest gratitude to the Region Hauts-de-France for providing the necessary resources to conduct this study.

References

1. Adhikari, R.: A neural network based linear ensemble framework for time series forecasting. Neurocomputing **157**, 231–242 (2015)
2. Aiwansedo, K., Badreddine, W., Bosche, J.: Trade-off clustering approach for multivariate multi-step ahead time-series forecasting (2023)
3. Al Amin, M.A., Hoque, M.A.: Comparison of ARIMA and SVM for short-term load forecasting. In: 2019 9th Annual Information Technology, Electromechanical Engineering and Microelectronics Conference (IEMECON), pp. 1–6. IEEE (2019)
4. Asadi, R., Regan, A.C.: A spatio-temporal decomposition based deep neural network for time series forecasting. Appl. Soft Comput. **87**, 105963 (2020)
5. Bandara, K., Bergmeir, C., Smyl, S.: Forecasting across time series databases using recurrent neural networks on groups of similar series: a clustering approach. Expert Syst. Appl. **140**, 112896 (2020)
6. Ceperic, E., Ceperic, V., Baric, A.: A strategy for short-term load forecasting by support vector regression machines. IEEE Trans. Power Syst. **28**(4), 4356–4364 (2013)
7. Cerqueira, V., Torgo, L., Soares, C.: Machine learning vs statistical methods for time series forecasting: size matters. arXiv preprint arXiv:1909.13316 (2019)
8. Challu, C., Olivares, K.G., Oreshkin, B.N., Garza, F., Mergenthaler-Canseco, M., Dubrawski, A.: N-hits: neural hierarchical interpolation for time series forecasting. arXiv preprint arXiv:2201.12886 (2022)
9. Chandra, R., Goyal, S., Gupta, R.: Evaluation of deep learning models for multi-step ahead time series prediction. IEEE Access **9**, 83105–83123 (2021)
10. Chen, J.F., Wang, W.M., Huang, C.M.: Analysis of an adaptive time-series autoregressive moving-average (ARMA) model for short-term load forecasting. Electr. Power Syst. Res. **34**(3), 187–196 (1995)
11. Cheng, Y., Xu, C., Mashima, D., Thing, V.L.L., Wu, Y.: PowerLSTM: power demand forecasting using long short-term memory neural network. In: Cong, G., Peng, W.C., Zhang, W., Li, C., Sun, A. (eds.) ADMA 2017. LNCS, vol. 10604, pp. 727–740. Springer, Cham (2017). https://doi.org/10.1007/978-3-319-69179-4_51
12. Ding, Q.: Long-term load forecast using decision tree method. In: 2006 IEEE PES Power Systems Conference and Exposition, pp. 1541–1543. IEEE (2006)
13. Drezga, I., Rahman, S.: Short-term load forecasting with local ANN predictors. IEEE Trans. Power Syst. **14**(3), 844–850 (1999)
14. Du, S., Li, T., Yang, Y., Horng, S.J.: Multivariate time series forecasting via attention-based encoder-decoder framework. Neurocomputing **388**, 269–279 (2020)
15. Gong, M., Zhao, Y., Sun, J., Han, C., Sun, G., Yan, B.: Load forecasting of district heating system based on informer. Energy **253**, 124179 (2022)
16. Hibon, M., Evgeniou, T.: To combine or not to combine: selecting among forecasts and their combinations. Int. J. Forecast. **21**(1), 15–24 (2005)

17. Kong, W., Dong, Z.Y., Jia, Y., Hill, D.J., Xu, Y., Zhang, Y.: Short-term residential load forecasting based on LSTM recurrent neural network. IEEE Trans. Smart Grid **10**(1), 841–851 (2017)
18. Lim, B., Arık, S.Ö., Loeff, N., Pfister, T.: Temporal fusion transformers for interpretable multi-horizon time series forecasting. Int. J. Forecast. **37**(4), 1748–1764 (2021)
19. L'Heureux, A., Grolinger, K., Capretz, M.A.: Transformer-based model for electrical load forecasting. Energies **15**(14), 4993 (2022)
20. Montero-Manso, P., Hyndman, R.J.: Principles and algorithms for forecasting groups of time series: locality and globality. Int. J. Forecast. **37**(4), 1632–1653 (2021)
21. Oreshkin, B.N., Carpov, D., Chapados, N., Bengio, Y.: N-beats: neural basis expansion analysis for interpretable time series forecasting. arXiv preprint arXiv:1905.10437 (2019)
22. Oreshkin, B.N., Dudek, G., Pełka, P., Turkina, E.: N-beats neural network for mid-term electricity load forecasting. Appl. Energy **293**, 116918 (2021)
23. Pan, M., et al.: Water level prediction model based on GRU and CNN. IEEE Access **8**, 60090–60100 (2020)
24. Papacharalampous, G., Tyralis, H., Koutsoyiannis, D.: Univariate time series forecasting of temperature and precipitation with a focus on machine learning algorithms: a multiple-case study from Greece. Water Resour. Manag. **32**(15), 5207–5239 (2018)
25. Pavlidis, N.G., Plagianakos, V.P., Tasoulis, D.K., Vrahatis, M.N.: Financial forecasting through unsupervised clustering and neural networks. Oper. Res. Int. J. **6**(2), 103–127 (2006)
26. Sajjad, M., et al.: A novel CNN-GRU-based hybrid approach for short-term residential load forecasting. IEEE Access **8**, 143759–143768 (2020)
27. Sen, R., Yu, H.F., Dhillon, I.S.: Think globally, act locally: a deep neural network approach to high-dimensional time series forecasting. In: Advances in Neural Information Processing Systems, vol. 32 (2019)
28. Sfetsos, A., Siriopoulos, C.: Time series forecasting with a hybrid clustering scheme and pattern recognition. IEEE Trans. Syst. Man Cybern.-Part A Syst. Hum. **34**(3), 399–405 (2004)
29. Sheikh, S.K., Unde, M.: Short term load forecasting using ANN technique. Int. J. Eng. Sci. Emerg. Technol. **1**(2), 97–107 (2012)
30. Suvarnam, B., Ch, V.S.: Combination of CNN-GRU model to recognize characters of a license plate number without segmentation. In: 2019 5th International Conference on Advanced Computing & Communication Systems (ICACCS), pp. 317–322. IEEE (2019)
31. Tadayon, M., Iwashita, Y.: A clustering approach to time series forecasting using neural networks: a comparative study on distance-based vs. feature-based clustering methods. arXiv preprint arXiv:2001.09547 (2020)
32. Tang, B., Matteson, D.S.: Probabilistic transformer for time series analysis. In: Advances in Neural Information Processing Systems, vol. 34, pp. 23592–23608 (2021)
33. Vaswani, A., et al.: Attention is all you need. In: Advances in Neural Information Processing Systems, vol. 30 (2017)
34. Wan, R., Mei, S., Wang, J., Liu, M., Yang, F.: Multivariate temporal convolutional network: a deep neural networks approach for multivariate time series forecasting. Electronics **8**(8), 876 (2019)
35. Wong, K.K., Song, H., Witt, S.F., Wu, D.C.: Tourism forecasting: to combine or not to combine? Tour. Manag. **28**(4), 1068–1078 (2007)
36. Xiuyun, G., Ying, W., Yang, G., Chengzhi, S., Wen, X., Yimiao, Y.: Short-term load forecasting model of GRU network based on deep learning framework. In: 2018 2nd IEEE Conference on Energy Internet and Energy System Integration (EI2), pp. 1–4. IEEE (2018)
37. Yongchun, L.: Application of Elman neural network in short-term load forecasting. In: 2010 International Conference on Artificial Intelligence and Computational Intelligence, vol. 2, pp. 141–144. IEEE (2010)

38. Yu, J., Zhang, X., Xu, L., Dong, J., Zhangzhong, L.: A hybrid CNN-GRU model for predicting soil moisture in maize root zone. Agric. Water Manag. **245**, 106649 (2021)

39. Zhang, H.T., Xu, F.Y., Zhou, L.: Artificial neural network for load forecasting in smart grid. In: 2010 International Conference on Machine Learning and Cybernetics, vol. 6, pp. 3200–3205. IEEE (2010)

40. Zhang, Y., Luo, L., Yang, J., Liu, D., Kong, R., Feng, Y.: A hybrid ARIMA-SVR approach for forecasting emergency patient flow. J. Ambient. Intell. Humaniz. Comput. **10**(8), 3315–3323 (2019)

Study on LSTM and ConvLSTM Memory-Based Deep Reinforcement Learning

Fernando Fradique Duarte[1]([envelope]) [iD], Nuno Lau[2] [iD], Artur Pereira[2] [iD],
and Luís Paulo Reis[3] [iD]

[1] Institute of Electronics and Informatics Engineering of Aveiro, University of Aveiro, Aveiro,
Portugal
fjosefradique@ua.pt
[2] Department of Electronics, Telecommunications and Informatics, University of Aveiro,
Aveiro, Portugal
{nunolau,artur}@ua.pt
[3] Faculty of Engineering, Department of Informatics Engineering, University of Porto, Porto,
Portugal
lpreis@fe.up.pt

Abstract. Memory-based Deep Reinforcement Learning (DRL) has been successfully applied to solve vision-based control tasks from high-dimensional sensory data. While most of this work leverages the Long Short-Term Memory (LSTM) as the memory module of the agent, recent developments have revisited and extended the original formulation of the LSTM. Some of these developments include the ConvLSTM, a convolutional-based implementation of the LSTM, the MDN-RNN, the combination of a Mixture Density Network with an LSTM and the GridLSTM, a multidimensional grid of LSTM cells. It seems however unclear how these different memory modules compare to each other in terms of agent performance, when applied in the context of DRL. This work aims to perform a comparative study of several memory-based DRL agents, based on the LSTM, ConvLSTM, MDN-RNN and GridLSTM memory modules. The results obtained seem to support the claim that in some cases these more recent memory modules can improve the performance of the agent, to varying degrees, when compared to a baseline agent based on an LSTM. The experimental results were validated in the Atari 2600 videogame platform.

Keywords: Deep reinforcement learning · Long short-term memory ·
Convolutional long short-term memory · Mixture density network · Grid long
short-term memory

1 Introduction

Memory-based Deep Reinforcement Learning (DRL) has been successfully applied to solve vision-based control tasks, such as videogames, directly from high-dimensional sensory data [1–7]. Most of this work leverages the Long Short-Term Memory (LSTM) [8] as the memory module of the agent. The LSTM is a very popular Recurrent Neural

A. P. Rocha et al. (Eds.): ICAART 2023, LNAI 14546, pp. 223–243, 2024.
https://doi.org/10.1007/978-3-031-55326-4_11

Network (RNN), featuring a specialized architecture designed to overcome the error backflow problems found in other RNN designs.

Recent developments have revisited and extended the original LSTM design. Some examples of this work include the Convolutional LSTM (ConvLSTM) [9], a convolutional-based implementation of the LSTM, the Mixture Density Network (MDN) [10] combined with an LSTM (MDN-RNN) [6, 7] and the GridLSTM [11], a multidimensional grid of LSTM cells. These memory modules aim to solve a wide range of diverse problems, such as: preserving spatial information, which may prove to be a crucial factor when dealing with vision-based control tasks (in the case of the ConvLSTM), endowing the agent with the ability to act instinctively on predictions of the future, without the need to explicitly plan ahead (in the case of the MDN-RNN) and generalizing the advantages of LSTMs to the context of Deep Neural Networks (DNNs) (in the case of the GridLSTM).

While each of these different memory modules tries to solve specific and dissimilar problems, they can all be applied to memory-based Reinforcement Learning (RL), see [5–7] for some examples of this. However, it is unclear how these different memory modules compare to each other in terms of performance and specifically when used in the context of DRL. The original work proposed in [12], which the present work aims to extend, tried to provide some insight into this issue by presenting a comparative study of the LSTM, ConvLSTM, MDN-RNN and GridLSTM memory modules in the context of DRL. The four main research questions originally proposed were the following:

- **Q1.** Can the learning process be improved by preserving the spatial information inside the memory module of the agent, when solving vision-based control tasks directly from high-dimensional sensory data (e.g., raw pixels)?
- **Q2.** What are the advantages or disadvantages of using a contextual memory (e.g., LSTM) as opposed to a predictive one (e.g., MDN-RNN)?
- **Q3.** Do different memory modules play significantly different roles concerning the decision making of the trained agent?
- **Q4.** Can the learning process be improved by using separate memory sub-modules in parallel to process different information (e.g., GridLSTM)? In this work this question is replaced by **Q4.1**, see Sect. 3.1 for more details.

While these research questions continue to be the focus of the present work, there are some noticeable changes to the original work, both in terms of the implementation of the agents and the experimental methodology used. These changes include:

- **C1 (Implementation).** The implementation of the MDN-RNN-based agent was revised. This allowed the number of trainable parameters of the agent to be roughly halved. This also presented the opportunity to test different versions of the predictive model, specifically: (1) the model only predicts the next state, (2) the model predicts both the next state and the next action and (3) the model predicts the next state, the next action, and the next reward.
- **C2 (Implementation).** This work only uses one of the two originally proposed versions of the GridLSTM-based agent. The rationale for this is twofold. On the one hand the performance results obtained in the original work did not seem to indicate a clear difference between the two versions tested. On the other hand, this work

proposes a different research question focused on the flow of memory through the different dimensions of the GridLSTM. Stated more specifically: *how does the flow of memory through the depth dimension impact the learning process and the performance of the agent?* Two scenarios are considered to answer this question. In the first scenario, memory is not allowed to flow through the depth dimension, similarly to the original formulation proposed in [11]. In other words, the depth dimension is memoryless. In the second scenario considered, memory is allowed to flow through the depth dimension. In this case the depth dimension keeps its own memory between consecutive steps. This is in contrast with the original work, which proposed a more implementation driven research question based on the different types of information flowing through the GridLSTM.

- **C3 (implementation).** The format of the experience tuples integrated by the memory module changed from (z_t, a_t) to (z_t, a_{t-1}, r_{t-1}). The use of experience information from the previous time step, namely a_{t-1} and r_{t-1} is required due to change **C4** below, whereas the inclusion of r_{t-1} allows the agent to potentially integrate more information into memory, which may be beneficial to the learning process.

- **C4 (methodology).** In the original work, the memory module did not participate in the optimization process of the encoder module. The rationale for this was to isolate the memory module from any possible interference from the encoder module, so that it could be analyzed in isolation. Unfortunately, some of the memory modules (e.g., ConvLSTM) proved to be sensitive to this methodology choice and performed poorly in some of the games (e.g., ChopperComand). Therefore, in this work the memory module participates in the optimization of the encoder module.

- **C5 (methodology).** The number of games tested was increased from 2 to 3 with the inclusion of the game SpaceInvaders.

Finally, in a similar fashion to the original work, the visualization technique proposed in [13] was used to visualize the saliency maps of the agents implemented, in an effort to derive further insight into their decision process. These visualizations are presented and discussed in Sect. 4. Also, this work does not address external memory-based DRL such as in [14] and [15]. As before, the Atari 2600 videogame benchmark was used to validate all the experiments.

The remainder of the paper is structured as follows. Section 2 presents the related work, including a brief overview of the technical background. Section 3 discusses the experimental setup. The discussion first lays out the main differences concerning the original work, both in terms of focus and research goals, implementation details, and overall methodology. This is followed by the presentation of the methods proposed and the training setup used. Section 4 presents the experiments carried out and discusses the results obtained and finally Sect. 5 presents the conclusions.

2 Related Work

This section first presents the notation used throughout the paper and some common terminology used in the RL literature, followed by a high-level overview of the related work and technical background pertinent to this work.

2.1 Notation and Terminology

In the RL literature, the agent-environment interaction is considered to occur at discrete intervals or time steps. The current time step is usually denoted as t, $t - 1$ is used to denote the previous time step and $t + 1$ is used to denote the next time step. At each time step t, the agent observes a state s_t (or observation o_t or z_t when denoting the state as processed by an encoder), chooses and action a_t to act on the environment, receives a reward signal r_{t+1} and the environment transitions to the next state s_{t+1}. Each time step of this interaction is often represented as a tuple of experience of the form $(s_t, a_{t+1}, r_{t+1}, s_{t+1})$. A trajectory τ, induced by a policy π, comprises a sequence of these tuples, see Fig. 1(a).

When presenting the memory modules, the hidden state of the RNN is usually denoted as a tuple of the form (h_t, c_t), where h_t denotes the hidden state and c_t denotes the hidden cell state. This hidden state is usually updated using some input, for example the experience tuple (z_t, a_{t-1}, r_{t-1}), together with the previous hidden state (h_{t-1}, c_{t-1}). For simplicity, (h_{t-1}, c_{t-1}) is usually considered to be implicitly included in the input to the RNN and may be omitted.

In the equations, W_i is used to denote the trainable weights and b_i is used to denote the bias terms of the ith layer of the DNN. σ denotes the sigmoid function, *tanh* denotes the function by the same name and $\otimes$ represents the Hadamard product. Also, when it is said that the size of a linear layer is for example 128, and assuming an input vector of size I, then W_i is a matrix of size [I, 128] and b_i is a vector of size [128], see Fig. 1(b). Lastly, a 3D tensor denotes a tensor of the form [C, H, W], which can be thought of as a volume with C channels of height H and width W, see Fig. 1(c).

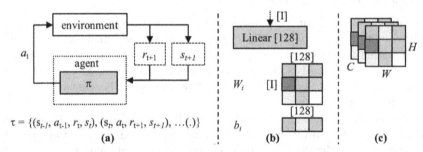

Fig. 1. (a) The agent-environment interaction. (b) Weight matrix W_i and bias vector b_i of a linear layer of size 128, assuming an input vector of size I. (c) A 3D tensor.

2.2 Memory-Based Deep Reinforcement Learning

Many control problems, such as videogames, must be solved in partially observable environments. This means that at each time step, the true underlying state of the environment, (e.g., the videogame), cannot be fully observed in its entirety by an external sensor, (e.g., the agent). The problem of partial observability arises frequently in vision-based control tasks. Occlusions, missing information about the velocities of objects and limitations associated to the vision sensors, such as restricted field-of-view or limited bandwidth, are some of the most common factors contributing to this [2].

One possible way to tackle the partial observability issue is to model the dynamics of the environment using the Partially Observable Markov Decision Process (POMDP) framework, wherein the agent maintains a belief state over the true world state given the observations it has received so far [1, 2]. See also [16] for a more formal and detailed discussion. However, maintaining a belief state can be both computationally costly and error prone.

Two other approaches commonly used to solve the partial observability issue, listed in order of ascending complexity include: 'manually' encoding the current state so that it satisfies the Markov property and dynamically learning memories while interacting with the environment [2]. Both approaches allow the environment to be modeled and solved using the Markov Decision Process (MDP) framework, therefore eschewing the complexities associated with POMDPs.

Concerning the 'manual' approach, in some cases (e.g., many Atari 2600 videogames) the current state can be trivially crafted to satisfy the Markov property, by simply providing multiple frames at each time step. This was the approach used in [17], where the last $k = 4$ past observations (i.e., game screens) were used as a 'sufficient' description of the state of the environment at each time step. The main drawback of this technique is its reliance on the value of k, which must be derived manually and is task dependent [1].

These issues may be addressed by dynamically learning memories, instead. In this case, the sequences of experience tuples derived from the agent-environment interactions can be dynamically integrated into a contextual memory. This memory is optimized jointly with the remaining modules composing the agent and requires no special learning setup. RNNs, such as the LSTM, are well suited to work with sequences and can be leveraged as the memory module in this case. This presents several advantages over the 'manual' solution. First, k is no longer necessary, since in this case the agent only needs access to the current state of the environment at each time step. Second, the agent can dynamically learn and determine what a 'sufficient' history is, according to the needs of the task. This may imply keeping a compressed history spanning more than k past observations. Examples of this work include [1–4].

2.3 Long Short-Term Memory

Early RNN designs were very unstable and hard to train, particularly when dealing with longer sequences. More specifically, these early designs suffered from error backflow problems, where the error signals would either vanish or blow-up during the optimization process. Therefore, these RNNs were of limited use and could not be used to solve complex problems. The LSTM [8] was introduced to solve these issues and is at the core of many of the recent successes in Artificial Intelligence (AI) research. Since its introduction the LSTM has gained widespread popularity in many domains of application such as speech recognition [18], machine translation [19], video sequence representation [20], language modeling and sentiment analysis [21]. Equation (1) below, presents the formulation of the LSTM as implemented in Pytorch [22], where i_t, f_t and o_t denote the input, forget, and output gates, respectively.

$$i_t = \sigma(W_{ii}x_t + b_{ii} + W_{hi}h_{t-1} + bh_i)$$
$$f_t = \sigma\left(W_{if}x_t + b_{if} + W_{hf}h_{t-1} + bh_f\right)$$
$$g_t = tanh\left(W_{ig}x_t + b_{ig} + W_{hg}h_{t-1} + bh_g\right) \qquad (1)$$
$$o_t = \sigma(W_{io}x_t + b_{io} + W_{ho}h_{t-1} + bh_o)$$
$$c_t = f_t \otimes c_{t-1} + i_t \otimes g_t$$
$$h_t = o_t \otimes tanh(c_t)$$

2.4 Convolutional Long Short-Term Memory

Despite their great success, LSTMs do not preserve spatial information, which may be important in vision-based tasks. The ConvLSTM [9] was proposed to address this issue. The original formulation of the ConvLSTM is based on the Peephole LSTM [23] variant, with the caveat that all the involved tensors are 3D, namely, the inputs, the hidden state of the RNN and the gates, see Eq. (2) below. An example of this work can be found in [5], where the authors used a ConvLSTM in their vision core to implement an attention-augmented RL agent.

$$i_t = \sigma(W_{xi}x_t + W_{hi}h_{t-1} + W_{ci} \otimes c_{t-1} + b_i)$$
$$f_t = \sigma(W_{xf}x_t + W_{hf}h_{t-1} + W_{cf} \otimes c_{t-1} + b_f)$$
$$c_t = f_t \otimes c_{t-1} + i_t \otimes tanh(W_{xc}x_t + W_{hc}h_{t-1} + b_c) \qquad (2)$$
$$o_t = \sigma(W_{xo}x_t + W_{ho}h_{t-1} + W_{co} \otimes c_t + b_o)$$
$$h_t = o_t \otimes tanh(c_t)$$

2.5 Grid Long Short-Term Memory

Broadly speaking, GridLSTMs generalize the advantages of LSTMs to the realm of DNNs. More specifically, the GridLSTM [11] was proposed to address two main issues related to DNNs, particularly those comprising longer sequences of layers: (1) the vanishing gradient problem, similar to the one addressed by LSTMs, but applied to DNNs and (2) the inability of DNN layers to dynamically filter their input and select only the information considered to be relevant at each moment.

At a high-level, a GridLSTM is a DNN arranged in a grid with one or more dimensions. Layers communicate with each other directly through LSTM cells which can be placed along any (or all) of these dimensions, although some dimensions (denoted non-LSTM dimensions) may still contain regular connections between the layers. These dimensions may be prioritized as needed. The cells communicate with each other using an efficient N-way communication mechanism. Finally, GridLSTMs promote more compact models by allowing the weights to be shared among all the dimensions (Tied N-LSTMs).

2.6 MDN-RNN

The MDN [10] combines a Neural Network (NN) with a mixture density model, which in principle can represent arbitrary conditional probability distributions. More formally, given an input x and an output y and assuming that the generator of the data $y \in Y$ is a mixture model, such as a Gaussian Mixture Model, the probability density of the target data can be represented as in Eq. (3) below, where the mixing components $\alpha_i(x)$ can be considered as prior probabilities (i.e., the probability that the target y was generated from the ith component of the mixture) and the functions $\phi_i(y|x)$ denote the conditional density of the target y for the ith kernel.

$$p(y|x) = \sum_{i=1}^{m} \alpha_i(x)\phi_i(y|x) \tag{3}$$

The work in [6, 7] combined an MDN with an LSTM, referred to as MDN-RNN, to derive a predictive memory of the future $P(z_{t+1}|z_t, a_t, h_t)$, which can be queried by the agent to act without the need to plan ahead.

3 Experimental Setup

This section presents the experimental setup used, including the discussion of the main differences regarding the original work, the presentation of the baseline architecture of the agents and the various memory modules proposed, and finally the training setup used to perform the experiments.

3.1 Implementation and Methodology Changes

C1 (implementation). The implementation of the MDN-RNN-based agent was revised. This allowed the number of trainable parameters to be almost halved in comparison to the original implementation. This was achieved by switching the internal implementation from using two linear layers to using three convolutional layers (with batch normalization, except the last layer) to predict z_{t+1} and a single linear layer to predict a_{t+1} and r_{t+1}. The convolutional layers were configured with [64, 64, 32] input channels, [64, 32, 64] output channels, and kernel size 3 with stride and padding 1 to keep the size of the feature maps fixed. This revision also presented the opportunity to pose a new research sub-question:

- **Q2.1.** How do different predictive models affect the learning process and the performance of the agent?

Three predictive models were tested to assess this research question, namely: (1) a predictive model of the next state, (2) a predictive model of both the next state and the next action and (3) a predictive model of the next state, the next action, and the next reward. The results obtained are discussed in Sect. 4.

C2 (implementation). The implementation of the GridLSTM-based agent was also revised to assess a new research sub-question, namely:

- **Q4.1.** How does the flow of memory through the depth dimension impact the learning process and the performance of the agent?

Two scenarios were considered to answer this question. In the first scenario, memory was not allowed to flow through the depth dimension, similarly to the original formulation [11]. In other words, at each time step the input is projected into the hidden state of the LSTM cell of the first layer of the depth dimension. In this case the depth dimension is effectively memoryless. In the second scenario considered, memory was allowed to flow through the depth dimension. More specifically, the input is only projected into the h_t slot of the hidden state, and the previous memory state is allowed to flow through the c_t slot. In this case the depth dimension keeps its own memory between consecutive steps. The results obtained are discussed in Sect. 4.

C3 (implementation). Due to change **C4**, the format of the experience tuples integrated by the memory module was changed to (z_t, a_{t-1}, r_{t-1}). The inclusion of r_{t-1} allows the agent to potentially integrate more information into memory, which may be beneficial to the learning process. The results obtained are discussed in Sect. 4.

C4 (methodology). Originally, the memory module was isolated from the encoder module by not participating in its optimization process. Given that some of the memory modules proved to be sensitive to this methodology choice and performed poorly in some of the games tested, in this work the memory module participates in the optimization of the encoder module, see Table 1 and Table 2. While this means that the memory module can no longer be analyzed in isolation, the affected memory modules should now be less sensitive to this new methodology.

Table 1. Pseudocode for the old methodology.

```
z_t = encode(s_t)
a_t = act(h_t, z_t)
(h_t, c_t) = memorize(z_t.detach(), a_t, (h_{t-1}, c_{t-1}))
```

The MDN-RNN module is the exception. Since the MDN-RNN module is predicting z_{t+1}, which in turn is derived by the encoder, both modules cannot participate in each other's optimization. Also, the MDN-RNN has its own optimization process independently from the rest of the agent, see Table 3. As a side note, *detach()* is used in Pytorch to cut the flow of the gradients during backpropagation.

Table 2. Pseudocode for the new methodology.

```
z_t = encode(s_t)
(h_t, c_t) = memorize(z_t, a_{t-1}, r_{t-1}, (h_{t-1}, c_{t-1}))
a_t = act(h_t)
```

Table 3. Pseudocode for the MDN-RNN module (new methodology).

```
z_t = encode(s_t)
(h_t, c_t) = memorize(z_t.detach(), a_{t-1}, r_{t-1}, (h_{t-1}, c_{t-1}))
a_t = act(z_t, h_t.detach())
```

3.2 Agent Architecture

The architecture used to compose the agents is similar to the one proposed in the original work [12]. More specifically, the architecture comprises three main blocks or modules, namely: (1) the encoder, responsible for processing the 2D high-dimensional inputs, (2) the memory, responsible for compressing the sequence of agent-environment experiences into a 'sufficient' memory of past interactions and (3) the policy, responsible for choosing the actions to perform on the environment.

More concretely, at each time step t, the encoder receives a single observation o_t, representing the current state of the game and encodes it into a set of feature maps z_t. The memory module integrates the next experience tuple (z_t, a_{t-1}, r_{t-1}) and updates its hidden state, which is used by the policy module to choose the action a_t to perform at that time step, see Fig. 2(a).

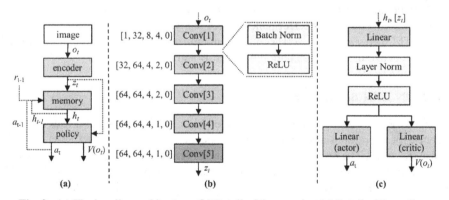

Fig. 2. (a) The baseline architecture. (b) Detail of the encoder. (c) Detail of the policy.

Due to implementation details, the input to the policy module of the MDN-RNN-based agent comprises both h_t and z_t, whereas all other agents use h_t only. Also, since the underlying learning algorithm used belongs to the actor-critic family of RL algorithms, the policy module also outputs the value function of the states $V(o_t)$.

While this architecture is common to all the agents tested, the implementation of the different modules may vary and shall be presented when appropriate. The exception to this is the policy encoder which is similar in all agents. Specifically, the policy comprises a linear layer with size 128 followed by layer normalization [24] and a Rectified Linear Unit (ReLU) nonlinearity, which feeds into two other linear layers, the actor and the critic, responsible for choosing the actions a_t and computing the values of the states $V(o_t)$, respectively, see Fig. 2(c).

3.3 Baseline Agent

The baseline agent, referred henceforth as *LSTM*, follows the original implementation [12]. Namely, the encoder is composed of $l = 5$ convolutional layers configured with (1, 32, 64, 64, 64) input channels, (32, 64, 64, 64, 64) output channels, kernel sizes (8, 4, 4, 4, 4), strides (4, 2, 2, 1, 1) and no padding, respectively. Each convolutional layer is followed by batch normalization [25] and a ReLU nonlinearity, see Fig. 2(b). In this case, the choice of $l = 5$ convolutional layers as opposed to $l = 4$ was made solely for the purpose of decreasing the number of trainable parameters (by approximately 1 million), since preliminary tests did not find any significant difference in terms of performance. The memory module comprises an LSTM with size 256.

3.4 ConvLSTM-Based Agent

The ConvLSTM-based agent, referred henceforth as *ConvLSTM*, also follows the original implementation. In this case, the encoder is composed of $l = 4$ convolutional layers. The reason for this is twofold. On the one hand some quick empirical tests seemed to indicate that the ConvLSTM performed better with $l = 4$. On the other hand, using $l = 4$ allowed the number of trainable parameters of both the LSTM and the ConvLSTM-based agents to be almost identical, therefore excluding this as a possible explanatory factor when comparing the agents performance wise. Finally, the memory module comprises a ConvLSTM with size [64, 8, 5]. The implementation used is similar to Eq. (1), converted to 3D inputs and using concatenation between x_t and h_{t-1}.

3.5 MDN-RNN-Based Agent

The MDN-RNN-based agent, henceforth referred to as *MDN-RNN*, also uses an $l = 4$ encoder, for the reasons already mentioned, since it is based on a ConvLSTM memory of size [64, 8, 5]. The remaining implementation details, except for those mentioned in Sect. 3.1, follow [10] and [6, 7]. The two main reasons to implement both the MDN-RNN and the GridLSTM modules using a ConvLSTM were the following: 1) the ConvLSTM has been less explored in the literature when compared to the LSTM and 2) because the ConvLSTM preserves spatial information. This allows a better inspection of the role of memory in the decision making of the trained agent, via visualization techniques such as [13].

3.6 GridLSTM-Based Agent

The GridLSTM-based agent, henceforth referred to as 2-*GridLSTM*, also uses an $l = 4$ encoder and is based on a ConvLSTM memory of size [64, 8, 5]. As already stated in Sect. 3.1 this agent differs from the original both in terms of implementation and research questions (**Q4.1** was added to the original set of research questions proposed and replaces **Q4**). The implementation used shares weights across dimensions and prioritizes the depth dimension.

3.7 Training Setup

In terms of pre-processing steps, the input image at each time step is converted to grayscale and cropped to 206 by 158. No rescaling is performed. All agents are trained for a minimum of 16,800,000 frames, which can be extended until all current episodes are concluded, similarly to what is proposed in [26]. In this context an episode is a set of m lives. A total of eight training environments were used in parallel to train the agents using the Advantage Actor-Critic (A2C) [27]. Adam [28] was used as the optimizer. The learning rate is fixed and set to 1e−4. The loss was computed using Generalized Advantage Estimation [29] with $\lambda = 1.0$. An entropy factor was added to the policy loss with a scaling factor of 1e−2, the critic loss was also scaled by a factor of 0.5, rewards were clipped in the range $[-1, 1]$ and a discount factor of $\gamma = .99$ was used. No gradient clipping was performed. The environment versions used during training implemented the frame skipping mechanism in-built in OpenAI Gym [30].

At the beginning of training the internal state of the memory component is set to an empty state (i.e., all zeros) representing the state of no previous knowledge. And is never reset to zero during the remainder of the training procedure. Finally, the number of trainable parameters for each of the memory modules implemented is as follows (for Riverraid): LSTM 1,206,899, ConvLSTM 836,019, MDN-RNN 2,785,807 and 2-GridLSTM 840,243.

4 Experimental Results

The experimental results were obtained using the following methodology. Each memory module implemented was trained using three agents initialized with different seeds. The training results were computed at every 240,000[th] frame over a window of size $w = 50$ and correspond to the averaged return scores obtained during training in the last w fully completed episodes. After the training process was completed, each of the three agents played 100 games for a total of 300. The scores obtained were used to derive the test results. The statistical significance tests were carried out using the one-way ANOVA and the Kruskal-Wallis H-test for independent samples, with $\alpha = 0.05$. The null hypothesis $H0$ considers that all agents have the same return mean results.

The Atari 2600 videogame platform, available via the OpenAI Gym toolkit, was the benchmark used to perform and validate the experiments. The three games used for the experiments were: RiverRaid, ChopperCommand and SpaceInvaders. These games were selected since they provide a wide range of different challenges. All agents were implemented in Pytorch. The results obtained are presented next.

234   F. F. Duarte et al.

4.1 Preliminary Results

Figure 3 and Fig. 4 below present the preliminary results regarding research sub-questions **Q2.1** and **Q4.1**, respectively. Regarding **Q2.1**, predictive model (2) achieved the best results, whereas predictive model (3) performed the worst. Given these results it seems to be the case that endowing predictive models with a broader scope (i.e., predicting more aspects of the environment dynamics besides the next state) can improve both the learning process and the agent's performance.

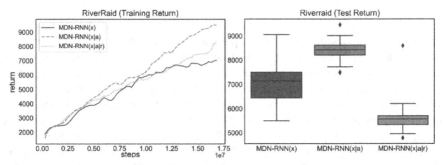

Fig. 3. Training and test results for Q2.1 (Riverraid). MDN-RNN(x), MDN-RNN(x|a) and MDN-RNN(x|a|r) denote predictive model (1), (2) and (3), respectively.

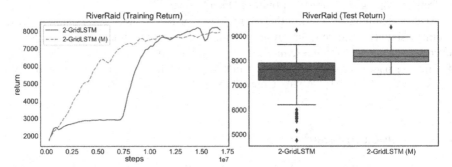

Fig. 4. Training and test results for Q4.1 (Riverraid). In 2-GridLSTM memory is not allowed to flow through the depth dimension. In 2-GridLSTM (M) memory flows through this dimension.

However, as exemplified by the results obtained by predictive model (3), this is not a straightforward process. On the one hand, not all aspects of the dynamics of the environment may be equally informative or even beneficial to the learning process. On the other hand, as the scope of the predictive model becomes broader, its internal architecture may become the real performance bottleneck. In this work, all models were tested out-of-the-box. Concerning **Q4.1**, it appears that allowing memory to flow through the depth dimension of the GridLSTM, agent 2-*GridLSTM* (*M*), can improve both the learning process and the performance of the agent. All results were statistically significant in both experiences. *MDN-RNN*(x|a) and 2-*GridLSTM* (*M*) were used in the following experiments.

4.2 Comparative Results

Revising the implementation of some of the models and adopting a new methodology opened the opportunity to compare the results obtained for both methodologies. As depicted in Fig. 5, overall, the performance of all agents improved when using the new methodology and the revised implementations. The ConvLSTM-based agent benefited the most with the new methodology, whereas the LSTM-based agent suffered a bit in terms of performance, particularly in Riverraid ($H0$ is not rejected for ChopperCommand with p-value 0.7 (ANOVA) and 0.18 (H-Test)). The results obtained by *MDN-RNN* and 2-*GridLSTM*, although encouraging, seem to indicate that these architectures need further finetuning. The original results can be found in [12].

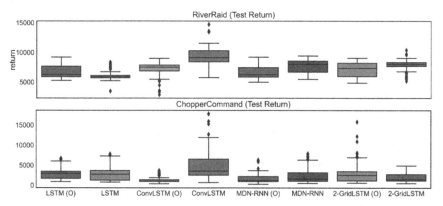

Fig. 5. Test results for the old methodology, models annotated with the (O) marker, and for the new methodology with revised implementations, models with no additional annotation. The games used were Riverraid and ChopperCommand.

4.3 Test Results

Figure 6 depicts the test results obtained for all agents under the new methodology and revised implementations. Overall *ConvLSTM* outperformed all other agents in all the games tested. *MDN-RNN* and 2-*GridLSTM* were able to outperform *LSTM* in Riverraid but underperformed on the remaining games. This may be evidence indicating the need to further finetune the architecture of these models in order to improve their performance in a wider range of games. All results are statistically significant.

Figure 7 depicts the 'reward per step' results. Overall, these results agree with the results depicted in Fig. 6. Nevertheless, the results obtained by 2-*GridLSTM* in Riverraid may seem a bit surprising, at least at first. The average number of steps (not depicted) tells the whole story: *LSTM* (1228), *ConvLSTM* (1740), *MDN-RNN* (1492) and 2-*GridLSTM* (1407). So, while in Riverraid 2-*GridLSTM* is more efficient per step than the other models it is only slightly better than *LSTM* in terms of how far it can progress in the game. The results for *LSTM* and *ConvLSTM* in ChopperCommand and SpaceInvaders are also related to this issue. In terms of efficiency both models are indistinguishable, since

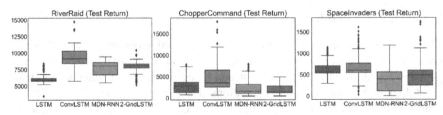

Fig. 6. Overall test results.

$H0$ cannot be rejected, p-value $= 0.54$ (ChopperCommand) and 0.16 (SpaceInvaders) for the H-test. However, ConvLSTM is able to progress further in both games: *LSTM* (987), *ConvLSTM* (1602) for ChopperCommand and *LSTM* (1208), *ConvLSTM* (1316) for SpaceInvaders.

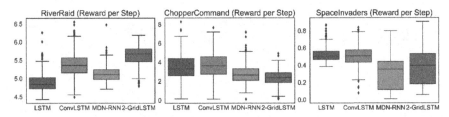

Fig. 7. Overall 'reward per step' results.

4.4 Image Saliency Visualization

The saliency metric proposed in [13] was leveraged to gain better insight into the decision process of the different agents implemented. The saliency maps used were derived using both image and memory perturbation. This section presents the image perturbation visualizations. The saliency visualizations reported were derived by taking the best trained agent for each memory module, running it over 20 games and choosing the best run. In the images, the policy network is displayed in blue whereas the value network is displayed in red.

Riverraid. Overall, the agents seem to focus on the main elements of the game, namely: the enemies, the riverbank and the agent's projectile. None of the agents seems to have learned to refuel in a consistent way, although their value networks indicate clear value in states of low fuel. Generally speaking, the difference in performance observed can be mostly explained by the way the agents prioritize their targets and how assertive they are at destroying or avoiding their enemies. The *ConvLSTM* agent seems to be better at this, and in particular in the way it steers its projectile to destroy a further away enemy while positioning itself to destroy a nearby enemy. The remaining agents seem to have more trouble choosing their targets, miss more shots, seem to be more undecisive at times, and get too close to their enemies, making them more prone to collisions. A side effect of this indecisiveness and inaccuracy is that sometimes these agents end up inadvertently refueling, see Fig. 8.

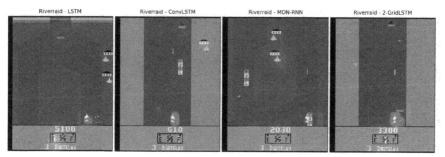

Fig. 8. From left to right: (**1**) The value network of the LSTM agent (colored in red) is focused both on the agent and the fuel indicator, which is almost completely depleted. However, the agent does not attempt to refuel. This is common to all other agents. (**2**) The ConvLSTM agent is very efficient at guiding its projectile to destroy a further away enemy while positioning itself to destroy a nearby target. (**3**) Due to inaccuracy or indecisiveness the MDN-RNN agent does not destroy all the fuel depots and ends up inadvertently refueling sometimes. The LSTM and 2-GridLSTM agents exhibit similar behavior. (**4**) Again, due to indecisiveness or inaccuracy, the 2-GrisLSTM agent suffers from various near miss scenarios, making it more prone to collisions with its enemies. The LSTM and MDN-RNN agents exhibit similar behavior (Color figure online).

ChopperComand. Overall, the agents seem to focus on the main elements of the game, namely: the enemies, the radar display, and the agent. although to varying degrees. There are some noticeable differences, however. The *ConvLSTM* agent seems to be the only agent that sometimes notices the enemies' bullets, although it is still killed by them, on occasion. The 2-*GridLSTM* agent on the other hand focuses on the game score, which is irrelevant for the most part. Similarly to Riverraid, the difference in performance observed can be mostly explained by the way the agents prioritize their targets and how assertive they are at destroying or avoiding their enemies. The *ConvLSTM* agent is clearly better at it, and it also seems to have better focus on the important aspects of the game. The other agents are inaccurate, fail to focus on their enemies at times, can be hesitant when prioritizing their targets and are prone to collisions. The *MDN-RNN* and 2-*GridLSTM* agents seem to be particularly prone to this kind of behavior, see Fig. 9.

SpaceInvaders. Overall, the agents seem to focus on the main elements of the game, namely: the alien enemies, the stationary defense bunkers, the agent itself. and the enemies' projectiles. The *MDN-RNN* agent also focuses on the surrounding areas near the agent, where the enemy projectiles fall, see Fig. 10.

The saliency visualizations also reveal some traces of planned behavior, given that sometimes it can be distinctively seen that the alien enemy highlighted also becomes the next target. Similar findings were reported in [13]. In this case the agents display very distinct behaviors, which explain the differences in performance observed. The *LSTM* and the *ConvLSTM* agent destroy their enemies more evenly across all the columns of enemies, whereas the *MDN-RNN* and the 2-*GridLSTM* agents exhibit a riskier behavior, preferring to destroy columns of enemies. This leaves them exposed as the defense bunkers are removed once the alien enemies have reached them.

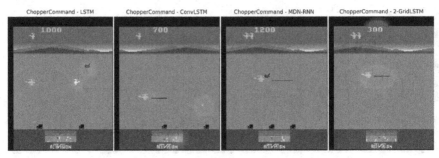

Fig. 9. From left to right: (**1**) The LSTM agent focuses on the main aspects of the game, but fails to recognize the enemies' bullets, and ends up being killed by them sometimes. (**2**) The ConvLSTM agent is the only agent that recognizes the enemies' bullets, although not all the time and this fact does not prevent it from still dying from being hit. (**3**) The MDN-RNN agent fails to focus on its enemies and is prone to collisions. (**4**) The 2-GridLSTM agent focuses on irrelevant aspects of the game such as the game score.

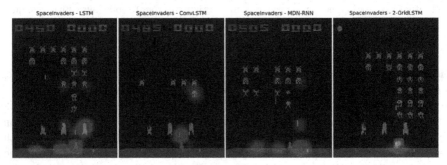

Fig. 10. From left to right: (**1**) The LSTM agent focuses on the main aspects of the game, namely the alien enemies, their projectiles, the defense bunkers, and the agent itself. All the other agents exhibit similar behavior, to varying degrees. (**2**) At times, traces of internal planning behavior can be distinctively observed, where the enemy highlighted becomes the next target. (**3**) The MDN-RNN agent placed strong focus on the enemies' projectiles and the areas surrounding the agent where these projectiles hit. (**4**) The 2-GridLSTM agent exhibits a riskier behavior by choosing to destroy columns of enemies as opposed to destroying the enemies more evenly across all columns. This leaves it exposed, as the defensive bunkers are removed once the enemies have reached them. The MDN-RNN agent exhibits similar behavior.

These visualizations also show another interesting trait of memory-based agents, contextual tracking. The SpaceInvaders game suffers from flickering, this means that objects may disappear between consecutive frames. One way to address this problem is to combine several frames (or game screens) together, as in the 'manual' approach described in Sect. 2.2 and take their maximum. In memory-based RL, however, only one frame is used at each time step. As a result of this the agent must track the trajectories of the objects as they vanish and reappear (flicker) between consecutive frames. And this is what is happening with the flickering projectiles of the enemies. While at times failing miserably, several instances of daring dodges can be observed throughout the course of the game. One such example is presented for the *ConvLSTM* agent in Fig. 10.

4.5 Memory Saliency Visualization

This section presents the memory perturbation visualizations, see Fig. 11, Fig. 12 and Fig. 13. This is made possible by the fact that ConvLSTM preserves spatial information. Memory perturbation was achieved, similarly to image perturbation, by zeroing out the memory positions. More specifically, at each time step the updated hidden state of the RNN h_t, was perturbed using a similar process to the one used to perturb the images, before being passed as input to the policy module.

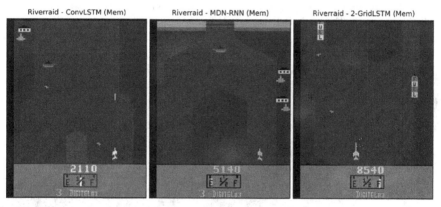

Fig. 11. Memory perturbation visualizations from left to right (Riverraid): (**1**) The ConvLSTM agent. (**2**) The MDN-RNN agent. (**3**) The 2-GridLSTM agent.

Overall, the images obtained are hard to interpret. This may be expected, given that the memory model is no longer isolated from the encoder and must integrate not only temporal information but also visual information. In the original work, given that the memory model was completely isolated from the encoder model, only the temporal information needed to be encoded, since the visual information could be encoded by the state representation. In that case, memory could be seen as a residual (i.e., temporal information only), which in turn provided clearer images. Unfortunately, some of the models proved to be sensitive to this methodology.

Nevertheless, these images provide some interesting observations. First, there seems to be evidence of the use of temporal information by way of an observed pattern, denoted here as 'sneaky' behavior, wherein the agent remains still, waiting for the enemy to reach a given position, at which point the agent fires and destroys the enemy. Evidence of this behavior can be observed in the *ConvLSTM* and 2-*GridLSTM* agents in SpaceInvaders (the images obtained for *MDN-RNN* are unfortunately too faded to discern this). Figure 13 depicts one such example of this behavior for the ConvLSTM agent.

The second evidence of the existence of temporal information consists of the image retention patterns observed in all the games. Examples of this can be seen in most of the

ChopperCommand - ConvLSTM (Mem)   ChopperCommand - MDN-RNN (Mem)   ChopperCommand - 2-GridLSTM (Mem)

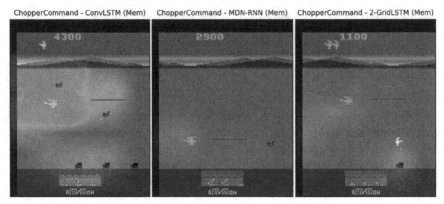

Fig. 12. Memory perturbation visualizations from left to right (ChopperCommand): (**1**) The ConvLSTM agent. (**2**) The MDN-RNN agent. (**3**) The 2-GridLSTM agent.

SpaceInvaders - ConvLSTM (Mem)   SpaceInvaders - MDN-RNN (Mem)   SpaceInvaders - 2-GridLSTM (Mem)

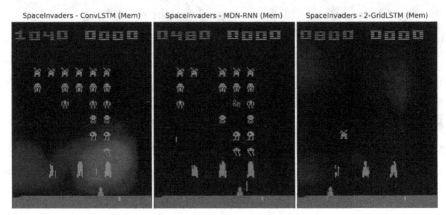

Fig. 13. Memory perturbation visualizations from left to right (SpaceInvaders): (**1**) The ConvL-STM agent. (**2**) The MDN-RNN agent. (**3**) The 2-GridLSTM agent.

images in Fig. 11, Fig. 12 and Fig. 13. As a concrete example, in Fig. 13, the memory perturbation for the 2-*GridLSTM* agent presents clear evidence of image retention, spanning most of the area where the enemies used to be. This is also an instance of a 'sneaky' attack. Interestingly these image retention marks disappear once the game is restarted even thou the internal state of the memory module is never reset programmatically.

4.6   Discussion

Given the results obtained, the proposed research questions can now be answered. Concerning **Q1**, the new methodology seems to have demonstrated that, at least in the games tested, preserving the spatial information can indeed improve the learning process and the quality of the trained agents. The fact that *ConvLSTM* outperformed *LSTM* on all the games tested provides evidence to support this claim. This conclusion is similar to the one stated in the original work, although the new methodology implemented in this work allows for a more informed and substantiated claim.

Regarding **Q2**, the results do not seem to support conclusive evidence that a predictive memory such as the MDN-RNN brings any benefit over the use of a contextual memory (e.g., LSTM). However, the preliminary results concerning **Q2.1**, seem to indicate that the predictive model is sensitive to the information it must predict and to the architecture used. Arguably, **Q2.1** seems to be a more important and interesting question to be answered by future research.

Concerning **Q3** it seems to be the case that different memory modules produce not only similar but also different behaviors. The 'sneaky' attack pattern observed in SpaceInvaders is an example of a shared behavioral trait among all the agents. The riskier behavior exhibited by the MDN-RNN and the 2-GridLSTM agents in SpaceInvaders is a mixed example of a shared behavioral pattern but at the same time in contrast to the safer approach exhibited by the LSTM and the ConvLSTM agents. Finally, regarding **Q4.1** it seems that the GridLSTM architecture can be further extended to the realm of RL, and this may be a topic of future research.

5   Conclusion

Memory-based DRL is an important research topic in AI development. As novel and evermore powerful memory architectures and designs are proposed and evolve over time, it is crucial to perform comparative studies to assess their capabilities and interpretability. This was the main focus of this work. By revising both the original methodology and the implementation of the memory modules tested, new research questions were able to emerge. The results obtained seem to indicate that better implementations together with better methodologies can impact the learning process and the performance of the agents and this is the most important result achieved by this work.

Acknowledgements. This research was funded by Fundação para a Ciência e a Tecnologia, grant number SFRH/BD/145723 /2019 - UID/CEC/00127/2019.

References

1. Hausknecht, M., Stone, P.: Deep recurrent Q-learning for partially observable MDPs. In: AAAI Fall Symposium - Technical Report, AI Access Foundation, pp. 29–37 (2015)
2. Heess, N., Hunt, J.J., Lillicrap, T.P., Silver, D.: Memory-based control with recurrent neural networks. arXiv:1512.04455, Preprint (2015)
3. Sorokin, I., Seleznev, A., Pavlov, M., Fedorov, A., Ignateva, A.: Deep attention recurrent Q-network. http://arxiv.org/abs/1512.01693, Preprint (2015)
4. Tang, Y., Nguyen, D., Ha, D.: Neuroevolution of self-interpretable agents. In: GECCO 2020: Genetic and Evolutionary Computation Conference, pp. 414–424. ACM, Cancún Mexico (2020)
5. Mott, A., Zoran, D., Chrzanowski, M., Wierstra, D., Rezende, D.J.: Towards interpretable reinforcement learning using attention augmented agents. In: Advances in Neural Information Processing Systems 32: Annual Conference on Neural Information Processing Systems 2019, NeurIPS 2019, Vancouver, BC, Canada, pp. 12329–12338 (2019)

6. Ha, D., Schmidhuber, J.: World models. http://arxiv.org/abs/1803.10122, Preprint (2018)
7. Ha, D., Schmidhuber, J.: Recurrent world models facilitate policy evolution. In: Advances in Neural Information Processing Systems 31: Annual Conference on Neural Information Processing Systems 2018, NeurIPS 2018, Montréal, Canada, pp. 2455–2467 (2018)
8. Hochreiter, S., Schmidhuber, J.: Long short-term memory. Neural Comput. **9**(8), 1735–1780 (1997)
9. Shi, X., Chen, Z., Wang, H., Yeung, D.-Y., Wong, W.-K., Woo, W.: Convolutional LSTM network: a machine learning approach for precipitation nowcasting. In: Advances in Neural Information Processing Systems 28: Annual Conference on Neural Information Processing Systems 2015, Montreal, Quebec, Canada, pp. 802–810 (2015)
10. Bishop, C.M.: Mixture Density Networks (1994)
11. Kalchbrenner, N., Danihelka, I., Graves, A.: Grid long short-term memory. In: 4th International Conference on Learning Representations, ICLR (2016)
12. Duarte, F.F., Lau, N., Pereira, A., Reis, L.P.: LSTM, ConvLSTM, MDN-RNN and GridLSTM memory-based deep reinforcement learning. In: Proceedings of the 15th International Conference on Agents and Artificial Intelligence, ICAART 2023, Lisbon, Portugal, pp. 169–179. SCITEPRESS (2023)
13. Greydanus, S., Koul, A., Dodge, J., Fern, A.: Visualizing and understanding Atari agents. In: Proceedings of the 35th International Conference on Machine Learning, ICML 2018, Stockholm, Sweden, pp. 1787–1796. PMLR (2018)
14. Graves, A., Wayne, G., Danihelka, I.: Neural turing machines. http://arxiv.org/abs/1410.5401, Preprint (2014)
15. Graves, A., et al.: Hybrid computing using a neural network with dynamic external memory. Nature **538**(7626), 471–476 (2016)
16. Kaelbling, L.P., Littman, M.L., Cassandra, A.R.: Planning and acting in partially observable stochastic domains. Artif. Intell. **101**(1–2), 99–134 (1998)
17. Mnih, V., et al.: Human-level control through deep reinforcement learning. Nature **518**(7540), 529–533 (2015)
18. Graves, A.: Generating sequences with recurrent neural networks. http://arxiv.org/abs/1308.0850, Preprint (2013)
19. Sutskever, I., Vinyals, O., Le, Q.V.: Sequence to sequence learning with neural networks. In: Advances in Neural Information Processing Systems 27: Annual Conference on Neural Information Processing Systems 2014, Montreal, Quebec, Canada, pp. 3104–3112 (2014)
20. Srivastava, N., Mansimov, E., Salakhutdinov, R.: Unsupervised learning of video representations using LSTMs. In: Proceedings of the 32nd International Conference on Machine Learning, ICML 2015, Lille, France, pp. 843–852. JMLR (2015)
21. Cheng, J., Dong, L., Lapata, M.: Long short-term memory-networks for machine reading. In: Proceedings of the 2016 Conference on Empirical Methods in Natural Language Processing, EMNLP 2016, Austin, Texas, USA, pp. 551–561. The Association for Computational Linguistics (2016)
22. Paszke, A., et al.: PyTorch: an imperative style, high-performance deep learning library. In: Advances in Neural Information Processing Systems 32: Annual Conference on Neural Information Processing Systems 2019, NeurIPS 2019, Vancouver, BC, Canada, pp. 8024–8035 (2019)
23. Graves, A., Mohamed, A., Hinton, G.E.: Speech recognition with deep recurrent neural networks. In: IEEE International Conference on Acoustics, Speech and Signal Processing, ICASSP 2013, Vancouver, BC, Canada, pp. 6645–6649. IEEE (2013)
24. Ba, L.J., Kiros, J.R., Hinton, G.E.: Layer normalization. https://arxiv.org/abs/1607.06450, Preprint (2016)

25. Ioffe, S., Szegedy, C.: Batch normalization: accelerating deep network training by reducing internal covariate shift. In: Proceedings of the 32nd International Conference on Machine Learning, ICML 2015, Lille, France, pp. 448–456. JMLR (2015)
26. Machado, M.C., Bellemare, M.G., Talvitie, E., Veness, J., Hausknecht, M.J., Bowling, M.: Revisiting the arcade learning environment: evaluation protocols and open problems for general agents. Artif. Intell. **61**, 523–562 (2018)
27. Mnih, V., et al.: Asynchronous methods for deep reinforcement learning. In: Proceedings of the 33nd International Conference on Machine Learning, ICML 2016, New York City, NY, USA, pp. 1928–1937. JMLR (2016)
28. Kingma, D.P., Ba, J.: Adam: a method for stochastic optimization. In: 3rd International Conference on Learning Representations, ICLR 2015, San Diego, CA, USA (2015)
29. Schulman, J., Moritz, P., Levine, S., Jordan, M.I., Abbeel, P.: High-dimensional continuous control using generalized advantage estimation. In: 4th International Conference on Learning Representations, ICLR 2016, San Juan, Puerto Rico (2016)
30. Brockman, G., et al.: OpenAI Gym. CoRR (2016)

Spatial Representation and Reasoning About Fold Strata: A Qualitative Approach

Yuta Taniuchi and Kazuko Takahashi[✉]

Kwansei Gakuin University, 1, Gakuen, Uegahara, Sanda 669-1330, Japan
{hcs57846,ktaka}@kwansei.ac.jp

Abstract. This paper proposes the method that handles strata based on qualitative spatial reasoning. We make a model for typical fold structure projected onto a two-dimensional plane, extracted by a rectangle. We give a symbolic representation to the model with the features of qualitative configuration and qualitative shape, and propose a reasoning method on this representation. First, we define the validity required of the representation and show the correspondence between the model and its representation. Next, we define operations such as rotation and symmetric transitions on the representation and show that they preserve the validity. Finally, we define the rules of connecting the models, and show reasoning on construction of global data by applying them. When multiple local data collected in distant locations are given, we can find global data by inserting missing parts. The approach based on qualitative spatial reasoning provides a logical explanation of the processes involved in strata-generation prediction, which in the field of structural geology have been examined manually to date, and enables to find results that manual analysis may overlook.

Keywords: Qualitative spatial reasoning · Knowledge representation · Logical reasoning · Shape information

1 Introduction

Natural disasters and topographical changes are closely related. Landslides and floods caused by heavy rain can be predicted from the lanscapes, and it is required to investigate the topography for safety when doing civil engineering and construction work. The structure of strata and its formation process are important factors to know the temporal change of topography.

In structural-geology research [9], the shapes and structures of strata are analyzed using data at various scales, from the micro level, such as collected small sample data measured in tens of centimeters, or slices that can be observed by microscopy, to the macro level at the out-crop scale of several-hundred meters, or aerial photos of larger regions. Regardless of scale, the entire shape of a stratum is estimated by integrating local data collected from multiple locations, since it is rarely exposed in a real landscape. There is no systematic approach in this estimation process, and human error may exist.

In this study, we propose a systematic approach using qualitative spatial reasoning (QSR), which is a subfield of artificial intelligence. QSR represents spatial entities

A. P. Rocha et al. (Eds.): ICAART 2023, LNAI 14546, pp. 244–266, 2024.
https://doi.org/10.1007/978-3-031-55326-4_12

symbolically without using concrete numerical data, and enables reasoning on the representation [3,4,13,16]. Representation focuses on specific aspects or properties of an object or the relation of objects, depending on the user's purpose, such as mereological relations, the relative positions or directions of objects, rough shapes, and on. Avoiding the need for precise values enables a small computational burden, and declarative representation suits human recognition. So far, lots of works have been done depending on the focused aspects of spatial data. Here, we focus on the shapes and configuration of objects.

Although it is rather difficult to consider shape in QSR, several researchers have proposed handling the shape of an object by projecting it onto a two-dimensional plane [1,2,5–8,10–12,15,18]. In most of these works, a set of primitives was introduced and the shape of the object was represented by arranging these primitives in the order of their occurrence when tracing the outline of the object. This process indicates that the target is essentially one-dimensional spatial data.

On the other hand, for our application, we have to consider representation based on local data extracted from a stratum, since the entire data do not comprise a closed curve. Moreover, we have to represent not only the shapes of layers that become regions of a two-dimensional plane but also their interconnections. Therefore, we cannot apply existing methods.

In this study, we propose representation and reasoning for a fold as a relatively simple strata structure. To apply QSR to the shapes of strata, there are two primary requirements: one layer continues in one direction if there is no fault, and the relations of inter-layer connections remain unchanged even if a stratum rotates or bends.

First, we define a model for local fold data and the language to describe it. Next, we define the validity required of the representation, and show that the model representation is valid and that a figure can be drawn on a two-dimensional plane for the valid representation. Moreover, we define operations on the representation corresponding to rotation and symmetric transitions, and show that the validity is preserved. Finally, we discuss the interconnection of models that have the same strata configurations. We show the process in which global data is obtained by connecting multiple local data, which was not sufficiently discussed in our previous work [17]. There, we mainly described the horizontal connection because of the page limit. In this paper, we formalize vertical connection precisely and discuss a sequence of connections as the reasoning process on this representation. We also show an application of predicting global data from multiple local data collected at different locations to solve the questions such as "Are they parts of the same large global strata?" or "Can we infer an ancient global stratum by connecting these local data?" It leads to the derivation of spatial relations among multiple local data collected in different places or at different times.

This study provides a mechanical treatment of strata using symbolic representation that focuses on their features. The approach based on qualitative spatial reasoning can provide logical explanations of processes that may be involved in future morphological changes that manual analysis may overlook.

This paper is organized as follows. In Sect. 2, we identify our target fold and the model. In Sect. 3, we define a description language. In Sect. 4, we provide a procedure to generate a representation for a model, and show that the representation and the model have a one-to-one relation. In Sect. 5 we define operations on this representation. In Sect. 6, we discuss reasoning on this representation. In Sect. 7, we compare our study with related works. Finally, in Sect. 8, we show our conclusions and future works.

2   Model

We describe a typical form of fold strata such as that shown in Fig. 1(a) [14]. We assume that there is no fault or hole, and that the curvature of all the layers is the same. We model a vertical cross section of the fold projected onto a two-dimensional plane. We derive the local data extracted from the global data by a rectangle that satisfies the following conditions **[COND]**. Based on these conditions, the fold is divided into regions using multiple smooth continuous curves (called *layer-borderlines*). Pairs of layer-borderlines do not intersect and there is no self-intersection. We treat this figure as our model.

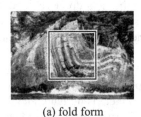
(a) fold form

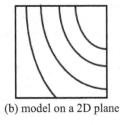
(b) model on a 2D plane

Fig. 1. A model for a fold [17].

[COND]

1. All layers and any space (a region containing no layer) in the global data appear to be connected regions in the local data.
2. The end-points of each layer-borderline are not located on a corner of the rectangle.
3. Each layer-borderline is a smooth curve with neither an extremum nor an inflection point.

For example, part of the fold shown in Fig. 1(a) is modeled as the figure in Fig. 1(b). In the model, the bottom-left point is regarded as the origin and the inclination of the curve is determined to be either increasing or decreasing.

We refer to the borderlines between layers as *layer-borderlines* to discriminate them from the borderline of the rectangle.

Note that since this is a qualitative model, we focus only on the side on which end-points of layer-borderlines occur and the order of the locations, ignoring their precise positions. As for the shape of a layer-borderline, we focus only on its inclination and convexity, ignoring its precise shape. As a result, several figures are regarded as the same model.

Example 1. In Fig. 2, (b) is regarded as same as (a), whereas (c) and (d) are not.

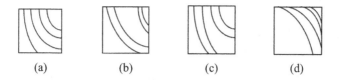

(a)   (b)   (c)   (d)

Fig. 2. Qualitative treatment of models [17].

3 Description Language

3.1 Language

We define two kinds of description languages Lang1 and Lang2 to represent the model for local data.

Lang1 is used to describe the configuration of a stratum. This is defined as Lang1 = $\{A_1, \ldots, A_n\} \cup \{\theta\}$ where $A_1, \ldots, A_n$ are the names of the layers and θ denotes the outside of the stratum. $A_1, \ldots, A_n$ and θ are called *layer-symbols*.

Lang2 is used to describe the shape of a layer-borderline. This is defined as Lang2 = $\{\text{↗}, \text{↘}, \text{↗}, \text{↳}\}$ where ↗, ↘, ↗ and ↳ indicate convex upward and increasing, convex upward and decreasing, convex downward and increasing, and convex downward and decreasing, respectively. ↗, ↘, ↗ and ↳ are called *shape-symbols*. We define the sets $Up = \{\text{↗}, \text{↗}\}$ and $Dn = \{\text{↘}, \text{↳}\}$.

Let $\sigma = e_1 \ldots e_k$ be either a sequence of symbols in Lang1 or that of those in Lang2. If σ is the null sequence, then we denote it as ϵ. For each i ($1 \le i \le k$), we denote $e_i \in \sigma$, and also denote $first(\sigma) = e_1$, $last(\sigma) = e_k$, $tail(\sigma) = e_2 \ldots e_k$ and $\sigma^{-1} = e_k \ldots e_1$. If $k = 1$, $tail(\sigma) = \epsilon$.

Definition 1 (local data description, layer-sequence). Local data description is defined as a pair (L, C), where L and C are finite sequences that include symbols in Lang1 and Lang2, respectively. L consists of four segments in the form $(\sigma^1)(\sigma^2)(\sigma^3)(\sigma^4)$ with auxiliary symbols '(' and ')'. The sequence of symbols without the auxiliary symbols '(' and ')' is called *a layer-sequence* of L.

A layer-sequence is considered as cyclic data, that is, for a layer-sequence $e_1 \ldots e_k$, e_k is considered as e_0, and $e_i \ldots e_k e_1 \ldots e_{i-1}$ are considered to be equivalent for all i ($1 \le i \le k$).

Definition 2 (sequence-of-transitions). For a local data description (L, C), let $I = e_1 \ldots e_k$ be a layer-sequence of L, where $k \ne 1$. Then the sequence $c_1 \ldots c_k$ where for each i ($1 \le i \le k$), $c_i = e_{i-1}/e_i$, $e_i \in \sigma_i$, $\sigma_i \in \{\sigma^1, \sigma^2, \sigma^3, \sigma^4\}$ is said to be a *sequence-of-transitions* of L. And $chgpt(c_i, \sigma_i)$ shows that c_i appears in σ_i.

Example 2. For $L = (A\theta)()(ABC)(B)$, the layer-sequence of L is $I = A\theta ABCB$, the sequence-of-transitions of L is $B/A\ A/\theta\ \theta/A\ A/B\ B/C\ C/B$, and $chgpt(A/\theta, \sigma^1)$ and $chgpt(\theta/A, \sigma^3)$ hold.

3.2 Validity

For a local data description, we introduce the term 'inclination of a layer-borderline' that relates L and C.

Definition 3 (inclination of a layer-borderline). *Let (L, C) be a local data description where $L = (\sigma^1)(\sigma^2)(\sigma^3)(\sigma^4)$. For each pair of layer-symbols X and Y, for which $chgpt(X/Y, \sigma)$ and $chgpt(Y/X, \sigma')$ where $\sigma \neq \sigma'$ hold, the inclination of the layer-borderline C_{XY} is defined depending on the pair of σ and σ' as follows:*

- **if** (σ, σ') **is either** $(\sigma^1, \sigma^2), (\sigma^2, \sigma^1), (\sigma^3, \sigma^4)$ **or** (σ^4, σ^3), **then** $C_{XY} = dn$
- **if** (σ, σ') **is either** $(\sigma^1, \sigma^4), (\sigma^2, \sigma^3), (\sigma^3, \sigma^2)$ **or** (σ^4, σ^1), **then** $C_{XY} = up$
- **otherwise**, $C_{XY} = any$.

Definition 4 (validity). *If a local data description (L, C) satisfies the following conditions, then it is said to be* a valid representation.
    Let $L = (\sigma^1)(\sigma^2)(\sigma^3)(\sigma^4)$ and its layer-sequence $I = e_1 \ldots e_k$.

v1. *For any pair X and Y of layer-symbols, if $chgpt(X/Y, \sigma)$ holds, then the sequence-of-transitions of L includes exactly one Y/X, and $chgpt(Y/X, \sigma')$ where $\sigma \neq \sigma'$, $\sigma, \sigma' \in \{\sigma^1, \sigma^2, \sigma^3, \sigma^4\}$ holds.*
v2. *I is $X_n\theta$ or in the form of $X_1 \ldots X_{n-1}X_nX_{n-1} \ldots X_1\theta$ where $X_i \neq X_j$ ($1 \leq i < j \leq n$).*
v3. *$|C| = 1$.*
v4. – *If for all C_{XY}, $C_{XY} = up$ or any, then $C \in Up$.*
       – *If for all C_{XY}, $C_{XY} = dn$ or any, then $C \in Dn$.*
       – *otherwise, $C \in Up \cup Dn$.*

From [v2], the following proposition holds.

Proposition 1. *Let (L, C) be a valid representation and I be the layer-sequence of L. Then I is equivalent to I^{-1}.*

4 Representation for a Model

We provide the representation for a model. We show that it is valid; and that conversely there exists a model of a valid representation and we can draw a figure satisfying **[COND]**.

4.1 Representation for a Model

When a model M of local data is given, starting from the top-left of M, trace the borderline of M in a clockwise manner to obtain a sequence of the layer-symbols that are encountered, and place parentheses around each side of the rectangle. Then we set $L = (\sigma_t)(\sigma_r)(\sigma_b)(\sigma_l)$, where $\sigma_t, \sigma_r, \sigma_b$ and σ_l are the sequence of upper side, right side, lower side and left side of the rectangle, respectively. We set C to correspond to the shape of the layer-borderline. (Note that the shape of all the layer-borderlines is the same.) Then (L, C) is said to be *the representation for M*.

Example 3. The representation for the model shown in Fig. 3 is $((A\theta)()(ABC)(B), \curlywedge)$. The sequence of layer-symbols starts not from layer-symbol B, but from A, although this may seem unnatural. If the sequence were to start from B, the layer-symbol occupying the top-left corner would appear in both σ_t and σ_l. To avoid such a situation and to treat the sequence cyclically, the sequence starts from A, the layer-symbol that is encountered first on tracing.

Fig. 3. Representation for a model [17].

Let (L, C) be the representation for a model M. The sequence-of-transitions $c_1 \ldots c_k$ of L shows the order of occurrence of the end-points of each layer-borderline on tracing the borderline of M. And for each i $(1 \leq i \leq k)$, $chgpt(c_i, \sigma_i)$ indicates that the end-point c_i of a layer-borderline is on the side corresponding to σ_i.

4.2 Validity and Drawability

Theorem 1 (validity of the model). *The representation for a model is valid.*

Proof. For any pair X and Y of layer-symbols in L, $chgpt(X/Y, \sigma)$ and $chgpt(Y/X, \sigma')$ show that the two end-points of the layer-borderline of X and Y are in σ and σ', respectively. From the first condition of **[COND]**, each layer-borderline of M does not intersect with itself or another layer-borderline. It has exactly two end-points on the borderlines, which are not on the same side of M, in accordance with the third condition of **[COND]**. Therefore, $\sigma \neq \sigma'$. Thus, validity [v1] holds.

The length of each layer-sequence is even, since each layer-borderline has exactly two end-points. Let $e_1 \ldots e_{2k}$ be the layer-sequence of L. If there is only one layer-borderline, then the layer-sequence of L is $X\theta$ where X is a layer-symbol. If there is more than one layer-borderline, then let $e_0 = e_{2k} = \theta$, $e_1 = X_1, \ldots, e_k = X_k$, where $X_i \in \mathrm{Lang1}$ $(1 \leq i \leq k)$. For each i, j $(0 \leq i < j \leq k - 1)$, if the end-points X_i/X_{i+1} and X_j/X_{j+1} occur in this order in the sequence-of-transitions of L, then X_{j+1}/X_j and X_{i+1}/X_i occur in this order in the sequence-of-transitions of L, since layer-borderline pairs should not intersect. Moreover, if we assume that $X_i = X_j$ $(i \neq j)$ holds, then the layer X_i should appear more than twice in L, indicating that it is a disconnected region; this contradicts the first condition of **[COND]**. Therefore, $X_i \neq X_j$. Thus, validity [v2] holds.

Validity [v3] holds from the assumption of the model. Therefore, C_{XY} are defined uniquely and consistently for all pairs of X and Y. Thus, validity [v4] holds.

Theorem 2 (drawability of the representation). *There exists the model of a valid representation.*

Proof. Let (L, C) be a valid representation and $L = (\sigma^1)(\sigma^2)(\sigma^3)(\sigma^4)$.

Let $c_1 \ldots c_{2k}$ be a sequence-of-transitions of L, since the lengths of sequence-of-transitions of L are even from validity [v2]. We locate each $c_i \in \sigma_i$ ($\sigma_i \in \{\sigma^1, \sigma^2, \sigma^3, \sigma^4\}$) ($1 \leq i \leq 2k$) on the borderline of the rectangle in the clockwise direction: locate the elements σ^1, σ^2, σ^3 and σ^4 on the upper side, right side, lower side and left side, respectively, in accordance with the order of occurrence in the sequence-of-transitions. Then, we can draw each layer-borderline so that its two end-points are not on the same side, and not on a corner, for the following reason.

For any pair X and Y of layer-symbols, we can draw a line between the end-points corresponding to X/Y and Y/X in the sequence-of-transitions. Validity [v1] indicates that a line connecting the two points exists; and validity [v2] indicates that lines do not intersect, and have no extremum or inflection point. Therefore, a region encircled by layer-borderlines and the borderlines of the rectangle is a connected region.

The inclination of all layer-borderlines is the same, which can be determined from validities [v3] and [v4]. Therefore, we can draw a smooth curve according to C.

Therefore, the model for a valid representation exists, which means that we can draw a figure corresponding to the model.

5   Operation

Our goal is to derive spatial relations among multiple local data collected in different locations or at different times. To achieve this, we define operations on the local data description and check for changes in the model resulting from these operations.

Let S_0 be a set of representations for models of local data. From Theorem 1, any element of S_0 is valid.

Here, we define three operations: rotation, horizontal flip and vertical flip on S_0 (Fig. 4). For $D = (L, C) \in S_0$, we define the operation o on $D = (L, C)$ as $o(D) = (o(L), o(C))$.

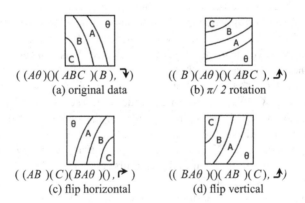

$((A\theta)()(ABC)(B), \blacktriangledown)$
(a) original data

$((B)(A\theta)()(ABC), \blacktriangleright)$
(b) $\pi / 2$ rotation

$((AB)(C)(BA\theta)(), \curvearrowright)$
(c) flip horizontal

$((BA\theta)()(AB)(C), \blacktriangleright)$
(d) flip vertical

Fig. 4. Operations on S_0 [17].

5.1 $\pi/2$ Rotation

Let r be the operation that rotates the model by $\pi/2$ clockwisely. This is defined as follows.

For $L = (\sigma_t)(\sigma_r)(\sigma_b)(\sigma_l)$, $r(L) = (\sigma_l)(\sigma_t)(\sigma_r)(\sigma_b)$.

For C, $r(\text{↱}) = \text{↴}, r(\text{↴}) = \text{↰}, r(\text{↰}) = \text{↳}, r(\text{↳}) = \text{↱}$.

Example 4. The representation for the model in Fig. 4(a) is $D = ((A\theta)()(ABC)(B), \text{↴})$. If we draw $r(D) = ((B)(A\theta)()(ABC), \text{↰})$, then we can obtain the model shown in Fig. 4(b), which corresponds to $\pi/2$ clockwisely rotated with respect to the original model shown in Fig. 4(a).

Proposition 2.

1. *The model corresponding to $r(D)$ is a figure that is $\pi/2$ clockwisely rotated relative to that corresponding to D.*
2. *For each D in S_0, $r(D)$ is valid.*
3. *$r(r(r(r(D)))) = D$.*

Proof. This can easily be proved, since the operation is only shifting segments.

5.2 Horizontal Flip

Let h be the operation that flips the model horizontally.

First, we detect the layer which will occupy the top-left corner of the model after applying the operation. This is said to be *a delimiter* and is defined as follows.

For $L = (\sigma_t)(\sigma_r)(\sigma_b)(\sigma_l)$,

$$delimiter(L) = \begin{cases} last(\sigma_t) \text{ (if } \sigma_t \neq \epsilon) \\ last(\sigma_l) \text{ (if } \sigma_t = \epsilon, \sigma_l \neq \epsilon) \\ last(\sigma_b) \text{ (if } \sigma_t = \sigma_l = \epsilon). \end{cases}$$

Let $I = e_1 \ldots e_k$ be the layer-sequence of L and e_z be its delimiter ($1 \leq z \leq k$). Let $I' = e_{z-1}e_{z-2} \ldots e_1 e_k e_{k-1} \ldots e_z$.

Then we set $h(L) = (\sigma_t')(\sigma_r')(\sigma_b')(\sigma_l')$, by dividing I' into four segments by inserting the symbols '(' and ')' so that $|\sigma_t'| = |\sigma_t|$, $|\sigma_r'| = |\sigma_l|$, $|\sigma_b'| = |\sigma_b|$ and $|\sigma_l'| = |\sigma_r|$.

For C, $h(\text{↱}) = \text{↴}, h(\text{↴}) = \text{↱}, h(\text{↰}) = \text{↳}, h(\text{↳}) = \text{↰}$.

Example 5. The representation for the model in Fig. 4(a) is $D = (L, C) = ((A\theta)()(ABC)(B), \text{↴})$. $I = A\theta ABCB$, and $delimiter(L) = \theta$, since $\sigma_t \neq \epsilon$. Therefore, $I' = ABCBA\theta$. The numbers of elements on each segment are $|\sigma_t'| = |\sigma_t| = 2$, $|\sigma_r'| = |\sigma_l| = 1$, $|\sigma_b'| = |\sigma_b| = 3$ and $|\sigma_l'| = |\sigma_r| = 0$. Therefore, by cutting I' by these numbers, we get $h(L) = (AB)(C)(BA\theta)()$. In addition, $h(C) = \text{↱}$. As a result, we obtain $h(D) = ((AB)(C)(BA\theta)(), \text{↱})$, shown in Fig. 4(c), which corresponds to the horizontally flipped original model shown in Fig. 4(a).

Proposition 3.

1. *The model corresponding to $h(D)$ is a figure that is horizontally flipped relative to that corresponding to D.*
2. *For each D in S_0, $h(D)$ is valid.*
3. *$h(h(D)) = D$.*

Proof. 1. Considering cyclicity, I' is equivalent to I^{-1}. The encountered order of layers on tracing the borderline of the model for $h(L)$ is the inverse of that in the original model. Moreover, the numbers of end-points on each side of the original model are the same as those on the corresponding sides of the model for $h(L)$, since $|\sigma|$ indicates the number of end-points on the side σ.

2. Assume that L is valid.

   I' is equivalent to I^{-1}. In addition, for any pair X and Y of layer-symbols $chgpt(X/Y, \sigma)$ and $chgpt(Y/X, \sigma')$ are mapped to $chgpt(Y/X, \tau)$ and $chgpt(X/Y, \tau')$, respectively, by h. Then $\tau \neq \tau'$ holds since $\sigma \neq \sigma'$ holds, from the definition of h. Therefore, validity [v1] holds.

   Validity [v2] holds, since I' is equivalent to I^{-1}.

   Validity [v3] trivially holds.

   We show that validity [v4] holds as follows. We show the case of $C \in Dn$. Since the inclinations of all the layer-borderlines are either dn or any, we consider a case in which $chgpt(X/Y, \sigma_b)$ and $chgpt(Y/X, \sigma_l)$ hold where the inclination is $C_{XY} = dn$. In this case, the pair is mapped to $chgpt(Y/X, \sigma'_b)$ and $chgpt(X/Y, \sigma'_r)$, by h. Their inclination is up. Similarly, for the other layer-borderlines, the inclination of dn is mapped to up, and any to any. Therefore, $h(C) \in Up$ holds. It follows that validity [v4] holds in this case. We can prove the other cases similarly.

3. Let I, I' and I'' be layer-sequence of $L, h(L)$ and $h(h(L))$, respectively. And let e_z be a delimiter of L $(1 \leq z \leq k)$.

   $$I = e_1 e_2 \ldots e_{z-1} e_z e_{z+1} \ldots e_{k-1} e_k$$
   $$I' = e_{z-1} \ldots e_2 e_1 e_k e_{k-1} \ldots e_{z+1} e_z$$

   (a) When $delimiter(L) = last(\sigma_t)$, $delimiter(h(L)) = last(\sigma'_t) = e_k$, since $|\sigma_t| = |\sigma'_t|$. Therefore,
   $$I'' = e_1 e_2 \ldots e_{z-1} e_z e_{z+1} \ldots e_{k-1} e_k.$$
   Therefore, $h(h(L)) = L$.

   (b) When $delimiter(L) = last(\sigma_l)$, $last(\sigma_l) = last(I) = e_k$. Then the layer-sequences are as follows.
   $$I = e_1 e_2 \ldots e_{k-1} e_k$$
   $$I' = e_{k-1} \ldots e_2 e_1 e_k$$
   If $\sigma'_l \neq \epsilon$, $delimiter(h(L)) = last(\sigma'_l)$ and $last(\sigma'_l) = last(I') = e_k$, since $\sigma'_t = \epsilon$. If $\sigma'_l = \epsilon$, $delimiter(h(L)) = last(\sigma'_b)$ since $\sigma'_t = \epsilon$, and $last(\sigma'_b) = e_k$. Therefore, $delimiter(h(L)) = e_k$. Therefore,
   $$I'' = e_1 e_2 \ldots e_{k-1} e_k$$
   Therefore, $h(h(L)) = L$.

   (c) When $delimiter(L) = last(\sigma_b)$, $last(\sigma_b) = last(I) = e_k$. Then $delimter(L) = delimiter(h(L)) = e_k$ holds by the same discussion with that in the above case.

   Therefore, $h(h(L)) = L$.

   As for C, $h(h(C)) = C$ holds trivially from the definition of h.

   Thus, we $h(h(D)) = D$ holds.

5.3   Vertical Flip

Let v be the operation that flips the model vertically. In this case, the delimiter is defined as follows.

For $L = (\sigma_t)(\sigma_r)(\sigma_b)(\sigma_l)$,

$$delimiter(L) = \begin{cases} last(\sigma_b) \ (\text{if } \sigma_b \neq \epsilon) \\ last(\sigma_r) \ (\text{if } \sigma_b = \epsilon, \sigma_r \neq \epsilon) \\ last(\sigma_t) \ (\text{if } \sigma_b = \sigma_r = \epsilon). \end{cases}$$

Let $I = e_1 \ldots e_k$ be the layer-sequence of L and e_z be its delimiter ($1 \leq z \leq k$). Let $I' = e_{z-1}e_{z-2} \ldots e_1 e_k e_{k-1} \ldots e_z$.

Then we set $v(L) = (\sigma_t')(\sigma_r')(\sigma_b')(\sigma_l')$, by dividing I' into four segments by inserting the symbols '(' and ')' so that $|\sigma_t'| = |\sigma_b|$, $|\sigma_r'| = |\sigma_r|$, $|\sigma_b'| = |\sigma_t|$ and $|\sigma_l'| = |\sigma_l|$.

For C, $v(\text{↱}) = \text{↳}, v(\text{↰}) = \text{↴}, v(\text{↲}) = \text{↰}, v(\text{↳}) = \text{↱}$.

Example 6. The representation for the model in Fig. 4(a) is $D = ((A\theta)()$ $(ABC)(B), \text{↰})$. If we draw $v(D) = ((BA\theta)()(AB)(C), \text{↴})$, then we can obtain the model shown in Fig. 4(d) which corresponds to the vertically flipped original model shown in Fig. 4(a).

Proposition 4.

1. *The model corresponding to $v(D)$ is a figure that is vertically flipped relative to that corresponding to D.*
2. *For each D in S_0, $v(D)$ is valid.*
3. *$v(v(D)) = D$.*

Proof. Similar to the proof regarding h.

5.4   Combination of Operations

Proposition 5. *Let S_0 be a set of representations for models of local data. For $D_1, D_2 \in S_0$ where $D_1 = (L_1, C_2)$ and $D_2 = (L_2, C_2)$, if D_2 can be obtained from D_1 by applying the operations r, h and v finite times, then the layer-sequences of L_1 and L_2 are equivalent.*

Proof. Let $L_1 = (\sigma_t)(\sigma_r)(\sigma_b)(\sigma_l)$. Then layer-sequence of L_1 is $I = \sigma_t\sigma_r\sigma_b\sigma_l$. The layer-sequence of $r(L_1) = (\sigma_l)(\sigma_t)(\sigma_r)(\sigma_b)$ is $\sigma_l\sigma_t\sigma_r\sigma_b$, which is equivalent to I because of its cyclicity. The layer-sequences of $h(L_1)$ and $v(L_1)$ are equivalent to $I' = e_{z-1}e_{z-2} \ldots e_1 e_k e_{k-1} \ldots e_z$, where e_z is the delimiter of L_1. Therefore, they are equivalent to I. Thus, the layer-sequences of L_1 and L_2 are equivalent.

The following property holds with respect to the combination of the operations, which can be proved similarly as the proof of Proposition 3.

Proposition 6. $r(r(D)) = h(v(D)) = v(h(D))$.

6   Reasoning Based on Connections of Models

6.1   Interconnection of Models

For a pair of representations for models, if the adjacency between the layers appearing in them is the same, then the configuration of the stratum is the same.

Definition 5 (same configuration). *For a pair of representations for models $D_1 = (L_1, C_1)$ and $D_2 = (L_2, C_2)$, let I_1 and I_2 be layer-sequences of L_1 and L_2, respectively. If I_1 is equivalent to I_2, then it is said that D_1 and D_2 have* the same configuration.

Example 7. In Fig. 5, (a), (b) and (c) have the same configuration, whereas (d) does not.

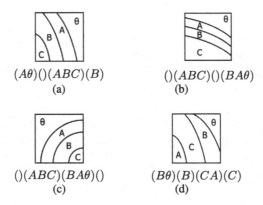

$(A\theta)()(ABC)(B)$
(a)

$()(ABC)()(BA\theta)$
(b)

$()(ABC)(BA\theta)()$
(c)

$(B\theta)(B)(CA)(C)$
(d)

Fig. 5. Same/different configuration [17].

Let S_0 be a set of representations for models of local data. When $D_1, D_2 \in S_0$ have the same configuration, we make a new model D by connecting them horizontally or vertically.

For a sequence of layer-symbols $L = (\sigma_t)(\sigma_r)(\sigma_b)(\sigma_l)$, we denote $set(L)$ as a set of the layer-symbols appearing in L, that is, $set(L) = \{e|e \in \sigma_t\} \cup \{e|e \in \sigma_r\} \cup \{e|e \in \sigma_b\} \cup \{e|e \in \sigma_l\}$.

For a sequence of shape-symbols C, $cend(C)$ shows the symbol to be connected, that is either $last(C)$ or $first(C)$ depending on the locations of the end-points. If $|C| = 1$, then $cend(C) = C$.

Table 1(a) shows a horizontal connection and Table 1(b) shows a vertical connection of a pair of shape-symbols. In these tables, 'ng' indicates that the connection cannot generate a smooth curve. $^T(C_1C_2)$ indicates that the curve is obtained by applying a vertical connection of C_1 and C_2. The symbol 'T' means the transpose of the sequence. If $|C| = 1$, $^TC = C$.

For example, in Table 1(a), the cell in the first row, first column shows that the result of connecting ↱ and ↱ is a single ↱; the cell in the first row, third column shows that the result of connecting ↱ on the left side and ↴ on the right side is the lined-up of these

Table 1. Connection of shape symbols.

left\right	↱	↰	↳	↴
↱	↱	↱↰	↱↳	ng
↰	↰↱	↰	ng	ng
↳	ng	ng	↳	↳↴
↴	ng	↴↰	↴↳	↴

(a) horizontal connection

top\bottom	↱	↰	↳	↴
↱	↱	T(↱↰)	ng	T(↱↴)
↰	T(↰↱)	↰	ng	ng
↳	ng	T(↳↰)	↳	T(↳↴)
↴	ng	ng	T(↴↳)	↴

(b) vertical connection

symbols, which indicates a maximal point. Similarly, the cell in the last row, second column shows that the result of connecting ↴ in the left side and ↰ on the right side is the lined-up of these symbols, which indicates a minimal point. On the other hand, in Table 1(b), T(↱↴) and T(↳↰) are the extrema, since the curve is traced from top to bottom.

There are two issues to note.

First issue is the order of tracing the layer-borderline.

Compare Table 1(a) and (b). Focus on the second row, first column of these tables, which shows a connection of ↰ and ↱. The shapes of these connections are different, although both of the results are ↰↱. Figure 6(a) shows the model obtained by the horizontal connection, whereas Fig. 6(b) shows the one obtained by the vertical connection. We use the symbol 'T' to discriminate these shapes.

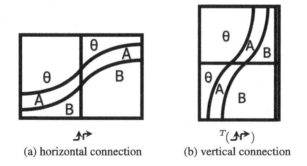

(a) horizontal connection ↰↱   (b) vertical connection T(↰↱)

Fig. 6. Different shapes of layer-borderlines with the same sequence.

Second issue is the nondeterminacy of the shapes. We cannot determine the shape of the composed layer-borderline only from the sequence of shape-symbols.

Consider T(↱↴) in the first row, fourth column in Table 1(b). There are two models for the representation T(↱↴) shown in Fig. 7(a) and (c). Similarly, there are two models for the representation T(↳↰) shown in Fig. 7(b) and (d). As we cannot determine the shape of the composed layer-borderline only from the sequence of shape-symbols, we identify it by checking the sequence of the layer-symbols.

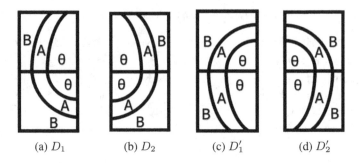

(a) D_1 (b) D_2 (c) D_1' (d) D_2'

Fig. 7. Two kinds of shapes of curves for the same sequence of shape-symbols.

6.2 Horizontal Connection of a Pair of Local Data

First, we show the horizontal connection of a pair of local data.

Let S_0 be a set of representations for models of local data. For a pair of $D_1 = (L_1, C_1)$ and $D_2 = (L_2, C_2)$ in S_0 that have the same configuration, we can connect the right side of D_1 to the left side of D_2 which is denoted by $D_1 || D_2$, if the following two conditions are satisfied.

all layers occurrence. Let $L_1 = (\sigma_t)(\sigma_r)(\sigma_b)(\sigma_l)$ and $L_2 = (\tau_t)(\tau_r)(\tau_b)(\tau_l)$. Take elements c_i of the sequence-of-transitions of L_1 that satisfy $chgpt(c_i, \sigma_r)$, and put them in the order of their appearance to make the sequence $c_1 \ldots c_k$. Similarly, take elements c_j' of the sequence-of-transitions of L_2 that satisfy $chgpt(c_j', \tau_l)$, and put them in their order of appearance to make the sequence $c_1' \ldots c_{k'}'$. Then, (i) if $c_i = e_{i-1}/e_i$ then $c_i' = e_{k+1-i}/e_{k-i}$ for each i ($1 \le i \le k$), (ii) $k = k' = |L_1|/2 = |L_2|/2$, (iii) $set(L_1) = set(L_2) = \cup_{1 \le i \le k}\{e \mid e$ appears in $c_i\} = \cup_{1 \le j \le k'}\{e \mid e$ appears in $c_j'\}$.

smooth curve. Either of the following holds. Note that $|C_1| = |C_2| = 1$.
1. $cend(C_1), cend(C_2) \in Up$
2. $cend(C_1), cend(C_2) \in Dn$
3. $cend(C_1) = $ ↗ and $cend(C_2) = $ ↘
4. $cend(C_1) = $ ↘ and $cend(C_2) = $ ↗

The condition of all layers occurrence means that all the end-points occurring on two connecting sides coincide, and that all the layer-symbols appear exactly once on both connecting sides. This avoids the case in which the figure corresponding to the resulting representation could contain a disconnected region. We will explain this later in Example 11. The condition of smooth curve means that the shapes of all the connected layer-borderlines are smooth.

If both conditions are satisfied, then $L = (\sigma_t \tau_t)(\tau_r)(\tau_b \sigma_b)(\sigma_l)$. $C = C_1$ if $C_1 = C_2$, and $C = C_1 C_2$ otherwise. And we can connect D_1 and D_2 horizontally to generate the representation $D = (L, C)$. In horizontal connection, the shape of the connected layer-borderlines is represented by tracing it from left to right.

Example 8. The representations for the models in Fig. 8(a) and (b) are $D_1 = (()(ABC)()(BA\theta), $ ↗$)$ and $D_2 = (()(A)(BC)(BA\theta), $ ↘$)$, respectively. (i) Take the specified elements from the layer-transitions $c_1 = \theta/A, c_2 = A/B, c_3 = B/C,$ $c'_1 = C/B, c'_2 = B/A, c'_3 = A/\theta,$ (ii) $|L_1|/2 = |L_2|/2 = 3,$ (iii) $set(L_1) = set(L_2) = \cup_{1 \le i \le 3}\{e \mid e \text{ appears in } c_i\} = \cup_{1 \le j \le 3}\{e \mid e \text{ appears in } c'_j\} = \{A, B, C, \theta\}.$ Therefore, the condition of all layers occurrence is satisfied. Moreover, the third condition of the smooth curve is satisfied. Thus, their horizontal connection $D_1 \| D_2$ is computed as $(()(A)(BC)(BA\theta), \text{↗↘}),$ which corresponds to the representation for the model in Fig. 8(c).

  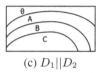

(a) D_1	(b) D_2	(c) $D_1 \| D_2$

Fig. 8. Horizontal connection of a pair of local data [17].

6.3 Vertical Connection of a Pair of Local Data

Next, we show the vertical connection of a pair of local data.

Let S_0 be a set of representations for models of local data. For a pair of $D_1 = (L_1, C_1)$ and $D_2 = (L_2, C_2)$ in S_0 that have the same configuration, we can connect the lower side of D_1 to the upper side of D_2 which is denoted by $D_1 + D_2$, if the following two conditions are satisfied.

all layers occurrence. Let $L_1 = (\sigma_t)(\sigma_r)(\sigma_b)(\sigma_l)$ and $L_2 = (\tau_t)(\tau_r)(\tau_b)(\tau_l)$. Take elements c_i of the sequence-of-transitions of L_1 that satisfy $chgpt(c_i, \sigma_b)$, and put them in the order of their appearance to make the sequence $c_1 \ldots c_k$. Similarly, take elements c'_j of the sequence-of-transitions of L_2 that satisfy $chgpt(c'_j, \tau_t)$, and put them in their order of appearance to make the sequence $c'_1 \ldots c'_{k'}$. Then, the same conditions with the (i)~(iii) stated in the horizontal connection should be satisfied.

smooth curve. Either of the following holds. Note that $|C_1| = |C_2| = 1.$
1. $cend(C_1), cend(C_2) \in Up$
2. $cend(C_1), cend(C_2) \in Dn$
3. $cend(C_1) = \text{↗}$ and $cend(C_2) = \text{↳}$
4. $cend(C_1) = \text{↘}$ and $cend(C_2) = \text{↗}$

If both conditions are satisfied, then $L = (\sigma_t)(\sigma_r \tau_r)(\tau_b)(\tau_l \sigma_l).$ $C = C_1$ if $C_1 = C_2$, and $C =^T (C_1 C_2)$ otherwise. And we can connect D_1 and D_2 vertically to generate the representation $D = (L, C)$. In vertical connection, the shape of the connected layer-borderlines is represented by tracing from top to bottom.

Example 9. The representations for the models in Fig. 9(a) and (b) are $D_1 = ((A\theta)()(ABC)(B), \text{↘})$ and $D_2 = ((BA\theta)(AB)(C)(), \text{↳}),$ respectively, and their vertical connection can be computed as $D_1 + D_2 = ((A\theta)(AB)(C)(B),^T(\text{↘↳}))$ which corresponds to the representation for the model of Fig. 9(c).

In the subsequent two subsections, we discuss a composed connections of multiple local data.

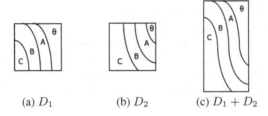

(a) D_1 (b) D_2 (c) $D_1 + D_2$

Fig. 9. Vertical connection of a pair of local data [17].

6.4 General Horizontal Connection

Consider general horizontal connection.

Let $L = (\sigma_t)(\sigma_r)(\sigma_b)(\sigma_l)$. One end-points of all layer-borderlines should be located in σ_r or σ_l. When we connect (L, C) horizontally, the connecting shape-symbol $cend$ can be determined only from C. However, when we connect $(L, {}^T C)$ horizontally, we have to determine $cend$ by checking the location of the other end-points. We refer the value of $cend$ as fol, which stands for 'first or last', in case of connecting $(L, {}^T C)$, in the following explanation. The value of $fol(C)$ is $first(C)$ or $last(C)$ depending on the case: if at least one of the other end-points is located in σ_t, then $cend(C) = last(C)$; if at least one of the other end-points is located in σ_b, then $cend(C) = first(C)$; otherwise, it is not always determined whether $cend(C) = last(C)$ or $cend(C) = first(C)$, and we can execute for each possibility.

Let D_1 and D_2 be the data obtained by horizontal/vertical connection of local data. We can connect the right side of D_1 to the left side of D_2.

- If $D_1 = (L_1, C_1)$ and $D_2 = (L_2, C_2)$, then $cend(C_1) = last(C_1)$, $cend(C_2) = first(C_2)$.
- If $D_1 = (L_1, C_1)$ and $D_2 = (L_2, {}^T C_2)$, then $cend(C_1) = last(C_1)$, $cend(C_2) = fol(C_2)$.
- If $D_1 = (L_1, {}^T C_1)$ and $D_2 = (L_2, C_2)$, then $cend(C_1) = fol(C_1)$, $cend(C_2) = first(C_2)$.
- If $D_1 = (L_1, {}^T C_1)$ and $D_2 = (L_2, {}^T C_2)$, then $cend(C_1) = fol(C_1)$, $cend(C_2) = fol(C_2)$.

If we apply only horizontal connections repetitively, then only the case of $cend(C_1) = last(C_1)$, $cend(C_2) = first(C_2)$ appears.

Let $L_1 = (\sigma_t)(\sigma_r)(\sigma_b)(\sigma_l)$ and $L_2 = (\tau_t)(\tau_r)(\tau_b)(\tau_l)$. If the same conditions as in the case of horizontal connection of a pair of local data are satisfied, then we can connect D_1 and D_2 horizontally to get $D = (L, C)$ where $L = (\sigma_t \tau_t)(\tau_r)(\tau_b \sigma_b)(\sigma_l)$, and C is defined as follows.

- In case of $cend(C_1) = last(C_1)$ and $cend(C_2) = first(C_2)$
  - if $cend(C_1) = cend(C_2)$, then $C = C_1 tail(C_2)$
  - otherwise, $C = C_1 C_2$
- In case of $cend(C_1) = last(C_1)$ and $cend(C_2) = last(C_2)$

- if $cend(C_1) = cend(C_2)$, then $C = C_1 tail(C_2^{-1})$
- otherwise, $C = C_1 C_2^{-1}$
- In case of $cend(C_1) = first(C_1)$ and $cend(C_2) = first(C_2)$
  - if $cend(C_1) = cend(C_2)$, then $C = C_1^{-1} tail(C_2)$
  - otherwise, $C = C_1^{-1} C_2$
- In case of $cend(C_1) = first(C_1)$ and $cend(C_2) = last(C_2)$
  - if $cend(C_1) = cend(C_2)$, then $C = C_1^{-1} tail(C_2^{-1})$
  - otherwise, $C = C_1^{-1} C_2^{-1}$

Example 10. Consider the horizontal connection of $D_1 = (L_1, {}^T C_1) = ((A\theta)(AB)()(), {}^T(\text{⟳}))$ and $D_2 = (L_2, {}^T C_2) = ((AB)()()(A\theta), {}^T(\text{⟲}))$ shown in Fig. 7(a) and (b), respectively. Let $L_1 = (\sigma_t)(\sigma_r)(\sigma_b)(\sigma_l)$. As $cend(C_1) = fol(C_1)$, we check the location of the end-points other than $\sigma_r = AB$. Then, as $\sigma_t = A\theta \neq \epsilon$, there exists an end-point on σ_t. Therefore, $cend(C_1) = last(C_1)$. Similarly, $cend(C_2) = last(C_2)$. Thus, the conditions of all layers occurrence and smooth curve are satisfied, and we obtain $C = C_1 C_2^{-1} = \text{⟳}(\text{⟲})^{-1} = \text{⟳⟳}$. Therefore, $D_1 \| D_2 = ((A\theta AB)()()(), \text{⟳⟳})$.

On the other hand, consider the horizontal connection of $D_1' = (L_1, {}^T C_1) = (()(A\theta)(AB)(), {}^T(\text{⟳}))$ and $D_2' = (L_2, {}^T C_2) = (()()(A\theta)(AB), {}^T(\text{⟲}))$ shown in Fig. 7(c) and (d), respectively. As $cend(C_1) = first(C_1)$ and $cend(C_2) = first(C_2)$, we obtain $C = C_1^{-1} C_2 = (\text{⟳})^{-1}\text{⟲} = \text{⟳⟲}$. $D_1' \| D_2' = (()()(A\theta AB)(), \text{⟳⟲})$.

6.5   General Vertical Connection

Next, consider general vertical connection.

Let $L = (\sigma_t)(\sigma_r)(\sigma_b)(\sigma_l)$. One end-points of all layer-borderlines should be located in σ_t or σ_b. When we connect $(L, {}^T C)$ vertically, the connecting shape-symbol $cend$ can be determined only from C. However, when we connect (L, C) vertically, we have to determine $cend$ by checking the location of the other end-points. We refer the value of $cend$ as fol, which stands for 'first or last', in case of connecting (L, C), in the following explanation. The value of $fol(C)$ is $first(C)$ or $last(C)$ depending on the case: if at least one of the other end-points is located in σ_r, then $cend(C) = first(C)$; if at least one of the other end-points is located in σ_l, then $cend(C) = last(C)$; otherwise, it is not always determined whether $cend(C) = last(C)$ or $cend(C) = first(C)$, and we can execute for each possibility.

Let D_1 and D_2 be the data obtained by horizontal/vertical connection of local data. We can connect the lower side of D_1 to the upper side of D_2.

- If $D_1 = (L_1, {}^T C_1)$ and $D_2 = (L_2, {}^T C_2)$, then $cend(C_1) = last(C_1)$, $cend(C_2) = first(C_2)$.
- If $D_1 = (L_1, {}^T C_1)$ and $D_2 = (L_2, C_2)$, then $cend(C_1) = last(C_1)$, $cend(C_2) = fol(C_2)$.
- If $D_1 = (L_1, C_1)$ and $D_2 = (L_2, {}^T C_2)$, then $cend(C_1) = fol(C_1)$, $cend(C_2) = first(C_2)$.
- If $D_1 = (L_1, C_1)$ and $D_2 = (L_2, C_2)$, then $cend(C_1) = fol(C_1)$, $cend(C_2) = fol(C_2)$.

If we apply only vertical connections repetitively, then only the case of $cend(C_1) = last(C_1)$, $cend(C_2) = first(C_2)$ appears.

Let $L_1 = (\sigma_t)(\sigma_r)(\sigma_b)(\sigma_l)$ and $L_2 = (\tau_t)(\tau_r)(\tau_b)(\tau_l)$. If the same conditions as in the case of vertical connection of a pair of local data are satisfied, then we can connect D_1 and D_2 vertically to get $D = (L, {}^T C)$, where $L = (\sigma_t)(\sigma_r \tau_r)(\tau_b)(\tau_l \sigma_l)$, and C is defined as same as in the general horizontal connection.

6.6 Succeeding Connections

Let S_0 be a set of representations for models of local data. We define S_1 as a union of the set of representations for the horizontally/vertically connected models and S_0.
$$S_1 = \{\, D \mid D = D_1 || D_2, D_1, D_2 \in S_0 \,\}$$
$$\cup \{\, D \mid D = D_1 + D_2, D_1, D_2 \in S_0 \,\}$$
$$\cup \, S_0.$$
We repeat this process by generating S_n from S_{n-1} for $n > 1$.
$$S_n = \{\, D \mid D = D_1 || D_2, D_1, D_2 \in S_{n-1} \,\}$$
$$\cup \{\, D \mid D = D_1 + D_2, D_1, D_2 \in S_{n-1} \,\}$$
$$\cup \, S_{n-1}.$$
In general, $D \in S_n$ is not always a valid representation, since a layer-borderline of D may include an extremum or an inflection.

Instead of validity, the following properties hold.

Theorem 3 (Property of Extended Representation). $D = (L, C) \in S_n$ *satisfies the following properties.*

Let $L = (\sigma_t)(\sigma_r)(\sigma_b)(\sigma_l)$, *the layer-sequence of* L, $I = e_1 \ldots e_k$ *and* $C = q_1 \cdots q_m$.

p1. *For any pair* X *and* Y *of layer-symbols, if* $chgpt(X/Y, \sigma)$ *holds, then the sequence-of-transitions of* L *includes exactly one* Y/X, *and* $chgpt(Y/X, \sigma')$ *where* $\sigma, \sigma' \in \{\sigma_t, \sigma_r, \sigma_b, \sigma_l\}$ *holds.*

p2. I *is* $X_n \theta$ *or in the form* $X_1 \ldots X_{n-1} X_n X_{n-1} \ldots X_1 \theta$, *where* $X_i \neq X_j$ $(1 \leq i < j \leq n)$.

p3. *For any* i $(1 \leq i \leq m - 1)$, $q_i \neq q_{i+1}$ *holds.*

We can apply a combination of horizontal/vertical connection to obtain the sequence $S_0, S_1, \ldots, S_n$. However, we have to choose the order of application because of the conditions of the connection.

Example 11. In Fig. 10, D_1 and D_2 cannot be horizontally connected, since they do not satisfy the first condition of horizontal connection. If they were horizontally connected, disconnected regions would appear. On the other hand, $D_3 + D_1$ and $D_4 + D_2$ can be generated since the pair D_3 and D_1, and the pair D_4 and D_2 satisfy the conditions of vertical connection, respectively. In addition, $(D_3 + D_1) || (D_4 + D_2)$ can be generated since the pair $D_3 + D_1$ and $D_4 + D_2$ satisfy the conditions of horizontal connection.

As a result, a representation for the global data that may contain a maximal point is obtained.

This example indicates that the properties stated in Theorem 3 are preserved on applying the connections in an appropriate order.

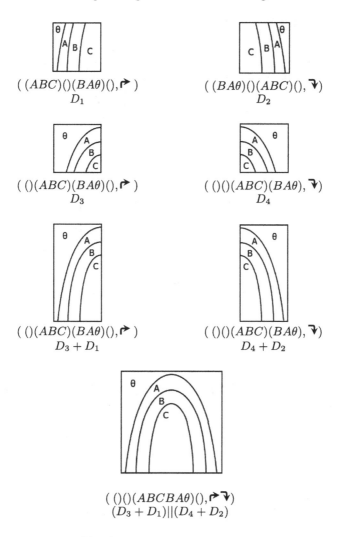

Fig. 10. Process of connections [17].

6.7 Prediction of Global Data

Actually, there is seldom found a stratum of which the entire shape is completely exposed. When multiple data are collected at distant locations, if they have the same configuration, then we can find several possible ways to connect them, by inserting several local data between them and applying the above reasoning.

Example 12. Assume that D_1 and D_2 are collected at distant locations (Fig. 11(a)), does a global stratum exist that contains both of them? One possible solution is shown in Fig. 11(b), which shows that there should exist D_3 and D_4 (Fig. 11(a)) to connect D_1 and D_2. Such intermediate data are often missing, and we infer the possibility that the global stratum exists, which changes in the long term as a result of crustal movements.

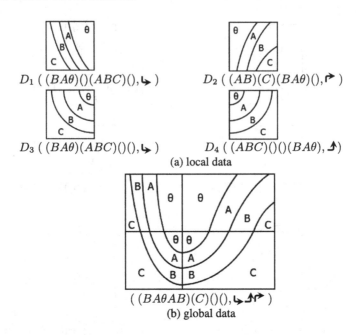

(a) local data

(b) global data

Fig. 11. Prediction of global data [17].

In this example, the right two rectangles are wider than the left ones in Fig. 11(b). Actually, the sizes of collected local data are not always same or distances between their locations are different. Here, we focus on the end-points of layer-borderlines and their shapes both of which are treated qualitatively. Therefore, we can make a model for a global data by changing the size or ratio of sides of rectangles of the models for local data.

Example 13. Assume that local data P, Q and R are collected at distant locations shown in Fig. 12. Does a global stratum exist that connects p_b and r_b, q_l and r_l, respectively?

In this case, we have a solution $(D_1 || D_2) + (D_3 || D_4) + ((D_5 + D_6) || D_7)$ shown in Fig. 13(a), which is obtained by the operations $||$ and $+$ repetitively. In this figure, the local data D_5, D_2 and D_4 correspond to P, Q and R, respectively. The representation for this model is $((\,)(ABC)()(BA\theta),^T(\text{↴↱↴ ↴↲↴↴↱}))$. There is another solution $(D_1 || D_2) + ((D_5 + D_6) \,||\, ((D_3 || D_4) + D_7))$ shown in Fig. 13(b) for which the representation is the same. This example shows that global structure can be generated by the reasoning procedure, and that multiple solutions can be found.

7 Related Works

To the best of the authors' knowledge, there has been almost no research on strata that uses symbolic representation and logical reasoning.

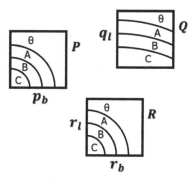

Fig. 12. Collected local data.

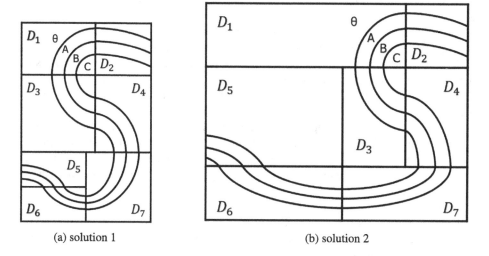

(a) solution 1   (b) solution 2

Fig. 13. A global data obtained by repetitive horizontal/vertical connections.

To combine AI techniques and structural geology, application of machine learning using big data is one possibility. However, the currently available strata-data archives are quite small and the stored data are not sufficiently categorized. Moreover, in most data archives, figures and landscapes are stored using numerical data.

On the other hand, in the QSR research field, several methods for symbolic treatment of shapes have been proposed. Almost all of them treat spatial data on a two-dimensional plane.

Leyton proposed a grammar that represents changes in the shape of a closed curve, starting from a simple smooth curve. He explained changes in shape based on a force acting from inside or outside the curve [12]. He showed that any shape of a smooth closed curve can be represented using language based on the proposed grammar. Tosue et al. extended the grammar so that it can represent phenomena such as the creation of a tangent point and division of the curve [18]. They applied the method to a process of organogenesis. Galton et al. proposed another grammar that can apply not only to a smooth curve but also to a straight line or a curve with cusps [8]. They showed that objects of various shapes can be symbolically represented by connecting a finite number of primitive segments. They also referred to transformation between representations differing in granularity. Cabedo et al. proposed a representation for the borderline of an object with further information such as relative lengths and relative angles, and also showed the juxtaposition of objects [1, 2]. Falomir et al. extended this representation to develop a new language for a qualitative shape representation of a two-dimensional object. They also considered the connection of the objects and formalized the composition of qualitative lengths, angles and convexities. Falomir et al. also defined similarity between qualitative shapes described in their extended model [6]. They focused only on the shape of the boundary of an object, whereas we treat the inner configuration of an object, which consists of multiple regions in a single object as well as the shape of the regions. They used straight lines to represent a shape, whereas we use curves, which is another difference.

All of these expressions adopted methods that represent the shape of an object by connecting primitive segments when tracing its borderline. On the other hand, Cohn took a different approach to represent a concave object [5]. He regarded differences in the closure and the object itself as regions and represented the spatial relations of these regions. Kumokawa et al. also proposed a different representation for a concave shape using closure [11].

A study by Kulik et al. applied QSR to landscape silhouettes [10]. They proposed a description language for the shape of an open line. They defined several primitives comprising two consecutive vectors depending on relative lengths and angles; regarded the borderline of a silhouette of a landscape as a pattern of connections between these primitives; and deduced landscape features, including mountain, valley, and plateau. They also proposed a transformation from the refined level to the abstract level. The differences between Kulik's method and ours are: first, he used straight lines as primitives, whereas we use curves; second, his target silhouette was always in the vertical direction, whereas our method can be applied to rotated forms; third, he neither formalized the method nor discussed the validity of the representation, whereas we both define the validity of the representation and prove one-to-one relation with the model.

In addition, while all existing studies treated the essentially one-dimensional data of a borderline, we treat the two-dimensional data of a stratum consisting of multiple regions.

8   Conclusions

We have discussed qualitative representation and reasoning for strata.

We provided a model for local data from a typical form of fold strata, and proposed its representation in the form of a pair of sequences of symbols that stand for the configuration of a layer and the shapes of the borderlines between layers. This representation is suitable to show the main features of strata: one layer extends in one direction if there is no fault, and the relations of interconnections between layers are unchanged even if the width of a layer, shape, or axis of a fold changes.

We defined the validity of the representation, and then proved that the representation for a model is valid and that conversely, there exists the model of a valid representation. Moreover, we defined several operations on the representation, and showed that they preserve the validity. We also showed reasoning about the connection of local data. We formalized the connection and showed that global data connecting several local data can be constructed.

This enables derivation of relations among multiple local data collected in different locations or at different times. Our main contribution is to show symbolic treatment of strata and provide a basis for logically explaining the process of landscape generation.

In future studies, we intend to identify sets of representations obtained from repetitive application of connections of local data. We are considering a relaxation of the condition of all layers occurrence for the connection so that more flexible reasoning is available. We are also considering the formalization needed to explain the strata-generation process, as well as a qualitative simulation for possible future morphological changes.

Acknowledgement. This research is supported by JSPS Kakenhi JP21K12020. The authors would like to thank Motohiro Tsuboi for giving useful advice from the field of geology.

References

1. Cabedo, L.M., Abril, L.G., Morente, F.V., Falomir, Z.: A pragmatic qualitative approach for juxtaposing shapes. J. Univ. Comput. Sci. **16**(11), 1410–1424 (2010)
2. Cabedo, L.M., Escrig, M.T.: A qualitative theory for shape representation and matching for design. In: Proceedings of the Sixteenth European Conference on Artificial Intelligence, ECAI 2004, pp. 858–862 (2004)
3. Chen, J., Cohn, A.G., Liu, D., Wang, S., Ouyang, J., Yu, Q.: A survey of qualitative spatial representations. Knowl. Eng. Rev. **30**, 106–136 (2013)
4. Cohn, A., Renz, J.: Qualitative spatial representation and reasoning. In: Handbook of Knowledge Representation, Chap. 13. Elsevier (2008)
5. Cohn, A.G.: Hierarchical representation of qualitative shape based on connection and convexity. In: Spatial Information Theory: Cognitive and Computational Foundations of Geographic Information Science (COSIT 1995), pp. 311–326 (1995)
6. Falomir, Z., Abril, L.G., Cabedo, L.M., Ortega, J.A.: Measures of similarity between objects based on qualitative shape descriptions. Spat. Cogn. Comput. **13**(3), 181–218 (2013)
7. Falomir, Z., Pich, A., Costa, V.: Spatial reasoning about qualitative shape compositions: composing qualitative lengths and angles. Ann. Math. Artif. Intell. **88**, 589–621 (2020)
8. Galton, A., Meathrel, R.: Qualitative outline theory. In: Proceedings of the Sixteenth International Joint Conference on Artificial Intelligence, pp. 1061–1066 (1999)
9. Kano, K., Murata, A.: Structural Geology. Asakura Publishing Co., Ltd. (1998). (in Japanese)
10. Kulik, L., Egenhofer, M.J.: Linearized terrain: languages for silhouette representations. In: Spatial Information Theory. Foundations of Geographic Information Science, International Conference, COSIT 2003, pp. 118–135 (2003)
11. Kumokawa, S., Takahashi, K.: Qualitative spatial representation based on connection patterns and convexity. In: AAAI08 Workshop on Spatial and Temporal Reasoning, pp. 40–47 (2008)
12. Leyton, M.: A process-grammar for shape. Artif. Intell. **34**, 213–247 (1988)
13. Ligozat, G.: Qualitative Spatial and Temporal Reasoning. Wiley, Hoboken (2011)

14. Nishimura, Y., et al.: Earth Science (High School Textbook, in Japanese). Daiichi Gakushusha Co. (2021)
15. Pich, A., Falomir, Z.: Logical composition of qualitative shapes applied to solve spatial reasoning tests. Cogn. Syst. Res. **52**, 82–102 (2018)
16. Sioutis, M., Wolter, D.: Qualitative spatial and temporal reasoning: current status and future challenges. In: Proceedings of 30th International Joint Conference on Artificial Intelligence, pp. 4594–4601 (2021)
17. Taniuchi, Y., Takahashi, K.: Qualitative spatial representation and reasoning about fold strata. In: Proceedings of the 15th International Conference on Agents and Artificial Intelligence (ICAART 2023), pp. 211–220 (2023)
18. Tosue, M., Takahashi, K.: Towards a qualitative reasoning on shape change and object division. In: Spatial Information Theory. 11th International Conference, COSIT 2019, pp. 7:1–7:15 (2019)

Ranking-Based Partner Selection Strategy in Open, Dynamic and Sociable Environments

Qin Liang[1,3]([envelope]), Wen Gu[2], Shohei Kato[3], Fenghui Ren[1], Guoxin Su[1], Takayuki Ito[4], and Minjie Zhang[1]

[1] University of Wollongong, Wollongong, Australia
ql948@uowmail.edu.au, {fren,guoxin,minjie}@uow.edu.au
[2] Japan Advanced Institute of Science and Technology, Nomi, Japan
wgu@jaist.ac.jp
[3] Nagoya Institute of Technology, Nagoya, Japan
shohey@nitech.ac.jp
[4] Kyoto University, Kyoto, Japan
ito@i.kyoto-u.ac.jp

Abstract. Agents with limited capacities need to cooperate with others to fulfil complex tasks in a multi-agent system. To find a reliable partner, agents with insufficient experience have to seek advice from advisors. Currently, most models are rating-based, aggregating advisors' information on partners and calculating averaged results. These models have some drawbacks, like being vulnerable to unfair ratings under a high ratio of dishonest advisors or dynamic attacks and locally convergent. Therefore, this paper proposes a Ranking-based Partner Selection (RPS) model, which clusters honest and dishonest advisors into different groups based on their different rankings of trustees. Besides, RPS uses a sliding-window-based method to find dishonest advisors with dynamic attack behaviours. Furthermore, RPS utilizes an online-learning method to update model parameters based on real-time interaction results. According to experiment results, RPS outperforms ITEA under different kinds of unfair rating attacks, especially in two situations: 1) there is a high ratio of dishonest advisors; 2)dishonest advisor takes dynamic attack strategies.

Keywords: Advisor · Partner selection · Unfair rating attacks · Ranking · Sliding window

1 Introduction

In open, large, and dynamic multi-agent systems (MASs), agents usually need to cooperate with others to accomplish complex tasks. To avoid being deceived by dishonest agents [4,5,8], agents need to estimate the trustworthiness of others and select a reliable partner, which is still a challenging problem. MASs are usually huge, making most agents need more interactions to construct direct trust of others [6], especially for newcomers. To solve this problem, agents usually seek information from third-party advisors to calculate the indirect trust of others. However, this incurs a new issue of unfair ratings. Unfair ratings are brought by dishonest advisors (e.g. attackers), who give distorted ratings to mislead the decisions of agents seeking partners [7, 10, 13]. There are various attack strategies, such as Camouflage, whitewashing, and Sybil. Moreover, attackers employ composite attacks to make it more difficult to detect attacks. [7], like Sybil camouflage attacks and Sybil whitewashing attacks.

There are many classical models published to address the issue of unfair ratings [3–6, 9]. For instance, BRS [1] and TRAVOS [2] use Beta distribution to reduce the negative effect of deceptive advice. Based on BRS, Zhang [4] proposed a personalized model, which considers personal experience and advisor advice for trust evaluation. The iCLUB [5] cluster buyers into different clubs and filter unfair testimonies. The HABIT [6] model studies the relationships between behaviours among groups of trustees to deal with advisors' disruptive, or incorrect information. The MET [7] model applies an evolutionary approach to establish a reliable network over time. The ACT model [9] utilizes a reinforcement learning technique to handle prejudiced testimonies.

Currently, traditional models still have three kinds of drawbacks: 1) when dishonest advisors are the majority (called worst-case unfair ratings [13]), rating-based models' accuracy would be decreased. For example, ITEA performs poorly under a high ratio of Fully Random and Selective Badmouthing dishonest advisors [14, 15]; 2) under dynamic unfair ratings, some models' accuracy decreases. For example, BRS and iCLUB cannot cope with Sybil attacks; TRAVOS and HABIT are unable to resist Camouflage attacks; The personalized model [4] fail to solve Sybil Whitewashing attacks. 3) some models are locally convergent, which cannot always select the best partner. For example, when the number of interactions is limited, the performance of the second-best partner may not differ significantly from that of the best partner. In this situation, some models tend to stop looking for other partners when finding the second-best partner is also reliable.

To solve the above three problems, we propose a Ranking-based Partner Selection (RPS) model. RPS has four advantages: 1) introduces the ranking of trustees as a supplement for rating data, which helps to distinguish between honest and dishonest advisors; 2) proposes a clustering-based method that automatically groups advisors based on their ranking of trustees and selects the first-order trustee based on group aggregation, which helps to reduce noises brought by advisor aggregation and prevent the locally-convergent problem; 3) proposes a sliding-window-based method, which helps to monitor abnormal behaviours of dishonest advisors; 4) introduces an online learning method, which helps to update model parameters based on interaction results in real-time.

The rest of this paper is organized as follows. Section 2 introduces related work. Section 3 describes the problem and presents the formal definitions. Section 4 describes the principle of the model and gives the detailed design of the Partner Selection and Parameter Adjustment modules. Section 5 demonstrates experiment settings and results. Section 6 concludes the paper and outlines future work.

This paper is extended from the 2023 ICAART conference paper [18]. We made three modifications. Firstly, we propose a sliding-window-based method to detect dishonest advisors' abnormal behaviours (e.g. In Camouflage attacks, dishonest advisors pretend to be honest first and give distorted ratings later), shown in Sect. 4.2. Secondly, we add group density into group weight calculation to filter out some dishonest groups where advisors with little similarities with each other (e.g. Partly Random advisors give distorted ratings randomly and thus have little similarity with others), as shown in Sect. 4.2. Thirdly, we add some new experiments to test the model's robustness, shown in Sect. 5.

2   Related Work

Some researchers have employed information theory in recent years to address the challenges posed by unfair rating attacks. For instance, the ITC model [10] utilizes two information-theoretic to evaluate the recommendation accuracy, which considers the advisor's true interactions with sellers and the seller's true trustworthiness. In addition, ITC compares two kinds of worst-case unfair rating attacks. Experimental results demonstrate that the recommendations can provide useful information even under the worst-case unfair ratings. Therefore, ITC has good performance than TRAVOS [2], BLADE [3], and MET [7], which failed to resist worst-case unfair ratings.

Wang et al. [13] uses a probabilistic model to cope with unfair ratings, which calculates attack impact based on the information theory. The paper contains two components. Firstly, the model studies unfair ratings caused by honest and objective advisors based on the probabilistic and information-leakage methods. Then, the model finds the worst-case attacks. Secondly, the model first investigates attacks caused by honest but subjective advisors and compares results with the earlier ones. Experiment results demonstrate that the truth is easier to hide by attackers under subjectivity, which cause the model to be vulnerable to unfair rating attacks.

Furthermore, some researchers propose robust models to deal with unfair ratings. Like the ITEA model [14, 15], which proforma well in Resolving dishonest agents. ITEA aggregates predictions from experts (e.g. advisors) based on the weighted average method and adjusts weights based on the latest feedback. ITEA uses advisor weights to represent their past performance and thus does not need to record individual losses of advisors at each time point. Therefore, ITEA is simpler and more robust than traditional models like TRAVOS, MET, and ACT. Since the ITEA model is easy to implement and performs better than other existing models, it is used as a benchmark for comparison.

3   Problem Definitions and Description

3.1   Definitions

The partner selection environments comprise three kinds of agents: *trustor*, *trustee* and *advisor*, whose formal definitions are presented below.

Definition 1. *Trustees represent agents willing to offer services to perform tasks, defined as $S = \{s_j | j = 1, ..., m\}$. Each trustee s_j has a reliability $rb_j \in [0, 1]$, representing the probability of s_j to provide qualified services.*

Table 1. A sample of worst-case unfair ratings [18].

(a) Reliability of trustees

	s_1	s_2	s_3'	s_4'
rb	0.9	0.8	0.3	0.4

(b) Advisors' ratings of trustees

	a_1	a_2'	a_3'	a_4'	a_5'	a_6'	$\bar{r}$
s_1	0.9	0.1	0.05	0.1	0.1	0.05	0.22
s_2	0.8	0.2	0.1	0.2	0.07	0.2	0.26
s_3'	0.3	0.3	0.3	0.3	0.3	0.3	0.3
s_4'	0.4	0.4	0.4	0.4	0.4	0.4	0.4

Definition 2. *Trustors represent agents seeking service to perform tasks, defined as* $B = \{b_i | i = 1, ..., x\}$.

Definition 3. *Advisors represent agents having direct interactions with trustees and willing to share information with trustors, defined as* $A = \{a_k | k = 1, ..., n\}$. *Each advisor has a label* $c \in \{0, 1, ..., y\}$, *where* $c = 0$ *(resp.* $c = y$) *representing it is honest (resp. it is dishonest and takes the y-th attack strategy).*

Definition 4. *An Interaction represents a process where an agent requests services from another agent and gets an outcome, defined as* $I = (v, s_j, o)$. v *represents a trustor* b_i *or an advisor* a_k, *and* s_j *represents a trustee.* $o \in \{0, 1\}$ *represents the interaction outcome between* v *and* s_j, *where 1 (resp. 0) denotes a successful (resp. unsuccessful) result.*

3.2 Problem Description

Unfair rating attacks are caused by dishonest advisors who give distorted ratings to increase (resp. decrease) the reputation of dishonest (resp. honest) trustees. Traditional models [1,2,5,6] are vulnerable to unfair rating attacks, particularly in scenarios where most advisors are dishonest (e.g. worst-case attacks [13]). The worst-case attacks render majority-rule-based models invalid. Table 1 shows an example of worst-case unfair ratings. There are one honest advisor (e.g. a_1) and five dishonest advisors (e.g. a_2', a_3', a_4', a_5' and a_6') in environment. The honest advisor gives true ratings of trustees. In comparison, dishonest advisors take the "Selective Badmouthing" attack strategy by giving distorted ratings for trustees whose reliability $rb \geq 0.5$. The averaged ratings (e.g. $\bar{r}$) based on all the advisors show that the dishonest trustee s_4' has the highest rating, which is unreliable.

The RPS model introduces the ranking of trustees as a supplement to rating data. Table 1 and Table 2 shows an example of the ranking of trustees based on ratings. The ranking of trustees of honest advisors (e.g. a_1) is the same as the trustor (e.g. b_1). In contrast, The ranking of trustees of dishonest advisors (e.g. a_2', a_3', a_4', a_5' and a_6') are

Table 2. Ranking of trustees based on ratings [18].

	Rankings of Trustees
b_1	$s_1 > s_2 > s_4' > s_3'$
a_1	$s_1 > s_2 > s_4' > s_3'$
a_2'	$s_4' > s_3' > s_2 > s_1$
a_3'	$s_4' > s_3' > s_2 > s_1$
a_4'	$s_4' > s_3' > s_2 > s_1$
a_5'	$s_4' > s_3' > s_1 > s_2$
a_6'	$s_4' > s_3' > s_2 > s_1$

different with the trustor. However, there are similarities between dishonest advisors. They have the same top two trustees (e.g. s_3' and s_4'). Therefore, the RPS model utilizes the different rankings of trustees to distinguish honest and dishonest advisors apart. Besides, introducing the ranking of trustees helps to alleviate local convergence problems. For instance, the two honest trustees (e.g. s_1 and s_2) have close reliability values (e.g. 0.9 and 0.8). Some classical models may struggle to find the best partner between s_1 and s_2 under limited interactions. Typically, these models cease searching for other trustees once they have found a reliable trustee s_2, which causes missing the best trustee s_1. In comparison, RPS choose the first-order trustee of rankings, which prevents local convergence.

Dynamic unfair ratings are more difficult to prevent in partner selection. Firstly, the changing behaviours of dishonest advisors result in a slower decrease rate of their weights and thus reduce model accuracy. For example, in Camouflage attacks, dishonest advisors pretend to be honest first to establish their reputation and then give distorted ratings later. Therefore, it takes more time to decrease their reputation. Secondly, it is difficult to monitor the abnormal behaviours of dishonest advisors based on limited storage and time. For example, storing all the rating values in a period may take a lot of space when there are many advisors and trustees in the environment. Similarly, it takes a lot of time to calculate these rating data. The RPS model proposes a sliding-window-based method that records only one value based on the ranking of trustees per advisor at each time point, which saves a lot of storage and time in monitoring dynamic behaviour, which will be introduced in Sect. 4.2.

4   Detailed Design of the RPS Model

4.1   Overview of the RPS Model

The objective of the Ranking-based Partner Selection (RPS) Model is to assist the trustor in identifying the best partner from a set of trustees (e.g. honest and dishonest trustees are represented as white and shadow nodes in Fig. 1) by leveraging information provided by advisors (e.g. honest and dishonest advisors are represented as white and shadow nodes in Fig. 1). As shown in Fig. 1, the RPS Model contains two modules: 1) Partner Selection (PS) module clusters honest and dishonest advisors into different

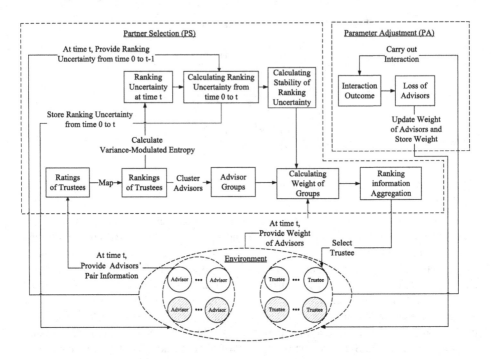

Fig. 1. Snapshot of the RPS model at time t. [18].

groups; 2) the Parameter Adjustment (PA) module aggregates group information to recommend a partner and then adjusts advisor weights based on the interaction result.

4.2 Partner Selection Module

At the time t, the trustor seeks advisors to share their information about trustees and then receives a set of pair information $\{(ps^t_{k,j}, ng^t_{k,j})|j = 1, ..., m\}$ from advisor a_k, where $ps^t_{k,j}$ and $ng^t_{k,j}$ represent the number of success and failure interactions between a_k and trustee s_j. Then, the set of pair information is first transmitted to the Partner Selection (PS) module to calculate a set of ratings $\{r^t_{k,j}|j = 1, ..., m\}$ by using the BRS model [1], shown in Eq. 1.

$$r^t_{k,j} = BRS(ps^t_{k,j}, ng^t_{k,j}) = \frac{ps^t_{k,j} + 1}{ps^t_{k,j} + ng^t_{k,j} + 2} \qquad (1)$$

Secondly, the PS module computes advisors' rankings of trustees based on ratings by interpreting the ranking of trustees as the likelihood of selecting a partner from the trustees. For example, the probability vector $\mathbf{p}^t_k = [p^t_{k,1}, ..., p^t_{k,m}]$ represents advisor a_k's partner selection probability on m trustees at time t. Besides, we assume there exist correlations between ratings and rankings.

Assumption 1: Advisors tend to select trustees with high ratings as partners. For example, in Table 1, advisor a_1's ratings on trustees are $[0.9, 0.8, 0.3, 0.4]$. Therefore, $p_{1,1} > p_{1,2} > p_{1,4} > p_{1,3}$ and $p_{1,1} + p_{1,2} + p_{1,3} + p_{1,4} = 1$.

Specifically, $p_{k,j}^t$ represents the partner selection likelihood of advisor a_k on trustee s_j at time t, as shown in Eq. 2, where $\mu = 10$:

$$p_{k,j}^t = \frac{e^{\mu r_{k,j}^t}}{\sum_{j=1}^{m} e^{\mu r_{k,j}^t}} \tag{2}$$

Thirdly, the PS module considers the ranking vector $\mathbf{p}_k^t$ as the advisors' characteristics for partner selection. Besides, we propose an assumption about the rankings of trustees.

Assumption 2: The rankings of trustees from honest and dishonest advisors are different. For instance, in an e-commerce environment, honest reviewers' rankings are generally consistent with the truth based on true ratings. In contrast, dishonest reviewers' rankings diverge from the truth due to distorted ratings.

Then, the PS module uses the DBSCAN algorithm [16] to cluster honest and dishonest advisors into different groups based on the ranking of trustees. We assume there are z groups $\{G_1^t, ..., G_z^t\}$ at time t.

Fourthly, the PS module computes group weights $w_{G_z}^t$ at time t, which is affected by two factors: 1) advisor weights in the group; 2) the evolution of advisors' rankings on trustees from time 0 to t.

We calculate the ranking uncertainty $\lambda(\mathbf{p}_k^t)$ to measure how informative advisors' rankings are rather than storing entire rankings, which saves a lot of storage and calculation time. The calculation of ranking uncertainty refers to the MASA model [17]. Specifically, we treat rankings $\mathbf{p}_k^t$ as a discrete distribution and use Eqs. 3, 4 to calculate entropy $H(\mathbf{p}_k^t)$ and variance $\sigma^2(\mathbf{p}_k^t)$ of rankings. Then, calculating the ranking uncertainty $\lambda(\mathbf{p}_k^t)$ based on entropy and variance, as shown in Eq. 5, where 1 (resp. 0) indicates absolute certainty (resp. complete uncertainty).

$$H(\mathbf{p}_k^t) = -\sum_{j=1}^{m} p_{k,j}^t \cdot \log_m^{p_{k,j}^t} \tag{3}$$

$$\sigma^2(\mathbf{p}_k^t) = \sum_{j=1}^{m} p_{k,j}^t \cdot (j - \frac{\sum_{j=1}^{m} j}{m})^2 \tag{4}$$

$$\lambda(\mathbf{p}_k^t) = (1 - H(\mathbf{p}_k^t))^{\frac{12\sigma^2(\mathbf{p}_k^t)}{m^2 - 1}} \tag{5}$$

The uncertainty of honest and dishonest advisors would differ because their rankings are different. In addition, we propose an assumption about the stability of ranking uncertainty.

Assumption 3: Honest advisors have more stable ranking uncertainty than dishonest advisors over time. For instance, in an e-commerce system, honest reviewers tend to give stable ratings for products when they have sufficient interaction experiences. In contrast, dishonest reviewers greatly change their ratings based on dynamic attack strategies. For instance, dishonest reviewers who adopt the Periodic Behavior attack strategy constantly switch between honest and distorted ratings. Rating changes incur ranking changes and finally cause a change of ranking uncertainty.

To calculate the stability of ranking uncertainty, the PS module first calculates the ranking uncertainties from time 0 to t, which is an uncertainty vector: $\mathbf{u}_k^t = [\lambda(\mathbf{p}_k^0), ..., \lambda(\mathbf{p}_k^t)]$.

Then, the PS module proposes a sliding-window-based method to monitor the dynamic changes of ranking uncertainty, shown in Fig. 2. The time series represents an advisor's uncertainty vector (e.g. $[0.65, 0.65, 0.65, 0.42, 0.42, 0.42]$) between times 0 to 5. The PS module uses a window of size 2, which slides along the time series and divides it into five-time sequences of length 2. Then, the PS module calculates the Mean Absolute Deviation (MAD) of each sequence, shown in Eq. 6.

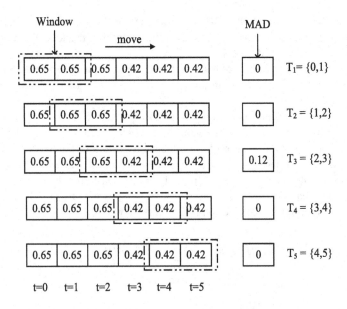

Fig. 2. Snapshot of the sliding-window-based method.

The Mean Absolute Deviation (MAD) of time sequence $\mathbf{u}_k^T$ represents the changes of ranking uncertainty of advisor a_k in time period T. The larger the MAD, the greater the range of change.

$$MAD(\mathbf{u}_k^{T_x}) = \frac{\sum_{t' \in T_x}\left|\lambda(\mathbf{p}_k^{t'}) - \frac{\sum_{t'=0}^{t}\lambda(\mathbf{p}_k^{t'})}{t}\right|}{t}, \quad x = 1, ..., t-1 \wedge t > 0 \quad (6)$$

According to Fig. 2, the advisor only changes the ranking uncertainty value at time 3. Therefore, the sequence MAD in period T_3 is the highest (e.g. 0.12). This situation may appear in camouflage attacks, where dishonest advisors pretend to be honest first and then change to dishonest behaviour at a certain point, providing distorted rankings thereafter. This situation may also appear in Periodic Behavior attacks, where dishonest advisors periodically switch between honest and dishonest behaviours.

Besides, to focus on the latest changes, the PS module uses an Exponentially weighted moving average (EWMA) method to calculate the weights of sequence MADs where sequences closer to the current time will be assigned higher weights, shown in Eq. 7. m is a smoothing factor; we set $m = 0.2$ to make the recent sequences have higher weights. Take Fig. 2 as an example; the weight of T_5 is higher than the others.

$$
\begin{cases}
w(\mathbf{u}_k^{T_x}) = \frac{1}{\sum w(\mathbf{u}_k^{T_x})} & \text{if } x = 1 \\
w(\mathbf{u}_k^{T_x}) = \frac{m \cdot w(\mathbf{u}_k^{T_{x-1}}) + (1-m) \cdot x}{\sum w(\mathbf{u}_k^{T_x})} & \text{if } x = 2, ..., t-1 \wedge t > 0
\end{cases}
\tag{7}
$$

Then, the PS module calculates an averaged MAD based on all time sequences, representing the stability of advisor a_k's ranking uncertainty from time 0 to t, shown in Eq. 8. Advisors with a higher average MAD tend to have more unstable rating behaviours and thus have a greater likelihood of being dishonest.

$$
\overline{MAD}_k^t = \sum_{x=1}^{t-1} w(\mathbf{u}_k^{T_x}) \cdot MAD(\mathbf{u}_k^{T_x}), \quad x = 1, ..., t-1 \wedge t > 0
\tag{8}
$$

After that, the PS module calculates the advisor weights, which are influenced by the stability of advisors' ranking uncertainty $\overline{MAD}_k^t$, shown in Eq. 9. Advisors with high average MAD would be assigned lower weights because their dynamic behaviours are similar to the attack patterns of honest advisors, where $\beta = 10$ in our paper.

$$
\begin{cases}
w_k^t = \frac{1}{k} & \text{if } t = 0 \\
w_k^t = w_k^t \cdot e^{-\beta \overline{MAD}_k^t} & \text{if } t > 0
\end{cases}
\tag{9}
$$

Then, the PS module calculates the weights of groups $w_{G_z}^t$ based on three factors: 1) the weights of advisors w_k^t in the group; 2) the size of advisor sets A_z in the group G_z, which reflect group influence in some extent, for example, groups with more users show stronger influence on social networks; 3) the density of groups. Groups with higher density have lower noise brought by the clustering process. We estimate the density group using the Sum of Squared Errors (SSE), shown in Eq. 10.

$$
SSE_z = \sum_{a_k \in A_z} (a_k - \frac{\sum_{a_k \in A_z} a_k}{|A_z|})^2
\tag{10}
$$

For each group G_z, SSE_z calculates the sum of the squares of the distances from each advisor a_k to the group centre. A smaller SSE represents that the advisors are closer to the group's centre and that the group is more densely clustered. Therefore, the group weight is calculated as shown in Eq. 11:

$$w^t_{G_z} = \frac{\sum_{a_k \in A_z} w^t_k}{|A_z|} \cdot \sqrt{|A_z|} \cdot e^{-SSE_z} \tag{11}$$

Later, the PS module calculates an averaged ranking $\overline{\mathbf{p}}^t$ based on groups, shown in Eq. 12.

$$\overline{\mathbf{p}}^t = \frac{\sum^z_{z'=1} w^t_{G'_z} \cdot \frac{\sum_{a_k \in A_z} w^t_k \cdot \mathbf{p}^t_k}{\sum_{a_k \in A_z} w^t_k}}{\sum^z_{z'=1} w^t_{G'_z}} \tag{12}$$

Finally, the PS module selects the top-rank trustee s_j with the highest probability value $\overline{p}^t_j$ as the partner (e.g. $max(\overline{\mathbf{p}}^t) = \overline{p}^t_j$).

4.3 Parameter Adjustment Module

When a partner is chosen, the trustor b_i will interact with partner s_j and get results $o^t_{i,j}$. Then, the PA module calculates two kinds of advisor losses based on interaction results: 1) the prediction loss; 2) the recommendation loss, as shown in Eqs. 13 and 14.

$$\begin{cases} P\{o^t_{i,j} = 1\} = rb_j \\ P\{f^t_{k,j} = 1\} = r^t_{k,j} \\ pl^t_k = |f^t_{k,j} - o^t_{i,j}| \end{cases} \tag{13}$$

The prediction loss pl^t_k is calculated based on the difference between advisors' prediction outcome $f^t_{k,j}$ and the trustor's true interaction outcome $o^t_{i,j}$. The trustor b_i (resp. advisor a_k) predicts partner s_j has a probability of rb_j (resp. $r^t_{k,j}$) to achieve a successful interaction, where rb_j and $r^t_{k,j}$ are the trust estimation of s_j from trustor and advisor, respectively.

$$\begin{cases} rl^t_k = -1, & if \ max(\mathbf{p}^t_k) = p^t_{k,j} \wedge o^t_{i,j} = 1 \\ rl^t_k = 1, & if \ max(\mathbf{p}^t_k) = p^t_{k,j} \wedge o^t_{i,j} = 0 \end{cases} \tag{14}$$

The recommendation loss rl^t_k is calculated for advisors whose top-rank trustees are the same as the selected partner. When outcome $o^t_{i,j} = 1$ (resp. $o^t_{i,j} = 0$), the advisors' prediction is accurate (resp. inaccurate). Then, the relevant advisors' weights would be increased (resp. reduced) by setting $rl^t_k = -1$ (resp. $rl^t_k = 1$).

Finally, the PA module adjusts advisor weights based on the two losses, as shown in Eq. 15, which refers to the weight updating process of ITEA [14,15], where $\eta = \sqrt{8 \cdot ln(n)/T}$, n is the advisor number, and T is the total interaction number between the trustor and partner.

$$w^t_k = w^{t-1}_k \cdot e^{-\eta pl^t_k} \cdot e^{-\eta rl^t_k}, \quad t > 0 \tag{15}$$

The detailed procedures of the RPS model are demonstrated in Algorithm 1.

Step 1: (Line 1–3) Initializing model parameters. At the time 0, assigning an averaged weight to each advisor: $w^0_k = \frac{1}{n}$, and using an empty array to represent advisors' ranking uncertainty: $\mathbf{u}^0_k = []$. At the beginning of time point t in time period $[1, T]$, the

---

Algorithm 1. The RPS Model [18].

Data: Trustors $\{b_i | i = 1, ..., x\}$, trustees $\{s_j | j = 1, ..., m\}$, advisors $\{a_k | k = 1, ..., n\}$,
and interaction numbers T

1 Sets advisors' weights at time $0 : w_k^0 = \frac{1}{n}, 1 \leq k \leq n$;

2 Sets advisors' ranking uncertainty at time $0 : \mathbf{u}_k^0 = []$;

3 **for** $t = 1$ **to** T **do**

4   b_i receives advisors' pair information of trustees: $(ps_{k,j}^t, ng_{k,j}^t), 1 \leq k \leq n, 1 \leq j \leq m$;

5   Calculates advisors' ratings of trustees: $r_{k,j}^t \in [0, 1]$;

6   Calculates advisors' rankings of trustees $\mathbf{p}_k^t = [p_{k,1}^t, ..., p_{k,m}^t]$;

7   Clusters advisors into z groups: $G_1^t, ..., G_z^t$;

8   Calculates of advisors' ranking uncertainty: $\lambda(\mathbf{p}_k^t)$;

9   Calculates the ranking uncertainty from time 0 to $t : \mathbf{u}_k^t = \mathbf{u}_k^{t-1}.\text{append}(\lambda(\mathbf{p}_k^t))$;

10   Calculates advisors' ranking stability: $\overline{MAD}_k^t$;

11   Calculates advisors' weights w_k^t ;

12   Calculates density of groups $SSE_z, 1 \leq z' \leq z$;

13   Calculates weights of groups: $w_{G_{z'}}^t, 1 \leq z' \leq z$;

14   Calculates an averaged ranking based on groups $\overline{\mathbf{p}^t} = [\overline{p_1^t}, ..., \overline{p_m^t}]$;

15   Select s_j with the highest $\overline{p_j^t}$ as partner ;

16   Observes interaction outcome $o_{i,j}^t \in \{0, 1\}$ between b_i and s_j;

17   Calculates advisors' prediction loss pl_k^t and recommendation loss rl_k^t ;

18   Updates weights of advisors w_k^t at time $t, 1 \leq k \leq n$;

19 **end**

---

trustor b_i receives advisors' pair information, where $(p_{k,j}^t, n_{k,j}^t)$ represents advisor a_k about its success and failure interaction numbers with trustee s_j. Then, b_i transmits pair information to the PS module.

Step 2: (Line 3–7) Clustering advisors into groups based on their rating data. Firstly, the PS module calculates the advisor's ratings of trustees based on Eq. 1, where $r_{k,j}^t$ represents advisor a_k's trust estimation of trustee s_j. Secondly, the PS module map rating data to ranking data based on Eq. 2, where $p_{k,j}^t$ represents advisor a_k's probability of selecting trustee s_j as a partner. Thirdly, the PS module utilizes the DBSCAN algorithm to cluster advisors based on rankings into z groups: $G_1^t, ..., G_z^t$. This step aims to allocate honest and dishonest advisors into different groups.

Step 3: (Line 8–15) Selecting a partner based on groups' rankings. Firstly, the PS module calculates the stability of advisors' ranking uncertainty from time 0 to t to find dishonest advisors with dynamic attack behaviours. Specifically, the PS module calculates the ranking uncertainty based on Eqs. 3, 4 and 5, where $\lambda(\mathbf{p}_k^t)$ represents advisor a_k's ranking uncertainty at time t. Then, the PS module records the ranking uncertainties from time 0 to t as a vector $\mathbf{u}_k^{t-1}$. Later, the PS module calculates advisors' ranking stability $\overline{MAD}_k^t$ based on Eqs. 6, 7 and 8. After that, the PS module uses Eq. 9 to calculate the weights of advisors based on $\overline{MAD}_k^t$. Then, it calculates the group density SSE_z using Eq. 10. Later, it calculates group weights (e.g. $w_{G_1}^t, ..., w_{G_z}^t$) based on the advisor weights, advisor numbers, and group density. Finally, the PS module calculates an averaged ranking $\overline{\mathbf{p}^t}$, and selects the trustee s_j with the highest probability $\overline{p_j^t}$ as the partner.

Step 4: (Line 16–18) Parameter adjustment is constructed based on interaction results. Specifically, the PA module first records the interaction outcome $o_{i,j}^t$ between trustor b_i and partner s_j, where $o_{i,j}^t = 1$ represents success (resp. $o_{i,j}^t = 0$ represents failure). Then, the PA module uses Eq. 13 to calculate the prediction loss pl_k^t by comparing advisors' prediction outcome and the trustor's interaction outcome. Then, the PA module uses Eq. 14 to calculate the recommendation loss rl_k^t by giving a reward (resp. a punishment) to advisors whose top-rank trustee is the selected partner when interaction results are successful or failure. Finally, based on the two losses, the PA module updates the advisor weights using Eq. 15.

5 Experiment

There exists one trustor, ten trustees (half honest, half dishonest), and 100 advisors in the environment. The reliability value of trustees is sampled uniformly and randomly from the set $\{0.1, 0.2, ..., 0.9\}$, where honest (resp. dishonest) trustees' trustworthiness is higher than or equal to (resp. lower than) 0.5. Before formal interactions, we set a pretreatment stage, letting advisors interact with the trustees three million times to gain sufficient experience. In each pretreatment interaction, randomly select an advisor and a trustee from the environment and record the success and failure interaction numbers, stored as positive results p and negative results n. The honest advisors will share true pair information (p, n). By contrast, dishonest advisors will give distorted pair information (p', n') based on various attack strategies shown in Sect. 5.1.

5.1 Dishonest Advisors and Dynamic Attacks

The experiments consider 10 dishonest advisors and four dynamic attack strategies. The first 10 settings refer to the conference paper [18] to test the model accuracy under different distorted ratings. Setting 11–14 refer to the ITEA model [14, 15] to test the model accuracy under dynamic attacks.

Setting 1: Partly Random (PR) Advisors. Each PR advisor $a_k \in DA$ first chooses trustees s_j for which it will offer distorted pair information based on a 50% probability. Then, randomly creating a rating value $r \in (0, 1)$ and computing the corresponding distorted pair (p, n) based on Eq. 1. For the remaining trustees, a_k will offer honest pair information.

Setting 2,3: BM(Badmouthing)/BS(Ballot-Stuffing) Advisors. For each BM/BS advisor $a_k \in DA$, it first randomly chooses trustees s_j for which it will offer distorted advice based on a 50% probability. Then, it selects the distorted pair (p, n) with the lowest(highest) $BRS(p_j, n_j)$ value among s_j's all the interaction experiences during the pretreatment process. For the remaining trustees, a_k will offer honest advice.

Setting 3,4: Additive BM/BS (ABM/ABS) Advisors. For each ABM advisor $a_k \in DA$, it gives a distorted pair for each trustee s_j. a_k first randomly creates a rating value $r \in (0.8, 1)$, and calculate a new rating value $r' = \frac{p_{k,j}+1}{p_{k,j}+n_{k,j}+2} - r$ based on its own experiences with trustee s_j. When $r' > 0$, creating distorted pair (p, n) with $BRS(p, n) = r'$. Otherwise, creating distorted pair $(0, p_{k,j} + n_{k,j})$. For each ABS advisor $a_k \in DA$, it calculates a value $r' = \frac{p_{k,j}+1}{p_{k,j}+n_{k,j}+2} + r$. When $r' < 1$, creating distorted pair (p, n) with $BRS(p, n) = r'$. Otherwise, creating distorted pair $(p_{k,j} + n_{k,j}, 0)$.

Setting 5,6: All-Negative/All-positive (AN/AP) Advisors. Each AN and AP advisor $a_k \in DA$ gives pair $(0, 10000)$ and pair $(10000, 0)$ for each trustee s_j, respectively.
Setting 7,8: Fully random (FR) Advisors. Each FR advisor $a_k \in DA$ works like PR advisors in Setting 1, but it will offer distorted information for all trustees.

Setting 9,10: Selective BM/BS (SBM/SBS) Advisors. For each SBM advisor $a_k \in DA$, it gives distorted pair $(0, p_{k,j} + n_{k,j})$ for trustees s_j when $BRS(p_{k,j}, n_{k,j}) > 0.5$, and gives honest advice for the remain trustees. For each SBS advisor $a_k \in DA$, it gives distorted pair $(p_{k,j} + n_{k,j}, 0)$ for trustees s_j when $BRS(p_{k,j}, n_{k,j}) < 0.5$, and gives honest advice for the remain trustees.

Setting 11: Camouflage. Advisors pretend to be honest in the first ten interactions and give true ratings and change to dishonest later and give distorted ratings.

Setting 12: Good-Bad-Good. Advisors behave honestly in the first ten interactions, then change to dishonest in the next ten interactions, and keep honest for the rest interactions.
Setting 13: Periodic Behavior. Advisors periodically switch between hoenst and dishonest states. Specifically, advisors behave honestly first and change to dishonest later, then repeat the previous operations.

Setting 14: Random Behavior. Every advisor randomly selects to behave honestly or dishonestly in each interaction.

5.2   Evaluation Metrics

1) Relative Frequency of Unsuccessful Interactions (RFU). RFU is referred to the ITEA model [14, 15] to test model accuracy by considering the ratio of negative interactions and total interactions, as shown in Eq. 16, where n_{it} and p_{it} represents the number of failed and successful interactions.

$$RFU = \frac{n_{it}}{n_{it} + p_{it}} \tag{16}$$

2) Relative Frequency of Unsuccessful Partner Selections (RFUPS). RFU is proposed to avoid locally convergent problems. For instance, trustees with a trustworthiness of 0.9 are usually treated as highly reliable, but it still has a likelihood of 0.1 to come up with failed interactions. Especially in limited interactions, the performances of trustees with a reliability of 0.9 and 0.8 might be similar. Therefore, we calculate the failure rate of selecting the best partner with the highest reliability, called the Relative Frequency of Unsuccessful Partner Selections (RFUPS), shown in Eq. 17, where

n_{ps} and p_{ps} represent the number of failed and successful number of the best partner selection.

$$RFUPS = \frac{n_{ps}}{n_{ps} + p_{ps}} \tag{17}$$

5.3   Results and Discussions

For each experiment, we select three ratios of the dishonest advisors (e.g. 90%, 50% and 10%), representing three scenarios of unfair rating attacks: worst-case, moderate-case and light-case. Furthermore, we set ten kinds of dishonest advisors (e.g. PR, BM, BS, ABM, ABS, AN, AP, FR, SBM, and SBS) and four kinds of dynamic attack strategies (e.g. Camouflage, Good-Bad-Good, Periodic Behavior, and Random Behavior). We execute 50 interactions for each setting to calculate the interaction and partner selection results and use RFU and RFUPS to test model accuracy. Besides, we repeat the experiment 50 times and calculate an average result to prevent noise.

Table 3. RFU/RFUPS for 50 interactions without dynamic attacks.

		90%	50%	10%
PR	RPS	0.142/**0.062**	0.135/0.000	0.126/0.000
	ITEA	**0.130**/0.080	0.130/0.001	0.128/0.000
BM	RPS	0.128/**0.057**	0.119/**0.021**	0.132/0.018
	ITEA	0.135/0.119	0.127/0.033	**0.116**/0.000
BS	RPS	0.133/0.000	0.114/0.000	**0.145**/0.000
	ITEA	0.132/0.000	0.119/0.000	0.162/0.000
ABM	RPS	0.143/0.000	0.122/0.000	0.130/0.000
	ITEA	**0.133**/0.000	0.121/0.000	0.124/0.000
ABS	RPS	0.112/0.000	0.156/0.000	**0.118**/0.000
	ITEA	0.109/0.000	**0.137**/0.000	0.134/0.000
AN	RPS	0.134/0.000	0.116/0.000	0.128/0.000
	ITEA	0.142/0.000	0.123/0.000	0.123/0.000
AP	RPS	0.131/0.000	0.128/0.000	0.110/0.000
	ITEA	0.134/0.000	0.130/0.000	0.113/0.000
FR	RPS	**0.143/0.165**	0.133/**0.022**	0.135/0.000
	ITEA	0.165/0.303	0.130/0.049	0.135/0.000
SBM	RPS	**0.359/0.576**	0.142/**0.034**	0.109/0.000
	ITEA	0.572/0.924	0.146/0.064	0.116/0.000
SBS	RPS	**0.136/0.043**	0.156/0.016	**0.124**/0.000
	ITEA	0.203/0.156	0.167/0.019	0.134/0.000

Table 3 shows the results without dynamic attacks, where RPS and ITEA models cope with unfair rating attacks brought by ten kinds of dishonest advisors. To reduce the bias, we set a threshold in the result comparison. When the RFU and RFUPS differences between the two models are higher than 0.01, we treat the winner as a significant performance advantage. Otherwise, we treat the performance of the two models as equal. The significant winner will be set in bold in the table.

According to Table 3, the RPS model performs well in most of the worst-case unfair rating attacks. For instance, when there are 90% PR and BM advisors in the environment, RPS shows better partner selection accuracy with a lower RFUPS. When there are 90% FR, SBM and SBS advisors in the environment, RPS has much better performance than ITEA in both RFU and RFUPS. For instance, RPS has a failure rate of 0.359 (resp. 0.576) in achieving success interactions (resp. in selecting partners) under 90% SBM advisors. In contrast, ITEA's failure rate is 0.572 (resp. 0.924), which is much worse than RPS. On the other hand, RPS has better RFUPS in most situations, even in cases with bad RFU. For example, under 90% PR advisors, RPS outperforms ITEA on RFUPS but is worse than ITEA on RFU, which may be caused by inaccurate estimates due to insufficient interaction. Generally speaking, when we find the best partner, the interaction failure rate would be decreased over time. Therefore, RFUPS helps to measure model accuracy under limited interactions.

Table 4. RFU/RFUPS for 50 interactions under Camouflage attacks.

		90%	50%	10%
PR	RPS	**0.118/0.002**	0.117/**0.000**	0.133/0.000
	ITEA	0.136/0.094	0.125/0.041	0.130/0.000
BM	RPS	**0.135/0.000**	0.136/**0.000**	0.137/0.000
	ITEA	0.157/0.219	0.130/0.039	0.140/0.000
BS	RPS	0.141/0.000	0.124/0.000	**0.121**/0.000
	ITEA	0.132/0.000	0.127/0.000	0.137/0.000
ABM	RPS	0.125/0.000	**0.110**/0.000	0.137/0.000
	ITEA	0.128/0.000	0.127/0.000	**0.126**/0.000
ABS	RPS	0.135/0.000	0.115/0.000	0.135/0.000
	ITEA	0.126/0.000	0.116/0.000	0.140/0.000
AN	RPS	**0.124**/0.000	**0.117**/0.000	0.124/0.000
	ITEA	0.134/0.000	0.130/0.000	**0.113**/0.000
AP	RPS	0.114/0.000	0.128/0.000	0.132/0.000
	ITEA	0.110/0.000	**0.118**/0.000	**0.120**/0.000
FR	RPS	**0.117/0.001**	0.156/**0.000**	0.126/0.005
	ITEA	0.172/0.329	0.164/0.077	0.122/0.000
SBM	RPS	**0.126/0.006**	**0.133/0.000**	0.121/0.000
	ITEA	0.599/0.951	0.179/0.13	0.112/0.000
SBS	RPS	**0.161/0.065**	0.136/0.005	0.118/0.000
	ITEA	0.221/0.169	0.129/0.004	0.119/0.000

Tables 4, 5, 6 and 7 shows the results under four kinds of dynamic attacks (e.g. Camouflage, Good-Bad-Good, Periodic and Random Behavior). According to Tables 4, 5, 6 and 7, the RPS model outperforms ITEA in most of the worst-case and moderate-case unfair ratings, especially in coping with FR, SBM and SBS advisors, demonstrating significant advantages. For example, in Camouflage attacks, when there are 90% FR advisors in the environment, RPS has a failure rate of 0.117 (resp. 0.001) in achieving successful interactions (resp. in selecting partners). By contrast, ITEA has a higher failure rate of 0.172 (resp. 0.329). Besides, the model accuracy under dynamic attacks increased compared with static attacks. The RFUPS in Tables 4, 5, 6 and 7 decreased a lot compared with Table 3, especially in dealing with PR, FR, SBM and SBS advisors, which might be because RPS uses a sliding-window-based method to reduce the weights of dishonest advisors with dynamic behaviours.

Table 5. RFU/RFUPS for 50 interactions under Good-Bad-Good attacks.

		90%	50%	10%
PR	RPS	**0.119/0.002**	0.138/**0.000**	**0.124**/0.000
	ITEA	0.134/0.085	0.143/0.072	0.136/0.000
BM	RPS	0.124/**0.003**	0.126/ **0.000**	0.113/0.000
	ITEA	0.133/0.098	0.129/0.034	0.116/0.000
BS	RPS	**0.123**/0.000	0.138/0.000	0.122/0.000
	ITEA	0.138/0.000	0.138/0.000	0.114/0.000
ABM	RPS	0.120/0.000	0.126/0.000	0.128/0.000
	ITEA	0.122/0.000	0.122/0.000	0.132/0.000
ABS	RPS	0.120/0.000	0.146/0.000	0.116/0.000
	ITEA	0.124/0.000	**0.136**/0.000	0.122/0.000
AN	RPS	0.136/0.000	0.115/0.000	0.129/0.000
	ITEA	0.134/0.000	0.126/0.000	0.130/0.000
AP	RPS	**0.123**/0.000	0.123/0.000	0.118/0.000
	ITEA	0.144/0.000	0.121/0.000	0.123/0.000
FR	RPS	**0.125/0.012**	0.124/**0.000**	0.124/0.000
	ITEA	0.204/0.407	0.130/0.058	0.121/0.000
SBM	RPS	**0.112/0.000**	**0.127/0.000**	0.127/0.000
	ITEA	0.600/0.985	0.204/0.134	0.122/0.000
SBS	RPS	**0.140/0.043**	0.138/0.010	0.124/0.000
	ITEA	0.185/0.132	**0.128**/0.006	**0.112**/0.000

Table 6. RFU/RFUPS for 50 interactions under Periodic Behavior attacks.

		90%	50%	10%
PR	RPS	0.119/**0.001**	0.120/**0.000**	0.131/0.000
	ITEA	0.120/0.128	0.112/0.040	0.137/0.000
BM	RPS	0.125/**0.002**	0.130/**0.000**	0.129/0.000
	ITEA	0.129/0.176	**0.120**/0.020	0.132/0.000
BS	RPS	0.138/0.000	0.124/0.000	0.133/0.000
	ITEA	**0.116**/0.000	0.123/0.000	0.133/0.000
ABM	RPS	0.130/0.000	0.128/0.000	0.110/0.000
	ITEA	0.126/0.000	0.124/0.000	0.113/0.000
ABS	RPS	0.130/0.000	0.152/0.000	0.125/0.000
	ITEA	0.129/0.000	**0.141**/0.000	0.128/0.000
AN	RPS	0.126/0.000	0.120/0.000	0.135/0.000
	ITEA	0.131/0.000	0.113/0.000	0.136/0.000
AP	RPS	0.132/0.000	0.123/0.000	0.116/0.000
	ITEA	0.138/0.000	0.122/0.000	0.118/0.000
FR	RPS	**0.141/0.018**	0.115/0.000	0.136/0.000
	ITEA	0.196/0.367	0.120/0.004	0.143/0.000
SBM	RPS	**0.13/0.020**	**0.127/0.001**	0.135/0.000
	ITEA	0.566/0.925	0.152/0.070	**0.116**/0.000
SBS	RPS	**0.145/0.027**	**0.132/0.000**	0.132/0.000
	ITEA	0.209/0.171	0.145/0.016	0.126/0.000

However, ITEA slightly outperforms the RPS model in some moderate-case and light-case dynamic unfair ratings. For instance, in Table 4, under the ratio of 10% ABM, AN and AP advisors, ITEA demonstrates a lower RFU than RPS. In Table 5, under 50% ABS and SBS advisors, ITEA has lower RFU values. Similar results can be found in Tables 6 and 7, which might be because reliability estimates are not very accurate under limited interactions. Even the best partner with the highest reliability will likely execute failure interactions in each round. Therefore, the RFU would be more precise in sufficient interactions.

Although the RPS model shows great performances in experiments, our datasets are created through a simulation like traditional papers [9, 14, 15]. In the future, we will execute the RPS model on more real-world datasets to test its effectiveness.

Table 7. RFU/RFUPS for 50 interactions under Random Behavior attacks.

		90%	50%	10%
PR	RPS	**0.118/0.000**	0.133/**0.000**	0.134/0.000
	ITEA	0.136/0.082	0.127/0.019	0.139/0.000
BM	RPS	0.123/**0.000**	0.141/0.000	0.122/0.000
	ITEA	0.132/0.100	**0.121**/0.006	0.120/0.000
BS	RPS	0.140/0.000	0.130/0.000	0.138/0.000
	ITEA	**0.123**/0.000	0.130/0.000	**0.121**/0.000
ABM	RPS	**0.131**/0.000	0.126/0.000	**0.124**/0.000
	ITEA	0.147/0.000	0.122/0.000	0.134/0.000
ABS	RPS	0.147/0.000	0.124/0.000	0.124/0.000
	ITEA	0.144/0.000	0.129/0.000	**0.113**/0.000
AN	RPS	**0.114**/0.000	0.126/0.000	0.132/0.000
	ITEA	0.124/0.000	0.125/0.000	0.135/0.000
AP	RPS	0.134/0.000	0.107/0.000	0.143/0.000
	ITEA	0.140/0.000	0.126/0.000	**0.123**/0.000
FR	RPS	**0.121/0.000**	**0.128/0.000**	0.134/0.000
	ITEA	0.187/0.397	0.146/0.043	0.132/0.000
SBM	RPS	**0.148/0.008**	**0.133/0.001**	0.125/0.000
	ITEA	0.570/0.926	0.218/0.206	0.120/0.000
SBS	RPS	**0.138/0.005**	**0.115**/0.000	0.120/0.000
	ITEA	0.216/0.163	0.133/0.005	0.126/0.000

6 Conclusion

This paper proposes a Ranking-Based Partner Selection (RPS) model to solve the partner selection problem under dynamic unfair rating attacks. Compared with traditional methods, RPS introduces the ranking of trustees, which helps to figure out dishonest advisors. Besides, RPS proposes a clustering method to divide honest and dishonest advisors into different groups. Moreover, the RPS model proposes a sliding-window-based method to find dishonest advisors with dynamic behaviours. In addition, RPS is an online-learning method that helps to update model parameters based on interaction results in real time.

In experiments, the PRS model outperforms ITEA in most of the worst and moderate cases of unfair ratings, especially when coping with the FR, SBM and SBS advisors. Besides, in most cases, the PRS model performs well in partner selection, shown as a lower RFUPS. However, ITEA slightly outperforms RPS in some moderate and light cases of unfair ratings, shown as a lower RFU.

References

1. Josang, A., Ismail, R.: The beta reputation system. In: Proceedings of the 15th Bled Electronic Commerce Conference, vol. 5, pp. 2502–2511 (2002)
2. Teacy, W.L., Patel, J., Jennings, N.R., Luck, M.: TRAVOS: trust and reputation in the context of inaccurate information sources. In: Proceedings of Autonomous Agents and Multi-agent Systems, vol. 12, no. 2, pp. 183–198 (2006)
3. Regan, K., Poupart, P., Cohen, R.: Bayesian reputation modeling in e-marketplaces sensitive to subjectivity, deception and change. In: Proceedings of the National Conference on Artificial Intelligence, vol. 21, no. 2, pp. 1206–1212 (2006)
4. Zhang, J., Cohen, R.: Evaluating the trustworthiness of advice about seller agents in e-marketplaces: a personalized approach. Electron. Commer. Res. Appl. **7**(3), 330–340 (2008)
5. Liu, S., Zhang, J., Miao, C., Theng, Y.L., Kot, A.C.: iCLUB: an integrated clustering-based approach to improve the robustness of reputation systems. In: Proceedings of the 10th International Conference on Autonomous Agents and Multiagent System, vol. 3, pp. 1151–1152 (2011)
6. Teacy, W.L., Luck, M., Rogers, A., Jennings, N.R.: An efficient and versatile approach to trust and reputation using hierarchical Bayesian modelling. Artif. Intell. **193**, 149–185 (2012)
7. Jiang, S., Zhang, J., Ong, Y.S.: An evolutionary model for constructing robust trust networks. In: Proceedings of International Conference on Autonomous Agents and Multiagent Systems, vol. 13, pp. 813–820 (2013)
8. Fang, H.: Trust modeling for opinion evaluation by coping with subjectivity and dishonesty. In: Proceedings of Twenty-Third International Joint Conference on Artificial Intelligence (2013)
9. Yu, H., Shen, Z., Miao, C., An, B., Leung, C.: Filtering trust opinions through reinforcement learning. Decis. Support Syst. **66**, 102–113 (2014)
10. Wang, D., Muller, T., Irissappane, A.A., Zhang, J., Liu, Y.: Using information theory to improve the robustness of trust systems. In: Proceedings of International Conference on Autonomous Agents and Multiagent Systems, pp. 791–799 (2015)
11. Wang, X., Ji, S.J., Liang, Y.Q., Leung, H.F., Chiu, D.K.: An unsupervised strategy for defending against multifarious reputation attacks. Appl. Intell. **49**(12), 4189–4210 (2019)
12. Zhou, X., Murakami, Y., Ishida, T., Liu, X., Huang, G.: ARM: toward adaptive and robust model for reputation aggregation. IEEE Trans. Autom. Sci. Eng. **17**(1), 88–99 (2019)
13. Wang, D., Muller, T., Zhang, J., Liu, Y.: Information theoretical analysis of unfair rating attacks under subjectivity. IEEE Trans. Inf. Forensics Secur. **15**, 816–828 (2019)
14. Parhizkar, E., Nikravan, M.H., Zilles, S.: Indirect trust is simple to establish. In: Proceedings of International Joint Conference on Artificial Intelligence, pp. 3216–3222 (2019)
15. Parhizkar, E., Nikravan, M.H., Holte, R.C., Zilles, S.: Combining direct trust and indirect trust in multi-agent systems. In: Proceedings of International Joint Conference on Artificial Intelligence, pp. 311–317 (2020)
16. Ester, M., Kriegel, H.P., Sander, J., Xu, X.: A density-based algorithm for discovering clusters in large spatial databases with noise. In: Proceedings of the Second International Conference on Knowledge Discovery and Data Mining, vol. 96, no. 34, pp. 226–231 (1996)
17. Zeynalvand, L., Zhang, J., Luo, T., Chen, S.: MASA: multi-agent subjectivity alignment for trustworthy Internet of Things. In: Proceedings of 21st International Conference on Information Fusion (FUSION), pp. 2013–2020 (2018)
18. Liang, Q., et al.: Partner selection strategy in open, dynamic and sociable environments. In: Proceedings of the 15th International Conference on Agents and Artificial Intelligence, vol. 2, pp. 231–240 (2023)

Weight Re-mapping for Variational Quantum Algorithms

Michael Kölle[✉], Alessandro Giovagnoli, Jonas Stein, Maximilian Balthasar Mansky,
Julian Hager, Tobias Rohe, Robert Müller, and Claudia Linnhoff-Popien

LMU Munich, Oettingenstraße 67, 80538 Munich, Germany
michael.koelle@ifi.lmu.de

Abstract. Inspired by the remarkable success of artificial neural networks across
a broad spectrum of AI tasks, variational quantum circuits (VQCs) have recently
seen an upsurge in quantum machine learning applications. The promising outcomes shown by VQCs, such as improved generalization and reduced parameter training requirements, are attributed to the robust algorithmic capabilities
of quantum computing. However, the current gradient-based training approaches
for VQCs do not adequately accommodate the fact that trainable parameters (or
weights) are typically used as angles in rotational gates. To address this, we
extend the concept of weight re-mapping for VQCs, as introduced by Kölle et al.
[9]. This approach unambiguously maps the weights to an interval of length 2π,
mirroring data rescaling techniques in conventional machine learning that have
proven to be highly beneficial in numerous scenarios. In our study, we employ
seven distinct weight re-mapping functions to assess their impact on eight classification datasets, using variational classifiers as a representative example. Our
results indicate that weight re-mapping can enhance the convergence speed of the
VQC. We assess the efficacy of various re-mapping functions across all datasets
and measure their influence on the VQC's average performance. Our findings
indicate that weight re-mapping not only consistently accelerates the convergence
of VQCs, regardless of the specific re-mapping function employed, but also significantly increases accuracy in certain cases.

Keywords: Variational quantum circuits · Variational classifier · Weight
re-mapping

1 Introduction

In past decades, machine learning (ML) has become an indispensable tool for tackling a wide range of problems in both science and industry. Overcoming previously
intractable computational problems, ML has nevertheless been faced with intrinsic limitations, such as the curse of dimensionality [1]. The successes of quantum computing
and machine learning have given rise to quantum machine learning (QML), now a central topic in both artificial intelligence and quantum computing. QML is an approach
to ML based on the laws of quantum mechanics. The basic unit of quantum information, the qubit, can be exploited to encode information and through quantum manip-
ulations problems can be solved computationally faster than on a classical computer.

© The Author(s), under exclusive license to Springer Nature Switzerland AG 2024
A. P. Rocha et al. (Eds.): ICAART 2023, LNAI 14546, pp. 286–309, 2024.
https://doi.org/10.1007/978-3-031-55326-4_14

In some cases, such techniques provide a quantum advantage, as seen in quantum algorithms used to solve systems of linear equations [8]. Specifically, this topic often centers around the acceleration of basic linear algebra subroutines. A major focus in the field of QML is Variational Quantum Computing (VQC) which employs quantum gates. Considering a qubit as the basic unit of information—a 2-dimensional complex vector in a Hilbert space—quantum gates can be represented as complex unitary operators, rotating or reflecting the vector on a unitary sphere. Every quantum gate can be decomposed into rotations and reflections [14]. Concatenating quantum gates gives rise to a quantum counterpart of the classical neural network: a quantum function approximator. The use of a qubit as a basic information unit allows for exponentially larger information encoding, as the space it occupies expands exponentially with the dimensions.

Aside from the previously discussed quantum advantage, QML, compared to its classical counterpart, benefits from the need for far fewer parameters in its function approximators [5]. However, there are still many issues and difficulties that need to be studied and properly addressed when dealing with quantum parameterized circuits, such as the barren plateau phenomena or the fact that adding more layers of gates increases the noise. Another major issue is the fact that the natural domain to which the rotational weights belong is the periodic interval $[0, 2\pi]$. The best way to deal with the periodicity of the weights, considering that they are updated with a standard gradient update rule and thus could assume ambiguous values, remains unclear. Similar to how data re-scaling or normalization techniques have significantly improved performance in classical ML cases [17], an approach has been introduced to re-map the parameters of a Variational Quantum Circuit, as illustrated in Fig. 1 [9]. More specifically, weight re-mapping functions have been introduced in the architecture of a variational quantum circuit to re-scale the parameters from the real domain to the compact interval $[\pi, \pi]$. In this work, we not only elaborate on this approach but also expand upon it by studying a broader range of weight re-mapping functions and testing them on a larger set of datasets. Our experimental results demonstrate that using a VQC equipped with a weight re-mapping function invariably guarantees a faster convergence compared to a VQC where no such function is employed.

In this study, we begin with a review of relevant literature and an explanation of the concept of weight re-mapping. This is followed by a detailed exposition of our research methodology and experimental design. Subsequently, we present our findings and engage in a comprehensive discussion of the results. The paper concludes with a summary of the study, an examination of its limitations, and suggestions for future research. All experimental data, along with a PyTorch implementation of the weight re-mapping functions utilized in this study, are accessible via this link[1].

2 Related Work

This work is an extension of Kölle et al. [9] which first introduces weight re-mapping for variational quantum circuits. We expand on this approach providing a wider range of evaluation and adding a new re-mapping function. Besides that, there are not many

---

[1] https://github.com/michaelkoelle/qw-map.

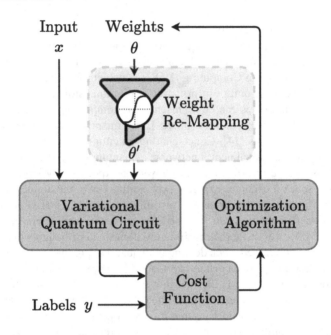

Fig. 1. Overview of the variational quantum circuit training process with weight re-mapping by Kölle et al. [9].

works in the literature focusing on on the embedding of data from the classical domain of $\mathbb{R}^n$ in the quantum one $SU(2^n)$. Mostly they rely on local or global mappings [10] which add an additional classical computation in the process of VQC evaluation. The classical embedding used is also data-specific and it must thus be adapted to every new dataset. The standard practice when it comes to local embeddings is to map each dimension of the dataset of interest to an interval, usually as $[\min(\text{data}), \max(\text{data})] \rightarrow [0, 1]$. This interval is then used to map each value to a rotation axis to the qubit. The different techniques that could be employed are single-qubit axis [19], multi-qubit embedding [11] and random linear maps [2,21].

3   Weight Re-mapping

In this section, we first describe the idea behind the weight mapping technique as introduced in [9] applied to variational quantum circuits. Then we proceed to illustrate the chosen architecture used for the task of classification and the different datasets used to test the VQC. While this study employs weight re-mapping in the context of classification tasks, it's important to underscore that this technique can be readily adapted for other machine learning paradigms, including unsupervised learning and reinforcement learning.

The standard training procedure of a classical neural network consists in updated the multi-dimensional vector $\vec{\theta} \in \mathbb{R}^n$ containing the weights of the connections between each neuron. Through the back-propagation the gradient of the loss function $\mathcal{L}$ con be computed and the weights are updated according to 1.

$$\vec{\theta}_i = \vec{\theta}_{i-1} - \alpha \nabla_{\vec{\theta}_{i-1}} \mathcal{L}(\vec{\theta}_{i-1}) \tag{1}$$

This represents the classical update step, which implicitly assumes that the space to which the weights belong and in which we follow the gradient direction is $\mathbb{R}^n$. This is true for a classical neural network where a weight can take any value of the real line $\mathbb{R}$. The same doesn't hold for a variational quantum circuit, where a parameter encodes a rotation around a specific axis of the Bloch sphere. Although technically every value of the real line could be assumed by a parameter, we must remember that a rotation of angle θ has a period of 2π, so that $R(\hat{v}, \theta) = R(\vec{v}, \theta + 2\pi)$. The whole $\mathbb{R}$ domain is thus redundant and letting the parameter take any real number may result in undesired behaviors, since moving according to the gradient of the loss function may lead the parameter in an adjacent interval, meaning that actually we are moving in the opposite direction with respect to the desired one. For these reasons it is natural to select a periodic interval $[\phi, \phi + 2\pi]$ as the parameter space of a variational quantum circuit. $\phi \in \mathbb{R}$ is a generic phase, and we choose $\phi = -\pi$ so that the chosen interval is centered around 0 and the parameters of a VQC result in $\vec{\theta} \in [-\pi, \pi]^n$. The weight re-mapping technique is employed to address the described mismatch between classical and quantum weights, so to constrain the classical real weights into the periodic interval. More in general a *mapping function* φ behaves by mapping the real line into a compact interval as

$$\varphi : \mathbb{R} \to [a, b] \tag{2}$$

More specifically, according to what has been discussed above, we choose $a = -b = -\pi$, so that $\varphi : \mathbb{R} \to [-\pi, \pi]$. The weight mapping function is introduced in such a way that, before a forward pass is performed, every rotation parameter inside the VQC will first be remapped. We can thus picture every rotation gate of the architecture working as follows

$$\boxed{R(\varphi(\theta))}$$

Only during the forward pass are thus the weights constraint to the periodic interval. Otherwise they are indeed free to take any value in the real domain. The update process will thus be adapted as

$$\vec{\theta}_i = \vec{\theta}_{i-1} - \alpha \nabla_{\vec{\theta}_{i-1}} \mathcal{L}(\varphi(\vec{\theta}_{i-1})) \tag{3}$$

which stresses the fact that during the computation of the loss function $\mathcal{L}$, so during the forward pass of the VQC, the weight mapping function φ is indeed applied. It is not though during the updated step.

3.1   Re-mapping Functions

We tested seven mapping functions to see which embedding into the periodic domain leads to better performances. Equations 4, 5, 6, 7, 8, and 9 were taken from Kölle et al.

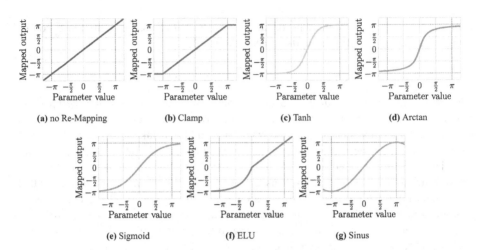

Fig. 2. Weight re-mapping functions [9].

[9]. Similarly to Kölle et al. [9], we use the identity function as a baseline, which has the same effect as if no function had been applied, as it can be seen in Fig. 2a.

$$\varphi_1(\theta) = \theta \tag{4}$$

The first mapping function we introduced is the one in Fig. 2b. Here all the parameters above π or below $-\pi$ are clamped to, respectively, π and $-\pi$. The values in between the two extrema are instead left untouched.

$$\varphi_2(\theta) = \begin{cases} -\pi & \text{if } \theta < -\pi \\ \pi & \text{if } \theta > \pi \\ \theta & \text{otherwise} \end{cases} \tag{5}$$

The next function we selected is the hyperbolic tangent, which is steeper around the 0 value but smoother around the values $-\pi$ and π, as shown in Fig. 2c. This means that the values around the bounds of the interval will not be widely differentiated.

$$\varphi_3(\theta) = \pi \tanh(\theta) \tag{6}$$

To conduct further studies on how the steepness of the mapping function affects the embedding of the real weights into the period, we scale the inverse of the tangent function by a factor of 2. The graph is shown in Fig. 2d.

$$\varphi_4(\theta) = 2 \arctan(2\theta) \tag{7}$$

We then tested a function with a steepness in between the two previous one, namely the sigmoid function. This needs obviously to first be rescaled with a factor of 2π in such a way that the bounds match the $[-\pi, \pi]$ interval. The result can be seen in Fig. 2e.

$$\varphi_5(\theta) = \frac{2\pi}{1 + e^{-\theta}} - \pi \tag{8}$$

The Exponential Linear Unit (ELU) has been tested as an example of an asymmetric function. To make it converge at least on the lower bound we set $\alpha = \pi$. The result can be seen in Fig. 2f.

$$\varphi_6(\theta) = \begin{cases} \pi(e^\theta - 1) & \text{if } \theta < 0 \\ \theta & \text{otherwise} \end{cases} \tag{9}$$

Lastly we introduce a new re-mapping function based on sinus. The graph is shown in Fig. 2g It has been properly scaled in such a way that its period is 4π and its amplitude 2π.

$$\varphi_7(\theta) = \pi \sin \frac{\theta}{2} \tag{10}$$

3.2   Variational Circuit Architecture

For the variational classifier used in our study, we have designed a three-component variational quantum circuit, illustrated in Fig. 3. Next, we will discuss this standard design with its three parts individually.

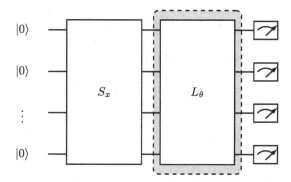

Fig. 3. Abstract variational quantum circuit used in this work. Dashed blue area indicates repeated layers. [9] (Color figure online).

State Preparation. The first component of our variational quantum circuit handles the state preparation S_x, which embeds a feature vector into a quantum circuit. The feature vector is composed of real values from the Euclidean space, which become mapped into the Hilbert space during the embedding process. The most common and general-purpose embedding techniques are the Angle Embedding and Amplitude Embedding. *Angle Embedding* is a technique used to encode n real-valued entries of the feature vector into the n qubits we use. This encoding starts by initializing the qubits as $|0\rangle$, followed by the embedding of information from the feature vector through the rotation angles, using rotational Pauli-X and Pauli-Y gates. The applied angles thereby represent the feature amplitudes to be encoded, illustrated below, using a single-axis rotational gate.

$$R_i(x_j)$$

The angle $x_j \in \mathbb{R}$ represents the j-th element of feature vector to encode, while the gate R_i, with $i \in \{X, Y\}$, represents the rotational gate applied on the i-th axis. The application of these rotational gates perform the respective embedding process. A rotation around the z-axis is unnecessary here, as the qubits were initialized with $|0\rangle$, a vector along the z-axis, which cancels out any effect of such a rotation. All our experiments with Angle Embedding are done using RX-Gates.

Amplitude Embedding consists in embedding the features into the amplitudes of the qubits. Since we can make use of superposition, we can embed 2^n features into n qubits. For Example, if we want to embed feature vector $x \in \mathbb{R}^3$ in to a 2 qubit quantum state $|\psi\rangle = \alpha |00\rangle + \beta |01\rangle + \gamma |10\rangle + \delta |11\rangle$ such that $|\alpha|^2 + |\beta|^2 + |\gamma|^2 + |\delta|^2 = 1$, we need to first pad our feature vector so that it matches 2^n features where n is the number of qubits used. Next, we need to normalize the padded feature vector y such that $\sum_{k=0}^{2^n-1} \frac{y_k}{\|y\|} = 1$. Lastly, we use a technique like the state preperation by Mottonen et al. [12] to embed the padded and normalized feature vector into the amplitudes of the qubits state.

Variational Layers. After conducting the quantum state preparation, the circuit implements iteratively layers of gates. Each layer, L_θ, consists of three single qubit rotations, as well as CNOT gates, used as entanglers. The number of iteratively implemented layers is determined by the layer-count L. In Fig. 3 the blue dashed area represents a single layer of gates which is then repeated L times. The implementation was inspired by the circuit-centric classifier design [16], exemplary shown as three qubit implementation below.

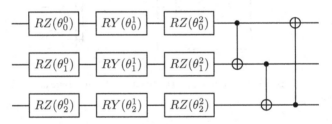

The trainable parameters θ_i^j, get applied on the i-th qubit and the j-th rotational gate, whereby $j \in \{0, 1, 2\}$. For simplicity, the shown graphic does omit the index of the respective layer. For the CNOT gates, responsible for the entanglement, the target bit is calculated by $(i + l) \bmod n$, which reveals the dependency on the respective layer-number l. This way of construction ensures for layer $l = 1$ a circular entanglement, as the control and target qubits are direct neighbors, exceptional of the last CNOT-gate, which constructs the circular character of entanglement. For the second layer, $l = 2$, control and target qubits are partly separated by another qubit. The index of the respective target qubit of the first qubit ($i = 0$) is here the third qubit ($i = 2$).

Measurement. Looking at our circuit architecture, the last part of the variational circuit consists of a measurement layer. Here, the expectation values of the first k qubits, where k depends on the classes to determine, is measured in their computational basis (z).

Afterwards, we add a bias to each of the measured expectation values, as those biases are also part of the parameters and updated accordingly. Ending the experiment, the softmax of the measurement is computed to normalize the respective probabilities.

3.3 Data Re-uploading Architecture

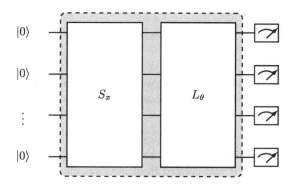

Fig. 4. Variational quantum circuit with data re-uploading used in this work. Dashed blue area indicates repeated encoding and layers. (Color figure online)

Originally introduced in Pérez-Salinas et al. [15], data re-uploading gets its name from the fact that the data is re-uploaded into the quantum circuit multiple times, at each layer of the circuit. This allows for a more expressive quantum circuit, as it can generate a richer set of transformations on the input data. The data re-uploading strategy is particularly useful for variational quantum classifiers because it allows the quantum circuit to learn complex, non-linear decision boundaries. This process effectively increases the expressivity of the quantum circuit, enabling it to capture more complex patterns in the data. In the context of our work, we utilize data re-uploading to enhance the performance of our variational quantum classifier. By re-uploading the data at each layer of the circuit, we are able to construct a more expressive quantum model that can better capture the intricacies of our dataset. This is particularly important for our investigation into the performance of the weight re-mapping method on more expressive circuits, as it allows us to explore the full potential of this technique. In terms of circuit construction, a circuit with data re-uploading is built from alternating embedding and variational layers (Fig. 4). The embedding layers, denoted as S_x, are responsible for mapping the classical data onto the quantum state space, while the variational layers, denoted as L_θ, apply a series of parameterized quantum gates that transform the quantum state. By alternating between these two types of layers, we are able to repeatedly re-upload and transform the data, thereby increasing the expressivity of the circuit. The structure of a data re-uploading circuit can be represented as follows:

$$U(\theta, x) = L_{\theta_n} S_{x_n} \ldots L_{\theta_1} S_{x_1} \tag{11}$$

where $U(\theta, x)$ is the total unitary operation representing the data re-uploading circuit, θ and x are the sets of parameters and input data respectively, and n is the number of layers in the circuit.

4 Experimental Setup

In the Experimental Setup section, we detail the methodology employed to evaluate the performance of the variational classifier, as described in Sect. 3.2. This includes the datasets used for testing, the baselines against which the classifier was compared, the metrics used to assess performance, and the hyperparameters and training procedures applied.

4.1 Datasets

In this section, we present the datasets that were used to assess the variational classifier from Sect. 3.2. We chose two popular datasets that pose a simple supervised learning classification task.

Abalone Dataset. The Abalone dataset is a well-known dataset in the field of machine learning and data mining. It was created from physical measurements of abalones, a type of marine snail, with the goal of predicting the age of the abalone from these measurements [13]. The dataset includes three classes, each representing a different sex of the abalone: Male, Female, and Infant. Each feature vector in the dataset contains eight attributes: length, diameter, height, whole weight, shucked weight, viscera weight, shell weight, and rings. The Abalone dataset is not balanced. The number of instances for each class are as follows: Male: 1528, Female: 1307, and Infant: 1342.

Banknote Authentication Dataset. The Banknote Authentication dataset is a popular dataset for binary classification tasks. It was created from images of genuine and forged banknote-like specimens, using an industrial camera usually used for print inspection [6]. The images were then processed using a wavelet transform tool to extract features from them. The dataset includes two classes, representing genuine and forged banknotes. Each feature vector in the dataset contains four attributes: variance of Wavelet Transformed image, skewness of Wavelet Transformed image, curtosis of Wavelet Transformed image, and entropy of image. These features capture the essential characteristics of the banknote images, making them suitable for the task of banknote authentication. The Banknote Authentication dataset roughly balanced, with 762 instances for the genuine class and 610 instances for the forged class.

Glass Identification Dataset. The Glass Identification dataset is a multi-class classification dataset that was created from the analysis of different types of glass. The dataset was collected for the purpose of forensic science to identify the type of glass found at crime scenes [6]. The dataset includes seven classes, each representing a different type of glass: building windows float processed, building windows non-float processed, vehicle windows float processed, containers, tableware, headlamps, and an undefined category. Each feature vector in the dataset contains nine attributes: refractive index, Sodium (Na), Magnesium (Mg), Aluminum (Al), Silicon (Si), Potassium (K), Calcium (Ca), Barium (Ba), and Iron (Fe). These features represent the chemical composition of the glass, which varies depending on the type of glass. The Glass Identification dataset is not balanced. The number of instances for each class are as follows: building windows float processed: 70, building windows non-float processed: 76, vehicle windows float processed: 17, containers: 13, tableware: 9, headlamps: 29, and undefined: 6.

Heart Disease Dataset. The Heart Disease dataset is a widely used dataset in the field of medical informatics and machine learning. It was created from several different studies and has been used in numerous research papers to develop and test algorithms for binary classification [4]. The dataset includes two classes, representing the presence and absence of heart disease. Each feature vector in the dataset contains 13 attributes: age, sex, chest pain type, resting blood pressure, serum cholesterol, fasting blood sugar, resting electrocardiographic results, maximum heart rate achieved, exercise induced angina, ST depression induced by exercise relative to rest, the slope of the peak exercise ST segment, number of major vessels colored by fluoroscopy, and thalassemia. The Heart Disease dataset is balanced, with 165 instances for the class representing the presence of heart disease and 138 instances for the class representing the absence of heart disease.

Iris Dataset. The Iris dataset, first introduced in an article by Fisher in 1936 [7], has since become a standard benchmark in the field of classification, and continues to be widely used in literature. For this study, we have used an updated version of the dataset, which corrects two minor discrepancies found in the original publication. This dataset is composed of three distinct classes, each representing a type of iris plant: Iris Setosa, Iris Versicolour, and Iris Virginica. Each class contains 50 instances, where every instance is characterized by a four-dimensional feature vector including sepal length, sepal width, petal length, and petal width (all measurements are in centimeters). While the first two classes (Setosa and Versicolour) can be linearly separated, the latter two (Versicolour and Virginica) are not linearly separable, posing a greater challenge for classification. We also use a version with the first two classes, resulting in a easier classification task.

Pima Indians Diabetes Dataset. The Pima Indians Diabetes dataset is a widely used dataset in the field of medical informatics and machine learning. It was created by the National Institute of Diabetes and Digestive and Kidney Diseases and aims to predict whether or not a patient has diabetes based on certain diagnostic measurements [18]. The dataset includes two classes, representing the presence and absence of diabetes. Each feature vector in the dataset contains eight attributes: number of times pregnant, plasma glucose concentration, diastolic blood pressure, triceps skin fold thickness, 2-hour serum insulin, body mass index, diabetes pedigree function, and age. The Pima Indians Diabetes dataset is not balanced, with 500 instances for the class representing the absence of diabetes and 268 instances for the class representing the presence of diabetes.

Seeds Dataset. The Seeds dataset is a commonly used dataset in the field of pattern recognition. It was created from measurements of geometrical properties of kernels belonging to three different varieties of wheat: Kama, Rosa, and Canadian [3]. The dataset includes three classes, each representing a different variety of wheat. Each feature vector in the dataset contains seven attributes: area, perimeter, compactness, length of kernel, width of kernel, asymmetry coefficient, and length of kernel groove. The Seeds dataset is balanced, with 70 instances for each class, resulting in a total of 210 instances.

Wine Dataset. The Wine dataset was produced from a chemical analysis of wines grown in the same region of Italy, which are derived from three different grape varieties [20]. This analysis was conducted in July 1991, originally examining 30 constituents. Unfortunately, the comprehensive details of these constituents have been lost over time, and the surviving dataset now comprises 13 chemical properties: Alcohol content, Malic acid, Ash, Alkalinity of ash, Magnesium, Total phenols, Flavanoids, Nonflavanoid phenols, Proanthocyanins, Color intensity, Hue, OD280/OD315 of diluted wines, and Proline. This dataset is not evenly distributed across the three classes, which represent the different grape varieties. The current composition is as follows: class 1 contains 59 instances, class 2 includes 71 instances, and class 3 encapsulates 48 instances.

4.2 Baselines

In our experiments, we compared our models against the following baselines: a variational quantum classifier (VQC) without re-mapping and, in the last experiment, a classical neural network (Classical NN).

Variational Quantum Classifier Without Re-mapping. The first baseline is a VQC without any re-mapping. This model uses a circuit with 6 layers and a varying embedding method. The embedding methods used include amplitude embedding, angle embedding, and amplitude embedding with data re-uploading. This baseline allows us to evaluate the impact of the re-mapping technique on the performance of the VQC.

Classical Neural Network. The second baseline is a classical NN, which we only used in the last experiment with the 2-class Iris Dataset. The architecture of this NN consists of an input layer with 4 nodes, a hidden layer with 6 nodes followed by an Exponential Linear Unit (ELU) activation function, and an output layer with a single node followed by a Sigmoid activation function. The choice of 6 nodes in the hidden layer was made to ensure a similar number of parameters to the VQC approach, allowing for a more direct comparison.

4.3 Metrics

In our experiments, we used two primary metrics besides the loss to evaluate the performance of our models: accuracy and the point of convergence.

Accuracy. The accuracy is a common metric used in classification tasks. It is defined as the proportion of correct predictions made by the model out of all predictions. In mathematical terms, if y_i is the true label and $\hat{y}_i$ is the predicted label, the accuracy is given by:

$$\text{Accuracy} = \frac{1}{N} \sum_{i=1}^{N} \delta(y_i, \hat{y}_i) \tag{12}$$

where N is the total number of samples, and $\delta(y_i, \hat{y}_i)$ is the Kronecker delta, which is 1 if $y_i = \hat{y}_i$ and 0 otherwise.

We distinguish between training, validation, and test accuracy. Training accuracy is calculated on the same data that was used for training the model. It gives an indication of how well the model has learned the training data, but it does not necessarily reflect how well the model will perform on unseen data. Validation accuracy is calculated on a separate set of data not used in training. It is used to tune hyperparameters and to get an estimate of the model's performance on unseen data while training. Test accuracy is calculated on another separate set of data after the model has been fully trained. It gives an unbiased estimate of the model's performance on unseen data.

Point of Convergence. The point of convergence (POC) is a metric that indicates when the model's learning process has stabilized. It is defined as the minimum step t at which the difference in validation loss falls below a threshold. The threshold is defined as the product of a factor k and the standard deviation of the validation loss. Mathematically, this is represented as:

$$\text{POC} = \min_t \{ t : \Delta\mathcal{L}_{\text{valid}}(\theta_t) < k \cdot \sigma(\mathcal{L}_{\text{valid}}(\theta)) \}$$

In our experiments, we chose $k = 1$. This choice means that the POC is the point at which the change in validation loss is less than one standard deviation of the validation loss. This is a valid way to determine the point of convergence because it ensures that the model's learning process has stabilized to within the normal variation of the validation loss. It provides a balance between waiting for the model to fully converge and stopping early to prevent overfitting.

4.4 Hyperparameters and Training

In all of our experiments, we used a consistent set of hyperparameters to ensure a fair comparison between different approaches. The learning rate was set to 0.01 and the batch size was set to 5 for all experiments. For the variational quantum classifier approaches, we used a circuit with 6 layers. The embedding method varied between experiments, with amplitude embedding, angle embedding, and amplitude embedding with data re-uploading being used. For the classical neural network approach, we used a hidden layer size of 6. This was chosen to ensure a similar number of parameters to the VQC approach, allowing for a more direct comparison. All experiments used the cross entropy loss function and the stochastic gradient descent (SGD) optimizer. Each experiment was repeated 10 times, with seeds ranging from 0 to 9, to ensure the robustness of our results.

5   Experiments

In this section we present the results of the experiments that we have carried out to benchmark the impact of the weight re-mapping functions. In principle our approach can be applied to any machine learning task relying on a Variational Quantum Circuit, such as Quantum Reinforcement Learning, The Quantum Approximate Optimization Algorithm, and so on. Here we chose supervised classification as our case study: a VQC has been used to classify 8 datasets and the re-mapping functions have been applied to see how the convergence of the classifier is improved.

We trained the classifier on the following datasets: Banknote Authentication, Glass Identification, Heart Desease, Pima Indians Diabetes, Iris, Seeds, Wine and Abalone dataset. The details of the training can be found in Sect. 4.4. We first show and comment more in detail in Sect. 5.1 the results relative to the different dataset to see how the functions affect the convergence speed. In doing so, we separate the two different encodings: amplitude and angle embedding. We only comment the top three performing functions. Then we show in Sect. 5.2 how each weight re-mapping function affects the convergence performance on average, considering all the datasets at once. We also studied the test accuracy and we perform an ANOVA test to check if and how the final performance, measured once the training is completed, is affected by the different functions. The results are shown in Sect. 5.3. In conclusion, as a small comparison with the classical counterpart, a classical neural network has been evaluated and compared with a variational quantum circuit in Sect. 5.4.

5.1   Convergence Results

In this section we show and comment more in details, for each type of embedding, four of the eight datasets. For each dataset the top three performing re-mapping functions are shown. The complete results can be seen in the Appendix in Fig. 9 and Fig. 10. The selected results for Amplitude and Angle embedding are shown respectively in

Table 1. Difference in validation accuracy compared to VQC at point of convergence using Amplitude Embedding.

approach dataset	VQC-arctan	VQC-clamp	VQC-elu	VQC-sigmoid	VQC-sin	VQC-tanh
abalone	0.016	0.000	0.013	−0.003	**−0.003**	0.016
banknote	0.060	0.000	0.008	0.002	0.002	0.019
glass	−0.241	0.000	−0.085	0.068	0.068	**−0.284**
heart_deasease	**−0.123**	0.000	−0.019	−0.086	−0.085	−0.117
indian_diabetes	**−0.017**	0.000	−0.003	0.002	0.000	0.002
iris	**−0.189**	0.000	−0.009	−0.121	−0.121	−0.141
seeds	−0.164	0.000	−0.235	−0.129	−0.137	**−0.389**
wine	**−0.443**	0.000	−0.070	−0.043	−0.043	−0.419
∅	−0.138	0.000	−0.050	−0.039	−0.040	**−0.164**

Table 2. Difference in validation accuracy compared to VQC at point of convergence using Angle Embedding.

approach dataset	VQC-arctan	VQC-clamp	VQC-elu	VQC-sigmoid	VQC-sin	VQC-tanh
abalone	**−0.165**	0.000	0.000	0.000	0.000	−0.133
banknote	−0.228	0.000	−0.201	−0.235	**−0.236**	−0.227
glass	**−0.247**	0.000	−0.079	−0.151	−0.180	−0.125
heart_deasease	**−0.166**	0.000	−0.105	−0.126	−0.124	−0.081
indian_diabetes	**−0.035**	0.000	−0.005	−0.035	−0.035	−0.015
iris	−0.222	0.000	−0.195	−0.124	−0.131	**−0.282**
seeds	**−0.684**	0.000	−0.543	−0.272	−0.277	−0.451
wine	**−0.133**	0.000	0.075	0.024	0.024	−0.022
∅	**−0.235**	0.000	−0.132	−0.115	−0.120	−0.167

Fig. 5 and Fig. 6. It can be seen how in both cases the convergence when applying the appropriate weight re-mapping function is much faster with respect to the VQC without any function applied. In order to properly estimate the impact that each re-mapping function has on the convergence of the VQC we propose a metric consisting in the difference in percentage between the validation accuracy of the VQC without and with a re-mapping function, as defined in Sect. 4.3. This metric has been calculated for each re-mapping function and for each dataset. The results can be seen in Table 1 for the Amplitude Embedding and in Table 2 for the Angle Embedding. We can see that in both cases the VQC-clamp has a difference of 0 with respect to the baseline, meaning that their performance is exactly the same. This is due to the fact that the weights here initialized and updated all are in the $[-\pi, \pi]$ range, where the Clamp function behaves as an identity function, thus not affecting the performance of the VQC. Excluding the Clamp function we can see that, in both tables, averaging on all the datasets all the values are negative, meaning that the accuracy of the baseline is always smaller than the one of each approach at its point of convergence. Also for each dataset, apart from some exceptions, it can be seen the negative percentage, resembling a higher accuracy. In the case of Angle Embedding, which is usually the most common encoding, it can be seen how averaging on all the datasets at least an improvement of 10% in convergence is always guaranteed.

5.2   Average Performance of Re-mapping Functions

As a further analysis we studied the different re-mapping functions averaging the accuracy and loss on all the datasets. In Fig. 7 the results can be seen. Both for Angle and Amplitude embedding the faster convergence due to the re-mapping functions can be seen. With respect to the normal VQC, adding a re-mapping function increases the performances os the classifier. A more detailed insight is given in Table 1 and 2, in particular in the last row, where the improvement in performance has been averaged on all the datasets. It can be seen that, depending on the chosen Embedding, the re-mapping function that on average performs the best is different: in the case of Amplitude Embedding,

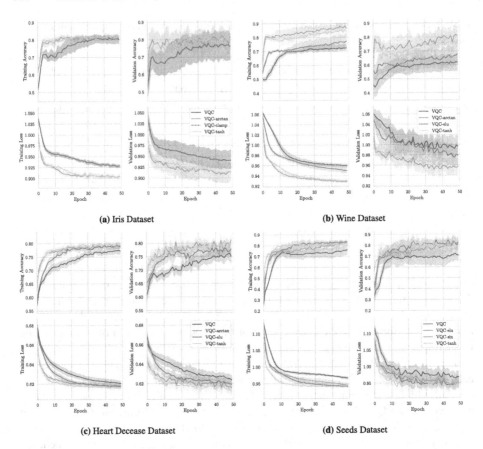

(a) Iris Dataset

(b) Wine Dataset

(c) Heart Decease Dataset

(d) Seeds Dataset

Fig. 5. Training and validation curves of the top 3 approaches for datasets Iris, Wine, Heart Desease and Seeds with Amplitude Embedding. In each epoch the algorithm processes 75% of the total samples of each dataset for training.

the tanh function has the faster convergence, while in the case of Angle Embedding the best function is arctan. Apart from these specific values which depend on the embedding and on the eight chosen datasets, the trend clearly indicates an improvement in the convergence speed of the classifier when constraining the weights of the VQC in their natural domain using an appropriate weight re-mapping function.

5.3 Test Accuracy

At the end of each training the final accuracy has been tested. In order to evaluate the impact on the final performance of the different weight re-mapping functions an ANOVA test of the test accuracies has been performed (Table 3 and 4).

Angle Embedding: The ANOVA test has been first carried out averaging first across all the datasets. The results show a statistical difference and significance in the approaches,

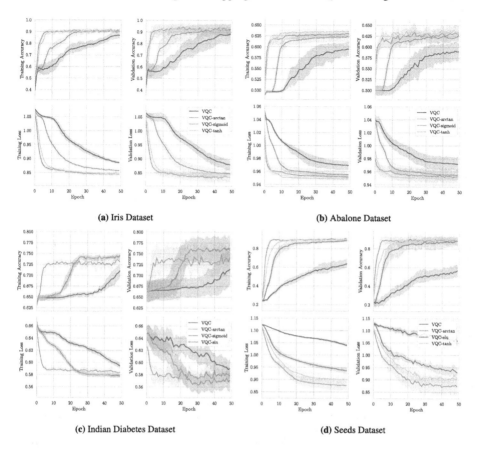

(a) Iris Dataset

(b) Abalone Dataset

(c) Indian Diabetes Dataset

(d) Seeds Dataset

Fig. 6. Training and validation curves of the top 3 approaches for datasets Iris, Abalone, Diabetis and Seeds with Angle Encoding. In each epoch the algorithm processes 75% of the total samples of each dataset for training.

Table 3. Test Accuracy and 95% confidence interval of tested mapping functions with Amplitude Embedding.

approach dataset	VQC	VQC-arctan	VQC-clamp	VQC-elu	VQC-sigmoid	VQC-sin	VQC-tanh
abalone	**0.524 ± 0.014**	0.520 ± 0.014	**0.524 ± 0.014**	0.523 ± 0.014	0.522 ± 0.014	0.521 ± 0.014	0.522 ± 0.014
banknote	**0.701 ± 0.022**	0.684 ± 0.022	**0.701 ± 0.022**	0.698 ± 0.022	0.690 ± 0.022	0.690 ± 0.022	0.690 ± 0.022
glass	0.400 ± 0.059	0.437 ± 0.060	0.400 ± 0.059	0.411 ± 0.059	0.422 ± 0.059	0.422 ± 0.059	**0.441 ± 0.060**
heart_deasease	0.753 ± 0.024	**0.776 ± 0.023**	0.753 ± 0.024	0.760 ± 0.023	0.759 ± 0.023	0.757 ± 0.023	0.767 ± 0.023
indian_diabetes	0.655 ± 0.030	0.652 ± 0.030	0.655 ± 0.030	**0.657 ± 0.030**	0.655 ± 0.030	0.655 ± 0.030	0.653 ± 0.030
iris	0.768 ± 0.061	**0.826 ± 0.054**	0.768 ± 0.061	0.747 ± 0.062	0.732 ± 0.064	0.742 ± 0.063	0.821 ± 0.055
seeds	0.711 ± 0.054	0.778 ± 0.050	0.711 ± 0.054	0.789 ± 0.049	0.774 ± 0.050	**0.793 ± 0.049**	0.781 ± 0.050
wine	0.643 ± 0.062	**0.848 ± 0.047**	0.643 ± 0.062	0.726 ± 0.058	0.683 ± 0.061	0.678 ± 0.061	0.804 ± 0.052
∅	0.644 ± 0.041	**0.690 ± 0.037**	0.644 ± 0.041	0.664 ± 0.040	0.655 ± 0.040	0.657 ± 0.040	0.685 ± 0.038

since we get $F(6, 63) = 18.440, <= 0.001$. The performance of the approaches was further analyzed on individual datasets. On most of the datasets there were no signif-

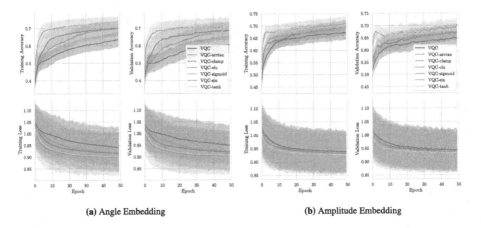

(a) Angle Embedding   (b) Amplitude Embedding

Fig. 7. Training and validation curves for every weight re-mapping function averaged on all the datasets.

Table 4. Test Accuracy and 95% confidence interval of tested mapping functions with Angle Embedding.

approach dataset	VQC	VQC-arctan	VQC-clamp	VQC-elu	VQC-sigmoid	VQC-sin	VQC-tanh
abalone	0.600 ± 0.013	0.635 ± 0.013	0.600 ± 0.013	0.624 ± 0.013	0.630 ± 0.013	0.628 ± 0.013	$\mathbf{0.639 \pm 0.013}$
banknote	0.936 ± 0.012	0.949 ± 0.010	0.936 ± 0.012	0.946 ± 0.011	0.949 ± 0.010	0.949 ± 0.010	$\mathbf{0.952 \pm 0.010}$
glass	0.315 ± 0.056	$\mathbf{0.459 \pm 0.060}$	0.315 ± 0.056	0.426 ± 0.059	0.363 ± 0.058	0.363 ± 0.058	$\mathbf{0.459 \pm 0.060}$
heart_deasease	0.518 ± 0.027	0.677 ± 0.026	0.518 ± 0.027	0.625 ± 0.026	0.623 ± 0.026	0.622 ± 0.026	$\mathbf{0.691 \pm 0.025}$
indian_diabetes	0.711 ± 0.029	0.736 ± 0.028	0.711 ± 0.029	0.733 ± 0.028	$\mathbf{0.751 \pm 0.027}$	0.747 ± 0.028	0.733 ± 0.028
iris	0.832 ± 0.054	0.884 ± 0.046	0.832 ± 0.054	0.858 ± 0.050	0.879 ± 0.047	0.879 ± 0.047	$\mathbf{0.900 \pm 0.043}$
seeds	0.526 ± 0.060	0.893 ± 0.037	0.526 ± 0.060	0.863 ± 0.041	0.852 ± 0.043	0.856 ± 0.042	$\mathbf{0.904 \pm 0.035}$
wine	0.422 ± 0.064	$\mathbf{0.517 \pm 0.065}$	0.422 ± 0.064	0.404 ± 0.064	0.430 ± 0.064	0.435 ± 0.065	0.509 ± 0.065
∅	0.607 ± 0.039	0.719 ± 0.036	0.607 ± 0.039	0.685 ± 0.037	0.685 ± 0.036	0.685 ± 0.036	$\mathbf{0.723 \pm 0.035}$

icant differences in performance among the approaches: for Iris we get $F(6, 63) = 0.534, p = 0.780$, for the Pina Indian Diabetes $F(6, 63) = 1.186, p = 0.325$, for the Banknote Authentication Dataset $F(6, 63) = 1.205, p = 0.315$, for the Wine Dataset $F(6, 63) = 1.474, p = 0.202$. Statistical significance in the impact of the different approaches is instead obtained with the Abalone Dataset, with $F(6, 63) = 3.138, p = 0.009$, glass dataset, $F(6, 63) = 3.362, p = 0.006$, Heart Deseases, where $F(6, 63) = 23.078, p =< 0.00$ and the Seeds dataset, where $F(6, 63) = 35.402, p < 0.001$.

Amplitude Embedding: The ANOVA revealed instead no significant differences between the final performance of the approaches using Amplitude Embedding, $F(6, 63) = 0.70$, $p = 0.65$. The performance of the approaches was also here further analyzed on individual datasets. On the abalone dataset, there were no significant differences in performance among the approaches, $F(6, 63) = 0.056, p = 0.999$. Similar results were observed for the banknote dataset, $F(6, 63) = 0.38$, $p = 0.89$, the glass dataset, $F(6, 63) = 0.31$, $p = 0.93$, the heart disease dataset, $F(6, 63) = 0.32$, $p = 0.92$, and the Indian diabetes dataset, $F(6, 63) = 0.016$, $p = 1.00$. On the iris dataset, there was a trend towards a difference in performance, but this did not reach statistical significance, $F(6, 63) = 1.55$, $p = 0.18$. The results were similar for the seeds dataset, $F(6, 63) = 1.17$, $p = 0.34$. However, on the wine dataset, there was a significant difference in performance between the approaches, $F(6, 63) = 4.01$, $p = 0.002$.

These results suggest that adding an appropriate weight re-mapping function may not only improve the convergence speed of the classifier, as previously discussed, but also has an impact on its final accuracy. In our experiments this improvement in the final accuracy is significant when using the Angle Embedding as an encoding method, while not so much when using the Amplitude Embedding.

However, our results also highlight the importance of dataset characteristics in determining the performance of the different approaches, since it can be seen, with both types of embeddings, that the statistical significance varies on each dataset. Al already shown in the previous section, and here once again confirmed, the impact of the re-mapping functions depends on the chosen set of data. In light of these findings, researchers and practitioners might need to consider both the properties of their dataset and try different re-mapping functions to improve their performance. Further studies are needed to understand the dataset features and the techniques that could predict the relative performance of the different approaches.

Once again we highlight the fact that these ANOVA tests refer to the *final* accuracy performance. Even though is some cases, like with Amplitude Embedding, this does not show a major improvement, the main result of introducing re-mapping functions, namely speeding up the convergence, still holds, as discussed in Sect. 5.1.

5.4 Comparison to Classical Neural Network

One of the recurring questions when dealing with VQCs is how their performances compare to classical neural networks with a similar amount of parameters. In this section we thus compare with a small case study a VQC, a VQC-tanh, so with a weight re-mapping function, a classical neural network and a VQC-tanh with data re-uploading. More precisely, we trained the VQC on the 2-D Iris dataset, a reduced version of the Iris dataset already described where only two classes are employed instead of three. Since two qubits have been used to encode the information with Amplitude Embedding and the depth is of six layers, we get a total of 36 parameters. In order to give a classical neural network the same amount of parameters, we introduced only one hidden layers of 6 neurons.

We can see the results in Fig. 8. It's easy to see how the classical neural network and the VQC roughly have the same validation accuracy, even though the first converges slightly faster. Once the VQC is equipped with a re-mapping function though, the convergence once again increases dramatically, with the data re-uploading architecture performing slightly better than the other. This can also be seen more clearly in through the Validation Loss, where the most striking result is how the classical neural network reaches much lower losses than the quantum approximators. This results in a much smaller variance in the accuracy at the point of convergence, which instead does not shrink in the quantum case.

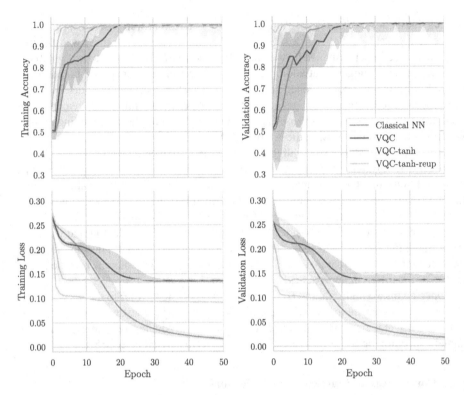

Fig. 8. Comparison of the VQC without weight re-mapping, VQC-tanh, VQC-tanh with data re-uploading and a classical neural network, evaluated on the two-class iris dataset.

6   Conclusion

In this paper, we build upon the work of [9], studying weight re-mapping functions in greater detail. This approach consists of re-scaling the weights of a variational quantum circuit so that they belong to their natural rotational domain, namely the $[-\pi, \pi]$ interval. We expand the scope of the work by integrating additional re-mapping functions into the VQC. Moreover, we study the performance of each function used in a classifier on eight different datasets, in contrast to the initial two proposed in the original work.

Our key contribution lies in demonstrating that the weight re-mapping approach consistently accelerates the convergence speed. This convergence speed varies depending on the dataset, but we also tested the impact of each function by averaging across all datasets. It can be seen that functions that are steeper around the initialization point, like arctan or tanh, have a higher speedup in convergence. This is a particularly important result in the field of Quantum Machine Learning. In all practical applications of the NISQ era, the resources needed to train or evaluate a VQC are still very costly, and enhancing the convergence of a quantum circuit translates into substantial energy savings. We further demonstrate that, in certain cases, weight re-mapping can notably enhance test accuracy.

An intriguing question emerging from this work is: which dataset features influence the selection of the re-mapping function? As already mentioned, depending on the dataset structure, certain functions may be more effective than others. Further studies should be conducted to understand how the underlying properties of a dataset relate to the choice of the re-mapping function. As an alternative or complementary approach, one could examine various optimizers that factor in the periodicity of the weights in the rotational realm. Ultimately, this approach should be applied to other traditional machine learning tasks-such as Quantum Reinforcement Learning-to assess its efficacy in addressing more generalized problems.

Acknowledgements. Datsets used were taken from the UCI Machine Learning Repository [6]. This paper was partially funded by the German Federal Ministry of Education and Research through the funding program "quantum technologies—from basic research to market" (contract number: 13N16196).

A   Appendix

In this section, we present the full evaluation results for all eight datasets and seven approaches. In Fig. 9, we show the experiments for circuits with Angle Embedding (x-axis). Furthermore, the experiments for the Amplitude Embedding circuits can be found in Fig. 10.

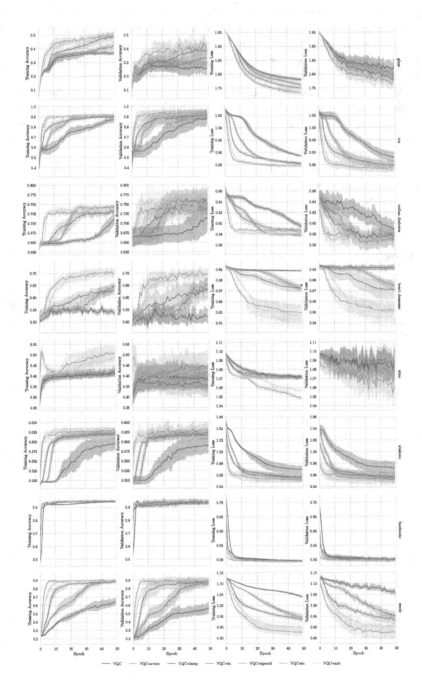

Fig. 9. Training and validation curves for each dataset and approach using Angle Embedding (x-axis).

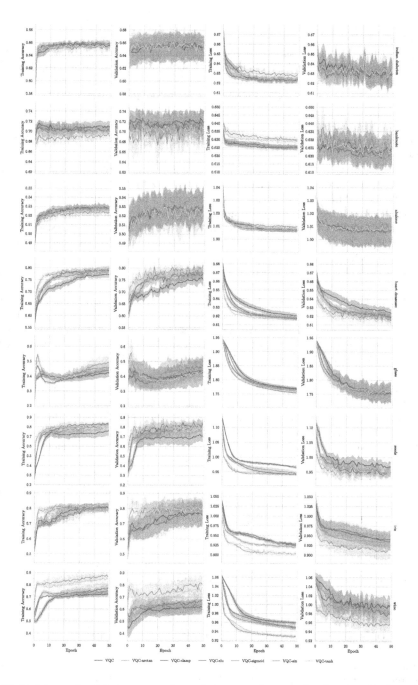

Fig. 10. Training and validation curves for each dataset and approach using Amplitude Embedding.

References

1. Bellman, R.: Dynamic programming. Science **153**(3731), 34–37 (1966)
2. Benedetti, M., Lloyd, E., Sack, S., Fiorentini, M.: Parameterized quantum circuits as machine learning models. Quantum Sci. Technol. **4**(4), 043001 (2019). https://doi.org/10.1088/2058-9565/ab4eb5
3. Charytanowicz, M., Niewczas, J., Kulczycki, P., Kowalski, P.A., Łukasik, S., Żak, S.: Complete gradient clustering algorithm for features analysis of X-ray images. In: Piętka, E., Kawa, J. (eds.) Information Technologies in Biomedicine. Advances in Intelligent and Soft Computing, vol. 69, pp. 15–24. Springer, Heidelberg (2010). https://doi.org/10.1007/978-3-642-13105-92
4. Detrano, R.: International application of a new probability algorithm for the diagnosis of coronary artery disease. Am. J. Cardiol. **64**, 304–310 (1989)
5. Du, Y., Hsieh, M.H., Liu, T., Tao, D.: Expressive power of parametrized quantum circuits. Phys. Rev. Res. **2**(3), 033125 (2020). https://doi.org/10.1103/physrevresearch.2.033125
6. Dua, D., Graff, C.: UCI machine learning repository (2017). https://archive.ics.uci.edu/ml
7. Fisher, R.A.: The use of multiple measurements in taxonomic problems. Ann. Eugen. **7**(2), 179–188 (1936)
8. Harrow, A.W., Hassidim, A., Lloyd, S.: Quantum algorithm for linear systems of equations. Phys. Rev. Lett. **103**(15), 150502 (2009). https://doi.org/10.1103/physrevlett.103.150502
9. Kölle, M., Giovagnoli, A., Stein, J., Mansky, M.B., Hager, J., Linnhoff-Popien, C.: Improving convergence for quantum variational classifiers using weight re-mapping. In: Rocha, A.P., Steels, L., van den Herik, H.J. (eds.) Proceedings of the 15th International Conference on Agents and Artificial Intelligence, ICAART 2023, Volume 2, Lisbon, Portugal, 22–24 February 2023, pp. 251–258. SCITEPRESS (2023). https://doi.org/10.5220/0011696300003393
10. Lloyd, S., Schuld, M., Ijaz, A., Izaac, J., Killoran, N.: Quantum embeddings for machine learning (2020). https://arxiv.org/abs/2001.03622. arXiv:2001.03622
11. Mitarai, K., Negoro, M., Kitagawa, M., Fujii, K.: Quantum circuit learning. Phys. Rev. A **98**, 032309 (2018). https://doi.org/10.1103/PhysRevA.98.032309
12. Mottonen, M., Vartiainen, J.J., Bergholm, V., Salomaa, M.M.: Transformation of quantum states using uniformly controlled rotations (2004)
13. Nash, W.J., Sellers, T.L., Talbot, S.R., Cawthorn, A.J., Ford, W.B.: The population biology of abalone (haliotis species) in tasmania. i. blacklip abalone (h. rubra) from the north coast and islands of bass strait. Sea Fisheries Division, Technical Report 48, p. 411 (1994)
14. Nielsen, M.A., Chuang, I.L.: Quantum Computation and Quantum Information: 10th Anniversary Edition. Cambridge University Press (2010). https://doi.org/10.1017/CBO9780511976667
15. Pérez-Salinas, A., Cervera-Lierta, A., Gil-Fuster, E., Latorre, J.I.: Data re-uploading for a universal quantum classifier. Quantum **4**, 226 (2020). https://doi.org/10.22331/q-2020-02-06-226
16. Schuld, M., Bocharov, A., Svore, K.M., Wiebe, N.: Circuit-centric quantum classifiers. Phys. Rev. A **101**(3), 032308 (2020). https://doi.org/10.1103/physreva.101.032308
17. Singh, D., Singh, B.: Investigating the impact of data normalization on classification performance. Appl. Soft Comput. **97**, 105524 (2019). https://doi.org/10.1016/j.asoc.2019.105524
18. Smith, J.W., Everhart, J.E., Dickson, W., Knowler, W.C., Johannes, R.S.: Using the ADAP learning algorithm to forecast the onset of diabetes mellitus. In: Proceedings of the Annual Symposium on Computer Application in Medical Care, p. 261. American Medical Informatics Association (1988)

19. Stoudenmire, E., Schwab, D.J.: Supervised learning with tensor networks. In: Lee, D., Sugiyama, M., Luxburg, U., Guyon, I., Garnett, R. (eds.) Advances in Neural Information Processing Systems, vol. 29. Curran Associates, Inc. (2016). https://proceedings.neurips.cc/paper/2016/file/5314b9674c86e3f9d1ba25ef9bb32895-Paper.pdf

20. Vandeginste, B.: Parvus: an extendable package of programs for data exploration, classification and correlation, M. Forina, R. Leardi, C. Armanino and S. Lanteri, Elsevier, Amsterdam, 1988, Price: US $645 ISBN 0-444-43012-1. J. Chemometr. **4**(2), 191–193 (1990). https://doi.org/10.1002/cem.1180040210. https://analyticalsciencejournals.onlinelibrary.wiley.com/doi/abs/10.1002/cem.1180040210

21. Wilson, C.M., et al.: Quantum Kitchen Sinks: An algorithm for machine learning on near-term quantum computers (2019). https://doi.org/10.48550/arXiv.1806.08321. arXiv:1806.08321

Effective Adaptive Strategy Selection Using Extended Fine-Tuning and CNN-Based Surrogate Model in Repeated-Encounter Bilateral Automated Negotiation

Shengbo Chang$^{(\boxtimes)}$ and Katsuhide Fujita

Department of Electrical Engineering and Computer Science,
Tokyo University of Agriculture and Technology, Tokyo, Japan
s215450r@st.go.tuat.ac.jp, katfuji@cc.tuat.ac.jp

Abstract. In this study, we tackle the challenges of repeated-encounter bilateral automated negotiation (RBAN) by introducing a fine-tuning approach to improve surrogate model-based strategy selection methods. To make this fine-tuning process more effective, we consider two policies: firstly, the aggregating policy, which reduces training parameters, and secondly, the complete-preference integration policy, which improves the use of past negotiation information. Moreover, we propose a convolutional neural network (CNN)-based surrogate model (CSM) to predict a strategy's performance by analyzing the distribution of utility values in negotiation outcomes. We evaluate the prediction capability of the CSM and the impact of the two policies on both CSM and fine-tuning approach. The experimental results demonstrate that the CSM outperforms existing expert-feature-based opponent models in terms of prediction accuracy. Ablation studies in RBANs reveal the superiority of combining the fine-tuning approach with both policies over using fine-tuning alone or with just one policy. Ablation studies in independent negotiations show that applying either or both policies on the CSM also improves the CSM's performance in independent negotiations, although the two policies are not initially designed for this context.

Keywords: Automated negotiation · Strategy selecting method · Surrogate model · Fine-tuning · Repeated-encounter bilateral automated negotiation

1 Introduction

Repeated-encounter bilateral automated negotiation (RBAN) frequently occurs in real-world scenarios, where parties negotiate multiple times across different domains [18]. Examples include retailers negotiating with suppliers for various products each season or companies revisiting contract terms with their partners as market conditions change. In these cases, learning from past experiences and adapting negotiation strategies to address the same opponent effectively becomes crucial.

In the context of automated negotiation, no single strategy can dominate all possible settings [12]. The optimal negotiation strategy may vary depending on the negotiation

Supported by JSPS KAKENHI Grant Numbers 22H03641, 19H04216 and JST FOREST (Fusion Oriented REsearch for disruptive Science and Technology) Grant Number JPMJFR216S.

A. P. Rocha et al. (Eds.): ICAART 2023, LNAI 14546, pp. 310–332, 2024.
https://doi.org/10.1007/978-3-031-55326-4_15

scenario and the opponent [1,5,24]. Therefore, selecting the best strategy for each scenario is essential. Surrogate models, generally used in algorithm selection, predict the outputs for unknown algorithm parameter inputs by regressing the known inputs with outputs. A surrogate model for strategy selection in automated negotiation typically uses negotiation scenario features and a strategy configuration as input, with the output being the predicted evaluation value [12,17]. In one-shot negotiation, where both the opponent's strategy and preference profile are unknown, the surrogate model assigns a higher value to the strategy that performs averagely well.

However, facing the same opponent in RBAN presents a promising direction for improving each negotiation by revising the surrogate model based on our experience with the opponent. Although several studies [1,8,9,11–13,17,20,23] have investigated strategy selection in automated negotiation, few have specifically considered the problem of RBAN. Our study addresses this gap by proposing a novel surrogate-model-based strategy selection method that utilizes fine-tuning to learn from the experience with the opponent online in RBAN. The fine-tuning approach adapts the surrogate model to the opponent by incorporating the latest negotiation results.

To enhance the performance of the fine-tuning approach in an online learning context, we introduce a policy for reducing the trainable parameters. This policy aggregates multiple surrogate models, each trained with a unique opponent. This policy restricts the aggregation layer as the only trainable part, effectively reducing the parameter space for training, thereby allowing the fine-tuning method to adjust the surrogate model more efficiently. As a result of this efficient adjustment, the surrogate model can provide a more accurate assessment of strategies. Additionally, it offers a robust initial choice when the opponent is unknown, taking into account the potential of facing various opponents.

Furthermore, we consider utilizing the learned opponent's preferences post-negotiation to make the adjustment of fine-tuning more accurate, thus introducing a complete-preference integration policy. In each negotiation, an agent can estimate the opponent's preferences using an opponent preference learning model [14,22], which processes the bidding trace of the opponent. This additional knowledge about past scenarios can aid the fine-tuning method in further refining the surrogate model. Unfortunately, existing surrogate models typically use only the features from public information and our own preference profile, which may result in lower learning efficiency. One possible solution is to apply surrogate models that incorporate the opponent's preferences. However, since the opponent's private preference profile is inaccessible before a negotiation, those surrogate models cannot be directly used for making predictions. The complete-preference integration policy resolves this issue by coordinating these surrogate models, which requiring complete scenario information, with the Monte Carlo Method. This involves randomly sampling the opponent's preference profile space and making predictions based on these samples.

Additionally, existing surrogate models often use expert scenario features to predict the performance of a strategy configuration for a given negotiation scenario [12,17,18]. Since these features are based on human intuition, the prediction accuracy may be somewhat lost. The 2-dimensional outcome space matrix of a negotiation scenario, which represents the distribution of the outcome based on our preferences and those of the opponent, can provide a comprehensive representation of the scenario. Convolutional neural networks (CNNs) can be trained to automatically extract useful features from the matrix, overcoming the limitations of reliance on human intuition. Consequently, we implement a CNN-based surrogate model that uses this matrix for prediction, ensuring the richness of the extracted features and thereby enhancing prediction accuracy.

We extend our previous publication [6] by delving further into the combination of the fine-tuning method, the aggregating policy, the complete-information integration policy, and the CNN-based surrogate model (CSM). We also demonstrate the additional experiments with various settings. In the experiments, we first validate the superiority of CSM by comparing it with expert-feature-based models. Subsequently, we evaluate the individual and combined efficacy of the aggregating and complete-information integration policies. We conduct a series of ablation studies that assess the impact of these policies on both the fine-tuning process and the CSM. These ablation studies are conducted in two separate contexts: the effect of the policies on fine-tuning is explored within the context of RBAN. At the same time, their impact on the CSM is investigated in the context of independent negotiation.

The contributions of this extended version are as follows:

– We propose a novel surrogate-model-based strategy selection method utilizing fine-tuning to learn from the opponent online in RBAN.
– We introduce two policies to enhance the fine-tuning method. The first policy, referred to as the aggregating policy, aggregates multiple surrogate models trained with diverse opponents, thereby reducing the parameter space for fine-tuning. The second policy, the complete-preference integration policy, operates by utilizing a surrogate model that requires complete information, thus allowing fine-tuning to utilize the learned opponent's preferences from past negotiations. This policy manages scenarios with incomplete information by sampling the opponent's private utility function.
– We propose a CNN-based surrogate model (CSM), which applies a CNN to a discrete, fixed-size outcome utility distribution matrix to extract scenario features. The matrix represents the number of outcomes falling within bins of a predefined utility range. This model effectively circumvents the limitations of human intuitive features.
– In our experiments, we initially justify the superiority of the proposed CSM by comparing it with existing expert-feature-based models. Subsequently, we validate the positive impact of the two proposed policies on fine-tuning through ablation studies in the context of RBAN. Lastly, through ablation studies conducted in the context of independent negotiations, we discover that applying the two policies can also enhance the performance of the CSM in these negotiations, even though the policies were not originally designed for this purpose.

The structure of this paper is as follows: Sect. 2 reviews related work and discusses key contributions and limitations of existing approaches; Sect. 3 introduces the concept of RBAN and elaborates on the specific challenges it presents; Sect. 4 describes the surrogate-model-based strategy selection method that utilizes fine-tuning extended with the two policies; Sect. 5 details the proposed CNN-based surrogate model; Sect. 6

presents experimental evaluations, assessing the CSM by comparing it to its corresponding existing model, conducting a series of ablation studies that evaluate the impact of these policies on both the fine-tuning process and the CSM. Finally, Sect. 7 concludes this work and shows several future directions.

2 Related Work

This work focuses on strategy selection for each negotiation scenario in RBAN, primarily related to strategy selection in automated negotiation.

[12] proposed a Meta-agent with a strategy portfolio used in ANAC and introduced several expert features to construct surrogate models for evaluating negotiation strategies in given scenarios. They also extended this to an online reinforcement learning version for flawed learned models. They trained the surrogate model to predict average performance against a set of opponents. Building on their work, [17] introduced a sequential model-based optimization mechanism for general algorithm configuration to select strategy parameters for a dynamic agent under various opponents and domains. The mechanism searches the configuration space accelerated by an expert-feature-based surrogate model. They also applied AutoFolio to create a strategy selector using domain and opponent features [18]. These studies rely on feature-based surrogate models, whereas our study explores extracting negotiation setting features with CNN.

[9] proposed estimating the opponent's strategy and preference in multiple negotiations to achieve better Pareto efficiency. [13] employed a reinforcement learning method inspired by [12] to select strategies for multiple negotiations. [21] suggested a strategy for the repeated prisoner's dilemma game using a recurrent neural network to predict future interactions and optimize the next moves. These works are applicable for repeated negotiations with a fixed opponent and negotiation domain. [11] applied boosting to bidding and acceptance strategies, proposing two versions of boosting learning: strategy selection and output combination of different strategies. [20] proposed an adaptive strategy switching mechanism for their autonomous negotiating agent framework that could classify opponents in a negotiation scenario and use expert recommendations to select coping strategies, outperforming most existing genius negotiators. Similarly, [23] introduced a negotiating agent framework that leverages Bayesian policy reuse in negotiations, recognizing opponents and providing coping policies or building new policies for unseen opponents. These works focus on coping strategies for opponents in a negotiation scenario but do not consider the RBAN case.

In this study, we concentrate on learning about the opponent from one negotiation scenario to another related to opponent modeling. Opponent modeling was introduced in [4] as a foundational component of the negotiation agent. Numerous studies have investigated learning the opponent's bidding strategy, utility function, and acceptance strategy, as reviewed in [2]. These studies primarily focus on learning within individual negotiation scenarios, whereas our work emphasizes learning from the opponent in RBAN across multiple negotiation scenarios.

3   Repeated-Encounter Bilateral Automated Negotiation

In this work, we focus on selecting a strategy from a strategy portfolio for an agent in RBAN. Each negotiation in RBAN involves a bilateral automated negotiation consisting of a negotiation protocol, a negotiation scenario, and two negotiators. The negotiation protocol and scenario settings in this paper adhere to the bilateral negotiation settings commonly used to evaluate negotiation strategies in the literature [1,12,17,18,20,23].

The negotiation protocol follows the Alternating Offers Protocol (AOP) [19], in which negotiators alternate making offers, accepting offers, or walking away until the deadline is reached or one negotiator agrees or walks away. The deadline can be measured by the number of rounds or real-world time. The negotiation scenario includes a negotiation domain and two preference profiles. The domain is public information, while a preference profile is unique and private, known only to its corresponding negotiator.

A domain D defines a set of issues $\mathcal{I} = \{I_1, \ldots, I_i, \ldots, I_{n_I}\}$ with possible values $V_i = \{v_1^i, \ldots, v_j^i, \ldots, v_{k_i}^i\}$, where n_I is the number of issues and k_i is the number of values for issue I_i. A set of values for each issue is referred to as an outcome ω. Ω is the set of all possible outcomes. A preference profile maps each outcome to a real value in the range $[0, 1]$, typically in the form of a utility function. This paper employs the linear additive utility function $U(\omega) = \sum_{i=1}^{n_I} w_i e_i(\omega[i])$, where w_i is the weight of issue I_i ($\sum_{i=1}^{n_I} w_i = 1$); $e_i(\cdot)$ is a function mapping the values of issue I_i to real numbers in the range $[0, 1]$; a negotiator will obtain 0 utility if no agreement is reached.

RBAN consists of a sequence of negotiations with the same opponent under AOP. A negotiation in RBAN can be denoted as a function $\pi(\theta, S)$ of a strategy θ and a scenario $S = (\Omega, U_{n_1}, U_{n_2})$, where U_{n_1} and U_{n_2} are a pair of utility function assigned to the two negotiators. The strategy selection problem for a negotiation scenario S_l in an RBAN negotiation sequence $\Pi = < \pi_1, \ldots, \pi_l, \ldots, \pi_{n_N} >$, including n_N negotiations, is defined as:

$$\operatorname{argmax}_{\theta \in \Theta} \{ U_{our}^i (\omega_l) \, | \omega_l \leftarrow \pi_l (\theta, S_l) \,, \, \Pi_l \}$$

where $\Pi_l = < \pi_1, \pi_2, \ldots, \pi_{l-1} >$ is a subset of Π, representing the negotiations before π_l; $\Theta = \theta_1, \theta_2, \ldots, \theta_{n_S}$ is the agent's strategy space, where n_S is the number of strategies; and, θ is a strategy configuration containing a set of numerical or categorical parameters.

4   Extended Fine-Tuning Method

In RBAN, adapting negotiation strategies based on previous encounters with the same opponent is critical for success. Fine-tuning is the process of training a model for a specific application using a well-established model from similar applications rather than training a model entirely from scratch. This approach offers better convergence than traditional learning technologies by leveraging knowledge acquired from other domains.

We apply the fine-tuning concept to the surrogate-model-based strategy selection, as illustrated in Fig. 1, where the surrogate model predicts our strategy's performance within a given negotiation setting. The application of fine-tuning involves three primary procedures:

Fig. 1. Application of the fine-tuning concept in RBAN with n negotiation scenarios.

1. **Initialization of the Surrogate Model.** We start by initializing the surrogate model.
2. **Strategy Selection.** We then use the surrogate model to select a strategy.
3. **Post-Negotiation Fine-Tuning:** After each negotiation, we fine-tune the surrogate model based on the most recent negotiation results.

This process enhances the model's ability to accurately predict the performance of our strategy in future negotiations with the same opponent. The improved predictive ability enables us to select more suitable strategies for subsequent negotiations.

However, our approach differs from the typical application of fine-tuning, which is often applied offline after training with all available data. We apply fine-tuning in an online learning situation, where training occurs whenever new data become available. This approach necessitates rapid convergence and a robust initial model.

A significant challenge is that the surrogate model's parameter space is usually vast, and the models for addressing different opponents can vary substantially. To mitigate this, we introduce an aggregation policy to reduce the parameter space and provide a more generalized initial surrogate model.

Moreover, utilizing the opponent's preferences learned in past negotiations for fine-tuning is beneficial for convergence. To further enhance the process, we propose a policy that encourages using surrogate models requiring complete scenario information. This policy provides a solution for applying these surrogate models when the opponent's private preference information is unknown.

Subsequently, we first introduce the aggregating policy and the complete-preference integration policy. We then detail the extended fine-tuning method coordinating the referred concepts and policies.

4.1 Aggregating Policy

The aggregating policy reduces the parameter space for training by aggregating multiple surrogate models. Each model is pre-trained with a unique opponent, and the trainable parameters are limited to the combined weights. This policy selects a set of candidate surrogate models, each possessing a unique set of strengths and weaknesses for predicting agreement utility when facing different opponents. The models are then combined using a weighted average, with weights fine-tuned during RBAN. This aggregated model, used as a starting point for the fine-tuning process, accelerates the adaptation process. Furthermore, this aggregated model is more generalized and robust, as it initially considers the potential of facing various opponents when the opponent's information is unknown.

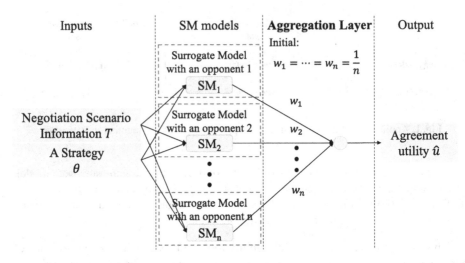

Fig. 2. Structure of the aggregating policy application. SM with opponent i indicates it was trained with negotiation data against opponent i.

Figure 2 presents a structure named the Aggregated Surrogate Model (ASM), which implements the aggregating policy. The ASM incorporates several pre-trained surrogate models in parallel through an input layer and consolidates their outputs with an aggregating layer. The output of the aggregating layer represents the predicted agreement utility.

The *aggregating layer* is a sigmoid-activated neuron, which ensures the output is scaled to the range $[0, 1]$. Its output is positively correlated with the weighted summation of the outputs of the aggregated surrogate models (Eq. 1). The weights of this layer are online trainable parameters, which balance the aggregated SMs. The ASM is expected to adapt to different opponent agents by adjusting these weights.

$$\hat{u}_\theta = \mathrm{ASM}(T, \theta)$$
$$= \mathrm{sigmoid}(\sum_{i=1}^{n} w_i \mathrm{SM}_i(T, \theta)) \propto \sum_{i=1}^{n} w_i \mathrm{SM}_i(T, \theta) \tag{1}$$

where T represents the scenario information required by the surrogate model; $\mathrm{SM}_i(\cdot)$ denotes a surrogate model trained against opponent agent i, and n is the number of aggregated surrogate models.

4.2 Complete-Preference Integration Policy

The complete-preference integration policy promotes the use of surrogate models that require complete scenario information, thus enabling more accurate adjustments using preferences learned from previous negotiations. It also provides a solution for applying these models when the opponent's private preference information is unknown. This solution generates random samples from the preference profile space to create a set of possible opponent preferences. A strategy's evaluation is then calculated based on these samples.

Table 1. Restrictions when sampling the opponent's preference profile.

Name of restriction	Equation
Each weight range	$0 < w_i < 1$
Total weights	$\sum_{i=1}^{n_I} w_i = 1$
Value mapping function	$0 \leq e_i(v_j^i) \leq 1$
First proposal	$e_i(v_j^i) = 1 \; if \; v_j^i \; in \; \omega_{first}, \; j = 1, \dots, k_i, \; i = 1, \dots, n_I$

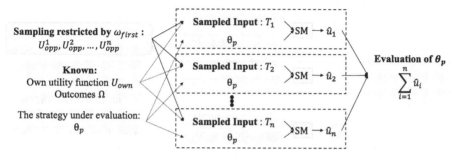

Fig. 3. Evaluation of $\theta_p \in \Theta$ in a negotiation scenario under the Complete-Preference Integration Policy. ω_{first} denotes the first bid from the opponent.

The complete-preference integration policy addresses the challenge of implementing a model that requires full information in negotiations where only partial information is available (i.e., the opponent's preference is unknown) with the Monte Carlo method. This method begins by randomly sampling the unknown opponent's utility function. It then predicts the performance of a strategy on the samples and selects the one with the best mean value. In the case of multiple-issue linear additive utility, a sampling assigns a weight w_i and generates a mapping function $e_i(v_j^i)$, $v_j^i \in V_i$ for each issue $I_i \in \mathcal{I}$ under certain restrictions (Table 1). The $e_i(v_j^i)$ maps a random number to each possible issue value $v_j^i \in V_i$. The first proposal restriction assumes that an opponent would propose the bid that maximizes its utility at the first step [1,5,24].

After sampling (as shown in Fig. 3), the sampled opponent's preference profiles, coordinated with known information, are processed into the input format T for the surrogate model. Finally, each strategy $\theta_p \in \Theta$ is evaluated using the surrogate model on all the samples. The average output on the samples is viewed as the predicted performance of a strategy. The best evaluated strategy is then applied to this negotiation scenario.

4.3 Extended Fine-Tuning Method Incorporating the Two Policies

In this section, we describe the procedures of the extended fine-tuning method, which incorporates both the aggregating policy and the complete-preference integration policy.

The first step involves initializing the aggregated surrogate model. By the complete-preference integration policy, we train a set of surrogate models, each requiring complete scenario information and each associated with a unique opponent. Then, consid-

---

Algorithm 1. Enhanced Fine-tuning after a negotiation π_k.

Ω_k is the outcome space, θ^k is the used strategy, ω_k is the agreement outcome, if no ω_k then $U_{own}^k(\omega_k) = 0$, BH_k is the opponent bidding history, α is the learning rate, U_{own}^k is own utility function, HOM is the hardheaded opponent model, Formate$(\cdot)$ is the function for processing the scenario information into the surrogate model's input format.

Require: $\Omega_k, \theta_k, \omega_k, BH_k, \alpha, U_{own}^k, \text{ASM}^k, \text{HOM}$
Ensure: ASM^k

$\hat{U}_{opp}^k \leftarrow \text{HOM}(BH_k)$

$\hat{T}_k \leftarrow \text{Formate}\left(\hat{U}_{opp}^k, U_{own}^k, \Omega_k\right)$

$\text{ASM}^{k+1} \leftarrow \text{ASM}^k - \alpha * \Delta\left(U_{own}^k(\omega_k), \text{ASM}^k\left(\hat{T}_k, \theta^k\right)\right)$

---

ering the aggregating policy, we initialize an aggregated surrogate model (ASM) that combines the individually trained surrogate models.

The second step pertains to strategy selection for a given negotiation scenario, where the opponent's preference profile is unknown. We apply the complete-preference integration policy to randomly sample the unknown opponent's preference profile. We then evaluate all strategies within the strategy profile and ultimately select the strategy with the best average performance.

The final step is the post-negotiation fine-tuning of the surrogate model, which is adjusted based on the most recent negotiation results. The enhanced fine-tuning method adjusts the weights of the aggregating layer of the ASM after each negotiation, as detailed in Algorithm 1. We use the Hardheaded Opponent Model (HOM) [22] to estimate the opponent utility function $\hat{U}_{opp}^k$ based on the opponent's bidding history BH_k. We then calculate $\hat{T}_k$ based on $\hat{U}_{opp}^k$ to fit the input format of the surrogate model. Finally, a back-propagation optimizer (e.g., Adams) fine-tunes the aggregating layer of the ASM using T_k as input, with the actual utility achieved in π_k as the expected output. Assuming the surrogate models of the ASM exhibit sufficient diversity, it is likely that the behavior pattern of an encountered opponent will resemble that of one or a combination of the training opponents. Therefore, adjusting the weights of the ASM's aggregating layer could enable it to adapt to an unknown opponent.

5   CNN-Based Surrogate Model

In this section, we propose a surrogate model with improved prediction accuracy to further enhance strategy selection - a Convolutional Neural Network (CNN)-based Surrogate Model (CSM). The CSM is designed to work in conjunction with the complete-preference integration policy. It extracts features from a matrix representing the distribution of outcomes' utilities, where each cell corresponds to the number of outcomes within a predefined utility range. By leveraging the power of CNNs, the CSM can automatically identify relevant features within the data, resulting in a richer set of extracted features that can improve the model's accuracy.

A CSM, denoted as CSM$(\cdot)$ in Eq. 2, takes scenario information and a strategy as inputs, and outputs the predicted agreement utility of applying the input strategy to the

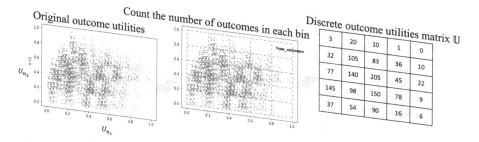

Fig. 4. Example of transforming the original outcome utilities to $\mathbb{U}$ (5×5). Each index on the axis corresponds to a utility range of the negotiator. The integers within the matrix indicate the number of outcomes in the corresponding utility bin.

input negotiation scenario. The strategy configuration θ can be represented as real numbers representing real-valued strategies or one-hot encoded vectors representing categorical strategies. The scenario information for input is represented as a discrete, size-fixed outcome distribution map, denoted as $\mathbb{U}\,(m \times m)$. Figure 4 provides an example of transforming the outcome space to $\mathbb{U}\,(5 \times 5)$. The discrete outcome-utilities matrix $\mathbb{U}\,(m \times m)$ is derived from the outcome utilities. Each element, $\mathbb{U}_{j,k(1 \leq j \leq m, 1 \leq k \leq m)}$ in $\mathbb{U}$, indicates the number of outcomes in the corresponding utility bins and can be calculated using Eq. 3.

$$\hat{u}_{\theta_j} = \text{CSM}(\mathbb{U}, \theta_j), j = 1, \ldots, n_s \qquad (2)$$

$$\mathbb{U}_{j,k} = \left| \{ \omega_i \in \Omega \; if \; b_{n_1,j}^{lower} \leq U_{n_1}(\omega_i) \leq b_{n_1,j}^{upper} \; and \; b_{n_2,k}^{lower} \leq U_{n_2}(\omega_i) \leq b_{n_2,k}^{upper} \} \right|$$

$$b_{n_1,j}^{lower} = (j-1) \times \frac{1}{m}, \; b_{n_1,j}^{upper} = j \times \frac{1}{m}, \; b_{n_2,k}^{lower} = (k-1) \times \frac{1}{m}, \; b_{n_2,k}^{upper} = k \times \frac{1}{m}$$

$$(j = 1, 2, \ldots, m; \; k = 1, 2, \ldots, m) \qquad (3)$$

where $\mathbb{U}_{j,k(1 \leq j \leq m, 1 \leq k \leq m)}$ is an element in $\mathbb{U}$ that shows the number of outcomes in the corresponding utility bin; U_{n_1} and U_{n_2} indicate the two utility functions of the negotiation scenario.

Mapping the outcome utility distribution to a size-fixed matrix, which indicates the number of outcomes within predefined utility bins, allows the CSM to be applied to domains of varying sizes. Additionally, this approach reduces the computational cost associated with convolution. Applying a CNN to this representation enables the model to identify patterns and relationships between utility values, leading to more accurate predictions about the opponent's preferences.

6 Experiments

In our previous paper, we compared a method that combines a Convolutional Neural Network (CNN)-based surrogate model with two policies against a traditional expert-feature-based neural network surrogate model. Our experiments, conducted in the context of independent negotiation, demonstrated the superior performance of the combined method. We further validated the benefits of applying the fine-tuning method on the combined method within the context of RBAN.

In this extension, we provide further evidence supporting the superiority of using a Convolutional Neural Network (CNN) to extract features from the negotiation scenario instead of using expert-features. Furthermore, we emphasize the significance of the combined method by conducting ablation studies that evaluate the individual contributions of each element in both independent negotiations and RBANs.

In the following sections, one of our primary objectives is to present experimental results showcasing the performance comparison between our proposed Convolutional Neural Network-based surrogate model (CSM) and the existing expert-feature-based surrogate models (ESM). Another is to evaluate the collaborative effect of fine-tuning, the aggregating policy, the complete-information integration policy, and the CSM by conducting ablation studies in both independent negotiations and RBANs.

6.1 Experimental Setup

We evaluated the strengths of surrogate models based on their testing losses, which indicate their prediction and generalization abilities, thereby implying the quality of the extracted features.

We evaluated the combined methods using the achieved agreement utility in negotiations by considering a scenario where we must select a parameter for a time-dependent agent using only a time-dependent strategy. This time-dependent strategy, which significantly impacts negotiation outcomes, is widely adopted by many advanced agents [24]. The time-dependent strategy, as referenced in [7], is governed by the function $U_t = 1 - \left(\frac{t}{T}\right)^e$, where T represents the maximum negotiation time, and e is a factor that controls the concession pattern during the negotiation process. A lower value of e implies faster concessions at the beginning and slower concessions towards the end, and vice versa. The strategy space is restricted to a specific range: $e \in [0.1, 10.0]$, with intermediate values including 0.1, 0.2, 0.3, 0.4, 0.5, 0.6, 0.7, 0.8, 0.9, 1, 1.11, 1.25, 1.62, 2.5, 3.33, 5, and 10. The concession curves calculated with these parameters exhibit mostly symmetry relative to the curve calculated with $e = 1$, resulting in an approximately uniformly distributed strategy space.

For our evaluation, we employed the same 45 negotiation scenarios as in [3]. These scenarios can be differentiated based on certain attributes such as domain size, bid distribution, or opposition, details of which are provided in Table 2.

Table 2. Scenarios with different features.

Domain	Size	Opposition	Distribution
ItexVsCypress	Small(180)	Low, medium, and high	Low, medium, and high
Employer	Small(3125)		
ADG	Medium(15625)		
Supermarket	Large(98784)		
Travel	Large(188160)		

Table 3. Opponent agents used in this experiment.

Type	Agent Name	Year of ANAC/Strategy
Testing	AgentK	2010
	Hardheaded	2011
	TheFawkes	2013
	Atlas3	2015
Training and testing	Time dependent	$e = 0.1$
	Time dependent	$e = 1.0$
	Time dependent	$e = 5.0$
	Tit-For-Tat	$\delta = 1$
	Tit-For-Tat	$\delta = 2$
	Tit-For-Tat	$\delta = 3$

We used ten different opponent agents for the experiments (Table 3), including four ANAC champions [5,10,16,24] and six basic agents [7].

6.2 Demonstrating Superiority of CNN-Based Surrogate Models

This section justifies the superiority of the proposed CSM compared with existing expert-feature-based surrogate models. The superiority of CSM further implies that using CNN to extract negotiation scenario features is more accurate for automated negotiation. We evaluated them based on their performance in testing losses.

We categorized the evaluation by the opponent, as we aim to investigate the performance against different opponents. We trained and tested the models on datasets from the same opponent. These datasets were obtained by enumerating all strategy parameters in negotiation with the opponent, and the output was the agreement utility using the strategy for a scenario against that opponent.

To test the generalization ability in terms of negotiation scenarios, we selected 18 out of the 45 scenarios for training and used the remaining scenarios for testing. Each scenario was unique in at least one feature. The training set included all *Employer* and *Supermarket* scenarios. The batch size for training was set to 100. For each negotiation setting, we repeated the training process 20 times with early stopping, and the model with the lowest validation loss was used for computing the testing losses.

In this experiment, the models used the complete scenario information for training and testing. The expert features used in the surrogate models, as referred to in [12] and [17], are presented in Table 4. We have also added extra features based on [15], which indicate the relationship between our preference and the opponent's preference. We classified the features into four categories based on the information utilized. The *Domain* category uses information about the structure of the outcomes space. The *Own Preference* and *Opponent's Preference* categories calculate features based on our and the opponent's preference profile, respectively. The *Preference Relationship* category includes features indicating the relationship between our preference profile and the opponent's preference profile.

Table 4. Features used in expert feature-based surrogate models. U denotes own utility function [6].

Type	Feature
Domain	Number of issues
	Average number of values
	Number of outcomes
Own Preference	Standard deviation of weights
	Average utility of Ω
	Standard deviation utility of Ω
Opponent's Preference	Standard deviation of weights
	Average utility of Ω
	Standard deviation utility of Ω
Preference Relationship	Conflict Level
	Win-Win Level
	Opposition Level: the distance of the outcome utilities to $(1, 1)$
	The opponent's utility toward our best outcome
	The opponent's utility toward our worst outcome
	Our utility toward the opponent's best outcome
	Our utility toward the opponent's worst outcome

Table 5. Testing losses of CSM, ESM-D, and ESM-N regarding each opponent. Hard denotes the HardHeaded agent. T4T denotes the tit-for-tat agent, Time denotes the time-dependent agent, and the number below them means the strategy parameter.

	Hard	AgentK	TheFawkes	Atlas3	T4T 1	T4T 2	T4T 3	Time 0.1	Time 1	Time 5
CSM	**0.039**	**0.069**	**0.087**	**0.044**	**0.184**	**0.089**	**0.189**	**0.029**	**0.052**	**0.067**
ESM-D	0.075	0.108	0.089	0.177	0.194	0.112	0.193	0.110	0.142	0.145
ESM-N	0.072	0.093	0.094	0.081	0.193	0.100	0.192	0.050	0.069	0.081

To prevent overfitting on domain features, since the models were trained only on scenarios of two different sizes, we implemented two versions of the expert-feature-based model: one includes the domain features as input, denoted ESM-D, and another neglected the domain features, denoted ESM-N.

The shape of $\mathbb{U}$ was set to 100×100, which was found to be a good balance between training time and performance based on our previous work [6]. The architectures of CSM and ESM inherited the structures tested in our previous paper [6], as shown in Fig. 5 (a) and (b).

Table 5 presents the testing losses of CSM, ESM-D, and ESM-N against various opponents. The testing opponents include the HardHeaded agent, AgentK, TheFawkes, Atlas3, as well as agents following tit-for-tat (T4T) and time-dependent (Time) strategies with differing strategy parameters. An examination of the testing loss across all opponents reveals that the CSM consistently achieves the lowest loss, indicative of its

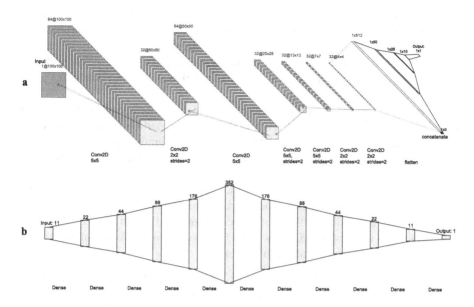

Fig. 5. The schematic diagram of CSM (a) and ESM (b) [6].

superior performance in these scenarios when compared to other models. This superiority is further underlined by the boldface applied to the lowest testing loss achieved with each opponent, where CSM outperforms in every case. In addition, the ESM-N model demonstrates a lower testing loss than ESM-D against almost all types of opponents. This implies that the domain-related features contribute less to the final agreement utility, usually deteriorating the training. The only exception is *TheFawkes*, where the difference is subtly compared. One reason could be that this *TheFawkes* agent may be more sensitive to the scenario size.

To summarize, these results indicate that the CSM model presents an advantageous approach for regressing the negotiation scenario and the applied strategy with the agreement utility across different opponent types. Furthermore, the stronger regression ability of the CSM model reflects the presence of richer and more representative features.

6.3   Ablation Study in Independent Negotiations

In the independent negotiations experiment part of our previous work, we have presented the experimental results of comparing the surrogate model, which combines the CSM with both the aggregating policy and the complete-information integration policy, denoted ACSM, with an existing expert feature-based neural network surrogate model (NNSM) [6]. We have found that the hypotheses that *ACSM outperforms NNSM in terms of agreement utility by 0.027%, in terms of social welfare by 0.253%, and in terms of agreement ratio by 0.335%* are significant at $\alpha = 0.1$ according to the Mann-Whitney U test ($p = 0.095$). These results have indicated that using ACSM is able to select more advantageous strategies than using NNSM.

In this section, we present the ablation studies applying the policies on the surrogate model in independent negotiations to assess their impacts on the model's performance. Although the two policies - the aggregating policy and the complete-information integration policy - are designed to enhance fine-tuning, they can also operate independently within the surrogate model. We conducted ablation studies to evaluate the effect of applying each policy individually.

We provided surrogate models with different policy configurations to perform the ablation studies. Because the CSM relies on complete scenario information, it cannot be applied independently of the complete-information integration policy. To assess the effect of removing the complete-information integration policy, we implemented a modified version of CSM that does not utilize complete scenario information to make predictions. We refer to this modified version as OCSM, which utilizes a one-dimensional CNN on a one-dimensional matrix. The matrix is calculated based solely on our own preference profile and indicates the number of outcomes falling within our utility slots.

By combining the proposed CSM with OCSM, we obtained four versions of surrogate models for conducting the ablation studies:

- ACSM: This surrogate model combines the CSM with the aggregating and complete-information integration policies. Initially, we train multiple CSMs using the complete scenario dataset specific to each opponent agent. These pre-trained CSMs are then aggregated to form an initial surrogate model. Finally, the surrogate model randomly samples the opponent's preference profile in the strategy selection phase. It then predicts the performance of each strategy based on these samples, selecting the one with the highest average predicted performance.
- CSM-A: This model combines the CSM with only the complete information integration policy, trained based on the average of previously aggregated opponents' data. Here, we train a single CSM with complete scenario information, utilizing a dataset representing an average across various opponents. This trained CSM serves as the initial surrogate model. Similar to ACSM, when applying the surrogate model to select a strategy for a negotiation, it predicts the performance of each strategy based on the samples.
- AOCSM: This model solely employs the aggregating policy. Implementation involves training several OCSMs on unique opponent-specific datasets under partial scenario information, comprising our preference profile and public domain information. Similar to ACSM, we aggregate the pre-trained OCSMs to create the initial surrogate model. When applying the surrogate model to select a strategy for a negotiation, it uses the available information to predict the performance of each strategy directly.
- OCSM-A: This model utilizes neither the aggregating nor the complete-information integration policy. It is trained on partial scenario information using an average dataset from aggregated opponents. Here, we train an OCSM, using partial scenario information and a dataset representing an average across various opponents. The trained OCSM then serves as the initial surrogate model. The strategy's performance for a negotiation scenario is predicted directly based on the available information.

In the previous section on testing the CSM, we trained ten CSMs, each with a unique opponent. Six of these CSMs, trained with basic agents (T4T1, T4T2, T4T3, Time0.1,

Table 6. Ablation experimental results of independent negotiation. Showing the obtained agreement utility of applying ACSM, CSM-A (with the aggregating policy ablated), AOCSM (with the complete-information integration policy ablated), and OCSM-A (with both policies ablated) regarding different negotiation scenario features. The bold text showed the model performed averagely best in the negotiation scenarios obtaining this feature. The data was tested to be significant at the $\alpha = 0.05$ level according to a Mann-Whitney U test.

Model	Size			Opposition			Distribution		
	Small	Medium	Large	Low	Medium	High	Low	Medium	High
ACSM	**0.678**	**0.720**	**0.615**	**0.769**	**0.685**	**0.529**	**0.582**	0.678	**0.723**
CSM-A	**0.678**	0.719	0.612	0.762	**0.685**	**0.529**	0.572	**0.680**	0.721
AOCSM	0.662	0.706	0.612	0.759	0.669	0.524	0.569	0.675	0.708
OCSM-A	0.652	0.718	0.570	0.715	0.667	0.515	0.566	0.643	0.687

Time1, and Time5), were used for aggregation in the ACSM. Similarly, we realized the AOCSM. We trained the CSM-A and OCSM models using the average value of the datasets from the six opponents used for the aggregation. We chose to use 20 Monte Carlo samples for computational efficiency, which strikes a good balance between computing cost and efficiency.

Table 6 presents the results of our ablation studies conducted in an independent negotiation context. The table provides insights into the effects of applying ACSM, CSM-A (uses only the complete-information integration policy), AOCSM (uses only the aggregation policy), and OCSM-A (uses neither the aggregation nor the complete-information integration policy.) across various negotiation scenario features. These features are segmented into three categories: Size, Opposition, and Distribution, each with Low, Medium, and High subcategories. The data from this table underwent a Mann-Whitney U test, confirming the statistical significance of the results at an alpha level of 0.05.

The ACSM model demonstrated superior performance, achieving the highest agreement utility across most negotiation scenarios. This highlights the importance of the aggregation and complete-information integration policies. Notably, the ACSM model performed best in negotiation scenarios of all sizes (Small, Medium, and Large), all levels of opposition (Low, Medium, and High), and Low and High levels of distribution.

Despite the absence of the aggregating policy, the CSM-A model managed to match the performance of the ACSM model in scenarios with Small size and Medium opposition and even slightly surpassed it in scenarios with a Medium distribution level. However, despite these instances, ACSM generally exhibited a modest advantage over CSM-A, implying the value of its additional aggregating policy. This distinction between the two models' training methodologies may explain these performance differences. ACSM is trained individually on each opponent, thereby potentially achieving superior convergence and extracting deeper, opponent-specific scenario information. On the other hand, CSM-A is trained on averaged data, which may obscure individual opponent characteristics, possibly making convergence more challenging. Consequently, ACSM's approach, which integrates the individually trained models' outputs, may offer enhanced fitting ability compared to the direct averaging method used by CSM-A. Overall, these findings indicate that training models on individual opponents could yield higher predictive accuracy than using averaged data.

Compared to the ACSM and CSM-A models, the AOCSM model, which lacks the complete-information integration policy, is noticeably outperformed. This performance differential underscores the considerable benefits of the complete-information integration policy employed by ACSM and CSM-A. This policy manages uncertainty in stages where the opponent's preferences in negotiation scenarios are unknown by randomly sampling these unknown factors and making predictions based on these samples. Although this approach may initially sacrifice some degree of precision, it can compensate for this loss by ensuring a sufficient number of samples, thus delivering superior predictions. In contrast, AOCSM, while avoiding this precision loss by making predictions based directly on known scenario information, fails to yield equivalent predictive performance. The strength of the complete-information integration policy lies in its requirement to train the model using complete scenario information, promoting enhanced model convergence and deeper extraction of scenario-specific data. Conversely, AOCSM's approach trains the model based on scenario information that excludes the opponent's preference profile, which may obscure critical distinctions between these profiles. This can potentially compromise the model's ability to extract key underlying features, negatively affecting the prediction accuracy in the final application. Therefore, despite the precision trade-off in the sampling process, the complete-information integration policy proves more beneficial for predictive performance when supplied with adequate samples.

Finally, the OCSM-A model, which lacks both policies, generally exhibits the lowest performance across all scenarios. This outcome underscores the advantages of implementing both policies in independent negotiations. Considering the marginal improvement introduced by the policies, applying the complete-integration policy to the OCSM-A results in an average agreement utility increase of 4.04%, while its application to the AOCSM yields a 1.56% increment. Similarly, implementing the aggregating policy on the OCSM-A leads to a 2.65% enhancement, but only a 0.2% improvement when applied to the CSM-A. These findings reveal that the complete-integration policy typically delivers a higher marginal improvement than the aggregating policy. Furthermore, applying any policy to the OCSM-A model tends to result in a noticeably superior enhancement, likely attributable to the greater room for improvement inherent in a model with lower initial performance.

In summary, the experimental results demonstrate the effects of the proposed policies in independent negotiation settings. The ACSM model, incorporating both policies, consistently outperforms the others. The complete-information integration policy enhances the surrogate model's efficiency, as demonstrated by the comparatively weaker performance of the AOCSM. This policy allows for comprehensive negotiation scenario information and promotes improved feature extraction under the two-dimensional input. The aggregating policy further augments the performance of the surrogate model by integrating a variety of models, each specifically trained with individual opponents, thereby offering more accurate predictions. Thus, the concurrent application of both policies, as exemplified by ACSM, presents the optimal approach for enhancing the efficacy of surrogate model-based strategy selection methods in independent negotiations. It is worth noting that while the two policies were not specifically designed for independent negotiations, this experiment aims to demonstrate the overall effectiveness of ACSM.

6.4   Ablation Studies in RBANs

In our previous work's RNANs experiment section, we presented experimental results demonstrating the effectiveness of fine-tuning in enhancing the ACSM's performance against different opponent agents [6]. This success observed even when the aggregated CSMs were not trained with the ANAC agents, suggests that fine-tuning enables ACSM to adapt effectively to the specific opponent agent encountered in a given RBAN session.

This section delves further into ablation studies in RBANs. Each model mentioned in the previous section has a fine-tuned version for application in RBANs, denoted respectively as F-ACSM, F-AOCSM, F-CSM-A, and F-OCSM-A. For F-ACSM and F-AOCSM, which include an aggregating layer, only the parameters of this layer are trainable, hence, fine-tuning applies solely to this layer. For F-CSM-A and F-OCSM-A, all parameters are trainable, allowing fine-tuning across the entire model.

In addition, F-ACSM and F-CSM-A (which require complete scenario information) were fine-tuned based on the learned opponent's preference after each negotiation, while F-AOCSM and F-OCSM-A used only the initially known incomplete scenario information. We conducted 60 RBAN sessions for testing, each encompassing all 45 scenarios in varying orders.

Figure 6 displays the obtained utilities from applying the models in RBANs. Similar to independent negotiations, F-ACSM, integrating all proposed methods and policies, consistently outperforms all other models. F-CSM-A, applying only the complete-information integration policy, exhibits the second-best performance by the end of the RBAN sessions, indicating the efficacy of fine-tuning even with longer surrogate model adjustment periods. The performance of F-AOCSM is nearly identical to AOCSM, implying a marginal effect of applying to fine-tune when the model only cooperates with the aggregating policy. F-OCSM-A, which employs no policy, performed the worst.

Additional results presented in Fig. 7 delineate the impact of fine-tuning more starkly. The y-axis represents the percentage difference in results achieved by each model with and without fine-tuning. Of all the models, F-ACSM showed the greatest improvement as the number of experienced scenarios increased. Despite the superior initial performance of ACSM-which theoretically leaves less room for improvement-fine-tuning brought about the most significant enhancements, emphasizing the superiority of jointly applying the two policies.

F-CSM-A initially experienced a slight performance decrement due to fine-tuning but demonstrated significant improvement towards the end of the RBAN sessions. This initial deterioration may be attributed to the challenge of adjusting the extensive parameter space appropriately during fine-tuning. However, as the model was continually adjusted with increasingly relevant information, it began to adapt better to the opponent. When comparing F-CSM-A with F-ACSM, the improvement exhibited by F-ACSM was both faster and more stable, indicating that the aggregating policy can expedite

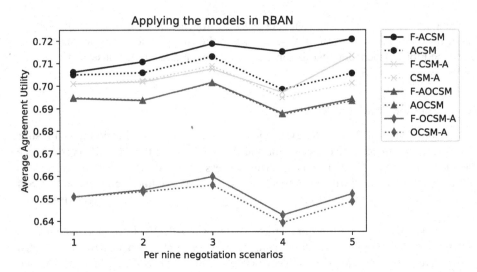

Fig. 6. Performance of F-ACSM, F-CSM-A, F-AOCSM, and F-OCSM-A. The dashed lines represent their respective models without fine-tuning. The value is the average utility obtained for every nine negotiation scenarios across the 60 RBAN sessions.

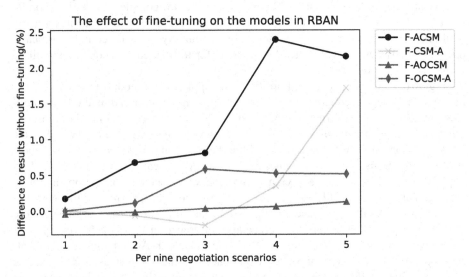

Fig. 7. Performance of F-ACSM, F-CSM-A, F-AOCSM, and F-OCSM-A relative to their non-fine-tuned counterparts. The value is the average for every nine negotiation scenarios across the 60 sessions.

the fine-tuning process by reducing the parameter space. On comparing F-CSM-A with F-AOCSM and F-OCSM-A-both lacking the complete-information policy-F-CSM-A displayed superior long-term improvement, despite the theoretically lesser room for improvement due to its initial high performance. This fact implies that incorporating the opponent's preference from previous negotiations to construct complete scenario information is beneficial for fine-tuning the surrogate model.

The slight improvement observed for F-AOCSM indicates that the aggregating policy, by limiting the number of trainable parameters, may make it difficult for the model to learn valuable information, particularly when using incomplete scenario information as input. In comparison to F-OCSM-A, which does not use any policy, fine-tuning had a lesser impact on AOCSM. This outcome could be attributed to a smaller improvement margin in AOCSM compared to OCSM-A, coupled with the constraints of the aggregating policy resulting in fewer trainable parameters.

In the case of F-OCSM-A, which does not employ either of the two policies, we found that fine-tuning provided a noticeable benefit, despite its generally low performance, as shown in Fig. 6. This implies that the model could still capture advantageous features from the opponent through fine-tuning, even with initially known incomplete scenario information. Particularly, given its initially low performance, F-OCSM-A had more room for improvement compared to other models.

In terms of the marginal improvement brought about by the policies, implementing either the aggregating policy or the complete-information policy independently only made a slight difference to the benefits of fine-tuning, although the overall agreement utility was higher. However, the combined application of both policies, as seen when comparing the performance of F-ACSM with that of F-CSM-A and F-AOCSM, significantly amplified the benefits of fine-tuning. This underscores the criticality of the collaborative application of the two policies when employing fine-tuning in RBAN.

To summarize, the model combining fine-tuning with the two policies outperformed the others, and the cooperative work of the two policies significantly enhanced the fine-tuning process, exceeding the isolated impact of either policy. While the individual application of either the aggregation or the complete-information integration policy can improve the agreement utility during RBAN, incorporating only one of the policies produces less pronounced effects on fine-tuning. Furthermore, in the context of RBAN, the complete-information integration policy contributes more to fine-tuning than the aggregating policy.

7   Conclusion and Future Work

This paper advances strategy selection in automated negotiation in two significant ways. Firstly, it introduces a novel surrogate model, termed CSM, for predicting strategy performance in automated negotiations. The CSM uses a convolutional neural network (CNN) to extract negotiation scenario features, thereby facilitating more accurate predictions compared to those based solely on expert features. Secondly, the paper proposes an enhanced fine-tuning approach for effectively adapting the surrogate model to specific opponents in Repeated-encountering Bilateral Automated Negotiations (RBAN). This approach incorporates two policies: an aggregating policy that reduces trainable parameters and a complete-information integration policy that improves fine-tuning efficiency by leveraging learned opponent preferences from past RBANs.

The efficacy of these contributions was validated through comprehensive experimental evaluation against a variety of scenarios and opponents. The CSM demonstrated superior prediction accuracy and generalization capabilities compared to existing expert feature-based neural network surrogate models. Moreover, ablation studies conducted within the RBAN context confirmed the collaborative effect of the two proposed policies on fine-tuning. While each policy independently improved fine-tuning marginally, their combined application substantially amplified the benefits of fine-tuning.

Interestingly, we discovered that these policies also enhanced the surrogate model in independent negotiations, a context they were not initially designed for. This discovery was corroborated by additional ablation studies assessing the impact of applying the two policies on the surrogate model in independent negotiations. The findings suggested that the concurrent application of both policies optimally enhanced the efficacy of surrogate model-based strategy selection methods in independent negotiations.

In future work, we plan to address the issue of overfitting-specifically, performance degradation caused by fine-tuning, particularly in late-stage RBAN. Developing early-stopping or dynamic learning rate rules for fine-tuning may be beneficial; however, the uncertainties inherent in negotiation scenarios make it challenging to accurately calculate the current accuracy of the opponent model and assess its performance post-tuning. Another promising direction involves designing additional selection methods that apply the two policies, for example, reinforcement learning. This direction is particularly promising, as the two policies have demonstrated beneficial features for fine-tuning.

References

1. Baarslag, T., et al.: Evaluating practical negotiating agents: results and analysis of the 2011 international competition. Artif. Intell. **198**, 73–103 (2013). https://doi.org/10.1016/j.artint.2012.09.004
2. Baarslag, T., Hendrikx, M., Hindriks, K., Jonker, C.: Measuring the performance of online opponent models in automated bilateral negotiation. In: Thielscher, M., Zhang, D. (eds.) AI 2012. LNCS, pp. 1–14. Springer, Heidelberg (2012)
3. Baarslag, T., Hendrikx, M., Hindriks, K., Jonker, C.: Predicting the performance of opponent models in automated negotiation. In: 2013 IEEE/WIC/ACM International Joint Conferences on Web Intelligence (WI) and Intelligent Agent Technologies (IAT), vol. 2, pp. 59–66. IEEE (2013). https://doi.org/10.1109/WI-IAT.2013.91
4. Baarslag, T., Hindriks, K., Hendrikx, M., Dirkzwager, A., Jonker, C.: Decoupling negotiating agents to explore the space of negotiation strategies. In: Marsa-Maestre, I., Lopez-Carmona, M.A., Ito, T., Zhang, M., Bai, Q., Fujita, K. (eds.) Novel Insights in Agent-based Complex Automated Negotiation. SCI, vol. 535, pp. 61–83. Springer, Tokyo (2014). https://doi.org/10.1007/978-4-431-54758-7_4
5. Baarslag, T., Hindriks, K., Jonker, C., Kraus, S., Lin, R.: The first automated negotiating agents competition (ANAC2010). In: Ito, T., Zhang, M., Robu, V., Fatima, S., Matsuo, T. (eds.) New Trends in Agent-Based Complex Automated Negotiations, pp. 113–135. Springer, Heidelberg (2012). https://doi.org/10.1007/978-3-642-24696-8_7
6. Chang., S., Fujita., K.: A fine-tuning aggregation convolutional neural network surrogate model of strategy selecting mechanism for repeated-encounter bilateral automated negotiation. In: Proceedings of the 15th International Conference on Agents and Artificial Intelligence - Volume 2: ICAART, pp. 277–288. INSTICC, SciTePress (2023). https://doi.org/10.5220/0011701300003393

7. Faratin, P., Sierra, C., Jennings, N.R.: Negotiation decision functions for autonomous agents. Robot. Auton. Syst. **24**(3), 159–182 (1998). https://doi.org/10.1016/S0921-8890(98)00029-3

8. Fujita, K.: Automated strategy adaptation for multi-times bilateral closed negotiations. In: Proceedings of the 2014 International Conference on Autonomous Agents and Multi-Agent Systems, pp. 1509–1510. AAMAS 2014, International Foundation for Autonomous Agents and Multiagent Systems, Richland, SC (2014)

9. Fujita, K.: Compromising adjustment strategy based on TKI conflict mode for multi-times bilateral closed negotiations. Comput. Intell. **34**(1), 85–103 (2018). https://doi.org/10.1111/coin.12107

10. Fujita, K., Ito, T., Baarslag, T., Hindriks, K., Jonker, C., Kraus, S., Lin, R.: The second automated negotiating agents competition (ANAC2011). In: Ito, T., Zhang, M., Robu, V., Matsuo, T. (eds.) Complex Automated Negotiations: Theories, Models, and Software Competitions, pp. 183–197. Springer, Heidelberg (2013). https://doi.org/10.1007/978-3-642-30737-9_11

11. Güneş, T.D., Arditi, E., Aydoğan, R.: Collective voice of experts in multilateral negotiation. In: An, B., Bazzan, A., Leite, J., Villata, S., van der Torre, L. (eds.) PRIMA 2017. LNCS, pp. 450–458. Springer, Cham (2017)

12. Ilany, L., Gal, Y.: Algorithm selection in bilateral negotiation. Auton. Agents Multi-Agent Syst. **30**(4), 697–723 (2016). https://doi.org/10.1007/s10458-015-9302-8

13. Kawata, R., Fujita, K.: Meta-strategy based on multi-armed bandit approach for multi-time negotiation. IEICE Trans. Inf. Syst. **E103.D**(12), 2540–2548 (2020). https://doi.org/10.1587/transinf.2020SAP0003

14. Matsune, T., Fujita, K.: Weighting estimation methods for opponents' utility functions using boosting in multi-time negotiations. IEICE Trans. Inf. Syst. **E101.D**(10), 2474–2484 (2018). https://doi.org/10.1587/transinf.2018EDP7056

15. Mohammad, Y., Nakadai, S., Greenwald, A.: NegMAS: a platform for automated negotiations. In: Uchiya, T., Bai, Q., Marsá Maestre, I. (eds.) PRIMA 2020. LNCS, vol. 12568, pp. 343–351. Springer, Heidelberg (2020). https://doi.org/10.1007/978-3-030-69322-0_23

16. Mori, A., Ito, T.: Atlas3: a negotiating agent based on expecting lower limit of concession function. In: Fujita, K., et al. (eds.) Modern Approaches to Agent-based Complex Automated Negotiation. SCI, vol. 674, pp. 169–173. Springer, Cham (2017). https://doi.org/10.1007/978-3-319-51563-2_11

17. Renting, B.M., Hoos, H.H., Jonker, C.M.: Automated configuration of negotiation strategies. In: Proceedings of the 19th International Conference on Autonomous Agents and MultiAgent Systems, p. 1116–1124. AAMAS'20, International Foundation for Autonomous Agents and Multiagent Systems, Richland, SC (2020)

18. Renting, B.M., Hoos, H.H., Jonker, C.M.: Automated configuration and usage of strategy portfolios for mixed-motive bargaining. In: Proceedings of the 21st International Conference on Autonomous Agents and Multiagent Systems, pp. 1101–1109. AAMAS 2022, International Foundation for Autonomous Agents and Multiagent Systems, Richland, SC (2022)

19. Rosenschein, J.S., Zlotkin, G.: Rules of Encounter: Designing Conventions for Automated Negotiation Among Computers. MIT Press, Cambridge (1994)

20. Sengupta, A., Mohammad, Y., Nakadai, S.: An autonomous negotiating agent framework with reinforcement learning based strategies and adaptive strategy switching mechanism. In: Proceedings of the 20th International Conference on Autonomous Agents and MultiAgent Systems, pp. 1163–1172. AAMAS 2021, International Foundation for Autonomous Agents and Multiagent Systems, Richland, SC (2021)

21. Taiji, M., Ikegami, T.: Dynamics of internal models in game players. Physica D **134**(2), 253–266 (1999). 10.1016/S0167-2789(99)00115-3, https://www.sciencedirect.com/science/article/pii/S0167278999001153

22. Van Krimpen, T., Looije, D., Hajizadeh, S.: Hardheaded. In: Ito, T., Zhang, M., Robu, V., Matsuo, T. (eds.) Complex Automated Negotiations: Theories, Models, and Software Competitions. SCI, vol. 435, pp. 223–227. Springer, Heidelberg (2013). https://doi.org/10.1007/978-3-642-30737-9_17

23. Wu, L., Chen, S., Gao, X., Zheng, Y., Hao, J.: Detecting and learning against unknown opponents for automated negotiations. In: Pham, D.N., Theeramunkong, T., Governatori, G., Liu, F. (eds.) PRICAI 2021. LNCS, pp. 17–31. Springer, Cham (2021). https://doi.org/10.1007/978-3-030-89370-5_2

24. (Ya'akov) Gal, K., Ilany, L.: The fourth automated negotiation competition. In: Fujita, K., Ito, T., Zhang, M., Robu, V. (eds.) Next Frontier in Agent-based Complex Automated Negotiation. SCI, vol. 596, pp. 129–136. Springer, Tokyo (2015). https://doi.org/10.1007/978-4-431-55525-4_8

A Novel Bagged Ensemble Approach for Accurate Histopathological Breast Cancer Classification Using Transfer Learning and Convolutional Neural Networks

Fatima-Zahrae Nakach[1] and Ali Idri[1,2(✉)]

[1] Faculty of Medical Sciences, Mohammed VI Polytechnic University, Marrakech-Rhamna,
Benguerir, Morocco
`Ali.Idri@um6p.ma`
[2] Software Project Management Research Team, ENSIAS, Mohammed V University,
Rabat-Salé-Kénitra, Rabat, Morocco

Abstract. This paper introduces a novel bagged ensemble approach for a binary classification using convolutional neural networks (CNNs) and transfer learning strategies. The CNN is trained independently on different bootstrapped samples (bags) of the training data, and the predictions are aggregated using majority voting to obtain the final classification result of the deep bagging ensemble. The BreakHis dataset, encompassing four magnification factors ($40\times$, $100\times$, $200\times$, and $400\times$), is used for evaluation, and in addition to the four-metrics (accuracy, precision, sensitivity, and F1-score), the Scott-knot statistical test and Borda count voting method are employed to comprehensively assess the performance of the different models and rank them. Experimental results demonstrated that the proposed approach achieved high values over the four metrics for breast cancer classification. The comparative analysis highlights the ability of the deep bagging ensembles to capture diverse and complementary features from different bags, and it showcases their superiority compared to the single CNNs and the hybrid bagging ensembles, where the pre-trained deep learning models are only used for feature extraction. The findings suggested that the simplicity and effectiveness of combining fine-tuned CNNs with bagging ensembles, make the proposed approach an attractive choice for practical implementation, as it holds a promise for accurate and reliable classification of histopathological breast cancer images. Furthermore, this approach can potentially be applied to other medical image classification tasks, providing a more efficient and accurate diagnosis for a range of diseases.

Keywords: Breast cancer · Bagging · Convolutional neural networks

1 Introduction

Breast cancer has become the most prevalent form of cancer worldwide in 2021, affecting over 2.1 million women and causing over one million deaths annually [1]. Early detection and accurate diagnosis of breast cancer can improve patient survival rates [2].

A. P. Rocha et al. (Eds.): ICAART 2023, LNAI 14546, pp. 333–352, 2024.
https://doi.org/10.1007/978-3-031-55326-4_16

Although histopathology biopsy imaging is currently the gold standard for identifying breast cancer in clinical practice [3], some intricate visual patterns are still difficult to categorize as benign or malignant [4]. Machine learning (ML) models can aid pathologists in automatically detecting cancer, improving accuracy, and speeding up the diagnosis process [5]. Before a patient can receive a better treatment plan that increases their chances of survival, the tumor type must be identified, hence, ML models must initially differentiate between benign and malignant tumors [3]. Predictive models have been developed using several ML classifiers in cancer research [6], but none of them have been proven to outperform the others in all cases [7]. Bagging, an ensemble learning method introduced by [8], aims to reduce the variance and enhance the performance of a given algorithm by aggregating the decisions of different predictors trained on different bags (subsets of the dataset) [9].

Convolutional Neural Networks (CNNs) have become a highly successful method for classifying histopathological images accurately and robustly by automatically extracting pertinent features from raw pixel data [10]. CNNs learn hierarchical representations that capture progressively more complex and abstract features, local patterns, and spatial relationships within the images by applying convolutional and pooling layers [11]. CNNs pose limitations in terms of high computational requirements, demanding significant computational resources both in terms of memory and processing power, and they typically require large datasets for effective training, which may be challenging to obtain in certain domains or applications [12]. To overcome these limitations of training deep CNNs, two transfer learning methods can be utilized: "feature extraction" and "fine-tuning" methods [11]. The hybrid architecture employs the first transfer learning method with CNNs, where the features of the images are extracted using the activation values of hidden neurons in pre-trained networks which allows the classification to be performed using ML-supervised learning models [13]. On the other hand, the deep architecture refers to the use of CNNs with the second transfer learning method for both feature extraction and classification, the pre-trained network is fine-tuned according to given labels by updating the weights of the later layers while keeping the earlier layers frozen [14].

In a recent study, Nakach et al. [15] proposed the use of bagging ensembles and hybrid architectures, combining deep learning (DL) techniques and ML classifiers, for binary classification of breast cancer histological images. To extend this approach, this paper aims to investigate if the performance of deep bagging ensembles can be further improved by incorporating other transfer learning techniques such as fine-tuning. This would involve using a single DL model, particularly a CNN, for both feature extraction and classification, and then combining multiple models trained on different bags based on their predictions on the classification task. The advantage of this approach is that it can potentially reduce the loss of information caused by using separate feature extraction and classification stages, resulting in a more efficient and effective diagnosis of breast cancer from histopathological images. Moreover, the performance of the deep bagging ensembles will be compared to that of single CNNs, as well as to the hybrid bagging ensembles, to evaluate the effectiveness of the approach and to confirm or refute the usefulness of the deep or hybrid architecture when using the bagging technique for binary classification of breast cancer histopathological images over the BreakHis dataset. To achieve this objective, the study examines four research questions:

1. **How does the bagging ensembles perform in comparison with their base learners?**
2. **What is the best number of base learners to use for the deep bagging ensembles?**
3. **Do deep bagging ensembles outperform the single CNN model?**
4. **What transfer learning method performs the best with the bagging ensemble technique: feature extraction or fine-tuning**?

The remainder of the paper is structured as follows: Sect. 2 explores existing research and literature relevant to the use of bagging ensemble for the classification of breast cancer images. Section 3 provides a detailed overview of the methodology employed in this study, outlining the architecture of the bagging ensembles, the experimental process, the evaluation metrics and the statistical evaluation. Section 4 presents the empirical findings in relation to the research question, followed by a rigorous discussion and interpretation of the results. Finally, Sect. 5 summarizes the key findings, and highlights the contributions of the study.

2 Related Work

To tackle the binary classification of histopathological images in breast cancer, several studies have explored the use of bagging ensembles using CNNs:

- The paper [16] introduced an Ensemble Bagging Weighted Voting Classification (EBWvc) method for breast cancer classification. The proposed method was evaluated through comparative analysis, and the results showed that EBWvc achieved significant improvements in classification performance compared to existing techniques. Specifically, EBWvc exhibited higher accuracy, precision, sensitivity, and F1-score values. For example, the accuracy of EBWvc was measured at 95%, outperforming Ensemble Machine Learning (92%), Support Vector Machine (SVM) (88%), Bagging-SVM (90%), AdaBoost Classifier (88%), and RF (87%). Similar patterns were observed in precision, sensitivity, and F1-score measurements. The study concluded that the proposed EBWvc method demonstrated superior performance compared to existing classification techniques. It also suggested future improvements, such as incorporating medical image fusion for diagnosing various diseases in humans.
- Guo et al. [17] proposed a new histopathology image recognition scheme that employs bagging and hierarchy voting to reduce generalization error and improve performance. They used a hybrid CNN architecture based on GoogleNet, with local and global features of images to achieve better classification accuracy. The proposed method achieved a classification accuracy of 87.5% for four categories of breast cancer.
- Kassani et al. [18] developed a bagging ensemble using pre-trained CNNs such as MobileNetV2, VGG19, and DenseNet201 for automatic binary classification of breast histopathological images. The study found that the proposed multi-model ensemble method outperformed single classifiers and ML algorithms, achieving an accuracy of 98.13% for the BreakHis dataset.

– Wang et al. [19] designed a bagging decision tree (DT) ensemble and a subspace discriminant classifiers ensemble for classifying the images of the BreakHis dataset. The DT bagging ensemble achieved the highest accuracy rate of 89.7% compared to single classifiers. For multi-classification, the subspace discriminant classifier ensemble gave an accuracy of 88.1%.
– Zhu et al. [20] used hybrid CNN models to construct bagging ensembles for classifying the BreakHis dataset and the BACH dataset. The results showed that combining multiple compact CNNs led to an improvement in classification performance.
– The study [15] aimed to verify the efficacy of hybrid bagging ensembles in detecting breast cancer and to compare their performance with that of single ML classifiers. The authors found that bagging hybrid DL was an effective approach for classifying histopathological breast cancer images. The study aimed to compare the effectiveness of bagging ensembles to single ML classifiers for diagnosing breast cancer. Specifically, the authors developed and evaluated 48 different bagging hybrid architecture ensembles for binary classification of breast cancer histopathological images using the BreakHis dataset at various magnification factors ($40\times$, $100\times$, $200\times$, and $400\times$). These ensembles were composed of three recent DL techniques for feature extraction through transfer learning [21], including DenseNet201 [22], MobileNetV2 [23], and InceptionV3 [24], along with three popular ML classifiers as base learners, which were Multilayer Perceptron (MLP), K-Nearest Neighbors (KNN), and SVM. Additionally, the bagging ensembles were composed of different numbers of base learners, ranging from 3 to 9 estimators with a step of 2.

3   Approach

This section provides a detailed overview of the methodology employed in this study, outlining the architecture of the bagging ensembles, the experimental process, the evaluation metrics and the statistical evaluation.

3.1   Methodology

The present paper explores the use of the bagging ensemble technique with pre-trained DL models for binary classification of breast cancer histological images. The proposed approach involves constructing different ensembles that benefit from reduced variance and improved generalization compared with their single models (trained on all the training dataset) and base learners (trained on bags), since each individual CNN within the ensemble captures different patterns and contributes diverse insights due to training process performed on different bootstrapped samples.

Figure 1 and 2 depict the flowchart of the bagging ensemble to classify histopathological images using the deep and hybrid architecture, respectively:

- For the deep bagging ensemble's architecture, multiple models based on the same CNN are trained independently on different bootstrapped samples (bags) of the training dataset, and the deep bagging ensembles are then constructed by combining the predictions of the different base models to obtain the final prediction on the testing dataset.

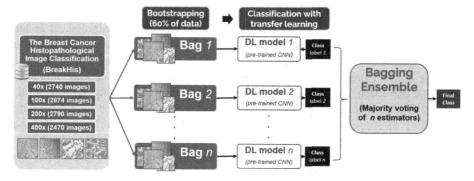

Fig. 1. Architecture of the deep bagging ensemble.

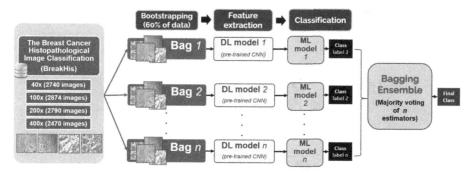

Fig. 2. Architecture of the hybrid bagging ensemble.

- For the hybrid bagging ensemble's architecture, multiple models based on the same CNN are applied on different bootstrapped samples (bags) of the training dataset to extract the features of the images, the extracted features over each bag are then used as inputs on a traditional ML model. The bagging ensembles are then constructed by combining the predictions of the different base learners to obtain the final prediction on the testing dataset.

3.2 Experimental Process

In this study, four bagging ensembles are constructed for the classification of benign and malignant breast cancer tumors over the four-magnification factor (MF) values of the BreakHis [25] dataset: $40\times$, $100\times$, $200\times$, and $400\times$. Each deep bagging ensemble employs a different number of bags (3, 5, 7 and 9) that represent 60% of the training dataset and use as a base learner the pre-trained CNN based on fine-tuning. DenseNet201 is used as a pre-trained CNN in this study, Fig. 3 depicts its architecture, it has been chosen due to it is high performance compared to other pre-trained CNNs for the classification of breast cancer histopathological images [15]. The predictions of the different variations of the base learners are aggregated utilizing majority voting to obtain the final classification result. In order to investigate the effectiveness of this approach and determine the most suitable strategy for bagging in breast cancer histopathological image classification, the performance of the deep bagging ensembles will be compared with that of single DL model (DenseNet201 trained on all the dataset) and hybrid bagging ensemble from the previous study [15], where the pre-trained DL models are only used for feature extraction, and the bagging ensembles are constructed using traditional ML models (SVM and MLP), Fig. 4 depicts the empirical design of the hybrid bagging ensembles [15]. Additionally, the present study aims to use other ML classifiers as base learners, specifically LightGBM and XGBoost (XGB), to explore the potential of boosting techniques combined with bagging ensembles in improving the binary classification of breast cancer histological images. Since boosting techniques have already been proven to be effective for the classification of the BreakHis dataset using the features extracted with pre-trained CNNs [26]. The empirical evaluations of the deep bagging ensembles involve seven steps as shown in Fig. 5. For the purpose of comparison, in this study, the preprocessing of the BreakHis dataset incorporates a similar approach as described in [15].

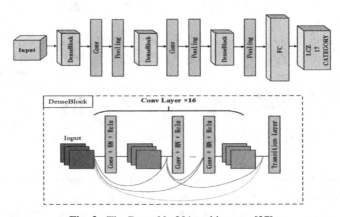

Fig. 3. The DenseNet201 architecture [27].

3.3 Evaluation Metrics

The evaluation criteria used to assess bagging ensembles, as well as their base learners and individual models, include accuracy, precision, sensitivity, and F1-score. These metrics are commonly employed in classification tasks [28]. Mathematically, they are represented by Eqs. 1 to 4:

$$\text{Accuracy} = (TP + TN)/(TN + TP + FP + FN) \tag{1}$$

$$\text{Precision} = TP/(TP + FP) \tag{2}$$

$$\text{Sensitivity} = TP/(TP + FN) \tag{3}$$

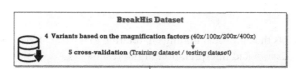

BreakHis Dataset

4 Magnification Factors (MF) (40X/100X/200X/400X)
↓
Feature extraction with 3 Deep Learning techniques (DenseNet 201 MobileNet V2, Inception V3)
12 Variants
↓
4 Machine Learning Classifiers (MLP, DT, SVM, KNN)
48 Variants

Step 1: For each **MF** and **FE** assess the performance in terms of accuracy, precision, sensitivity and F1 score of each variant of classifiers,

---

Step 2: For each **MF** and each **FE** model construct 9 bags (60% of the Dataset with replacement), and for each bag assess the performance in terms of accuracy of each variant of classifiers.

Step 3: For each **MF**, each **FE** model, and for each classifier construct 4 Bagging homogenous ensembles depending on each number of estimators (3, 5, 7 and 9) using the bags constructed before.

Step 4: For each **MF**, each **FE** model, and each classifier, compare the **4 Bagging homogenous ensembles with their singles** using SK test based on the accuracy and Borda count based on the best SK clusters in terms of accuracy, precision, sensitivity and F1 score.

Step 5: For each **MF**, each **FE** model, and each classifier, compare the **4 Bagging homogenous ensembles with different number of estimators** using SK test based on the accuracy and Borda count based on the best SK cluster in terms of accuracy, precision, sensitivity and F1 score.

Step 6: For each **MF**, each **FE** model, and each classifier, compare the **best Bagging ensemble with the simple classifier** using SK test based on the accuracy and Borda count based on the best SK cluster in terms of accuracy, precision, sensitivity and F1 score.

Step 7: For each **MF**, compare the **best Bagging ensemble of each classifier and FE to each others** using SK test based on the accuracy and Borda count based on the best SK cluster in terms of accuracy, precision, sensitivity and F1 score.

Step 8: Compare **the best Bagging ensemble** of each **MF to each others** using SK test based on the accuracy and Borda count based on the best SK cluster in terms of accuracy, precision, sensitivity and F1 score.

Fig. 4. Experimental Design of [15].

BreakHis Dataset

4 Variants based on the magnification factors (40x/100x/200x/400x)
↓
5 cross-validation (Training dataset / testing dataset)

Step 1: Assess the performance of the CNN model based on all the dataset in terms of accuracy, precision, sensitivity and F1 score to classify the histopathological images of breast cancer tumors benign or malignant.

Step 2: Construct 9 bags using 60% of the training dataset (with replacement), train 9 CNN independently on each bag and assess the performance of the CNN models on the testing dataset.

Step 3: Construct **4** deep bagging with different number of base learners (3, 5, 7 and 9) by aggregating the the the predictions of the CNNs trained on the bags constructed before using majority voting.

Step 4: Compare the **4 Bagging deep ensembles with their base learners** using SK test based on the accuracy and Borda count based on the best SK clusters in terms of accuracy, precision, sensitivity and F1 score.

Step 5: Compare the **4 Bagging deep ensembles with different number of base learners** using SK test based on the accuracy and Borda count based on the best SK cluster in terms of accuracy, precision, sensitivity and F1 score.

Step 6: Compare the **best Bagging ensemble** (found in step 5) **with the single CNN models** (from step 1) using SK test based on the accuracy and Borda count based on the best SK cluster in terms of accuracy, precision, sensitivity and F1 score.

Step 7: Compare the **deep bagging ensembles with the hybrid bagging ensembles** that use the CNN model for feature extraction and a machine learning model for classification using SK test based on the accuracy and Borda count based on the best SK cluster in terms of accuracy, precision, sensitivity and F1 score.

Fig. 5. Experimental Design of the present study.

$$F1 - score = 2 \times (Sensitivity \times Precision)/(Sensitivity + Precision) \quad (4)$$

Here, TP refers to a correctly identified malignant case, FP represents a benign case incorrectly identified as malignant, TN denotes a correctly identified benign case, and FN signifies a malignant case incorrectly identified as benign.

3.4 Statistical Evaluation

To ensure the integrity of the binary classification task, a 5-fold cross-validation approach was employed. This technique can help mitigate the risk of overfitting and increase the robustness of your predictions as it guarantees that each observation from the original dataset has an opportunity to appear in both the training and test sets. Furthermore, for each fold, the images selected for testing purposes were not utilized during training. To draw the conclusion, a combination of statistical tests was employed to ensure a comprehensive and robust assessment of the models' performance across multiple datasets (each MF of the BreakHis dataset is considered as an independent dataset). The SK statistical test [29] was utilized to cluster the models based on their accuracy over the five folds, the best SK cluster comprises one or more models that exhibit the highest accuracy and are statistically similar. If multiple models are identified, they are ranked using the Borda Count voting system [30], which considers four performance measures: accuracy, sensitivity, precision, and F1-score.

4 Results and Discussion

This section presents the empirical findings in relation to the research question, followed by a rigorous discussion and interpretation of the results.

4.1 How Does the Bagging Ensembles Perform in Comparison with Their Base Learners?

As it was mentioned it the empirical design, 9 base learners were used to construct the four deep bagging ensembles that contain 3, 5, 7, and 9 bags respectively. Each base learner was trained on a different bag, the objective of this subsection is to evaluate the performance of each deep bagging ensemble and compare it with the performance of the N base learners that construct it. Figure 6, 7, 8 and 9 show the mean accuracy value of the base learners in comparison to the mean accuracy value of the ensembles over the four MFs respectively. The best base learner achieved an accuracy of 91.53%, 90.54%, 92.47 and 90,52% for MF 40×, 100×, 200× and 400× respectively. The worst accuracy value of the base learners was 90%, 89.42%, 91.25% and 89.03% for MF 40× , 100×, 200× and 400× respectively. The best deep bagging ensemble achieved an accuracy of 91.53%, 92.07%, 93.47 and 91,82% for MF 40×, 100×, 200× and 400× respectively. The worst accuracy value of the deep bagging ensembles was 92.01%, 91.16%, 92.58% and 91.62% for MF 40×, 100×, 200× and 400× respectively. In general, the deep bagging ensemble consistently achieves higher accuracy compared to all individual base learners that contribute to the ensemble.

The SK test based on accuracy was employed over each MF to check whether there was a notable difference between the performance of the bagging ensembles and their base learners. Figure 10, 11, 12 and 13 show the SK results test of the four deep bagging ensembles compared with their base learners over MF 40×. It was found that the SK tests over all the MFs contain one cluster, which implies that the accuracy of the deep bagging ensembles is statistically similar to the accuracy of their base learners.

In order to identify which model is the best for each MF, the models of the best SK cluster were then ranked by the Borda Count voting system based on accuracy, sensitivity, F1-score and precision. It was found that the deep bagging ensembles are always ranked first as they outperform all their base learners over all the MFs.

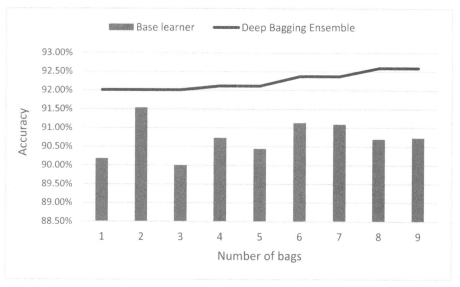

Fig. 6. Mean accuracy values of the deep bagging ensembles in comparison to their base learners over MF 40×.

4.2 What is the Best Number of Base Learners to Use for the Deep Bagging Ensembles?

This subsection aims to evaluate the impacts of the bags on the performances of the deep bagging ensembles they construct in order to identify the best number of base learners (3, 5, 7 or 9), over the four MF values: 40×, 100×, 200× and 400×. Table 1 summarizes the testing mean values of the best deep bagging ensembles with the number of bags used over each MF. The SK test based on accuracy was employed over each MF to check whether there was a notable difference between the performance of the four deep bagging ensembles. Figure 14 shows the SK results test of the four deep bagging ensembles over MF 40×. It was found that the SK tests over all the MFs contain one cluster, which implies that regardless the number of base learners used the accuracy of the four deep bagging ensembles is statistically similar.

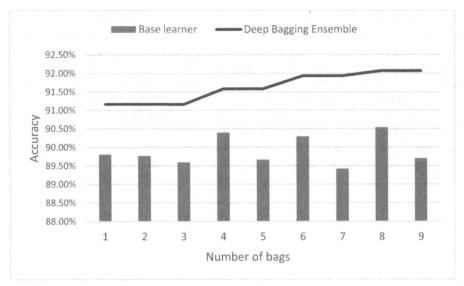

Fig. 7. Mean accuracy values of the deep bagging ensembles in comparison to their base learners over MF 100×.

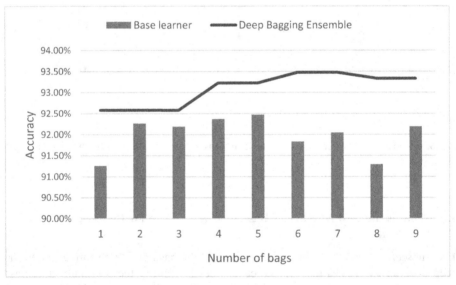

Fig. 8. Mean accuracy values of the deep bagging ensembles in comparison to their base learners over MF 200×.

In order to identify which deep bagging ensemble is the best for each MF, the models of the best SK cluster were then ranked by the Borda Count voting system based on accuracy, sensitivity, F1-score and precision. Table 2 presents the ranks of the different deep bagging ensembles over each MF using the Borda Count method. For MF

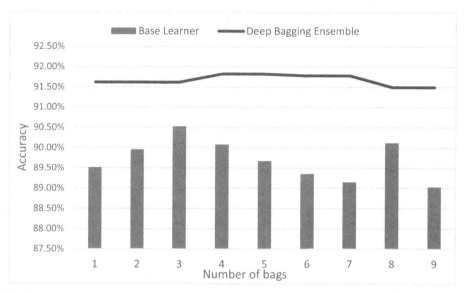

Fig. 9. Mean accuracy values of the deep bagging ensembles in comparison to their base learners over MF 400×.

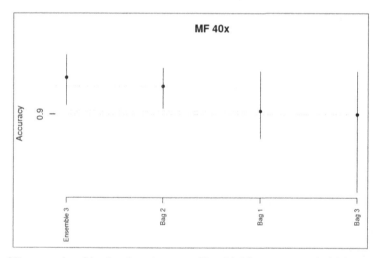

Fig. 10. SK test results of the deep bagging ensemble with 3 bags compared with its base learners over MF 40×.

40× and MF 100×, the deep bagging ensembles respect an ascending order: the deep bagging ensemble of 9 base learners was ranked first, the deep bagging ensemble of 7 base learners was ranked second, the deep bagging ensemble of 5 base learners was ranked third, and the deep bagging ensemble of 3 base learners was ranked last. For MF 200× and 400×, it was found that adding more bags does not always guarantee a higher performance, as an example for MF 200× the deep bagging ensemble of 7 base learners

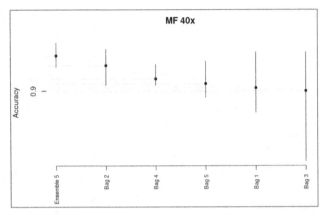

Fig. 11. SK test results of the deep bagging ensemble with 5 bags compared with its base learners over MF 40×.

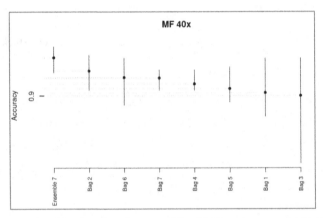

Fig. 12. SK test results of the deep bagging ensemble with 7 bags compared with its base learners over MF 40×.

was ranked first, the deep bagging ensemble of 9 base learners was ranked second, while for MF 400×, the deep bagging ensemble of 5 base learners was ranked first, the deep bagging ensemble of 7 base learners was ranked second, and the deep bagging ensemble of 9 base learners was ranked third.

4.3 Do Deep Bagging Ensembles Outperform the Single CNN Model?

This subsection compares the single CNN model (trained on all the training dataset) and the deep bagging ensembles of each MF. Table 3 summarizes the testing mean values of the single CNN model over each MF in terms of accuracy, precision, sensitivity, and F1-score. Figure 15, 16, 17 and 18 show the SK results test of the four deep bagging ensembles compared with the single DL model (DenseNet201) for each MF. It was found

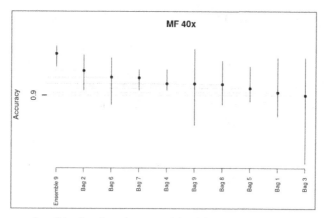

Fig. 13. SK test results of the deep bagging ensemble with 9 bags compared with its base learners over MF 40×.

Table 1. Performance values of the deep bagging ensembles over each MF.

MF	Number of bags	Accuracy (%)	Precision (%)	Sensitivity (%)	F1-score (%)
40 ×	3	92,01	92,27	89,66	95,18
	5	92,12	92,31	90,26	94,53
	7	92,37	92,51	90,77	94,38
	9	**92,59**	**92,74**	**90,81**	**94,82**
100 ×	3	91,16	91,26	90,62	92,13
	5	91,58	91,73	90,43	93,18
	7	91,93	92,10	90,32	94,02
	9	**92,07**	**92,22**	**90,66**	**93,88**
200 ×	3	93,23	93,40	91,94	95,00
	5	93,23	93,40	91,94	95,00
	7	**93,47**	**93,66**	**91,83**	**95,64**
	9	93,33	93,50	91,93	95,21
400 ×	3	91,62	91,68	90,53	92,93
	5	**91,82**	**91,86**	**91,01**	**92,77**
	7	91,78	91,78	91,36	92,29
	9	91,50	91,51	90,97	92,12

that the SK tests over all the MFs contain one cluster, which implies that the accuracy of the deep bagging ensembles is statistically similar to the single DL model.

Table 2. Ranks of the deep bagging ensembles over the 4 MF using Borda Count.

MF	Ensemble with 3 bags	Ensemble with 5 bags	Ensemble with 7 bags	Ensemble with 9 bags
40 ×	4th ranked	3rd ranked	2nd ranked	1st ranked
100×	4th ranked	3rd ranked	2nd ranked	1st ranked
200×	4th ranked	3rd ranked	1st ranked	2nd ranked
400×	4th ranked	1st ranked	2nd ranked	3rd ranked

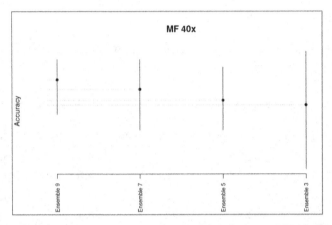

Fig. 14. SK test results of the four deep baggings over MF 40×.

After using the Borda Count voting method, it was found that for MF 40×, the single CNN model outperforms all the deep bagging ensembles. Contrarily, for MF 100×, MF 200× and 400×, the best deep bagging ensemble outperform the single CNN model.

Table 3. Performance values of single pre-trained DL model and the deep bagging ensembles.

MF	Accuracy (%)	Precision (%)	Sensitivity (%)	F1-score (%)
40×	92,77	92,94	91,32	94,82
100×	91,96	91,85	92,58	91,23
200×	93,08	93,23	91,75	94,79
400×	91,05	90,86	92,46	89,36

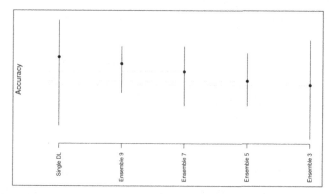

Fig. 15. SK test results of the four deep bagging ensemble compared to the single DL model over MF 40×.

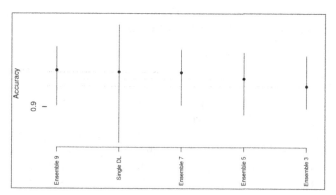

Fig. 16. SK test results of the four deep bagging ensemble compared to the single DL model over MF 100×.

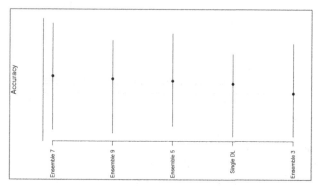

Fig. 17. SK test results of the four deep bagging ensemble compared to the single DL model over MF 200×.

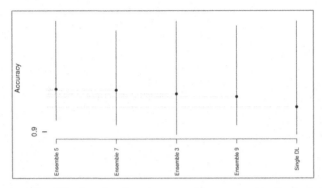

Fig. 18. SK test results of the four deep bagging ensemble compared to the single DL model over MF 400×.

4.4 What Transfer Learning Method Performs the Best with the Bagging Method: Feature Extraction or Fine-Tuning?

This subsection compares the best deep bagging ensembles over each MF with the hybrid bagging ensembles constructed using ML classifiers as base learner. XGBoost, LightGBM, MLP, and SVM were chosen for the bagging ensemble with 9 estimators due to their superior performance in previous studies [15, 26], surpassing that of other classifiers. It was found that the deep bagging ensembles outperform the hybrid bagging ensembles with SVM, XGBoost and Light GBM as base learners. Thus, this paper recommends to not use ML classifiers based on boosting methods as base learners for the hybrid architecture of the bagging ensemble due to their poor performance compared to the other hybrid bagging ensembles. On the other side, it was found that the hybrid bagging ensembles that use MLP as a base learner have a similar performance to the best deep bagging ensembles and slightly outperform them for MF 100× and 200× . Table 4 summarizes the testing mean values of the best hybrid bagging ensembles over each MF in terms of accuracy, precision, sensitivity, and F1-score. It was found that the deep bagging ensembles outperform the hybrid bagging ensembles, this novel approach not only mitigates potential information loss associated with separate feature extraction and classification stages but also benefits from reduced variance and improved generalization.

Overall, empirical evidence has shown that deep bagging ensembles based on CNNs yield remarkable results compared to the base learners, single CNN models, and the hybrid bagging ensembles for the classification of the BreakHis dataset over the four MFs. By training multiple models, each with its own biases and variances, the ensemble's aggregated prediction tends to reduce the impact of individual model errors, leading to improved overall performance and enhanced generalization capabilities which helps mitigate the risk of overfitting. The combination of diverse predictions from multiple models enables the bagging ensemble to achieve higher accuracy, better robustness against noise and outliers, and increased stability in predictions.

Table 4. Performance values of the hybrid bagging ensembles over each MF.

MF	Base learner	Accuracy (%)	Precision (%)	Sensitivity (%)	F1-score (%)
40×	**MLP**	92,55	92,64	91,65	93,65
	XGBoost	90,07	90,34	88,06	92,77
	SVM	91,24	91,40	89,87	92,99
	LGBM	90,73	91,05	88.30	93,94
100×	**MLP**	92,10	92,23	90,83	93,67
	XGBoost	89,56	89,82	87,59	92,21
	SVM	90,47	90,64	89,00	92,34
	LGBM	89,84	90,14	87,56	92,90
200×	**MLP**	93,62	93,69	92,99	94,43
	XGBoost	90,72	91,07	87,99	94,43
	SVM	88,85	89,46	85,17	94,29
	LGBM	90,57	90,95	87,70	94,50
400 ×	**MLP**	91,34	91,29	91,39	91,23
	XGBoost	88,95	89,31	86,28	92,61
	SVM	86,03	86,81	82,09	92,13
	LGBM	88,83	89,19	86,21	92,45

5   Conclusion and Future Work

In conclusion, this study presented and discussed a novel approach for binary classification of breast cancer histological images using bagging ensembles with a widely-used pre-trained DL model (DenseNet201). This study aims to provide reliable and meaningful insights into the proposed methodology's effectiveness and applicability by employing rigorous evaluation techniques, and utilizing established performance metrics. Training each model independently on different bootstrapped samples and aggregating their predictions through majority voting, achieved a high accuracy in breast cancer classification. The findings highlight the effectiveness of fine-tuned CNN models combined with bagging ensembles for accurate and reliable classification of histopathological breast cancer images, and demonstrate the superiority of the deep bagging ensembles over individual CNN models and hybrid architectures. This approach shows promise for practical implementation, offering a simple yet powerful solution for the accurate diagnosis of breast cancer from histological images. Moreover, bagging ensembles can help capture more complex relationships within the data, enhancing the model's ability to handle intricate patterns and achieve superior performance on challenging tasks.

However, to enhance the understanding of the potential of the proposed approach and provide valuable insights into the strengths and weaknesses of the deep bagging ensembles, future research could explore the application of this method using alternative CNN models. For further improvement, the approach could be extended by applying feature bagging instead of sampling dataset samples for each base learner. The robustness and generalization ability of the classification models can be enhanced by feature bagging, as variance is reduced and the identification of the most informative features is facilitated. Potential issues such as feature redundancy and overfitting can be addressed through this approach, ultimately leading to an improvement in the performance of the classification task.

Acknowledgments. This work was conducted under the research project "Machine Learning based Breast Cancer Diagnosis and Treatment", 2020–2023. The authors would like to thank the Moroccan Ministry of Higher Education and Scientifc Research, Digital Development Agency (ADD), CNRST, and UM6P for their support.

References

1. Sung, H., et al.: Global cancer statistics 2020: GLOBOCAN estimates of incidence and mortality worldwide for 36 cancers in 185 countries. CA: Cancer J. Clin. **71**, 209–249 (2021). https://doi.org/10.3322/caac.21660
2. Clegg, L.X., et al.: Impact of socioeconomic status on cancer incidence and stage at diagnosis: selected findings from the surveillance, epidemiology, and end results: national longitudinal mortality study. Cancer Causes Control **20**, 417–435 (2009). https://doi.org/10.1007/s10552-008-9256-0
3. Kumar, V., Abbas, A.K., Aster, J.C.: Robbins Basic Pathology E-Book. Elsevier Health Sciences, Edinburgh (2017)
4. Gupta, V., Bhavsar, A.: Breast cancer histopathological image classification: is magnification important? In: 2017 IEEE Conference on Computer Vision and Pattern Recognition Workshops (CVPRW), pp. 769–776. IEEE, Honolulu, HI, USA (2017). https://doi.org/10.1109/CVPRW.2017.107
5. din, N.M. ud, Dar, R.A., Rasool, M., Assad, A.: Breast cancer detection using deep learning: Datasets, methods, and challenges ahead. Computers in Biology and Medicine. 149, 106073 (2022). https://doi.org/10.1016/j.compbiomed.2022.106073
6. Saxena, S., Gyanchandani, M.: Machine learning methods for computer-aided breast cancer diagnosis using histopathology: a narrative review. J. Med. Imaging Radiat. Sci. **51**, 182–193 (2020). https://doi.org/10.1016/j.jmir.2019.11.001
7. Nemade, V., Pathak, S., Dubey, A., Barhate, D.: A review and computational analysis of breast cancer using different machine learning techniques (2022). https://doi.org/10.46338/ijetae0322_13
8. Breiman, L.: Bagging predictors. Mach. Learn. **24**, 123–140 (1996). https://doi.org/10.1007/BF00058655
9. Hosni, M., Abnane, I., Idri, A., de Gea, J.M.C., Alemán, J.L.F.: Reviewing ensemble classification methods in breast cancer. Comput. Methods Programs Biomed. **177**, 89–112 (2019). https://doi.org/10.1016/j.cmpb.2019.05.019
10. Davri, A., et al.: Deep learning on histopathological images for colorectal cancer diagnosis: a systematic review. Diagnostics. **12**, 837 (2022). https://doi.org/10.3390/diagnostics12040837
11. Hou, L., et al.: Automatic histopathology image analysis with CNNs. In: 2016 New York Scientific Data Summit (NYSDS), pp. 1–6 (2016). https://doi.org/10.1109/NYSDS.2016.7747812
12. Alzubaidi, L., et al.: Review of deep learning: concepts, CNN architectures, challenges, applications, future directions. J. Big Data. **8**, 53 (2021). https://doi.org/10.1186/s40537-021-00444-8

13. Zerouaoui, H., Idri, A., Nakach, F.Z., Hadri, R.E.: Breast fine needle cytological classification using deep hybrid architectures. In: Gervasi, O., Murgante, B., Misra, S., Garau, C., Blečić, I., Taniar, D., Apduhan, B.O., Rocha, A.M.A.C., Tarantino, E., Torre, C.M. (eds.) ICCSA 2021. LNCS, vol. 12950, pp. 186–202. Springer, Cham (2021). https://doi.org/10.1007/978-3-030-86960-1_14

14. Zerouaoui, H., Idri, A.: classifying breast cytological images using deep learning architectures. In: Presented at the 15th International Conference on Health Informatics (2022)

15. Nakach, F.-Z., Idri, A., Zerouaoui, H.: Deep hybrid bagging ensembles for classifying histopathological breast cancer images. In: Presented at the 15th International Conference on Agents and Artificial Intelligence (2023)

16. Ponnaganti, N.D., Anitha, R.: A novel ensemble bagging classification method for breast cancer classification using machine learning techniques. TS. **39**, 229–237 (2022). https://doi.org/10.18280/ts.390123

17. Guo, Z., Li, X., Huang, H., Guo, N., Li, Q.: Deep learning-based image segmentation on multimodal medical imaging. IEEE Trans. Radiat. Plasma Med. Sci. **3**, 162–169 (2019). https://doi.org/10.1109/TRPMS.2018.2890359

18. Kassani, S.H., Kassani, P.H., Wesolowski, M.J., Schneider, K.A., Deters, R.: Classification of histopathological biopsy images using ensemble of deep learning networks. arXiv:1909.11870 (2019)

19. Wang, J., Zhu, T., Liang, S., Karthiga, R., Narasimhan, K., Elamaran, V.: Binary and multiclass classification of histopathological images using machine learning techniques. J. Med. Imaging Health Inform. **10**, 2252–2258 (2020). https://doi.org/10.1166/jmihi.2020.3124

20. Zhu, C., Song, F., Wang, Y., Dong, H., Guo, Y., Liu, J.: Breast cancer histopathology image classification through assembling multiple compact CNNs. BMC Med. Inform. Decis. Mak. **19**, 198 (2019). https://doi.org/10.1186/s12911-019-0913-x

21. Pan, S.J., Yang, Q.: A survey on transfer learning. IEEE Trans. Knowl. Data Eng. **22**, 1345–1359 (2010). https://doi.org/10.1109/TKDE.2009.191

22. Wang, S.-H., Zhang, Y.-D.: DenseNet-201-based deep neural network with composite learning factor and precomputation for multiple sclerosis classification. ACM Trans. Multimedia Comput. Commun. Appl. **16**, 1–19 (2020). https://doi.org/10.1145/3341095

23. Sandler, M., Howard, A., Zhu, M., Zhmoginov, A., Chen, L.-C.: MobileNetV2: inverted residuals and linear bottlenecks. In: 2018 IEEE/CVF Conference on Computer Vision and Pattern Recognition, pp. 4510–4520. IEEE, Salt Lake City, UT (2018). https://doi.org/10.1109/CVPR.2018.00474

24. Szegedy, C., Vanhoucke, V., Ioffe, S., Shlens, J., Wojna, Z.: Rethinking the inception architecture for computer vision. In: Presented at the Proceedings of the IEEE Conference on Computer Vision and Pattern Recognition (2016)

25. Spanhol, F.A., Oliveira, L.S., Petitjean, C., Heutte, L.: A dataset for breast cancer histopathological image classification. IEEE Trans. Biomed. Eng. **63**, 1455–1462 (2016). https://doi.org/10.1109/TBME.2015.2496264

26. Nakach, F.-Z.: Hybrid deep boosting ensembles for histopathological breast cancer classification. Health Technol. 18

27. Jelihovschi, E., Faria, J.C., Allaman, I.B.: ScottKnott: a package for performing the scott-knott clustering algorithm in R. Tend. Mat. Apl. Comput. **15**, 003 (2014). https://doi.org/10.5540/tema.2014.015.01.0003

28. Zerouaoui, H., Idri, A.: Reviewing machine learning and image processing based decision-making systems for breast cancer imaging. J. Med. Syst. **45**, 8 (2021). https://doi.org/10.1007/s10916-020-01689-1

29. Emerson, P.: The original Borda count and partial voting. Soc Choice Welf. **40**, 353–358 (2013). https://doi.org/10.1007/s00355-011-0603-9
30. Hemant Kumar, A.V., Tripathi, S., Agrawal, R., Kumar, S.: Transfer learning and supervised machine learning approach for detection of skin cancer: performance analysis and comparison. DCTH, **10**, 1845–1860 (2021)

UTP: A Unified Term Presentation Tool for Clinical Textual Data Using Pattern-Matching Rules and Dictionary-Based Ontologies

Monah Bou Hatoum[1] , Jean Claude Charr[1(✉)] , Alia Ghaddar[2] ,
Christophe Guyeux[1] , and David Laiymani[1]

[1] University of Franche-Comte, 90000 Belfort, France
`jean-claude.charr@univ-fcomte.fr`
[2] Department of Computer Science, International University of Beirut,
P.O. Box 146404, Beirut, Lebanon

Abstract. Clinical textual data such as discharge summaries and chief complaints summarize the patient's medical history and treatment plan. These unstructured complex data include ambiguous medical terms, abbreviations, diagnostic investigation values and dates which pose significant challenges for human and machine learning tasks to process them. This paper proposes a novel approach that transforms clinical text with different writing styles into a uniform and standard presentation using pattern-matching rules and JSON dictionary-based ontologies. The main goal of the proposed approach is to improve the communication between healthcare parties or professionals by improving the quality of the clinical textual data and reducing its heterogeneity and ambiguity. In addition, this data quality improvement enhances the performance of machine learning downstream tasks. Our approach identifies the abbreviations, medical terms, negations, dates, and investigation values from the unstructured textual data. Then, it replaces the detected entities with their corresponding unified and normalized presentation based on pattern-matching rules that relies on the linguistic features, pattern-matching rules, and JSON dictionaries. The inductive content analysis method was followed to generate the pattern-matching rules with the help of a medical team. Its role is to validate the accuracy of the detected entities. Finally, the proposed approach was applied to a massive real-world dataset in order to evaluate its impact on the performance of various machine learning models. The results show a significant improvement in performance after preprocessing the clinical textual data using our approach.

Keywords: Deep learning · Natural Language Processing (NLP) · Computer-Aid diagnosis · Chief complaints · Text mining · Abbreviations · Medical phrases · ChatGPT 4

1 Introduction

Clinical discharge summaries are crucial documents that comprehensively summarize the patient's medical history and treatment plan. These summaries serve as a vital source of information for healthcare providers, helping them make informed decisions about

A. P. Rocha et al. (Eds.): ICAART 2023, LNAI 14546, pp. 353–369, 2024.
https://doi.org/10.1007/978-3-031-55326-4_17

patient care. However, using different medical terms, abbreviations, and ways of presenting diagnostic investigation values and dates in the discharge summary poses significant challenges for human and machine learning tasks [11].

Table 1. Example of disorders that have different synonyms.

Medical Term	Synonyms
Dyspnea	Shortness of breath, difficulty breathing
Edema	Swelling, Fluid retention
Hypercholesterolemia	High cholesterol, High blood cholesterol
Hypertension	High blood pressure, Elevated blood pressurehigh BP, HBP, HTN
Hypoglycemia	Low blood sugar, Low blood glucose
Hyperglycemia	High blood sugar, High blood glucose
Epistaxis	Nosebleed, Nasal bleeding
Conjunctivitis	Pink eye, Conjunctival inflammation
HyperPyrexia	Fever
Rhinorrhea	Runny nose

One of the significant challenges in clinical discharge summaries is using different medical terms which refer to the same disease or health condition. For Example, a sudden coronary artery blockage that causes the heart muscle to stop beating can be called a *heart attack, myocardial infarction, coronary artery disease*, and *cardiac arrest*. Table 1 shows more examples of diseases with many synonyms. This variety of medical terms can be confusing for non-medical personnel and machine learning models because they sound like they describe different things. The medical staff should know the importance of using the standard vocabulary when communicating with non-medical personnel and patients to avoid misinterpretation [16]. Moreover, machine learning algorithms usually look for patterns in the data to classify them. Using different synonyms for the same diseases can make it more difficult for machine learning models to identify these patterns [1,11,14].

Another challenge in clinical discharge summaries is the use of abbreviations. Abbreviations are commonly used in clinical documentation to save time and space. However, many abbreviations could be ambiguous, especially when the same abbreviation has different meanings in different medical specialties [21]. For Example, *MS* refers to *Multiple Sclerosis* in the Neurology department and *Mitral Stenosis* in the Cardiology and Radiology departments [8]. In addition, some abbreviations use different short terms with the same meaning. For Example, *HTN* refers to *hypertension* and *HBP* refers to *high blood pressure*, which complicates the learning of patterns' identification for machine learning models.

Furthermore, presenting diagnostic investigation values and dates in discharge summaries also presents a significant challenge. Investigation values are numerical data that provide critical information about a patient's health. However, how these values are presented in the discharge summary can vary depending on the physician. For instance, some physicians may present the values in a numeric form while others may use descriptive terms such as *normal, elevated*, or *high*. For example, a *RBC: 4.3* for a female patient is considered as a *normal Red Blood Cell count*, whereas it is low for a male patient. These numerical values might confuse the medical staff and could lead to misinterpretations.

In addition, physicians might write the date formats in various ways, as shown in Table 2. Using dates inside the discharge summary is usually related to the episode of care or some past medical history. Machine learning tasks cannot understand the context of dates presented in the discharge summary. One way to address this problem is to convert the dates in the text into periods like *two days before* or *one week before* based on the detected date and the encounter date (visit date). This workaround will make it easier for machines to understand the dates' context and identify patterns in the data.

Table 2. An example of some different date formats physicians use in clinical textual data.

Date Format	Example
dd MMM yyyy	14 Feb 2023, 23 Mar 2023
dd/MM/yyyy	14/02/2023, 23/03/2023
dd-MM-yyyy	14-02-2023, 23-02-2023
yyyy-MM-dd	2023-02-14, 2023-02-23
dd.MM.yyyy	14.02.2023, 23.02.2023
Period	before one week, after two days

This paper proposes a novel "Unified Term Presentation" (UTP) approach for processing clinical textual data that transforms them into an easily readable, less complex, and ambiguous unified presentation. UTP is based on pattern-matching rules and dictionary-based ontologies for term recognition and uses domain-specific knowledge to transform clinical texts into a unified representation. UTP applies several changes to the input unstructured textual data by transforming all dates with their different formats into periods, replacing all the abbreviations with their complete expanded forms, replacing all the diagnostic test values with categorical values based on the normal ranges for the detected diagnostic terms and unifying the negation terms. UTP improves the quality of care by ensuring that all clinicians' data are standard and use the same terminology. In addition, Machine-learning algorithms can then use this representation to generate more accurate predictions. The main contributions of this paper on clinical textual data transformation are two-fold:

- Providing a novel approach (tool) that healthcare providers can use to unify the input data from physicians and apply data preprocessing for machine learning tasks.
- Providing an empirical study on a massive real-world dataset with over 9.5M records before and after applying our approach.

The paper is organized as follows: Sect. 2 presents a general overview of the data preprocessing paradigm. Section 3 provides in-depth information on the Unified Transformation Presentation model. Section 4 shows the experimental setup and results. Section 5 discusses our findings and the approach limitations. The paper ends with a conclusion and some perspectives.

2   Related Works

Research about clinical text mining has gained more significant interest recently. The development of machine learning and deep learning techniques helped address many complicated healthcare problems, such as extracting medical terms and valued information from clinical textual data. This section provides a general overview of some existing clinical textual data preprocessing methods.

2.1   Feature Extraction

Clinical Feature Extraction (CFE) and Clinical Named Entity Recognition (CNER) are NLP methods for extracting relevant and entity information from clinical textual data. Feature extraction methods are vital in improving the performance of machine learning training tasks. It eliminates the non-relevant data from the corpus and reduces the vocabulary size. Feature extraction is a widely explored topic, and there are many tools with impressive performance, such as *SciSpacy* [18], *Med-Flair* [7], and *CT-BERT* [13]. However, the amount of noise in the data and the data diversity significantly impact the performance of the CFE and CNER methods.

2.2   Deep Learning Techniques

In recent years, NLP using Deep Learning techniques has achieved impressive results, especially with transformer-based technologies [20]. *BERT* (Bidirectional Encoder Representations from Transformers) [6] is a natural language processing model. It generates contextualized word embeddings and was trained on language modeling and the next sentence prediction tasks to generate a pre-trained model. It was published in 2018 and achieved state-of-the-art performance in NLP tasks. Currently, *BERT* pre-trained models are used for transfer learning by fine-tuning these models on specific domain datasets. *Clinical BERT* [2] and *BioBERT* [12] are two examples of transfer learning. However, Some studies showed that the non-contextualized techniques surprisingly performed better than *BERT* in industrial datasets [3].

2.3   Existing Solutions

Natural Language Processing Tools. Several popular NLP libraries are used for different purposes. *spaCy* [10] is a widely used NLP library known for its speed and accuracy. It uses statistical and machine learning techniques to perform tasks such as named entity recognition, part-of-speech tagging, and dependency parsing. *scispaCy* [18] contains set pretrained models on medical datasets that were built on top of *spaCy*. On the other hand, *coreNLP* [15] is a Java-based NLP library that provides features like tokenization, POS tagging, and named entity recognition. *NLTK* [4] is another popular NLP library based on Python and provides features like tokenization, POS tagging, named entity recognition, and sentiment analysis. These NLP tools use linguistic features and pattern-matching rules to process text. However, they may have some limitations when handling complex and nuanced language used in clinical settings and keeping up with the rapid expansion of medical terminology.

ChatGPT 4. *ChatGPT 4* is an AI chatbot developed by OpenAI. It can carry on open-ended conversations, summarize factual topics, and create stories. It is more accurate and informative than previous chatbots and has the potential to be used in a variety of applications, such as customer service, education, and entertainment. The main challenges to AI chatbots adoption are safety, trust, and cost. ChatGPT is a promising new development in AI chatbots, but these challenges must be addressed before it can be used to preprocess clinical textual data.

Rule-Based Approach. Authors in [8] provided a cleansing approach called *EMTE* that removes the irrelevant data from the clinical textual data using rule-based pattern rules. Their approach replaces the abbreviations with their expanded form and detects negations and medical terms. Then, they concatenate the tokens in the detected medical term using underscores. As a result, they were able to reduce the vocabulary size, and they achieved an F1-score of 69.68%. However, their approach have some limitations. For example, their approach did not tackle the different medical terms that have same meaning, which can be reduced more. Also, concatenating medical terms does not effectively reduce the vocabulary size. For example, as shown in Fig. 1, there are nine different possible generated vocabularies for two medical terms (*high blood pressure*, *low blood pressure*), where it could be only four vocabularies (*high*, *low*,*pressure*, and *blood*) if the medical term concatenation was not used.

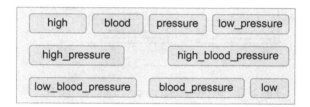

Fig. 1. An example of the possible generated vocabularies from two medical terms (*high blood pressure* and *low blood pressure*) using *EMTE*.

3   Model

We aim to provide a tool that removes confusion and prevents misinterpretation by non-specialized physicians (such as medical staff, technicians, and patients) when reading clinical textual documents. This confusion can arise due to the extensive use of abbreviations by physicians from different specialties, complex medical terms that might be unfamiliar to other medical staff, and investigation values embedded with the clinical textual data. We propose a tool called *UTP* (Unified Term Presentation) that transforms complex clinical textual data into more readable and easy-to-understand medical textual data. *UTP* detects and converts the diagnostic values into categorical ranges based on the requested investigation and the patient demographical data. The categorical values contain (below range, within normal range, above range, negative, and positive).

Also, *UTP* expands the detected abbreviations into their full form based on the physician's specialty. Moreover, *UTP* transforms complex medical terms into more general and readable terms by other nonspecialized individuals. In addition, *UTP* can transform the detected dates in the clinical textual data into a period presentation based on the visit date information, reducing the complexity of the machine-learning tasks.

Figure 2 shows the architecture of the *UTP* tool that consists of four processing components: *Date to Period*, *Investigation values*, *Abbreviations*, and *Medical Terms*. All these components are customized pipes added to the *spaCy* [10] tool. They override the existing *NER*(Named Entity Recognition) of *spaCy*. The *UTP* tool employs the existing features in *spaCy* tool, like the linguistic features (*POS,TAG*, and *DEP*) and the pattern-matching rules engine in both detection and transformation processes.

This section presents in detail every feature of UTP and their importance for human and machine-learning readability and their impact on vocabulary size reduction while mitigating the term-learning confusion (e.g. using one unified term *high blood pressure* instead of multiple different terms like *hypertension*, *high blood pressure*, and *HTN*).

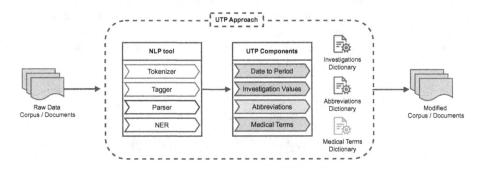

Fig. 2. The preprocessing proposed approach *UTP*.

3.1 Date to Period Transformation

Physicians extensively use dates in their medical documents to explain the chronological development of the patient's care during admissions. It is also very important in outpatient departments, especially in the obstetrics and gynecology department where the "last menstrual period" *LMP* and "estimated due date" *EDD* play important roles during a patient's pregnancy and maternity. However, having dates without any reference in the clinical textual data is confusing for machine learning tasks, especially when no information is provided on the patient's visit date. Also, the patient's visit date is confidential and should not be shared. Therefore, transforming the dates found in clinical textual data into a period presentation is essential since it preserves patient confidentiality and helps reduce vocabulary size and confusion for the training tasks.

UTP detects different date styles found in the corpus and transforms the dates into periods compared to the document's effective date. For example, a patient visited the obstetrics and gynecology department on the 19th of June 2022, and the physician wrote the following chief complaint (LMP: 01 Jun 2022, EDD: 08/03/2023). *UTP* converts this data into (LMP: before 2 weeks and 5 days, EDD: after 37 weeks and 3 days) since the obstetrics and gynecology department physicians prefer to track the pregnancy in weeks. Also, *UTP* can present the period in months like (EDD: 8 months, two weeks and 3 days).

3.2 Abbreviations and Investigation Values Transformation

The abbreviations used in clinical textual data can be either medical disorders (*ADD*, which stands for Attention deficit disorder), procedures (*SVD*, which stands for Spontaneous vaginal delivery), investigation results (*Hbg: 11.9*, *Hbg* stands for Hemoglobin), and general abbreviations (*hx*, which stands fro History of, *rx*, which stands for prescription) that have no restrictions for usage unlike other types.

Investigation Values. Investigation value is a combination of an abbreviation with a value. The abbreviation represents a laboratory or imaging test, and the value is the test result. Every test has a normal range that helps the physicians diagnose if the patient's test result is outside this normal range. The normal ranges are very critical since they strictly depend on the machines used in the given hospital. Every machine has its configuration, and every test has a different normal range based on the patient demographical data and the used standard units of measure. For example, normal range values of the "High-sensitive cardiac troponin (hs-cTn)" laboratory test should be less than 14 ng/ml or 4000 pg/ml. So, the value *hs-cTn: 150* is considered very high if the unit of measure is "ng/ml," and it is normal if the ussed unit of measure in the machine was "pg/ml".

UTP uses a JSON-based dictionary containing all the hospital's laboratory and imaging tests. Every entry contains the following information (abbreviation, fully expanded form, list of normal ranges based on the age restriction and gender restriction). *UTP* automatically builds pattern-matching rules using *SpaCy* to detect the investigation abbreviations and the values that come after these abbreviations. Then, based on the normal range of the detected investigation, *UTP* transforms the abbreviation into its expanded form and the value into a categorical value, leading to a unified and readable format. For example, *UTP* transforms *"Hbg: 11.9"* into *"hemoglobin below range"* for a male sample and into *"hemoglobin within normal range"* for a female sample.

Abbreviations Transformation. Working with the disorders and procedural abbreviations is ambiguous since the same abbreviation might have different meanings in different specialties. *UTP* uses a JSON-based dictionary that contains a list of abbreviations used in the considered hospital with the following information structure (abbreviation, fully expanded form, list of specialties). The list of specialties can be empty, which means the given abbreviation can be used in all departments without any confusion. *UTP* transforms the abbreviations into their expanded form by eliminating all abbreviations unrelated to the given sample's specialty, which mitigates the abbreviation ambiguity. For example, *UTP* transforms *"MS"* into *"multiple sclerosis"* for a sample from the neurology department and into *"mitral stenosis"* for a sample from the cardiology specialty.

3.3 Medical Terms Transformation

Physicians extensively use medical disorders' scientific names, making it difficult to understand by nonspecialized individuals like para-medical, nurses, and patients. *UTP* relies on both linguistic features and pattern-matching rules using the *SpaCy* tool to detect the medical terms loaded from a JSON-based dictionary that stores medical terms with their synonyms and the preferred term to be used. The JSON-based dictionary was built by extracting the medical terms with their synonyms from the *snomed-CT* database, then validated by a medical team to ensure its accuracy and properly identify the preferred term to be used.

Figure 3 shows how our approach *UTP* detects the the entities from a clinical textual data. The image shows the raw data, the detected entities, and the transformation results. There are different types of detected entities: *ABBR* stands for *Abbreviations*, *LAB_VALUE* stands for *Investigation values*, *MEDICAL* stands for *Medical Terms*, *PERIOD* stands for the *DATES*, and *NEG* stands for *NEGATIONS*. UTP were able to transform the detected entities into more readable clinical textual data. For example, the detected abbreviation *ga* was correctly transformed into *gestational age* depending on the specialty of the sample. the medical term *dysuria* was transformed into *painful urination*, which is more readable by nonspecialized individuals. Also, *UTP* was able to detect the investigation values *Hbg 12* and *wbc 14* correctly as *LAB_VALUE* entities. Then, *UTP* correctly transformed them based on the gender of the patient into *hemoglobin normal range* since the range for adult females is between 12 and 14. Moreover, the *wbc 14* was correctly transformed into *white blood cell count above range* since the range for adult females is between 4 and 11. Furthermore, *UTP* transformed the dates based on the encounter date into the period as depicted in Fig. 3.

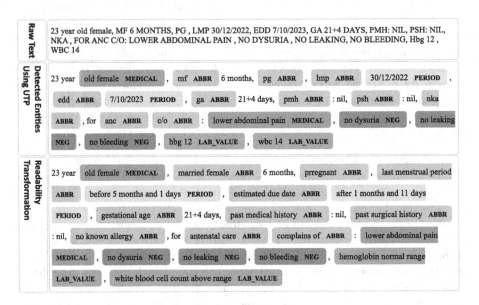

Fig. 3. An example from Obstetrics & Gynecology department of how the *UTP* tool detects and transform a clinical textual data into more readable clinical textual data.

4   Experiments and Results

The proposed approach improves the readability of clinical textual data by transforming and converting the terms that are potentially causing conflicts either when communicating between professionals in healthcare institutes or when working on machine learning tasks. To evaluate the performance of this approach, several experiments were conducted to solve a multilabel classification problem for ICD-10 prediction on clinical textual data preprocessed by *UTP*. This section represents the experimental setup with their results.

4.1   Experiment Setup

ICD-10 prediction is a well-known multilabel classification problem where the input data are the textual data (chief complaints, history of present illness, discharge summaries), and the ICD-10 codes are the labels. ICD-10 codes are hierarchical alphanumeric codes [5,17,19]. The number of ICD-10 codes used by hospitals differs depending on the available covered specialties. For example, in dental clinics, physicians mainly use codes in the range [K00–K14] that cover teeth and jaw problems. While in the Obstetrics & Gynecology department, the physicians mainly use the codes that start with *O* that cover delivery-related cases and *Z34*, Z35** that cover pregnancy-related cases. Also, there are some age and gender restrictions in the ICD-10 codes. For example, all codes that start with *P* are allowed only for newborn cases.

4.2   Medical Dataset

The dataset, used in the experiments, was retrieved from a private Saudi hospital and consists of over 9.6 M records with over 3,100 ICD-10 codes. The dataset contained data from 24 different specialties. Figure 4 shows the different specialties with their relative proportions. Data from the Internal medicine department makes up to 23.7% of the total data samples while data from Obstetrics & Gynecology department makes up to 13.2% which reflects how much the data is imbalanced. It is worth mentioning that the data collected from the hospital was anonymized.

4.3   JSON Dictionaries

Abbreviation Dictionary. In most hospitals, the medical staff is required to follow standards and regulations when documenting patients' information. One such standard is to avoid using ambiguous abbreviations, such as *LFT* that can stands for either *Lung Function Test* or *Liver Function Test* [9]. To avoid confustion, hospitals issue an internal standard list of allowed common and specialty specific abbreviations. It is worth noting that some abbreviations might have different meanings in different hospitals or specialties and departments depending on the defined list of standard abbreviations and conventions. Therefore, it is important to transform the abbreviations into their expanded form when communicating with other institutes, such as Healthcare Isurance Companies. For the sake of the experiment, we built the abbreviation JSON dictionary while taking into consideration the internal policy of the hospital regarding the allowed abbreviation usage. The structure of the dictionary is similar to the one used in [8].

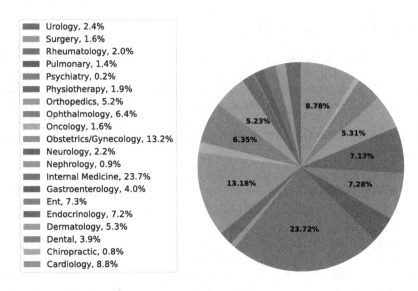

Urology, 2.4%
Surgery, 1.6%
Rheumatology, 2.0%
Pulmonary, 1.4%
Psychiatry, 0.2%
Physiotherapy, 1.9%
Orthopedics, 5.2%
Ophthalmology, 6.4%
Oncology, 1.6%
Obstetrics/Gynecology, 13.2%
Neurology, 2.2%
Nephrology, 0.9%
Internal Medicine, 23.7%
Gastroenterology, 4.0%
Ent, 7.3%
Endocrinology, 7.2%
Dermatology, 5.3%
Dental, 3.9%
Chiropractic, 0.8%
Cardiology, 8.8%

Fig. 4. The chart shows the relative proportion of the 24 specialties.

Diagnostic Values. Diagnostic tests help physicians to diagnose a patient's condition or monitor the progression of the disease. The test results help physicians to manage the patient's medical problems, if any. The test results are either numerical values (measurements) or categorical (findings). For example, blood tests can measure the amount, size, and concentration of different cells and substances in the blood. Most of these laboratory tests are reported with numerical values compared to standard range values (also known as normal range values or reference values). Moreover, these standard values setups directly depends of the used machine in the laboratory or radiology department.

On the other hand, pregnancy tests detect the presence of the hormone (human chorionic gonadotropin (hCG)) in women's urine or blood. The result of such a test is either positive (indicating pregnancy) or negative (indicating no pregnancy). We focused on tests that have numerical values since these values might vary from one patient to another depending on the gender and age of the patient and other conditions. The standard normal values for the diagnostic tests were retrieved from the hospital's database and were stored in a JSON-based dictionary.

Medical Terms Synonyms. A custom *medical_term_detector* was built using the spaCy python library and the linguistic features (DEP, POS, TAG) that detect and annotate the possible medical terms. Then, the unique discovered medical terms were extracted and added to a new corpus that contains only medical terms. Afterwards, the available *snomedct* database from the UMLS website was used to extract all the available synonyms for each term in the new corpus. Then, the inductive content analysis method was followed to remove all found words from the generated corpus of unique medical terms. The resulting medical terms are those that contain typos, those that have no synonyms, and those that have synonyms not listed in the *snomedct* database. With the help of a medical team, a total of 23,671 medical terms were checked and validated.

4.4   Machine Learning Task

The *Clinical_BERT* and *BioBERT* pretrained models were used as a baseline to compare the performance of the ICD-10 prediction classification task before preprocessing the clinical textual data using our approach *UTP* and after. The experiments setup was using *Clinical_BERT* and *BioBERT* as an embedding layer, in addition to a classifier layer. Then both models were fine-tuned using two corpora (Raw Data corpus, Data processed corpus using *UTP*).

Table 4 shows the hyperparameters used in the experiments. Moreover, the data was split into a training dataset with 70% of the data, a validation dataset with 10%, and a testing dataset with 20%. All experiments were run on *Colab Pro+* from Google. The data was processed and tokenized locally using the hospital servers, and the training tasks were done on *Colab Pro+* using the numerical data and labels. The data was converted from text to numerical values using *BERTTokenizer*. Moreover, *Colab Pro+* has a maximum of 24 h execution time allowed. This limitation was overcomed using a 12-folds cross-validation approach to avoid repeating the whole experiment.

In assessing the efficacy of the Unified Term Presentation (UTP) method, Table 3 offers crucial insights by showcasing a substantial reduction in vocabulary complexity. Before UTP implementation, the corpus comprised 553,712 unique terms, which, after applying UTP's normalization techniques, including date conversions, categorization of diagnostic values, abbreviation expansions, and medical term standardization, was significantly reduced to 310,514 terms. This reduction underscores UTP's role in enhancing data readability and simplification, which is essential for improving machine learning models' interpretability and performance in clinical applications.

Table 3. The steps of the UTP approach on a corpus which contains over 9.5M samples with 553,712 unique words.

Corpus	Unique Words	Change	Total Change
Raw Data	553,712	-	-
Dates to period	482,124	−12.93%	−12.93%
Diagnostic values to categorical	434,002	−9.98%	−21.62%
Abbreviations to expanded form	359,891	−17.08%	−35.00%
Medical terms normalization	310,514	−13.72%	−43.92%

Table 4. *Clinical_BERT* and *BioBERT* models hyperparameters.

Learning Rate	2e-5
Batch Size	32
Epsilon	1e−8
K-fold	12
Optimizer	Adam
Loss function	Binary cross entropy

Table 5. The f1-micro scores when applying the various individual transformations on data from four different departments.

F1-Micro scores						
Department	Raw Data	Date	Abbreviation	Investigation Values	Medical Terms	UTP
Obstetrics & Gyneocology	85.36%	89.10%	85.98%	86.15%	87.01%	91.05%
Pediatrics	81.78%	83.39%	82.24%	82.44%	83.33%	84.74%
Emergency Room	39.74%	39.85%	40.49%	40.84%	40.98%	41.12%
Internal Medicine	47.21%	47.22%	48.13%	48.21%	48.57%	48.68%
F1-Micro gain score using gain% = (After - Before)/Before						
Department	Raw Data	Date	Abbreviation	Investigation Values	Medical Terms	UTP
Obstetrics & Gyneocology	–	4.38%	0.73%	0.93%	1.93%	6.67%
Pediatrics	–	1.97%	0.56%	0.81%	1.90%	3.62%
Emergency Room	–	0.28%	1.89%	2.77%	3.12%	3.47%
Internal Medicine	–	0.02%	1.95%	2.12%	2.88%	3.11%

In order to know the contribution of every individual transformation (dates, investigations, abbreviations, and medical terms) of *UTP*, several experiments were conducted to measure the f1-micro of the raw data compared to an individual transformation.

Table 5 shows the contributions made by individual transformation on four different specialties datasets using f1-micro score performance value and the gain value. The results show that the *Date* transformation improved the f1-micro score by *4.38%* and *1.79%* on data from the *"Obstetrics & Gynecology"* and *"Pediatrics"* departments, respectively. In contrast, the contribution of the *Date* transformation was low on data from the *"Emergency Room"* and *"Internal Medicine"* departments. The reason behind the low contribution is due to the fact that dates are not expensively used in these departments compared to the *"Obstetrics & Gynecology"* and *"Pediatrics"* departments.

Table 6 presents the results of the experiments of supervised learning on the multilabel classification problem using a large real-world dataset. The conducted experiments used two different BERT models *Clinical BERT* and *BIO BERT*. The results of the ICD-10 predictions from clinical textual data results are shown for the *Training*, *Validation*, and *Testing* datasets. The columns represents the recall, and F1-score (micro and weighted) evaluation metrics. The experiments that used the corpus modified by *UTP* outperformed the results of the raw data corpus for all the considered metrics. For example, the *UTP+Bio BERT* experiment gave *micro-F1* score around *74.64 ± 2.28 e−03* for the for from the test dataset compared to *68.11 ± 2.17 e−03* achieved by *Bio BERT*. Similarly, the *UTP+ Clinical BERT* achieved a *micro-F1* score around *73.25 ± 2.11 e−03* compared to the *67.16 ± 2.18 e−03* score achieved by *Clinical BERT*.

4.5 Comparison with ChatGPT 4 Tool

In this subsection, the *UTP* approach, built using pattern-matching rules and JSON-based dictionaries, is compared to *ChatGPT 4* that can do the same work using machine

Table 6. The result of two well-known specific domain BERT models on the large real-world dataset before and after applying *UTP*.

Training Results			
Experiments	Recall	micro-F1	weighted-F1
Clinical BERT	65.51 $\pm$ 8.66 $e-03$	76.89 $\pm$ 7.92 $e-03$	73.14 $\pm$ 9.18 $e-03$
Bio BERT	65.21 $\pm$ 8.31 $e-03$	76.47 $\pm$ 8.06 $e-03$	73.05 $\pm$ 8.03 $e-03$
UTP + Clinical BERT	72.88 $\pm$ 6.57 $e-03$	84.03 $\pm$ 6.18 $e-03$	84.94 $\pm$ 7.13 $e-03$
UTP + Bio BERT	72.19 $\pm$ 6.12 $e-03$	83.75 $\pm$ 5.81 $e-03$	84.31 $\pm$ 6.52 $e-03$
Validation Results			
Experiments	Recall	micro-F1	weighted-F1
Clinical BERT	58.64 $\pm$ 6.81 $e-03$	67.92 $\pm$ 7.32 $e-03$	65.20 $\pm$ 6.19 $e-03$
Bio BERT	59.13 $\pm$ 6.07 $e-03$	68.38 $\pm$ 6.82 $e-03$	65.71 $\pm$ 6.64 $e-03$
UTP + Clinical BERT	66.87 $\pm$ 5.78 $e-03$	73.77 $\pm$ 5.98 $e-03$	71.01 $\pm$ 5.01 $e-03$
UTP + Bio BERT	67.33 $\pm$ 5.06 $e-03$	74.32 $\pm$ 5.79 $e-03$	71.33 $\pm$ 5.77 $e-03$
Testing Results			
Experiments	Recall	micro-F1	weighted-F1
Clinical BERT	58.07 $\pm$ 3.43 $e-03$	67.16 $\pm$ 2.18 $e-03$	65.95 $\pm$ 2.81 $e-03$
Bio BERT	59.97 $\pm$ 3.31 $e-03$	68.11 $\pm$ 2.17 $e-03$	65.43 $\pm$ 2.80 $e-03$
UTP+ Clinical BERT	66.08 $\pm$ 2.21 $e-03$	73.25 $\pm$ 2.11 $e-03$	71.09 $\pm$ 2.09 $e-03$
UTP+ Bio BERT	67.83 $\pm$ 2.88 $e-03$	74.64 $\pm$ 2.28 $e-03$	72.01 $\pm$ 2.20 $e-03$

Table 7. Comparison between *UTP* and *ChatGPT 4* while preprocessing 5,000 chief complaints form the Obstetrics & Gynecology department.

Experiments	Accuracy	Recall	Micro-F1	Weighted-F1
Raw	91.43%	82.84%	90.56%	88.95%
UTP	92.16%	83.13%	91.05%	89.27%
ChatGPT	92.29%	83.75%	91.32%	89.70%

learning techniques. The comparison with *ChatGPT 4* was conducted on a dataset consisting of 5000 samples with 7 ICD-10 codes labels from the *"Obstetrics & Gynecology"* department. This department was chosen because its physicians frequently use dates, investigation values, abbreviations, and medical terms in their clinical data. In order to preserve the patient's confidential medical data while using *ChatGPT 4*, all the sensitive information was removed from the dataset. The updated visit date was added to the textual data with a tag called *"reference_date"*. Then, the *ChatGPT 4* API was used to prompt the following questions : *"Change the dates found in the text into periods, change the investigation values into categorical values as normal, below range, and above range. Finally, convert the complex medical terms into a more readable format that patients can easily read"*. *ChatGPT 4* results were very impressive.

It converted most of the samples on the first try. Also, it included additional sentences to better explain the chief complaints. However, some issues were detected during the experiment that are discussed in the next section.

Table 7 compares the results obtained while using *ClinicalBERT* on *Raw Data* (without any modification on the clinical textual data), preprocessed data using *UTP* and preprocessed data using *ChatGPT 4*. The results show that *ChatGPT 4* gives slightly better results than *UTP*. *ChatGPT 4* did not only replace the terms in the clinical textual data, but also rephrased the sentences with different words. Sentence rephrasing is an impressive capabilities that *ChatGPT 4* can accomplish. However, in some samples, the *ChatGPT 4* included bias and irrelevant information to the patient's case, which gives nonrealistic diagnosis that might affect the patient's care if this tool was used in production.

5 Discussion

The *UTP* tool transforms medical textual data into more readable data by humans and machine learning algorithms. Moreover, unlike the pre-trained models, *UTP* does not require retraining or additional resources (Memory and GPU/TPU). Retraining the deep learning models is a major challenge in real-world healthcare applications since it requires a large number of samples and additional resources. This section discusses the results of the experiments using BERT pre-trained models on a huge dataset. The experiments were run on raw data before any transformation and on preprocessed data using *UTP*.

5.1 Advantages

In general speaking, *UTP* transformed the information from a complex presentation into more easy-to-understand and less confusing for human and machine learning models. Moreover, *UTP* succeeded in reducing the vocabulary size of the corpus and unified the medical terms, which is very helpful for machine learning. For example, replacing all the synonyms of *"high blood pressure"* with *"hypertension"* reduces the complexity of the training of the deep neural network by reducing the vocabulary size. Furthermore, *UTP* is flexible and maintainable because it is easy to add and update the JSON files to include new terms or abbreviations definitions. However, other machine learning techniques require obtaining samples and retraining the model if machine learning approaches were implemented.

5.2 Limitations

During the experiments, we mainly focused on the clinical textual data (discharge summaries and chief complaints) to predict the ICD-10 codes. However, in some specialties, physicians rely on the ICD-10 codes more than the documentation. For example, traumatic cases in the emergency room require including information on when, where, and how to describe the cause of trauma, the activity, and the location. Physicians include all this information by selecting the related ICD-10 codes without having a detailed medical documentation, leading to low prediction performance as shown in Table 5. On the other hand, when a department uses a wide range of ICD-10 codes, it decreases the prediction performance, such as in the Internal Medicine department. Also, diseases like diabetes and hypertension can be confusing since they might appear together. The first as the primary diagnosis and the second as the secondary one and vice versa, leading to confusion in training and hence a low performance.

5.3 ChatGPT 4 Limitations

Although *ChatGPT 4*, which uses a machine-learning approach, gives impressive results. However, an additional and time-consuming work on the dataset was required to be able to send it to *ChatGPT 4*. Moreover, *ChatGPT 4* was trained on public datasets. Therefore, it is exposed to a wider range of biases and inaccuracies than a private pre-trained model has. During the experiment, it was detected that in some samples, non-sensical and nonrelevant sentences were generated by *ChatGPT 4*. Furthermore, the data had to be manually cleaned and the dates obfuscated before using the APIs, which is time-consuming and not applicable to real-world applications in healthcare.

6   Conclusion

In this paper, we proposed a new tool called *UTP* that transforms the clinical textual data into more readable and easy-to-understand for human and machine learning tasks. *UTP* uses JSON-based dictionaries and linguistic features to build pattern-matching rules for their flexibility and maintainability. *UTP* unifies medical terms, replaces investigation values with categorical values, converts abbreviations into expanded forms, and transforms dates into periods. Experiments showed the effectiveness of *UTP* on vocabulary reduction without losing information. Also, we demonstrated its positive impact on the performance of machine learning models (micro-F1 reached 74.64% in testing results). In addition, *UTP* was compared to the most recent machine learning tools that can do the same tasks *ChatGPT 4*. As a result of this study, the *UTP* tool is now integrated with the Saudi *"Specialized Medical Center"* hospital systems. Several recommendations were raised to improve the medical documentations, especially the traumatic cases in the emergency service. In future work, we aim to work on improving the accuracy of the ICD-10 prediction by exploring more vital input features. We would also like to investigate the relationships among the ICD-10 labels themselves to improve the ICD-10 predictions. We believe that using a graph-based classifiers which takes into consideration the labels' relationships can improve furthermore the accuracy of the training.

References

1. Abrahamsson, E., Forni, T., Skeppstedt, M., Kvist, M.: Medical text simplification using synonym replacement: adapting assessment of word difficulty to a compounding language (2014). https://doi.org/10.3115/v1/w14-1207

2. Alsentzer, E., et al.: Publicly available clinical Bert embeddings (2019). https://doi.org/10. 48550/ARXIV.1904.03323, https://arxiv.org/abs/1904.03323
3. Arora, S., May, A., Zhang, J., Ré, C.: Contextual embeddings: when are they worth it? (2020). https://doi.org/10.18653/v1/2020.acl-main.236, http://dx.doi.org/10.18653/v1/2020. acl-main.236
4. Bird, S., Klein, E., Loper, E.: Natural language processing with Python: analyzing text with the natural language toolkit. "O'Reilly Media, Inc." (2009)
5. Chen, P.F., et al.: Automatic ICD-10 coding and training system: deep neural network based on supervised learning (2021). https://doi.org/10.2196/23230
6. Devlin, J., Chang, M.W., Lee, K., Toutanova, K.: Bert: pre-training of deep bidirec- tional transformers for language understanding (2018). https://doi.org/10.48550/ARXIV. 1810.04805, https://arxiv.org/abs/1810.04805
7. ElDin, H.G., AbdulRazek, M., Abdelshafi, M., Sahlol, A.T.: Med-flair: medical named entity recognition for diseases and medications based on flair embedding. Proc. Comput. Sci. **189**, 67–75 (2021). https://doi.org/10.1016/j.procs.2021.05.078, https://www.sciencedirect.com/ science/article/pii/S1877050921011753. aI in Computational Linguistics
8. Hatoum, M., Charr, J.C., Guyeux, C., Laiymani, D., Ghaddar, A.: EMTE: an enhanced medical terms extractor using pattern matching rules (2023). https://doi.org/10.5220/ 0011717300003393
9. Holper, S., Barmanray, R., Colman, B., Yates, C.J., Liew, D., Smallwood, D.: Ambiguous medical abbreviation study: challenges and opportunities (2020). https://doi.org/10.1111/ imj.14442, http://dx.doi.org/10.1111/imj.14442
10. Honnibal, M., Montani, I., Van Landeghem, S., Boyd, A.: spaCy: industrial-strength natural language processing in python (2020)
11. Leaman, R., Khare, R., Lu, Z.: Challenges in clinical natural language processing for automated disorder normalization (2015). https://doi.org/10.1016/j.jbi.2015.07.010, http:// dx.doi.org/10.1016/j.jbi.2015.07.010
12. Lee, J., et al.: Biobert: a pre-trained biomedical language representation model for biomedi- cal text mining (2019). https://doi.org/10.48550/ARXIV.1901.08746
13. Liu, X., Hersch, G.L., Khalil, I., Devarakonda, M.: Clinical trial information extraction with Bert (2021). https://doi.org/10.48550/ARXIV.2110.10027
14. Maciejewski, M.L., Weaver, E.M., Hebert, P.L.: Synonyms in health services research methodology (2010). https://doi.org/10.1177/1077558710372809, http://dx.doi.org/10.1177/ 1077558710372809
15. Manning, C.D., Surdeanu, M., Bauer, J., Finkel, J., Bethard, S.J., McClosky, D.: The Stanford CoreNLP natural language processing toolkit. In: Association for Computational Linguistics (ACL) System Demonstrations, pp. 55–60 (2014)
16. Martin, A.K., Green, T.L., McCarthy, A.L., Sowa, P.M., Laakso, E.L.: Healthcare teams: terminology, confusion, and ramifications (2022). https://doi.org/10.2147/jmdh.s342197
17. Moons, E., Khanna, A., Akkasi, A., Moens, M.F.: A comparison of deep learning methods for ICD coding of clinical records (2020). https://doi.org/10.3390/app10155262, http://dx. doi.org/10.3390/app10155262
18. Neumann, M., King, D., Beltagy, I., Ammar, W.: Scispacy: fast and robust models for biomedical natural language processing (2019). https://doi.org/10.48550/ARXIV.1902. 07669, https://arxiv.org/abs/1902.07669

19. Sammani, A., et al.: Automatic multilabel detection of icd10 codes in Dutch cardiology discharge letters using neural networks (2021). https://doi.org/10.1038/s41746-021-00404-9
20. Singh, S., Mahmood, A.: The NLP cookbook: Modern recipes for transformer based deep learning architectures (2021). https://doi.org/10.1109/access.2021.3077350, http://dx.doi.org/10.1109/ACCESS.2021.3077350
21. Vermeir, P., et al.: Communication in healthcare: a narrative review of the literature and practical recommendations (2015). https://doi.org/10.1111/ijcp.12686, http://dx.doi.org/10.1111/ijcp.12686

Fault Tolerant Robust Adaptive Workload Orchestration in Pure Edge Computing

Zahra Safavifar[1] , Charafeddine Mechalikh[2(✉)] , and Fatemeh Golpayegani[1(✉)]

[1] School of Computer Science, University College Dublin, Dublin, Ireland
zahra.safavifar@ucdconnect.ie, fatemeh.golpayegani@ucd.ie
[2] New Technologies of Information and Telecommunication,
University Kasdi Merbah, Ouargla, Algeria
charafeddine.mechalikh@gmail.com

Abstract. Pure Edge Computing (PEC) emerges as a solution to meet the increasing demand for time-sensitive and data-driven applications by bringing cloud applications and services closer to end users. Nevertheless, the mobile nature of edge devices and their inherent computing limitations pose several challenges in supporting urgent and computationally intensive tasks. Tasks become worthless and can lead to serious safety issues if they fail to meet the deadline. Furthermore, device crashes can trigger significant system failures. Hence, it is crucial for such systems to handle failures and be fault tolerant to maximise the completion of latency-sensitive tasks in accordance with available resources.

This paper proposes a Fault-Tolerant Robust Adaptive Workload Orchestration (FTR-AdWOrch) that handles uncertainties caused by resource failures in dynamic environments. Resource prioritization and a reallocation mechanisms are designed to minimize the number of missed deadlines for task completion and data loss. We propose a fault-tolerant orchestrator that utilises a backup node to prevent any potential orchestrator node failure, which plays a vital role in workload management and the system performance. The simulation results show that FTR-AdWOrch can minimize missed deadlines of urgent tasks while minimizing the data loss of lower priority tasks regardless of dynamic conditions.

Keywords: Workload orchestration · Reinforcement learning · Pure edge computing · Adaptive model · Robust model · Fault tolerant · Dynamic environment

1 Introduction

The exponential growth of active Internet of Things (IoT) devices and their applications produces vast data at the network edge. According to "Data Age" projections, an astounding 175 zettabytes of data will be generated annually by 2025, with 30% requiring real-time processing. The availability and popularity of these devices have given rise to a wide range of critical IoT applications, including intelligent transport systems [6],

---

Supported by Science Foundation Ireland.

A. P. Rocha et al. (Eds.): ICAART 2023, LNAI 14546, pp. 370–386, 2024.
https://doi.org/10.1007/978-3-031-55326-4_18

emergency systems [7], and critical infrastructure monitoring [12]. Using cloud computing for IoT data and application processing involves some challenges such as high latency, unreliable connection, and lack of real-time response. To address these limitations, Edge Computing has emerged to bring cloud computing close to the end user by providing small-scale data centers at the edge of the network. However, increasing the number of such data centers by increasing the data produced at the edge is not a solution, and we need to shift toward Pure Edge Computing (PEC) to minimize the use of high-capacity servers and harness currently available resources at the edge devices.

IoT applications can involve private data, latency sensitivity tasks, or generate large amounts of data with fast processing requirements. Failure to meet critical deadlines can result in fatalities and substantial losses [3,9,18]. This highlights the critical role of resource management and scheduling in edge computing, where incoming requests with various Service Level Agreements (SLA) and deadlines should be accommodated by resource-constraint devices. Existing literature proposes various approaches to accommodate tasks with different degrees of time sensitivity in Edge Computing. However, some of these approaches oversimplify the problem by neglecting certain dynamic aspects of the real-world environment. These oversimplifications include assuming homogeneity among computing nodes and tasks [3,17], disregarding the impact of bandwidth fluctuations on delay [3,5,17], and neglecting mobility of devices [1,3,5,11,17,20].

Fault tolerance is another concern in distributed platforms encompassing mission-critical IoT applications, particularly when the intended edge node encounters a functional failure. Since IoT applications usually are real-time, not managing such failures can have disastrous consequences. Furthermore, when an application's components are deployed on a single node, the overall service reliability is at a notable risk. Consequently, it becomes imperative to introduce a mechanism that effectively addresses the vulnerabilities associated with a single point of failure. This mechanism is essential to enhance the reliability of the application, ensuring its resilience against potential service failures. Therefore, Several studies have addressed fault tolerance in different aspects of edge and cloud computing, including fault-tolerant task scheduling mechanism [21], a fault-tolerant data offloading technique [8] and fault tolerant for a critical component failure [2].

A wide range of IoT applications are currently running on edge computing platforms, among which healthcare applications have captured the attention of both researchers and industry professionals. Edge computing is being employed to improve healthcare services. The data on these platforms pertains to human health and safety, making it highly sensitive to latency and changes in network dynamics such as available bandwidth [19] By harnessing nearby edge devices as a computational resource, Pure Edge Computing enables the provision of low-latency services, making it an ideal option for deploying healthcare platforms.

In this paper, we considered workload orchestration in the healthcare platforms of a nursing home, where the health signals of elderly people with various health conditions are monitored and analyzed. The platform is facilitated by Pure Edge Computing, where an array of heterogeneous edge devices such as smartphones, laptops, PCs, wearables, and sensors, along with a private Edge server are in the area. The varying urgency and priority of the data generated by these devices result in the creation of Hard-Real-Time (HRT) tasks such as vital sign monitoring and Soft-Real-Time (SRT) tasks such as camera data management. Given the unpredictable and dynamic nature of the PEC environment, a robust model is necessary to handle workload orchestration, especially in emergency situations. This includes scenarios where few devices are available in the environment or when there is a high workload request, or when the orchestrator node fails.

This paper is an extension of our previous works [15,16]. A Reinforcement Learning (RL)- based Adaptive Workload Orchestration (AdWOrch) was proposed, which uses Q-learning to adapt to the environment dynamics. This paper proposes an extension for AdWOrch to achieve a Fault Tolerant Robust Adaptive Workload Orchestration (FTR-AdWOrch) that can operate in various unpredictable and dynamic environments in the PEC. The objective is to prevent entire system failure along with minimizing the missing deadline of SRT tasks while meeting almost all HRT tasks and minimizing data loss of NRT tasks, even in emergency situations such as sparse or crowded areas. This is achieved by introducing a backup orchestrator, task priority definition, and reallocation mechanisms. Our contributions to this paper are as follows:

– Designing a fault tolerance central orchestrator.
– Reshaping the reward function to minimize the delay for HRT and SRT tasks.
– Developing a resource reallocation mechanism to prevent task failure when there are no accessible resources or the resource is unable to execute the assigned task.
– A prioritization mechanism for different tasks.

The remainder of this paper is organized as follows. The literature is reviewed in Sect. 2. An overview of PEC and Real-Time systems and AdWOrch is presented in Sect. 3. The problem and environment characteristics are described in Sect. 4. Workload orchestration using the FTR-AdWOrch model is presented in Sect. 5. Section 6 evaluates the proposed model through extensive simulations. In Sect. 7, the paper is concluded by giving an outline of the future directions of this work.

2   Related Work

Edge computing is a powerful driver for IoT applications, but its limited resources available at edge devices/servers pose challenges. Moreover, these applications requested tasks at different levels of urgency, and prioritizing tasks imposes further challenges to task scheduling problems. Researchers have developed various task-scheduling methods, both preemptive and non-preemptive, to efficiently schedule various tasks based on their characteristics and requirements [11].

Dai et al. [3] has developed the Best-Fit Replacement algorithm for edge servers to prioritize time-sensitive tasks for autonomous vehicles based on urgency level. Tasks are categorized into three levels of urgency based on vehicle speed, weather, number of passengers, and road section. Sharif et al. [17], presented a priority-based resource allocation algorithm where tasks are classified into two priority levels (normal and priority tasks). the authors aimed to reduce response time and enhance resource utilization.

A Game Theory based algorithm for computation offloading in Multi-access Edge Computing (MEC) is proposed in [20]. It predicts server waiting time based on its task queue and accordingly arranges task processing time, sequence, and frequency. Lee and Park [11] presented a Software-Defined Networking (SDN)-based scheduling algorithm to reduce the transmission delay of emergency data in MEC environments. It assumes two predefined priority levels: periodic data, and emergency data. Fadahunsi et al. [5] presented a two-stage scheduling strategy that matches the real-time tasks to a set of edge computing resources. Their model considers three types of tasks: hard real-time, soft real-time (or interactive), and batch tasks. The two-stage architecture prioritizes real-time tasks with a global scheduler in the first stage, then incorporates non-real-time tasks in the second stage. This approach maximizes completion rates for both batch and real-time tasks.

In the aforementioned studies, the focus was on task scheduling based on urgency levels, resulting in a significant reduction in response time. However, none of these studies took into account the PEC environment and the allocation of tasks to various edge devices with limited resources, which may be either mobile or stationary.

In addition to managing tasks with different urgency levels, ensuring fault tolerance is crucial in distributed platforms operating in dynamic environments. This is especially important in edge computing when components such as edge nodes with crucial responsibility experience a functional failure for any reason.

Zhou et al. [21] addressed the critical challenge of scheduling fault-tolerant mixed-criticality systems and ensuring the safety of tasks of varying critical levels in the face of transient faults. They utilized task re-execution as their chosen fault-tolerant technique to accomplish this goal. Kaur et al. [8] proposed a technique for fault-tolerant offloading of data by IoT devices such that the data collected is transferred to the cloud with minimal loss. The proposed technique employs opportunistic contacts between IoT and mobile fog nodes to provide a fault-tolerant enhancement to the IoT architecture. Chattopadhyay et al. [2] have developed Aloe, an innovative SDN orchestration framework that reduces flow-setup delay and improves availability by replacing service-grade SDN controller applications with lightweight instances. Aloe provides fault tolerance with recovery from network partitioning by employing self-stabilizing placement of migration-capable controller instances. The fault-tolerant controller orchestration ensures the liveness of the system even in the presence of multiple simultaneous devices or network faults.

Previous studies have suggested solutions for fault-tolerant task scheduling and data offloading in cloud and fog environments. However, fault tolerance design for the PEC environment still has received less attention. While the mobility and distribution of devices in the PEC lead to a highly dynamic and unpredictable environment, which increases the risk of faults and failures.

3   Background

This section includes a brief introduction of concepts and description of systems focused on this paper.

3.1   Pure Edge Computing

Pure Edge Computing takes place at the bottom layer of the network architecture. It aims to harness the distributed vast computational power present at edge devices, such as smartphones, laptops, tablets, etc., and minimize the use of high-capacity servers at the edge. According to the study from Carnegie Mellon University, computing at the distributed edge layer is more efficient in terms of energy consumption and latency for specific applications, compared to computing in the distant cloud [4].

However, PEC is a network of diverse and resource-limited devices that can be either stationary or mobile. As a result, a wide range of IoT applications, each with varying time sensitivity, are produced in an unpredictable and fluctuating workload. To operate in such an environment, an orchestrator that can adapt to different situations and dynamics is required.

3.2   Real-Time and Non-Real-Time Systems

A real-time system is one whose basic specification and design correctness arguments must include its ability to meet its timing constraints [10]. In contrast, non-real-time systems have no strict deadlines, and their tasks can be failed and repeated if they are not complete. Three levels of time sensitivity systems and tasks are defined: Systems that operate in real-time are required to meet strict timing constraints [10]. On the other hand, non-real-time systems do not have such strict deadlines and can afford to fail and repeat tasks if necessary. Time-sensitive systems and tasks are categorized into three levels as follows:

Hard-Real-Time (HRT): It is crucial to adhere to strict deadlines when completing tasks in specific systems, such as aviation control, fire alarm systems, and specific sub-systems of the healthcare system. Failure to meet task deadlines in these systems can result in severe consequences, including harm to the system or its environment, as well as potential injury or loss of life. These types of systems are referred to as hard real-time systems.

Soft-Real-Time (SRT) tasks are characterized by flexible deadlines, where any delays or failures in execution may result in a downgrade of the SLA. Examples of soft real-time systems include video streaming and online gaming.

Non-Real-Time (NRT): There are no strict deadlines for these tasks, and the system can tolerate their failure. Examples of applications in this category include weather forecasting and road maintenance data collection.

Real-world smart platforms usually consist of different types of tasks that should be managed based on their priority.

3.3   AdWOrch

The Adaptive Workload Orchestration (AdWOrch) model has been designed based on the Fuzzy Decision Tree (FDT) algorithm, which was introduced in [13]. FDT has been enhanced with a new reward function and resource selection strategy in AdWOrch to improve the workload orchestration operation.

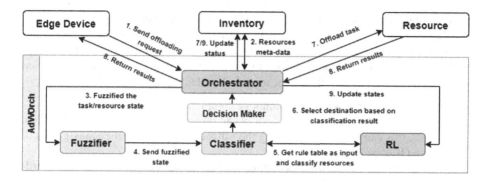

Fig. 1. AdWOrch Components and task offloading flow.

Figure 1 [16] demonstrates the AdWOrch process and components. In the first step, the edge device sends an offloading request to the central orchestrator. Then, the orchestrator retrieves the characteristics of all nearby resources from the inventory. It then combines resources' characteristics with the attributes of the tasks to create a state observation, which is then sent to the fuzzifier.

Since tasks and resources are heterogeneous and their parameters have a broad range of values and change frequently. Hence, instead of describing resources by their crisp values, each value will be fuzzified and defined by a language phrase such as "low", "medium", or "high" to facilitate such variations. After the fuzzification phase, in the classification phase, using a decision tree, resources are classified to estimate how much each resource is reliable for offloading the task. The Q-table generated by the RL component is utilized to build the decision tree. Then the decision-maker component selects a nearby device with sufficient reliability.

Once the tasks are offloaded to their destination, the resource status in the inventory is promptly updated. After the task is complete the task execution outcome is sent to the orchestrator, which subsequently sends it to the source device. Moreover, when the result is returned, the device's resource status in the inventory is updated again and the task execution result is sent back to the RL component. Moreover, the RL component receives the rewarding result (i.e. success or failure) once the result is returned. The resource status in the inventory is updated again simultaneously. Finally, the RL component updates the Q-table based on the received rewarding results by the reward function.

4   Problem Statement

The objective of this study is to propose a model that fulfills three crucial requirements that are essential for models designed for dynamic environments. These requirements are fault-tolerant, robustness, and adaptiveness. Therefore, to minimize missed soft real-time deadlines while meeting almost all hard real-time in a PEC environment, a fault-tolerant robust adaptive workload orchestration model is proposed.

In the PEC environment, resource-constrained devices should handle a variety of tasks with different levels of urgency and SLA. Additionally, devices come in different forms and can be stationary or mobile. Mobile devices can easily move within or enter/leave the area. Battery-powered devices vary in their remaining battery level and locations. In such an environment, various types of failures occur, the orchestrator node might be failed for any reason and leads to system crash. Moreover, tasks can be failed due to different reasons as follows that must be handled:

- **Failure due to Latency:** A task cannot be completed before its deadline.
- **Failure due to Mobility:** Mobile devices can move across and join or exit the area. However, this can cause issues during the offloading process as they may go out of range and lose connection.
- **Failure due to Incompatible Hardware/Software:** Devices are have different hardware and software capabilities, leading to varying scopes. However, these allocated scopes may not always be compatible with a task due to differing requirements. As a result, the mismatch can ultimately lead to task failure due to insufficient resources.
- **Failure due to no Available Resources:** In a PEC environment, a device may become isolated and unable to locate nearby devices to offload. This can lead to the failure of the task due to a lack of available resources.
- **Failure due to a Dead Device:** This failure is resulting from situation that a battery-operated device runs out of energy and cannot executes assigned tasks.

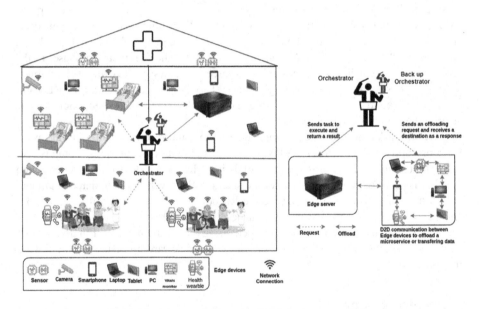

Fig. 2. Health care platform in a PEC environment [16].

5   Model Design

A Fault-Tolerant Robust Adaptive Workload Orchestration (FTR-AdWOrch) model is proposed based on the AdWOrch model [15]. Using reinforcement learning, it aims to achieve fault-tolerance and robustness along with adaptability in unpredictable and dynamic PEC environments, which can accommodate resource constraints in dense or sparse areas.

5.1   Fault Tolerant Orchestrator

A centralized, powerful RL-based orchestrator entity is introduced to allocate or real-locate tasks to the available resources by considering the type of the tasks (i.e., HRT, SRT, NRT) by minimizing the delay and failure in the system. However, relying on a single central orchestrator carries the risk of system crashes in the event of failure. To mitigate this risk, a backup orchestrator instance is included in our model design to ensure fault tolerance. In case of the primary orchestrator's failure, this backup instance will be activated immediately to facilitate in task orchestration.

5.2   RL Model

This paper employs a Q-learning-based RL model. The state, action, and reward for the RL algorithm are defined as follows:

State Representation: AdWOrch utilizes two feature sets to represent the state at timestamp t, the attributes of tasks, and the characteristics of resources. The task's attributes are represented in the Table 1. The resource characteristics are demonstrated in Table 2.

Table 1. Task attributes at timestamp t.

Attributes	Description
t_{siz}	The size of the task
t_{lat}	The maximum acceptable latency for the task
t_{mob}	Mobility state of the device that generated the task
t_{typ}	task type

Table 2. Devices' characteristics at timestamp t.

Attributes	Description
d_{mips}	The total MIPS available in the device
d_{cu}	Current CPU utilization of the device
d_b	Remaining battery (for battery-based devices)
d_{ql}	Number of task waiting for execution at the device
d_{mob}	The mobility state of the device

In order to enhance the learning process and decrease size of q-table, we shift our focus from CPU utilization to the device's current load, d_l. This metric is calculated by dividing the queue length of pending tasks awaiting execution on the device, d_{ql}, by the number of CPU cores present on the device, d_{cc}, see Eq. 1.

$$d_l = d_{ql}/d_{cc} \qquad (1)$$

Also, the expected execution time, t_{et}, which is calculated by the task size, t_s, divided by the MIPS size, d_m, is replaced with device MIPS size and task size. See Eq. 2.

$$t_{et} = t_{siz}/d_{mips} \tag{2}$$

Action Space: The action space $A = \{0, 1\}$ is the set of all possible resource selection strategies. For the resource that has been selected for a given task $A = 1$ and for other resources in the environment $A = 0$.

Reward: After taking action a at time step t, the orchestrator receives an immediate reward from the environment. This reward is represented as either 1 for success or 0 for failure of the task. This research aims to ensure that HRT deadlines are met almost always while minimizing the failure rate of SRT tasks. To achieve this, AdWorch [15] introduced a delayed penalty in the reward function that helps to minimize the failure caused by missing deadlines. Additionally, this work incorporates further penalties for SRT and HRT task failures as can be seen in Eq. 3.

$$R(s, a) = R_s - (w * D_p) \tag{3}$$

$$D_p = T_d/T_l \tag{4}$$

The task outcome, R_s, can be represented in the set of $\{0, 1\}$ to indicate either a success or a failure. The delay penalty D_p is calculated by dividing the delay time T_d by the task latency time T_l (see Eq. 4). Although exceeding 1 is possible, it's an uncommon occurrence. The weight of the penalty, w, varies for different types of tasks with a value of 3 for HRT tasks, 1.5 for SRT tasks, and 1 for NRT tasks.

5.3 FTR-AdWOrch Model

To achieve robustness for the designed model a two-tier architecture is proposed in which edge devices and sensors operate as primary computational resources and generate tasks. In emergency circumstances, as a proactive action plan, the edge server in the second layer is responsible for facilitating the required resources for HRT and SRT tasks.

Figure 3 shows how FTR-AdWOrch manages various types of tasks (i.e., HRT, SRT, NRT) to minimize task failure for different reasons as listed in Fig. 3. FTR-AdWOrch has incorporated the red components in the flowchart, which helps to improve the AdWOrch process to achieve robustness. When a task has been received by FTR-AdWOrch a task, the first step is to use the AdWOrch orchestrator to find an optimum resource from nearby devices. If AdWOrch finds a suitable resource, the task will be offloaded to it. Otherwise, if there are no resources currently available, this will result in two situations: i) a case the task is an NRT, it will fail immediately due to the "no available resources". ii) in the case that the task is an HRT or SRT, it will be sent to the Edge server directly to prevent failure due to "No available resources". In this step, the FTR-AdWOrch disregards all NRT tasks for two specific reasons: i) Since during a disaster, limited resources and bandwidth are available, the real-time tasks should

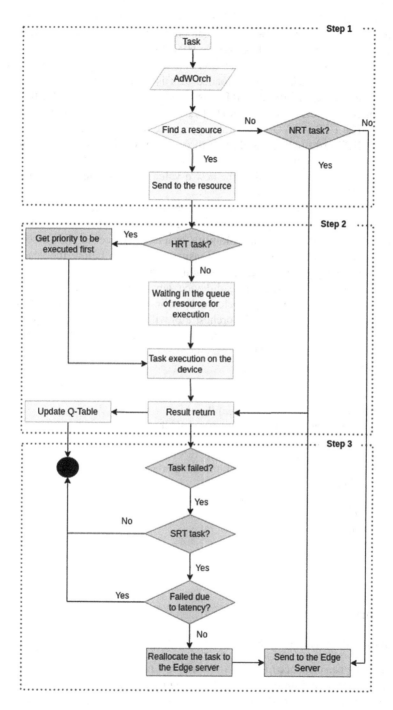

Fig. 3. Task offloading process by R-AdWOrch [16].

be handled with higher priority. ii) Sending too many NRT tasks on the Edge server caused an overload of the bandwidth and computing resources, which could result in a long response time and ultimately cause the HRT task to fail.

In step 2, once the destination selection and task offloading have been completed, the FTR-AdWOrch checks if the offloaded task is an HRT. If it is, it will be given priority and executed before any SRT or NRT tasks that are waiting in the device's execution queue. Hence, the chance of HRT tasks failure due to "missing deadline" will be reduced. The FTR-AdWOrch operates on a preemptive system, which enables the execution of NRT tasks to be paused and returned to the queue, allowing incoming HRT tasks to be executed immediately. Once the execution is completed, the outcome (i.e. success, failure) is used to calculate the new q-value based on the reward function and update the q-table (see Sect. 5.2).

In step 3 when the FTR-AdWOrch has received a task failure result, it will check if the task is an SRT and if the failure was caused by reasons other than latency, such as incompatible hardware or software, mobility, or a dead device. In such cases, the task will be reallocated to the Edge server to ensure completion before the deadline. The result will then be returned after execution at the Edge server.

To prevent failure caused by a dead device, any SRT and NRT tasks will be reallocated once the battery level falls below a specific threshold. However, current HRT tasks will proceed as planned, but the orchestrator will avoid any future tasks from being offloaded to this device. Algorithm 1 demonstrates more details on task reallocation in cases of low remaining battery [16].

```
while running do
    if offloading request (task, device) then
        if remaining energy(device) < threshold then
            if task ≠ HRT then
                reallocate(task,INSUFFICIENT_POWER);
                /*reallocate due to insufficient power*/
            else
                addToExecutionQueue(t);
            end
        end
    end
end
```

Algorithm 1. Tasks reallocation for low battery edge devices.

6   Performance Evaluation

6.1   Simulation Settings

To evaluate the performance of FTR-AdWOrch in a pure edge environment, we employ PureEdgeSim [14]. We simulate a smart nursing home that accommodates senior citizens with varying health conditions. There are individuals who are bedridden, whereas others are in relatively good health and can perform daily activities. Different healthcare sensors gather various vitals and transmit the data for analysis and diagnosis. The level of urgency for each data varies; for instance, the vitals of a severely ill patient take precedence over those of a healthy individual. Along with health sensors, other devices such as cameras are utilized to capture people's actions in the area, while other sensors gather historical data from the surroundings and equipment. The characteristics of these devices are summarized in Table 3.

Table 3. Types of edge devices.

Types	Laptops	Smartphones	Gateways	Stationary sensors	Mobile sensors
Generate tasks	No	Yes	No	Yes	Yes
Ratio (%)	11	18	11	28	32
Mobility	No	Yes	No	No	Yes
Speed (m/s)	–	1.4	–	–	1.4
Battery-powered	Yes	Yes	No	No	Yes
Battery-capacity (Wh)	56.2	18.75	–	–	–
Idle energy consumption (W)	1.7	0.2	3.8	–	–
Max energy consumption (W)	23.6	5	5.5	–	–
CPU (GIPS)	110	25	16	–	–
CPU cores	8	8	4	–	–

In the event of a telecommunication incident at the smart nursing home mentioned an emergency may occur. It leads to disconnecting half of the edge devices from the main network while still having access to the internal network. Furthermore, if the number of individuals is increased, the system experiences a significant increase in workload, as indicated in Table 5. There is a private Edge server available in the area, and devices can connect to it using the main network. This server will have a computing capacity of 400 GIPS (Giga Instruction Per Second). The monitoring of vital signs of critically ill patients is considered an HRT task, while the analysis of vital signs and processing of camera data in healthy individuals falls under SRT tasks. Historical data collection tasks are considered NRT tasks (see Table 4). All devices can access via the internal network to the central orchestrator and access the Edge server through the main network.

Table 4. The types of applications.

Application types	Latency(ms)	Size (MI)
HRT	15	200
SRT	500	5000
NRT	30000	10000

Moreover, in order to evaluate the importance of fault tolerance design, we simulated the 10 min scenarios where the orchestrator experiences a power outage lasting 2 min for different ranges of device numbers in the area.

Table 5. Scenarios profile.

Number of devices	HRT[a]	SRT[a]	NRT[a]
50	135	135	270
100	135	135	270
300	135	135	270

[a]Requested task for each device per minute.

To evaluate the performance of the proposed model, the results are compared to AdWOrch [15]. For each of the explained scenarios, a simulation of 30 min is run 5 times.

6.2 Evaluation Metrics

We define two evaluation metrics. The **task success rate** for each task type is calculated by the number of successful tasks divided by the total number of generated tasks. The **average delay time** for each type of task is calculated by dividing the total delay time by the number of generated tasks. The total delay time is calculated by summing up the total network time, total execution time, and total waiting time. Furthermore, we assessed how effective the **reallocation** mechanism is by calculating how many tasks are reallocated due to low battery power, mobility, and incompatible resources.

For **fault tolerance** scenario, the evaluation metric is percentage of **tasks lost** during orchestrator node downtime.

6.3 Results and Discussion

Average Delay: Figure 4(a-c) demonstrates that FTR-AdWOrch significantly decreases the delay of HRT tasks when the device density is low (i.e., 50 devices) compared to the baseline. Moreover, FTR-AdWOrch delivers comparable results in all other scenarios. This reduction in delay can be attributed to the additional penalty in the reward function for failing HRT and SRT tasks. If an HRT task exceeds the deadline, the RL component receives a heavily weighted penalty. Furthermore, HRT tasks take priority over non-HRT tasks. There are two ways to ensure this: i) HRT tasks will be placed at the front of the queue of the device for execution; ii) when an HRT task arrives at a device, if no free computational resource is available, executing NRT tasks are paused and resources are allocated to HRT tasks. These allow fast execution even in resource-constrained scenarios.

Success Rate: As can be seen in Fig. 4d, FTR-AdWOrch yields a significantly higher success rate for HRT tasks compared to the baseline. This improvement is a result of applying two prioritization approaches to prevent HRTs failure: i) when there is not sufficient battery power to complete all tasks on the device queue, the device redelegates non-HRT tasks to other devices; ii) as explained in Sect. 5.2, the heavily weighted delay penalty for the HRT helps the algorithm to be more sensitive to HRT failures compared with SRT and NRT tasks. Furthermore, according to Fig. 4e success rate for SRT tasks

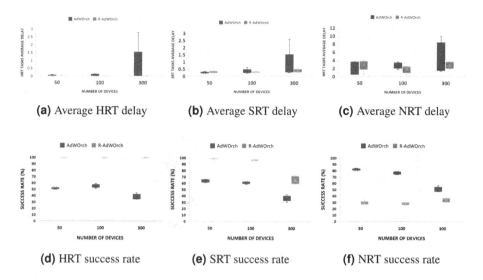

(a) Average HRT delay   **(b)** Average SRT delay   **(c)** Average NRT delay

(d) HRT success rate   **(e)** SRT success rate   **(f)** NRT success rate

Fig. 4. The simulation results for different scenarios [16].

in FTR-AdWOrch is significantly higher than the AdWOrch. The primary cause is the allocation strategy used for SRT tasks that fail for reasons other than latency. By reallocating these tasks to the edge server, they have a second chance to meet the deadline and succeed.

Task Lost: Figure 5 shows the percentage of tasks lost in a 10-min scenario with 2-min orchestrator downtime. As can be seen across all scenarios, an average of 20% of tasks were lost due to the absence of backup orchestration nodes. This highlights the importance of having a fault-tolerant design and backup orchestrator nodes.

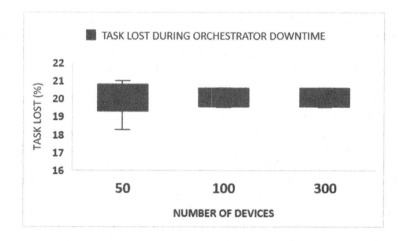

Fig. 5. Task lost during the orchestrator node downtime.

The pie chart shown in Fig. 6a illustrates how each of the proposed methods including priority, reallocation, SRT/HRT delay penalty, and edge server have contributed to enhancing the success rate of tasks. FTR-AdWOrch accounts for 60% of the success rate in emergency scenarios, while AdWOrch only accounts for 40%.

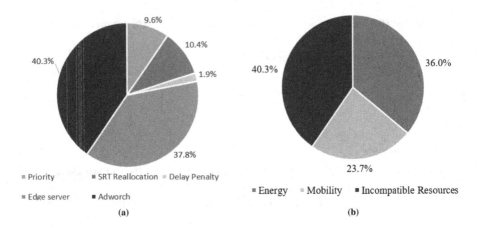

Fig. 6. (a) The contribution of R-AdWOrch methods in the success rate. (b) The contribution of reallocation reasons [16].

The pie chart in Fig. 6b shows the quantity of SRT tasks that were reallocated and the reasons for their reallocation. The FTR-AdWOrch reallocates SRT tasks to avoid data loss in case of a failed task due to "mobility" or "incompatible hardware/software," and to prevent task failure caused by a battery-powered device dead.

7   Conclusions

This paper proposed a Fault-Tolerant Robust Adaptive Workload Orchestration (FTR-AdWOrch) system for a PEC environment, with inherent uncertainties. The objective of the proposed method is to handle system failure while meeting almost all HRT tasks and minimizing SRT task deadline misses. The model was applied to a healthcare application and compared to the baseline model (AdWOrch). According to the simulation results, FTR-AdWOrch demonstrated higher success rates in both HRT and SRT tasks while decreasing delay times compared to the baseline. Additionally, the system can resist failure of the orchestrator node, which is no longer a single point of failure.

Although this research achieved a high task success rate for HRT and SRT tasks, improving the success rate of NRT tasks is a gap that can be addressed in the future work of our research. Furthermore, the orchestration of dependent tasks poses a significant challenge in this area that we must overcome in future work. Additionally, using a backup node to manage failure is not always feasible in resource constrained systems. In this paper, we have shown the importance of fault tolerance mechanism in PEC environment and future works can include more innovative approaches for workload management at the uncertain times.

Acknowledgements. This publication has emanated from research supported in part by a grant from Science Foundation Ireland under Grant number 18/CRT/6183. For the purpose of Open Access, the author has applied a CC BY public copyright license to any Author Accepted Manuscript version arising from this submission.

References

1. Azizi, S., Shojafar, M., Abawajy, J., Buyya, R.: Deadline-aware and energy-efficient IoT task scheduling in fog computing systems: a semi-greedy approach. J. Netw. Comput. Appl. **201**, 103333 (2022)
2. Chattopadhyay, S., Chatterjee, S., Nandi, S., Chakraborty, S.: Aloe: fault-tolerant network management and orchestration framework for IoT applications. IEEE Trans. Netw. Serv. Manag. **17**(4), 2396–2409 (2020). https://doi.org/10.1109/TNSM.2020.3008426
3. Dai, H., Zeng, X., Yu, Z., Wang, T.: A scheduling algorithm for autonomous driving tasks on mobile edge computing servers. J. Syst. Archit. **94**, 14–23 (2019)
4. Drolia, U., et al.: The case for mobile edge-clouds. In: 2013 IEEE 10th International Conference on Ubiquitous Intelligence and Computing and 2013 IEEE 10th International Conference on Autonomic and Trusted Computing, pp. 209–215. IEEE (2013)
5. Fadahunsi, O., Ma, Y., Maheswaran, M.: Edge scheduling framework for real-time and non real-time tasks. In: Proceedings of the 36th Annual ACM Symposium on Applied Computing, pp. 719–728 (2021)
6. Ghanadbashi, S., Golpayegani, F.: Using ontology to guide reinforcement learning agents in unseen situations: a traffic signal control system case study. Appl. Intell. **52**(2), 1808–1824 (2022)
7. Golpayegani, F., Ghanadbashi, S., Riad, M.: Urban emergency management using intelligent traffic systems: challenges and future directions. In: 2021 IEEE International Smart Cities Conference (ISC2), pp. 1–4. IEEE (2021)
8. Kaur, P.: Fault tolerant data offloading in opportunistic fog enhanced IoT architecture. Multiagent Grid Syst. **18**(2), 107–118 (2022)
9. Khan, M.A.: A survey of security issues for cloud computing. J. Netw. Comput. Appl. **71**, 11–29 (2016)
10. Kim, Y.K., Son, S.H.: Predictability and consistency in real-time database systems. Adv. Real-time Syst. 509–531 (1995)
11. Lee, C.H., Park, J.S.: An SDN-based packet scheduling scheme for transmitting emergency data in mobile edge computing environments. Hum. Cent. Comput. Inf. Sci **11**, 28 (2021)
12. Malekjafarian, A., OBrien, E.J., Quirke, P., Cantero, D., Golpayegani, F.: Railway track loss-of-stiffness detection using bogie filtered displacement data measured on a passing train. Infrastructures **6**(6), 93 (2021)
13. Mechalikh, C., Taktak, H., Moussa, F.: A fuzzy decision tree based tasks orchestration algorithm for edge computing environments. In: Barolli, L., Amato, F., Moscato, F., Enokido, T., Takizawa, M. (eds.) Advanced Information Networking and Applications. AINA 2020. AISC, vol. 1151, pp. 193–203. Springer, Cham (2020). https://doi.org/10.1007/978-3-030-44041-1_18
14. Mechalikh, C., Taktak, H., Moussa, F.: Pureedgesim: a simulation framework for performance evaluation of cloud, edge and mist computing environments. Comput. Sci. Inf. Syst. **00**, 42–42 (2020)
15. Safavifar, Z., Ghanadbashi, S., Golpayegani, F.: Adaptive workload orchestration in pure edge computing: a reinforcement-learning model. In: 2021 IEEE 33rd International Conference on Tools with Artificial Intelligence (ICTAI), pp. 856–860. IEEE (2021)

16. Safavifar, Z., Mechalikh, C., Golpayegani, F.: A robust adaptive workload orchestration in pure edge computing. In: 15th International Conference on Agents and Artificial Intelligence, ICAART 2023, pp. 325–333. SCITEPRESS (2023)

17. Sharif, Z., Jung, L.T., Ayaz, M.: Priority-based resource allocation scheme for mobile edge computing. In: 2022 2nd International Conference on Computing and Information Technology (ICCIT), pp. 138–143. IEEE (2022)

18. Uddin, M., Ayaz, M., Mansour, A., Aggoune, E.H.M., Sharif, Z., Razzak, I.: Cloud-connected flying edge computing for smart agriculture. Peer-to-Peer Netw. Appl. **14**(6), 3405–3415 (2021)

19. Wang, H., Gong, J., Zhuang, Y., Shen, H., Lach, J.: Healthedge: task scheduling for edge computing with health emergency and human behavior consideration in smart homes. In: 2017 IEEE International Conference on Big Data (Big Data), pp. 1213–1222. IEEE (2017)

20. Xu, J., Hu, Z., Zou, J.: Computing offloading and resource allocation algorithm based on game theory for IoT devices in mobile edge computing. Int. J. Innov. Comput. Inf. Control **16**(6), 1895–1914 (2020)

21. Zhou, J., et al.: Fault-tolerant task scheduling for mixed-criticality real-time systems. J. Circuits Syst. Comput. **26**(01), 1750016 (2017)

Exploring Narrative Economics: An Agent-Based Co-Evolutionary Model Featuring Nonlinear Continuous-Time Opinion Dynamics

Arwa Bokhari[1,2](✉) [ID] and Dave Cliff[1] [ID]

[1] Department of Computer Science, University of Bristol, Bristol BS8 1UB, U.K.
{oc21380,csdtc}@bristol.ac.uk
[2] Information Technology Department, College of Computers and Information Technology, Taif University, Taif, Saudi Arabia
a.bokari@tu.edu.sa

Abstract. The efficient market hypothesis has been a leading theory of financial economics for decades. This theory states that financial markets are efficient, in that the price of an asset reflects all available information about its value. However, there are phenomena in financial markets that are difficult to explain using this theory alone. In 2017, Robert Shiller, a Nobel Laureate, introduced the concept of *Narrative Economics* as an approach to explain these difficult-to-understand economic phenomena. According to this approach, narratives, or stories that participants in asset markets hear, believe, and tell each other, play a crucial role in shaping economic outcomes, such as the price dynamics of digital assets that hold little value. Shiller argues that narratives are critical to understanding seemingly irrational behaviors, such as investing in highly volatile cryptocurrency markets, as people invest based on their beliefs and opinions about the prospects of the asset, which they express in the form of narratives. By incorporating narratives into economic analysis, narrative economics offers a new lens through which to view financial markets and understand the complex behaviors of market participants. This paper extends the work on narrative economics by building upon the agent-based modeling platform developed by Bokhari and Cliff [5] in which the interplay between narratives and price dynamics is achieved by employing the PRDE adaptive zero-intelligence trader strategy introduced by Cliff [11], and the continuous-time real-valued nonlinear opinion dynamics model reported by Bizyaeva et al. [4]. This paper presents a series of meticulously designed experiments aimed at examining the influence of different opinion types on trader behavior, particularly when traders hold neutral opinions. The primary objective of these experiments is to simulate the reciprocal influence between narratives and the dynamism of the market. Our experiments revealed that our simulated market system was able to achieve stability in a controlled environment. Furthermore, we found that the opinions of the entire population of 60 traders could be influenced by just a single trader. This paper contributes to the ongoing dialogue in narrative economics by presenting a robust and reliable experimental platform that facilitates comprehensive empirical studies.

© The Author(s), under exclusive license to Springer Nature Switzerland AG 2024
A. P. Rocha et al. (Eds.): ICAART 2023, LNAI 14546, pp. 387–410, 2024.
https://doi.org/10.1007/978-3-031-55326-4_19

Keywords: Narrative economics · Opinion dynamics ·
Co-Evolutionary systems Adaptive markets · Financial markets ·
Automated trading · Agent-Based computational economics

1   Introduction

Economic discourse has traditionally been dominated by models and theories centered on quantifiable data and empirical analysis. However, another crucial factor drives economic outcomes: narratives. Narrative economics, a term coined by Nobel laureate Robert J. Shiller [33,34], proposes that popular narratives, stories that spread through society, significantly influence economic behavior and, consequently, economic phenomena. In particular, Shiller argues that phenomena which are difficult to explain in any other way, such as cryptocurrency price fluctuations, can best be explained by reference to the narratives in play in the cryptocoin markets. Given the contemporary digital communication age, where information and narratives disseminate swiftly and extensively, acknowledging the impact of narratives within the sphere of economics is gaining recognition. This growing field of study provides a new perspective to interpret economic events and predict economic trajectories. Nonetheless, despite its potential, the empirical exploration of narrative economics remains underdeveloped, indicating the need for more research to understand its implications and overall significance.

In their notable work, Lomas & Cliff [29] introduced a convincing perspective that narratives can be viewed as expressions of opinion. Utilizing this idea, they linked agent-based models of financial markets and the enduring field of social sciences known as Opinion Dynamics (OD). The primary focus of OD research is to understand the mechanisms by which individuals in a population can influence others to change their opinions, and how they might revise their own opinions under the influence of external factors. Lomas & Cliff integrated an elementary and outdated OD models method, that have been in existence for two decades, into their agent-based computational economics model, essentially as a proof-of-concept. In their model, traders engage in asset trading by submitting bid or ask orders to an automated central financial exchange (such as a real-life stock exchange or a cryptocurrency exchange website). They demonstrated how alterations in a trader-agent's opinions could be reflected in the dynamics of market prices. However, they did not explore the mutual influence – how market prices can reshape traders' opinions.

In today's financial markets, most financial instruments are traded using adaptive automated trading systems, which adjust their trading strategies in real-time so that they can maximize their profits, given the current distribution of other trading strategies on the market against which they compete. Since both of these competing strategies are constantly being adjusted to remain profitable, contemporary financial markets are co-evolving systems. Understanding the dynamics of today's financial markets is crucial, considering the obvious concerns about their stability and efficiency; it is, however, a challenging undertaking since market systems have so many nonlinearly interconnected elements. When exploring contemporary markets, researchers typically either analyze and model fine-grained data from real-world systems (in the context of financial exchanges), this means both real-time data and historical data. This approach is known as the study of market microstructure; [31]. However, experiments conducted on various types of simplified situations under controlled conditions - a method referred to as experimental economics [35] - have increasingly used agent-based models (ABMs).

Similar to OD research, studies involving ABMs of economic and financial systems have been ongoing for several decades. It is an adequately mature field with its own term: *Agent-Based Computational Economics* (ACE: refer to, for example, [7,27,39]). In ACE models, a simulated economic or financial system is created and populated by a certain number of independent agents, with each agent following a specific algorithm or strategy for interacting with other agents in the system. It has been consistently shown that ACE models using only the simplest trader strategies can be surprisingly informative. These so-called *zero intelligence* (ZI) trading strategies are now regularly employed to demonstrate and investigate various economic and market phenomena. The paper that pioneered the establishment of markets populated by ZI traders as valuable subjects of study is [24]; for reviews of the influence and effectiveness of ZI studies in ACE, see [2,19,28].

Very recently, Cliff introduced the *PRDE* (**P**arameterized-**R**esponse zero-intelligence with **D**ifferential **E**volution) trading strategy [11] as an example of an effective ZI trading strategy capable of adaptive modifications. This adaptive zero-intelligence strategy has the potential to adjust its trading behavior to better correspond with current market conditions, with the intention of maximizing its personal profitability consistently. Cliff's PRDE is an enhancement of his prior PRZI (**P**arameterized-**R**esponse **Z**ero-**I**ntelligence) trading strategy, which was created to counter a problem revealed in the original Lomas & Cliff work. The adapted ZI trading strategies by Lomas & Cliff did incorporate traders' opinions into their trading behavior. However, it could generate scenarios where the opinionated traders all settled into a condition where no further market transactions were possible, resulting in a completely inactive market. For a comprehensive explanation of this, see the discussion in [12]. PRZI and later PRDE were presented as solutions to this problem in Lomas & Cliff's 2021 paper. In our preceding paper [5], we introduced the BFL-PRDE model in which we show how market's dynamics can affect traders' opinions. Our model not only addresses the limitations of Lomas & Cliff's proposal but also includes a mathematically intricate OD model that enriches its modeling capabilities even further. This enhancement enables a more thorough investigation of various elements within the field of narrative economics.

This paper extends our prior research by increasing the depth and breadth of our experimental scope. Specifically, we delve into scenarios where traders are neutral. Moreover, we investigate the potential influence of market prices on shaping these traders' opinions, questioning whether fluctuations in market prices can affect traders' opinions. A comparative analysis of PRDE and BFL-

PRDE is conducted to underscore the enhancements introduced by BFL-BRDE. Lastly, we aim to identify the minimal number of participants necessary to trigger significant price shifts - this involves determining the required number of traders for substantial changes in market prices to occur.

In Sect. 2, we provide further details about the background of our work, focusing on explaining the PRDE trader strategy. In Sect. 3, we demonstrate how the BFL OD model can be customized for PRDE integration. Section 4 outlines the integration process of BFL into PRDE traders. In Sect. 5, we present the details of our experiments and discuss the results. Lastly, in Sect. 6, we explore future directions and discuss the implications of our findings.

2   Background

Shiller highlighted the significance of narrative analysis in economic processes. He suggested that epidemic spread models, like the Kermak-McKendrick model, provide a great analogy for examining narratives in economics, comparing financial crises and market bubbles to epidemics, both driven by specific accepted narratives. These narratives follow identifiable patterns. The study of "opinion dynamics" observes public sentiment formation and spread across social networks. Lomas & Cliff suggested that Shiller's "narrative" is an opinion expression, linking financial market behavior with social dynamics and implying the potential use of opinion dynamics tools for understanding economic phenomena.

2.1   Simulated Financial Markets

The study of simulation models of financial markets has been known for a long time as a means of exploring the fine-grained dynamics of various form of market. Such models very often require populating a market mechanism with a number of trader-agents: autonomous entities that work independently within the framework of the particular market mechanism being simulated. According to the market simulation literature reviewed here, traders in the market are typically assigned specific roles, either as buyers or sellers. Each buyer or seller is given an order to purchase or sell a specific quantity of an abstract commodity traded in the market. Additionally, they are provided with a private *limit price*, which is the highest price a buyer can pay or the lowest price a seller can accept for the item. The *profit*, also known as *utility* or *surplus*, is calculated as the difference between the transaction price and the trader's limit price. Over the 30 years or so that ACE has been the topic of active development, a few specific trader-agent algorithms are notable for their longevity in the literature: SNPR [32]; ZIC [24]; ZIP [8]; GD [22]; MGD [38]; GDX [37]; HBL [23]; and AA [40]. The seminal ZIC developed by Gode and Sunder (1993) is highly stochastic however it shows surprisingly human-like market dynamics. In a landmark paper by IBM researchers [14], GD and ZIP were the first to be demonstrated to consistently show superior performance to human traders (see also: [15–17]), and the IBM result is widely cited as initiating the rise of algorithmic trading in real-world financial markets. All of the these strategies, except for SNPR and ZIC, use some form of machine learning (ML) or artificial intelligence (AI) to modify their responses over time, better-adapting their trading behavior to the market conditions they find themselves in, and the details of these algorithms have often been published in major AI/ML conferences and journals.

Recently, Cliff proposed the PRZI [12] trading algorithm: PRZI traders are firmly in the ZI tradition but they each have a scalar real-valued *strategy* parameter $s \in [-1, +1] \in \mathbb{R}$ which governs their response to market events: when a PRZI trader has $s = 0$ its trading behavior is identical to the seminal ZIC of [24], but when $s > 0$ it becomes more "urgent", quoting prices that are more likely to find a counterparty and lead to a transaction, but for which the expected profitability of the transaction will be reduced relative to the prices quoted when $s = 0$; and similary when $s < 0$ the PRZI trader is more "relaxed" quoting prices that are more profitable if they do lead to a transaction, but less likely to lead to a transaction than the prices quoted when $s = 0$. At the extremes, when a PRZI trader i has $s_i = -1.0$ its trading strategy is equivalent to the maximally relaxed *Shaver* (abbreviated SHVR) strategy proposed in [9,10]; and when $s_i = +1.0$ it is acting as the maximally urgent *Give-away* (GVWY) strategy, also described in [9,10]. As thus defined, an individual PRZI trader is non-adaptive: it is assigned an s-value at creation, and keeps that same s value for all of its lifetime. However, in subsequent work PRZI traders have been extended to adapt their s-values dynamically, as market conditions change, attempting to always increase or maintain their profitability as market circumstances alter. This allows populations of adaptive PRZI traders to be used as a tool for simulation modelling of contemporary real-world financial markets, in which all traders are simultaneously adapting their trading strategies, each seeking to maximize their own profitability, while burdened by the complexity and uncertainty of adapting to a market environment where every other trader is simultaneously adapting, continuously adjusting its strategy in real-time.

The most recent and currently most efficient adaptive PRZI trader was described in [11]: *PRzi with Differential Evolution* (PRDE), which makes use of Differential Evolution (DE: see e.g. [3,36]) as its optimization strategy. Each PRDE trader maintains a population of size $k \geq 4$ candidate s-values, and iterates over an infinite loop in which on each iteration it evaluates each of the k candidates in turn, and then uses a basic DE process to create a new candidate s-value, which is also evaluated: if that new candidate is better than one of the four in the original population, it replaces that one; if not, it is discarded; and the loop iterates again. Evaluation of any one candidate s-value involves the PRDE trader operating in the market using only that s-value for some period of time, and then calculating the profit-per-unit-time for that s-value as its "fitness" score in the DE process. For all our experiments reported here, we used the Python PRDE reference implementation published on Github as part of the freely-available *BSE* platform for agent-based modelling of contemporary financial markets, available as [9].

3   Market Model

In all of our experiments reported here we used BSE in its default configuration, where it allows for the definition of some number of buyer-agents N_B, and some number of seller-agents N_S. Each buyer (seller) is periodically issued with assignments to buy (sell) a unit of the exchange's tradeable asset at a price no higher (lower) than that trader's given private limit price, and to find a willing seller (buyer) as a trading counte-party via interacting within a continuous double auction (CDA) running on a centralised financial exchange that operates a Limit Order Book (LOB), by submitting bid (ask) orders to the exchange. The CDA is an auction mechanism in which any buyer can submit a bid order to the exchange at any time, and any seller can submit a sell order at any time, and the exchange continuously runs a *matching engine* to pair up buyers and sellers whose orders are compatible – e.g. if a seller S1 quotes an ask of $100 for a unit of the asset and a buyer B1 then quotes a bid price of more than $100, the exchange matches B1 and S1 as counter-parties to a transaction and S1 then sells to B1 for $100, because that was the earlier-quoted of the two prices. However, whenever a trader quotes a price that cannot be matched with a counter-party, that quote "rests" at the exchange and is entered on the LOB; with the exchange publishing an updated LOB to all market participants every time the LOB changes. The published LOB shows a summary of the array of all unmatched buyer orders resting at the exchange (on the *bid-side* of the LOB) and all unmatched seller orders (on the *ask-side*) of the LOB, with the two sides of the LOB sorted in price-order from best (highest bid, lowest ask) to worst (lowest bid, highest ask). All major financial exchanges around the world for stocks/shares, currencies, commodities, and digital assets run LOB-based CDAs, so in this respect BSE is an excellent model of real-world exchanges. For further details of CDAs and LOBs, see e.g. [1,20,25]. Limit prices on the trader's assignments were drawn from a pair of supply and demand curves that we specified, allowing us to control the equilibrium price and quantity in each market session. In our exploration of narrative economics, we define the elements of this market model, highlighting how each component functions within the narrative framework and how it subsequently influences traders' behavior as follows:

3.1   Trader Model

Below are the definitions of the trader and the trader social network.

Definition 1 (Trader). Each trader i is represented as a vector $\langle \alpha, \beta, \lambda, \omega, x, d, u \rangle$. Here, $\alpha = \{-1, 0, +1\}$ signifies the trader's role where $+1$ represents a seller, -1 a buyer, and 0 an idle trader. $\beta \in \mathbb{N}_0$ and $\omega \in \mathbb{N}_0$ depict the amount of money acquired and the number of shares held by a trader during a session, respectively. $\lambda \in \mathbb{N}$ denotes a trader's limit price, setting selling and buying thresholds. $x \in \mathbb{R} \in [-1, +1]$ represents the trader's opinion on future price movements of the tradable asset. $d \in \mathbb{R}^+$ and $u \in \mathbb{R}^+ \cup \{0\}$ respectively show the trader's resistance to opinion change and the attention paid to external opinions.

Definition 2 (Trader Social Network). A signed directed graph $G = (V, E)$ represents the agent-based social network of N traders. Here, each vertex in set V symbolizes an individual trader, and each edge (i, j) in set E denotes the one-way relationship from trader i to trader j. The adjacency matrix $A = [a_{ij}] \in \mathbb{R}^{N \times N}$ encodes the network topology. The relationship between traders i and j is characterized by the elements a_{ij} of the adjacency matrix. Specifically, a_{ij} is greater than zero when there's a trust relationship between traders i and j, zero when there's no relationship, and less than zero when there's a suspicious relationship between the two traders.

3.2   BFL: Nonlinear OD Model

Consider a network of N trading agents forming opinions $x_1, ..., x_N \in \mathbb{R}$ about the price of a tradable asset, and $M \geq 0$ communication sources (such as mass media), offering static opinions $c_1, ..., c_M \in \mathbb{R}$ about the same asset. Consider x_i, the real-valued opinion variable of trader i, where negative values indicate a decline in prices, while positive values indicate an increase. The same is true for the value of the opinions from the communication sources; for instance, c_k denotes the opinion from communication source k regarding the asset's price.

Let x_i be the opinion state of agent i and $X = (x_1, ..., x_N)$ the opinion state of the agent network. Agent i is neutral if $x_i = 0$. The origin $X = 0$ is called the network's neutral state. Agent i is unopinionated if its opinion state is small, i.e., $\|x_i\| \leq \vartheta$ for a fixed threshold $\vartheta \approx 0$. Agent i is opinionated if $\|x_i\| \geq \vartheta$. Agents can agree and disagree. When two agents have the same qualitative opinion state (e.g., they both favor the same option), they agree. When they have qualitatively different opinions, they disagree.

The conventional approach to modeling opinion formation depends on the concept of weighted averaging, a principle initially propounded by DeGroot [18]. Nevertheless, this linear weighted-average model has a significant disadvantage: it consistently leads to consensus. According to Mei [30], the strength of attraction between agents i and j increases linearly as their opinion differences widen, creating a paradox in the context of opinion formation. To address this limitation, we have adopted the model proposed by Bizyaeva [4] which is a robust, nonlinear, and tuneable opinion dynamics model. This sophisticated model enables us to control the behavior of the system and accurately simulate required market conditions. This will allow us to experiment with different scenarios and explore the effects of various external factors on the system. In this model, agents' opinions are assumed to evolve continuously over time. It is our objective in this study to tailor the model to best suit the trading market in which it will be implemented. The following is a detailed description of the parameters and specifications relevant to our application:

- Saturated opinion exchanges. The linear weighted-average paradox is effectively overcome by saturated interactions between traders [4]. The saturation of interactions restricts the influence of highly connected individuals, resulting in a more accurate representation of the collective opinion prevailing within the market's population.

- Local opinion. A trader's local opinion within the network is formed through a weighted sum of opinions expressed by all other traders, using the adjacency matrix A. There are two types of interactions in the network: self-reinforcing interactions, which are weighted by a_{ii}, and neighbor interactions, weighted by a_{ij}. In both cases, the sign of the adjacency weight determines the nature of the interaction. The weights within the adjacency matrix A are subject to updates based on the trustworthiness of each trader, establishing a dynamic feedback loop. This loop continually modifies the influence each trader's opinion has on the network. This updating process can be modeled using the following equation: $a_{ij}(t + 1) = a_{ij}(t) + \delta(a_{ij})$. In this equation, $\delta(a_{ij})$ is a function representing the perceived honesty of trader j during their last interaction. If trader j exhibited honesty, $\delta(a_{ij})$ is positive and increases the weight a_{ij}. Conversely, if trader j was dishonest, $\delta(a_{ij})$ is negative, resulting in a decrease in the weight a_{ij}. Such an adaptive model can be used to effectively adjust the influence of each trader's opinion based on their historical behavior. This provides a dynamic system where each trader's influence is self-regulated.
- Opinions from communication sources. The impact of communication sources, such as the mass media, on a trader's opinion is captured by a weighted linear sum of the static opinions of these sources. This sum is weighted by the weight matrix $B = [b_{ik}] \in \mathbb{R}^{N \times M}$, which identifies to what extent each trader can be influenced by a given communication source.
- Attention. The trader's attention or susceptibility to exchange its opinion can be a variable parameter. Specifically, the attention parameter, denoted as u_i, is linked to the profitability of a trader. If a trader incurs a loss, the trader's attention increases. Conversely, if the trader does not experience a loss, the attention remains constant. This implies that a trader who experiences a loss becomes more alert to its neighboring traders and communication sources. Let $\pi(t)$ represent the trader's profit at time t and $\pi(t - 1)$ be the profit at the previous time period $t - 1$. The attention of the trader is then updated according to the following rules:

$$u_i(t + 1) = \begin{cases} u_i(t) + \xi & \text{if } \pi_i(t) - \pi_i(t - 1) < 0, \\ u_i(t) & \text{if } \pi_i(t) - \pi_i(t - 1) \geq 0. \end{cases} \tag{1}$$

Here, ξ represents an incremental value that increases as the market session approaches the end.

- Resistance. A trader's resistance parameter d_i represents its willingness to change its opinion. In some cases, traders are extremely resistant and refuse to change their initial opinions (also known as "stubborn agents") as in [21]. For example, a financial expert might form her opinion solely based on the state of the market. Agents like these are considered influencers. They can be represented by setting their parameters as follows: $d = 1$ (the highest), $u = 0$ (the lowest). As opposed to this, we can model truth seekers on the other side of the spectrum who do not trust their own opinion and seek the opinion of other agents by setting $d = 0$ (the lowest), $u = 1$ (the highest). The majority of traders can be represented by ordinary agents in the middle. In situations in which the resistance parameter is dominant over the attention parameter, the agent pays less attention to other agents' opinions and communication sources. On the other hand, if the attention parameter is dominant, the agent pays close attention to the opinions of other agents and to the communication sources. As the market session approaches the end, agents move from a weakly attentive state to a strongly attentive state due to an increasing sense of urgency (the market session is drawing to a close), so they become more attentive to their neighbors and their communication sources and less resistant.

– Inputs. It is important to note that agents have exogenous inputs. In this context, "exogenous" refers to inputs received from the agents' environment "market". Two input parameters g_i and e_i are introduced for each agent, which represents an environment-based input signals. In this case, the first input parameter g_i represents the collective opinion of the market, as summarised by public data shown on a central financial exchange, such as the market's current mid-price or micro-price, which is analogous to the global opinion in the work of [26], the second input parameter e_i is on the other hand represents some indication of the likelihood of a specific opinion proving to be true at a future point in time – what [26] referred to as the "event opinion". In the ABM model of [26], the events that agents held opinions on were simulated horse-races, and specifically each agent held an opinion on the likely winner of a particular race – each race involved only a small number of horses (typically fewer than 10), and once a race was underway the agents' opinions would change in ways affected by the relative track-positions and speeds of the set of horses competing in the race, and the likelihood at time t_0 of any particular horse winning the race was estimated by running multiple simulations, each projecting forward from the competitors' track positions at t_0 to the race end-time t_{end}, and using the results from these simulations to estimate a probability function over the space of possible outcomes. In the context of an accurate model of a financial market with potentially very many traders interacting at sub-second time-resolution in market sessions that could last for hours, doing multiple fine-grained simulations to estimate the likelihood of the possible final outcomes would be an extremely computationally expensive way of delivering less than two bits of information (i.e., there are only three possible outcomes – Rise, Fall, and Unchanged – which are encodable in two binary digits), using a sledgehammer to crack a nut. Instead, the event opinion can be computed as follows: individual traders manage different transaction histories, varying in length based on a uniform distribution between 2 and the total number of transaction records. Traders update their records asynchronously at different time intervals. Upon reaching a specified record length and update time, each trader performs calculations on their data. They randomly select either the Simple Moving Average (SMA) or Exponential Moving Average (EMA) for the "price" to determine an average that prioritizes recent prices (EMA) or equally weighs all prices (SMA). The most recent price and selected average are then used to compute the event opinion, as a basic trading signal indicating whether the last price is higher (positive signal), lower (negative signal), or equal (neutral signal) to the chosen average. Let P_t represent the price at time t, and let L be the record length. For SMA, the equation is: $SMA = \frac{1}{L} \sum_{t=1}^{L} P_t$. For the EMA, the equation is: $EMA_t = P_t * \alpha + EMA_{t-1} * (1 - \alpha)$, where $\alpha = \frac{2}{(L+1)}$ is the smoothing factor, and EMA_{t-1} is the EMA at time $t - 1$. The initial EMA value could be set as the first price or calculated using SMA for the initial period. Next, the event opinion is computed. This is a simple trading signal determined by comparing the current price P_t with a chosen average. If P_t exceeds the chosen average, the event opinion is set to 1. If P_t is less than the chosen average, the event opinion is set to -1. If P_t equals the chosen average, the event opinion is set to 0. Where P_t is the last (or the most recent) price in the prices' record $P_1, P_2, ..., P_{t-1}, P_t$, and the chosen average is either the SMA or the EMA, randomly selected. As an alternative, supply, and demand data can be used to predict whether prices will rise or fall. In the event that there is an excess of supply relative to demand, the price of the asset will fall and vice versa. A simple way to do this is by taking the difference between the current market mid-price, denoted here by $p_m(t) = (p_{bid}^*(t) + q_{ask}^*(t))/2$, and the current market micro-price based on [6], denoted here by $p_\mu(t)$, where

$$p_\mu(t) = \frac{p_{ask}^*(t) q_{bid}^*(t) + p_{bid}^*(t) q_{ask}^*(t)}{q_{bid}^*(t) + q_{ask}^*(t)} \tag{2}$$

in which $p_{ask}^*(t)$ is the price of the best ask at time t (i.e., the price at the top of the bid side of the CDA market's limit order book (LOB); $p_{bid}^*(t)$ is the price of the best bid at time t (i.e. the price at the top of the ask side of the LOB); $q_{bid}^*(t)$ is the total quantity available at $p_{bid}^*(t)$; and $q_{ask}^*(t)$ is the total quantity available at $p_{ask}^*(t)$. In the case of zero supply/demand imbalance at the top of the LOB (i.e., Eq. 2 reduces to the equation for the market midprice, and therefore the difference between the two prices, denoted by $\triangle_m(t) = p_\mu(t) - p_m(t)$ is zero). Accordingly, a positive imbalance (i.e. $\triangle_m(t) >> 0$) indicates that the subsequent transaction prices are likely to increase, and a negative imbalance (i.e. $\triangle_m(t) << 0$) indicates that subsequent transaction prices are likely to fall.

As per [4], the networked opinion dynamics are as follows:

$$\dot{x}_i = -d_i x_i + u_i (S_1 (s_A) + S_2 (s_B)) + (g_i + e_i) \tag{3}$$

where $s_A = \sum_{j=1}^{N_T} A_{ij} x_j$ and $s_B = \sum_{k=1}^{M} B_{ik} c_k$.

The evolution of agent i's opinion is determined by four terms. These terms are the linear damping term d_i, the saturated network interaction term $S_1 (s_A)$, the saturated communication source influence term $S_2 (s_B)$, and the environmental signal terms g_i and e_i. Here, $S_1, S_2 : \mathbb{R} \rightarrow \mathbb{R}$ are bounded saturation functions satisfying $S(0) = 0$, $S(0)' = 1$, $S(0)'' = 0$, $S(0)''' \neq 0$ with an odd symmetry $S(-y) = -S(y)$; S_1 saturate the network interactions, S_2 saturates the communication sources influence; the damping coefficient $d_i > 0$ represents a trader's reluctance to form a strong belief since it drives the values $\dot{x}$ to the neutral point, which implies that higher d_i indicates that the trader will be more resistant to forming an opinion, however, the parameter $u_i \geq 0$ indicates how attentive agents are to their social interactions, which affects the degree to which their opinions are socially influenced. Environment inputs e_i, g_i represent opinions derived from the environment, which are independent of the other agents' opinions.

3.3 Minimal Opinion Network Model

The role of complex network interactions among trading agents, the effect of communication sources, and the impact of introducing information from the market environment on traders' opinion formation and market dynamics are studied here using a homogeneous regime of model Eq. 3, thus imposing restrictions on the following parameters: $d_i = d > 0$, $u_i = u > 0$, $and \; S_1 = S_2 = tanh$. In this regime, we consider a fully connected and homogeneous network of agents. To illustrate, let's consider a primitive network consisting of five traders. Here, the groups $\{T_1, T_2\}$ and $\{T_3, T_4, T_5\}$ represent two distinct communities that exhibit higher levels of trust among their members compared to other traders in the network. The initial parameters are set according to [4], where $u_i = 0.5$, $d_i = 1$ for all traders $i = 1, 2, \ldots, 5$. The initial opinion state is denoted as X_{t_0}, consisting of the values: $0.9, -0.4, 0.4, 0.1, -0.8$. Figure 1 depicts a scenario where traders, in the absence of external communication sources and market influences, shape their opinions through interaction with their social network. This process results in opinion clustering at convergence: one with traders T_1 and T_2 developing positive sentiments, and the other with traders T_3, T_4, and T_5 forming negative perceptions. The formation of these opinions is depended upon initial opinions. In a subsequent experiment, using the same setup, we incorporated environmental inputs. The inputs, represented by g_i and e_i, which were uniformly set to 0.5 for all traders, suggesting a universally positive expectation of price increase given the current market state. As displayed in Fig. 2, the opinions align towards a positive consensus. This indicates that the environmental input's value overpowers the influence of inter-network communication among the trading communities. However, the introduction of an attention model – as detailed in Sect. 3.2 – created a different scenario. In this model, each trader pays more attention to their neighbors and communication sources when experiencing losses or as the market session nears its end. As shown in Fig. 3, this leads to polarization in opinions. This suggests that traders pay more attention to their social networks, which, in turn, becomes the primary force shaping their opinions.

Figure 4 shows the opinion formation taken a sparse opinion distribution when information from one communication source is introduced. Each trader trusted the same information source, differently based on the weight matrix B. However, when we introduce a positive input from the environment, we can see in Fig. 5 that the opinions are moved toward the positive, which indicates that input from the environment dominates the opinions' formation even in the presence of an information source. Finally, in Fig. 6, we set T_3 to have a positive opinion equals +1 from time $t2$ and onward. It can be seen that T_4 and T_5 opinions are influenced by their trusted neighbor T_3 and shift their opinions to the positive side while T_1 and T_2 shift their opinion away from them to the negative side as they are in the untrusted neighboring community. Overall, these results suggest that using the homogeneous regime, both external market inputs and internal network dynamics play crucial roles in shaping traders' opinions. The relative influence of these factors varies based on specific market conditions and individual trader parameter settings.

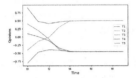 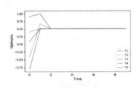 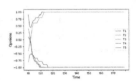

Fig. 1. Clustering with no communication or market input.

Fig. 2. Positive consensus with positive market input and no communication.

Fig. 3. Polarization in the absence of communication and market input.

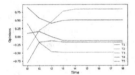 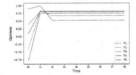 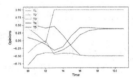

Fig. 4. Opinion formation with varied weight in matrix B and no market input.

Fig. 5. Opinion formation with communication sources, varying weight in matrix B, and positive market input.

Fig. 6. Change in opinion when T_3 adopts a positive opinion from t_2 onward.

4   Adding BFL to PRDE

PRZI [12], the ancestor of PRDE [11], was specifically designed to enable traders to adapt effectively to shifting market conditions, aligning their actions with their designated roles as either buyers or sellers. Nevertheless, PRDE traders are unable to predict market trends. Consequently, PRDE traders, whether acting as buyers or sellers, establish quote prices based on the value of their specific strategy. Within this framework, a trader's approach can range from urgent to relaxed or even neutral, all in accordance with its strategy's value. Importantly, this value isn't static—it co-evolves in response to the strategies employed by other market participants. In this study, we give PRDE traders a real-valued opinion variable. This addition implies that opinionated PRDE (BFL-PRDE) buyers and sellers will exhibit divergent behaviors, even within the same market conditions. For example, when the consensus opinion anticipates rising prices, BFL-PRDE buyers, functioning as a hybrid of GVWY and ZIC, will respond with increased urgency. Consequently, they will set their quote prices based on strategy values influenced by these opinions. In contrast, BFL-PRDE sellers will exhibit a more relaxed approach, quoting prices based on strategy values that resembles a ZIC and SHVR hybrid. The same logic applies when the prevailing opinion forecasts falling asset prices. To clarify, consider the relationship between the opinion x_i and the PRDI $s_i - value$. If trader i forms an opinion that prices will ascend, and i is a buyer, the trader should skew its PMF toward urgency. Conversely, if i is a seller, the trader should incline its PMF toward relaxation. The same logic holds if the trader anticipates a price drop.

By this point, it should be obvious that we require some function that maps from trader i's opinion variable x_i to its PRDE strategy s_i, i.e., $s_i = F_i(x_i)$. Considering the simplest case, since both s_i and $x_i \in [-1, +1] \in \mathbb{R}$, it is possible for the mapping to be the identity function, or its opposite, depending upon whether i is a buyer or a seller. A buyer's simplest F_i is identity function: $F_i(+1) = +1, F_i(-1) = -1$, whereas a seller's simplest F_i is negative identity function: $F_i(+1) = -1, F_i(-1) = +1$. It should be noted, however, that this fairly rapidly shifts the trader's strategy to the extremes (either SHVR or GVWY) as $|x| \to 1$; therefore, this may not always be the most effective approach: because at the extremes, buyers usually lose. Consider, for example, a buyer playing SHVR. It will be moving away from its minimum price to its limit price, which means it ends up quoting high quote prices. In contrast, a seller playing SHVR moves from its maximum price while still making high quote prices, and generates more profit as a result. Additionally, when a buyer plays GVWY, it loses since its limit price is its maximum price. At the extremes, a buyer only has a chance of winning when the seller plays GVWY. It is due to the fact that the seller will maintain its limit price as its minimum price. This results in the deal being in favor of the buyer, even if the buyer is bidding higher than its limit price.

In [11], it is assumed that each PRDE trader maintains a private local population of potential strategy-values of population-size $NP \geq 4$, which for trader i can be represented by $s_{i,1}, s_{i,2}, ..., s_{i,NP}$. Since PRDE traders use just a single real scalar value to specify their bargaining behavior, every individual in the DE population is a single value. Consequently, the conventional DE concept of crossover (i.e., selecting alleles from two parents, one allele per dimension of the genomes) is not applicable: PRDE constructs a genome entirely by operating on the base vector. In its current configuration, PRDE applies the basic "vanilla" DE/rand/1 where, after evaluating a particular strategy $s_{i,x}$, three other s-values are randomly selected from the population: $s_{i,a}, s_{i,b},$ and $s_{i,c}$ where $x \neq a \neq b \neq c$, and therefore a new candidate strategy $s_{i,y}$ is created s.t. $s_{i,y} = max(min(s_{i,a}+F_i(s_{i,b}-s_{i,c}),+1),-1)$ where F_i represents the trader's differential weight coefficient (in the experiments reported here, $F_i = 0.8; \forall i$), using the min and max functions, the candidate strategy is kept within the range $[-1.0, +1.0]$. In BFL-PRDE we introduce the trader's opinion $s_{i,o}$ as a new candidate strategy. Then the fitness of $s_{i,y}$ and $s_{i,o}$ are evaluated and the best strategy replaces $s_{i,x}$, otherwise, it is discarded; and then the next strategy $s_{i,x+1}$ is evaluated.

5   Evaluation

In this section, we aim to evaluate the BFL-PRDE extension of PRDE by answering the following four questions: firstly, we consider how the opinion dynamics of BFL-PRDE traders affect market prices. Secondly, we question if the distribution of prices can impact the opinions of traders. Thirdly, we make comparisons between markets populated only by BFL-PRDE traders and those populated solely by PRDE traders. Lastly, we seek to identify the minimum size of a trader group, if any, that can effectively induce significant price inflation in a given asset, thus potentially disrupting market stability.

5.1   Implementation Details

In the subsequent experiments, we employ the BSE platform to simulate a single-commodity financial market. The simulation involves a total of $N = 60$ traders, comprising an equal number of buyers and sellers ($N_B = N_S = 30$ each). It is important to note that traders are assigned a fixed role and cannot switch between buyer and seller positions. The only decision each trader can make is the price at which they are willing to quote. Each trader implements the BFL-PRDE strategy with $k = 5$. The simulation incorporates a pricing schedule to achieve perfect elasticity of supply and demand, ensuring that every seller can find a buyer who acts as a counterparty and vice versa. Specifically, buyers are assigned a maximum purchase price of \$140 per unit, while sellers are restricted to a minimum sale price of \$60 per unit. This pricing scheme is widely used in experimental economics research to ensure that no trader is given extra-marginal prices that would restrict their ability to find counterparties. When a transaction occurs, both traders' cash and stock assignments are depleted, and they become inactive for a random duration of up to five seconds before they receive fresh cash or stock, enabling them to resume trading.

To simulate continuous time, BSE employs a discrete time-slicing approach with a temporal step-size of $\Delta t = 1/N$, meaning that each trader can interact with the market at least once per second. Our experiments run for 150 days of round-the-clock 24×7 trading, even though the co-evolutionary dynamics play out over much longer periods. We calculate the profit per second (PPS) of each strategy s at time t by summing all profits generated during the time interval $[t - \Delta_E, t]$ and dividing that sum by the evaluation period Δ_E. We set Δ_E to 7200 s, and since there are $k = 5$ strategies, each trader requires 10 simulated hours to evaluate all its candidate strategies. Transaction profits are determined by the difference between the agreed-upon price and the buyer's and seller's individual limit prices. For example, if a transaction occurs at a price of $90, the buyer's profit on the trade is $50 (denoted as π_B), and the seller's profit is $30 (denoted as π_S), because all buyers have a limit price of $140, and all sellers have a limit price of $60.

In this paper, the primary focus is the internal dynamics of opinion formation amongst traders, specifically through the BFL opinion dynamics model. We have initialized the model with the following parameters: $u_i = 0.5$, $d_i = 1$ for all $i = 1$, $\ldots$, N, $A = [a_{ij}] = [1]$ for all $i, j = 1, \ldots, N$. Notably, we intentionally do not incorporate communication sources in this analysis. This is a strategic choice to study the self-contained opinion dynamics within the traders' network, free from the influence of external sources of information (not directly extracted from the market). This approach allows us to investigate the inherent behaviors and trends within the system itself, which can form a basis for understanding the more complex scenarios where external information sources come into play, a topic we plan to explore in subsequent works.

5.2   Market Reactions to Opinions

In this experiment, we present the impact of opinions on prices as observed in our simulations. Our first evaluation question is addressed by examining the results from extreme opinion distributions, such as those in which all traders hold extremely positive opinions, those in which all hold extremely negative opinions, those where all traders hold neutral opinions, i.e., the price is not expected to change.

Figure 7 displays results from 12 IID 150-day experiments. During these experiments, traders were exogenously given negative opinions for the first 45 days, neutral opinions for the next 60 days, and positive opinions for the final 45 days. Notably, transaction prices in a positive market-with each trader consistently holding a +1 opinion-ranged from $110 to $140. In contrast, in a negative market where every trader held a constant −1 opinion, prices fluctuated between $75 and $100. During the neutral phase, with opinions at 0, prices were between $115 and $125. The figure illustrates the reactive nature of market prices to these shifts in opinions. Intriguingly, transaction prices align closely with traders' opinions during all three phases, suggesting a causal relationship between opinions and price-quoting decisions. These outcomes align precisely with intuitive expectations, thus validating the functionality of the system under extreme conditions where opinions remain constant and when they shift.

Figure 8 complements these findings by presenting the corresponding changes in traders' profit per second (PPS) values. During the initial 45-day period, when all traders held negative opinions, sellers traded urgently and entered into transactions that yielded less profit for them, while buyers traded with less urgency and held out for more profitable prices. However, during the last 45 days, as the opinions shifted to positive, the fortunes of buyers and sellers reversed. Notably, during the neutral phase of opinions, traders quoted uniform random prices, and sellers predominantly benefited, this is because the most treated prices were relatively high, which means that usually, the deal ends up in the favor of the sellers. We observed that the most commonly agreed-upon price was \$140 in the positive phase, \$60 in the negative phase, and \$130 during the neutral phase. This sheds light on the reason behind the lower profits for buyers in the last two phases.

In our model of a financial market that uses opinionated agents, we observe a causal relationship between opinions and prices, which replicates the findings of [29]. However, in the following section, we show that our system goes beyond their work by demonstrating causality in the opposite direction. Specifically, we illustrate that changes in the distribution of prices within the market can impact the distribution of opinions among traders' population.

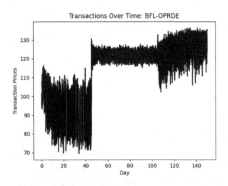 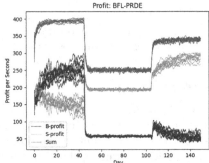

Fig. 7. Plot of transaction prices from 12 IID experiments. Illustrating prices' correlation with opinions shifts.

Fig. 8. Profitability-per-second (PPS) plot (from the same experiments in Fig. 7).

5.3   Price-Driven Shifts in Opinions

In the world of financial trading, the term *market impact* is often used to denote instances where the quoted price of a security changes in response to a proposed large trade, large enough to alter the supply or demand curve for the security. This price shift results in a less favorable price for the trader attempting to carry out the large trade, compared to the price quoted on the exchange when the order was initially placed. This means that the trader trying to execute the large trade gets a worse price than what was quoted on the exchange at the time that trader issued the order; and crucially this shift in price occurs *before any transaction has actually taken place.* For example if a real-world stock-trader issues a bid-quote to buy a single share of IBM, the price that trader is quoted by potential sellers of IBM will be very close to whatever the current best ask price is on the exchange's LOB for IBM; but if the trader instead issues a bid-quote for one million IBM shares, this sudden revelation of excess demand for IBM stock means that potential sellers of IBM are all likely to alter the prices they quote, shifting upward, to reflect the rise in IBM's share-price that the sellers anticipate occurring as an immediate consequence of the newly increased demand for that stock. Similarly, the arrival of a large ask order will prompt potential buyers to instantly revise their bid-prices down – and, in both cases, the price change happens before any transaction takes place.

In Sect. 3.2, we introduced $\Delta_m(t)$ as a way of measuring supply/demand imbalance at the top of the LOB and so in this experiment we add $\Delta_m(t)$ to the opinion dynamics model in Eq. 3 as the environment factor e_i. In consequence, BFL-PRDE traders alter their behavior in response to anticipated changes in price – that is, they will be sensitive to market impact, because their opinions will be affected by the distribution of prices (and quantities) on the LOB. For example, when prices are likely to rise, BFL-PRDE buyers should feel an increased sense of urgency and BFL-PRDE sellers should feel a decreasing sense of urgency. In contrast, when prices are likely to fall, BFL-PRDE sellers should increase their urgency, whereas BFL-PRDE buyers should reduce their urgency.

To test this, here we show results from 12 IID experiments in which the market is suddenly flooded with a large number of sell orders all priced at $60 during the period from day 60 to day 90, after which the excess sell orders are abruptly removed: this step-change in excess supply in the market causes an imbalance at the top of the LOB, resulting in a negative value of $\Delta_m(t)$, which indicates an expected near-term decline in the asset price. We found that buyers' strategies at this point clustering around –0.8, which means buyers are being relaxed and acting as a hybrid of ZIC and SHVR; on the other hand, sellers' strategies over the same period clustering around +0.8 i.e. acting urgently as a hybrid of ZIC and GVWY. As can be seen from Fig. 9, the change in strategies is reflected in the quoted prices, leading to a substantial decline in transaction prices during the period of excess supply. The same effect is shown in the PPS time series shown in Fig. 10: sellers have suffered significant losses, while buyers have made huge profits during the period of excess supply. This demonstrates that market dynamics have an impact on opinion dynamics. Thus, we are able to affirmatively answer our second evaluation question.

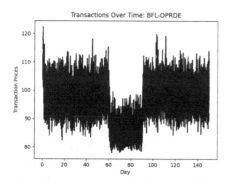
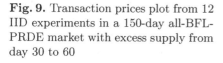
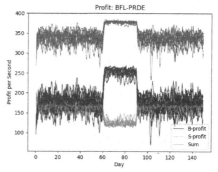

Fig. 9. Transaction prices plot from 12 IID experiments in a 150-day all-BFL-PRDE market with excess supply from day 30 to 60

Fig. 10. Profitability plot from 12 IID experiments with only BFL-PRDE traders (from the same experiments in Fig. 9)

A simplified version of BFL-PRDE is presented here. However, Eq. 2 has the weakness of being sensitive only to imbalances at the top of the LOB (the measure is not sensitive to imbalances at deeper levels of the LOB, thus being quite fragile). Multi-level order flow imbalance (MLOFI) is an alternative metric that can be used to measure imbalance as proposed by [13], which takes into account multiple levels of the LOB when determining LOB supply/demand imbalance.

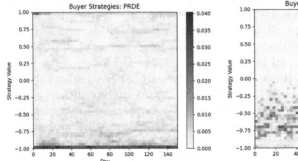

Fig. 11. Heatmap of PRDE buyers strategy distribution from one of the experiments in Fig. 14.

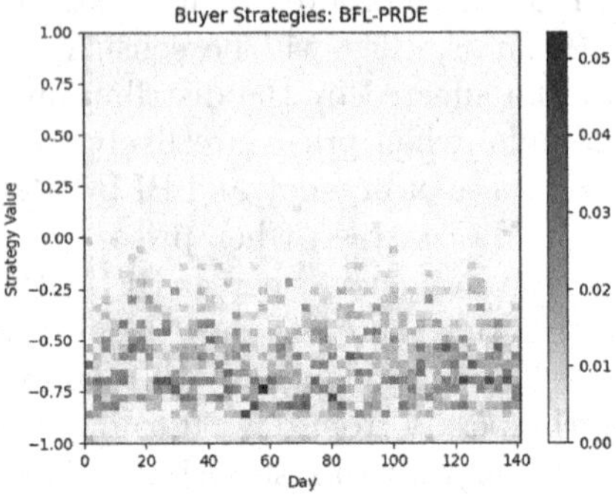

Fig. 12. Heatmap of BFL-PRDE buyers strategy distribution from the same experiment as Fig. 13

5.4   A Side-by-Side Look at BFL-PRDE and PRDE

Here we compare the performance of PRDE and BFL-PRDE over twelve IID trials, each lasting 150 days. To illustrate the co-evolutionary dynamics under the BFL OD model at the level of individual traders' strategies, Fig. 11 shows heatmaps illustrating the elite s-values of the 30 buyers in a 150-day experiment conducted in a market populated by PRDE. Similarly, Fig. 12 depicts the heatmaps illustrating the elite s-values of the 30 buyers in a 150-day experiment conducted in a market populated by BFL-PRDE. for which the corresponding PPS is shown in Figs. 14 and 13. Both experiments assigned initial strategy values at $(t = 0)$ randomly from a uniform distribution over the range $[-1.0, +1.0]$. Upon visual inspection, it is clear that BFL-PRDE traders are moving in a more diverse strategy space than PRDE traders. Note that sellers' s-values are the inverse of the buyers'.

Figure 13 presents a PPS plot for 12 IID experiments conducted in a market populated by BFL-PRDE traders. Despite the total profit extracted (i.e., $\pi_T(t)$) by these traders being less than that of PRDE traders-as Fig. 14 demonstrates-there is a distinctive pattern of profit-making. Notably, BFL-PRDE buyers and sellers generate profits interchangeably. This fluctuating profit dynamic is markedly different from the consistent losses experienced by PRDE buyers, suggesting that BFL-PRDE traders, being opinionated, are adapting faster than PRDE traders. Since BFL-PRDE and PRDE differ only in the use of OD, this increase in performance can be directly related to OD. The third evaluation question was thus clarified.

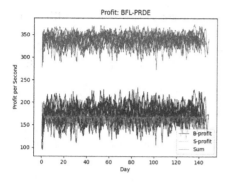
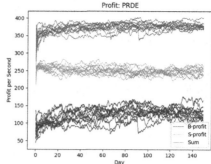

Fig. 13. A profitability plot of 12 IID 150-day experiment for a market populated exclusively with BFL-PRDE traders (i.e., under BFL OD model).

Fig. 14. Plot of profitability data from 12 IID experiments 150-day experiment in a market populated entirely by PRDE traders.

5.5   Market Dynamics: Stability and Influence

As mentioned in the previous experiments, we operate within an idealized economic environment, hypothesizing perfectly elastic supply and demand curves in a market at a stable equilibrium. This model allows for a controlled examination of market disruption, as minor shifts can have substantial implications. Perfect elasticity indicates infinite responsiveness from both buyers and sellers to any price changes, keeping the market in a static equilibrium state.

Figure 15 showcases the results from twelve experimental trials conducted using a bounded randomized regime setting, with attention incrementally increasing over time. The term "bounded" in this context refers to the use of a uniform distribution confined to the same values as in the homogeneous regime from our previous experiments. For example, the network weights are bounded between -2 and $+1$; attention values are limited within the range 0.1 to 0.5, and resistance values are constrained between 0.1 and 1.0. Figure 15 visual

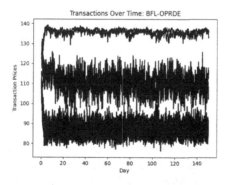

Fig. 15. Transaction prices of 12 IID of the bounded randomized regime with attention incremented over time, showing the stable market state.

representation aids in understanding how the market sustains its equilibrium, despite variations in trial parameters and network weights within their limits. It is important to note that during these experiments, all traders receive the same input/signal from the market/environment in terms of the event and the global opinions e and g.

In order to address our fourth research question in the upcoming experiment, we intend to intentionally disrupt this stability, thus creating an environment that helps us investigate market instability factors. As proposed by Zigrand et al. [41], market instability can be primarily attributed to nonlinear sensitivities to changes, incomplete information, and internal or "endogenous" risks emanating from system feedback loops. Nonlinear sensitivities to changes suggest that seemingly minor modifications can precipitate significant market responses, potentially inducing instability. Incomplete information introduces disparities in knowledge distribution among market participants, thereby making some better informed than others, which can lead to uneven responses to changes and thereby cause market volatility. In addition, endogenous risks, born from internal feedback loops within the system, may destabilize the market even further. Such feedback loops may amplify or diminish the effects of the initial market disturbance, leading to unpredictable market behaviors. These factors intertwine to produce complex market dynamics that are challenging to understand and predict.

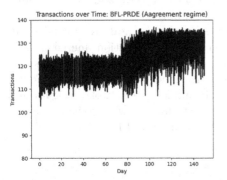 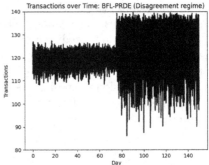

Fig. 16. Transaction prices of 12 IID experiments showing the influence of one trader over a fully connected trusted network: $A = [a_{ij}] = 1$ for all i, j.

Fig. 17. Transaction prices of 12 IID experiments showing the influence of one trader over a fully connected conflicted network: $A = [a_{ij}] \in [-2, 1]$ for all i, j.

Our objective in this experiment is to determine the minimum group size of informed traders that can significantly disturb market stability. This initial exploratory research lays the foundation with a basic experiment, with the plan to incrementally introduce more complexity in future papers. The first experiment, represented in Fig. 16 and 18, uses an agent network that is fully connected, with each connection having an equal weight of 1. The experiment is initiated with traders' opinions being in the neutral state $X_{t_0} = (0)$, then mid-way through the trial, a chosen group of traders is externally informed about a forthcoming price change. Our results interestingly show that the influence of a single trader can affect a group of 60 traders. Notably, in the middle of the trial period, transaction prices began to rise, mirroring the positive opinion $(+1)$ of the informed trader; concurrently, we observed a positive shift in the traders' opinions resulting in a total agreement among traders. The second experiment, illustrated in Fig. 17 and 19, involves modifying the network weights to be drawn from a uniform distribution between -2 and 1, suggesting varied trust levels among traders. This test further emphasizes the substantial impact a single trader can exert, affirming that one trader can indeed influence a group of 60 traders. However, it also revealed considerable fluctuations in transaction prices. Despite the informed trader maintaining a positive opinion of $+1$, prices showed significant variability. This variation can be attributed to traders who has a negative (or suspicious) relationship, diverging in their responses to the informed trader's positive opinion, as well as the traders swayed by it. This outcome underscores how diverse relationships among traders within the network can significantly influence market behavior. The opinion forming a bifractation can be observed in Fig. 19 with each group moving apart from the other, the one influenced by the trader and the other influenced to move away from it. It is worth noting that the current population consists of only 60 traders, which is relatively small. However, we recognize the importance of conducting future experiments with a significantly larger number of traders. By increasing the sample size, we can enhance the reliability and confidence in the results obtained.

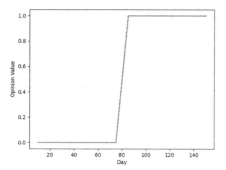 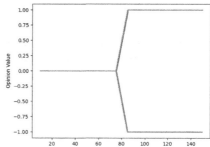

Fig. 18. Collective Opinion forming a consensus by the influence of one informed trader in the agreement regime.

Fig. 19. Collective opinion forming a symmetric bifurcation influenced by one informed trader in the disagreement regime.

6   Discussion and Conclusions

In this research, we have expanded upon the experimental framework for agent-based narrative economics models, first introduced in our earlier work [5]. In doing so, we have reviewed the model's underlying rationale and mechanics more deeply and have undertaken additional exploration of a variety of the simulated market system-related aspects. These market systems were able to exhibit a reciprocal network of interactions where narratives (opinions) influence prices. Conversely, fluctuations in prices can impact and reshape opinions (narratives). One key area of focus was to identify the minimal size of an informed group that could profoundly impact market stability. Our findings were surprising, revealing that the influence of a single trader could significantly alter the dynamics within a pool of 60 traders. These results contribute to our understanding of market dynamics, demonstrating how a single agent's actions can ripple through an interconnected system, significantly altering its behavior. As we move forward, we plan to incrementally introduce more complexity in our future experiments to further uncover market instability factors.

Shiller's seminal proposal for work on narrative economics argues that empirical research should collect data on the narratives individuals share about economic matters, which subsequently shape their anticipations of future economic events, and in turn, significantly influence economic dynamics. The work we have presented here proposes an alternative, yet complementary, experimental approach to Shiller's. Our approach offers experimentalists the opportunity to access agent-based simulations via our platform, enabling a deeper understanding of the dynamic interplay between opinions, the expression of these opinions, and the resulting economic outcomes. To facilitate other researchers in replicating and building upon our results, we will provide our system's source code as a freely available open-source repository on GitHub[1]. We are excited to observe the varied applications our system will serve in future research.

A key limitation of this study is its predominant focus on simulations conducted in a homogeneous regime with predefined parameters. This holds true even in randomized scenarios where these parameters were still stringently controlled. Our next step will be to integrate dynamic feedback into the OD model parameters. We aim to develop feedback mechanisms that enable the model to adapt to fluctuating market conditions. This, in turn, will promote a robust dynamical transition between distinct opinion patterns.

References

1. Abergel, F., Anane, M., Chakraboti, A., Jedidi, A., Toke, I.: Limit Order Books. Cambridge University Press, Cambridge (2016)
2. Axtell, R.L., Farmer, J.D.: Agent-based modeling in economics and finance: past, present, and future. J. Econ. Lit. (2022)
3. Bilal, Pant, M., Zaheer, H., Garcia-Hernandez, L., Abraham, A.: Differential evolution: a review of more than two decades of research. Eng. Appl. Artif. Intell. **90**, 103479 (2020)
4. Bizyaeva, A., Franci, A., Leonard, N.E.: Nonlinear opinion dynamics with tunable sensitivity. IEEE Trans. Autom. Control (2022)

---

[1] https://github.com/NarrativeEconomics/OD.

5. Bokhari, A., Cliff, D.: Studying narrative economics by adding continuous-time opinion dynamics to an agent-based model of co-evolutionary adaptive financial markets. In: Proceedings of the 15th International Conference on Agents and Artificial Intelligence - Volume 2: ICAART, pp. 355–367. INSTICC, SciTePress (2023). https://doi.org/10.5220/0011797000003393

6. Cartea, Á., Jaimungal, S., Penalva, J.: Algorithmic and High-Frequency Trading. Cambridge University Press, Cambridge (2015)

7. Chen, S.H.: Agent-Based Computational Economics. Routledge, London (2018)

8. Cliff, D.: Minimal-intelligence agents for bargaining behaviours in market-based environments. Technical report. HPL-97-91, HP Labs Technical report (1997)

9. Cliff, D.: Bristol stock exchange: open-source financial exchange simulator (2012). https://github.com/davecliff/BristolStockExchange

10. Cliff, D.: BSE: a minimal simulation of a limit-order-book stock exchange (2018). ArXiv:1809.06027

11. Cliff, D.: Metapopulation differential co-evolution of trading strategies in a model financial market. In: Proceedings of the 2022 IEEE Symposium Series on Computational Intelligence (SSCI) (2022)

12. Cliff, D.: Parameterised response zero intelligence traders. J. Econ. Interact. Coord. 1–54 (2023)

13. Cont, R., Cucuringu, M., Zhang, C.: Price impact of order flow imbalance: multi-level, cross-sectional and forecasting (2021). ArXiv:2112.13213

14. Das, R., Hanson, J.E., Kephart, J.O., Tesauro, G.: Agent-human interactions in the CDA. In: Proceedings of the IJCAI2001, pp. 1169–1178 (2001)

15. De Luca, M., Szostek, C., Cartlidge, J., Cliff, D.: Studies of interaction between human traders and algorithmic trading systems. Technical report, UK Government Office for Science, London, September 2011

16. De Luca, M., Cliff, D.: Agent-human interactions in the CDA, redux. In: Proceedings of the ICAART-2011 (2011)

17. De Luca, M., Cliff, D.: Human-agent auction interactions: adaptive-aggressive agents dominate. In: Proceedings of the IJCAI 2011 (2011)

18. DeGroot, M.H.: Reaching a consensus. J. Am. Stat. Assoc. **69**(345), 118–121 (1974)

19. Farmer, J.D., Patelli, P., Zovko, I.: The Predictive Power of Zero Intelligence in Financial Markets. PNAS **102**(6), 2254–2259 (2005). https://doi.org/10.1073/pnas.0409157102

20. Friedman, D., Rust, J. (eds.): The Double Auction Market. Addison-Wesley, Boston (1992)

21. Ghaderi, J., Srikant, R.: Opinion dynamics in social networks with stubborn agents: equilibrium and convergence rate. Automatica **50**(12), 3209–3215 (2014)

22. Gjerstad, S., Dickhaut, J.: Price formation in double auctions. Games Econ. Behav. **22**(1), 1–29 (1998)

23. Gjerstad, S., et al.: The impact of pace in double auction bargaining. University of Arizona, Department of Economics Working Paper, p. 03 (2003)

24. Gode, D.K., Sunder, S.: Allocative efficiency of markets with zero-intelligence traders: market as a partial substitute for individual rationality. J. Polit. Econ. **101**(1), 119–137 (1993)

25. Gould, M., Porter., M., Williams, S., McDonald, M., Fenn, D., Howison, S.: Limit order books. Quant. Financ. **13**(11), 1709–1742 (2013)

26. Guzelyte, R., Cliff, D.: Narrative economics of the racetrack: an agent-based model of opinion dynamics in in-play betting on a sports betting exchange. In: Rocha, A.P., Steels, L., van den Herik, J. (eds.) Proceedings of the 14th International

Conference on Agents and Artificial Intelligence (ICAART2022), vol. 1, pp. 225–236. Scitepress (2022)

27. Hommes, C., LeBaron, B. (eds.): Computational Economics: Heterogeneous Agent Modeling. North-Holland (2018)

28. Ladley, D.: Zero intelligence in economics and finance. Knowl. Eng. Rev. **27**(2), 273–286 (2012)

29. Lomas, K., Cliff, D.: Exploring narrative economics: an agent-based modeling platform that integrates automated traders with opinion dynamics. In: Rocha, A.P., Steels, L., van den Herik, J. (eds.) Proceedings of the 13th International Conference on Agents and Artificial Intelligence (ICAART2021), vol. 1, pp. 137–148. SciTePress (2021)

30. Mei, W., Bullo, F., Chen, G., Hendrickx, J., Dörfler, F.: Rethinking the microfoundation of opinion dynamics: rich consequences of an inconspicuous change. arXiv preprint arXiv:1909.06474 (2019)

31. O'Hara, M.: Market Microstructure Theory. John Wiley & Sons, Hoboken (1998)

32. Rust, J., Miller, J., Palmer, R.: Behavior of trading automata in a computerized double auction market. In: Friedman, D., Rust, J. (eds.) The Double Auction Market, pp. 155–198. Addison-Wesley (1992)

33. Shiller, R.: Narrative economics. Am. Econ. Rev. **107**(4), 967–1004 (2017)

34. Shiller, R.: Narrative Economics: How Stories Go Viral & Drive Major Economic Events. Princeton (2019)

35. Smith, V.: Papers in Experimental Economics. Cambridge University Press, Cambridge (1991)

36. Storn, R., Price, K.: Differential evolution: a simple and efficient heuristic for global optimization over continuous spaces. J. Glob. Optim. **11**, 341–359 (1997)

37. Tesauro, G., Bredin, J.: Sequential strategic bidding in auctions using dynamic programming. In: Proceedings of the AAMAS2002 (2002)

38. Tesauro, G., Das, R.: High-performance bidding agents for the continuous double auction. In: Proceedings of the 3rd ACM Conference on E-Commerce, pp. 206–209 (2001)

39. Tesfatsion, L., Judd, K. (eds.): Handbook of Computational Economics, vol. 2: Agent-Based Computational Economics. North-Holland (2006)

40. Vytelingum, P., Cliff, D., Jennings, N.R.: Strategic bidding in continuous double auctions. Artif. Intell. **172**(14), 1700–1729 (2008)

41. Zigrand, J.P., Cliff, D., Hendershott, T.: Financial stability and computer based trading. The Future of Computer Trading in Financial Markets. Working paper, pp. 6–23 (2011)

GaSUME: A BERT-Covered Genetic Algorithm for Text Summarization

Imen Tanfouri[1] and Fethi Jarray[1,2(✉)]

[1] LIMTIC Laboratory, UTM University, Tunis, Tunisia
fjarray@gmail.com
[2] Higher Institute of Computer Science of Medenine, Tunis, Tunisia

Abstract. Automatic Text Summarization (ATS) is a fundamental task in natural language processing (NLP), it deals to reduce text size by deleting extraneous data while keeping the original text's semantic structure. Lately, transformer-based models have achieved remarkable success in ATS and have been regarded as state-of-the-art models for various NLP applications. In this study, we are interested in extractive summarization for a single text, where the purpose is to extract a selection of sentences that best expresses the document's summary. For automatic text summarization, we propose a combination of Bidirectional Encoder Representations from Transformers (BERT) and a Genetic Algorithm (GA) called GaSUME an improved extension of GaSum system [1], where GA is used as a search space approach and BERT is utilized as a fitness metric. We evaluate our model on the CNN Daily Mail and PubMed available datasets, Our results showed that GaSUME achieves a ROUGE-1 score of 55.89% on the CNN Daily Mail dataset and outperforms the state-of-the-art methods by a significant margin in terms of the rouge score.

Keywords: Document summarization · Natural language processing · Bert model · Genetic algorithm · Triplet loss function

1 Introduction

Automatic text summarization is the process of generating a short version of a larger text while retaining the most important information and overall meaning. This process is usually carried out by a computer program or algorithm that analyzes the text and extracts the most relevant sentences or phrases, which are then assembled into a shorter summary.

Text summarization can be useful in a variety of contexts, such as news articles, research papers, and legal documents, where there is a need to quickly extract key information from a large amount of text. There are two main types of text summarization: extractive summarization [5,6], which selects and combines sentences directly from the original text, and abstractive summarization [2–4] which generates new sentences based on the meaning of the original text. ATS systems can also be classified as single-document or multi-document summarization systems according to the number of input documents. The former produces the summary from a single document, whereas the latter generates the summary from a group of documents.

A. P. Rocha et al. (Eds.): ICAART 2023, LNAI 14546, pp. 411–424, 2024.
https://doi.org/10.1007/978-3-031-55326-4_20

Automated text summarization can save time and effort for individuals who need to read and understand large amounts of text, and can also be used to enhance search engine results and improve the efficiency of natural language processing tasks. However, the accuracy and effectiveness of automated text summarization still pose a challenge, as it requires a deep understanding of language and context to accurately capture the main ideas and relevant details of a text.

Over the years, researchers have developed various approaches to tackle this challenging problem, including traditional methods like rule-based algorithms and statistical approaches. However, recent advancements in deep learning have brought new possibilities, with techniques such as the integration of Genetic Algorithms (GA) and Bidirectional Encoder Representations from Transformers (BERT) showing promising results in text summarization.

In this contribution, we focus on an extractive summary-level approach, and we aim to fix its issues by proposing a Genetic Algorithm (GA) wrapped BERT method. This paper extends our recent article, GaSUM: A Genetic Algorithm Wrapped BERT for Text Summarization [1], where different crossover and mutation operators are implemented. In addition, we add the PubMed dataset [29] in the evaluation step. The contribution of this work can be summarized as follows:

1. Propose GaSUME: a hybrid approach of GA and BERT for extractive summary level approach for single document summarization.
2. Wrap the MatchSUM approach and run it inside a GA structure.
3. Validate our method on the CNN/Daily Mail and PubMed available dataset and achieve state-of-the-art performance.

The remainder of this paper is structured as follows. Section 2 reviews the related work on ATS. Section 3 explains our GaSUME proposed method for ATS. Section 4 details the experiments and the results. Section 5 concludes this paper and mentions some future extensions.

2   Related Works

Extractive text summarization approaches can be divided into traditional machine learning (ML) models that need handcrafted feature extraction and deep learning models that combine feature extraction and prediction into a single network. classical ML approaches include statistically based systems [7,8], support vector machine (SVM) [9], Latent Semantic Analysis (LSA) and Latent Dirichlet Allocation (LDA) [6,10–12], boosting [13], Reinforcement Learning [23], Sequence to Sequence models [24], and meta-heuristic approaches [14–16]. According to the approach used, an extractive summarization procedure can be either a sentence-level [19,24,25] or a summary-level [26]. An extractive sentence level consists of assigning a score for each sentence of the document, then selecting or extracting sentences with the highest score to create the final summary. The main drawback of this method is the fact that it does not take into account the semantics of a complete summary when selecting sentences independently. In order to cope with this challenge, Zhong [22] proposed MatchSUM, a summary-level approach that jointly learns salience and redundancy in extractive summarizing. They cast the summarization task as a semantic text-matching problem rather than the commonly used sequence labeling model. It consists of creating summaries and returning the summary with the greatest score. They modeled the scoring phase as a semantic textual matching problem and built a BERT-based framework to solve it. MatchSUM, on the other hand, becomes impractical when the search space is large, like in the case of long documents. They used a Siamese-based neural network to assess the semantic similarity between the original document and a candidate summary. They employed triplet loss, which requires that a good summary be semantically similar to the source content. They also received a 44.41 ROUGE-1 score on the CNN/DM dataset. Despite the fact that we have based our proposed solution on this, MatchSUM's fundamental drawback is the lack of a search strategy, which decides how to explore the search area in order to obtain a decent summary. One of our contributions is the development of a genetic algorithm to address the exploration problem.

Nada et al. [18] suggested a BERT-based method for clustering the embedded data vectors after embedding the phrases with BERT. Finally, sentences closer to the centroids are chosen for creating the summary. The fundamental disadvantage of this method is that the phrases are encoded separately into fixed-sized embeddings. Yang Liu [19] presented BERTSUM, an extension of BERT for extractive summarization, to address this issue. It is the first extractive sentence-level summarization model based on BERT. In contrast to the previous BERT release, which could only handle two sentences, it can accommodate numerous sentences by introducing a [CLS] token before each one. It earns a ROUGE-1 score of 30.01 on the CNN/DM dataset [3,20].

LEAD [21] presents a neural model for single-document summarization based on joint extraction and syntactic compression. This is a neural network model that encodes a source document, picks sentences from that document, and applies discrete compression options. They choose phrases from the document, find potential compressions using constituency parsing, then score those compressions using a neural model to provide the final summary. On the CNN/DM dataset, it gets a ROUGE-1 score of 40.43.

3   GaSUME Proposed Method

In this paper, we consider the extractive summarization task as an optimization problem, in which we try to extract the best subset of sentences that represent a coherent summary and maximize the evaluation score.

Our approach consists of two parts (see Fig. 1): a local search-based genetic algorithm (GA) to explore the search space and provide the best summary, and a BERT-based semantic textual similarity model (Fitness-BERT) to calculate a fitness score that represents the similarity between the original document and a proposed summary. We compute a global score of the selected summary, as opposed to the sentence-level summary approach.

We suppose that:

D is the input text created by N sentences, C is the candidate summary built of k sentences extracted from D, $\mathcal{C}$ presents the search space, i.e. the space of all feasible solutions or summaries, C^* is the human-annotated or golden summary of D, $f(D, C)$

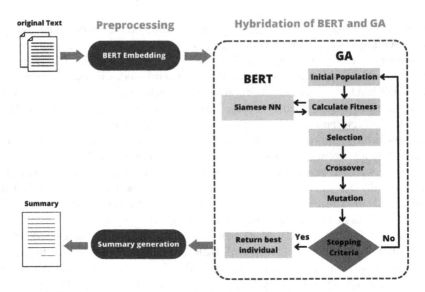

Fig. 1. GaSUME flowchart is created by a local search-based genetic algorithm to identify the best summary and a BERT-based fitness function to compute a summary's fitness score [1].

the similarity score of C according to D and $\hat{C}$ is the candidate summary with the highest score, i.e. the best summary according to the score [1]. Where:

$$\hat{C} = \arg\max_{C \in \mathcal{C}} score(C, D) \tag{1}$$

The most important issue in text summarization is the calculation of summaries' scores according to the original document. In this contribution, we use a similarity measurement based on BERT.

3.1 Fitness-BERT Component

We defined C and D similarity as Semantic Textual Similarity (STS) tasks. STS tries to measure the degree of similarity between the input texts D and the candidate summary C. We design a neural network known as a Siamese neural network (SNN) to determine how closely two texts are similar (see Fig. 2) [1].

SNN consists of two identical subnetworks, a.k.a. twin networks, that output the embedding of the given two input sentences. Each sub-network implements the BERT embedding. We feed the document D and the candidate summary C to SNN and take r_D and r_C as their token representations [CLS], respectively. We use cosine between r_D and r_C to measure the similarity between D and C [1],

$$f(D, C) = cosine(r_D, r_C) \tag{2}$$

SNN is commonly trained with the triplet loss function [28], which ensures that the gold summary is closer to the document than any other candidate summary. In its terminology, D is the anchor, C^* is the positive sample, and C is the negative sample [22]. Mathematically, it is stated as follows:

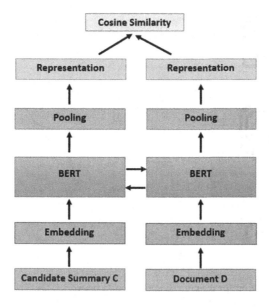

Fig. 2. A Siamese neural network (SNN) architecture that outputs the semantic similarity between the candidate summary and the original text [1].

$$L_1 = max(0, f(D, C) - f(D, C^*) + \gamma_1 \qquad (3)$$

where an γ_1 is a margin value (see Fig. 3).

We assume that the candidate summaries are sorted in decreasing order of ROUGE scores with the gold summary. Zhong et al. [22] added a pairwise margin loss for all the candidate summaries as a regularization term. The reasoning for this is that the candidate pair with the greatest rank gap should have the greatest score margin. Mathematically, it can be expressed as follows:

$$L_2 = max(0, f(D, C_j) - f(D, C_i) + (j - i)\gamma_2 \quad i < j \qquad (4)$$

where c_i denotes the candidate summary number i and γ_2 is a hyper parameter. Finally, the margin-based triplet loss can be expressed as Eq. (7)

$$L = L_1 + L_2 \qquad (5)$$

The most difficult aspect of using triplet loss is determining how to construct negative examples, i.e. the set of all summaries. In this case, we use the proposed pruning methodology [22], in which we first use a filtering operation to remove extraneous phrases and then use a brute-force method to construct all possible summaries [1].

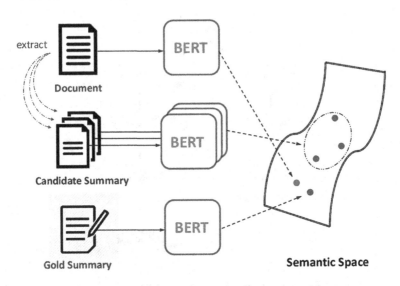

Fig. 3. Triplet loss function for training Siamese neural network [22]. The golden summary C^* should be semantically closer to the source document than any other candidate summary.

3.2 GA Component

The inference phase consists of selecting the highest score summary of document D.

$$\hat{C} = \arg\max_{C \in \mathcal{C}} f(D, C) \tag{6}$$

Since $\mathcal{C}$ is a very huge space, we propose GA to explore it. A genetic algorithm (GA) is a search-based algorithm for solving combinatorial optimization problems in machine learning, computer vision [27], and natural language processing. It initially creates a set of possible solutions known as population and then iteratively generates better and better individuals with regard to a fitness function or criterion by selecting, crossing, and mutating them (see Fig. 4). One of the main advantages of GA is that it does not need derivative computation. The most difficult aspect of using triplet loss is determining how to construct negative examples, i.e. the set of all summaries. In this case, we use the proposed pruning methodology [22], in which we first use a filtering operation to remove extraneous phrases and then use a brute-force method to construct all possible summaries [1].

Initial Population. This stage starts by generating a set of ps random individuals (chromosomes) as the initial population P. Each individual of P represents a potential solution (summary) to the problem at hand (text summarization). Each chromosome has n genes, where n is the total number of sentences in the document. Each gene represents a sentence, and it can take the value 1 if the sentence will participate in the summary or 0 otherwise.

For example, if we have a document with five sentences $n = 5$ and suppose that the population size $ps = 3$ the initial population may be as follows $P = ([01101], [10101],$

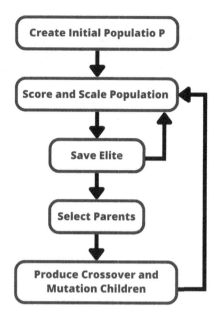

Fig. 4. Flowchart of genetic algorithm [1]. Which is composed of initial population generation, fitness scoring, parent selection, and diversification operators such as crossover and mutation.

[01101]). The selection of the population size Ps is a relevant issue because if the population is too small, the GA may converge too rapidly to a poor solution, and if it is too large, the algorithm may take a very long time to converge, particularly if the fitness function is time-consuming.

Next, if our initial population is created we assign a fitness value to each chromosome based on a predefined fitness function, which measures how well the solution solves the summarization task.

Elitism. This step consists to preserve the best individuals of the current population and pass them along unchanged to the following generation. This makes sure that the best solutions so far discovered are not lost in the course of evolution. This method greatly improves genetic algorithms, because it allows saving the best solutions when we create a new population.

Selection. The selection step involves choosing individuals with the best scores and allowing them to pass on their genes to the following generation. There are many ways to choose an individual from a population, including tournament selection, rank selection, and roulette wheel selection. The tournament selection strategy consists of selecting k individuals randomly from the population and keeping the best one, where k is the tournament size parameter. This process is repeated until we have the required number of individuals to successfully reproduce.

The tournament candidates are chosen in two variants: with or without replacement. In our experimental setting, we applied the tournament selection strategy with replacement. Once the selection of individuals to form the parents is performed, the next phase is the application of diversification operators such as crossover and mutation.

Crossover. Crossover is the process that consists of combining the genetic information of two individuals (parents) to produce new offspring (children). There are different techniques of swapping parents to get offspring such as one-point, two-point, and uniform crossover strategies (see Fig. 5). Uniform crossover supposed as a more general version of the multi-point crossover, where each bit (gene) is randomly swapped between the parents.

In this work, we adopt the uniform crossover strategy.

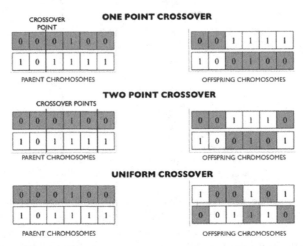

Fig. 5. Crossover strategies [1]. From top to bottom: select a pivot point and swap the tails of the two parents to get two new offspring, select two pivots and swap the middle substring of both parents and uniformly (probability 0.5) select each bit from parent 1 or parent 2.

Mutation. Mutation creates offspring by randomly altering some genes of individual parents. This helps in exploring new regions of the solution space that may lead to better solutions. There are different variants of mutation such as swap, insertion, inversion, and displacement mutation 6. In this manuscript, we adopt the insertion strategy.

Summary Generation. In the summarization task, after the execution of the genetic algorithm, we get the best individual with the highest fitness score. The final step is to decode this individual to get the final summary. We take the positions of genes with value 1, and we concatenate sentences of these positions in the same order as the original text [1].

Toy Example. Figure 7 shows a toy example of a document summarization. Table 1 presents the scores of similarity between the original and the generated summary.

The final summary returned by GaSUME is evaluated using the Recall-Oriented Understudy for Gisting Evaluation (ROUGE) metric which considers both Recall and Precision between candidate (model-generated) summary and reference (golden-annotated) summary. It is branched into ROUGE-1, ROUGE-2, and ROUGE-L scores.

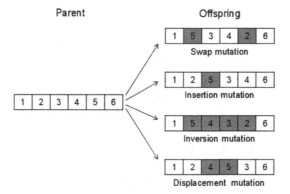

Fig. 6. Mutation strategies [1]. From top to bottom; exchange the values of two bits, randomly select a bit and randomly insert it, invert the values of a sequence of bits, and displace a sequence of bits.

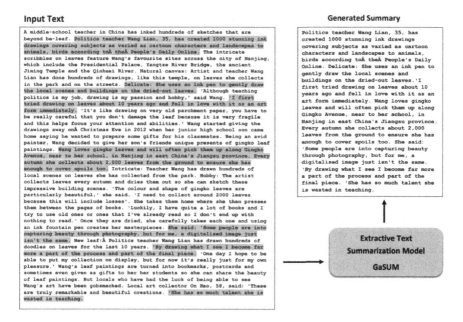

Fig. 7. Example of running GaSUME algorithm over a toy example. The extracted sentences are highlighted in the original document.

In ROUGE-1 precision and recall compare the similarity of uni-grams (each token of comparison is a single word) between reference and candidate summaries.

In ROUGE-2 precision and recall compare the similarity of bi-grams (each token of comparison is 2 consecutive words) between reference and candidate summaries.

In ROUGE-L precision and recall measure the Longest Common Sub-sequence (LCS) words between reference and candidate summaries.

Table 1 presents ROUGE-score for the toy example in terms of recall, precision, and F-score.

Table 1. ROUGE score for the toy example.

ROUGE Metric	Precision	Recall	F-score
ROUGE_1	0.72	0.57	0.63
ROUGE_2	0.53	0.37	0.47
ROUGE_L	0.68	0.50	0.59

4   Experiments and Results

In this section, we describe the evaluation metric and datasets used for text summarization and present our implementation of the GaSUME Method.

4.1   Evaluation Metric

We evaluate the quality of our system using the ROUGE metric, which stands for Recall-Oriented Understudy for Gisting Evaluation.

It evaluates the quality of a generated summary by comparing it to a golden summary created by humans.

$$ROUGE - N = \frac{\sum_{S \in Summ_{ref}} \sum_{N-grams \in S} Count_{match}(N - gram)}{\sum_{S \in Summ_{ref}} \sum_{N-grames \in S} Count(N - gram)} \qquad (7)$$

where:

- N is the length of $n - grams$ i.e. ROUGE-1: uni-gram metric and ROUGE-2: Bi-gram metric.
- $Count_{match}$ represents the maximum number of the matching $N - grams$ between the reference summary ($Summ_{ref}$) and the generated summary,
- $Count_{N-gram}$ is the total number of $n - grams$ in the reference summary.

To evaluate how accurate our machine-generated summaries are, we calculate the Precision, Recall, and F-measure for these metrics.

ROUGE precision refers to how many candidate summary words are relevant. It is calculated according to the following equation:

$$P = \frac{|grams_{ref} \cap grams_{gen}|}{grams_{gen}}, \qquad (8)$$

ROUGE recall refers to how many words of the candidate summary are extracted from the reference summary. The recall value is calculated according to the following equation:

$$R = \frac{|grams_{ref} \cap grams_{gen}|}{grams_{ref}} \qquad (9)$$

where $grams_{gen}$ are grams of generated summary and $grams_{ref}$ are the grams of reference summary.

F measure provides the complete information that recall and precision provide separately using the equation below:

$$F_{score} = \frac{2PR}{P + R} \qquad (10)$$

4.2 Summarization Dataset

We carried out experiments on the CNN/DailyMail and PubMed extractive datasets. The former is a large English dataset of more than 300,000 news articles written by journalists at CNN and the Daily Mail. Each document is paired with 3–4 golden summaries. PubMed [29] is a dataset of scientific articles in which the abstract is considered the summary of the ground truth and the rest of the article the original document.

4.3 Implementation Details

We implement the genetic algorithm under the parameters presented in Table 2.

Table 2. Parameters of genetic algorithm.

Description	Value
Population size	50
Tournament size	32
Selection strategy	tournament
Tournament variant	by replacement
Crossover strategy	uniform
Iteration number	1000
Crossover Probability	0.6
Mutation Probability	0.2

For the fitness-BERT component, we used the BERT-biased Siamese network fine-tuned in [22]. Concerning the GA component, we run a genetic algorithm with the following parameters: 1000 generations, population size 50, tournament selection as a selection strategy, crossover probability 0.6, and mutation probability 0.2.

The performance of our proposed method is evaluated using the ROUGE metric. ROUGE stands for Recall-Oriented Understudy for Gisting and is a well-known summary evaluation method. It counts the number of overlapping n-grams between the golden summary and the machine summary. Table 3 shows a performance comparison between our GaSUME model and the state-of-the-art.

The experimental result shows that GaSUME outperforms the state-of-the-art approaches including LEAD [21], MatchSUM [22], and GaSUM [1] models according to R-1, R-2, and R-L metrics. Moreover, GaSUME is faster and more intelligent in

Table 3. Comparison of numerical results on CNN/Daily Mail dataset and PubMed dataset through R_1, R_2 and R_L ROUGE metrics.

Dataset	CNN/DailyMail			PubMed		
Model	R-1	R-2	R-L	R-1	R-2	R-L
MatchSUM (BERT-base)	44.22	20.62	40.38	41.21	14.97	36.75
MatchSUM (RoBERTa-base)	44.41	20.86	40.55	–	–	–
LEAD	40.43	17.62	36.67	34.00	8.60	27.10
GaSUM	55.75	44.98	54.32	–	–	–
GaSUME	**55.89**	**45.07**	**54.91**	**49.56**	**27.00**	**42.66**

the search for the optimal summary. In addition, GaSUME can be embedded in other metaheuristics, such as particle swarm optimization (PSO). This outperformance is due to the use of the GA approach that efficiently explores the search space in order to find near-optimal solutions. In fact, the search space is exponential in the document size, and we have to choose the search strategy carefully to avoid discarding some regions or exhaustively searching for the best summary.

5   Conclusion

In this research, we suggest a hybrid strategy for extracting summary at the summary level using genetic algorithm exploration (GaSUME) and BERT representation. We demonstrate the effectiveness of BERT-based Siamese networks for summary scoring and the utility of genetic algorithms as an exploration technique to identify the best summary. On the CNN-Daily Mail and PubMed datasets, GaSUME beat the state-of-the-art performance. Future directions for this work include adding an attention mechanism to the Siamese network to further enhance the performance of our method.

References

1. Tanfouri, I., Jarray, F.: GaSUM: a genetic algorithm wrapped BERT for text summarization. In: ICAART (2) (2023)
2. Paulus, R., Xiong, C., Socher, R.: A deep reinforced model for abstractive summarization. arXiv preprint arXiv:1705.04304 (2017)
3. Nallapati, R., et al.: Abstractive text summarization using sequence-to-sequence RNNs and beyond. arXiv preprint arXiv:1602.06023 (2016)
4. Bai, Y., Gao, Y., Huang, H.: Cross-lingual abstractive summarization with limited parallel resources. arXiv preprint arXiv:2105.13648 (2021)
5. Liu, Y.: Fine-tune BERT for extractive summarization. arXiv preprint arXiv:1903.10318 (2019)
6. Tanfouri, I., Jarray, F.: Genetic algorithm and latent semantic analysis based documents summarization technique (2022)
7. Al-Hashemi, R.: Text summarization extraction system (TSES) using extracted keywords. Int. Arab. J. Technol. **1**(4), 164–168 (2010)

8. Haboush, A., et al.: Arabic text summarization model using clustering techniques. World Comput. Sci. Inf. Technol. J. (WCSIT) **2**(3) (2012). ISSN 2221-0741

9. Boudabous, M.M., Maaloul, M.H., Belguith, L.H.: Digital learning for summarizing Arabic documents. In: Loftsson, H., Rögnvaldsson, E., Helgadóttir, S. (eds.) NLP 2010. LNCS (LNAI), vol. 6233, pp. 79–84. Springer, Heidelberg (2010). https://doi.org/10.1007/978-3-642-14770-8_10

10. Froud, H., Lachkar, A., Ouatik, S.A.: Arabic text summarization based on latent semantic analysis to enhance Arabic documents clustering. arXiv preprint arXiv:1302.1612 (2013)

11. Al-Khawaldeh, F., Samawi, V.: Lexical cohesion and entailment based segmentation for Arabic text summarization (LCEAS). World of Comput. Sci. Inf. Technol. J. (WSCIT) **5**(3), 51–60 (2015)

12. Mohamed, M., Oussalah, M.: SRL-ESA-TextSum: a text summarization approach based on semantic role labeling and explicit semantic analysis. Inf. Proces. Manage. **56**(4), 1356–1372 (2019)

13. Belkebir, R., Guessoum, A.: A supervised approach to Arabic text summarization using AdaBoost. In: Rocha, A., Correia, A.M., Costanzo, S., Reis, L.P. (eds.) New Contributions in Information Systems and Technologies. AISC, vol. 353, pp. 227–236. Springer, Cham (2015). https://doi.org/10.1007/978-3-319-16486-1_23

14. Al-Abdallah, R.Z., Al-Taani, A.T.: Arabic single-document text summarization using particle swarm optimization algorithm. Procedia Comput. Sci. **117**, 30–37 (2017)

15. Jaradat, Y.A.: Arabic single-document text summarization based on harmony search. Diss. Yarmouk University (2015)

16. Tanfouri, I., Tlik, G., Jarray, F.: An automatic Arabic text summarization system based on genetic algorithms. Procedia Comput. Sci. **189**, 195–202 (2021)

17. Miller, D.: Leveraging BERT for extractive text summarization on lectures. arXiv preprint arXiv:1906.04165 (2019)

18. Abu Nada, A.M., et al.: Arabic text summarization using AraBERT model using extractive text summarization approach (2020)

19. Liu, Y., Lapata, M.: Text summarization with pretrained encoders. arXiv preprint arXiv:1908.08345 (2019)

20. Hermann, K.M., et al.: Teaching machines to read and comprehend. In: Advances in Neural Information Processing Systems, vol. 28 (2015)

21. Xu, J., Durrett, G.: Neural extractive text summarization with syntactic compression. arXiv preprint arXiv:1902.00863 (2019)

22. Zhong, M., et al.: Extractive summarization as text matching. arXiv preprint arXiv:2004.08795 (2020)

23. Keneshloo, Y., Ramakrishnan, N., Reddy, C.K.: Deep transfer reinforcement learning for text summarization. In: Proceedings of the 2019 SIAM International Conference on Data Mining. Society for Industrial and Applied Mathematics (2019)

24. Nallapati, R., Zhai, F., Zhou, B.: SummaRuNNer: a recurrent neural network based sequence model for extractive summarization of documents. In: Proceedings of the AAAI Conference on Artificial Intelligence, vol. 31, no. 1 (2017)

25. Jia, R., et al.: Deep differential amplifier for extractive summarization. In: Proceedings of the 59th Annual Meeting of the Association for Computational Linguistics and the 11th International Joint Conference on Natural Language Processing (Volume 1: Long Papers) (2021)

26. Gong, S., et al.: CSSS: a novel candidate summary selection strategy for summary-level extractive summarization

27. Jarray, F., Costa, M.-C., Picouleau, C.: Approximating hv-convex binary matrices and images from discrete projections. In: Coeurjolly, D., Sivignon, I., Tougne, L., Dupont, F. (eds.) DGCI

2008. LNCS, vol. 4992, pp. 413–422. Springer, Heidelberg (2008). https://doi.org/10.1007/978-3-540-79126-3_37

28. Schroff, F., Kalenichenko, D., Philbin, J.: FaceNet: a unified embedding for face recognition and clustering. In: Proceedings of the IEEE Conference on Computer Vision and Pattern Recognition (2015)

29. Cohan, A., et al.: A discourse-aware attention model for abstractive summarization of long documents. arXiv preprint arXiv:1804.05685 (2018)

Segmented Glioma Classification Using Radiomics-Based Machine Learning: A Comparative Analysis of Feature Selection Techniques

Amal Jlassi[1]([✉]), Amel Omri[2], Khaoula ElBedoui[1,3], and Walid Barhoumi[1,3]

[1] Université de Tunis El Manar, Institut Supérieur d'Informatique, Research Team on Intelligent Systems in Imaging and Artificial Vision (SIIVA), LR16ES06 Laboratoire de Recherche en Informatique, Modélisation et Traitement de l'Information et de la Connaissance (LIMTIC), 2 Rue Abou Rayhane Bayrouni, 2080 Ariana, Tunisia
amal.jlassi1991@hotmail.com

[2] Ecole Nationale d'Ingénieurs de Tunis (Enit), LR RISC, Tunis, Tunisia

[3] Université de Carthage, Ecole Nationale d'Ingénieurs de Carthage, 45 Rue des Entrepreneurs, 2035 Tunis-Carthage, Tunisia

Abstract. Accurate classification of glioma grades is crucial for effective treatment planning and patient prognosis. In this extended study, we propose a comprehensive approach combining radiomics features and machine learning techniques to classify glioma grades. We explore the effectiveness of different feature selection methods, including Recursive Feature Elimination (RFE), Minimum Redundancy - Maximum Relevance (MRMR), and k-best, in identifying relevant features from segmented glioma for accurate classification. To achieve this, a deep learning approach that combines Convolutional Neural Networks (CNN) based on the hybridization of U-Net and SegNet is investigated in this study.

The evaluation of the proposed approach involves training and testing machine learning models, including Linear Regression, Random Forest and XGBoost, using the selected features from each feature selection technique. The obtained results show that XGBoost with k-best feature selection achieves the highest accuracy and Area Under the Curve (AUC) for distinguishing between Low-Grade Gliomas (LGG) and High-Grade Gliomas (HGG). This indicates the effectiveness of the k-best feature selection method in capturing the most discriminative information for glioma grade classification. To the best of our knowledge, this is the first study to incorporate machine learning with RFE, MRMR, and k-best feature selection methods for predicting glioma grade. The proposed approach demonstrates improved accuracy compared to existing methods, highlighting the potential of radiomics and machine learning in glioma classification.

Keywords: Glioma grade · Hybrid CNN · Segmentation · Classification · Radiomics

A. P. Rocha et al. (Eds.): ICAART 2023, LNAI 14546, pp. 425–447, 2024.
https://doi.org/10.1007/978-3-031-55326-4_21

1   Introduction

Glioma is the predominant type of primary brain tumor, constituting around 51% of all tumors affecting the central nervous system [1]. In fact, glioma refers to a type of brain tumor that originates from glial cells, which are supportive cells in the brain [2]. Gliomas can be broadly categorized into two main groups based on their grade or aggressiveness: Low-Grade Gliomas (LGG) and High-Grade Gliomas (HGG) (Fig. 1). On the one hand, according to the World Health Organization (WHO), LGG are a class of grade I and grade II brain tumors. Contrary to LGG grade I, which is frequently curable by surgical resection, LGG grade II is infiltrative and reach to reproduce the higher-grade lesion [3]. Furthermore, and as reported by WHO also, an increasing number of LGG grade II has been incidentally found through cervical MRI (Magnetic Resonance Imaging); however 3.8% to 10.4% of patients do not have obvious tumor-related symptoms. According to the 2021 edition of the WHO classification of tumors of the Central Nervous System (CNS), LGG and glioneuronal tumors account for over 30% of pediatric central nervous system neoplasms, leading them to be the most often encountered brain tumors in children. Furthermore, in its fifth edition of classification of tumors of the CNS, the WHO affirms that LGG and glioneuronal tumors account for more than 30% of pediatric neoplasms of the central nervous system. Thus, LGG is one of the most commonly encountered brain tumors among children, and the number of affected children may dramatically rise. Indeed, as per the data published on the site cancer.net, it is estimated that approximately 5, 900 brains will be diagnosed with brain tumors in children aged 0 to 19 years in the United States. On the other hand, HGGs, which encompass grade III and grade IV brain tumors, are characterized by an infiltrative nature [4] and have a tendency to progress to higher-grade lesions, unlike grade I gliomas which are typically curable through surgical resection. Additionally, WHO reports an increasing incidence of grade II HGGs incidentally detected through cervical MRI. However, it is worth noting that a significant proportion of patients with HGG grade II may not exhibit obvious tumor-related symptoms. These aggressive tumors, including grade III and grade IV gliomas, are associated with a poor prognosis and challenging treatment

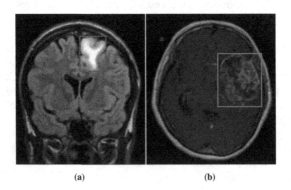

(a)   (b)

Fig. 1. A sample of MRI scans from BraTS dataset: (a) An example where LGG is framed in red, (b) An example where HGG is framed in green. (Color figure online)

options. Generally, while HGGs can occur in individuals of all ages, they are more commonly diagnosed in adults compared to children. Among pediatric brain tumors, LGG, which include grade I and grade II tumors, are more prevalent [5]. Alongside LGGs, glioneuronal tumors are also frequently encountered in the pediatric central nervous system.

Furthermore, in terms of diagnosis, MRI is usually used throughout the neuro-oncology patient's treatment [6] since routine structural imaging provides particular anatomical and pathological information. However, predicting patient outcomes based only on MRI data for glioma tumors are imprecise and suffers from the clinicians' inter-variability issue, radiomics as a new research direction in this field, aims to explore the relationship between tumor genomic characteristics and medical imaging such as MRI [7]. In fact, radiomics is a methodology that involves the transformation of medical images into high-dimensional quantitative data, which provide insights into the underlying pathophysiology, particularly the heterogeneity of tumors. By extracting a wide range of quantitative features from medical images, radiomics enable a more comprehensive characterization of tumor properties and their spatial distribution [8]. Recently, radiomics has gained significant attention due to their potential for predicting genetic status and survival outcomes in individuals diagnosed with brain tumors [22,23]. This emerging field has garnered interest from researchers and clinicians alike. Moreover, combining radiomics with machine learning techniques could further enhance the effectivness of extracting and analyzing a multitude of quantitative imaging features from gliomas' MRI scans [11]. In fact, the first step in extracting tumor features is commonly the manual segmentation of MRI by neuroradiologists or clinicians. However, manual segmentation is costly, and time-consuming, and results often lead to inter-observer variability, which can significantly sway the diagnosis. In an effort to overcome these limitations, automatic glioma segmentation seems to be one of the effective solutions. Recently, progress in Deep Learning (DL) for automatic brain segmentation has reached a level that achieves the performance of skilled radiologists. Nevertheless, most of the existing DL works have been focused on glioblastoma, comparatively to LGG [12]. Several studies suggest that glioma can be associated with different genomic subtypes, which are significant factors in determining the course of treatment. Based on the recent literature, there is no noninvasive approach identifying radiomic subtypes, although that some studies have demonstrated a correlation between glioma shape characteristics and subtypes [13]. In fact, this could lead to conducting radiogenic analysis and enhances inferences about these correlations. However, there still exists a gap in our knowledge regarding the utility of imaging to identify the HGG from the LGG.

Overall, distinguishing between LGG and HGG in brain tumors is crucial for determining treatment strategies and prognosis. The aggressiveness and infiltrative nature of the tumor significantly impact therapeutic decisions and patient outcomes. Nevertheless, the differentiation between LGG and HGG is challenging due to the wide range of glioma grades and the subjective nature of radiological interpretation. Currently, differentiation relies on radiologists' interpretation of semantic radiological features, which can be subjective and dependent on their experience. This subjectivity and inter-observer variability in differentiating glioma grades, using preoperative MRI-based radiologic features, can impact treatment decisions and prognostication in clinical practice. To address this issue, we propose to investigate machine learning classifiers in order to model radiomic features extracted from automatically segmented radiological images, specifically MRI scans. By using machine learning algorithms, radiomics-based glioma classification aims to objectively distinguish between LGG and HGG. In fact, we have studied many relevant machine learning classifiers to model the extracted radiomic features from segmented glioma. Thus, the grade of glioma can be determined non-invasively, while classifying the grade of gliomas based on the radiomics features obtained from the segmented data. We sought to explore the accuracy of tumor radiomics using various machine learning classifiers in predicting glioma grades. The main contribution of the proposed method resides in the fact that the extraction of radiomic features from segmented glioma is performed accurately using an hybrid Convolutional Neural Network (CNN). Then, these features are used to build a fairly robust model to classify LGG from HGG using three different and relevant machine learning classifiers in the test cohort.

The remainder of this paper is organized as follows. Section 2 describes the state of the art whereas Sect. 3 presents the proposed model for glioma grade classification based on radiomics that are extracted from automatically segmented glioma. Then, in Sect. 4 we show results for the classification models. In Sect. 5 we produce a conclusion with some directions.

2   Related Work

Various segmentation approaches have been developed in the litterature in order to delineate low-grade glioma as well as high-grade glioma on MRI scans. These approaches can be categorized based on the type of data. Indeed, LGG and HGG are two distinct types of brain tumors with different characteristics and prognoses, requiring tailored approaches for accurate detection and segmentation. In what follows, we analyze and compare the existing methods that specifically address LGG and HGG tumors, while focusing on their algorithmic techniques, performance metrics, and limitations. In fact, this section provides an overview of relevant methods that deal with glioma tumors' (LGG as well as HGG) diagnosis, while highlighting the importance of the accurate detection and segmentation in the diagnosis and treatment planning of these tumors.

2.1   Methods for LGG Detection and Segmentation

This section presents a brief review of methods that have been specifically developed for the detection and segmentation of LGG tumors in MRI scans. In fact, various methods, mainly based on machine learning and deep learning models, are discussed. Segmentation of LGG in MRI scans presents several challenges due to the nature of these tumors and the characteristics of the imaging data. On the one hand, LGGs can exhibit high variability in terms of size, shape, intensity, and texture, making it challenging to accurately segment them. The presence of heterogeneous tumor regions, such as necrosis, edema, and infiltrative margins, further complicates the segmentation process. On the other hand, LGGs are often surrounded by normal brain tissue, resulting in class imbalance during the segmentation task. Indeed, the majority of the image voxels correspond to non-tumor regions, while the tumor regions are relatively sparse. This imbalance can affect the performance of segmentation algorithms and lead to biased results.

A-Deep Learning. In recent years, CNN models have shown promising performances in glioma diagnosis not only in terms of accuracy but also in terms of efficiency. For instance, Pereira et al. [14] have developed two different structures with dissimilar depths to deal with the LGG diagnosis. Similarly, Dvorak et al. [15] have evaluated the effectiveness of different patch selection techniques based on the segmentation results of CNNs. Havaei et al. [16] have proposed a multiscale CNN structure in order to enhance the use of local and global information. A combination of a Random Forest (RF) classifier and the final output of CNNs has been used to produce better classification results. Likewise, Zhao et al. [17] have introduced a method that combines an FCNN architecture and a Conditional Random Forest (CRF) classifier. The main advantage of this method is that it treats the issue of unbalanced data. The patches are randomly extracted wile controlling their number per class. However, the size or quality of the patches can easily affect LGG segmentation. For example, a patch of small size cannot have all the spatial information, whereas a patch of considerable size needs more computational resources. To address these problems, recent studies used CNN-based encoder-decoder networks. For instance, Buda et al. [13] have recently proposed a fully automatic way to quantify LGG characteristics using U-Net architecture and test whether these characteristics are predictive of tumor genomic subtypes. Due to the excellent performance of U-Net, other segmentation networks based on the U structure of U-Net are produced such as UNet++. In this context, Xu et al. [18] have suggested an LGG segmentation tool based on the UNet++ model, while adopting nested dense skip connections to reduce the semantic gap between encoder and decoder caused by the U-Net model. Moreover, Naser et al. [19] have combined CNN based on the U-Net for LGG segmentation with transfer learning based on a pre-trained convolutional-base of VGG16 and a fully connected classifier. The latter U-Net architecture uses skip connections to the corresponding layers in the decoding part. Thus, it leads to a shortcut for gradient flow in shallow layers during the training task. Recently, two models, which are U-Net with a ResNeXt-50, have been investigated in [20]. This work has included analyzing LGGs through deep learning-based segmentation, shape feature extraction, and statistical analysis to identify correlations between selected shape features and genomic subtypes. More recently, a deep learning approach that combines CNN based on the hybridization of U-Net and SegNet has been developed in [21].

B-Radiomics and Machine Learning. Radiomics focus on extracting a large number of quantitative features from medical images. These features capture tumor heterogeneity and are then used as inputs to machine learning algorithms for LGG segmentation. The importance of radiomics in LGG segmentation lies in its ability to extract detailed and comprehensive information from medical images, allowing for a more comprehensive analysis of tumor characteristics. This information, combined with the power of machine learning algorithms, could enhance the segmentation accuracy, while facilitating better understanding and diagnosis of LGG tumors. On the one hand, the main contribution of the Deep Learning-based Radiomics (DLR) approach [22] in the context of LGG is its ability to extract deep information from multiple modalities of MRI for predicting the mutation status of Isocitrate DeHydrogenase 1 (IDH1). Furthermore, the DLR approach may used the Fisher vector encoding to encode the CNN features extracted from image slices of different sizes. This encoding technique has allowed for the effective representation of the extracted features, enabling the prediction of IDH1 mutation status in patients with LGG. On the other hand, some studies have aimed to investigate whether clinical MRI images can be used to stratify molecular subtypes of diffuse LGG [23]. In fact, to classify glioma subtypes, a three-level machine learning model based on multimodal MR radiomics has been proposed in [23]. Radiomic features have been extracted from the MRI scans, before being fed to machine learning algorithms in order to classify the tumors based on their molecular subtypes. Similarly, Sun et al. [24] have focused on the analysis of radiomic features and machine learning classifiers for glioma grading. They have compared different feature selection methods and machine learning algorithms to determine the most effective combination for accurate glioma grading. Furthermore, Choi et al. [25] have improved the prediction of survival outcomes in LGG using a combination of machine learning and radiomic phenotyping. The study has employed machine learning algorithms, including Support Vector Machines (SVM) and random forests, to develop predictive models based on the extracted radiomic features. The models were trained to classify LGG patients into different survival groups, enabling the prediction of patient outcomes. A multiparametric MRI radiomics model using CNNs has been investigated in [26] to predict the expression level of the synaptophysin (SYP) gene and prognosis in LGG patients. In fact, the CNN model was trained on the extracted radiomic features and the corresponding SYP gene expression levels and patient prognosis data. In a recent study, Lam et al. [27] have involved a dataset of LGG patients, including their MRI scans and molecular subtype information. In fact, machine learning algorithms were applied to the extracted radiomic features to develop a classification model. Moreover, the authors of [28] have developed a radiomics-based machine learning model for predicting Tumor Mutational Burden (TMB) in LGG. Radiomic features, which capture quantitative information about the tumor's characteristics, were extracted from the radiological images. Then, machine learning algorithms were applied to the extracted radiomic features to build a predictive model for TMB.

2.2 Methods for HGG Detection and Segmentation

Various methods have been developed for the detection and segmentation of HGG. In fact, both HGG and LGG tumors exhibit spatial and temporal heterogeneity, making accurate segmentation difficult. Infiltrative growth patterns and indistinct boundaries are common in both types, requiring precise delineation of tumor regions. However, HGG, such as glioblastoma, is considered more aggressive and malignant compared to LGG [29]. They have a higher propensity for growth, invasion, and recurrence. As a result, there is a greater clinical need for accurate segmentation of HGG to aid in treatment planning, monitoring disease progression, and assessing treatment response [30]. On the one hand, deep learning has emerged as a powerful tool in the field of medical imaging, particularly in the detection and segmentation of HGG. For instance, an elegant approach has been proposed in [31] to combine the power of faster Region-based

Convolutional Neural Network (R-CNN) and edge detection techniques from image processing algorithms. The faster R-CNN framework has allowed to effectively detect and localize glioma cells by leveraging its ability to learn discriminative features and perform precise object detection. Another method of automatic image segmentation based on Holistically Nested Neural Networks (HNN) has been introduced in [32] for HGG segmentation from MRI images. Similarly, Dong et al. [33] have proposed a U-Net architecture that consists of an encoder pathway that captures contextual information from the input image and a decoder pathway that reconstructs the segmented tumor regions. A multiparametric deep learning model has been also developed in [34]. It used various MRI sequences; including T1-weighted, T2-weighted, and fluid-attenuated inversion recovery (FLAIR) images; in order to improve the accuracy of glioblastoma segmentation. The model was trained and evaluated using a large dataset of heterogeneous MRI data obtained from routine clinical practice. On the other hand, the combination of radiomics with deep learning holds great promise for advancing the field of medical imaging analysis. In fact, in the context of HGG segmentation, the integration of radiomics with deep learning enables the development of multiparametric models that can investigate diverse MRI sequences to capture the rich information contained in the images. This combination allows for a more comprehensive and detailed analysis of the tumors, leading to enhanced segmentation accuracy and robustness. For instance, Choi et al. [35] have focused on predicting DH1 mutation status in glioblastoma using radiomics analysis based on MRI data. The study has compared the performance of a manual segmentation approach with a fully automated deep learning-based approach for tumor segmentation. The main objective was to evaluate the effectiveness of radiomic features extracted from MRI images in predicting the DH1 mutation status, which is an important molecular marker in glioblastoma. More recently, Bangalore Yogananda et al. [36] have proposed a CNN architecture to perform HGG segmentation. In addition to tumor segmentation, the deep learning model is employed to predict patient survival. In fact, radiomic features are extracted from the segmented tumors, before using them as input to a survival prediction model. This model has used machine learning algorithms to correlate the radiomic features with patient survival data, allowing for the estimation of survival outcomes.

2.3   Methods for LGG and HGG Detection and Segmentation

Segmenting both LGG and HGG is indeed a challenging task due to several reasons. In fact, both LGG and HGG exhibit significant intra-tumoral heterogeneity, meaning that different regions within the tumor can have varying characteristics. This heterogeneity can make it difficult to accurately delineate tumor boundaries and classify different tumor subregions. Moreover, LGG and HGG can vary widely in terms of size and shape. LGG tumors tend to be smaller and have more defined boundaries, while HGG tumors can be larger and infiltrative, with diffuse edges that blend into the surrounding healthy tissue. Accommodating this variability in size and shape is a challenge for segmentation algorithms. In this context, Amirmoezzi et al. [37] have proposed a knowledge-based system for brain tumor segmentation that relies solely on 3D FLAIR (Fluid-Attenuated Inversion Recovery) images. The system has used a combination of pre-existing knowledge and expert-defined rules to perform accurate segmentation of brain tumors. By leveraging the specific characteristics and information provided by 3D FLAIR images, the system has proved to be able to effectively identify and delineate tumor regions. Similarly, a technique based on CNN in accomplishing accurate brain tumor segmentation in multi-spectral MRI, has been designed in [38]. Likewise, Banerjee et al. [39] have investigated a combination of feature extraction, feature selection, and classification techniques in order to classify different regions based on their intensity, texture, and spatial characteristics. Differently, multi-planar images (axial, sagittal, and coronal) and CNN have been recently used for brain tumor segmentation in [40]. Furthermore, Zhou et al. [41] have proposed a 3D dense connectivity network with an atrous convolutional feature pyramid for brain tumor segmentation in MRI scans. More recently, U-Net has been investigated in [42]. This work includes the histogram-based nonparametric tumor localization method to identify the tumorous regions.

It is worth mentioning that these categorizations are not mutually exclusive, and there can be overlap between the approaches used for LGG and HGG segmentation. Additionally, advancements in medical imaging and machine learning techniques continue to expand the possibilities for accurate and robust segmentation of both LGG and HGG tumors.

3   Materials and Methods

In this section, we firstly present the dataset that we investigated in this work. Subsequently, the proposed method for glioma segmentation is discussed using the chosen dataset. In fact, radiomic features are extracted from the automatically segmented glioma regions to provide input for three relevant machine learning algorithms employed for glioma grade classification. Figure 2 illustrates the workflow, which outlines the steps involved in the proposed method for glioma grade classification using radiomics and machine learning models.

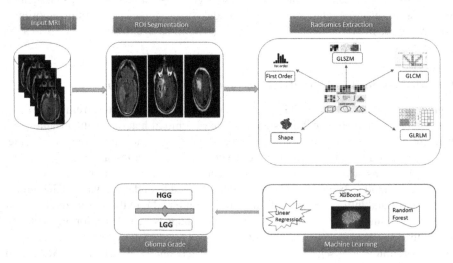

Fig. 2. Workflow of the proposed glioma grade classification method using radiomics and machine learning classifiers.

3.1 Materials

Datasets used in this study contain brain MR images together with manual segmentation masks. On the one hand, LGG images were obtained from The Cancer Imaging Archive (TCIA). These scans correspond to 110 patients included in The Cancer Genome Atlas (TCGA) LGG collection with fully FLAIR (Fluid-Attenuated Inversion Recovery) sequence and genomic cluster data available. The collection of patients comes from five different institutions (Thomas Jefferson University - 16 patients; Henry Ford Hospital - 45 patients; UNC - 1 patient; Case Western - 14 patients; and Case Western St. Joseph's - 34 patients), and the patients are distributed as 50 patients with Grade II and 58 patients with Grade III. Each MRI per patient is composed of 20 to 88 slices with a size of 256 pixels, illustrating cross-sectional areas of the brain as shown in Fig. 3. Tumor shape assessment was based only on the FLAIR abnormality since tumor enhancement in LGG is infrequent. The Ground Truth (GT) generated by tumor masks was performed by Buda et al. [13] using the FLAIR MRI images, and they made it publicly available for download on Kaggle (www.kaggle.com).

On the other hand, The BraTS (Brain Tumor Segmentation) dataset is a widely used benchmark for brain tumor detection and segmentation from MRI data. In particular, the BraTS 2019 dataset includes multi-parametric MRI scans of 150 patients, each with a labeled segmentation mask of the brain tumor regions. In fact, the dataset was annotated by expert radiologists using a range of imaging modalities; such as T1-weighted, T1-weighted post-contrast, T2-weighted, and FLAIR imaging; in order to provide accurate segmentation of the brain tumor regions. The used dataset contains both HGG and LGG

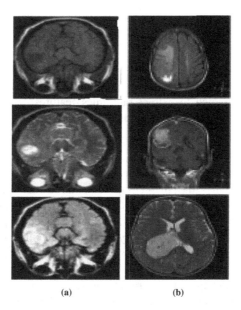

(a)   (b)

Fig. 3. A sample of MRI scans from the used datasets: (a) examples from theTCIA dataset, (b) examples from the Brats dataset.

brain tumors (Fig. 3). It is worth noting that the investigated datasets include various challenges, such as the presence of non-enhancing tumors and ambiguous boundaries between tumor and non-tumor regions, making it a challenging and realistic benchmark for brain tumor detection and segmentation. The details of the investigated datasets are summarized in Fig. 4.

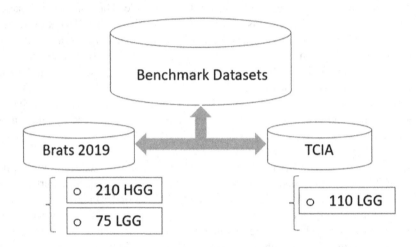

Fig. 4. Overview of the used benchmark datasets.

3.2 Methods

In this section, we introduce the proposed method, which builds upon previous work [21], to perform glioma segmentation using a hybrid CNN. The segmented glioma regions are then investigated to extract radiomics features, which are subsequently employed to train machine learning methods for accurate glioma grade classification.

Glioma Segmentation. An overview of the proposed approach used for glioma segmentation is shown in Fig. 5. In fact, the proposed fully automated method for glioma segmentation based on a hybrid CNN is composed of three main procedures: image preprocessing, data augmentation, and segmentation. Indeed, in order to reduce the unbalance between tumor and non-tumor classes, we have isolated empty slices that do not contain any brain or other tissue after applying the "Skull Stripping" process. Table 1 highlights the used preprocessing techniques to enhance the quality of the segmentation based on hybrid CNN [21].

In summary, the mentioned preprocessing techniques offer advantages such as improved accuracy, reduced noise, enhanced visualization, consistent intensity, improved comparability, increased robustness, augmented data, invariance to orientation, variation in object sizes, improved generalization, and feature invariance. These

Fig. 5. An overview of the proposed hybrid CNN.

Table 1. Preprocessing techniques.

Preprocessing Method	Advantages	Preprocessing Example
The "Skull Stripping"	Extracting brain tissue from the non-brain tissue	
Normalisation	Enhancing the tissue intensity	
Flip	Involving mirroring the data along a specified axis	
Scale by 4% –8%	Introducing variability in object sizes	
Rotation by 5°–15°	Exposing the model to different rotation angles	

techniques contribute to the reliability, robustness, and performance of machine learning models in analyzing and interpreting brain imaging data.

Furthermore, deep neural networks are nowadays payoff popularity among researchers and have shown outstanding performance with appreciated accuracy in medical image segmentation. In particular, CNN is a type of deep neural network that can learn and extract features from images. In fact, many researchers have used CNN for automatic brain tumor segmentation in MRI images. So, it is important to find the relevant advantages of each model in order to develop a hybrid architecture by inheriting the advantages of these models. It is noticeably expected that the hybrid architecture will give a more devoted result. Particularly, U-Net has achieved good results in medical image segmentation. Hence, it is the most commonly used in the glioma segmentation task. It has performed outstanding results in this challenge and it has overcome the problems of fewer data capacity, fuzzy boundaries, and high gray scales in medical image analysis. In fact, the U-Net method includes an encoder for processing input MRI scans and a decoder for generating outputs [43]. Firstly, the encoder decomposes the image into different levels of feature maps. Then, it extracts the coarse-grained features of the main feature maps. Next, the decoder restores the feature maps of each layer by an up-sampling process. The concatenation cascades the features of each layer of the encoder with the features obtained by the transpose convolution operation in the decoder. Thus, it reduces the loss of accuracy in the feature extraction process. The objective of the previous work [21] has been to combine popular deep CNN models, which are U-Net and SegNet, for the automatic segmentation of tumors in the brain MRI images, by exploring the advantages of each model. The proposed U-SegNet is a hybridization of U-Net architecture, which is widely used for LGG segmentation, along with the relevant Seg-Net architecture. Figure 6 shows the U-SegNet architecture which is an assembly model that combines the U-Net and SegNet architectures.

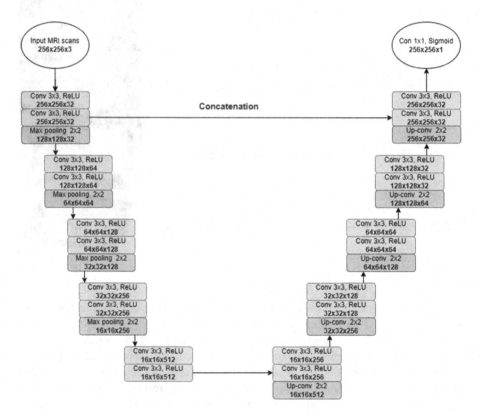

Fig. 6. U-SegNet architecture used for segmentation. Below each layer specification dimensionality of a single example that this layer outputs were provided [21]. (Color figure online)

Similarly to U-Net, the U-SegNet architecture is a U-shaped model with image features trained at different levels through a set of convolution and pooling layers. The decoder layer uses the pooling indices from the max-pooling step corresponding to the encoder layer's role to oversample the low-level feature maps instead of the deconvolution layers. We have used the same parameters of SegNet to implement U-SegNet. Additionally, we have used 10 encoder blocks and 10 decoder blocks. Batch normalization and ReLu activation functions were applied on the feature maps after the filters were applied in the encoder branch. A U-Net type hop connection is only provided at the upper layer, as shown in Fig. 6, in order to insert feature maps with fine detail. The jump connection helps us to introduce fine information without increasing the parameters as it was done in U-Net. Finally, a Sigmoid layer is used in order to produce class probabilities for each pixel independently. The hyperparameters adopted for the training process of this model are presented in Table 2.

Table 2. Hyperparameters for the U-SegNet model.

Hyperparamter	Value
Learning rate	0.0001
Epochs	100
Optimizer	Adam
Batch size	16
Momentum	0.5

The segmentation model used in this work was based on CNN with an hybrid architecture. In order to improve the learning performance, we have implemented the U-SegNet architecture. This architecture is a new model based on the SegNet model with a connection hop to the upper layer to retrieve the finer details of the feature map. Moreover, we have introduced dropout in the encoder layer which is a regulation technique in order to avoid overfitting (increase validation accuracy). We have chosen what gives the model a better opportunity to learn independent representations. Typically, using a small dropout value of 20–50% of neurons is sufficient, with 20% being a good starting point. Too low a value has minimal effect and too high a value leads to under-training of the network. As shown in Fig. 6, the U-SegNet consists of 5 blocks of layers which contain 2 convolution layers (in blue color) with ReLU activation function and one max pooling layer (in pink color) in the encoding (down-sampling) part and a similar 5 blocks of layers but with one convolution transpose layer (in pink color) instead of max pooling in the decoding (up-sampling) part. The number of filter channels and the image size are given at the bottom of each layer. The size of the input layer (in white color) is $256 \times 256 \times 3$ and the size of the output layer is $256 \times 256 \times 1$ which is a convolution layer with Sigmoid activation function.

Grade Classification Based on Radiomics. This study used radiomics to analyze glioma [44] from MR images. In fact, we extracted radiomic features from segmented glioma. A Python package called Pyradiomics (version 3.6.2, https://github.com/Radiomics/pyradiomics.git) [45], was used to extract several features. Thus, extracted features consisted of first-order, texture features and shape. First-order texture features are computed based on the average pixel value and intensity histogram analysis. These features provide information about the distribution of gray-level frequencies within ROI [46]. However, shape features are obtained through the process of three-dimensional surface rendering. These features encompass descriptors that characterize the size and shape of ROI in three dimensions. Shape features are not influenced by the distribution of gray-level intensities within the ROI. The GLCM (Gray-Level Co-occurrence Matrix) is a method that characterizes the joint probability function by representing the frequency of occurrence of different combinations of two neighboring pixels within a given area [47]. On the other hand, the GLSZM (Gray-Level Size Zone Matrix) quantifies the number of connected pixels within a matrix that have the same gray-level intensity. It provides insights into the size and distribution of these connected regions within the defined area [48]. Lastly, the GLRLM (Gray-Level Run Length Matrix) measures the lengths of successive pixels in a matrix that share the same gray-level value. It focuses on capturing the repetitive patterns and runs of pixels with identical gray-level values within the area [49]. These techniques offer valuable insights into the spatial relationships, connectivity, and distribution of gray-level intensities within a given region of interest, contributing to the comprehensive analysis of texture and structural characteristics in medical imaging applications.

Therefore, feature selection is an essential procedure aimed at reducing the number of parameters in a dataset while retaining maximum variance from the original data [50]. This step is typically carried out prior to training a machine learning model to prevent overfitting and enhance model performance [51]. Ultimately, the objective of feature reduction is to strike a balance between retaining valuable information and optimizing the model's predictive capabilities. In this context, Recursive Feature Elimination (RFE) method is performed [52]. In fact, RFE stands out as one of the most popular techniques due to its simplicity, flexibility, and effectiveness in identifying the most relevant features for predicting the target variable or endpoint. RFE is a wrapper-type algorithm that can be applied to any machine learning model to generate the optimal feature subset that yields the highest performance. In addition to RFE, another commonly used feature selection method is the k-best selection. The k-best selection approach aims to identify the K most informative features from a given dataset [53]. One of the feature selection methods that is widely used is Minimum Redundancy - Maximum Relevance (MRMR) [54]. In fact, MRMR aims to find a subset of features that have the maximum relevance to the target variable while minimizing redundancy between the selected features. In the present study, three machine learning methods such as Linear Regression (LR), Random Forest (RF) and XGBoost (XGB) are performed using mentioned feature selection methods. Figure 7 describes details of grade classification glioma based on radiomics.

After each cycle, the feature subset along with the corresponding model accuracy was recorded. This allows for the evaluation and comparison of different feature subsets.

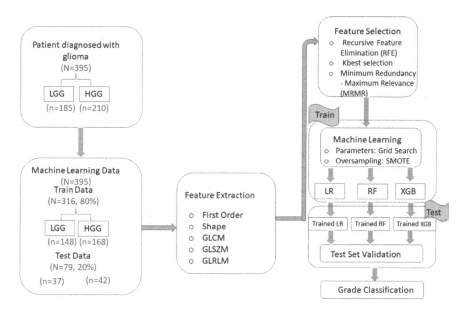

Fig. 7. Flowchart of the proposed framework for glioma grade classification.

We trained machine learning models to distinguish between LGG and HGG using the already-constructed training data. Three types of machine learning models were trained for comparisons: LR, RF, XGB. Logistic Regression (LR) is a statistical method commonly used for predicting probabilities by utilizing a linear combination of independent variables [55]. In LR, the aim is to classify or predict outcomes based on a binary or categorical response variable. Random Forest (RF) is an ensemble model that extends the decision tree method by constructing multiple decision trees and combining their results to determine the final prediction [56]. Each decision tree is trained on a different subset of the data using a random selection of features. The RF model then combines the predictions of all the individual trees through voting or averaging to make the final classification decision. On the other hand, XGBoost (Extreme Gradient Boosting) is a boosting algorithm that was developed to address the limitations of gradient boosting [57]. It is known for its fast execution speed and excellent prediction performance. XGBoost incorporates a form of overfitting regularization by performing internal cross-validation during each iteration. This helps to prevent overfitting and enhances the generalization ability of the model.

4   Models Evaluations on the Testing Datasets

The evaluation of models on testing datasets is a crucial step in assessing their performance and generalization capabilities. In this section, we present the results and analysis of the models' performance on the independent testing datasets. In order to evaluate the performance of each model (Random Forest, Logistic Regression, XGBoost) using the selected feature subsets obtained from the feature selection methods (RFE, MRMR, k-best), we calculated several evaluation metrics including accuracy, AUC (Area Under the Curve), and F1-score. Accuracy (1) is a commonly used metric that measures the overall correctness of the model's predictions. It is calculated as the ratio of the correctly classified instances to the total number of instances in the testing dataset.

$$Acc = \frac{TP + TN}{TP + TN + FP + FN} \tag{1}$$

AUC (2) is a metric commonly used for binary classification problems. It measures the overall discriminative power of the model by calculating the area under the Receiver Operating Characteristic (ROC) curve. Essentially, this area represents the proportion of correctly ordered pairs of objects, specifically those consisting of an object from class 1 and an object from class 0. In other words, it indicates the algorithm's ability to correctly rank the objects, ensuring that objects from class 1 are placed ahead of those from class 0 in the ordered list.

In the general case, AUC for a binary solution is as follows:

$$AUC = \frac{TP \cdot FP}{2} + TP \cdot (1 - FP) + \frac{(1 - TP) \cdot (1 - FP)}{2} = \frac{1 + TP - FP}{2} \tag{2}$$

F1-score (3) is a metric that combines precision and recall to provide a balanced measure of the model's performance. It takes into account both the false positives and false negatives in the predictions. F1-score is calculated as the harmonic mean of precision and recall, providing a single value that represents the model's overall performance.

$$F1 - score = \frac{2 \times TP}{2 \times TP + FP + FN} \tag{3}$$

where, TP, FP, and FN denote True Positive, False Positive, and False Negative, respectively, of the class for which the result is calculated.

For each classification model and feature selection method combination, we have calculated these evaluation metrics using the predictions made by the model on the testing dataset. This allows us to assess the accuracy, discriminative power, and overall performance of each model in classifying the glioma grade. By comparing the performance of the models across the different feature selection methods, we can identify which combination yields the best results in terms of accuracy, AUC, and F1-score. This analysis provides valuable insights into the effectiveness of the feature selection methods and their impact on the predictive performance of the models. Figure 8, Fig. 9 and Fig. 10 showcase the performance comparison of different models (LR, RF, XGB) when coupled with various feature selection methods (MRMR, RFE, KBest) based on accuracy (ACC), area under the curve (AUC), and F1-score.

Figure 8 displays the comparison of accuracy values among different models (LR, RF, XGB) when paired with various feature selection methods (MRMR, RFE, KBest). The results reveal that XGBoost, combined with the RFE method, achieves the highest accuracy. When combined with RFE, XGBoost benefits from the iterative feature selection process, which helps identify the most relevant features for the model's performance. In fact, RFE eliminates less informative features, allowing XGBoost to focus

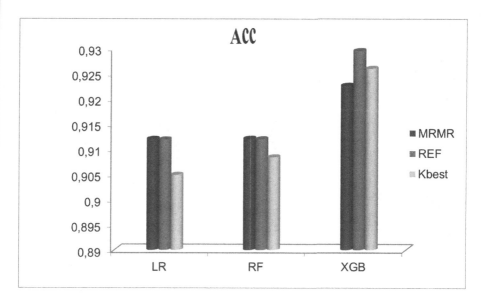

Fig. 8. Comparison of the average classification accuracy for different classification models with distinct feature selection methods.

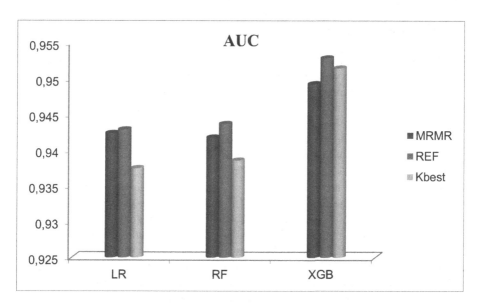

Fig. 9. Comparison of Average Classification AUC for Different Models with Feature Selection Methods.

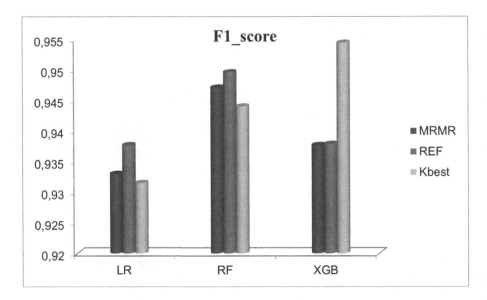

Fig. 10. Comparison of the average classification F1-score for different classification models with distinct feature selection methods.

on the most influential features and make more accurate predictions. This combination of XGBoost and RFE leads to improved model performance and higher accuracy compared to other models and feature selection methods in the evaluation.

Based on analysing the obtained results, XGBoost with RFE has recorded the highest AUC value among the evaluated models and feature selection combination (Fig. 9). This suggests that XGBoost, when combined with RFE, is effective in achieving a higher discrimination ability and better predictive performance compared to other model-feature selection combinations. Additionally, it is observed that RF with RFE performs comparatively well in terms of AUC compared to LR. This implies that RF, when combined with RFE, is capable of achieving a better discrimination ability and predictive performance than LR in this particular evaluation. In this case, it appears that k-best feature selection works well only with XGB and not as effectively with LR and RF. This could be the reason that LR and RF are both influenced by the presence of correlated features. If there are strong correlations among the selected features by k-best, it can adversely affect the performance of LR and RF, leading to sub-optimal results. XGB, on the other hand, is generally more robust to correlated features.

It is interesting to note that XGB with k-best feature selection performs the best in terms of F1-score (Fig. 10). This could be explained by the fact that using the selected features from k-best, XGB may be able to exploit the specific information contained in those features more effectively, leading to improved performance in terms of F1-score. Thus, XGBoost has outperformed all other algorithms. Furthermore, the confusion matrix is a relevant tool for evaluating the performance of a classification model. It provides a visual representation of the model's predictions compared to the actual ground truth values.

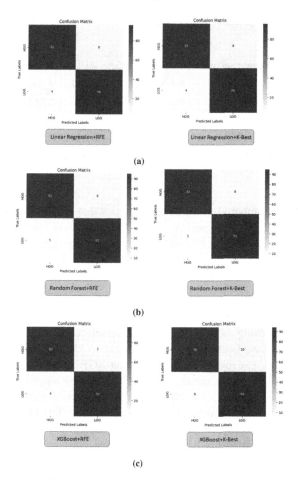

Fig. 11. Confusion matrix calculated from various machine learning algorithms for classifying LGG and HGG. (a) Confusion matrix of linear regression with RFE and k-best, (b) Confusion matrix of random forest with RFE and k-best, (c) Confusion matrix of XGBoost with RFE and k-best. (Color figure online)

Figure 11 a–c show the confusion matrices for the three classifiers. Within each matrix, the horizontal row represents the actual ground true class, while each column represents the predicted class. The main diagonal shown in high blue represents the number of data points that were classified correctly. Thus, confusion matrices show consistent and satisfactory performance across all classes (LGG and HGG), and it indicates that models are accurate in distinguishing between the different classes of gliomas. Because XGBoost has outperformed all other algorithms, we have continued evaluating the XGBoost model comparatively to other methods (Table 3). In fact, Table 3 summarizes the results of the performances from other studies performing the same task of classifying glioma. It shows the training accuracy, the testing accuracy, and the AUC of each model. It is clear that XGBoost with k-best performs the highest accuracy and

Table 3. Evaluation of the proposed model comparatively to state-of-the-art models (best values are in bold).

Models	Training accuracy	Testing accuracy	AUC	Algorithm
[25]	–	0.758	0.857	V-Net
[27]	0.8850	0.6905	0.812	XGBoost
[27]	–	0.8509	–	Random Forest
[36]	–	0.89	0.894	CNN
Current study	**0,9964**	**0.9295**	**0.9544**	XGBoost with k-best

AUC than the other compared models. It is obvious that adding k-best feature selection helps to improve the performance. Thus, XGBoost with k-best gave an average accuracy value of 0.9295. Also CNN models seem to be doing quite well.

5 Conclusion

This study has focused on the classification of glioma grades using radiomics features and machine learning models. Various feature selection methods; including RFE, MRMR, and k-best; have been investigated in order to identify the most relevant features for classification. The results have showed that XGBoost with k-best feature selection has achieved the highest accuracy and AUC, indicating its effectiveness in distinguishing between LGG and HGG. Furthermore, the evaluation of the confusion matrix has provided insights relating to the model's performance. The high values along the main diagonal of the matrix has demonstrated the correct classification of instances, while the off-diagonal elements have indicated miss-classifications. This highlights the importance of considering both true positive and false positive rates to evaluate the model's performance comprehensively. Overall, to the best of our knowledge, this study is the first to implement a machine learning-incorporated RFE, MRMR and k-best feature selection methods for predicting the glioma grade. The obtained results by this study prove that the proposed method could noninvasively predict glioma grade with more accurate performance compared to existing methods. In particular, the study has demonstrated the potential of radiomics and machine learning in glioma classification, providing valuable insights for clinicians and researchers in making accurate diagnoses and treatment decisions. However, further research is still needed to validate and refine the proposed solutions and to explore additional features and algorithms that can enhance the classification accuracy and predictive power. As a future work, we aim to explore additional predictive biomarkers. In addition to radiomics features, there are other potential biomarkers that can be considered for glioma classification, such as genetic markers, histopathological features, or clinical data. Future studies can investigate the integration of these biomarkers with radiomics features to enhance the predictive power of the machine learning models.

References

1. Bastian, M., Reifenberger, G.: Practical implications of integrated glioma classification according to the World Health Organization classification of tumors of the central nervous system 2016. Curr. Opin. Oncol. **28**(6), 494–501 (2016)
2. Usinskiene, J., et al.: Optimal differentiation of high-and low-grade glioma and metastasis: a meta-analysis of perfusion, diffusion, and spectroscopy metrics. Neuroradiology **58**, 339–350 (2016)
3. Villa, C., Miquel, C., Mosses, D., Bernier, M., Di Stefano, A.L.: The 2016 World Health Organization classification of tumours of the central nervous system. La Presse Médicale **47**(11–12) (2018)
4. Black, D., Kaneko, S., Walke, A., König, S., Stummer, W., Molina, E.S.: Characterization of autofluorescence and quantitative protoporphyrin IX biomarkers for optical spectroscopy-guided glioma surgery. Sci. Rep. **11**(1), 20009 (2021)
5. Ditto, A., Leone Roberti Maggiore, U., Evangelisti, G., Bogani, G., Raspagliesi, F.: Diagnostic accuracy of magnetic resonance imaging in the pre-operative staging of cervical cancer patients who underwent neoadjuvant treatment: a clinical-surgical-pathologic comparison. Cancers **15**(7), 2061 (2023)
6. Jlassi, A., ElBedoui, K., Barhoumi, W., Maktouf, C.: Unsupervised method based on probabilistic neural network for the segmentation of corpus callosum in MRI scans. In: VISIGRAPP (4: VISAPP) (2019)
7. Maciej, M.: Radiogenomics: what it is and why it is important. J. Am. Coll. Radiol. **12**(8), 862–866 (2015)
8. Scapicchio, C., Gabelloni, M., Barucci, A., Cioni, D., Saba, L., Neri, E.: A deep look into radiomics. Radiol. Med. **126**(10), 1296–1311 (2021)
9. Kickingereder, P., et al.: Radiomic profiling of glioblastoma: identifying an imaging predictor of patient survival with improved performance over established clinical and radiologic risk models. Radiology **280**(3), 880–889 (2016)
10. Zhang, B., et al.: Multimodal MRI features predict isocitrate dehydrogenase genotype in high-grade gliomas. Neuro-oncology **19**(1), 109–117 (2017)
11. Máté, M., et al.: Machine learning workflows to estimate class probabilities for precision cancer diagnostics on DNA methylation microarray data. Nat. Protoc. **15**(2), 479–512 (2020)
12. Thomas, B., et al.: Machine learning and glioma imaging biomarkers. Clin. Radiol. **75**(1), 20–32 (2020)
13. Mateusz, B., Mazurowski, M.: Association of genomic subtypes of lower-grade gliomas with shape features automatically extracted by a deep learning algorithm. Comput. Biol. Med. **109**, 218–225 (2019)
14. Thaha, M.M., Kumar, P.M., Murugan, Dhanasekeran, Vijayakarthick, Selvi, S.: Brain tumor segmentation using convolutional neural networks in MRI images. J. Med. Syst. **43**, 1–10 (2019)
15. Dingwen, Z., et al.: Exploring task structure for brain tumor segmentation from multi-modality MR images. IEEE Trans. Image Process. **29**, 9032–9043 (2020)
16. Mohammad, H., et al.: A convolutional neural network approach to brain tumor segmentation. In: Crimi, A., Menze, B., Maier, O., Reyes, M., Handels, H. (eds.) BrainLes 2015. LNCS, vol. 9556, pp. 195–208. Springer, Cham (2016). https://doi.org/10.1007/978-3-319-30858-6_17
17. Zhong, Y., et al.: WHU-Hi: UAV-borne hyperspectral with high spatial resolution (H2) benchmark datasets and classifier for precise crop identification based on deep convolutional neural network with CRF. Remote Sens. Environ. **250**, 112012 (2020)

18. Xu, D., et al.: Automatic segmentation of low-grade glioma in MRI image based on UNet++ model. J. Phys. Conf. Ser. **1693**(1) (2020)
19. Mohamed, N., Deen, M.J.: Brain tumor segmentation and grading of lower-grade glioma using deep learning in MRI images. Comput. Biol. Med. **121**, 103758 (2020)
20. Rohit, P., Paradkar, R.: Analysis of Lower-Grade Gliomas in MRI Through Segmentation and Genomic Cluster-Shape Feature Correlation. bioRxiv (2022)
21. Jlassi, A., ElBedoui, K., Barhoumi, W.: Brain tumor segmentation of lower-grade glioma across MRI images using hybrid convolutional neural networks. In: 15th International Conference on Agents and Artificial Intelligence ICAART (2023)
22. Zeju, L., et al.: Deep learning based radiomics (DLR) and its usage in noninvasive IDH1 prediction for low grade glioma. Sci. Rep. **7**(1), 1–11 (2017)
23. Chia-Feng, L., et al.: Machine learning-based radiomics for molecular subtyping of gliomas machine learning for molecular subtyping of gliomas. Clin. Cancer Res. **24**(18), 4429–4436 (2018)
24. Pan, S., et al.: Comparison of feature selection methods and machine learning classifiers for radiomics analysis in glioma grading. IEEE Access **7**, 102010–102020 (2019)
25. Choi, Y.S., et al.: Machine learning and radiomic phenotyping of lower grade gliomas: improving survival prediction. Eur. Radiol. **30**, 3834–3842 (2020)
26. Xiao, Z., et al.: Multiparametric MRI features predict the SYP gene expression in low-grade glioma patients: a machine learning-based radiomics analysis. Front. Oncol. **11**, 663451 (2021)
27. Lam, L.H.T., et al.: Molecular subtype classification of low-grade gliomas using magnetic resonance imaging-based radiomics and machine learning. NMR Biomed. **35**(11), e4792 (2022)
28. Lam, L.H.T., et al.: A radiomics-based machine learning model for prediction of tumor mutational burden in lower-grade gliomas. Cancers **14**(14), 3492 (2022)
29. Blionas, A., et al.: Paediatric gliomas: diagnosis, molecular biology and management. Ann. Transl. Med. **6**(12) (2018)
30. Qing, Z., et al.: Treatment response and prognosis evaluation in high-grade glioma: an imaging review based on MRI. J. Magn. Reson. Imaging **56**(2), 325–340 (2022)
31. Gunasekara, K., Dissanayake, M.B.: MRI based glioma segmentation using deep learning algorithms. In: 2019 International research conference on smart computing and systems engineering (SCSE). IEEE (2019)
32. Ying, Z., et al.: Brain tumor segmentation using holistically nested neural networks in MRI images. Med. Phys. **44**(10), 5234–5243 (2017)
33. Dong, H., et al.: Automatic brain tumor detection and segmentation using U-Net based fully convolutional networks. In: Valdés Hernández, M., González-Castro, V. (eds.) MIUA 2017. CCIS, vol. 723, pp. 506–517. Springer, Cham (2017). https://doi.org/10.1007/978-3-319-60964-5_44
34. Perkuhn, M., et al.: Clinical evaluation of a multiparametric deep learning model for glioblastoma segmentation using heterogeneous magnetic resonance imaging data from clinical routine. Investig. Radiol. **53**(11), 647 (2018)
35. Choi, Y., et al.: IDH1 mutation prediction using MR-based radiomics in glioblastoma: comparison between manual and fully automated deep learning-based approach of tumor segmentation. Eur. J. Radiol. **128**, 109031 (2020)
36. Bangalore Yogananda, C.G., et al.: Fully automated brain tumor segmentation and survival prediction of gliomas using deep learning and MRI. In: Crimi, A., Bakas, S. (eds.) BrainLes 2019. LNCS, vol. 11993, pp. 99–112. Springer, Cham (2020). https://doi.org/10.1007/978-3-030-46643-5_10
37. Yalda, A., et al.: A knowledge-based system for brain tumor segmentation using only 3D FLAIR images. Australas. Phys. Eng. Sci. Med. **42**, 529–540 (2019)

38. Sajid, I., et al.: Brain tumor segmentation in multi-spectral MRI using convolutional neural networks (CNN). Microsc. Res. Tech. **81**(4), 419–427 (2019)
39. Subhashis, B., Mitra, S.: Novel volumetric sub-region segmentation in brain tumors. Front. Comput. Neurosci. **14**, 3 (2020)
40. Wu, S., et al.: Three-plane-assembled deep learning segmentation of gliomas. Radiol. Artif. Intell. **2**(2), e190011 (2020)
41. Zhou, Z., et al.: 3D dense connectivity network with atrous convolutional feature pyramid for brain tumor segmentation in magnetic resonance imaging of human heads. Comput. Biol. Med. **121**, 103766 (2020)
42. Ilhan, A., Abiyev, R.: Brain tumor segmentation in MRI images using nonparametric localization and enhancement methods with U-net. Int. J. Comput. Assist. Radiol. Surg. **17**(3), 589–600 (2022)
43. Drozdzal, M., et al.: The importance of skip connections in biomedical image segmentation. In: Carneiro, G., et al. (eds.) DLMIA LABELS 2016. LNCS, vol. 10008, pp. 179–187. Springer, Cham (2016). https://doi.org/10.1007/978-3-319-46976-8_19
44. Philippe, L., et al.: Radiomics: the bridge between medical imaging and personalized medicine. Nat. Rev. Clin. Oncol. **14**(12), 749–762 (2017)
45. Van Griethuysen, J., et al.: Computational radiomics system to decode the radiographic phenotype. Cancer Res. **77**(21), e104–e107 (2017)
46. Lucas, C., Mortezaie, G.: Analysis of mammographic microcalcifications using gray-level images and neural networks (2002)
47. Meenakshi, G., Dhiman, G.: A novel content-based image retrieval approach for classification using GLCM features and texture fused LBP variants. Neural Comput. Appl. **33**, 1311–1328 (2021)
48. Yang, Y., et al.: Optimizing texture retrieving model for multimodal MR image-based support vector machine for classifying glioma. J. Magn. Reson. Imaging **49**(5), 1263–1274 (2019)
49. Şaban, Ö., Akdemir, B.: Application of feature extraction and classification methods for histopathological image using GLCM, LBP, LBGLCM, GLRLM and SFTA. Procedia Comput. Sci. **132**, 40–46 (2018)
50. Jundong, L., et al.: Feature selection: a data perspective. ACM Comput. Surv. (CSUR) **50**(6), 1–45 (2017)
51. Arafet, S., et al.: Adaptive feature selection in PET scans based on shared information and multi-label learning. Vis. Comput. **38**, 257–277 (2022)
52. Bharat, R., et al.: Diagnosis of Alzheimer's disease using universum support vector machine based recursive feature elimination (USVM-RFE). Biomed. Signal Process. Control **59**, 101903 (2020)
53. Fan, W., et al.: AutoFS: automated feature selection via diversity-aware interactive reinforcement learning. In: 2020 IEEE International Conference on Data Mining (ICDM). IEEE (2020)
54. Mesut, T., et al.: A deep feature learning model for pneumonia detection applying a combination of mRMR feature selection and machine learning models. IRBM **41**(4), 212–222 (2020)
55. Lynne, C.: Logistic regression. Medsurg Nurs. **29**(5), 353–354 (2020)
56. Schonlau, M., Yuyan, R.: The random forest algorithm for statistical learning. Stata J. **20**(1), 3–29 (2020)
57. Nalluri, M., et al.: A scalable tree boosting system: XG boost. Int. J. Res. Stud. Sci. Eng. Technol. **7**, 36–51 (2020)

RDC-Repair: Towards a Relevance-Driven Approach for Data and Constraints Repair

Nibel Nadjeh[(✉)], Sabrina Abdellaoui, and Fahima Nader

Laboratoire des Méthodes de Conception de Systèmes (LMCS), Ecole nationale Supérieure d'Informatique (ESI), BP, 68M Oued-Smar, 16270 Alger, Algeria
{n_nadjeh,s_abdellaoui,f_nader}@esi.dz

Abstract. Over the years data cleaning solutions have focused on modifying data in order to satisfy a set of integrity constraints (ICs). However, constraints may also be erroneous. Consequently, when dealing with an inconsistency, it becomes difficult to determine whether the data is dirty, the ICs or both. In this paper, we address three main challenges: (1) Uncertainty: Since both data and ICs could be dirty, it is difficult to detect the source of the inconsistency and how to repair it. We propose a new metric to evaluate the relevance degree of ICs (Functional Dependencies (FDs)). (2) ICs Accuracy: when repairing ICs, they could be transformed to overrefined ICs preventing errors detection or oversimplified ICs leading to clean data modification. We propose to extract possible FD repairs from association rules with limiting the number of LHS attributes to avoid overrefined FDs. Oversimplified FDs on the other hand, are avoided by allowing FD repairs only when the candidate is close enough to the FD. (3) Data Accuracy: Most existing solutions repairing both data and constraints, focus more on the simultaneous repair and less on the data repair algorithm, which affects the quality of the data updates. We propose to use CSP-DC which updates data when possible, and handles ambiguous repair cases by formulating the data cleaning problem as a constraint satisfaction problem, allowing all repairs to be consistent. Experiments show that our solution outperforms most renowned state-of-the-art approaches and provides accurate constraints and data repairs in a linear time.

Keywords: Data quality · Data consistency · Data cleaning · Data repair · Constraint repair · Constraint satisfaction problems

1 Introduction

Over the last few years, data has been widely used for prediction, analysis, and decision making. However, real data is usually of poor quality [2] and using it as it is may lead to bad decision-making. This can cause time and money losses, as well as serious repercussions in some critical application areas, like automotive and healthcare [30]. Consequently, data quality management has become crucial for both data scientists and decision makers [19].

To improve data quality, multiple data cleaning solutions were proposed. The most common method is to use a set of quality rules (QRs) to identify data errors also called

A. P. Rocha et al. (Eds.): ICAART 2023, LNAI 14546, pp. 448–468, 2024.
https://doi.org/10.1007/978-3-031-55326-4_22

violations, then find the modifications that minimally change the data and respect the QRs expressed as integrity constraints (ICs) such as: Functional Dependencies (FDs) [4], Conditional Functional Dependencies (CFDs) [9], Denial Constraints (DCs) [29], etc. [13]. However, quality rules may also be erroneous or outdated, which makes it difficult to know whether the data is dirty or the QRs that are incorrect or both [3, 6, 26, 28].

Existing approaches repairing data and quality rules select the repair that minimizes a cost model [3, 6, 26]. Chiang and Miller [6] proposed a unified model to evaluate the repair cost between data and FDs then, selects the one minimizing this cost (data or ICs). However, data and ICs cannot be equally trusted, Beskales et al. [3] proposed to repair data and FDs simultaneously based on the relative trust concept, which consists in applying constraints repairs that keeps the data repair cost under a predefined threshold. Unfortunately, looking for such repairs has a high time complexity. Instead of presetting a parameter to bound data changes, Song et al. [26] reduced the problem complexity by trying multiple constraints variations with different thresholds and selecting the DFs/DCs repairs having a reasonable data repair cost.

Although considering both data and rules repairs improved data quality, existing solutions tend to be less effective in terms of data repair quality when focusing on the simultaneous repairs [3, 6, 26]. Indeed, cleaning data is a challenging task and most of existing data repairing approaches apply the repairs having the minimal cost, which may add more noise to the data by modifying the wrong cells or selecting incorrect repair values [25, 30]. Furthermore, repairing cells that participate in several ICs is challenging, because their modification may affect the consistency of other ICs [19].

To improve the quality of repairs, external data like master data [11, 12] and knowledge bases (KBs) have been used to extract relevant data repairs [1, 8]. However, these approaches need human intervention to select one of the many possible repairs found [19].

In response to the problems listed above, we propose RDC-Repair, a new data cleaning solution that considers both data and constraints repair in an automatic way, while also allowing human intervention when necessary. This work is an extension of our previous work CSP-DC [19], which is a data cleaning system dedicated to repair data inconsistencies. In this work, we consider that both data and rules may be dirty and propose an algorithm to repair data, rules or both.

Unlike existing studies repairing constraints and data, which look for repairs that minimize a cost model, we propose a new model maximizing the degree of relevance of the constraints (FDs). The idea behind is to select from the closest FD-variants the one having the highest relevance score, which makes it more trustworthy.

Instead of testing all possible combinations, FD-variants are generated by constructing FDs from the association rules extracted from the dirty data. This allows us to reduce the number of comparisons, which makes the solution more efficient and adapted to datasets with a high number of attributes/or FDs. Since our repair method extracts potential FDs and evaluates them using our proposed metric, it could be used as a technique for FDs discovery, when no possible ICs are available for a given dataset.

After that, based on the updated FDs, data is repaired using CSP-DC [19], which automatically repairs data when possible or generates possible repairs otherwise.

Instead of involving the user to choose the appropriate repair, we propose a new solution to automatically handle ambiguous repair cases. Our solution is based on constraint satisfaction problems (CSP) [22]. They are usually used to solve problems under constraints, by finding values to variables while satisfying all constraints. In our case, it consists of finding repairs to dirty cells, which respect the entire set of integrity constraints simultaneously, allowing us to improve the data quality and guarantee the consistency of repairs. High data repair accuracy, on the other hand, is ensured by verifying all constraints before instantiating variables, which makes it a holistic choice [19]. When both constraints and data are dirty, inaccurate constraints are identified, repaired then, used to detect data violations and resolve them. We ensure high repair accuracy in this case, thanks to our proposed relevance metric, allowing us to identify dirty FDs and select relevant repairs. Data is then updated accurately as the repaired FDs allow to correctly detect violations, which helps the repair algorithm to update only dirty data cells and avoid generating more noise.

To achieve our goal, we face several challenges including:

- Using association rules to detect FD-variants in dirty data is challenging. FDs could be extracted from association rules when the data is consistent w.r.t the FDs but not when they are dirty.
- Looking for the FD repair from multiple variants may be time consuming, especially when dealing with a high number of constraints and/or attributes. Reducing the search space should be considered.
- Finding the right balance when repairing FDs to avoid both oversimplified and over-refined FDs. Indeed, removing too many attributes may create an oversimplified FD with a high number of violations which leads to modifying clean data and introducing more noise to it. On the other hand, adding attributes may transform the IC on an overrefined FD which prevents the detection of violations and the repair of dirty data.
- Solving a CSP consists of finding a repair that respects all constraints. Since a subset of the data is automatically repaired and used as an initialization of the CSP, their repair must be done carefully to avoid generating new violations, because the final result strongly depends on this step [19].
- Solving a CSP is NP-Complete [21]. In addition, the time complexity of the most known CSP solving algorithms is exponential [23] and depends on the number variables, constraints and the domains sizes [18]. As our problem has a large number of variables and values, it becomes challenging to solve it efficiently [19].

Contributions:

1. Proposing a new repair algorithm that considers data, constraints and a hybrid repair.
2. Instead of looking for the repair that minimizes a cost function, we favor constraints repair that increases the number of trusted patterns and decreases the number of unique and untrustworthy patterns.
3. Proposing a new metric to assess the quality of ICs and select the most relevant one.
4. Proposing to prune the search space of constraints' possible repairs, by transforming them to the FDs discovered using association rules, which allows us to reduce the complexity of the problem.

5. Proposing a strategy to avoid the generation of overrefined/oversimplified constraints by bounding the size of the FD-variants and the similarity between dirty FDs and FD-variants.
6. Preserving a high data repair quality by using CSP-DC which updates data only when there is enough evidence and generates possible repairs otherwise. Ambiguous repair cases are handled by formulating the data cleaning problem as CSP.
7. We conduct experiments to assess the effectiveness and the efficiency of RDC-Repair and compare it against some of the state-of-the-art works.

This paper will be organized as follows. Section 2 presents RDC-Repair architecture overview of RDC-Repair. Section 3 presents the details of our IC repair solution. Section 4 presents our data repairing solution. In Sect. 5, we discuss the results of our experimental study. Section 6 analyzes some data cleaning studies. Section 7 concludes our work and discusses some perspectives.

2 Solution Overview

Our Cleaning process is composed of three main phases as shown in Fig. 1:

1. **Violations Detection.** In this phase the RQs given as input and expressed as FDs are used to identify the violations (data that do not respect the FDs). A FD F: X → Y is violated if two tuples in the data share the same X (the left hand side (LHS)) and have different Y (the right hand side (RHS)). If data violates one or more FDs, a repair search for both FDs and data is triggered.
2. **Quality Rules Repair.** In this phase, we look for potential repairs to each FD and update it, if necessary, through the following steps:
   - FD discovery: In this step, a set of possible updates is extracted by means of association rules discovered from dirty data and translated into FDs.
   - Patterns' extraction: Here, for each FD, we select its patterns, which represent only the data units of a tuple that are covered by the concerned FD. After that, patterns are grouped into three groups: Trusted/Clean patterns, dirty patterns and unique patterns which are patterns appearing one time in the dataset.
     Trusted patterns are selected by grouping patterns sharing the same LHS value together and selecting the one having the maximum frequency value. If external data like knowledge bases or master data is available, trusted patterns could be extracted by verifying their presence in this external data as we proposed in [20]. Other patterns of each group are considered as dirty ones.
   - FD repairing: In this step, we select among multiple possible updates the most relevant one, if it exists. To do so, we calculate a score of relevance for each FD-variant (a discovered FD having a high similarity with the FD). The minimal similarity that a FD should have with its candidates is specified via a threshold. The score of relevance on the other hand, is calculated taking into account the number of trusted, dirty and unique patterns of each FD-variants (see more details in Sect. 3). At the end of this phase the updated FDs are returned.
3. **Data Repair:** This phase is composed of two principal steps:

– Violation detection and updates discovery: In this step, repaired FDs are used to detect violations. Then, CSP-DC selects repairs for violations that can be easily resolved and returns multiple possible fixes for ambiguous repair cases. To do this, any data repair algorithm could be used as long as it returns possible fixes when there is a confusion about the update to choose. As we proposed in [19], it is preferable to use a repair algorithm which exploits external data [1,8] to guarantee the good quality of the updates. To repair data, CSP-DC deals with three possible cases:

(a) Violations with one possible repair: in this case, data is automatically updated as the proposed repair is likely to be the good one.

(b) Violations with no possible repairs: here, the users are invited to repair the involved cells.

(c) Violations with multiple possible repairs: in this case, the concerned cells are annotated and their possible repair values are collected [19].

At the end of this phase, the consistency of data is verified. If new violations were triggered when repairing the first violations, another cleaning iteration is done [19].

– CSP Based Repair: In this step, CSP-DC transforms the updated data, repaired FDs, and possible repairs to define the problem as a CSP and initialize its elements. Variables referring to clean data are initialized, domains of annotated cells are constructed using the possible repairs, and the FDs are translated to constraints on variables. Finally, the CSP is solved by finding repair to annotated data using a backtracking search algorithm which returns the repaired data [19].

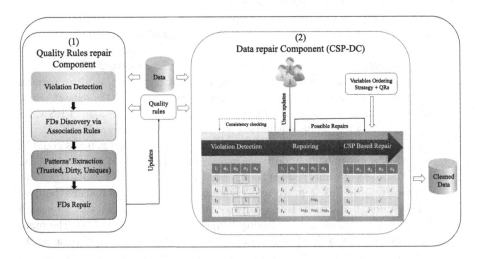

Fig. 1. The workflow of RDC-Repair.

3   Quality Rules Repair

In the following, we explain how FD-variants are extracted and how their relevance degree is evaluated before updating the FDs.

FD-Variants Discovery. In order to look for possible repairs to integrity constraints, we propose to discover constraints from dirty data using association rules. The idea behind is to create a pruned list of variants instead of evaluating all possible cases. In our work, we focus on the most used type of constraints which is functional dependencies (FDs). We believe that the solution can be generalized to cover other constraints like CFDs which have been widely discovered via association rules or using any other constraints discovery method (example [7] for DCs).

To discover FD-variants, we use Buranosky et al. solution called FDTool[1] [5], which allows the creation of FDs from clean data using association rules. In order to be able to use FDTool to extract FDs from dirty data, we modify the algorithm to allow it to generate rules that are not respected by all data. To do that, we allow the extraction of FDs that are respected by the majority of the data but not all of it. Technically, this comes to empirically fixing a lower threshold to bound the cardinality of candidates.

To avoid creating too overrefined rules, we bound the size of the discovered FDs by specifying their maximum number of attributes on LHS. This size limitation reduces the number of irrelevant discovered FDs, which in turn reduces the number of possible repairs of each dirty FD, and therefore the calculation time.

A discovered FD 'DF' is a variant of 'F' if the similarity between them is higher than a predefined threshold. The similarity is calculated by mapping the two FDs using Eq. 1 which takes into account the position of attributes. So, having a LHS attribute of F1 present in the RHS of F is not considered as a match.

$$sim(FD_i, FD_j) = \frac{(LHS_i \cap LHS_j) + (RHS_i \cap RHS_j)}{max(|FD_i|, |FD_j|)} \tag{1}$$

Measuring the similarity between FDs and their potential repairs enables the selection of only repairs that are sufficiently close. It reduces the risk of a major modification to the FD, which prevents the creation of oversimplified FDs by minimizing the deletion of attributes, thus preserving the FD repair quality. Moreover, this similarity measurement is a pruning process since only FD-variants are evaluated next. As a result, the computation time is reduced.

Patterns' Extraction. Extracting patterns comes to selecting the relevant part of each tuple by retrieving only the units covered by the FD. The purpose behind this step is to classify each pattern as trusted, dirty and unique. The patterns' extraction allows us to evaluate them more easily compared to tuples. Indeed, since in a dirty tuple (i.e. having some erroneous attribute values), some parts could be clean w.r.t a given FD and dirty w.r.t another one. Splitting tuples in multiple patterns, each one containing only the data units covered by one specific FD, allows us to extract the information about their quality.

---

[1] https://github.com/USEPA/FDTool.

To evaluate the quality of patterns, they are first gathered into groups, each one containing patterns sharing the same LHS value and different RHS values. This means that this group of patterns do not respect the FD (i.e. violation), consequently one of them must be correct and the others are dirty. In order to identify the trusted pattern of each group, we propose to verify their presence in external data like knowledge bases or master data, if they are available. Otherwise the pattern having the maximum frequency value in a group is the trusted one. The rest of the patterns of each group are considered dirty [20]. Unique patterns on the other hand, are those that appear only once in the data.

FD Repair. To select the appropriate updates to dirty FDs, a relevance score (Sr) of each candidate (FD-variant) is calculated using Eq. 2. The higher Sr, the more relevant the FD-variant is. The idea behind is to penalize the FD-variants that generate a high number of unique and dirty patterns compared to the initial FD and favor the FD-variants maximizing the number of trusted patterns. Penalizing candidates with a high number of unique patterns allows us to avoid transforming the FD into an overrefined FD.

$$Sr = 1 - ((\alpha * UniqueP + \beta * TrustedP + \gamma * DirtyP)/AllPatterns) \quad (2)$$
$$With (1 \geq \alpha, \gamma > 0), (\beta < 0) and (\alpha + \beta + \gamma) = 0$$

The FD repair process is described in Algorithm 1. It takes as input the Data, the FDs, the Dirty_FDs, the maximum length of the LHS of the discovered FDs max_length, a similarity threshold $sim\_thresehold$, the relevance threshold (th) used to prune FDs that we can consider as clean, the minimum relevance threshold (th_min) used to guarantee that the applied repairs have a very high relevance score, and the parameters to calculate Sr. First, a list of FDs is discovered, to be used as possible repairs for the dirty FDs. This list is pruned by removing the FDs given as input. After that, the dirty FDs are ordered using their SR. The idea behind is to repair first the most irrelevant FDs instead of looking for possible repairs to already clean ones. This prevents a clean FD from being transformed into the clean version to which a dirty DF is supposed to be transformed (because it has a slightly higher (Sr)), thus preventing the latter from being repaired/correctly repaired.

Next, for each FD from ($Dirty\_FDs$), the relevance score (Sr) is calculated, if the Sr is higher than the threshold (th), this means that the Sr is high enough to say that the FD is considered as clean. This step is crucial to reduce the run-time as it avoids looking for repairs to clean FDs.

Otherwise, if the FD is considered as dirty, its similarity is compared with the discovered FDs to select its FD-variants. The FD-variant having the maximal relevance score is selected as a repair. During the search, if a selected FD-variant has a relevance score higher than (th), it is returned as a repair of FD.

In some cases, the discovered FDs do not include the correct repairs of all dirty FDs due to the high data error rate. Consequently, no possible repair is found for them. If such a case occurs, we handle it by enriching the list of FD-variants progressively. First, we suggest removing one attribute at a time from the LHS, if this last contains more than one attribute. A repair is returned, once a FD-variant having the Sr value higher than (th) is found. If no repair is found, one attribute could be added at time (the maximal length value should be respected). Also, another iteration could be done

Algorithm 1. ConstraintsRepair.

Input: Dirty Data D, Dirty FDs $Dirty\_FDs$, Max LHS length max_length, Similarity threshold $sim\_thresehold$, α, β, $gama$, Minimum Relevance threshold th_min, Relevance threshold th
Output: $CleanedFDs$, $UrepairedFDs$

1:   $DiscoveredFDs \leftarrow$ FDsDiscovery(D, max_length)
2:   $Discovered\_FDs$.remove($Dirty\_FDs$) // Prunning
3:   $Dirty\_FDs \leftarrow$ Order($Dirty\_FDs$)
4: **for** FD **in** $Dirty\_FDs$ **do**
5:     N_unics, N_trusted, N_dirty $\leftarrow$ extractPatterns(D, FD)
6:     SR_max $\leftarrow$ RelevanceScore(FD, N_unics, N_trusted, N_dirty)
7:     **if** $(SR\_max > th)$ **or** $(V\_DF1 = 0)$ **then**
8:       Cleaned_FDs.append(FD)
9:     **else**
10:       **for** i in range (0, len(DiscoveredFDs)) **do**
11:         **if** Similarity(FD, DiscoveredFDs[i] $>= sim\_threshold$) **then**
12:           $FD\_variant \leftarrow$ DiscoveredFDs[i]
13:           N_unics, N_trusted, N_dirty $\leftarrow$ extract_patterns(D, $FD\_variant$)
14:           Sr = RelevanceScore(FD, N_unics, N_trusted, N_dirty)
15:           **if** $Sr > th$ **then**
16:             Cleaned_FDs.append(FD_variant)
17:             break;
18:           **else**
19:             scores.append(Sr)
20:             indexes.append(i)
21:           **end if**
22:         **end if**
23:       **end for**
24:       **if** (b = True) **and** (max(scores) > SR_max) **and** (max(scores) > th_min) **then**
25:         ind $\leftarrow$ selectIndexiMax(scores)
26:         Cleaned_FDs.append(DiscoveredFDs[indexes[ind]])
27:       **else if** (max(scores) < th_min) **and** (SR_min < th_min) **then**
28:         print("No possible repairs, please use a higher threshold when discovering FDs")
29:         UnrepairedFDs.append(FD)
30:       **else**
31:         Cleaned_FDs.append(FD)
32:       **end if**
33:     **end if**
34: **end for**
35: **return** $Cleaned\_FDs$, $Unrepaired\_FDs$

---

to select more candidates (discovered FDs) by changing the threshold bounding the cardinality of candidates, which generally helps to find releventt repairs.

Note that fixing the threshold (th) is not necessary, but it is helpful to speed up the search for FDs repairs.

For an easier and more relevant selection of both (th) and (t_min), we propose to first consult the relevant scores of all FDs, then, fix the adapted values.

After repairing FDs, they are used to detect violations and look for data repairs as shown in Algorithm 2. The used data repair algorithm is described in details in [19].

Algorithm 2. Data and Constraints Repair.

Input: Dirty Data D, Dirty FDs FDs, Max LHS length max_length, Similarity threshold $sim\_thresehold$, α, β, γ, Minimum Relevance threshold th_min, Relevance threshold th
Output: $Cleaned_Data$

1:   $Cleaned\_FDs \leftarrow$ ConstraintsRepair(D, FDs, max_length, $sim\_thresehold$, α, β, γ,
2:   $Cleaned\_Data \leftarrow$ DataRepair(D, $Cleaned\_FDs$)

---

4   Data Repair

In this section, we present our data repair process including the constraint satisfaction problems based solution. We explain how we translate the data cleaning problem into a CSP, how its elements are initialized, how the problem is solved, and how the exponential time complexity is avoided via our optimizations.

Our data repair process is composed of two main steps. The first one, uses a data repair algorithm to automatically repair data when possible and returns possible repairs when there is ambiguity about the cells to modify or the repair to choose. In the later case, cells are annotated. This process could be repeated until no violation is detected. During the repair process, the user could be invited to repair data with no possible fixes. The second step is the CSP-based repair solution, which consists in finding to annotated cells, repair values that respect all constraints at the same time by formulating the data cleaning as a CSP. In the following, we will mainly focus on this second step.

4.1   Data Cleaning Translation into Constraint Satisfaction Problem

The data cleaning problem is composed of two main elements: (1) Data that represents a list of tuples, each one contains multiple attribute values. (2) Integrity constraints that formulate a set of quality rules in order to ensure data consistency. We represent our problem as follows [19]:

- Variables (X): We consider every cell as a variable $Xi.j$, where "i" is the identifier of the tuple and "j" the attribute that the variable refers to.
- Domains (D): A domain represents the possible values of a variable.
- Constraints(C): are the translation of the FDs into conditions on variables. A variable may be under one or multiple constraints.

Once the problem representation is done, we initialize its elements. Variables related to the clean cells are initialized by assigning the value corresponding to the tuple "i" and the attribute "j" to the variable $X_{i.j}$ the rest of variables (related to annotated cells) are set to 'tags'. After that, the possible repairs returned for the annotated cells, are used in addition to their original values to construct their domains [19].

5   CSP Resolution to Find Data Repairs

In order to find repair values to annotated cells and guarantee the consistency of the repair (i.e. respect all FDs simultaneously), we solve the CSP previously initialized. For this purpose, we use a backtracking search algorithm which consists in assigning to each variable, a value from its domain and checking for each assignment, if all constraints are respected. In this case, this value is assigned to the current variable, otherwise if one or multiple constraints are violated, a backtrack is necessary in order to change the value of a previously instantiated variable that may cause this inconsistency. We refer the reader to the CSP-DC article [19] for more details about how the repair search is done.

5.1 Optimizations to Reduce the Complexity of the Problem

To avoid the exponential time complexity of the backtracking search, two optimizations were proposed. The first one consists in reducing the repair search space by pruning the variables' domains as well as the set of their neighbors, which are other variables on which constraints should be verified. The second optimization orders the variables to allow a more efficient search [19].

5.2 Neighbors and Domains Pruning

Pruning the List of Neighbors: Instantiating a variable implies a consistency verification w.r.t all ICs. This comes to a pairwise comparison between each non-instantiated variable and all the other variables concerned by the same constraint (i.e. neighbors). To avoid the pairwise comparison, we propose to extract for each IC, a non-redundant list of "n"-uplets with "n" the number of its attributes. This means that the comparison will be done only with one occurrence of the "n"-uplets instead of all of them, which avoids the comparison with the same data combination multiple times. If a variable corresponds to an attribute participating in multiple constraints, neighbors are selected considering all these constraints [19].

Pruning the List of Domains: The complexity of the backtracking search of the order $O(e * d^n)$ (with n the number of variables, e the number of constraints, and d the size of the largest domain) [18]. To avoid the exponential time complexity, we use the list of possible repairs returned in the first repair step, instead of using all the attribute's domain values. This reduces the number of values to be tested before finding the correct repair thus, reducing the repair time [19].

5.3 Variables Ordering

When solving a CSP, the backtracking search algorithm usually uses a variables ordering heuristic and a value ordering heuristic. However, existing heuristics are sometimes time consuming. We propose a new variables ordering technique adapted to our data cleaning problem. In consists in using the conflict score (cf_F) which determines the conflicts that a constraint F has with other constraints, based on the number of common attributes between them. Instead of calculating the cf_F score for constraints ordering like proposed in [6], we propose to use it also for attribute ordering since variables can be grouped using the attributes that they refer to. So, instead of having $n * m$ variables to order, we just define an order on the "m" groups, each one having "n" variables.

The selection of variables inside groups can be done randomly. Since they share the same constraints, the accuracy of repairs won't be affected. Variables are selected as follows [19]:

1. Select the constraint with the highest cf_F.
2. Select, in decreasing order, the most overlapping attributes of the chosen IC.
3. Select the LHS attribute of the chosen IC first.

6 Experimental Study

In this experimental study we aim to: (1) Assess the effectiveness and efficiency of our FD repair algorithm, (2) Show the data repair effectiveness and efficiency, (3) Evaluate the effectiveness of our proposed cleaning solution (RDC-Repair) when dealing with both data and rules errors, (4) Compare the accuracy provided by RDC-Repair against some if state-of-the-art cleaning approaches.

6.1 Setup

We run our experiments on a 64bit AMD Ryzen 75800H and 32 GB RAM.

Dataset. We use Hospital, a real-world dataset of 100k records. Errors were generated on the 8 attributes covered by the 8 FDs in Table 1.

Table 1. FDs used for experiments.

Id	FD
φ_1	$MeasureCode, State \rightarrow StateAvg$
φ_2	$ZIPCode \rightarrow State$
φ_3	$PhoneNumber \rightarrow ZIPCode$
φ_4	$ZIPCode \rightarrow City$
φ_5	$MeasureCode \rightarrow MeasureName$
φ_6	$MeasureCode \rightarrow Condition$
φ_7	$PhoneNumber \rightarrow City$
φ_8	$PhoneNumber \rightarrow State$

Errors. In our experiments, two types of errors were injected:

E1 (Errors from the active domain): This error type makes it harder for repair algorithms to find the right repair since multiple repair candidates may exist.

E2 (Random Errors): Are random errors that may or may not generate IC's violations. Following the same line of evaluating data repairing in [27, 29], errors were generated by randomly picking a character and change it to 'x'.

Metrics. The following metrics were used:

Data Precision. The number of correctly repaired cells over the total number of repaired cells.

Data Recall. The number of correctly repaired cells over the total number of dirty cells (annotated cells are considered as unprepared cells).

FD Precision. The number of attributes correctly added/deleted to LHS's/ RHS's of dirty FDs over the total number of removed/added attributes from clean FDs when constructing dirty FDs.

FD Recall. The number of attributes correctly added/removed to LHS's/ RHS's of dirty FDs over the total number of attributes removed/added from clean FDs when constructing dirty FDs.

F1-Score (F1). calculated as $2 * (P * R)/(P + R)$.

Note. As our data repair process is composed of two phases, we use in all our experiments that include data repairs, our repair algorithm proposed in [20]. It provides data updates only when there is enough evidence about their correctness, and annotated data cells otherwise.

6.2 Rules Repair Evaluation

Effectiveness Results. To study the effectiveness of our FDs repairing and the impact of the error rate on it, we varied the error rate from 2% to 10% on 20k records of the Hospital dataset. We also studied the impact of the variation of the error type.

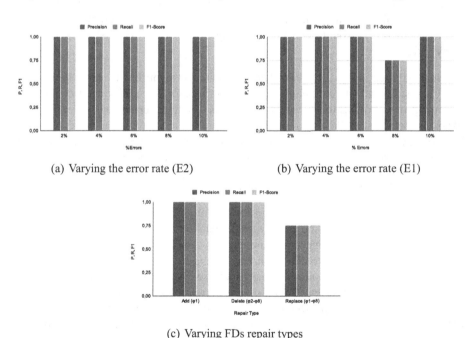

(a) Varying the error rate (E2)   (b) Varying the error rate (E1)

(c) Varying FDs repair types

Fig. 2. Effectiveness of FDs repairing.

We used 3 dirty FDs over 8 FDs, one needs attribute replacement ($State \rightarrow StateAvg$)), one needs attribute removing ($ZIPCode, StateAvg \rightarrow City$) and one needs attribute adding ($State \rightarrow Measurename$).

Figure 2(a) shows that our FDs repair algorithm preforms very well when dealing with random errors. Indeed, it returned 100% accurate repairs. Results also show that the F1-score (respectively precision and recall) were not affected by the error rate, which is due to the flexibility that the algorithm offers while selecting FD-variants (changing the thresholds when no repairs are available) as well as our proposed metric which allows to select the most relevant DF repair.

In Fig. 2(b), we show the FD repair performance results when the error rate is from the active domain (E1). Although the FD repair in E1 is high, repairing FDs was more difficult compared to E2. It required the user intervention to select each time adapted thresholds that bound Sr, in contrast to E2, where the same setting was used for all data errors. When the error rate is 8%, the F1 score decreases due to appending 'Measure-Name' to the LHS of the dirty FD ($State \rightarrow StateAvg$) instead of 'MeasureCode'.

We also assessed the effectiveness of the FD repairing algorithm when dealing oversimplified FDs, overrefined FDs and FDs that are oversimplified and overrefined at the same time (needs attribute replacement to be repaired). The evaluation is done by injecting 5% data errors on 20k records of the hospital dataset and generating dirty FDs as following:

- Removing 'MeasureCode' from φ_1 to evaluate the repair by adding attributes.
- Adding attributes to the LHS of (φ_2-φ_8) to assess the repair by removing attributes.
- Modifying 4 FDs from (φ_1-φ_8) by changing a random attribute to assess the repair by replacement.

Results illustrated in Fig. 2(c), show that our FD repair algorithm achieved high scores in all cases. Indeed, it returned 100% accurate repairs when FDs needed attributes appending or removing to be repaired and 75% accurate repairs when dealing with attributes replacement. We explain the lower score of the FD replacement repair by the fact that one FD among the 4 dirty ones was nor repaired, because no possible repair was returned when discovering FDs from dirty data. Although it was possible to try exhaustively all possible repairs of the remaining dirty FD (since the dataset has a moderate attributes number), we didn't consider this step in our experiments.

Run-Time Results. In Fig. 3, we report the run-time results of the FD repair process when varying the error rate, the error type and dataset size.

Results in Fig. 3(a) show that when the error is random (E2) our algorithm is fast. Indeed, We observe a linear curve when varying the error rate.

Unlike E2, the run-time of E1 does not increase linearly as the noise rate increases. We explain this by the fact that the run-time is correlated with the number of the generated candidates (discovered FDs). As illustrated in Fig. 3(c), the number of discovered FDs depends on the dataset but does not increase linearly. Indeed, the number of discovered FDs when the error rate is 4% is the highest one, which explains why it corresponds to the highest run-time.

We also studied the scalability of our FD reapir algorithm. In Fig. 3(d), we show the run-time result of our FDs repair process when varying the dataset size. They show that our algorithm scales well and repairs FDs in a linear time.

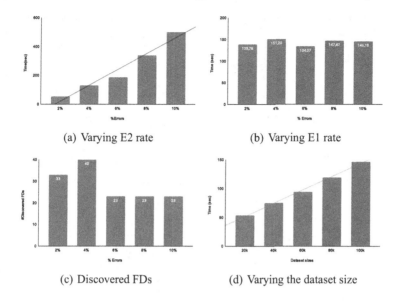

(a) Varying E2 rate

(b) Varying E1 rate

(c) Discovered FDs

(d) Varying the dataset size

Fig. 3. FDs repairing Run-time results.

6.3   Data Repair Evaluation

Effectiveness Results. To evaluate the performance of our data repairing process, we use 20k records from Hospital dataset and injected errors from the active domain (E1) on attributes covered by the following FDs:

$FD1 : ZIPCode \rightarrow State$

$FD2 : PhoneNumber \rightarrow ZIPCode$

$FD2 : ProviderNumber \rightarrow City, PhoneNumber$

In these experiments, we study a particularly difficult repair scenario, where data errors are from the active domain and FDs have overlapped attributes, which creates a high number of ambiguous cases to deal with.

Note. To create the ground truth, we modified the dataset to be consistent with the used FDs befor injecting errors.

Figure 4 illustrates the accuracy of the our data repairs in the first repair phase (before the CSP based repair) and after using the CSP based solution. The results in Fig. 4(a) show that the precision is stable and high. Indeed, the first repair phase returned a 100% accurate repairs which is due to the fact that data is carefully modified. The CSP based repair also returned a high precision score going beyond 99.8%. This means that annotated data cells were correctly updated, which is due to the strength of the CSP representation, allowing only consistent repairs. Although the consistency is guaranteed by our solution, it is not always possible to achieve 100% clean repairs. This happens when dealing with some special cases difficult to handle even by users. We refer the reader to the CSP-DC article [19] for more details.

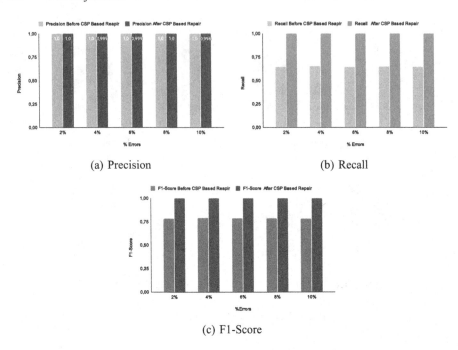

(a) Precision   (b) Recall

(c) F1-Score

Fig. 4. Effectiveness of data repairing when varying the data error rate.

The results in Fig. 4(b–c) show that the first repair phase returned a relatively low Recall and F1-score. This is due to the high number of annotated cells due to ambiguous repair cases. Both scores increase remarkably after applying the CSP based repair, which is explained by the instantiation of annotated cells by their good repair values.

Also, we notice that all scores remain stable when increasing the error rate, so we can conclude that our data repair accuracy is not affected by the error rate.

Run-Time Results. In Fig. 5(a–b), we report the run-time results of the CSP based repair when varying: 1) the error rate on 20k records and 2) the dataset size from 20k to 100k with the error rate fixed at 1%.

The reported error rate represents the initial error rate before the annotation.

Results show that our CSP based repair has a linear time when varying the error rate or the dataset size. This is due to our optimizations as well as the fact that the algorithm is designed to be executed in parallel.

To study the impact of the domains and neighbors pruning as well as our variables' ordering on the efficiency, we varied the dataset size from 5k to 20k and fixed error rate at 1%.

Results illustrated in Fig. 5 show that our proposed optimizations helped to accelerate the repair process. Indeed, when the dataset size reaches 20k our repair time is 300 times faster than the repair without the pruning and 1500 times faster than the repair without the pruning nor the variables' ordering (random selection). In other words the pruning process and the variables ordering allowed us to reduce the repair time by more than

21% and 78% respectively (i.e, 99% when used together) [19]. The results also show that our optimizations helped to reduce the complexity of the problem, as the more data there is, the larger the gap between the curves becomes. Indeed, neighbor pruning reduced the number of comparisons between variables by selecting as few neighbors as possible, the domain pruning reduced the search space when looking for repairs, and variable ordering helped us to converge quickly to the solution by avoiding dead ends and thus backtracks [19].

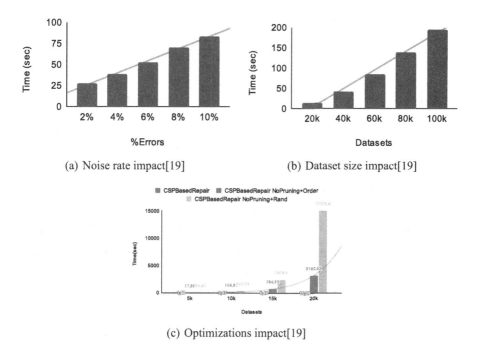

(a) Noise rate impact[19]   (b) Dataset size impact[19]

(c) Optimizations impact[19]

Fig. 5. Run-time results.

6.4 Rules and Data Repair Evaluation

To assess the effectiveness of RDC-Repair, we varied the error rate (E2) on 20k records of Hospital. We used 6 FDs ($\phi_1 - \phi6$), including 3 dirty with different repair cases as specified in the Rules Repair Evaluation.

Results illustrated in Fig. 6 show that RDC-Repair performs very well when dealing with both data and FDs errors. They also show that the F1 score is stable and higher than 96% with 100% correctly modified data cells (i.e. 100% precision). This is due to the fact that data is modified only when we are sure about its correctness which prevents the modification of data with erroneous values. This also could be explained by the fact that all dirty FDs where correctly repaired as show in Fig. 2(a), which helped to detect violations and repair them correctly. Note that some errors were not repaired because the injected noise creates outliers (by adding random characters). As a result, this errors cannot be detected, especially that some attributes participate only in the LHS of FDs like (MeasureCode).

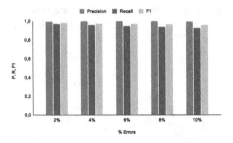

Fig. 6. Effectiveness of our cleaning process when both data and rules are dirty.

6.5   Comparison to Baselines

We compared the effectiveness RDC-Repair to two types approaches:

- Data repairing approaches: Holistic [29] and Vrepair [15].
- Rules and data repairing approaches: Unified [6], Relative [3] and CVtolerant [26].

We used the Hospital dataset with ($\phi_1 - \phi_6$) and followed the same experimental setup used in [26] to be able to use the results presented in Fig. 7.

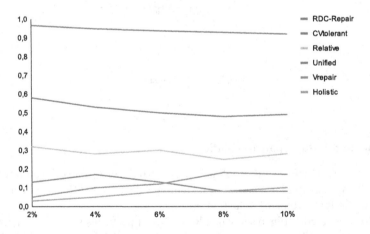

Fig. 7. Comparison to Baselines.

Since in [26] neither the used dirty FDs nor their error rate were specified, we used 6 dirty FDs, to evaluate our cleaning process effectiveness. This represents the worst case possible, but it allows us to make sure that the comparison is not unfair.

Results illustrated in Fig. 7 show that our approach outperforms significantly all the other approaches. Indeed, it achieved a high and stable F1-score going beyond 91.9% and up to 96.6%. We explain this by: (1) Our FD repair algorithm returned a high quality FDs. Indeed, most of them were 100% correctly repaired and the others were transformed to high quality FDs allowing to detect and repair correctly most of violations. (2) We particularly pay attention to the data repair process which updates data carefully and avoids new violations generation.

7 Related Work

Existing constraint-based data cleaning approaches have been focusing more on modifying data in order to respect the integrity constraints and less on constraints repair [4, 8, 10, 12, 14, 16, 17, 24, 29, 30].
Few works consider both data and constraints repairs [3, 6, 26, 28]. Some of them detect the source of the error (either data or constraints) then apply one type of repairs [6]. Others look simultaneously at ICs repairs that lead to minimal data repairs [3, 26].

Our work is positioned between these two methods, it first looks for repairs to dirty ICs, repairs them, then, looks for data repairs that respect the new set of ICs.

Existing approaches select the repair that minimize a cost model. Chiang and Miller. [6] used a unified model based on the description length, to evaluate the repair cost between data and FDs then, selects the one minimizing this cost (data or ICs). Beskales et al. [3] on the other hand, considered that data and rules should be relatively trusted. They proposed to apply constraints repairs that keeps the data repair cost under a predefined threshold τ. Song et al. [26] proposed to try multiple constraints variations with different thresholds and select the ICs repair leading to a reasonable data repair cost.

Instead of selecting Data/ ICs repair based on their repair cost, we propose to evaluate the relevance degree of FDs, repair dirty ones by selecting the update that maximizes the relevance score, then, repair data using clean FDs. Unlike other approaches trying all possible ICs combinations when looking for their repairs, we extract from data the ICs (FDs) that are more likely to be correct, which reduces the problem's complexity.

Most existing solutions lose in accuracy of repairs when repairing both sources. They either favor one source over another [6] or perform better when the error is in the constraints [3], but significantly lose in accuracy once the data is dirty [26]. Moreover existing approaches repairing generally looks for updates that minimally change original data and satisfy a set of ICs [4, 10, 12, 14, 29]. However, the minimal repair does not guarantee the accuracy of repairs nor the consistency of data especially, when unverified fixes are applied [11, 19].

For high-quality repairs, we perform automatic repairs, when possible, ask for human intervention to resolve violations with no possible repairs found, and annotate data cells involved violations with multiple possible repairs. Ambiguous repair cases are treated by formulating the problem as a constraint satisfaction problem and solving it. Compared to existing cleaning approaches, our solution provides higher repair accuracy.

8   Conclusion

In this article, we address the problem of uncertainty regarding the quality of both data and constraints. We propose RDC-Repair, a new data cleaning approach that takes into account constraints (FDs) and data repairs without trading off the quality of data updates, nor the efficiency of the repair process. To ensure high repair quality, our constraints repair is done by choosing the most trustworthy FD-variant instead of the one that minimizes a cost function. The selection is done by evaluating the degree of relevance of each FD-variant based on the number of its trusted, dirty, and unique patterns extracted from data and categorized using their frequency, or by leveraging external data such as knowledge bases and master data.

Instead of exhaustively testing all attribute combinations to repair dirty FDs, candidates are generated by extracting FDs using association rules discovered from the dirty data. This allows us to reduce the number of candidates, which in turn reduces the runtime. The generation of overrefined FDs is prevented by fixing an upper threshold limiting the number of possible attributes in the LHS of the discovered FDs. The same way, oversimplified FDs are avoided by fixing a lower threshold to bound the similarity between the dirty FD and its repair candidates.

For high-quality repairs, we used CSP-DC [19], which performs automatic repairs when possible, or generates multiple possible fixes when not. Violations for which no repairs were found, are repaired manually to ensure data consistency at this stage.

To deal with ambiguous repair cases, CSP-DC annotates the involved cells, collects their previously generated possible repairs and translates the search for their repairs into a CSP. A consistent repair is found using a CSP resolution algorithm, which selects only updates that satisfy all constraints at the same time. CSP-DC optimizes the repair search using a variable ordering technique and a pruning strategy to reach the solution quickly and avoid dead-ends.

Our experiments demonstrate that our repair algorithms improve both rules and data quality, achieving a high repair accuracy going beyond 91% and up to 100%. They also show that both FDs and data repairs are provided in a linear time. The evaluation of our proposal against some of the state-of-the-art approaches showed RDC-Repair significantly outperformed the existing solutions in terms of repair accuracy, while maintaining its efficiency.

In future work, we may focus on the generalization of our constraint repair algorithm in order to support other types of ICs like CFDs and DCs.

References

1. Abdellaoui, S., Nader, F., Chalal, R.: QDflows: a system driven by knowledge bases for designing quality-aware data flows. J. Data Inf. Q. **8**(3–4), 1–39 (2017). https://doi.org/10.1145/3064173. https://dl.acm.org/doi/10.1145/3064173
2. Berti-Equille, L.: Reinforcement Learning for Data Preparation with Active Reward Learning (2019)
3. Beskales, G., Ilyas, I.F., Golab, L., Galiullin, A.: On the Relative Trust between Inconsistent Data and Inaccurate Constraints (2013)

4. Bohannon, P., Fan, W., Rastogi, R., Flaster, M.: A Cost-Based Model and Effective Heuristic for Repairing Constraints by Value Modification (2005)

5. Buranosky, M., Stellnberger, E., Pfaff, E., Diaz-Sanchez, D., Ward-Caviness, C.: FDTool: a python application to mine for functional dependencies and candidate keys in tabular data. F1000Research **7** (2018)

6. Chiang, F., Miller, R.J.: A Unified Model for Data and Constraint Repair (2011)

7. Chu, X., Ilyas, I.F., Papotti, P.: Discovering denial constraints. Proc. VLDB Endow. **6**(13), 1498–1509 (2013)

8. Chu, X., et al.: KATARA: a data cleaning system powered by knowledge bases and crowd-sourcing. In: Proceedings of the 2015 ACM SIGMOD International Conference on Management of Data, Melbourne, Victoria, Australia, pp. 1247–1261. ACM (2015). https://doi.org/10.1145/2723372.2749431. https://dl.acm.org/doi/10.1145/2723372.2749431

9. Cong, G., Fan, W., Geerts, F., Jia, X., Ma, S.: Improving Data Quality: Consistency and Accuracy (2007)

10. Dallachiesa, M., et al.: NADEEF: a commodity data cleaning system. In: Proceedings of the 2013 International Conference on Management of Data - SIGMOD 2013, New York, USA, p. 541. ACM Press, New York (2013). https://doi.org/10.1145/2463676.2465327. http://dl.acm.org/citation.cfm?doid=2463676.2465327

11. Fan, W., Li, J., Ma, S., Tang, N., Yu, W.: Towards certain fixes with editing rules and master data. VLDB J. **21**(2), 213–238 (2012). https://doi.org/10.1007/s00778-011-0253-7

12. Geerts, F., Mecca, G., Papotti, P., Santoro, D.: The LLUNATIC data-cleaning framework. Proc. VLDB Endow. **6**(9), 625–636 (2013). https://doi.org/10.14778/2536360.2536363. https://dl.acm.org/doi/10.14778/2536360.2536363

13. Ilyas, I.F., Chu, X.: Trends in cleaning relational data: consistency and deduplication. Found. Trends® Databases **5**(4), 281–393 (2015). https://doi.org/10.1561/1900000045. http://www.nowpublishers.com/article/Details/DBS-045

14. Khayyat, Z., et al.: BigDansing: a system for big data cleansing. In: Proceedings of the 2015 ACM SIGMOD International Conference on Management of Data, Melbourne, Victoria, Australia, pp. 1215–1230. ACM (2015). https://doi.org/10.1145/2723372.2747646. https://dl.acm.org/doi/10.1145/2723372.2747646

15. Kolahi, S., Lakshmanan, L.V.S.: On approximating optimum repairs for functional dependency violations. In: Proceedings of the 12th International Conference on Database Theory - ICDT 2009, St. Petersburg, Russia, p. 53. ACM Press (2009). https://doi.org/10.1145/1514894.1514901. http://portal.acm.org/citation.cfm?doid=1514894.1514901

16. Konda, P., et al.: Magellan: Toward Building Entity Matching Management Systems (2016)

17. Mahdavi, M., Abedjan, Z.: Baran: effective error correction via a unified context representation and transfer learning. Proc. VLDB Endow. **13**(12), 1948–1961 (2020). https://doi.org/10.14778/3407790.3407801. https://dl.acm.org/doi/10.14778/3407790.3407801

18. Mouelhi, A.E., Jégou, P., Terrioux, C., Zanuttini, B.: Sur la complexité des algorithmes de backtracking et quelques nouvelles classes polynomiales pour CSP (2012)

19. Nadjeh, N., Abdellaoui, S., Nader, F.: CSP-DC: data cleaning via constraint satisfaction problem solving. In: Proceedings of the 15th International Conference on Agents and Artificial Intelligence, Portugal, vol. 2, pp. 478–488 (2023)

20. Nibel, N., Abdellaoui, S., Nader, F.: Bigcleaner: a new big data cleaning approach (under review). J. Data Inf. Qual. 1–25 (2023)

21. Pang, W., Goodwin, S.D.: A graph based backtracking algorithm for solving general CSPs. In: Xiang, Y., Chaib-draa, B. (eds.) Advances in Artificial Intelligence. LNCS, vol. 2671, pp. 114–128. Springer, Heidelberg (2003). https://doi.org/10.1007/3-540-44886-1_11

22. Poole, D.L., Mackworth, A.K.: Artificial Intelligence: Foundations of Computational Agents. Cambridge University Press (2010). google-Books-ID: B7khAwAAQBAJ

23. Razgon, I.: Complexity analysis of heuristic CSP search algorithms. In: Hnich, B., Carlsson, M., Fages, F., Rossi, F. (eds.) CSCLP 2005. LNCS, vol. 3978, pp. 88–99. Springer, Heidelberg (2006). https://doi.org/10.1007/11754602_7

24. Rekatsinas, T., Chu, X., Ilyas, I.F., Ré, C.: HoloClean: holistic data repairs with probabilistic inference. Proc. VLDB Endow. **10**(11), 1190–1201 (2017). https://doi.org/10.14778/3137628.3137631. https://dl.acm.org/doi/10.14778/3137628.3137631

25. Rezig, E.K., Ouzzani, M., Aref, W.G., Elmagarmid, A.K., Mahmood, A.R., Stonebraker, M.: Horizon: scalable dependency-driven data cleaning. Proc. VLDB Endow. **14**(11), 2546–2554 (2021). https://doi.org/10.14778/3476249.3476301. https://dl.acm.org/doi/10.14778/3476249.3476301

26. Song, S., Zhu, H., Wang, J.: Constraint-variance tolerant data repairing. In: Proceedings of the 2016 International Conference on Management of Data, San Francisco, California, USA, pp. 877–892. ACM (2016). https://doi.org/10.1145/2882903.2882955. https://dl.acm.org/doi/10.1145/2882903.2882955

27. Song, S., Zhu, H., Wang, J.: Constraint-variance tolerant data repairing. In: Proceedings of the 2016 International Conference on Management of Data, pp. 877–892 (2016)

28. Volkovs, M., Fei Chiang, Szlichta, J., Miller, R.J.: Continuous data cleaning. In: 2014 IEEE 30th International Conference on Data Engineering, Chicago, IL, pp. 244–255. IEEE (2014). https://doi.org/10.1109/ICDE.2014.6816655. http://ieeexplore.ieee.org/document/6816655/

29. Chu, X., Ilyas, I.F., Papotti, P.: Holistic data cleaning: putting violations into context. In: 2013 IEEE 29th International Conference on Data Engineering (ICDE), Brisbane, QLD, pp. 458–469. IEEE (2013). https://doi.org/10.1109/ICDE.2013.6544847. http://ieeexplore.ieee.org/document/6544847/

30. Yakout, M., Elmagarmid, A.K., Neville, J., Ouzzani, M., Ilyas, I.F.: Guided data repair. arXiv preprint arXiv:1103.3103 (2011)

Developing Image-Based Classification Techniques to Analyse Customer Behaviour

Ryan Butler[1(✉)] and Edwin Simpson[2]

[1] Department of Engineering Mathematics, University of Bristol, Bristol, UK
ryan@butlermail.co.uk
[2] Intelligent Systems Labs, University of Bristol, Bristol, UK

Abstract. Banks, investment firms and other financial service providers are required to safeguard customers from unsuitable financial products under Know Your Customer (KYC) regulation, such as FCA Sect. 5.2. Recent work has proposed to model a customer's risk profile as a heatmap, which can be used to calculate a risk score by classifying the image via a CNN and extracting geometric features from it using contour detection. This provides an interpretable approach to analysing customer spending behaviour. However, there is a lack of comparative evaluation in the literature of alternative classification techniques to the heatmap representation, which is the focus of our paper. The heatmap model evaluated by this study achieved an F1 score of 94.6% when classifying heatmap geometry, far outperforming other configurations, including state-of-the-art algorithms typically employed for TSC such as HIVE-COTE, as well as alternative image-transform techniques such as Gramian angular fields. Our experiments used a transactional dataset produced by Lloyds Banking Group, a major UK retail bank, via agent-based modelling (ABM). This data was computer generated and at no point was real transactional data shared. This study shows that a grouped CNN model paired with the heatmap representation is superior to conventional time series classification and image-transform methods at classifying customer spending.

Keywords: Simulated transactional data · Grouped convolutional neural network · Agent-based modelling · Know your customer

1 Introduction

In countries such as the UK, firms offering financial services are required by law to assess a customer's risk before offering financial products. This falls under the Financial Conduct Authority's (FCA) *Know Your Customer* guidance (FCA Handbook, Sect. 5.2 [15]). KYC requires firms to assess a customer's credit risk, safeguard them from unsuitable products, and carry out anti-money laundering and fraud assessments [19]. These checks come at a high cost: it is estimated that the average bank spends £55m annually on KYC [36], and that cumbersome manual KYC checks lead to 25% of bank applications being abandoned, causing banks to lose out on substantial revenue. Online checks do not fare much better, with failure rates of up to 20%, as they rely on data provided by customers that is often of low quality. Outsourcing to dedicated compliance

© The Author(s), under exclusive license to Springer Nature Switzerland AG 2024
A. P. Rocha et al. (Eds.): ICAART 2023, LNAI 14546, pp. 469–491, 2024.
https://doi.org/10.1007/978-3-031-55326-4_23

platforms, such as Pass Fort [37], is costly, while non-compliance leads to hefty fines. For example, Deutsche Bank was fined £163m and Barclays fined £72m for failures under EU law [36]. There is therefore a clear need for reliable, low cost methods for assessing customer risk.

Several applications of Machine learning (ML) have previously been proposed to reduce the friction and cost of KYC checks. Khandani et al. [22] were able to predict consumer credit default and delinquency 3–12 months ahead with high accuracy from transactional data. To detect fraud, Sinanc et al. [39] converted credit card transactions into an image using Gramian angular fields (GAF), then applied a convolutional neural network (CNN) [25] classifier. Their approach achieved an F1 score of 85.49%, outperforming alternative methods [39]. However, only Butler et al. [8] and Butler and Simpson [9] have developed techniques to ascertain customer risk to determine whether they should be offered specific products (FCA Sect. 5.2 [15]).

The limited work on customer risk can be attributed to the availability of datasets: most available datasets contain gold labels only for credit events and fraud [22,39], not spending behaviour. A key reason is that firms cannot provide real transactional data for research purposes due to the General Data Protection Regulation (GDPR) [45]. An alternative is to produce synthetic data using ABM [23], but to date only Butler et al. [8] and Butler and Simpson [9] have used data produced by ABM for the customer safeguarding aspect of KYC, while earlier work applied ABM to fraud detection [23]. This paper therefore addresses the research gap by using ABM-generated data to predict and evaluate risk for safeguarding individual customers.

To provide a human-interpretable classifier, Butler et al. [8] proposed to convert transactional data to a heatmap image, before classifying its geometric components. Butler and Simpson [9] extended this method to identify more complex geometric patterns in the heatmaps, which indicate spending behaviour patterns and can help to quantify impulsivity. The geometric features were used to compute risk scores for different spending categories, which could inform a decision on whether to offer a customer a particular financial product. For example, if an individual's scores indicate impulsive spending in the takeaway or restaurant categories, it would be inappropriate and contrary to FCA Sect. 5.2 [15] to offer them a cashback card that incentivises eating out.

While Butler and Simpson [9] demonstrated the potential of the heatmap technique, the previous work lacks a comparison with alternative Time Series Classification (TSC) and image-transform algorithms. Therefore, this paper extends their prior work and compares their algorithm to state-of-the-art TSC algorithms, such as HIVE-COTE [1], and alternative image-transform techniques, such as the use of recurrence plots (RPs) [20]. Furthermore, we provide a comprehensive literature survey of TSC algorithms, which was omitted from prior work [9]. Lastly, the previous evaluation of generated risk scores relies on the qualitative similarity between their risk score distributions and a theoretical normal distribution. This paper provides a more thorough, quantitative assessment using normal probability plots [11] to show how strongly their risk scores approximate this distribution.

1.1 Aims and Objectives

The objectives of this study are:

- Explore contemporary TSC techniques in the literature, as well as current ML approaches.
- Show how the heatmap representation is superior to a conventional feature vector used during TSC, as well as to advanced TSC techniques such as HIVE-COTE.
- Demonstrate how the heatmap representation is superior to alternative image-transform techniques such as GAF.
- Illustrate the performance of the risk score algorithm using normal distribution plots.

2 Literature Review

2.1 Overview of Time Series Classification Techniques

Time series data is composed of "a sequence of data points indexed in time order" [6]. A commonly used baseline for TSC is the nearest neighbour classifier (K-NN) with the dynamic time warping distance metric [14]. A large body of TSC literature is focused on developing techniques to outperform this baseline, such as the use of random forests to classify time series [17], which have shown strong performance in TSC problems [31]. This approach has been developed further in the diverse representation canonical interval forest classifier (DrCif), which expands the random forest technique by extracting randomised intervals from a time series, as well as the 22 canonical time-series characteristics (Catch22) [28], resulting in significant improvements over conventional time series random forests [31,33]. Another approach to outperform the K-NN baseline is the temporal dictionary ensemble (TDE) [32], which discretises and approximates windows over a time series to produce words. These are then used to form a bag of words representation of the time series, before being classified [32].

The most successful attempts to outperform this baseline have involved the use of ensemble methods, such as the development of the collective of transformation-based ensembles (COTE) [2], which consists of several classifiers trained on multiple time series representations of the training data [2]. Lines et al. further developed COTE by producing HIVE-COTE, which uses a new hierarchical structure with probabilistic voting that outperforms the former. According to Bagnall et al. [1], HIVE-COTE is regarded as state-of-the-art in the academic community for TSC. However, to achieve its state-of-the-art performance, it is computationally very expensive, as it requires training 37 different classifiers and cross-validating each hyperparameter used in its constituent classifiers. In particular, the shaplet transformation classifier [21] has a time complexity of $O(n^2 \times l^4)$, where n is the number of time series in the dataset and l is the length of each time series. This renders the algorithm unfeasible for confronting the large datasets commonly found in big data problems [14]. This is especially true when analysing transactional data due to the volume of transactions a bank receives [35]. For context, there were 2.1 billion credit and debit card transactions in the UK during August 2022 alone [42]. COTE and HIVE-COTE also suffer from a lack of interpretability, as the output of one of their individual classifiers can be difficult for an expert to analyse [14]. Therefore, when many of these classifiers are combined in an ensemble method, the interpretability of the model is significantly hindered [14].

2.2 Using Deep Neural Networks for TSC

Deep neural networks (DNNs) are far better suited for big data problems, as they can be run via parallel computations that utilise multiple graphical processing units (GPUs) [27]. This enables DNNs to handle data with high dimensionality and be less susceptible to the curse of dimensionality [14]. DNNs are neural networks that possess at least two hidden layers between the input and output layers (see Fig. 1) [26]. DNNs provide an alternative route for TSC, yet literature examining this application is limited [14]. A key example is that DNNs are not discussed in Bagnall et al.'s [1] 2017 review of existing TSC algorithms. DNN models can be split into generative and discriminative models. A discriminative model draws a boundary in the data space to discriminate between class labels, while a generative model attempts to model how the data is placed in the space (i.e. how the data was generated) [3]. In the literature, discriminative models are generally regarded as more accurate than generative models for TSC [1, 34]; therefore, they will be the focus of this review henceforth.

Discriminative models can be further divided into end-to-end models and models that have a bespoke feature extraction step. End-to-end models directly learn features from the dataset [16]. An overview of deep learning techniques for TSC can be found in Fig. 2.

The advantage of end-to-end techniques over TSC techniques that require a domain-specific feature engineering stage is that their performance is not dependent on the quality of the designed feature, thereby removing any potential bias that may occur during the feature-designing stage [14]. These models, however, have limited interpretability, as they learn features directly from the training data that can make them difficult to improve or modify [16]. The image-transform technique bridges the gap between these two approaches by providing a domain-agnostic and interpretable technique for TSC [14].

2.3 Image-Transform for TSC

Image-transform involves the conversion of time series data into an image, which is then classified by a CNN [14]. This means the feature vector (i.e. the image) is not influenced by the time series data's domain, nor is it handcrafted, removing any potential bias from the domain or the user. The features present in an image are also easier for a human to interpret than a raw time series. Moreover, raw time series data typically possesses long temporal correlations, which can be challenging for conventional TSC algorithms to learn [44]. Lastly, image-transform leverages the extensive computer vision research carried out in the past decade for use in TSC [14, 20].

An example of an image-transform technique is the production of recurrence plots (RPs) [12, 20]. These are graphical representations of time series data that indicate which points return to their previous state; hence, they are a 2D representation of the data's recurrences [12]. RPs have been shown to produce competitive results on the UCR (University of California, Riverside) time series archive, a collection of datasets commonly used as a benchmark for TSC performance, to state-of-the-art TSC algorithms [20]. However, recurrence plots require training to derive insights from, as they are highly complex [29]. Alternatively, the Gramian angular fields (GAF) image-transform technique is far more human-interpretable because temporal dependency is

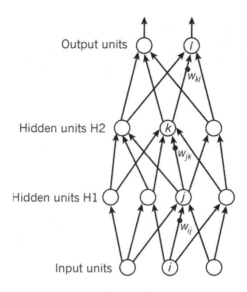

Fig. 1. DNN architecture [25].

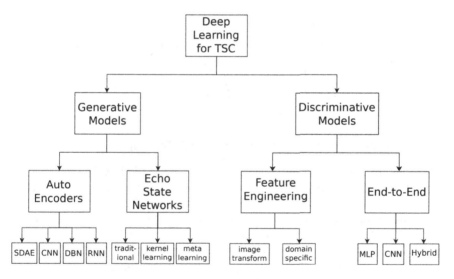

Fig. 2. Overview of deep learning techniques for TSC [14].

maintained; time increases from the top left to the bottom right of the image [44]. The GAF representation first involves the scaling of the time series data to $[-1, 1]$ using a min-max scaler [44]. The data is then converted into the polar coordinate system before computing the gram matrix of that data, assuming that n 2D vectors have a norm of 1 (see Eqs. 1 and 2), and using a custom inner product function (see Eqs. 3 and 4) [44]. This produces an image where the data along the diagonal from the top left to the bottom right is the original value of the scaled time series at that time step, and the data points vertically below and to the right of this value represent the custom inner product function of that value and the values in the future time steps (see Fig. 3). This process converts a complex dynamic system into an interpretable image, enabling a ML algorithm to easily learn the long temporal correlations typically present in the time series data, as well as for a human to derive insights directly from the image.

$$G = \begin{pmatrix} \langle u_1, v_1 \rangle & \langle u_1, v_2 \rangle & \cdots & \langle u_1, v_n \rangle \\ \langle u_2, v_1 \rangle & \langle u_2, v_2 \rangle & \cdots & \langle u_2, v_n \rangle \\ \cdots & \cdots & \cdots & \cdots \\ \langle u_n, v_1 \rangle & \langle u_n, v_2 \rangle & \cdots & \langle u_n, v_n \rangle \end{pmatrix} \tag{1}$$

$$G = \begin{pmatrix} \cos(\phi_{1,1}) & \cos(\phi_{1,2}) & \cdots & \cos(\phi_{1,n}) \\ \cos(\phi_{2,1}) & \cos(\phi_{2,2}) & \cdots & \cos(\phi_{2,n}) \\ \cdots & \cdots & \cdots & \cdots \\ \cos(\phi_{n,1}) & \cos(\phi_{n,2}) & \cdots & \cos(\phi_{n,n}) \end{pmatrix} \tag{2}$$

$$x \oplus y = \cos(\theta_1 + \theta_2) \tag{3}$$

$$\begin{aligned} \cos(\theta_1 + \theta_2) &= \cos(\arccos(x) + \arccos(y)) \\ &= \cos(\arccos(x) \cdot \arccos(y)) - \sin(\arccos(x)) \cdot \sin(\arccos(y)) \\ &= x \cdot y + \sqrt{1 - x^2} \cdot \sqrt{1 - y^2} \\ &= \langle x, y \rangle - \sqrt{1 - x^2} \cdot \sqrt{1 - y^2} \end{aligned} \tag{4}$$

2.4   Issues with Contemporary Image-Transform Techniques

While GAFs are more human-interpretable than RPs, it can still be difficult for a human to relate their geometric features back to the original data and derive insights. This is because, in a GAF representation, time increases in a one-dimensional fashion along the diagonal of the image. In addition, spatially, the pixels to the right and below a given pixel on the diagonal are the custom inner product (see Eq. 3) of the data points from the time step of the given diagonal pixel up until the last time step (see Fig. 3). As a result, the geometric features are difficult to relate intuitively back to the data because the spatial position of a pixel is not directly related to the timestep of the data. Alternatively, a heatmap image representation [8] that possesses two time dimensions is far easier for a human to interpret. This is because the time dimensions affect the spatial position of the geometric features, making it easier for a human to intuitively understand what the features represent and derive insights from them.

2.5   Overview of the Heatmap Representation

The heatmap representation is an image-transform technique for time series data [8], where the Cartesian coordinates of a pixel represent the time step (e.g. day of the week

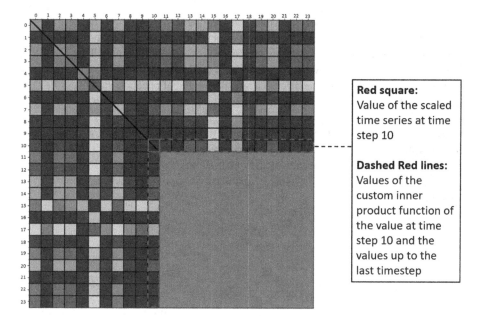

Red square:
Value of the scaled time series at time step 10

Dashed Red lines:
Values of the custom inner product function of the value at time step 10 and the values up to the last timestep

Fig. 3. How to interpret a Gramian angular fields plot. NB: The original scaled time series values are the pixels along the diagonal marked with a black line starting at (0,0) and ending at time step 10 (10,10). The pixels either side of this line represent which pair of timesteps are used in the custom inner product calculation up to time step 10. The green square obscures data where the timestep is >10. (Color figure online)

vs week number) of the time series, while the value of the pixel itself aggregates the values at that time step [9]. Compared to RPs and GAFs, the images created by the heatmap technique are far more interpretable, as the position of a pixel in a heatmap corresponds to the time step of the data (see Fig. 4) [9]. As a result, complex temporal relationships, which are a key challenge for conventional TSC algorithms [44] to analyse, can be more easily derived from a heatmap [9].

2.6 Previous Uses of the Heatmap Representation

The first use of the heatmap representation was in Butler et al. [8], in which the authors used a transactional dataset produced by Lloyds Banking Group to produce several per category 9×31 (i.e. 9 months by 31 days) heatmaps. These heatmaps could be divided based upon whether there was a line in the heatmap ("line") or if its payments were more random ("spotty"). A CNN classifier was then trained to label these two data-types. This classification in conjunction with statistical analysis of the individual's spending was then used to summarise a customer's spending behaviour. However, Butler et al. [8] has several limitations including, training the CNN on a basic geometric feature, using a single CNN architecture, and a reliance on statistical analysis to infer spending behaviour when directly using the heatmap geometry could reveal more unique insights [9].

These limitations were addressed in the second paper covering the heatmap representation in Butler and Simpson [9]. In their paper, they created an algorithm to determine customer risk using the geometric features present in a heatmap. This algorithm outputted several per-category risk scores, which could be by a firm to determine whether an individual should be offered a specific financial product. However, they did not analyse the performance of the heatmap representation in relation to alternative image-transform techniques, as well as commonly used TSC techniques. As a result, a comparative evaluation of these techniques and the heatmap approach will be carried out in this study. Furthermore, the performance of their risk score algorithm was determined by the qualitative similarity of their risk scores to a normal distribution. This can be examined more robustly using a quantitative approach, such as using normal probability plots [11].

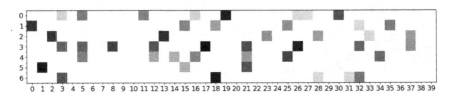

Fig. 4. Example 7×40 heatmap i.e., 7 days of the week by 40 weeks, depicting the normalised sum of an individual's transactions per day in the time period [9].

3 Summary of Related Literature

To summarise, DNNs are superior to conventional TSC techniques when addressing big data problems, such as analysing transactional data. Discriminative DNN techniques also typically perform better than generative techniques in the literature [1,34]. Of the discriminative DNN techniques, image-transform is superior to end-end architectures and techniques that require a domain-specific feature engineering stage, as it is both domain-agnostic and human-interpretable.

Of the image-transform techniques, the heatmap representation is superior from a human interpretability standpoint, as the spatial position of geometric features in the image is directly related to the time dimension.

Lastly, the literature currently lacks a comparison of the heatmap technique to alternative image-transform approaches and conventional TSC algorithms.

4 Methodology

4.1 Dataset Simulation

The dataset used in this study was a simulated dataset provided by Lloyds Banking Group. This dataset was produced by their in-house, agent-based model (ABM) [23] through modelling the transactions in a theoretical town containing 1,304 unique agents, which were divided into customers and vendors. Each customer-agent possessed traits which influenced the chance of them carrying out a transaction. These traits were randomly allocated based the agent's initial parameters, which were chosen based on expert knowledge from the retail banking community. Consequently, it is assumed that the data produced by this method is an accurate representation of real transactional data [8].

4.2 Algorithm Structure

The algorithm used in this study can be seen in Fig. 5. It takes as an input a customer's transactional data, which it converts into several RGB heatmaps split by transaction category. These heatmap images are classified by a CNN [25], as well as, broken down into their constitute geometric features utilising contour detection [40]. The output of both these processes are then used to produce several per-category risk scores for a given customer.

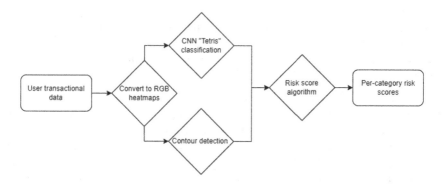

Fig. 5. Overall algorithm [9].

4.3 Heatmap Feature Vector Design

Through manual sorting of vendor names, customer transactions were split into 15 transaction categories. As in Butler and Simpson [9] there were 40 weeks present in the utilised dataset. Consequently, the transactions for each category were used to create a 7×40 RGB (Red-Green-Blue) image. The R layer contained a Boolean value which showed there was a payment on a given day, the B layer the normalised sum of transactions for that day, and lastly, the G layer the normalised standard deviation of payments.

The R layer was selected as it showed the high level structure of payments in the 7×40 time period, while the G layer revealed the proportion of payments, in a transaction category, carried out on a given day. Finally, the B layer showed the spread of payments within a day's spending.

4.4 1D Conventional Feature Vector

In order to compare the efficacy of the heatmap feature vector to conventional TSC algorithms, a 1D time series was produced for each transaction category. These feature vectors were 280 time steps (i.e. the number of days in the dataset) long and possessed a 1 on a given day if there was a transaction and 0 if not.

4.5   Image-Transform Feature Vectors

To compare the heatmap technique to alternative image-transform techniques, a 35×35 GAF representation was produced for each of the conventional feature vectors. This GAF geometry was chosen as any greater dimensionality causes intractable run times for the chosen classification algorithms. Furthermore, a recurrence plot was also produced for each conventional feature vector.

4.6   Labelling Procedure

Similarly to Butler and Simpson [9], the heatmaps were labelled based on the geometric structure of their R layer and were split into those that possessed a clear geometric structure, i.e. "Tetris", and those that did not, i.e. "Non-Tetris". A example "Tetris" heatmap can be seen in Fig. 6, and a heatmap was labelled as such if it satisfied the following:

- Does it have at least one horizontal chain of three payments or one vertical chain of three payments? [9]
- Does it have geometric components that look like Tetris pieces, or does it look like a completed Tetris section? [9]

There were a total of 10,812 heatmaps to label, so to aid in the labelling process, we followed a similar method to that of Butler et al. [8]. The heatmaps were first clustered via UMAP [30]. However, as opposed to the manual cluster labelling in Butler and Simpson [9], this paper introduces an intermediary stage where density based clustering is performed via HDBSCAN [10], which automates the identification of clusters. Thereby limiting the influence of human error during this process. Afterwards, a random sample of 5 heatamps were extracted from each cluster, whose dominant geometric feature was used to label the remainder of heatmaps in that cluster. These labels were then manually checked for errors. This process was then repeated and any differences evaluated.

Identifying whether a heatmap has an underlying geometric structure ("Tetris") is critical for this study, because this can be used to infer overall spending behaviour. For example, horizontal rows in a heatmap represent consecutive daily spending, so, if that spending is 5 days in length from Monday to Friday in the Cafe category, you can deduce that the individual buys a daily coffee.

The 1D feature vectors detailed in Sect. 4.4 each relate to a specific per-category heatmap. Moreover, each GAF and RP image, outlined in Sect. 4.5, also has a corresponding heatmap image by extension. Thus, the same labels can be applied to each of these feature vector designs.

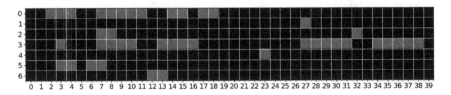

Fig. 6. Example Tetris heatmap [9].

4.7 Model Architectures

Baseline Models. The first baseline model used in this study is a simple rules-based classifier which labels a heatmap as "Tetris" if there is a vertical or horizontal chain of three payments. The second and third baseline models are K-NN classifiers (with $k = 1$) using the dynamic time warping metric and euclidean metric respectively. These were chosen as they are commonly used benchmarks for a TSC algorithm's performance [14].

Advanced TSC Models. Advanced TSC algorithms are also explored in this study to position the heatmap representation among conventional TSC algorithms. These are discussed in Sect. 2.1, and include TSF [17], DrCif [31], TDE [32] and HIVE-COTE [31].

Single Kernel CNN Model. The Single Kernel CNN model from Butler et al. [8] can be seen in Fig. 7. This model was evaluated in order to compare it to the advanced TSC algorithms and the grouped CNN architecture.

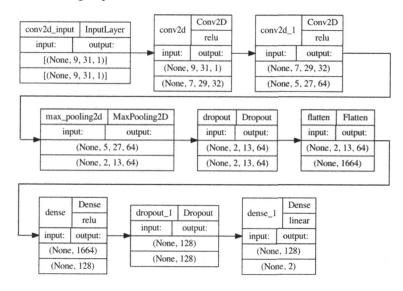

Fig. 7. Single kernel CNN model structure [8].

Grouped CNN Model. The grouped CNN structure can be seen in Fig. 8. The same grouped CNN architecture, as detailed in Butler and Simpson [9], was implemented. This was in order to compare the results of their study to the performances of alternative TSC algorithms.

Model Validation. A train-test split of 20% was used to divide the feature vector datasets into training and test datasets. Two paired bootstrap tests [13] using 1000000 virtual tests and a threshold of 0.01, were also performed on the single and grouped CNN architectures, as well as the grouped CNN and HIVE-COTE methods; this is in

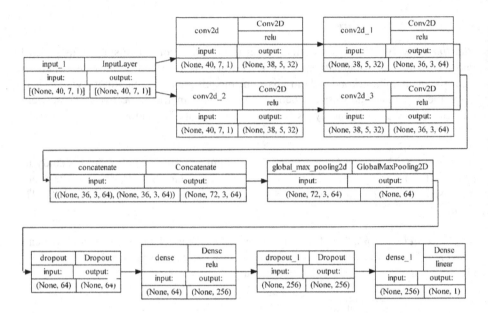

Fig. 8. Grouped CNN model structure [9].

order to determine if any increases in performances between the methods is accidental. Finally, a 10-fold cross-validation [24] of the grouped CNN was implemented to investigate how the model performed using random data splits.

4.8 Heatmap Image Analysis

Contour Detection. Contour detection [18] was performed on the heatmap images to show their high-level geometric features. As in Butler and Simpson [9], statistics about these features were then measured including:

- The max width of a contour, a, which indicates the largest chain of payments on consecutive days.
- The max height of a contour, b, which indicates the largest chain of payments on the same day of the week.
- The area of a contour, c, used to infer the number of payments within the contour.
- The median of the G layer (Sect. 4.3) in the contour (i.e. the median normalised sum payment of the contour), denoted d. This value represents the average size of a payment in a given contour.
- The median of the B layer (Sect. 4.3) in the contour (i.e. the median normalised standard deviation of payments of the contour), denoted f. This value yielded a measure of the average variation of payments on a given day within a contour.

These features can be used to derive insights about a customer's underlying spending behaviour and, as a result, determine that customer's risk [9].

Risk Score Algorithm. In order to calculate the risk score of a heatmap, Butler and Simpson's [9] risk score methodology was implemented. Firstly, the logit [4], x, from the grouped CNN's classification (see Fig. 8) is inputted into the sigmoid function to output a probability:

$$S(x) = \frac{1}{1 + e^{-x}}. \tag{5}$$

This probability, along with contour statistics, are then extracted from the image (see Sect. 4.8), and inserted into the following equation:

$$r = \left\| (a^\alpha b^\beta c^\gamma d^\delta)(1 + f)^\epsilon \right\| \times S(x), \tag{6}$$

where a to f are the statistics derived from each contour, and α to ϵ are hyperparmeter exponent weights for these statistics. These hyperparameters weight how important a particular contour statistic is in determining if a customer is exhibiting risky spending behaviour. These are calculated by first ranking the statistics in order of significance and then taking the reciprocal of that rank for the corresponding value of the hyperparameter exponent.

Lastly the output of Eq. 6 was then mapped to $[0, 1]$ using the following equation:

$$R = 1 - \frac{1}{1 + r} \tag{7}$$

Equation 7 produces a risk score and this was calculated for each customer in each of the transaction categories.

Interpreting and Evaluating the Risk Scores. The distribution of risk scores was explored in order to evaluate how well the risk score algorithm determines risk. This was measured by evaluating how closely the spread of risk scores, calculated from the test set of heatmaps, approximates a normal distribution, as this would indicate the algorithm was discriminating well between different degrees of risk. Both qualitative analysis comparing the histogram of risk scores to an ideal normal distribution, and quantitative analysis representing the scores as a normal probability plot [11] were carried out. This process was then repeated for subgroups within the population of risk scores, i.e. the "Tetris" and "Non-Tetris" labelled data, to determine the performance of the algorithm at discriminating risk between heatmaps of the same label. A threshold of risky spending behavior was then calculated using the mean (μ) and standard deviation (σ) of the population of risk scores [9]:

$$R_{cut} = \mu + 2\sigma \tag{8}$$

Equation 8 calculates the risk score value where 97.5% of the scores lie below by using the emprical rule [38].

5   Results

5.1   Final Datasets

During the labelling process described in Sect. 4.6, a UMAP projection [30] of the heatmaps along with cluster labels assigned by HDBSCAN [10] was produced, and can be seen in Fig. 9. This was then utilised to develop the final dataset of heatmaps, that contained 10,812 heatmaps broken down into 1,646 "Tetris" and 9,166 "Non-Tetris" labelled images. This is a very imbalanced class distribution, so the F1 score was chosen to measure performance of the classifiers [43]. The same labels were used for each heatmap's corresponding conventional 1D, GAF and RP feature vectors (see Sects. 4.4 and 4.5), producing a second, third and fourth dataset.

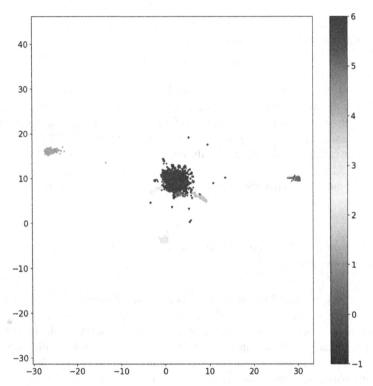

Fig. 9. UMAP projection of heatmap dataset along with HDBSCAN clusters. UMAP hyper-parameters: n_neighbors=20, min_dist=0.1, n_components=2, metric=Euclidean. HDBSCAN hyperparameters: min_samples=1, min_cluster_size=300.

5.2   Model Performances

From Table 1, the grouped CNN architecture classified the heatmaps in the test set with a greater F1 score than the image-baseline and single CNN model achieving an F1 score of 94.3%. Furthermore, the paired bootstrap test outputted a $p \ll 0.01$, indicating that the performance of the grouped CNN model in relation to the single CNN model is not a consequence of random chance.

Moreover, from Tables 1, 2, 3 and 5, for the single and grouped CNN architectures, the heatmap feature vectors showed far greater performances on the test set than the conventional, GAF and RP feature vectors. From Tables 1 and 4, the grouped CNN architecture using the heatmap feature vector also outperformed all of the alternative conventional TSC algorithms, including HIVE-COTE ($p \ll 0.01$, paired bootstrap test), which is considered state-of-the-art [1].

Table 1. Performance on the test set using heatmap feature vectors [9].

Model	Mean F1 score on test set (n = 10)
Image-Baseline	78.6%
Single CNN	86.1%
Grouped CNN	94.3%

Table 2. Performance on the test set using GAF features vectors.

Model	Mean F1 score on test set (n = 10)
Single CNN	67.2%
Grouped CNN	72.4%

Table 3. Performance on the test set using RP features vectors.

Model	Mean F1 score on test set (n = 10)
Single CNN	80.4%
Grouped CNN	75.8%

Table 4. Conventional TSC algorithms performance on 1D feature vectors.

Model	Mean F1 score on test set (n = 10)
K-NN(euc)	25.7%
K-NN(dtw)	57.6%
TRF	75.4%
DrCif	79.5 %
TDE	44.2 %
HIVE-COTE	82.9%

Table 5. DNN algorithms performance on 1D feature vectors [9].

Model	Mean F1 score on test set (n = 10)
Single CNN	80.4%
Grouped CNN	77.0%

Lastly, the grouped CNN achieved a high F1 score of 94.8% during cross validation with minimal overfitting (See Figs. 10 and 11).

5.3 Risk Score Algorithm Results

Hyperparameter Rankings. The same hyperparameter rankings that were assigned in Butler and Simpson [9] were also used during this study and are detailed in Table 6. α, δ and ϵ, were ranked as 1, because their corresponding contour statistics, i.e. maximum width, a, median normalised sum spending, d and median normalised standard deviation, f, were seen as the most significant in an individual showing risky spending

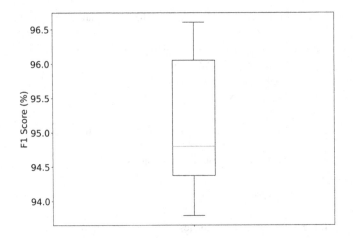

Fig. 10. 10-fold CV F1 score results. Median = 94.8%. IQR = 1.7% [9].

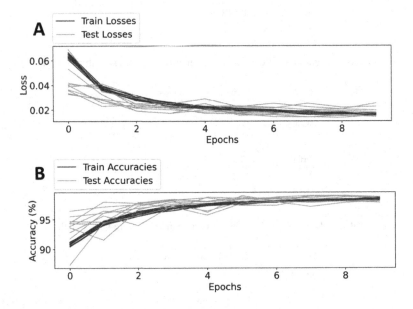

Fig. 11. 10-fold CV history. A: Loss vs epoch. B: Accuracy vs epoch [9].

behaviour. Alternatively, β and γ were ranked as 2 and 3 respectively, because their corresponding statistics, i.e. the max height of a contour (b) and area of a contour (c), were seen as less important.

Analysing the Risk Score Distribution. Figure 12, which shows the overall distribution of risk scores, is heavily right-skewed and does not approximate a normal distribution very well. This is because it is composed of two overlapping distributions of "Tetris" and "Non-Tetris" labelled heatmaps [9]. The distribution of Tetris scores in

Table 6. Hyperparameter importance (1 is highest.) [9].

Contour statistic	Hyperparameter	Rank
a	α	1
b	β	2
c	γ	3
d	δ	1
f	ϵ	1

Fig. 13 closely follows the least squares regression line with an $R^2 = 0.946$, indicating that these scores strongly approximate a normal distribution. Alternatively, the "Non-Tetris" scores in Fig. 14 follow the regression line less well with an $R^2 = 0.411$. Additionally, a large proportion of the scores are between 0 and 0.1, indicating a heavy positive skew to the distribution. Consequently, when these two datasets are combined the resulting distribution becomes predominately right skewed, owing to the significantly higher number of "Non-Tetris" labelled data. Finally, a cut-off point for risky spending behaviour was calculated, using Eq. 8, and the overall distribution statistics, shown in Fig. 12, at 0.512.

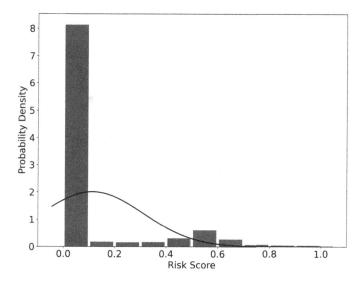

Fig. 12. Normalised distribution of risk scores in test set with approximate normal distribution overlaid. $\mu = 0.112$, $\sigma = 0.20$ [9].

Example Customer's Risk Scores per Spending Category. An example output of the risk score algorithm can be seen for a simulated customer in Table 7. This shows that this individual spends impulsively in the online shop, clothing shop, supermarket, and takeaway categories.

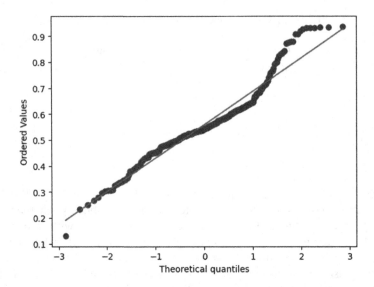

Fig. 13. Probability plot of "Tetris" labeled scores. Best fit line slope: 0.129, intercept: 0.559, and $R^2 = 0.946$.

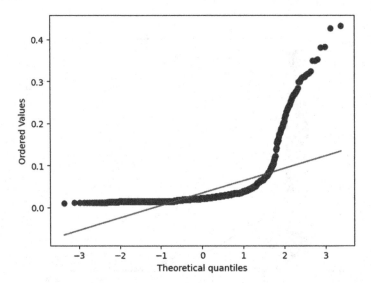

Fig. 14. Probability plot of "Non-Tetris" labeled scores. Best fit line slope: 0.030, intercept: 0.034, and $R^2 = 0.411$.

6   Discussion

6.1   Critical Findings

The results in Sect. 5.2 for heatmap image classification show that the grouped CNN model significantly outperformed both a simple rules-based classifier and a single ker-

Table 7. Risk scores for an example user in each category with corresponding risky spending behaviour labels [9].

Category	Risk Score	Risky Spending?
Finances	0.018	N
Entertainment	0.017	N
Online shop	0.536	Y
Exercise	0	N
Personal care	0.417	N
Clothing shop	0.523	Y
Restaurant	0	N
Cafe	0	N
Supermarket	0.59	Y
Education	0.062	N
Home Shop	0.026	N
Pub/Bar	0	N
Takeaway	0.928	Y
Sports shop	0	N
Family	0	N

nel CNN on both the test set and 10-fold cross validation over the training set. The grouped CNN architecture, using the heatmap feature vector, also outperformed contemporary TSC techniques including HIVE-COTE, which is considered state-of-the-art [1]. Consequently, this satisfies the second aim of this study, which was to demonstrate that superior performance can be achieved using geometric features extracted from a heatmap representation of a customer's spending, rather than conventional TSC features. Lastly, when using the GAF and RP representation, the single and grouped CNN architecture perform worse than when the heatmap representation is utilised, indicating that the heatmap technique is superior to these alternative image-transform approaches, satisfying the third aim of this study.

Section 5.3 described an algorithm for computing risk scores for different spending categories. We investigated the distribution of risk scores to determine whether they can discriminate between customers with different levels of risk. Figure 12 shows the overall distribution, which has a heavy positive skew. This distribution can be decomposed into two separate, overlapping distributions: one for the risk scores for heatmaps classified as "Tetris" (Fig. 13), and one for the "Non-Tetris" heatmaps (Fig. 14), which dominate the overall distribution as the dataset contains far more examples of this class. The "Non-Tetris" distribution has a strong right skew, reflecting that most "Non-Tetris" cases have lower risk scores. This arises because Eq. 6 weights the scores by the probability of "Tetris" classification. The "Non-Tetris" distribution therefore aligns with our intentions, as "Tetris" patterns are associated with impulsive spending, therefore "Non-Tetris" heatmaps are much less likely to include risky spending behaviour.

The "Tetris" distribution in Fig. 13 is a much better approximation to a normal distribution, suggesting that the risk score can assign different levels of risk to customers in the "Tetris" category. This is a promising outcome, as it is important to be able to discriminate between cases within the "Tetris" class to quantify different degrees of risky behaviour. The risk score also allows a financial service provider to quantify risk associated with particular spending categories. This would allow them to make fine-grained judgements, such as deciding not to offer a customer a cashback card for clothes shopping if the customer has a high risk score for that category.

6.2 Limitations and Recommendations

The experiments presented in this study should be seen as a proof of concept, showing how ABM and ML can be applied to KYC. The analysis of the risk score in this paper is limited by a lack of gold labels, which could be used to tune the hyperparameters in Eq. 6 and assess its accuracy. We recommend that these hyperparameters are tuned in future applications to maximise the correlation between the generated risk scores and a set of comparable gold-standard risk scores, which could be provided by expert human labellers. We also recommend future experimentation with real customer data before deploying the method, as the dataset used in this study is synthetic.

The spending categories used in this study were created manually to encompass the different vendors referenced in the dataset. A further limitation of our work is that manual categorisation may be impractical in a real-world application, since it would be challenging to classify all vendors by hand for all transactions that a bank processes [41]. Automated techniques for classifying vendors are therefore an important topic for future research.

6.3 Ethical Considerations

A danger of categorising individual spending patterns is the potential to unintentionally discriminate against certain groups of people. For example, compulsive buying disorder (CBD), defined as "excessive shopping cognitions and buying behaviour that leads to distress or impairment" [5], has been associated with attention deficit hyperactivity disorder (ADHD) [7]. Thus, risk scores based on impulsive spending may be predictors of neurodiversity. Future applications of the proposed method should therefore be limited to customer safeguarding and further research is needed to into the possible effects of any application of the method on different minority groups.

7 Conclusions

Firstly, contemporary TSC technqiues were explored in Sect. 2. This paper then evaluated the heatmap technique's performance against these state-of-the-art TSC algorithms and alternative image-transform techniques. The grouped CNN model utilised by this study was able to classify heatmaps with a clear geometric structure ("Tetris") and those without, achieving an F1 score of 94.6% on the test dataset. This model structure exceeded the performance of all the alternative architectures and feature vector designs tested including HIVE-COTE which is among the best performing TSC algorithms. Moreover, the use of normal probability plots [11] was able to quantitatively illustrate the performance of the risk score algorithm. Therefore, all the stated aims of this study were met. This work demonstrates how a grouped CNN architecture using the interpretable heatmap representation is superior to alternative models and feature vector designs at classifying customer spending behaviour.

7.1 Future Work

As discussed in Sect. 6.2, a key limitation of this study is the lack of golden labels to validate the risk score algorithm. Therefore, to further extend this study, ABM could be used to generate a dataset equivalent to that provided by Lloyds Banking Group with additional labels for customer spending behaviour per spending category. This would enable the performance of the risk score algorithm to be more accurately measured and validated.

Acknowledgments. The experiments for this paper were carried out on the high performance computing service of the University of Bristol (BluePebble).

References

1. Bagnall, A., Lines, J., Bostrom, A., Large, J., Keogh, E.: The great time series classification bake off: a review and experimental evaluation of recent algorithmic advances. Data Mining Knowl. Discov. **31**(3), 606–660 (2017). https://doi.org/10.1007/s10618-016-0483-9
2. Bagnall, A., Lines, J., Hills, J., Bostrom, A.: Time-series classification with cote: the collective of transformation-based ensembles. In: 2016 IEEE 32nd International Conference on Data Engineering (ICDE), pp. 1548–1549 (2016). https://doi.org/10.1109/ICDE.2016.7498418
3. Bishop, C.: Pattern recognition and machine learning. J. Electron. Imaging **16**, 140–155 (2006). https://doi.org/10.1117/1.2819119
4. Bishop, C.M.: Pattern Recognition and Machine Learning. Springer, New York (2016)
5. Black, D.W.: A review of compulsive buying disorder. World Psychiatry **6**(1), 14–18 (2007)
6. Bowerman, B.L., O'Connell, R.T.: Forecasting and Time Series: An Applied Approach, 3rd edn. Duxbury Press (1993)
7. Brook, J.S., Zhang, C., Brook, D.W., Leukefeld, C.G.: Compulsive buying: earlier illicit drug use, impulse buying, depression, and adult ADHD symptoms. Psychiatry Res. **228**(3), 312–317 (2015). https://doi.org/10.1016/j.psychres.2015.05.095
8. Butler, R., Hinton, E., Kirwan, M., Salih, A.: Customer behaviour classification using simulated transactional data. In: Proceedings of the European Modeling & Simulation Symposium, EMSS (2022). https://doi.org/10.46354/i3m.2022.emss.039
9. Butler, R., Simpson, E.: Analysing Customer Behaviour Using Simulated Transactional Data, pp. 499–510 (2023). https://www.scitepress.org/Link.aspx?doi=10.5220/0011902100003393
10. Campello, R.J., Moulavi, D., Sander, J.: Density-based clustering based on hierarchical density estimates. In: Pei, J., Tseng, V.S., Cao, L., Motoda, H., Xu, G. (eds.) PAKDD 2013. LNCS, vol. 7819, pp. 160–172. Springer, Heidelberg (2013). https://doi.org/10.1007/978-3-642-37456-2_14

11. Chambers, J.M.: Graphical Methods for Data Analysis. Chapman and Hall/CRC, New York (2017). https://doi.org/10.1201/9781351072304
12. Eckmann, J.P., Kamphorst, S.O., Ruelle, D.: Recurrence plots of dynamical systems. Europhys. Lett. **4**(9), 973 (1987). https://doi.org/10.1209/0295-5075/4/9/004
13. Efron, B., Tibshirani, R.J.: An Introduction to the Bootstrap. Springer, Boston (1993). https://doi.org/10.1007/978-1-4899-4541-9
14. Fawaz, H.I., Forestier, G., Weber, J., Idoumghar, L., Muller, P.A.: Deep learning for time series classification: a review. Data Mining Knowl. Discov. **33**(4), 917–963 (2019). https://doi.org/10.1007/s10618-019-00619-1
15. Financial Conduct Authority: Cob 5.2 Know Your Customer - FCA handbook (2004). https://www.handbook.fca.org.uk/handbook/COB/5/2.html?date=2007-10-31
16. Glasmachers, T.: Limits of end-to-end learning. In: Proceedings of the Ninth Asian Conference on Machine Learning, pp. 17–32. PMLR (2017). https://proceedings.mlr.press/v77/glasmachers17a.html. ISSN 2640-3498
17. Goehry, B.: Random forests for time-dependent processes. ESAIM Probab. Stat. **24**, 801–826 (2020). https://doi.org/10.1051/ps/2020015
18. Gong, X.Y., Su, H., Xu, D., Zhang, Z.T., Shen, F., Yang, H.B.: An overview of contour detection approaches. Int. J. Autom. Comput. **15**(6), 656–672 (2018). https://doi.org/10.1007/s11633-018-1117-z
19. GOV.UK: 'Know Your Customer' guidance (2016). https://www.gov.uk/government/publications/know-your-customer-guidance/know-your-customer-guidance-accessible-version
20. Hatami, N., Gavet, Y., Debayle, J.: Classification of time-series images using deep convolutional neural networks (2017). https://doi.org/10.48550/ARXIV.1710.00886. https://arxiv.org/abs/1710.00886
21. Hills, J., Lines, J., Baranauskas, E., Mapp, J., Bagnall, A.: Classification of time series by shapelet transformation. Data Mining Knowl. Discov. **28**, 851–881 (2013). https://doi.org/10.1007/s10618-013-0322-1
22. Khandani, A.E., Kim, A.J., Lo, A.W.: Consumer credit-risk models via machine-learning algorithms. J. Bank. Finance **34**(11), 2767–2787 (2010). https://doi.org/10.1016/j.jbankfin.2010.06.001
23. Koehler, M., Tivnan, B., Bloedorn, E.: Generating fraud: agent based financial network modeling. In: Proceedings of the North American Association for Computation Social and Organization Science (NAACSOS 2005), Notre Dame, IN, p. 5 (2005)
24. Kohavi, R.: A study of cross-validation and bootstrap for accuracy estimation and model selection. In: Proceedings of the 14th International Joint Conference on Artificial Intelligence - Volume 2, IJCAI 1995, pp. 1137–1143. Morgan Kaufmann Publishers Inc., San Francisco (1995)
25. LeCun, Y., Bottou, L., Bengio, Y., Haffner, P.: Gradient-based learning applied to document recognition. Proc. IEEE **86**(11), 2278–2324 (1998). https://doi.org/10.1109/5.726791
26. LeCun, Y., Bengio, Y., Hinton, G.: Deep learning. Nature **521**, 436–444 (2015). https://doi.org/10.1038/nature14539
27. Lu, J., Young, S., Arel, I., Holleman, J.: A 1 tops/w analog deep machine-learning engine with floating-gate storage in 0.13 μm cmos. IEEE J. Solid-State Circ. **50**(1), 270–281 (2015). https://doi.org/10.1109/JSSC.2014.2356197
28. Lubba, C.H., Sethi, S.S., Knaute, P., Schultz, S.R., Fulcher, B.D., Jones, N.S.: catch22: CAnonical time-series CHaracteristics. Data Mining Knowl. Discov. **33**(6), 1821–1852 (2019). https://doi.org/10.1007/s10618-019-00647-x
29. Marwan, N.: How to avoid potential pitfalls in recurrence plot based data analysis. Int. J. Bifurcat. Chaos **21**(04), 1003–1017 (2011). https://doi.org/10.1142/S0218127411029008. https://www.worldscientific.com/doi/10.1142/S0218127411029008

30. McInnes, L., Healy, J., Melville, J.: UMAP: uniform manifold approximation and projection for dimension reduction (2020)

31. Middlehurst, M., Large, J., Bagnall, A.: The canonical interval forest (CIF) classifier for time series classification. In: 2020 IEEE International Conference on Big Data (Big Data), pp. 188–195 (2020). https://doi.org/10.1109/BigData50022.2020.9378424. arXiv:2008.09172

32. Middlehurst, M., Large, J., Cawley, G., Bagnall, A.: The temporal dictionary ensemble (TDE) classifier for time series classification, vol. 12457, pp. 660–676 (2021). https://doi.org/10.1007/978-3-030-67658-2_38. arXiv:2105.03841

33. Middlehurst, M., Large, J., Flynn, M., Lines, J., Bostrom, A., Bagnall, A.: HIVE-COTE 2.0: a new meta ensemble for time series classification (2021). https://doi.org/10.48550/arXiv.2104.07551. arXiv:2104.07551

34. Nguyen, T.L., Gsponer, S., Ifrim, G.: Time Series Classification by Sequence Learning in All-Subsequence Space, pp. 947–958. IEEE Computer Society (2017). https://doi.org/10.1109/ICDE.2017.142. https://www.computer.org/csdl/proceedings-article/icde/2017/6543a947/12OmNBeRtO2. ISSN 2375-026X

35. Nobanee, H., Dilshad, M.N., Dhanhani, M.A., Neyadi, M.A., Qubaisi, S.A., Shamsi, S.A.: Big data applications the banking sector: a bibliometric analysis approach. SAGE Open 11(4), 21582440211067234 (2021). https://doi.org/10.1177/21582440211067234

36. Ogonsola, F., Pannifer, S.: AMLD4/AMLD5 KYCC: know your compliance costs (2017). https://www.fstech.co.uk/fst/mitek/Hyperion-Whitepaper-Final-for-Release-June2017.pdf

37. PassFort: Passfort (2015). https://www.passfort.com/

38. Ross, S.M.: Descriptive statistics. In: Introduction to Probability and Statistics for Engineers and Scientists, pp. 9–53. Elsevier (2009). https://doi.org/10.1016/b978-0-12-370483-2.00007-2

39. Sinanc, D., Demirezen, U., Sağıroğlu, c.: Explainable credit card fraud detection with image conversion. ADCAIJ Adv. Distrib. Comput. Artif. Intell. J. 10(1), 63–76 (2021). https://doi.org/10.14201/adcaij20211016376

40. Suzuki, S., Abe, K.: Topological structural analysis of digitized binary images by border following. Comput. Vis. Graph. Image Process. 30(1), 32–46 (1985). https://doi.org/10.1016/0734-189x(85)90016-7

41. UK Finance: Card spending update for august 2022 (2022). https://www.ukfinance.org.uk/data-and-research/data/card-spending

42. UKFinance: Card spending update for august 2022 (2022). https://www.ukfinance.org.uk/system/files/2022-11/Card%20Spending%20Update%20-%20August%202022.pdf

43. Umer, M., Imtiaz, Z., Ullah, S., Mehmood, A., Choi, G.S., On, B.W.: Fake news stance detection using deep learning architecture (CNN-LSTM). IEEE Access 8, 156695–156706 (2020). https://doi.org/10.1109/ACCESS.2020.3019735

44. Wang, Z., Oates, T.: Spatially encoding temporal correlations to classify temporal data using convolutional neural networks (2015). https://doi.org/10.48550/ARXIV.1509.07481. https://arxiv.org/abs/1509.07481

45. Wolford, B.: Regulation (EU) 2016/679 of the European Parliament and of the Council of 27 April 2016 on the protection of natural persons with regard to the processing of personal data and on the free movement of such data, and repealing Directive 95/46/EC (General Data Protection Regulation) (Text with EEA relevance) (2016). http://data.europa.eu/eli/reg/2016/679/2016-05-04/eng

Author Index

in the United States
& Taylor Publisher Services